The All-Party Oireachtas Committee was established on 17 December 2002. Its terms of reference are:

> *In order to provide focus on the place and relevance of the Constitution and to establish those areas where Constitutional change may be desirable or necessary, the All-Party Committee shall complete the full review of the Constitution begun by the two previous committees. In undertaking this review, the All-Party Committee will have regard to the following:*
>
> *a   the Report of the Constitution Review Group*
>
> *b   participation in the All-Party Committee would involve no obligation to support any recommendations which might be made, even if made unanimously*
>
> *c   members of the All-Party Committee, either as individuals or as Party representatives, would not be regarded as committed in any way to support such recommendations*
>
> *d   members of the All-Party Committee shall keep their respective Party Leaders informed from time to time of the progress of the Committee's work*
>
> *e   none of the parties in Government or Opposition would be precluded from dealing with matters within the All-Party Committee's terms of reference while it is sitting.*

The committee comprises ten TDs and four senators:

Denis O'Donovan, TD (FF), *chairman*
Senator Michael Finucane (FG), *vice chairman*
Barry Andrews, TD (FF)
James Breen, TD (IND)
Ciarán Cuffe, TD (GP)
Senator Brendan Daly (FF)
Senator John Dardis (PD)
Jimmy Devins, TD (FF)
Pádraic McCormack, TD (FG)
Arthur Morgan, TD (SF)
Senator Ann Ormonde (FF)
Jan O'Sullivan, TD (LAB)
Peter Power, TD (FF)
Senator Joanna Tuffy (LAB)

The secretariat is provided by the Institute of Public Administration:

Jim O'Donnell, *secretary*

While no constitutional issue is excluded from consideration by the committee, it is not a body with exclusive concern for constitutional amendments: the Government, as the executive, is free to make constitutional proposals at any time.

The All-Party Oireachtas Committee on the Constitution
Fourth Floor, Phoenix House
7-9 South Leinster Street
Dublin 2

Telephone: 01-662-5580
Fax: 01-662-5581
Email: info@apocc.irlgov.ie
Website: www.constitution.ie

Contents

Foreword

Having dealt with the right to life of the unborn in its *Fifth Progress Report: Abortion* in November 2000 and with private property provisions in its *Ninth Progress Report: Private Property* in April 2004, the committee continues its review of the Articles in the Constitution dealing with fundamental rights with this its *Tenth Progress Report: The Family*. Government concern with the issue was expressed by Frank Fahey TD, Minister of State, Department of Health and Children, in a letter to our then chairman Brian Lenihan TD, 20 June 1999 (see Appendix 1).

This report examines the changes that are occurring in Irish society and seeks to evaluate what, if any, changes are needed in the Constitution to enable the state to deal adequately with them.

I wish to thank the members of the public who made submissions to us and the witnesses who appeared at the oral hearings. I wish in particular to thank Dr Finola Kennedy and Gerard Hogan SC for their professional advice and help. I wish to thank the members of the committee for their dedicated participation in the work of this report and their unfailing courtesy at all times. The secretariat of the committee rendered us invaluable service.

Denis O'Donovan TD
Chairman
January 2006

THE FAMILY

Introduction

In order to provide the general context for its study of the family the committee invited written submissions from the public in a series of public notices in the national press (5–11 November 2004). The proposed deadline was 31 January 2005. A copy of the notice is reproduced in Appendix 2. The committee received 7,989 submissions, 7,886 from individuals, 103 from interest groups. It also received 16,143 petitions. The vast majority of these communications supported leaving the Articles related to the family unchanged. Some individuals and interest groups requested the committee to give them an opportunity to support their written submissions with oral presentations. The committee, anxious to inform itself as fully as possible, decided to hold hearings in public, availing of the recording facilities of the Houses of the Oireachtas. Accordingly the committee was reconstituted for the month of April 2005 as the Joint Committee on the Constitution by resolutions of both Houses of the Oireachtas.

The schedule for the public hearings was as follows:

Tuesday 19 April 2005
The Law Society of Ireland
Geoffrey Shannon
Joan O'Mahony
Rosemary Horgan
Colleen Farrell

Irish Society for the Prevention of Cruelty to Children
Paul Gilligan
Grace Kelly

Family Support Agency
Michael O'Kennedy SC
Muriel Walls
Pat Bennett

One Family
Dr Fergus Ryan
Karen Kiernan
Anne Bowen

Barnardos
Owen Keenan
Nora Gibbons
Geoffrey Shannon
Anne Conroy

AMEN
Mary Cleary
Frank McGlynn
Clem Roberts
Michael Scully

Kathy Sinnott, HOPE Project
Kathy Sinnott MEP

Wednesday 20 April 2005

Women's Health Council
Geraldine Luddy
Dr Cecily Kelleher
Alessandra Fantini

Adoption Board
John Collins
Kiernan Gildea
Patricia Smyth
Celia Loftus

TREOIR
Margaret Dromey
Eilish Craig
Margot Doherty
Natalie McDonnell

Thursday 21 April 2005

**Irish Episcopal Conference and Office of Public Affairs
of the Archdiocese of Dublin**
Mary Quinn
John Farrelly
Fr Paul Tighe
Fr Timothy Bartlett

Foróige
Sean Campbell
Seamus O'Brien
Dr Pat Dolan
Anne Marie Kelly

WITH (Women in the Home)
Catriona Lynch
Áine Uí Ghiollagáin

Mother & Child Campaign
Maria McMenamin
Niamh Ní Bhriain
Anne Green
Dr Seán Ó Domhnaill

GLUE
Mark Lacey
Dil Wickrcmasinghc
Adriana Avila
Mo Halpin

Immigrant Council of Ireland
Denise Charlton
Catherine Cosgrave

Irish Council for Civil Liberties
Aisling Reidy
Conor Power
Judy Walsh

Christian Solidarity Party
Cathal Loftus
Michael O'Brien

Friday 22 April 2005

AIM Family Services
Deirdre McDevitt
Maura Murray
Valerie O'Loughlin

Workers' Party
Pádraic Mannion
Mary Diskin
Andrew McGuinness
Gerry Grainger

Presbyterian Church in Ireland
Very Rev Dr Alistair Dunlop
Lindsay Conway OBE
Rev David Moore

Muintir na hÉireann
Richard Greene
Anne Shields
Dónal O'Driscoll
Colm Callanan

Men's Council of Ireland
Sam Carroll
Frank McGlynn

Gay Catholic Caucus
David Donnellan
Thomas Giblin
Michael Hayes

Brethern
David Joynt
Murray Robertson
Michael McMullan
Ben Watson
Dan Watson

European Life Network
Patrick Buckley
Olivia Connolly
Eleanor McFadden

Tuesday 26 April 2005

Ombudsman for Children
Emily Logan
Paul Bailey
Marianne Azema

Irish Human Rights Commission
Dr Maurice Manning
Suzanne Egan
Dr Alpha Connelly

Church of Ireland
Rt Rev MG Jackson
Sam Harper
Claire Burrows
Ven Robin Bantry White

IPPA, the Early Childhood Organisation
Irene Gunning
Marlene McCormack

Mothers at Home
Nora Bennis
Maire Burke
Theresa Heaney
Rose Ryan

Irish Senior Citizens' Parliament
Michael O'Halloran
Sylvia Meehan

Reformed Presbyterian Church of Ireland
Rev Mark Loughridge
Rev Raymond Blair

Wednesday 27 April 2005

National Women's Council of Ireland
Joanna McMinn
Marie Hainsworth
Orla O'Connor

Council for the Status of the Family
Louis Power
Lelia O'Flaherty
Eilis Bennett
David Bennett

Council on Social Responsibility of the Methodist Church in Ireland
Robert Cochran
Rev Rosemary Lindsay

Parental Equality
Liam Ó Gogáin
Paul Coleman
Jason Soraghan
Dominic McKevitt

National Youth Federation
Diarmuid Carney
Michael McLaughlin

Irish Foster Care Association
Anne Rennison
Pat Whelan

Family and Life
David Manly
Angela Keavney
Anna Maguire

Right Nation
Justin Barrett
Sinéad Dennehy
Denis O'Connor

Thursday 28 April 2005

Unmarried and Separated Fathers of Ireland
Ray Kelly
Donnacha Murphy
Dave Carroll
Eamonn Quinn

Age Action Ireland
David Stratton
Mary McColclough

Focus on the Family
Mervyn Nutley
Stephen Cardy
Cormac Ó Ceallaigh

Knights of St Columbanus
Charles B McDonald
Charles A Kelly

NCCRI
(National Consultative Committee on Racism and Interculturalism)
Philip Watt
Nobhule Nduka
Anna Visser

OPEN
Frances Byrne
Naomi Feeley

johnny
Pádraic Whyte
Conor Coughlan

Family and Media Association
W Ivo O'Sullivan
Gobnait Ó Grádaigh
Jacqueline Asgough

A number of interest groups that wished to appear before the committee but that could not do so in April were accommodated by the committee in meetings it arranged in its offices in Phoenix House, Dublin 2. The schedule of these meetings was as follows:

Thursday 26 May 2005

L.inc (Lesbians in Cork)
Mary Hogan
Angela O'Connell

Glen
Kieran Rose
Eoin Collins
Brian Sheehan
Keith O'Malley

Family First Association (Ireland)
Philomena Faughnan
Gerry Naughton
Maura McGurk
Edward Winter

The committee appreciates the generosity and forbearance of the staff of the Houses of the Oireachtas who undertook the extra substantial burden involved in the committee's public hearings: Kieran Coughlan, Clerk of the Dáil; Paul Conway, the Superintendent of the House; Ronan Lenihan and Gina Long, who acted as Clerks of the Joint Committee; Cliona O'Rourke, who directed the filming of the hearings, and Anne Robinson, the Editor of Debates. The committee is most grateful to Art O'Leary, Director of Committees, and Pádraic Donlon, who made a committee room in Leinster House available for the hearings.

Chapter 1

Changes in the demographic and social context of the family

This chapter sets out the demographic and social context of Articles 41 and 42 of the Constitution and presents the principal changes in family formation, marriage, births and other indicators of family life since 1937. It also examines the cultural context for the changes in family life, highlighting Irish entry into the EEC as a defining point of change. The changed nature of childhood and family life owing to extended participation in education is presented, because a shift has taken place from a low level of post-primary participation in 1937 to a point at which just 100 per cent of girls aged sixteen years and 91 per cent of boys aged sixteen years participate in full-time education. The consequences for the family of Articles 41 and 42 are considered, and finally, based on the material set out in the chapter, a number of key issues and questions relating to these Articles are raised.

1 Demographic and socio-economic context

The 1937 Constitution was embedded in the contemporary economic and social reality of a predominantly rural society in which agriculture provided the economic foundation. The bulk of the population was engaged in agriculture, either as farmers themselves, or as 'relatives assisting', that is family members effectively working for subsistence. In 1937, 100,000 holdings were between one and fourteen acres and family labour was vital. In 1937 the total population was just under 3 million. Today the population has exceeded 4 million for the first time since 1871. In 1937 the total labour force was 1.3 million; of those in employment, 614,000 or 50 per cent were in agriculture; 244,000 of those in agriculture were 'relatives assisting'. Seventeen per cent were engaged in industry and 33 per cent were in services. In 2003 the total labour force was 1.8 million; of those in employment only 6 per cent were in agriculture, while 28 per cent were in industry and 66 per cent were in services.

In every decade from the 1920s to the 1960s there was a substantial level of net emigration, that is a substantial excess of those leaving the country compared with those entering the country. This has had an impact on family formation. In the decade 1936 to 1946 average annual net migration was 19,000 or 190,000 for the decade. It has been estimated that two in every five children aged under fifteen years in 1945 had emigrated by 1971.[1] The fourteen-year

---

1   D. Garvey, 'The history of migration flows in the Republic of Ireland', *Population Trends* 39, Spring (1985), Table 3.

olds of the 1946 census would have reached their fiftieth birthdays by 1982. About 570,000 babies were born in Ireland in the 1930s. However, the 1981 census recorded just 313,000 people who were born in the 1930s. Among the many factors, including mortality, which affect the comparison, it is clear that emigration exerted a massive toll. With improved economic conditions in the 1960s, the outward flow of migration slowed and was reversed in the 1970s, a decade which experienced net immigration, including an inflow from Northern Ireland, in the wake of the crisis which erupted in Northern Ireland in 1969. Emigration resumed in the 1980s and by 1986 the net outflow just matched the natural increase in population, that is the excess of births over deaths, in that year. Between 1991 and 2002 the trend was reversed once more as a flow of immigrants began to exceed emigrants.[2]

Households

Before presenting the data on household formation the use of the term 'an teaghlach', or household, in the Irish text of the Constitution is considered. Two words for 'family' are used in the Irish text. They are 'an teaghlach' and, in the case of mothers of families, 'máithreacha clainne'. Turning first to 'an teaghlach', this word means both family and household, as it derives from the compound 'teg', a house, and 'slóg', a troop. In Article 41.2.1, 'teaghlach' is translated in English as 'home'; 'trína saol sa teaghlach' is translated by 'by her life within the home'. In Article 41.2.2, 'ar mháithreacha clainne', is translated by 'mothers', while 'dualgais sa teaghlach' is translated by 'duties in the home'. Turning to marriage, a comparison of the Irish and English texts throws up further matters relevant to the current discussion. Article 41.3.1 begins 'Ós ar an bPósadh atá an Teaghlach bunaithe', which is translated in English as, 'Since it is on Marriage that the Family is founded'.

Fergus Kelly in *A Guide to Early Irish Law* (1988), quoted in *A study of the Irish text*, by Micheál Ó Cearúil,[3] shows that several forms of sexual union (lánamhnas) are distinguished. In many of these unions property and sexual union are intimately linked. Kelly lists nine forms of sexual union and places at the top of the list 'union of joint property' into which both partners contribute movable goods. The woman in such a union is called a 'wife of joint authority'. Next come the 'union of a woman on man-property' into which the woman contributes little or nothing, and the 'union of a man on woman-property' into which the man contributes little or nothing. The fourth category is the 'union of a man visiting', a bit like cohabitation. In the fifth category the woman goes off with the man rather like an elopement, while in the sixth category the woman allows herself to be abducted. In the

---

2   Census, various.
3   Micheál O Cearúil (1999), *Bunreacht na hÉireann, A study of the Irish text*, p. 599, Stationery Office, Dublin.

seventh category the woman is secretly visited with her kin's consent, which is also given in the sixth category. The eighth and ninth unions are not marriage because they involve rape in one case and the union of the insane in the other.

It is worth noting that the word 'teaghlach' used in the Irish version of the Constitution for 'family' is a potentially inclusive word extending to kin, and coincides closely with definitions of 'family' in the census returns until 1979, whereby those resident in households on the census night were counted as a family, even though some blood relatives were excluded because they were absent on the night of the census. The wider concept of 'teaghlach' could also be viewed as including the extended family of grandparents and other relatives as distinct from the narrower concept of the 'nuclear' family.

The definition of the family used in the census at the time the Constitution was enacted, and for many subsequent decades, was closer to that of household. Writing in 1954, Dr R. C. Geary, Director of the Central Statistics Office, maintained that the term 'family', as used for census purposes, was a misnomer, and that it would be better to use the term 'household', and reserve the term 'family' for a group related by blood or marriage (consanguine or conjugal). According to the census a family was defined as 'any person or group of persons living in a single household ... and included in a separate census return as being in separate premises or part of premises'. Domestic servants and other employees who lived in the household, as well as temporary visitors, were included in the family, while on the other hand the family did not include members who might have been temporarily absent on the census night, e.g. as seasonal workers in Britain or children at boarding schools.[4] A revised definition of 'family' for census purposes was introduced in 1979 and this will be examined later in this chapter.

Table 1: Number and distribution of households in the state, 1936–2002

Size of household	1936 Number 000	1936 Per cent	2002 Number 000	2002 Per cent
One-person	60.6	9.4	277.6	21.6
Two-person	111.0	17.1	333.7	26.0
Three-person	111.5	17.2	227.8	17.7
Four-person	100.1	15.5	223.2	17.3
Five-person	82.9	12.8	134.9	10.5
Six-person and over	181.3	28.0	90.8	7.0
All Households	647.4	100	1,288.0	100

Source: CSO

4   R. C. Geary (1954/55), 'The Family in Irish Census of Population Statistics', *Journal of the Statistical and Social Inquiry Society of Ireland*, 19: 1–30.

Turning to the data, it emerges that between 1936 and 2002 the number of households in Ireland doubled, increasing from 647,000 in 1936 to 1,288,000 in 2002. Over the period the average size of the household fell from 4.31 persons to 2.94 persons. The number of households rose in every category from one-person to five-person households, but the number of households with six or more persons fell by half.

The most striking feature of the change in household composition is in the big increase in the share of one-person and two-person households and the decline in the share of the largest households. In 2002 the share of one-person and two-person households in total households had risen to just under 48 per cent from 26.5 per cent in 1936, that is a rise to close to one-half of all households from just over one-quarter in 1936. By contrast the share of households with six or more persons in total households fell from 28 per cent to 7 per cent over the period. The increase in one-person households reflects an increase both in young persons living separately from their families and an increase in elderly persons living alone.

Table 2: Composition of private households in 2002

Composition of household	000s	Per cent
One-person	277.6	21.6
Couple*	211.4	16.4
Couple* with children	489.5	38
Couple* with other persons	17.2	1.3
Couple* with children and other persons	44.3	3.4
Lone parent with children	131.2	3.4
Lone parent with children and other persons	19.4	1.5
Two or more family units	5.7	0.4
Non-family households	91.7	7.1
Total	1,288	100

Source: Census 2002
* Couples include both married and cohabiting couples

In 1936 about one in twelve persons aged sixty-five years and over lived alone compared with more than one in four in 2002. Partly reflecting the longer life expectancy of females almost one in three females over sixty-five now live alone. The largest category of households consists of couples, whether married or single, with children. They comprise over one in three of all households. The next largest category of households is that of single persons comprising one in five households. Elderly persons living alone represent an important component of one-person households, amounting to 41 per cent of all one-person households and accounting for nearly twenty-six per cent of persons aged sixty-five years and over.

Family units

The 1979 census was the first Irish census in which the population was classified by number and type of family unit. The family unit was defined as i) a man and wife, ii) a man and his wife together with one or more single children of any age, or iii) one parent together with one or more single children of any age. In 1986 the family unit was extended to include cohabitees with the addition of 'or couple' to the category 'man and wife'. The census definition of the family unit is both expansive and restrictive. It is expansive in that it includes couples who cohabit, a definition at variance with the Constitution. It is restrictive in so far as it excludes some consanguinous units which are not conjugal units. For example, a grandparent and a grandchild, or two sisters living in one household, do not constitute a family in the census definition, but, assuming the sisters were the fruits of a marriage union, they would constitute a family according to the Constitution. On the other hand, adopted children, resident in the family household on the night of the census, have always been counted as family members in the census, but because there was no legal adoption at the time of the Constitution in 1937, children who were adopted informally at the time could not be part of the constitutional family founded on the marriage of parents. From the time of The Adoption Act 1952 until The Adoption Act 1988, it was possible to adopt illegitimate children only, or orphans where both parents were dead. Under the 1988 Act it is possible to adopt children born within marriage in certain limited circumstances. Unlike adoption, fosterage has no place in the constitutional framework, yet it is vital to the family life for those directly concerned.[5]

Turning to the most recent census data on family units in 2002, as shown in Table 3, one quarter of family households with either a husband or wife or a cohabiting couple do not contain children. Over half of all family units contain a husband, wife and children while the remaining households are lone parent households or cohabiting couples with children. Of the 692,000 family units in which children are present, 73.5 per cent are composed of a husband, wife and children, while the other 26.5 per cent are composed of a lone mother with children (18.8%), lone father with children (3.4 %) and a cohabiting couple with children (4.3%). In 2002 a total of 325,305 children, or 22 per cent of children in family units, lived either in households where the adults were cohabiting or in lone parent households.

---

5 William Duncan, 1996, 'The constitutional protection of parental rights', *Report of the Constitution Review Group*, p. 622, Dublin, Stationery Office.

Table 3: Family units in private households, 2002

Type of family unit	Number of units	Per cent	Number of children	Per cent
Husband and wife without children	184,950	20	–	–
Cohabiting couple without children	47,907	5.2	–	–
Husband and wife with children	508,035	55	1,145,514	78
Cohabiting couple with children	29,709	3.2	51,725	3.5
Lone mother with children	130,364	14	233,516	16.0
Lone father with children	23,499	2.5	40,064	2.7
Total family units	924,464	100	1,470,819	100

Source: Census 2002

Marriage

The number of marriages taking place each year indicates the number of marriage-based family units which are formed. The majority of marriages are first-time marriages, but a number are marriages in which one or both partners had been married previously and where marriage ended either through death or divorce.

Table 4: Average annual number of marriages and marriage rate by decade since 1931

1931–40	14,359	4.9
1941–50	16,585	5.6
1951–60	15,742	5.4
1961–70	17,430	6.0
1971–80	21,562	6.8
1981–90	18,888	5.4
1991–95	16,345	4.6
1996–00	17,256	4.7
2003	20,302	5.1

Source: CSO

The number of marriages taking place in Ireland was at its lowest in the 1930s, a period of economic depression, intensified by the Economic War with Britain. The number picked up in the 1940s but dropped back in the 1950s as emigration soared. Marriage numbers and the marriage rate rose throughout the 1960s and into the 1970s, but in the 1980s marriage lost popularity and the number of marriages and the marriage rate continued to slide until the second half of the 1990s when marriage staged a recovery. The current level of marriages is at its highest point since the start of the 1980s. Some of the increase in marriage since the late 1990s may be due to a postponement factor from earlier years, as the average age of marriage has risen.

Cohabitation

There was a total of 77,600 family units comprising cohabiting couples in 2002 (Table 5), an increase of 31,300 on six years earlier. Almost two-thirds of these were childless couples, with a total of 51,700 children in the remaining one-third of the units.

The number of same-sex cohabiting couples was 1,300 in the 2002 census compared with 150 such couples in 1996. Two-thirds of these couples are male couples.

Table 5: Cohabiting couples by size of family unit, 2002

Number of children	000s
None	47.9
One	15.7
Two	8.8
Three or more	5.2
Total family units	77.6
Total children in family units	51.7

Source: CSO

Cohabiting couples accounted for 8.4 per cent of all family units in 2002 compared with 3.9 per cent in 1996. Those without children accounted for one in five of all childless couples in 2002, while those with children represented 5.5 per cent of all couples with children. The number of children living with cohabiting parents increased from 23,000 in 1996 to 51,000 in 2002. Just over three-quarters of cohabiting couples without children were unions in which both partners were single, while a further 5.8 per cent were separated. The corresponding proportions for cohabiting couples with children were 58.8 per cent and 11.5 per cent respectively in 2002.

Separation and divorce

An indication of the relative extent of marital breakdown is provided by expressing the number of separated and divorced persons as a percentage of the total number of ever-married persons. In 2002 this proportion stood at 7.5 per cent compared with 5.4 per cent six years earlier. Limerick City (11.7 per cent) had the highest rate of marital breakdown in the country followed by Dublin City (10.6 per cent), while Cavan (4.9 per cent) and Galway County (5.1 per cent) had the lowest rates in 2002.

Divorce was unavailable in Ireland prior to its legalisation in 1996. Divorce is now incorporated into the Constitution following the referendum in 1995. The 1986 Census was the first census to provide information on the breakdown of marriage. Prior to 1986, some information on marital breakdown was published in Labour Force Survey Reports since 1983 and in the *Report of the Joint Oireachtas Committee on Marital Breakdown*. In 1986 there were 37,000 separated persons, including a number who had obtained divorces elsewhere. By 1996 the number had grown to 88,000 and by 2002 the number had reached 134,000. It is clear that the number separated and divorced is growing rapidly. Between 1996 and 2002 the number married increased by 7.2 per cent, the number widowed grew by 1.3 per cent and the number separated, including divorced, grew by 53 per cent (Census 2002). Within the overall separated category the number of persons recorded as divorced more than trebled, from 9,800 to 35,1000, between 1996 and 2002, reflecting the legalisation of divorce in the state in 1996.

Lone-parent households

In 2002 there were 154,000 lone parent family units, of which 42 per cent were headed by a widowed person, 32 per cent by a separated/divorced person, and 24 per cent by a single person. Lone-parent families are not a new phenomenon. Because of the lower expectation of life in the early decades of the last century, many children grew up in one-parent households resulting from widowhood. Even though widowers are more likely to remarry than widows, in 1926, at the first census in the Free State, 8 per cent of fourteen-year-olds lived in households where the mother was dead and the father alive, so lone fathering is not an invention of the early twenty-first century. A second cause of lone parenthood is the break-up of existing marriages, which has been occurring with increasing frequency.

Lone parenthood also arises because of births outside marriage. However, many births outside marriage are to cohabiting couples. Compared with other EU countries, births outside marriage are above average in Ireland.[6] However, in a number of countries the proportion

---

6   M. Heanue (2000), 'Matters of Life and Death', in A. Redmond (ed.), *That was then, This is now. Change in Ireland, 1949–1999*, pp. 30–31, Central Statistics Office.

of births outside marriage is higher than in Ireland. At the turn of the millennium 65 per cent of births took place outside marriage in Iceland, a non-EU country, while the share is in the region of 50 per cent in Sweden, Norway and Denmark. In France the figure is just over 40 per cent and in Britain it is almost 40 per cent.

The spotlight is sometimes focused on births to young single mothers, so it is relevant to establish the facts. In Ireland the age of consent is 17 years and the age of marriage is 18 years. In 2002 there were just 300 births to women aged 16 years and under, all but 8 of which were non-marital births. With regard to the 8 marital births, it is possible that these births, or some of the births, were to women who had been married outside Ireland according to the laws prevailing in a different culture. Seven of the girls who gave birth in 2002 were aged 14 years; 56 girls were aged 15 years and 225 were aged 16 years. When births to girls aged 17 years are included, that is to girls below the legal age of marriage but not below the age of consent, there were close to 800 births, or 1.25 per cent of total births in 2002. All but 17 of these took place outside marriage.

Births at young ages are not a new phenomenon. Turning back to 1970 there was a total of 134 births to girls aged 16 years and under, almost evenly divided between marital and non-marital births. Until 1972, the permitted legal age for marriage for girls was 14 years. It was increased to 16 years in 1972 and to 18 years in 1986. Because the overall numbers of young teenage births are now predominantly outside marriage, it could be argued that there is some link between the increase in the marriage age and births to young women outside marriage. Shotgun weddings were not unknown in the past.

In order to marry below the age of eighteen years in Ireland, a court exemption is required. Exemptions are generally granted on cultural grounds, for example for members of the Travelling Community and for Romanies. Application may also be made to obtain recognition for what are sometimes called 'limping marriages'. In such cases a party to a marriage may be below the legal age required in Ireland, but meet the age requirements in the jurisdiction in which the marriage was performed, for example in Northern Ireland or the rest of the United Kingdom where the legal age for marriage is 16 years.[7]

Births

Total births fell fairly steadily from the early twentieth century until the 'baby boom' during World War II. The level rose sharply throughout the 1940s from 57,000 in 1940 to 69,000 in 1949 owing to a number of factors. Firstly, there was a reduction in emigration when war broke out. Secondly, a marked concentration of the increase in

---

7   Information from the Department of Health and Children.

registered births occurred in a single year, 1942, owing to the stemming of emigration in that year, a particularly unpleasant war year in Britain. The introduction of work permits contributed to a curbing of emigration, while the introduction of food rationing probably increased the accuracy of registration of births. The introduction of children's allowances for the third and each subsequent child in 1944 also provided an incentive to register births.

Table 7: Average annual number of births and birth rate per decade since 1931

Decade	Total number	Non-marital number	Total per 1,000	Non-marital as % of total
1931–40	57,105	1,893	19.3	3.3
1941–50	65,011	2,285	21.9	3.5
1951–60	61,700	1,220	21.2	2.0
1961–70	62,400	1,385	21.7	2.2
1971–80	69,400	2,633	21.8	3.8
1981–90	61,628	5,644	17.6	9.2
1991–95	50,044	9,656	14.1	19.3
1996–00	53,222	15,299	14.4	28.7
2003	61,517	19,313	15.5	31.4

Source: CSO

Births rose to a twentieth-century peak of 74,000 in 1980 and then fell continuously by more than one-third to below 48,000 in 1994. In 2003 there were 10,800 more births than there had been in 1996. Of these 4,300 were within marriage, and 6,500 were outside marriage. It is difficult to interpret the recent increase in births: while age-specific fertility of women in the age groups 20–24 and 25–29 has fallen in the 1990s, age-specific fertility for the age groups 30–34 and 35–39 has increased, reflecting a postponement factor. Some of the increase may be due to the return of former migrants as well as the inflow of foreign nationals.

The increase in births outside marriage has been very striking, rising from under 2,000 per annum in the 1930s to almost 20,000 in 2003, or from 3 per cent to 31 per cent of total births. The decline in births within marriage has been equally striking, falling from 70,700 to 42,200 between 1980 and 2003. In 1996 births within marriage increased for the first time in nearly twenty years. The overall drop in births is linked to the decrease in family size. In 1955, 21 per cent of births were first births. In 1998 first births accounted for 40 per cent (21,000 out of 53,000) of births. In 1955 31 per cent of births were fifth births compared with only 5 per cent in 1998. In 1962 there were 2,000 births to mothers with ten children and over, compared with 55 such births in 1998 (Heanue, ibid).

An increase in permanent childlessness is becoming evident, as has already occurred in continental countries and in the United Kingdom. In the UK the likelihood of childlessness has increased steadily over the past fifty years. It is estimated that 17 per cent of women born in the UK in 1955 are childless and that 21 per cent of those born in 1965 will remain childless. In Germany it is estimated that of women now entering their child-bearing years, 25 per cent will remain childless.

The average age of a mother at first birth fell in the 1960s considerably below the level of the 1930s and 1940s, but has been rising in recent decades. Overall it was above 28 years in 2003; 31 years within marriage and almost 25 years outside marriage. At the same time the absolute number of teen births has been rising. Ninety per cent of all births are to women aged 20–39. The age-specific fertility rate for 20–24 year old women began to decline in 1970 while for women aged 25–29 years the decline began in 1965. The fall in fertility is marked in the age group 25–29. In 1971 one-quarter in that age group gave birth compared with one-tenth in 1996 (Heanue, ibid). In both groups the decline has begun to taper off while the long-term decline in the age-specific fertility rate of women aged 30–34 and 35–39 was halted in 1994 and since then has moved upwards. The total fertility rate (TFR) declined from 4.03 in 1965 to 2.08 in 1989, the first year in which fertility fell below replacement level. The TFR fell further to 1.85 in 1995. Since then it increased to 1.93 in 1998.

Non-national births: In the period 1996–2002 net migration in the age bracket 25–44 years amounted to over 100,000 – 54,000 males and 52,300 females. Many of these were Irish persons living abroad who returned to Ireland. Many others were non-Irish-born immigrants. An increasingly important feature of the overall births picture is the increase in births to non-nationals. Data on births to non-nationals are not readily available from the CSO, but may be obtained directly from maternity hospitals. By definition this means that home births are excluded.

It is only in the past couple of years that maternity hospitals have produced separate figures for births to non-nationals. An idea of the significance of births to non-nationals may be gained from the following. Between 2001 and 2002 total births increased from 57,900 to 60,500, an increase of 2,600. In the same year births to non-nationals in the three major maternity hospitals in Dublin – the Coombe Women's Hospital, Holles Street and the Rotunda – increased by over 4,000. In those hospitals births to non-nationals accounted for 20 per cent of total deliveries or close to that share. In the main centres outside Dublin there was also a significant number of births to non-nationals.

Infant and maternal mortality: The *Report* of the Department of Local Government and Public Health for 1934–37 painted a bleak picture of infant and maternal mortality. Throughout the nineteen thirties deaths of infants below one year averaged about 4,000 per year. In 2002 the number of deaths to infants below one year was 305. The *Report* for 1934–37 highlighted the fact that infant mortality rates varied markedly according to whether the child was legitimate or illegitimate, possibly related to the poorer socio-economic conditions, as well as maternal health. In 1930 one out of every four illegitimate children died in the first year of life, their mortality rate being four times higher than that of children born of married parents. In 1934 a total of 2,030 children were born out of wedlock. One year later, 538, or more than one in four, were dead.

In 1951 infant deaths, at close to 3,000, exceeded deaths from tuberculosis by 800. Deaths from tuberculosis declined more rapidly than infant deaths so that in 1955 there were 2,264 infant deaths and 889 deaths from tuberculosis. Seventeen of the infant deaths were due to tuberculosis; the majority of infant deaths were due to congenital malformations, immaturity and pneumonia.

In 2002 there were five maternal deaths. In the 1930s maternal deaths averaged around 200 per year. In 1931 the number was 246 and in 1941 it was 182. From the 1950s onwards the use of penicillin and other drugs dramatically reduced maternal mortality. The causes of maternal mortality, which tended to be higher in rural than in urban areas due to poorer access to medical facilities, included haemorrhage at childbirth, toxaemia and puerperal infection.

Adoption: There was no legal adoption in Ireland at the time the Constitution was enacted. Legal adoption was introduced into Ireland with the passing of the Adoption Act 1952, which provided for the establishment of the Adoption Board, An Bórd Uchtála, with powers to make adoption orders. Prior to 1952 informal adoption, as well as fosterage, existed on a limited scale with adoptions being arranged through private adoption societies, usually affiliated to one of the Churches, most frequently the Catholic Church. The Adoption Act 1952, together with further Acts of 1964, 1974, 1976 and 1988, comprise the law governing adoption in Ireland. Since the passing of the 1952 Act, 40,000 adoption orders have been made, an average of 1,000 per year, with the annual number varying from a high point of almost 1,500 in 1967, to less than 300 in 2002. In 2002, 266 adoption orders were made, of which 167 orders related to family adoptions, that is by birth mothers and their husbands or other relatives.

The Adoption Act 1952 provided for the adoption of children born out of wedlock and for children both of whose parents were dead. The Act contained a condition which required that adopting parents 'were of the same religion as the child and his parents or, if the child is illegitimate, his mother'. In effect the measure prevented couples in a marriage where spouses were of different religions, from adopting a child. Subsequently, following a High Court case, this element of the Act was found to be unconstitutional in that it discriminated against those in so-called 'mixed marriages', that is marriages between persons from different Churches. A new Adoption Act in 1974 repealed the religious clause in the 1952 Act.

Illegitimacy was central to adoption. Adoption was largely a method of providing homes with a father and a mother for illegitimate children while at the same time meeting the needs of in general, but not exclusively, infertile couples. Between 1952 and the Adoption Act 1988 children born within marriage could only be adopted if both their father and their mother were dead. At the high point of adoption in 1967 when almost 1,500 adoption orders were made, the number of orders was almost identical with the number of illegitimate births in that year. In 1973 when the allowance was introduced for an unmarried mother who kept her child, the number of adoptions was over 1,400, not very different from the 1967 level. Gradually the number of adoption orders began to decline and, significantly, of the adoption orders made, the share of orders made in respect of family adoptions rose dramatically. Family adoptions refer to adoptions made by birth mothers and their husbands, and by other relatives including grandparents, brothers, sisters, uncles and aunts. Over the recent past the total number of adoption orders made fell from 715 in 1987 to 266 in 2002 of which a majority were family adoptions. In 2002 there were also 399 orders made for eligibility and suitability to adopt outside the state, that is for foreign adoptions.

The Adoption Board has expressed concern regarding the position of birth fathers in relation to adoption. The Board states in its *Report* for 2002:

> As noted in its 2000 and 2001 reports it remains the Board's view that adoption is not always the ideal solution in step-parent situations and that some other legal means should be devised for establishing the rights of the birth mother's husband without extinguishing those of the birth father ....

> The Board again calls on the Minister to explore the possibility of introducing amending legislation to allow the Board to attach conditions to the making of an adoption order to ensure that a birth father can have continuing access to his child after the making of an adoption order.[8]

---

8   *Report of An Bord Uchtála* (The Adoption Board), 2002, pp. 7–8, Dublin, Stationery Office.

Notwithstanding amending Acts, adoption procedures remain rooted in the 1952 Act and the nature of the adoption system derives from the attitudes and customs of the 1950s. Central to these attitudes was the supremacy of the marriage-based family, the constitutional cornerstone of society.

Men and women in the home and in the workforce

The model of family life incorporated into the Constitution is one in which the woman cares for home and children. This reflected the social reality of the time when few married women were in the workforce and priority was given to jobs for male breadwinners. A bar against married women national teachers was introduced in 1933. The Conditions of Employment Act 1936 set down quite stringent restrictions on the employment of women aged eighteen years and over and girls. In due course all these restrictions were lifted, mainly in the wake of Irish entry into the EEC.

In 2003 there were over 5,000 men classified as being on 'home duties'. As with women the number of men on 'home duties' has declined in recent years. The number was over 9,000 in 1999. In 2003, just over one million men were classified as 'at work'. However a strict division on the basis of 'Principal economic status' fails to convey the actual situation of those fathers and mothers who combine parenting and caring for others with participation in the workforce.

The changes in female labour force participation can be categorised into three phases: pre-1971; the twenty years from 1971 to 1991; and the more recent years. Much of the increase in the participation of women in the 1970s was associated with the abolition of the marriage bar against women in public sector jobs. Traditionally for women marital status has been an important determinant of whether a woman was or was not in the workforce or on 'home duties'. Five per cent of married women were in the paid workforce in 1937 compared with almost 50 per cent today. Of those aged 25–34 years and 35–44 years, 65 per cent and 63 per cent respectively of married women were in the workforce in 2003.

The proportion of women aged fifteen years and over who were in the workforce – just 33 per cent – changed little between 1936 and 1991, but increased sharply to 47 per cent in 2003. The proportion engaged in home duties in 1936 was only slightly higher than the proportion so engaged in 1991, but there was a marked drop between 1991 and 2003, to less than 35 per cent. The share of women on home duties had risen to a high of over 60 per cent in 1971 and so has almost halved since then.

Table 6: Females classified by principal economic status, 1936–2003 (per cent)

Economic status	1936	1971	1991	2003
Labour force	32.8	27.3	32.9	46.6
Not labour force, of which:	67.2	72.7	67.1	53.5
home duties	51.5	60.2	49.1	34.8
at school/students	3.8	8.6	11.6	12.5
retired and others	12.0	3.9	6.5	6.2

Source: Derived from Census data for 1936, 1971 and 1991, females aged fourteen years and over in 1936 and 1971, aged fifteen years and over in 1991; data for 2003 are from CSO *Statistical Yearbook*, 2004, females aged fifteen years and over.

Table 7 shows the labour force participation of women by marital status aged sixteen years and over since 1971. In 2003, 48 per cent of married women and 59 per cent of separated/divorced women were in the workforce. An increasing number of women in the workforce are mothers, including mothers of very young children. Over half of all mothers in Ireland with children aged from birth to sixteen years work; almost 28 per cent are in full-time employment. For mothers with very young children aged from birth to three years, the proportion in work is over 50 per cent, with 26 per cent in full-time employment.[9]

Table 7: Labour force participation of women by marital status, 1971–2003

Year	Single %	Married %	Widowed %	Separated/divorced %	Total %
1971	59.8	7.5	19.3	na	27.3
1981	56.4	16.7	11.4	na	29.7
2003	63.3	48.0	10.5	58.9	50.8

Source: CSO

The following is a brief summary of the main demographic changes since 1937.

- The total number of households has risen, with the biggest increase occurring in one-person and two-person households and a decline in households with five or more persons. One in ten households in 1937 was a one-person household, compared with more than one in five today.

9   W. Adema, 2003, *Babies and Bosses*, p. 48, Paris, OECD.

- In 1937 less than one in ten persons aged sixty-five years and over lived alone; today over one in four of the over sixty-fives live alone, with one in three women over 65 living alone.
- Of total family units in which children were present in 2002, just under three-quarters are composed of husband, wife and children, while over one-quarter are either lone parents with children or cohabiting couples with children.
- One of the few indicators which is closely similar then and now is the age of a woman at first marriage – just twenty-nine years in 1937 and slightly below twenty-nine years today.
- Both the marriage rate at 5.4 per 1,000, and the birth rate at 20.4 per 1,000, were higher in 1937 than they are today at 4.5 and 14.0 respectively.
- A striking feature with regard to marriage is the rise in marriage breakdown.
- Three per cent of births took place outside marriage, compared with 32 per cent today.
- Average family size was between 3 and 4 children compared with 1.6 today.
- The nature of adoption has changed with a majority of adoptions being family adoptions, and an increasing number of adoptions of children from outside Ireland.
- The proportion of women who work full time in the home has declined, especially in the past decade and especially among younger women.

2 Cultural context: State-Catholic Church consensus followed by split in consensus

While the rural and agricultural dominated the economic context in which the people lived and worked in the twenty-six counties of the Irish Free State in 1937, the Catholic ethos imbued the value system at a time when 93 per cent of the population was Catholic and participation in the Church, as measured by attendance at Sunday mass, was very high. The dominant social thinking of the time, pre-eminently as expressed in the papal encyclical, *Quadragesimo Anno*, published in 1931, favoured 'subsidiarity' – that the state should offer support or help (*subsidium*) to smaller groups, including the family, but should not supplant them.

But it was not only in Ireland, or specifically within the Catholic Church, that what would be nowadays regarded as a conservative vision of society could be found. In 1935, two years before the enactment of the Constitution, prohibition against the importation and sale of contraceptives had been introduced. But similar legislation had been introduced earlier in France, Belgium and Italy while there was provision for limited access in Britain. Restrictive legislation had yet to be introduced in Germany and Spain. Nor was emphasis on the traditional role of women in the home a specifically conservative Catholic view in 1937. In the same year as the Irish Constitution passed into law in 1937, *The Irish Times*, then the liberal Protestant newspaper, had this to say on its Leader page:

> Some day, please Heaven! The nation will be so organised that work will be available for every man, so that he may marry and assume the burdens of a home, and for every woman until she embarks upon her proper profession – which is marriage. In that more prosperous nation there will be no question of the woman who 'will not allow marriage to interfere with her career'.[10]

Looking back on the sixty-eight years that have elapsed since 1937, the period might be divided decade by decade for purposes of analysis, but a broader division also suggests itself, marked by the entry of Ireland into the EEC in 1973, at the midway point in the period. In 1972, the year before Ireland joined the EEC, the retirement took place of Dr John Charles McQuaid as Archbishop of Dublin. Dr McQuaid had been Archbishop of Dublin since 1940, just a few years after the enactment of the Constitution to which he had made some contribution. In some respects, he personified 'Catholic Ireland' and his retirement, followed shortly afterwards by his death, symbolised the passing of an era. In the years from 1937 until Ireland entered the EEC, there was a tendency to emphasise the differences between Ireland and Britain. Ireland was Catholic, rural and agricultural while Britain was Protestant, urban and industrial. The shift away from agriculture and the transformation of the economy began to narrow the differences on the economic front, while the changes in the Church after Vatican II led to a more ecumenical approach, as for example the dropping of the ban on attendance by Catholics at Trinity College Dublin. Furthermore the Catholic Church itself began to drop the title 'Catholic' from some of its organisations. For example the Dublin Institute of Catholic Sociology was rebranded as the Dublin Institute of Adult Education and the Catholic Marriage Advisory Council was rebranded as ACCORD. Notwithstanding the changes, 88 per cent of the population gave their religion as 'Catholic' at the 2002 census. Over 5 per cent of the population either declared that they had no religion or did not state their religion. Church of Ireland members accounted for less than 3 per cent of the population, while Muslims were less than 0.5 per cent. The presence of almost 20,000 Muslims adds a dimension to Irish society which did not exist in 1937.

From the perspective of family change in Ireland, entry into the EEC in 1973 represents a defining point. The year was a landmark year in regard to several aspects of the family. It was the year when the highest marriage rate for the twentieth century, 7.5 per 1,000,

10 *Irish Times*, 22 February, 1937.

was recorded (the absolute number of marriages peaked at just 23,000 in 1974). It was the year in which the marriage bar in the public service which obliged women to leave employment on marriage was removed. It was also the year in which judgment was granted in the McGee case, which led to legislation in 1979 to overturn the ban on contraceptives, in place since 1935. It was also the year in which an allowance for an unmarried mother who reared her child on her own was introduced. The school-leaving age was raised to fifteen years in 1972 and the following year, 1973, was the year in which the first cohort of beneficiaries of free post-primary education left school. These changes had a marked impact on the family in the past quarter century. In particular, they influenced the lifestyle choices and opportunities for women. Prior to EEC entry Ireland was still an agricultural society in which the family farm provided the basic livelihood for many, although the shift away from agriculture was already well under way. The agricultural policy of the EEC essentially encouraged the development of larger farms and hastened the demise of the traditional smaller family farm.

A number of changes are of particular significance:

1   the shift from values which sought to minimise the involvement of the state in the family to values which seek to involve the state through laws and supports in every aspect of family life from childcare facilities to care of older people
2   the provision for divorce in the Constitution under certain circumstances
3   the abolition of most of the consequences of illegitimacy
4   the major shift in policy from encouraging women to engage in 'home duties' to a prioritisation of workforce participation.

1   A shift in values

Articles 41 and 42 which deal with the Family and Education were among the most innovatory in the entire Constitution. The Constitution of 1922 which was replaced by that of 1937 contained nothing at all about the family and marriage and its references to education were more limited. Historian, Joe Lee, states that 'The social clauses of the constitution blended prevailing Catholic concepts with popular attitudes rooted in the social structure'.[11] The social thinking of the papal encyclical, *Quadragesimo Anno* (1931), which favoured 'subsidiarity', was published against a background in which the drums of bolshevism, communism and totalitarianism, including an attempt to abolish the family in Russia after the Russian Revolution, throbbed in the background.[12] In the general election campaign of 1932, Fianna Fáil included in its manifesto a statement to the effect that it had 'no leaning towards Communism

11 J. J. Lee (1989), *Ireland 1912–1985*, Cambridge, Cambridge University Press.
12 N. S. Timasheff (1946), *The Great Retreat*, Boston: MA, E. P. Dutton.

and no belief in Communist doctrines'.[13] The intention of Article 41 and Article 42 was to defend the family against unwarranted interference by the state. Any suggestion that the government might attempt to influence family size, for example, would have been anathema to the social thinking behind the Constitution.

That Article 41 sought to protect the family from external forces was the approach taken by Finlay CJ in *L v L* [1992] 2 IR 77:

> Neither Article 41.1.1° – 2° purports to create any particular right within the family, or to grant to any individual member of the family rights, whether property or otherwise, against other members of the family, but rather deals with the protection of the family from external forces.

From the foundation of the state to the enactment of the 1937 Constitution a broad consensus existed regarding the values which should inform laws and policies. This led to a close similarity, though not identity, between the laws of the Catholic Church and the state. Until the latter part of the twentieth century, the areas of marriage, homosexuality, contraception and abortion were ones in which the laws of the state supported the teaching of the Catholic Church, although in the case of marriage there were important differences, for example regarding age of marriage and nullity of marriage.

Church teaching on the nature of the family and the role of men and women fitted well into the agrarian context and into the domain of the traditional breadwinner-father family. When the people supported what the hierarchy and the clergy prescribed, it often coincided with economic imperatives. In a clear insight the historian, K. H. Connell, writing on the strict sexual code in the century following the Famine, makes the following statement:

> But, for all the power of Church and State, so formalised a code would hardly have been adopted so generally if it were at variance with social and economic needs: indeed, the peasant's respect for the Catholic code as transmitted to him has sprung, not least, from its compatibility with his patriarchal and material ambition.[14]

For at least the first half of the twentieth century, the emphasis in Church social teaching was on independent, self-reliant families, free from state intervention. Changes in emphasis in Church teaching coincided with changes in Church leadership, particularly with the advent of Pope John XXIII, following the death of Pope Pius XII in 1958. The effects of the Second Vatican Council

---

13 Fianna Fáil election manifesto 1932.
14 K. H. Connell (1968), 'Catholicism and Marriage in the Century after the Famine', in K. H. Connell, *Irish Peasant Society*, p. 158, Oxford, Clarendon Press.

continue to reverberate, as individual Catholics have been challenged to think more for themselves and as the blanket condemnation of state intervention in family life has withered. Public opinion moved in a more liberal direction, reflecting the growing liberalism of ordinary Catholics whose behaviour drifted steadily away from strict observance of Catholic tenets, especially in regard to patterns of sexual behaviour. Sunday is, for example, for an increasing number, another working day, and that has direct consequences for families. Rev Professor Liam Ryan, Emeritus Professor of Sociology at University College Maynooth, identifies three ways in which Vatican II was a major influence on the values and attitudes of Irish Catholics:

> ... it revealed to many Catholics the possibility of a private world of conscience and behaviour; it stressed that the Church was not merely the pope and bishops but the entire people of God whose common convictions carry an inner truth of their own; and it transformed religious thinking from being introverted and pessimistic to be outward-looking and optimistic.[15]

Legislation was gradually introduced, or earlier legislation repealed, so that the laws of the land reflect those of a pluralist society. Among the most significant of these changes from the point of view of the present discussion are the following: the legalisation of contraception on a limited basis in 1979 and subsequent expansion of availability in the 1980s; the abolition of most of the consequences of illegitimacy in 1987, the decriminalisation of homosexual relations in 1993, and the introduction of a provision in the Constitution which permits divorce, following a referendum in 1995.

2 Divorce

At the time of drafting the *Report of the Constitution Review Group* (the Whitaker Report), litigation on the divorce referendum was proceeding and so the position regarding divorce was unclear.[16] Provision for divorce came with the Family Law (Divorce) Act 1996 which became law on 27 February 1997. From the point of view of the family Articles in the Constitution, the introduction of divorce has been the most significant change since 1937, because it has effectively redefined marriage. Marriage according to the law is no longer 'til death us do part; rather it is until death or divorce. This point merits reflection. When it is stated that the family in the Constitution is based on marriage, it must be remembered that 'marriage' in 2005 differs from marriage in 1937 in the most

---

15 L. Ryan (1984), 'The Changing Face of Irish Values', in M. Fogarty et al (eds), *Irish Values and Attitudes. The Irish Report of the European Value Systems Study*, p. 104 Dublin.
16 *Report of the Constitution Review Group* (1996), pp. 320–321, Dublin, Stationery Office.

fundamental respect. Today marriage can be, and increasingly is, terminated by divorce. In this respect marriage has moved closer to cohabitation in that both can be terminated on the initiative of one of the parties, albeit subject to more restrictions in the case of marriage. Second or subsequent families resulting from marriage, including spouses and stepbrothers and stepsisters, as well as lone parents created following divorce, must now be part of the 'family' recognised by the Constitution, because they are creations of a constitutional provision. With easy divorce available in many jurisdictions, the dividing line between marriage and cohabitation is no longer so clearcut and, in the event of break-up, cohabitation presents less potential legal difficulty. The growth in cohabitation in Ireland has been marked, with close to 80,000 family units, or over 8 per cent of all family units, now based on cohabitation.

The intrinsic logic of Articles 41 and 42 of the 1937 Constitution, has been fractured by behavioural changes, but it received the coup de grâce with the introduction of divorce. The family in the Constitution is now based on a potentially temporary arrangement. The family in the Constitution has already been redefined.

3 Consequences of illegitimacy

Because the position of children is central to the family, it is worth reflecting further on the changes made following the Status of Children Act in 1987. Another reason for reflecting on the matter is because it touches closely on the position of fathers of children born outside marriage. In 1984 the Supreme Court ruled that illegitimate children had no succession rights in respect of their father's estate where their father died intestate. An unmarried man died intestate, leaving a daughter, sisters and a brother and it was argued on behalf of the daughter that the Succession Act 1965 should be interpreted to permit an illegitimate child to succeed to her father's estate. If this was not accepted, it was argued that the Act was unconstitutional in that it discriminated against the child. The Supreme Court held that the Succession Act distinguished between legitimate and illegitimate children, and that the Act gave no rights of succession to a father's estate to an illegitimate child. All persons had to be treated equally before the law but the distinction made between the rights of children born in and out of marriage had to be considered in the light of the Act, one of the purposes of which was to safeguard the inheritance rights of married persons and of the children of a marriage. The court ruled that the Oireachtas, by acting to protect the legitimate family was acting in accordance with Article 41 of the Constitution.

In 1983 the Law Reform Commission had argued that existing law could not be justified in protecting the institution of marriage by denying the rights of innocent persons, namely 'children born outside marriage,' and in the opinion of the Commission the

Constitution would not require such a conclusion. The Law Reform Commission made a far-reaching proposal 'that the legislation remove the concept of illegitimacy from the law and equalise the rights of children born outside marriage with those of children born within marriage'. The Commission was aware that this would mean the recognition of the parental relationship 'in cases which the law in many countries has been reluctant to recognise – namely where children are born as a result of adulterous or incestuous unions'. The Commission stated 'in our view it should be open to the mother, a man alleging that he is the father, the child, or any person with a proper interest, to take proceedings seeking a declaration as to parenthood'. The Commission recommended that in proceeding to establish parenthood the father and the mother should be compellable witnesses, and that it should be possible to ask for a declaration of parenthood 'at any time during the joint lives of the parent and child, and where either dies, within six years of the death, where a share in the estate is being claimed'.

The Status of Children Act was passed in 1987. The principle underlying this Act is to place children whose parents have not married each other on the same footing, or as nearly so as possible, as the children of married parents in the areas of guardianship, maintenance and property rights. The non-marital child will first have to prove his/her claim in court. The Act provides a means of appointing the father of a non-marital child as joint guardian with the child's mother by applying to a court. Where the mother consents and the father has been entered on the births' register as the father, joint guardianship can be effected with the minimum formality. The non-marital child of a testator is also given the right to apply for just provision under The Succession Act. It is worth noting that the Status of Children Act 1987 differs in at least one important feature from the recommendations of the Law Reform Commission on the matter of illegitimacy. The main difference is that the Law Reform Commission recommended prima facie that the father of an illegitimate child should be in the same position as the father of a legitimate child and it was up to the mother to apply to the court if this position was to be altered. The Status of Children Act puts the onus the other way.

The Constitution Review Group gave a number of reasons for not recommending the granting to non-marital fathers the same rights as those of non-marital mothers. Firstly, it would 'include fatherhood resulting from rape, incest, or sperm donorship'[17] and secondly, it might include fathers who have not had a 'stable relationship with the mother prior to birth, or subsequent to birth with the child' (ibid). Social researcher, Kieran McKeown, contests the first reason as relating to exceptional circumstances.[18]

17 *Report of the Constitution Review Group* (1996), p. 326, Dublin, Stationery Office.
18 K. McKeown (2001),'Families and Single Fathers in Ireland', *Administration*, 49, 1:15.

Presumably the point could also be made that rape and incest can occur within marriage and, likewise, a married couple could decide to avail themselves of donor sperm. But these must be regarded as highly unusual circumstances. With regard to the second reason, McKeown says that responsibility for the relationship between the parents rests on both the mother and the father, while with regard to the relationship with the child, it may not be possible for a father to establish a relationship if no right to establish such a relationship exists, because a father might be prevented from so doing.

4 Workforce participation

While the Constitution deplored the possibility that economic necessity might force a woman out of her home to take up employment, the Commission on Emigration which reported in 1954 remarked in a practical tone that if a woman could continue in work after marriage, the additional income might facilitate earlier marriage and give a sense of greater security: 'If, therefore, it were the custom here for women to remain in employment after marriage, it is probable that marriage rates would improve'.[19] However, it is worth noting that the Commission also suggested that the ultimate demographic effect of more widespread employment of married women was far from certain:

> . . . it is possible that the fertility rate would decrease. Indeed, the long-term social and even economic implications must remain matters of conjecture and controversy. The effect on the home and family has also to be remembered (ibid).

The Commission expressed the belief that the removal of the marriage bar in the civil service, the banks and for teachers would help to raise the marriage rate. All these changes occurred and the labour force participation of married women increased while marital fertility declined.

The removal of the restrictions on the employment of women, in particular of married women, began with the removal of the bar against married women national teachers in 1958. A series of significant changes in regulations governing the employment of women was introduced following Irish entry into the EEC in 1973. On 31 July 1973, shortly after Ireland entered the EEC, the marriage bar in the civil service was ended. The Anti-Discrimination (Pay) Act 1974 came into operation in December 1975 and established the right of men and women to equal pay for equal work. On 1 July 1977 the Employment Equality Act came into operation and prohibited discrimination on grounds of sex or marital status in

---

19 Commission on Emigration and Other Population Problems (1954), p. 81, Dublin, Stationery Office.

recruitment, training or provision of opportunities for promotion. Other important Acts were the Unfair Dismissals Act 1977, and the Maternity (Protection of Employees) Act 1981. The Unfair Dismissals Act protects employees, including pregnant employees, from unfair dismissal by laying down criteria and providing for an adjudication and redress system. The Maternity Act was of particular importance in ensuring the right of a woman to return to work following the birth of a child.

Changes in the system of taxation of married couples subsequent to the *Murphy* case in 1980 have facilitated the growth in dual earner married couples, or at any rate reduced the tax disincentives which existed prior to the *Murphy* judgment. The nub of the *Murphy* case was that for tax purposes the incomes of husband and wife were added together and taxed as a single income. The result was that the joint income of a married couple was subject to higher tax because it reached higher tax bands more quickly than the same total income if earned by two single people. In his High Court decision, Mr Justice Hamilton held that Section 192 of the Income Tax Act 1967, which obliged a husband and wife to pay more tax on their combined salaries than they would if they were single, was unconstitutional. In the 1980 Budget the benefits of the court decision were extended to *all* married couples by the then Minister for Finance, George Colley, by granting to married couples double the personal allowance of a single person, whether or not both husband and wife were in paid employment. In a change introduced in Budget 2000, Finance Minister, Charlie McCreevy, moved towards individualisation of the tax code by favouring couples with two incomes and rowing back on the manner in which Colley had implemented the *Murphy* judgment. The minister contended that the change would encourage more married women to participate in the workforce.

3 Education

Article 42 of the Constitution endorses the family as the primary and natural educator of the child. The Article, in keeping with the ethos of the Constitution to protect the family from state interference and as guardian of the common good, requires that children receive a certain minimum education, moral, intellectual and social. The 'certain minimum' is not defined in the Constitution. Article 42.4 says that the state shall provide for free primary education and shall endeavour to supplement and give reasonable aid to private and corporate educational initiative. In the small family farm context child labour was important and many children were drawn away from school into work. Under the School Attendance Act 1926 every child was required to attend school from the age of six to fourteen years. In 1937 the school leaving age was fourteen years and remained thus until 1972 when it was raised to fifteen years. An Inter-Departmental Committee on Raising the School-Leaving Age (IDCRA), which reported in 1935, found the position in Ireland closely similar to that in other European countries. A key issue for the Committee was the link between agricultural occupations and the school-leaving age, in particular 'how far juvenile labour is indispensable to the farming community'.[20] At the time there were several thousand juveniles, a majority of whom were boys aged fourteen and fifteen years, engaged in agriculture. The overwhelming majority of young persons in agricultural occupations were sons and daughters, or other relatives, of farmers. The bulk of these juveniles worked on farms under thirty acres in size. The importance of this juvenile or child labour varied considerably by area. Such labour was less important to farmers in areas where the holdings were larger, but it was of great importance on the small holdings along the Western seaboard. In County Clare, for example, there were large numbers of smallholders entirely dependent on family labour and 'many such farmers look forward to the time when the eldest boy will be 14 years old, and it would be a serious matter to them if the school-leaving age were raised'. The Committee viewed juvenile labour in agriculture as 'indispensable and its withdrawal would be a serious hardship to parents' (IDCRA, 1935: 16). An influential factor in deciding against a recommendation to raise the school-leaving age was the potential hardship that would ensue for poor parents who depended on the labour of their children. Another objection was the potential cost to the state:

> The most serious economic issue that would arise from the raising of the school-leaving age and the withdrawal of juveniles from employment would be the hardship which it would cause parents whose circumstances were poor.[21]

Furthermore, the Committee observed that if juveniles were compelled to go to school instead of to work, it would be almost inevitable that there would be a demand for maintenance allowances and that the cost of such a scheme would be prohibitive. Even if the cost were not prohibitive, there was a philosophical argument against such a scheme: 'We think it would be entirely wrong in principle to start young people in life with the conception that the State is responsible for their support'.

The importance of the contribution of children to family income was also remarked on by the Commission of Inquiry into the Reformatory and Industrial School System, which reported in 1936. The Commission's report stated that at a time when the statutory minimum period of detention in a reformatory was three years, justices were often reluctant to commit for three years a young person who, but for his sentence, might be contributing to family

20 IDCRA (1935), p. 26, Dublin.
21 IDCRA (1935), p. 26, Dublin.

income.[22] In the 1950s the Emigration Commission asserted that children remained an important resource as workers:

> In agriculture, the additional labour available in a large family, from the time children are able to work on the land until they obtain employment away from home, is a valuable aid to increased production.[23]

The question of the school-leaving age was also considered by the Commission on Youth Unemployment (CYU), which was established in May 1943 by Seán Lemass, Minister for Industry and Commerce, under the chairmanship of Dr John Charles McQuaid. The CYU reported in 1951 and recommended that the school-leaving age be raised ultimately to sixteen years, and as a first step to fifteen years. The Commission, aware of the economic hardship of poor families, favoured family support via children's allowances and maternity and child welfare services. The Commission dismissed the objection that such help would lessen parental responsibility:

> A difficulty seen by some is that helping the children tends to lessen the sense of responsibility of parents for the maintenance and upbringing of their offspring. But to the average poor mother of a growing family the assistance received encourages her to feel that she is not fighting a losing battle against circumstances, and the attitude of the children towards society, when they grow up, is not embittered by the recollection of early years of almost unbearable poverty.[24]

There is evidence that children were exploited for their labour in the past. Over the course of the nineteenth century, fundamental reforms, culminating in the Shaftesbury Acts, guaranteed minimum protection of children. In the late Victorian era an idealised version of childhood began to emerge and, to some extent, exist, among the privileged classes, but economic conditions in Ireland meant that a work-free childhood was the exception rather than the rule.

The changing economic position of children is linked with two factors in particular: the move away from agriculture and the extension of formal education which means that children are dependent on their parents for economic support for a longer period. A measure of the degree to which attitudes have changed is found in the view taken in the 1990s by researchers regarding the costs of children.[25] They maintain that there are two kinds of costs

---

22 *Report of the Commission of Inquiry into the Reformatory and Industrial School System* (1936), p. 15, Dublin, Stationery Office.
23 Report of the Commission on Emigration (1954), p. 99, Dublin.
24 CYU (1951), p. 29, Dublin.
25 C. Carney et al (1994), *The Cost of a Child: A report on the financial cost of child-rearing in Ireland*, Dublin: Combat Poverty Agency.

associated with children Firstly, there are the direct costs of food, clothing, education and other living costs. Secondly, there are indirect costs such as income forgone by parents who care for children, or the costs of childcare when parents do in fact work outside the home. There is no suggestion regarding income forgone *by the child*, or loss to family budget on that account, or to the loss of child labour on family farms, which was so important in earlier decades.

The growth in participation in education since 1937 has been striking. At that time participation rates in post-primary education were below 10 per cent.[26] In 1936 there were 386,000 young persons aged between twelve and eighteen years, and there were less than 50,000 post-primary places available in all the schools, including secondary and vocational schools. In other words there were places potentially available for less that 13 per cent of the age group. In 1971, following the introduction of free post-primary education there had been a very slight increase in the number of persons aged twelve to eighteen years to 396,000 but the number of post-primary places available had risen to 213,000, equivalent to places available for almost 54 per cent of the age group.[27]

Table 8: Participation rates in full-time education for ages 15–24, 2002–03

Age	Male As % of population	Female As % of population	Female Per cent points	Excess Per cent
15	97.5	100.0	2.5	2.6
16	91.0	99.5	8.5	9.3
17	77.9	88.2	10.3	13.2
18	56.5	72.8	16.6	29.4
19	44.5	61.5	17.0	38.2
20	39.2	51.6	12.4	31.6
21	30.6	37.5	6.9	22.5
22	20.5	22.5	2.0	9.8
23	11.2	11.9	0.7	0.6
24	7.5	8.2	0.7	0.9

Source: CSO Yearbook, 2004:102.

Some years earlier, *Investment in Education,* the 1965 report of the Commission on Higher Education, reported that in 1963, 36.8 per cent of sixteen year olds were in full-time education. By contrast in 2003,[28] 91 per cent of males and 99.5 per cent of females aged

26 Séamas Ó Buachalla (1988), *Education Policy in Twentieth Century Ireland*, Dublin: Wolfhound Press.
27 Ó Buachalla, ibid: 384, Table 13.2
28 Central Statistics Office, 2004, *Statistical Yearbook of Ireland*, 2004: 102, Table 5.2.

45

sixteen years were in full-time education. A significant feature of current participation rates is that female participation exceeds that of males at *every* age from fifteen years upwards, as shown in Table 8. The gap between male and female participation increases steadily up to age nineteen when girls are 38 per cent more likely to participate in full-time education than boys. The gap is also very wide at ages eighteen, twenty and twenty-one. Greater rates of female participation have consequences beyond education because higher participation rates are associated with higher rates of labour force participation and reduced as well as postponed fertility.

Policy in a number of European countries is currently being directed towards increasing fertility, and in that context policy makers are looking at time spent in education. There are at least two ways of affecting the mean age of childbearing which might result in an increase in fertility. These are to change the usual sequence of behaviour, for example to have children while still in third-level education, rather than following third-level education, or to reduce the actual period of time spent in full-time education. In a number of European countries discussion is taking place precisely regarding the reduction in years of study for certain qualifications. In Bavaria, the duration of high school was recently cut from nine to eight years. There is empirical evidence to show that reducing the years spent in full-time education leads to a younger age at childbirth and an increase in overall fertility.[29]

4 What have been the consequences for the family of the existence of Article 41 and Article 42?

The intention of Article 41 and Article 42 was to defend the family against unwarranted interference by the state. An attempt had been made in Russia to abolish the family after the Russian Revolution, and although it proved a failure, echoes of the policy still resounded.[30] Against such a backdrop the desire to protect the family against totalitarian onslaught is understandable, though Justice Catherine McGuinness, in the Kilkenny Incest case, suggested that emphasis on the rights of the family in the Constitution may have resulted in giving a higher value to the rights of parents over those of children. By contrast with seventy years ago, there are today unceasing pleas for the state to assume more and more the traditional tasks of the family, from childcare to care for the elderly.

The introduction of divorce into Article 41 has been referred to already. There have been cases argued on the basis of Article 41 and Article 42, for example the Sinnott case in relation to provision

29 Wolfgang Lutz and V. Skirbekk (2004), 'How would "Tempo Policies" Work? Exploring the Effect of School Reforms on Period Fertility in Europe'. Paper presented at the Annual Meeting of the Population Association of America, Boston: MA, April 1–3, 2004.
30 N. S. Timasheff (1946), *The Great Retreat*, Boston: MA, E. P. Dutton.

of education for a handicapped child. There have also been several important pieces of legislation ameliorating the position of spouses and children, including The Family Law (Maintenance of Spouses and Children) Act 1976, The Family Home Protection Act 1976 and The Family Law (Protection of Spouses and Children) Act 1981. At a time when the overwhelming bulk of property was held by men, the Succession Act 1965 was a vital piece of legislation to protect widows. While it could be argued that these pieces of legislation were introduced pursuant to the duty of the state to protect the family imposed by Article 41, that Article alone was not sufficient to afford any of these protections to spouses and children. But in a general way, it should be remembered that the threat envisaged in 1937 was of too much 'interference' by the state in the family.

The question now posed is what policies have been introduced which give practical backing to the sentiments expressed regarding support for the 'woman in the home'. An examination of tax and social welfare provisions to determine what policies are designed to protect and support the 'woman in the home' of the 1937 Constitution, yields little. The principal benefit appears to be the current freedom from capital taxation on the transfer of assets between spouses. But this was not always the case. For many years when estates were subject to death duties, it was possible that a widow might have to sell the home to pay the taxes due, so it cannot be held that the provisions in the Constitution were the basis for preferential tax treatment of spouses, but rather legislation.

Twenty years ago, Mr Justice Brian Walsh expressed astonishment that no one had brought a constitutional case on behalf of mothers who are forced into the labour market by economic necessity.[31] A seismic shift has occurred from the stated rhetoric of the Constitution to the practical reality of Budget 2000 which sought to incentivise the movement of women into the labour market and *out* of the home through the individualisation of personal income taxation. The position following the most recent budget, Budget 2005, is that a single person remains in the lower tax band up to income of €29,400 and a married two-earner couple may earn exactly twice that amount, €58,800, before becoming liable for the higher rate, but a married one-earner couple moves into the higher rate band at income of €38,400. This difference is ameliorated to some extent if one of the couple is a full-time carer at home by the payment of a home carer's tax credit of €770. This emphasis in policy must be judged successful because the numbers of mothers of young children in the workforce has climbed.

Changes in the taxation code following the *Murphy* case have been referred to earlier. The situation whereby the tax paid by two single

---

31 B. Walsh (1987), 'The Constitution and Constitutional Rights', in Frank Litton (ed.), The Constitution of Ireland 1937–1987, *Administration*, 35, 4:98, Dublin: Institute of Public Administration.

persons was increased following their marriage could be viewed both as a tax on marriage and as a disincentive for a married woman to enter the workforce. In implementing the judgment in the *Murphy* case a key decision was taken by the then Minister for Finance, George Colley, to extend the benefits of the judgment to *all* married couples, including those where one partner, generally the wife, was working full time in the home. What Mr McCreevy did in effect in Budget 2000 was to roll back the *optional* element in the implementation of the *Murphy* judgment as carried through by George Colley. This is probably why, despite talk of a constitutional challenge to the McCreevy Budget, no challenge ever emerged.

Some changes in the social welfare code might be said to have been inspired by Article 41, although such provisions are found in countries with no comparable constitutional provision. Also some important provisions were introduced prior to the enactment of the Constitution, including the introduction in 1935 of the widows' contributory pension and non-contributory pension for widows over sixty, and for younger widows with at least one dependent child under fourteen years. In 1970 a means-tested deserted wives allowance was introduced and in 1973 deserted wives' benefit was introduced at the same time as the allowance for unmarried mothers. Over the years there have been many changes in the social welfare code, some of which touched on the balance between marital and non-marital families, but again it is difficult to isolate any provision which was of relative benefit to the 'woman in the home'. The introduction of an allowance for an unmarried mother in 1973, subsequently expanded to an unmarried father caring for his child, was challenged in the courts in the *MacMathúna* case, as favouring the unmarried woman over the 'woman in the home', but it was rejected by the courts. Some progress was made towards recognising work done by homemakers for pension purposes. Under the Homemakers' Scheme introduced in April 1994 both men and women who take some years out of the workforce for the purpose of caring for young children at home can have those years counted towards pension purposes.

One consequence of the constitutional protection of the marriage-based family has been the marginalisation of the father of a child born outside marriage. This has consequences for the child. In practical, as distinct from rhetorical, terms the Constitution did, until the referendum in 1995, proscribe divorce. It does not appear to have resulted in much positive action for 'the woman in the home', while it has marginalised unmarried fathers and possibly sheltered abusive parents, if there is truth in the suggestion of Justice McGuinness in the Kilkenny Incest case.

5 Key issues

The family: how to define it

The most important issue – the strategic one – relates to the definition of the family. It is clear from the submissions to the committee that there is no unanimity as to what comprises a family. Definitions include the family based on the Catholic sacrament of matrimony, families formed subsequent to divorce and remarriage, as well as families not based on marriage.

Cohabiting heterosexual couples

A second issue is whether in view of the considerable and growing incidence of cohabitation the state can adequately deal with the problems that may arise in relationships if constitutional recognition is limited to relationships based on marriage.

Same-sex couples

A third issue is whether or not the definition of family in the Constitution should be extended to allow for same-sex marriage.

Children

A fourth issue is whether or not explicit protection for children should be written into Article 41 of the Constitution.

The natural or birth father

A fifth issue concerns the extent to which the Constitution should recognise the role of men, both their rights and responsibilities, in relation to their children born outside of marriage.

Lone parents

A sixth issue arises from the need to ameliorate the difficult position in which lone parents typically find themselves. Should the definition of the family be extended to provide protection for lone parents?

Woman in the home

A seventh issue concerns the extent to which it is exclusively the work of the 'woman in the home' which deserves recognition in the Constitution. Although the numbers of both men and women who work full time in the home have declined, men and women contribute to the life of the home, as well as to the workplace. As the thrust of policy is to move women out of the home and into the workforce, and as men are already predominantly engaged in the workforce, there is a possibility that children may be deprived of parental care in their most vulnerable years. Should the work of both men and women in the home receive constitutional protection?

6 Responsibilities and rights

Each of the seven issues listed may be analysed in the context of responsibilities and rights. Broadly, the responsibilities relate to the care of dependants. For example, if a person is a father or a mother, it is in the interest of the broader society to ensure that children are properly cared for by their parents. In ordinary circumstances it may not be the best approach to limit caring responsibilities to one parent. The Constitution places no responsibilities on unmarried fathers because such fathers are simply omitted from the Constitution.

An important aspect of the care of dependants from the point of view of society concerns the balance between generations. The balance between generations is at the core of society. Society depends on the emergence of a new generation to replace the one which is ageing, and society benefits if each new generation is reared in a nurturing environment. There is widespread concern throughout the EU regarding the demographic changes which are taking place in the EU and the associated demographic balance. In March 2005 the European Commission launched a Green Paper on demographic change. Figures published in the Green Paper show that by 2030 there will be a reduction of 6.8 per cent in the number of persons in the working-age group. In 2030 about two active people (15–64) will have to take care of one retired person (65+).

Depending on the assumptions, projections made by the Central Statistics Office in Ireland suggest a population which may reach 4.8 million in 2031. One element of the projections that seems well nigh certain is that the population will have a much greater number of over 65s. The over 65s are projected to increase from 435,000 at present to 850,000 in 2031.

An aspect of population balance which is of increasing importance is the provision of sufficient young persons to sustain and replace the older age group which is expanding rapidly. This balance hinges to some extent on the relations between children and grandparents – the 'support ratio'. The number of girls in the population aged 0–14 years fell by 105,000 from 508,000 to 403,000 between 1980, the peak year for births in the twentieth century, and 2002. This decline reduces the pool of child-bearing women in the future – other things being equal. In 2002, there were 156,529 young women aged 20–24 years, but there were only 128,200 young girls aged 5–9 years, i.e. a potential shortfall in fifteen years time of those aged 20–24 of 28,329, or 22 per cent below the present level. In the EU in 2000 there were 50 per cent more women aged 35–39 than there were girls aged 0–4.

If much is already known, there are three big uncertainties. These relate to life expectancy, fertility and migration. Life expectancy has increased markedly over the past one hundred years and it may increase further. Ireland has changed from having very high levels of emigration to receiving thousands of immigrants each year. But fertility is the unknown which is of most concern to the current discussion. Already the increase in the mean age of childbearing, due to postponement of births, has resulted in a lasting loss of births that contributes to the ageing of the population.

In the EU in 2003 the fertility rate fell to 1.48, well below the replacement level of 2.1 children per woman. An examination of fertility and live births out of wedlock for all the twenty-five EU countries yields an interesting result. If one expects that more traditional societies, where more children are born to married couples, have higher fertility rates, one would not find evidence to support this hypothesis. If a relationship can be identified it is the opposite, i.e. the countries today with the highest fertility rates – the Nordic countries, France, the UK and Ireland – have the highest proportion of births out of wedlock. The Mediterranean countries – Greece, Italy, Spain and Malta – have low proportions of children born out of wedlock, but these countries have the lowest fertility. This picture is somewhat distorted by the new member countries, with their combination of very low fertility and high proportion of births out of wedlock. Also countries with a higher proportion of women at work may have higher fertility perhaps because they may have better childcare provision.

The seven central issues raised may also be considered in the context of *rights*. A constitutional right to recognition may be regarded as a basic right. Many other rights, including succession rights to property, a right to enjoy tax benefits and certain other privileges and to claim pension rights, may stem from constitutional recognition. To what extent are certain benefits to be ring-fenced for married couples either in first or subsequent marriages, as distinct from cohabiting couples or consanguine units, such as a mother and daughter or two brothers, or other relationships of care?

Following the individualisation of the tax code in 2000, the position in the income tax code is similar for a two-income couple and for two individuals. However the position differs sharply with regard to inheritance tax and capital acquisitions tax and, of course, pensions. At the present time a surviving spouse can inherit an estate tax free and capital transfers between married couples are free from tax. By contrast if two sisters are living together and one dies, then the surviving sister will be subject to tax on her sister's estate, above a certain minimum threshold, although allowance is made if both sisters live in the same house. In the case of a lesbian couple, even if they have lived together for a number of years, they are strangers at law, and subject to inheritance tax on that basis. Furthermore, if one member of the couple were to die intestate, his or her blood relatives would stand to inherit under the Succession

Act. A related matter concerns the right to benefit from social welfare entitlements as a 'dependant' or a 'widow' or 'widower', or indeed as the 'partner' who may accompany a person who is entitled to a free travel pass.

Conclusion

It is almost seventy years since the Constitution was enacted. In that time every aspect of Irish life has changed. It may be contended that nowhere have the changes been more striking than in family life. Our initial exploration exposes the complexities our society is facing into. The committee's paramount concern is whether the Constitution is providing a basic context where Irish people can deal with those complexities – where they can use their freedom to develop a fulfilling lifestyle while observing the constraints the community believes are needed to ensure social stability and continuity. Chapter 2 explores how people feel about the definition of the family in the Constitution.

Chapter 2

The Family: how to define it

Article 41

1   1° *The State recognises
the Family as the
natural primary and
fundamental unit
group of Society, and
as a moral institution
possessing inalienable
and imprescriptible
rights, antecedent and
superior to all positive
law.*
2° *The State, therefore,
guarantees to protect
the Family in its
constitution and
authority, as the
necessary basis of
social order and as
indispensable to the
welfare of the Nation
and the State.*

2   1° *In particular, the
State recognises that by
her life within the
home, woman gives to
the State a support
without which the
common good cannot
be achieved.*
2° *The State shall,
therefore, endeavour to
ensure that mothers
shall not be obliged by
economic necessity to
engage in labour to the
neglect of their duties
in the home.*

In Chapter 1 we saw how demographic and social change has
made for the appearance of a far broader range of family forms
than the Constitution envisaged. Here we explore whether the view
of the family embraced by the Constitution is robust enough to
allow all family forms to be fairly treated or whether the
constitutional formulation needs to be extended. Article 41 contains
the main provisions relating to the family. Article 42 is closely
linked with Article 41 and has been construed by the courts as
containing in Article 42.5 a guarantee of children's rights which go
beyond education (*In re The Adoption (No2) Bill 1987* [1989] IR
656). Article 40.3 is also relevant, because the rights of an
unmarried mother in relation to her child and the rights of a child
born of unmarried parents have been held to be personal rights
protected by Article 40.3 (*The State (Nicolau) v An Bord Uchtála*
[1966] IR 567 and *G v An Bord Uchtála* [1980] IR 32.

The Constitution Review Group observed:

> Article 41 was a novel provision in 1937. The Constitution of
> 1922 contained no provision relating to family and marriage.
> It is generally considered that Articles 41and 42 were heavily
> influenced by Roman Catholic teaching and Papal encyclicals.
> They were clearly drafted with only one family in mind,
> namely, the family based on marriage.

It is generally acknowledged that these provisions were influenced
by contemporary Catholic social teaching. Taken in isolation,
however, the above statement might serve to create the misleading
impression that the provisions were exceptional in themselves.
Most continental constitutions contain similar provisions dealing
with the protection of the family, as does Article 8 of the European
Convention on Human Rights. A good example here is provided
by Article 6 of the German Basic Law:

(1) Marriage and family enjoy the special protection of the state.
(2) Care and upbringing of children are the natural right of the
     parents and a duty primarily incumbent on them. The state
     watches over the performance of this duty.
(3) Separation of children from the family against the will of the
     persons entitled to bring them up may take place only
     pursuant to a law, if those so entitled fail in their duty or if the
     children are otherwise threatened with neglect.

*3 1° The State pledges
itself to guard with
special care the
institution of Marriage,
on which the Family is
founded, and to
protect it against
attack.
2° A Court designated
by law may grant a
dissolution of marriage
where, but only where,
it is satisfied that
   i. at the date of the
   institution of the
   proceedings, the
   spouses have lived
   apart from one
   another for a period
   of, or periods
   amounting to, at
   least four years
   during the previous
   five years,
   ii. there is no
   reasonable prospect
   of a reconciliation
   between the spouses,
   iii. such provision as
   the Court considers
   proper having regard
   to the circumstances
   exists or will be made
   for the spouses, any
   children of either or
   both of them and
   any other person
   prescribed by law,
   and
   iv. any further
   conditions prescribed
   by law are complied
   with.
3° No person whose
marriage has been
dissolved under the
civil law of any other
State but is a subsisting
valid marriage under
the law for the time*

(4) Every mother is entitled to the protection and care of the community.

(5) Illegitimate children shall be provided by legislation with the same opportunities for their physical and spiritual development and their position in society as are enjoyed by legitimate children.

The special case of divorce aside, is there anything so different between these provisions of the German Basic Law and Article 41 of the Constitution?[32]

1 1° The State recognises the Family as the natural primary and fundamental unit group of Society, and as a moral institution possessing inalienable and imprescriptible rights, antecedent and superior to all positive law.
2° The State, therefore, guarantees to protect the Family in its constitution and authority, as the necessary basis of social order and as indispensable to the welfare of the Nation and the State.

2 1° In particular, the State recognises that by her life within the home, woman gives to the State a support without which the common good cannot be achieved.
2° The State shall, therefore, endeavour to ensure that mothers shall not be obliged by economic necessity to engage in labour to the neglect of their duties in the home.

3 1° The State pledges itself to guard with special care the institution of Marriage, on which the Family is founded, and to protect it against attack.

Moreover, Article 41 equally reflects the thinking of the earlier Weimar Constitution of 1919:

Article 119
Marriage, as the foundation of the family and the preservation and expansion of the nation, enjoys the special

---

32 It is true that, in the one case where case law based on Article 6 was relied on, *Murphy v Attorney General* [1982] IR 241, the Supreme Court rather tersely (and quite unconvincingly) said that this case law did not assist the plaintiffs' contentions. In *Murphy* the plaintiffs had challenged the constitutionality of provisions of the Income Tax Act 1967 which had aggregated the incomes of husbands and wives for tax purposes. Reliance was placed on a decision of the German Constitutional Court in 1957 which had held similar German legislation to be unconstitutional on the ground that it infringed Article 6(1) since it interfered with the right of married persons to make personal decisions, including the right of the wife to decide whether she would devote herself to the home or work outside the home. Because the legislature could not directly interfere with that right, the Constitutional Court held that it could not do so indirectly by means of tax measures designed to penalise working wives.
But it is not easy to see why the Supreme Court so fleetingly dismissed this (very convincingly) reasoned German authority, especially since the Supreme Court has in other key decisions recognised that the autonomy of family decision making from state interference is at the heart of Article 41: see for example *McGee v Attorney General* [1974] IR 284; *Re Article 26 and the Matrimonial Homes Bill 1993* [1994] 1 IR 305 and *North Western Health Board v HW* [2001] 3 IR 622.

being in force within the jurisdiction of the Government and Parliament established by this Constitution shall be capable of contracting a valid marriage within that jurisdiction during the lifetime of the other party to the marriage so dissolved.

Article 42

1 *The State acknowledges that the primary and natural educator of the child is the Family and guarantees to respect the inalienable right and duty of parents to provide, according to their means, for the religious and moral, intellectual, physical and social education of their children.*

2 *Parents shall be free to provide this education in their homes or in private schools or in schools recognised or established by the State.*

3 *1° The State shall not oblige parents in violation of their conscience and lawful preference to send their children to schools established by the State, or to any particular type of school designated by the State. 2° The State shall, however, as guardian of the common good, require in view of actual conditions that*

protection of the constitution. It is based on the equality of both genders.

It is the task of both the state and the communities to strengthen and socially promote the family. Large families may claim social welfare.

Motherhood is placed under state protection and welfare.

Article 120
It is the supreme obligation and natural right of the parents to raise their offspring to bodily, spiritual and social fitness; the governmental authority supervises it.

Article 121
Legislation has to create equal preconditions for children born out of wedlock, concerning their bodily, spiritual and social development, as they are given to legitimate children.

Article 122
Youth is to be protected against exploitation as well as against moral and spiritual dissipation, bodily neglect. State and communities have to take appropriate measures.

Measures which interfere by the means of force in the parents' right to raise their children may only be taken if based on a law.

Given that other provisions of the Constitution appear to have been clearly adapted from the Weimar model,[33] it seems reasonable to assume that these provisions of Weimar were at least examined by the drafters in 1937. With the exception of the special provisions of Article 121 dealing with children born out of wedlock, one could find a close fit between these provisions and Article 41 and, for that matter, much of Article 42. The reality probably is that Articles 41 and 42 represent a diverse jumble of sources, both religious and secular.

In any event, in the liberal democratic tradition to which it belongs, the Constitution, by giving a ringing endorsement of the family, bolstered the freedom of the individual against the claims of the state. It should be noted that when the Constitution was enacted in 1937 those parts of Europe controlled by totalitarian regimes, whether of the right or of the left, were making outrageous claims on the freedom of the individual.

The traditional family enshrined in the Constitution is the nuclear family consisting of a married couple, a man (the breadwinner) and

---

33 See for example the extremely close overlap between the provisions of Article 12 and Article 13 dealing with the powers and tenure of office of the President and Article 41 to Article 49 of the Weimar Constitution dealing with the powers of the German President: see Kelly, *The Irish Constitution* (Dublin, 2004), at 224–225. Note also the discussion in *Howlin v Morris* [2004] 2 ILRM 53 at 75–76 as to the extent to which the parliamentary privilege provisions in Article 15.10 and Article 15.12 were derived from the corresponding Weimar provisions.

the children receive a certain minimum education, moral, intellectual and social.

4   *The State shall provide for free primary education and shall endeavour to supplement and give reasonable aid to private and corporate educational initiative, and, when the public good requires it, provide other educational facilities or institutions with due regard, however, for the rights of parents, especially in the matter of religious and moral formation.*

5   *In exceptional cases, where the parents for physical or moral reasons fail in their duty towards their children, the State as guardian of the common good, by appropriate means shall endeavour to supply the place of the parents, but always with due regard for the natural and imprescriptible rights of the child.*

his wife (a mother concerned with her household duties) and their dependent children whose physical and moral development is based on the stable lifelong commitment of the parents and the values they transmit to their children. The traditional model is built on the lifelong union of a man and woman, formalised in a marriage ceremony; in its primary form the man assumed the role of the head of the family while the wife, dependent upon him for physical maintenance, established primacy in the care and upbringing of the children; the children were expected to absorb the values of their parents and be subservient to them. Certain conditions were identified which give the traditional family its status and its social context: the status of the family is based on natural law, not on the positive laws created by states or pronounced by judges as law givers; the prohibition of divorce and the lack of legal recognition of cohabitation supported the primacy of the family based on marriage; the prohibition of contraception promoted the fertility which produces children within the family and makes for the continuity of the state; the prohibition of homosexuality promoted fruitful heterosexual unions.

Most of the religious bodies that made submissions endorsed the paramount status given to the traditional family in the Constitution. In its submission, the Committee on the Family of the Irish Episcopal Conference and the Office of Public Affairs of the Archdiocese of Dublin (hereinafter referred to as the Irish Catholic Bishops' Conference) observes:

> Articles 41 and 42 of the Constitution, as originally drafted, represent a most important protection of marriage and the family. In striking contrast to the United States Constitution, for example, the Irish Constitution recognises the family as the natural unit of society and as a moral institution possessing inalienable and imprescriptible rights, antecedent and superior to all positive law. Under Article 41.3.1, the State pledged itself to guard with special care the institution of marriage, on which the family is founded, and to protect it against attack.

> In setting out this position, the Constitution is clearly recognising the importance of the family based on marriage and the vital contribution it makes to the well-being of society and the state. It is not the Constitution that creates the family or that defines it, rather it recognises an institution that is prior to it.

> In doing so, the Constitution recognises that in discussing the relationship between the family and society, there is much at stake. Marriage and the family are primary sources of stability, life and love in any society, they constitute a 'primary vital cell' from which the rest of society derives so

much of its own cohesion and potential success. This fact is recognised by our own Constitution when it describes the family 'as the necessary basis of social order and as indispensable to the welfare of the Nation and the State'.

The Presbyterian Church in Ireland supported and endorsed Article 41.1 of the Constitution on the status of the family:

> We believe the Constitution is right to describe the family as 'a moral institution possessing inalienable and imprescriptible rights, antecedent and superior to all positive law'. Its weakness is in failing to define what is meant by 'family'. While recognising that there is an increasing variety of living arrangements among the citizens of Ireland, we do not believe that the way for legislation to deal with this matter is by redefining the nature of the family in a way that is different from mainline Christian teaching as presented in scripture.

The Association of Baptist Churches in Ireland answers the question, how should the family be defined?, as follows:

> As one man and one woman committed in marriage to each other for life, together with any children of their marriage or adopted into it. This is the God-given building block of every society. The future stability of Irish society depends on a secure foundation. Healthy families are that secure foundation. To tamper with the definition of the family is to attack the foundations of the State.

The Association of Irish Evangelical Churches states:

> Marriage has historically been defined as a lifelong covenant union between a man and a woman that is witnessed by God and the community. This definition has enjoyed almost universal acceptance across time and cultures. Marriage is of such importance that it is uniquely protected in law and culture. It predates the law and any constitution, and is an anthropological and sociological reality, not primarily a legal one. No civilisation can survive without it, and those societies that allowed it to become irrelevant have faded into history. Christians believe that this definition of marriage originates with God. The first book of the Bible, Genesis, lays the foundation for the Christian and Jewish understanding of this covenant union between a man and a woman.

The Evangelical Alliance Ireland states:

> The family should continue to be seen as a man and a woman in a legally recognised marriage together with their

children. There is no other solid, tried legal basis on which to define 'family'. The institution of a legally recognised marriage covenant between a man and a woman has provided the basic unit for almost every society for millennia. This does not mean that there cannot be families that deviate from the norm. There are. But accepting the traditional family unit as the norm enables society to look at how to respond to situations that differ from the norm and ensure that people in those situations are treated fairly.

The Islamic Foundation of Ireland states:

> The provisions of the Irish Constitution in relation to the family enshrined in Articles 41.1.1, 41.1.2, 41.3.1 and 42.1 should be maintained. Any departure from the concept of the union of man and woman as being essential to the definition of family is unacceptable and repugnant to the religious beliefs of the vast majority of the Irish State. This would be the view of Jews, Muslims and Christians.

It should be noted that the Church of Ireland General Synod and the Council on Social Responsibility of the Methodist Church in Ireland qualified their view of the position the traditional family should have in the Constitution. The Church of Ireland states:

> The family protected by the Constitution is the family based on marriage. The present day understanding of the family, however, is something much broader than the traditional marriage based family. A clear distinction needs to be made between the definition of marriage and the definition of the family. We favour the inclusion in the Constitution of a broad definition of the family which will not only continue to protect the institution of marriage but will also allow the State to recognise the numerous units which are generally regarded as family units but which are not marriage based. The Church of Ireland, of course, continues to stress marriage as the optimum context, particularly for the nurture of children, but at the same time we feel that other domestic situations should be accommodated and legislative provision made for them.

The Council on Social Responsibility of the Methodist Church in Ireland states:

> We hold strongly to the view that the Constitution is not the place to determine detailed matters of social policy. Rather its role is to delineate general principles of public and social policy, which can then be instantiated in whatever detail is required through ordinary legislation, and revised from time to time as deemed necessary in the same manner. Thus for

this reason we opposed proposals to insert specific regulations in the Constitution regarding abortion, divorce, etc. quite apart from our views for or against those specific proposals. And so in the present case, we would argue that the Constitution should only state general principles relating to families and family rights. The existing text could therefore be streamlined and we would also oppose adding any new specific matters of detail.

Secondly, we have consistently argued that it is not the role of the Constitution to uphold or enforce the specific viewpoint of any church (or other faith or philosophy) *per se*, no matter how much we might agree or not with such a viewpoint. The general framework for social policy in the Constitution should be framed so as to be, as far as is feasible, objectively intended to maximise the common good. Whether or not we agree with the viewpoint in such a Constitution, or indeed the legislation implementing it, is our concern, not that of the state. Of course the religious tradition in Ireland will naturally influence the way these matters are considered, and that is right and proper, but a clear distinction needs to be made between that fact, and the actual endorsement of any specific religious perspective. Given the increasing multi-cultural nature of Irish society, this factor takes on an extra dimension and urgency at the current time.

Thirdly, turning to the current topic, it must be recognised that in relation to some aspects of it, and in particular to laws and issues around marriage, religious requirements and the requirements of the state have become heavily intertwined over the years. In considering these topics, we feel it is useful, and indeed important, to recognise that these two aspects are logically separate, and to keep the distinction clear as we discuss this matter.

And finally in these general comments, we note that while churches, or other faith communities, have in the past been seen as the primary determinants of moral values, that role has been increasingly taken up by the adoption within civil society of ethical and moral codes. The most prominent of these are of course the UN Convention on Human Rights. We as a church respect and endorse this trend, believing that it represents a maturing of human society and civilization. We would argue, however, that within this scenario, there is still a role for churches to articulate issues of morality and ethics on an ongoing basis, while accepting that we are just one voice among many and no longer have any privileged role in this regard (and which in our own case in the Methodist Church, we probably never had).

The overwhelming majority of the submissions received from individuals (close on 8,000) and of the over 16,000 petitions were trenchantly in support of leaving the Articles relating to the family unchanged and therefore were in support of the traditional family. A considerable number of the 130 submissions received from interest groups also supported that position.

Thus, the Mother & Child Campaign presents its position as follows:

> The family is the fundamental social unit. Article 43.1.1 of Bunreacht na hÉireann recognises the special position of the family and gives it inalienable and imprescriptible rights, antecedent and superior to all positive law. Article 41.3.1 pledges the State to guard with special care the institution of marriage, on which the Family is founded, and to protect it from attack. The Committee should not attempt to change or broaden this constitutional definition of the family.

> The Mother & Child Campaign does not accept the UN definition of the family, which, if used as a basis for any attempted changes to our constitution, would effectively remove the status of marriage (on which the family is based and which is constitutionally protected and generally recognised and accepted) as an institution and reduce it to one of the number of options, including – among others – homosexual units. We wholly reject any attempt to change, in any way, those articles of our constitution pertaining to the family based on marriage.

> The state has a duty to ensure that, for the future well-being of society, families be given such support as is necessary to maintain their acknowledged role in that society with dignity.

NEART (Coalition of Pro-Women's Rights, Pro-Family and Pro-Life Groups) maintains:

> The definition of the family as laid down in the Constitution, and as recognised in law, must be retained.

> The rights of the family as a unit and the rights of the individual members of the family are complementary. It is the duty and the obligation of the State, under the Constitution, to ensure a harmonious interaction between members of the family by ensuring that adequate support such as by way of finance, housing, etc, is made available to the family. The Constitution provides for instances where such material means do not adequately provide for harmonious relations within the family, and all other appropriate avenues for the maintenance of such relations have been tried and failed.

Right Nation defends the traditional family this way:

> In the first instance something needs to be stated which properly speaking ought not to be necessary: the family works. As an institution it performs the tasks set before it infinitely better than any alternative which has been suggested by anyone at any time. Reason and experience are the bedrock proofs of both its durability and its remarkable efficacy. This requires to be explicitly stated since, as is perhaps natural but unfortunate, we tend to think of the family when problems arise, and the issues raised in the media are generally those of family failure or dysfunction. Most families, however, are neither failing nor dysfunctional, but rather are the healthy and happy context in which children are born and develop, both physically and mentally, towards a maturity which allows them as adults to found their own family, equally healthy and happy.

Comhar Críostaí – The Christian Solidarity Party states:

> At the outset the Christian Solidarity Party reminds the committee that the Irish Constitution commences with an invocation to the most Holy Trinity and acknowledges all our obligations to Our Divine Lord, Jesus Christ. It is clear, therefore, that the Irish Constitution, in particular, expresses very strong support for the Christian understanding of both marriage and the family.

> The Christian understanding of the family is a family based on marriage, a voluntary union of one man and one woman to the exclusion of all others. The family is a community of persons: of husband and wife, of parents and children, of relatives. Such an understanding of the family is essential for the promotion of the common good. Because of the indispensable role of the family for society, constitutional protection of the family, as already exists in our Constitution, must be maintained.

Support for the traditional family, the predominant family form in the state, comes not from the statements and arguments found in the submissions only. Support also comes from the global community in the form of the United Nations and from widescale research in the social sciences.

Global support

The most recent global endorsement of the family as an institution came in November 2004 in the declaration of the Doha International Conference for the Family which was accepted as a

Resolution without a vote by the United Nations in December 2004 (see Appendix 4 for the complete text of the declaration). The declaration took into consideration the academic, scientific and social evidence collected for the Conference, which collectively demonstrates that the family is not only the fundamental unit group of society but is also the fundamental agent for sustainable social, economic and cultural development. Reiterating that strong, stable families contribute to the maintenance of a culture of peace and promote dialogue among civilisations and diverse ethnic groups, the declaration calls upon and encourages international organisations and members of civil society at all levels to take action to promote the family. It calls on international, national and voluntary organisations to, among other things,

- reaffirm the importance of faith and religious and ethical beliefs in maintaining family stability and social progress
- encourage and support the family to provide care for older persons and persons with disabilities
- observe, preserve and defend the institution of marriage
- take effective measures to strengthen the stability of marriage by, among other things, encouraging the full and equal partnership of husband and wife within a committed and enduring marital relationship and establishing effective policies and practices to condemn and remedy abusive relationships within marriage and the family, including the establishment of public agencies to assist men, women, children and families in crisis.

Research support

Those who support the traditional family cited a large volume of research as endorsing their views (see for example the European Life Network submission in Appendix 3). That organisation supplied a copy of *Why Marriage Matters*. From the Center of the American Experiment, *Why Marriage Matters* provides findings from the social sciences on an important range of marriage issues arising from American experience, findings on the relationship of marriage to family, economics, physical health and longevity, mental health and emotional wellbeing and crime and domestic violence. Its fundamental conclusion is that marriage is an important social good, associated with an impressively broad array of positive outcomes for children and adults alike.

For further research findings see the submission of Focus on the Family Ireland in Appendix 3. The committee did not receive comparable wide-ranging research on European experience.

The part played by the traditional model of the family in providing stability, happiness and continuity to society is almost universally acknowledged. Even those who would like to see the Constitution embrace all forms of family acknowledge that special protection should be accorded to the family based on marriage.

The Constitution, through its interpretation by the courts and the laws framed by the Oireachtas under it to serve the common good, seeks to respond to the needs and wishes of the citizens at each particular period. We have seen in Chapter 1 how the model of the family which was installed in the Constitution in 1937 subserved neatly the demography of the state and the ethos created by it. As demography and Irish society changed in the interim there have been a number of adjustments to the model. The common law, which continued to operate so long as it was not found repugnant to the new Constitution, acknowledged the father as the head of the family. In the 1950s the courts ruled that both the father and mother jointly managed the family. The *McGee* case [1974] IR 284 led to the legal change in regard to the use of contraceptives. The legal response to the *Norris* case in the European Court of Human Rights in 1988 has removed the legal prohibition on homosexual acts in private between consenting adults. In 1996 the Fifteenth Amendment of the Constitution provided for the dissolution of marriage in certain specified circumstances. However, many of the submissions received from interest groups suggest that these changes do not go far enough to meet the needs and wishes of contemporary society.

The formulation of Article 41 has been criticised on the following technical grounds:

- Natural law, upon which the position of the family is based through the use of the adjectives inalienable and imprescriptible, fails to yield legal precision – and therefore certainty – because there is no agreed source for determining what the natural law is in a particular case.

- The Article acknowledges the right of the family as a unit to govern itself. This places a barrier between the state and the family and protects the family from the state. But it concomitantly prevents the state from intervening to protect individual members of the family, in particular dependent children, unless extraordinary failures or abuse by parents become evident.

- By recognising only the family based on marriage the Constitution excludes non-marital families from constitutional recognition and from the privileges that flow from it.

The equality model

Another model of the family emerged in the developed world in the aftermath of World War I to embrace the independent and emancipated young women who made demands for equal work opportunities, sexual independence and an active life. The exigencies of the economic depression of the nineteen thirties limited the appeal of this model. Its ascendancy came after World War II. That cataclysm had drawn vast numbers of women into industrial production and made them independent wage-earners. It also created the powerful movement in Europe and the rest of the world towards the identification, protection and promotion of human rights, including gender equality, which endows the model with much of its practical appeal. Because of the salience of gender equality as the dynamic propelling adoption of the model we call it the equality model.

Ireland has not been immune from the conditions favouring this model. As the Constitution Review Group (1996) put it:

> The family in Irish society has been profoundly affected by social trends since 1937. The mores of Irish society have changed significantly over the past six decades. The traditional Roman Catholic ethos has been weakened by various influences including secularisation, urbanisation, changing attitudes to sexual behaviour, the use of contraceptives, social acceptance of premarital relations, cohabitation and single parenthood, a lower norm for family size, increased readiness to accept separation and divorce, greater economic independence of women.

> The most striking changes in the family in Ireland since 1937 are the 30% drop in the birth-rate from 18.6 to 13.4 per 1,000, the rise from 3% to 20% in the proportion of births outside marriage and the increase from 5.6% to 32.4% in the proportion of married women who work outside the home. The traditional family consisting of a husband, wife and four to five children has dwindled to husband, wife and two children.

A considerable number of the submissions from interest groups and organisations involved in family affairs favours the equality model. They believe that the state should extend its concern to non-marital families as well as to the predominant traditional family group. In the interest of equality, they believe those families should be treated the same way as the traditional family. Many of them look for a clear distinction to be made between the definition of marriage and the definition of the family. They favour the inclusion in the Constitution of a broad definition of the family which will not only continue to protect the institution of marriage but will also allow the state to recognise the numerous units which are generally regarded as family units but which are not marriage based. They favour the UN definition (International Year of the Family 1994):

> Any combination of two or more persons who are bound together by ties of mutual consent, birth and/or adoption or placement and who, together, assume responsibility for, inter alia, the care and maintenance of group members, the addition of new members through procreation or adoption, the socialisation of children and the social control of members.

Thus the Adoption Board says:

> The changing nature of Irish society is evident in the growth of individualism; the changing role of women; the changing social climate (marital breakdown and divorce); recent social legislation (legislation on homosexuality, equality); the changing economic and demographic climate (including greater labour mobility and immigration); the changing attitudes to religion and the changing nature and composition of families.

> In the light of these developments the Adoption Board recommends ... broadening the constitutional definition of the family in line with the UN definition of the family ... so as to more fully reflect the changing nature of Irish society in general and of adoption practice in particular.

The Irish Society for the Prevention of Cruelty to Children says:

> The definition of family needs to be developed ... in line with current social reality and thinking. Such a definition should focus on family structure and more on family function which sees the family as a unit of nurturance for children and adults based on positive communication rather than a relationship based on patriarchal power, authority, property relationships or the institution of marriage.

The Irish Council for Civil Liberties presents its view as follows:

> The ICCL submits that it is essential that the current reference to the family based on marriage in Article 41.3.1 is removed. The ICCL submits that it is preferable that the Constitution should not seek to define the family because for the purposes of international human rights law, and Ireland's obligations thereunder, it is clear that the family is defined by reference to close personal ties which are established between individuals and not a formal designation under national law. To unnecessarily impose a narrow definition

would run the risk of excluding and discriminating against some families, and members thereof, including children, in the recognition and protection of their rights. The ICCL submits that the approach of the European Court of Human Rights to defining what is family life is to be preferred.

The ICCL submits that not only can the Constitution recognise all families, whether based on marriage or not, but that it is imperative that it does. The ICCL recommends that the Constitution should include a commitment to recognise the family in its various forms as the primary and fundamental unit in society.

The National Women's Council of Ireland states:

The NWCI advocates using the definition of family as outlined by the United Nations ....

[The Constitution's] restricted view of the family has already placed Ireland in breach of its international human rights obligations. In the case of *Johnston and Others v Ireland* (1987) 9 EHRR 203, the European Court of Human Rights found that the inferior position at law of the Applicant, who was a non-marital child, violated the guarantee under Article 8 of the European Convention on Human Rights to respect for family life. Many of the inequalities faced by a non-marital child were rectified by the Status of Children Act 1987. In the case of *Keegan v Ireland* (1994) 18 EHRR 342 the European Court of Human Rights held that the Applicant's right to respect for his family life had been violated when he, as a natural father, had no right to be appointed guardian and thus to have had a role in the adoption proceedings concerning his child.

In order to comply with international human rights requirements, and to reflect the reality of family diversity the Constitution must therefore have due regard to the rights and concerns of all families.

The Women's Health Council states:

The definition of family implied in our Constitution as that based on marriage no longer reflects the reality of Irish society... [O]ne must look at the purpose of family life in order to legislate and formulate policies which will protect it and support it ...Participants at recent public consultations expressed their desire for official policy to see the family in terms of what it does – caring – and the kinds of relationships and values that comprise it rather than seeing the family in terms of structure or a group of people who are defined by a legal relationship. So, if one agrees that the main purpose of family life is to care for close personal relationships and especially children, then the state must encompass all family forms that carry out this task without discriminating on the basis of how they were constituted.

IPPA, the Early Childhood Organisation, states the following:

> We believe that the family transcends households, and that family relationships extend beyond and between households. The traditional notion of family is exclusive and one that, according to Daly (2004),[34] reporting on the Public Consultation Fora ... does not receive such widespread support. The call, from this forum, was for 'a more inclusive definition of family which can encompass all types of families'. The changing nature and function of family must be acknowledged. While the traditional views or understandings of 'family' can be maintained, the reality is somewhat different. Elkind (2002) suggests that the family can be viewed as a social organism that must adapt to the demands of its social habitat – when society changes so too must the family.

The Law Society takes the following view:

> Since the adoption of the Irish Constitution in 1937 the nature of the Irish family has changed dramatically. There is little doubt that the Irish family law system now requires nothing less than a major overhaul if it is to meet the increasing demands placed on it. The law must now root itself in reality and not emotive or traditional rhetoric.

> The time is now ripe to consider changing the law to facilitate a broader and more inclusive definition of the 'family' in a manner that will promote and foster the best interests of children. We need to adopt a more 'functional' approach to the family, an approach based on the fact of the parties living together rather than the nature of the relationship between the parties.

> We need to depart from a system of family law where legal status alone is the sole determinant of family rights and privileges.

A sharp division

It is evident from the submissions that there is sharp division between those who support the traditional model of the family and those who support the equality model. Many of those who support

---

34 Daly, M. (2004), *Families and Family Life in Ireland: Challenges for the Future*, Report of the Public Consultation Fora, Dublin: Department of Social and Family Affairs.

the traditional model would see any change in the constitutional position of the family based on marriage as a deadly blow against the family. Thus Family & Life:

> Family & Life is well aware of the changed social and economic conditions over the past half century, all of which have affected the family and family life in Ireland. We are also aware that certain lobby groups want changes in this area. But there is more. Over the past half century the very concept of the family has been subject to adverse criticism, especially by influential writers in the social sciences. Today, the family's negative image has filtered into mainstream opinion, especially in academic, professional and media circles. Before deciding that the constitutional definition of the family should change (be deleted, expanded or replaced?), the legislators should be aware of what has happened to the family in our western culture over the past fifty years.

It goes on to present that experience (for the full text of the submission see Appendix 3). It points out that there are two competing definitions of family – the traditional or normative family, which is precisely framed, and the families captured by what is called 'the United Nations' definition', a 'vague and general formulation which allows two or more people to combine by mutual or common consent to form a family'. It is a minimal definition, which dispenses with marriage and gender, lifelong commitment and exclusivity.

Those who support the equality model of the family in the main appreciate the contribution made by the traditional model – and wish support for it to continue – but they also wish to see the definition of the family extended so that all family forms can be dealt with equally.

A real issue

The Department of Social and Family Affairs, one of the state agencies most intimately involved in family affairs, in its submission indicates that its nationwide consultation process showed up a concern for clearer legal recognition and protection of other partnerships, apart from marriage but also a concern that such recognition might reduce the status of marriage:

> It is generally recognised that marriage makes a major contribution to promoting stability and continuity in family life, but that there have also been major changes affecting marriage in recent decades. These include:
>
> • a growing proportion of couples in recent years are co-habiting outside of marriage, although many marry if they

have, or decide to have, children

- married couples not having children or deciding not to have children
- couples having fewer children which, together with increasing longevity, means that the period of childrearing represents a much shorter period of a couple's life together than in the past
- greater equality between men and women, with women, as a result of growing female participation in the workforce, not being as economically dependent on their husbands as in the past, reinforced by couples having fewer children
- same-sex couples seeking the right to marry and obtain the legal protection and social recognition for their relationship it affords. Such couples are generally childless, but some may have children from previous relationships.

In the course of the consultation through the family fora, support was expressed for clearer legal recognition and protection of other partnerships, apart from marriage. There was also concern expressed from another perspective, however, that recognition of other partnerships could have the effect of reducing the status of marriage, and thereby weakening it as a key source of stability and continuity in family life.

The Department's report on the Public Consultation Fora, *Families and Family Life in Ireland – Challenges for the Future* (2004), states that support for the traditional view of the family:

> ... was much less widespread than for that calling for change, however. The view that Ireland is changing and therefore that we need to recognise this and plan our policies around it emerged spontaneously at every Forum and also in response to calls for the preservation of the more traditional view where they occurred. The main point being made here was that, in the context of increasing diversity in Irish society, we need an inclusive definition of family, one that can encompass all types of families. To be inclusive a definition should be capable of embracing such diverse family forms as those made up of grandparents and children, those consisting of foster parents and children, those of lone parents and children, those of unmarried partners and children as well as same-sex parents and children.

> Diversity was usually conceived in structural terms in that it related to what one might call the packaging or structure of the family – such as the number of parents in a family, the marital status of the adults vis-à-vis each other and the

identity of the adults vis-à-vis the children. Cultural diversity, in terms of different beliefs, values and practices as they relate to parenting, caring for elderly or ill family members and so forth, was much less often referred to. Hence, for example, the possibility that Ireland now contains people with quite different ideas about what is good family behaviour and the appropriate way to conduct family life was not that widely referred to. Some points about ethnic diversity were mentioned, however, at a number of Fora and in some of the submissions. In general, Irish society is seen to be exclusionary of these families and groups. 'Asylum seekers and refugees are at the margins in Ireland.'

Conclusion

There is a general belief that the traditional family contributes enormously to the common good and that it should be given special protection in the Constitution. Many of those who feel that other family forms should also be given constitutional protection believe that this can be achieved through giving recognition to family life in general but adding a provision that gives special protection to the family based on marriage. This is the approach favoured by the Constitution Review Group. This approach is rejected by those who feel that any extension of the definition of family inevitably dilutes the unique position of the family based on marriage.

Before deciding on the issue of definition the committee will examine in the six following chapters six major areas of concern that arise from the submissions and bear on the question of definition:
- cohabiting heterosexual couples
- same-sex couples
- children
- the natural or birth father
- lone parents
- woman in the home.

Chapter 3

Cohabiting heterosexual couples

While the traditional family predominates in the state, some 8.4% (census 2002) of families consist of cohabiting heterosexual couples. Cohabitation may be defined as the condition of two people who are living together as man and wife but are not legally married to each other.

AIM Family Services lists six kinds of cohabiting heterosexual couple:

- couples who cannot afford to marry because of the cost
- couples who don't want the commitment of marriage
- couples where one partner has had a church annulment and has re-married in the Roman Catholic Church only. These couples cannot sign the register after the ceremony, because without a civil annulment or divorce the partner is not free to remarry. (They are married in the eyes of the Church only and the marriage has no status in law.)
- couples where one partner has a foreign divorce that is not recognised in the state
- couples where one partner had a recognised but 'difficult' divorce and is loath to make that commitment again and so lives with his/her 'new' partner
- couples where one of the partners is married to someone else.

The Law Reform Commission in its consultation paper *Rights and Duties of Cohabitees* points to a variety of motives which have been suggested a couple may have in choosing to live together outside marriage.

- The couple may decide to move in together because they find each other sexually attractive, but they may not intend the arrangement to have any degree of permanence.
- The cohabitation may be viewed as a 'trial marriage'. It has been suggested that this is a key reason for cohabiting.
- The cohabitation may be viewed as an alternative to marriage because
  — marriage may not be an option: for example the cohabitees may be heterosexual persons who are already married
  — both or one of the partners may be idealogically opposed to marriage
  — both or one of the partners may be opposed to marriage for financial reasons. Perhaps they are already supporting a spouse, or an ex-spouse, or receiving support from a former partner, and do not want to jeopardise this

— another factor which seems to trigger cohabitation is unexpected pregnancy, and this type of cohabitation seems to have replaced the so-called 'shotgun wedding'.

John Mee in his book *The Property Rights of Cohabitees* (Hart 1999) puts the complexity of cohabitation as follows:

> The whole question is a very difficult one, since people's motives may change over time. Consider the case of a couple who move in together at an early stage in their relationship, seeing their cohabitation as a trial period before a possible marriage. If, for some reason (probably the reluctance of one partner) they never actually marry, they will not necessarily separate. Many of the cases in this area involve relationships which drift on for many years, even after it has become apparent that the originally envisaged marriage will never take place. Such a relationship begins as a 'trial marriage' and ends, in effect, as an alternative to marriage.

Article 41.3.1, with its reference to the institution of marriage 'on which the family is founded', precludes cohabiting heterosexual couples from the constitutional protection accorded to marital families. The Law Reform Commission's consultation paper points out:

> For example, cohabitees do not have the same property rights as spouses. In particular, the courts have no jurisdiction to make a property adjustment order in favour of a cohabitee on the termination of the relationship and cohabitees do not enjoy the protection of the Family Home Protection Act 1976. In addition, cohabitees do not have the same succession rights as spouses and they have no right to claim maintenance during or after the relationship. Similarly, cohabitees are unable to claim certain tax and social welfare benefits, which are available to spouses. Furthermore, State pensions and many older commercial pensions do not make provision for cohabitees. Cohabitees have no right to succeed to tenancies and cohabitees have no right to make decisions concerning the health of their partner, no matter how long they have lived together.

Many of the submissions supported the current position in relation to marriage:

European Life Network declared:

> For our children's well being, and to protect the fragile freedoms of religion, speech and association, we must not allow the creation of government-imposed counterfeit 'marriage' under any guise whatsoever ... marriage is

civilisation's primary institution, and we tamper with it at our peril.

Family Solidarity said:

> Trying to cater in the Constitution for cohabiting couples would damage the status of the traditional family. Siblings or other members living together need to have legislation introduced to regulate the distribution of property etc.

The Knights of St Columbanus said:

> The so called 'de facto' unions have been taking on special importance in recent years. The common element of such unions is that of being forms of cohabitation of a sexual kind, which are not marriage. Some recent initiatives propose the institutional recognition of 'de facto' unions and even their equivalence to families which have their origin in a marriage commitment. It is important to draw attention to the damage that such recognition and equivalence would represent for the identity of marriages traditionally understood.

Mothers at Home said:

> Every individual, because of their inherent human dignity, must be protected by the State. The family based on marriage is guaranteed protection under the Constitution and this must remain. It is not possible to give constitutional protection to families other than those based on marriage because the family is a union of a man and a woman in the lifelong convenant of marriage. Unions not based on marriage already have protection by the personal rights identified under Article 40.3. Where siblings or other family members reside together, some legal protection with regard to say, distribution of property etc, can be provided. The Constitution currently recognises that the family based on marriage offers the stability and security needed by society. This must not be weakened by affording the same status to other unions.

The Islamic Foundation of Ireland said:

> There seems to be a contradiction between the suggestion made by the Constitution Review Group of the state pledging to guard with special care the institution of marriage and protect it against attack on one side, and on the other hand affording recognition to families not based on marriage. It can also be argued that in accordance with the universally accepted concept of the state being the guardian of the common good – which is stated in the Constitution – the

state should be seen as promoting marriage (in the form of a union between a man and a woman) and discouraging relationships outside marriage in this sense as much as possible.

Muintir na hÉireann said:

> Every individual, because of their inherent human dignity, must be protected by the state. The family based on marriage is guaranteed protection under the Constitution and this must remain. It is not possible to give constitutional protection to families other than those based on marriage because the family is a union of a man and a woman in the lifelong convenant of marriage.

The Constitution Review Group (1996), in its concern to meet the needs of cohabiting heterosexual couples, concluded that legislation alone was not sufficient. It recommended a constitutional change which would extend constitutional protection to family life in general and retain especial regard for the family based on marriage. The relevant elements of its recommendation are:

i) recognition by the State of the family as the primary and fundamental unit of society

ii) a right for all persons to marry in accordance with the requirements of law and to found a family

iii) a pledge by the State to guard with special care the institution of marriage and protect it against attack, subject to a proviso that this section should not prevent the Oireachtas from legislating for the benefit of families not based on marriage or for the individual members thereof

iv) a pledge by the State to protect the family based on marriage in its constitution and authority

v) a guarantee to all individuals of respect for their family life whether based on marriage or not.

The CRG proposal would provide a constitutional basis for legislation that would extend 'marriage-like' protections to co-habiting heterosexual couples. Subsequent to the Constitution Review Group's report the Law Reform Commission in its consultation paper *Rights and Duties of Cohabitees* (2004) put forward the view that such protections could be provided by legislation without any need to amend the Constitution. It is of the view that the law as it stands allows the Oireachtas to legislate in respect of the non-marital family provided that it does not place such relationships in a more favourable position than the marital family:

> The seminal case here is *Murphy v Attorney General*. In this case, the Supreme Court held that a married couple, each of

whom was working, could not be taxed more severely, in terms of tax bands and tax allowances, than two single persons living together. Likewise, in *Hyland v Minister for Social Welfare*, the Supreme Court held that a married couple could not be paid less social welfare benefit or assistance than a cohabiting couple. In addition, in *Green v Minister for Agriculture*, Murphy J in the High Court struck down an administrative scheme providing compensation to persons farming in disadvantaged areas because the means test provided for the aggregation of the income of the married couple, but not of the cohabiting couple. In *MacMathuna v Ireland*, the plaintiffs, a married couple, challenged the constitutionality of legislation which gave a tax-free allowance to single parents in respect of the child or children living with them, on the basis that it treated single people more favourably than married people. Carroll J in the High Court rejected this claim on the basis that 'the position of a single parent is different to the position of two parents living together. The parent on his or her own has a more difficult task in bringing the children up single handedly because two parents living together can give each other mutual support and assistance.' However, Carroll J stressed that the legislation would have been unconstitutional if the allowance was payable while the woman was cohabiting. It seems probable that this line of authority would not prevent the legislature increasing the rights of cohabitees to bring them on a par with those of a married couple, as it only appears to prevent married couples being treated less favourably than cohabiting couples are.

The Law Society in its submission did not feel that constitutional amendment was necessary in order to meet the needs of cohabiting heterosexual couples:

> The Society recommends that the rights of cohabitees should be reflected in legislation rather than in the Constitution. It believes that legislation should be introduced facilitating registered partnership agreements, but does not see the need to change our fundamental law. In summary, the Law Society endorses the recommendations of the Law Reform Commission in its recent Consultation Paper *Rights and Duties of Cohabitees*.

The Irish Catholic Bishops' Conference, which does not wish to see the constitutional definition of the family changed, endorsed the need to care for cohabiting heterosexual couples through appropriate legislation:

> It is important that such units [non-marital family units], especially insofar as they include children, are offered

appropriate social and financial support as is already provided for by various statutory and regulatory measures. It is clear that such support can be, and is, offered in ways that do not undermine the position of the family based on marriage. The precise achievement of such a balance is a matter of prudent social policy judgements and is best achieved without specific constitutional direction... Questions concerning the rights of individual members of non-marital units are best considered as personal rights. If there were to be a guarantee to all individuals of respect for their family life whether based on marriage or not, as envisaged by the Review Group, it is arguable that said provision would effectively render meaningless any attempt to define the family in terms of marriage. In this context, it is appropriate to attend, albeit perfunctorily, to the recent Consultation Paper on the Rights and Duties of Cohabitees issued by the Law Reform Commission. It is interesting to note that the Commission was of the view that Article 41 does not prevent the Oireachtas legislating in respect of cohabitees, so long as the legislation does not grant cohabitees more extensive rights than those enjoyed by married couples. Whatever view one may hold about the actual proposals of the Commission, it is clear that the existing constitutional support for the family based on marriage would not seem to exclude extensive measures being taken in support of non-marital units.

Conclusion

It can be inferred that cohabiting heterosexual couples, who by definition have opted out of marriage, would expect the state nevertheless to respect their family life and protect it. The state agencies concerned with family affairs must acknowledge such families and seek to meet their needs. An extension of constitutional protection to family life in general would be welcomed by both the families themselves and the agencies that deal with them. However, it is clear that legislation could extend to such families the broad range of marriage-like privileges without any need to amend the Constitution.

Chapter 4

Same-sex couples

Those who support same-sex marriage are homosexuals who wish to be able to express mutual affection with the openness and esteem that heterosexuals can enjoy. They support therefore the equality model of the family which promises equal regard for every form of family life.

Supporters of the equality model of the family tend to support provision for same-sex marriage on the grounds that it is a requirement of the equality value, already enshrined in such legislation as the Equality Act 2004, the Equal Status Act 2000 and the Employment Equality Act 1998.

In its submission the Gay Catholic Caucus seeks empathy with society in general:

> Courageous science and research, as well as the dawning of gay consciousness across the globe, mean that, for an ever wider number of the world's population, homosexual relationships and homosexual sex are now seen as falling within the 'normal' range of human sexuality … We address overlapping audiences in what follows. Most widely, we speak to the straight community in Ireland. Our argument is that the gay marriage issue is not just a gay issue, but is an issue for all Irish people. Gay people are your sons, daughters, sisters, brothers, cousins, nephews, nieces, uncles, aunts, and even spouses; they are your co-workers, friends, neighbours, and co-citizens. Blithely to deprive these people, your relatives and friends, of the right to marry, says something profound about what kind of society you choose, and also deprives you of the resource that the full expression of gay love could be for Irish families and communities.

> Law can seem cold and abstract, but it has consequences for real flesh and blood people. For gay people who would like to marry, but are precluded from doing so by the Irish State, the law means that:
> • They pay higher income tax.
> • They pay higher capital gains tax.
> • They pay higher stamp duty.
> • They pay higher inheritance and gift tax if they make any gifts or bequests to each other.
> • Their non-Irish spouse cannot easily work and live in Ireland.

- They may face discrimination in pension benefits.
- In cases of domestic violence, they are less protected by the law because they cannot claim barring orders under the Domestic Violence Act 1996.
- They may not be recognised as next of kin if their partner is hospitalised.
- The partner of a deceased gay person will have no entitlement equivalent to that of a spouse, to a share of the estate of the deceased.
- In case of pregnancy, the partner of the pregnant person will not be entitled to parental leave.
- They can adopt but only as single people.
- The child of a gay couple is disadvantaged because he or she cannot legally be recognised as a child of both parents. The disadvantages relate to gifts, inheritance and custody.

Is this fair? We think not.

Johnny – Gay Peer Action Charity Group underscores the perceived injustice:

> This submission clearly outlines the current injustice and discrimination that Lesbian, Gay, Bisexual and Transgendered (LGBT) couples experience as a result of the state's prohibition of marriage for same-sex couples. The lack of recognition has led to grave inequality in accessing state services and other associated benefits of which only state recognised married couples can avail themselves. Consequently, we argue that the state does not recognise each member of our society as equal, fails to acknowledge the diverse nature of the family unit, does not provide for the protection and well-being of every child, and has policies that do not correspond to the progress made across Europe and the world to end this discrimination.

> In order to bring about equality, we ask for the introduction of legislation that allows for a wider interpretation of the term 'marriage' as used in the Constitution, and thus recognises civil marriage for same-sex couples.

GLEN – Gay and Lesbian Equality Network states:

> Based on the principle of equality of rights, duties and responsibilities, we are asking now that the law on civil marriage be amended so that it is open to any two people, irrespective of gender. It should be stressed that civil marriage is quite separate from a religious marriage and that what GLEN is calling for is marriage in the eyes of the state in a Registry Office as distinct from a religious marriage ceremony in a church. We make no comment or any request about the codes that apply to religious marriage ceremonies.

GLUE – Gay and Lesbian Unions Eire is concerned with the position of immigrants who are gay and lesbian:

> GLUE's primary concern ... is to ensure immigration rights be granted to committed same sex partnerships. We have highlighted the injustices that same sex couples must endure on a daily basis and we hope that this submission will assist in the creation of legislation to encompass our fast growing cosmopolitan community. We also hope that this will benefit heterosexual couples.

The Women's Health Council finds that legislative amendments are urgently needed:

> Lesbian women and gay men have been found to suffer from discrimination and prejudice resulting in disadvantage and exclusion from full participation in society (Gay and Lesbian Equality Network and Nexus Research Co-operative, 1995). They also experience poorer mental health because of the chronic stress associated with being a member of a stigmatised minority group (Meyer, 2003). This situation has been recently further exacerbated by the Irish government. Through the introduction of the Social Welfare (Miscellaneous) Bill 2004, which restricts the definition of 'spouse' or 'couple' to a married couple and to an opposite sex cohabiting couple for state welfare schemes, Ireland is now in breach of Article 14 (obligation not to discriminate) and Article 8 (right to respect for private and family life) of EHCR, and is the only EU country to have introduced deliberately discriminatory legislation against lesbians and gays for over a decade (Equality Coalition, 2004). Hence, legislative amendments are urgently needed to reverse this situation and to promote and support their full participation in all aspects of society, including legally recognised relationships and families.

Aim Family Services takes the following view:

> There is need for greater debate in this area. Firstly, we should ascertain the wishes of the majority of Irish gay people and devise a system of registration of domestic partnerships that would confer the rights at present unavailable to same sex and heterosexual cohabiting couples in the area of tax, social welfare and inheritance.

Labour LGBT – a group of members of the Irish Labour Party who identify as Lesbian, Gay, Bisexual or Transgendered – states:

> To date there has been no reasonable justification as to why the state should sanction heterosexual marriages and refuse

to do the same for non-heterosexual couples. For some the issue of procreation was an argument in favour of providing limited support to the non-recognition of non-heterosexual couples by the state. However it is well established that many heterosexual couples who have state recognised marriages are unable to conceive or have no intention of doing so. For others it is religious reasons, yet the state now allows for divorce. Labour LGBT feels there should be a separation of church and state and that old religious tradition can no longer discriminate against the LGBT minority. Others have used economic arguments that to provide same-sex couples with the same benefits as married couples would cost the taxpayer money. Our response is Gay Men and Lesbians pay PAYE and PRSI too, so why should we not be given these benefits?

Sinn Féin states:

The refusal to recognise same sex partnerships, regardless of equivalent permanency, denies lesbians and gays the access to a broad section of rights available to heterosexual married couples. We would like to bring to the committee's attention the fact that the High Court has cleared the way for a lesbian couple (Katherine Zappone and Louise Gilligan) to bring a legal action to have their Canadian marriage recognised in this state and to have the Revenue Commissioners treat them under the Tax Acts in the same way as a married couple. Zappone and Gilligan are arguing that the refusal of the Revenue to recognise them as a married couple in Irish law for tax purposes breaches their rights under the Constitution and the European Convention for the Protection of Human Rights and Fundamental Freedoms. In permitting the couple to proceed with such an action the High Court was satisfied that they had demonstrated an arguable case. The lack of protection for gay and lesbian partnerships has permitted the government to introduce provisions such as that introduced in the Civil Registration Bill 2003 specifically excluding same sex couples from the benefits of the legislation.[35]

Young Greens – Óige Ghlas states:

While extending the right to marry to same-sex couples would have financial implications for the exchequer, such considerations cannot be used to trump the basic equality argument. Same-sex marriage can in no way undermine religious rules as regards marriage, as it would only apply in

35 Sinn Féin introduced an amendment supporting equal rights of same-sex couples, in opposition to the government amendment specifically excluding them from the legislation. This was opposed by the government parties while Labour and Fine Gael abstained. Amendment No 5 by Sean Crowe TD to the Civil Registration Bill 2003 was defeated by 63 votes to 10.

the civil sphere. Indeed, some of the countries that allow same-sex couples to marry permit individual registrars to refuse to perform such ceremonies if it is against their personal beliefs.

Further, at a time of falling marriage rates, the Young Greens/Óige Ghlas believe that by opening the institution of marriage to a group of previously excluded people, the concept of marriage will be made firmer.

Irish Council for Civil Liberties (ICCL) explores the state's international commitments in regard to the issue:

The right to marry is protected under both Article 12 and Article 23 of the ECHR and the ICCPR respectively. Both Articles refer to the right of men and women to marry. To date, the UN Human Rights Committee has determined that the express reference to men and women in Article 23 means that the failure to provide for same-sex marriage will not lead to a violation of the prohibition on discrimination on grounds of sexual orientation under the Covenant.[36]

However, in *Goodwin v United Kingdom* and *I v United Kingdom*[37] the Court, in a unanimous decision, found that the UK was in breach of Articles 8 and 12 of the ECHR. The Court found that although the right to marry is subject to the national laws of the Contracting States the limitations on it must not restrict or reduce the right in such a way or to such an extent that the very essence of the right is impaired. The Court found that the UK laws, in prohibiting a post-operative transsexual from marrying a member of their former gender, impaired the very right to marry and was in violation of the Convention. The Court acknowledged that although the first sentence of Article 12 refers in express terms to the right of a man and woman to marry, in 2002 it could not be assumed that these terms must refer to a determination of gender by purely biological criteria, or required some pre-requisite capacity to procreate.

In the context of the submission to the Inter-Departmental Committee on Reform of Marriage the ICCL has already raised the fact that Irish law is in violation of the ECHR due to its denial of the right to marry to transsexuals,[38] except ironically where that marriage would be *de facto* between same-sex partners.

---

36 Communication No 902/1999: *Joslin v New Zealand* 30/07/2002. CCPR/C/75/D/9 02/1999.
37 Judgments 11 July 2002.
38 *Foy v Registrar of Births*, High Court, Irish Times Law Report, 10 July 2002.

Opposing views

Those who oppose same-sex marriage are supporters of the traditional model of the family. They regard same-sex marriage as a contradiction in terms – by definition marriage is a union of two persons of the opposite sex. Recognition of same-sex marriage would represent an attack on marriage. They repudiate the contention that to deny same-sex couples the right to marry is to discriminate against them. Marriage is open to everyone once they meet the necessary criteria: they are not already married and the other person is an adult, free to marry, not a close family member, and of the opposite sex. They oppose giving the right to adopt and rear children to same-sex couples on the grounds that it denies to children their natural right to be brought up in an environment in which they have both a male and a female role-model.

Right Nation states:

> The question of whether the state should allow homosexuals to marry is a logically absurd one since it isn't the state which created heterosexual marriage in the first instance, but it is as earlier pointed out a natural institution. Correctly put the state provides by its laws an acknowledgement and a registration of marriage but does not create it. The state, consequently, can no more create a homosexual marriage than it can make … [an] orange be an apple.

AMEN states:

> In addressing this question we must look at the purpose of marriage and why the institution of marriage was created. Essentially civil marriage exists for the protection of the next generation and to deal with succession rights etc. At present Irish law requires that one party to a marriage must be male and the other must be female … The position was further clarified in *Foy v An tArd-Chlaraitheoir* when McKenchie J stated that 'marriage as understood by the Constitution, by statute and by case law refers to the union of a biological man with a biological woman'. The Inter-Departmental Committee on the Reform of Marriage Law proposed that the definition of marriage should be that approved by the Supreme Court, i.e. 'the voluntary and permanent union of one man and one woman to the exclusion of all others for life'... Perhaps the best way to deal with the position of gay couples is that outlined by Archbishop Diarmuid Martin:
>
> > Church teaching stresses that marriage is exclusively between a man and a woman, because this is part of the basic structure of the complementarity of the sexes, something rooted in creation, and not simply a social or

cultural construct. It may, in certain circumstances, be in the public interest to provide legal protection to the social, fiscal and inheritance entitlements of persons who support caring relationships which generate dependency, provided always that these relationships are recognised as being qualitatively different from marriage and that their acceptance does not dilute the uniqueness of marriage.

European Life Network states:

Giving 'gay' relationships marital status will destroy marriage. Homosexual and lesbian pairings are not marriage and never can be. It is futile therefore to pretend that they can or should be given a special status or treatment equivalent to that of marriage ... Unlike race or ethnicity, homosexuality is in no way immutable or genetically determined. It is a chosen behaviour. People need not embrace unnatural feelings, and many homosexuals have overcome 'gay' desires and gone on to lead heterosexual lives, including getting married and having children. Science has produced no credible evidence of innate homosexuality. The most famous 'born gay' study, by Dean Hamer, a homosexual activist researcher, could not be replicated. Thus, comparisons to inter-racial marriage cases, such as *Loving v Virginia* (US Supreme Court, 1967), are irrelevant and misleading. The very soul of marriage – the joining of the two sexes – is never at issue in the *Loving v Virginia* case.

Focus on the Family Ireland states:

Marriage has never been defined or regulated according to sexual orientation; in fact, the idea of sexual orientations has never previously been an issue in stable society. It has only come about because of the political activity of the homosexual lobby in gaining legitimacy for their opinions. No scientific institution in the world has ever established the immutability of homosexuality. Many scientists have tried, but none has ever succeeded. Homosexuality cannot be compared to genealogy or ethnic heritage which cannot be changed. In fact, Columbia University researchers William Byrne and Bruce Parsons carefully analysed all the major biological studies on homosexuality. Finding no studies that supported a purely biological cause for homosexuality they found the origins of homosexual identification rooted in a 'complex mosaic of biological, psychological and social/cultural factors'.

The Reformed Presbyterian Church of Ireland states:

God has directed that families are comprised of male and female for good reason ... [I]n a survey of over 200 studies carried out over the last 15–20 years by reputable scientists and research facilities who were either positive or neutral towards homosexuality, it was found that the percentage of homosexual relationships that last past 5 years is so small as to be almost non-existent. Of those that last that long, virtually none are monogamous. The stereotype of the happy gay man and his lifelong loving partner is a myth. As a lifestyle homosexuality is extraordinarily destructive and dysfunctional (*Straight and Narrow: Compassion and Clarity in the Homosexual Debate* (1995), Thomas Schmidt, Leicester: Inter Varsity Press, 1995).

The Association of Baptist Churches in Ireland states:

One of the main purposes of marriage, if not the main one, is the birth and nurture of the next generation in an environment which provides both fatherhood and motherhood. By definition gay couples neither (a) produce children on their own, nor (b) provide both male and female role models. If gay couples are to be given some special legal status short of marriage, or special privileges and/or exemptions, then in fairness this should open the door to similar provisions for the benefit of all kinds of other domestic arrangements and commitments.

The Council for the Status of the Family states:

We believe that legal recognition of homosexual unions would obscure certain basic values and cause devaluation of the institution of marriage as it is at present understood and universally accepted ... The anecdotal evidence from elsewhere (e.g. since the beginnings of the AIDS crisis in the 1980s) confirms that long-term relationships between men are uncommon and that much of the male homosexual culture is more concerned with promiscuity, rivalry and conquest than with lifelong fidelity.

Statistics from that era reveal that, in San Francisco, 25% of male homosexuals had had over 1,000 sexual partners, another 25% more than 500 partners, while the remainder had had somewhat less. Lifetime relationships were very much the exception rather than the rule.

This Council considers that the use of vague abstract terms such as *growing recognition, popular support, new awareness, greater tolerance, diversity in family life* are not helpful in identifying the needs of real families based on marriage which are the bedrock of every civilised society.

Evangelical Alliance Ireland states:

> The introduction of gay marriage would effectively discriminate against other domestic relationships that are often as permanent and stable as a gay relationship, such as siblings living together or an unmarried child living with an elderly parent. There are issues of legal and financial protection requiring attention in many such relationships. These issues can and should be dealt with under law without undermining the uniqueness of marriage.

The Family First Association (Ireland) states:

> As gay couples do not have the biological means to 'create' a natural 'household' family then it would not be ethical to allow gay couples to marry ... Gay couples who are willing to make a lifetime commitment to each other should be allowed make a legal declaration/statement by way of an 'oath of fidelity', which would be State approved.

Plumbline Network of Churches in Ireland states:

> Homosexual couples should not be afforded the status of marriage. They are not able to produce children through their union and should not be allowed to adopt the children of others. Children deserve the best possible environment to develop, and the Constitution should do nothing which would deny the rights of children to a father and a mother with the distinctiveness that each brings to the parenting role ... Registered domestic partners may be an alternative course of action to deal with inheritance and property issues. There is no need to amend the Constitution to enact registered partnerships, which could also serve for all other sorts of domestic arrangements, which are not necessarily based on a sexual relationship.

In general those who support the traditional model of the family recognise that people who are homosexual must be shown tolerance. The Church of Ireland says:

> Marriage for us is understood as the joining together of a Man and a Woman in lifelong and exclusive commitment, in a covenant which in its purpose is relational, unitative and where possible procreative. A same-sex couple does not have of itself the capacity or potential to procreate and as such cannot under any circumstances fulfil this complete definition. A same sex union can and should be given Constitutional protection under the broad definition of the family favoured above [see the full text of this submission in

Appendix 3], but cannot in our view be considered a marriage, nor should the language and distinctive ceremonies of marriage be associated with it in civil law.

The Irish Catholic Bishop's Conference states:

Church teaching stresses that marriage is exclusively between a man and a woman, because this is part of the basic structure of the complementarity of the sexes, something rooted in creation, and not simply a social or cultural construct.

The Catholic Church remains committed to advocating and promoting the common good of everyone in our society. The Catholic Church teaches that homosexual people are to be 'accepted with respect, compassion and sensitivity'. The Church condemns all forms of violence, harassment or abuse directed against people who are homosexual ... The recognition of same-sex unions on the same terms as marriage would suggest to future generations and to society as a whole that marriage as husband and wife, and a same-sex relationship, are equally valid options, and an equally valid context for the bringing up of children. What is at stake here is the natural right of children to the presence normally of a mother and father in their lives. Given the legal changes that have already taken place and the fact that two people can make private legal provision covering many aspects of their lives together, including joint ownership of homes, living wills and powers of attorney, the argument that same-sex marriage is necessary to protect human rights becomes a redundant one. When it is balanced against the manner in which it will undermine such a fundamental institution as marriage and the family, it is difficult to see how such a development could be justified in terms of the Government's duty to defend marriage and the common good.

Some advances

Those who support same-sex marriage were cheered that such provisions were recently made in the Netherlands, Belgium, Spain and Canada. They would also have been cheered by the ruling in March 2005 made by Richard Kramer, a San Francisco Superior Court judge: 'No rational basis exists for limiting marriage in this state [California] to opposite-sex partners'. He said that to limit marriage in this way is anti-homosexual discrimination akin to racial discrimination (California's Supreme Court ruled in 1948 that the state's ban on interracial marriage violated the equal-protection clause of the United States Constitution). The judge rejected the view that the procreation and rearing of children by a man and a woman were the essential purpose of marriage: 'One does not have to be married in order to procreate, nor does one have to procreate in order to be married'. Heterosexual couples who are unable or unwilling to have children are free to marry but same-sex couples are singled out to be denied marriage. For health reasons the state can legitimately ban incestuous marriages but the judge said it cannot discriminate on the 'arbitrary classifications of group or races' citing the 1948 state Supreme Court ruling. The judge also rejected that discrimination would not exist if same-sex couples were given marriage-like rights through civil partnerships: 'The idea that marriage-like rights without marriage is adequate smacks of a concept long rejected by the [US] courts – separate but equal'. (The judge's ruling is subject to appeal to the Californian Supreme Court.)

However these successes have provoked strong opposition in many countries. Some homosexuals therefore are prepared to moderate their demand and settle for the legislative provision for same-sex unions or partnerships such as have been provided initially by Denmark, followed by Finland, France, Norway, Sweden, Germany and Britain. The committee received a submission from Senator David Norris which proposed a Civil Partnership Bill to allow same-sex and indeed heterosexual cohabiting couples a bundle of legal privileges matching but not exceeding those of married couples.

Conclusion

Provision for same-sex marriage would bring practical benefits. But it would require a constitutional amendment to extend the definition of the family. However, legislation could extend to such couples a broad range of marriage-like privileges without any need to amend the Constitution (as has been suggested in the case of cohabiting heterosexual couples).

Chapter 5

Children

Article 41

1   1° *The State
recognises the Family
as the natural
primary and
fundamental unit
group of Society, and
as a moral institution
possessing inalienable
and imprescriptible
rights, antecedent
and superior to all
positive law.*
*2° The State,
therefore, guarantees
to protect the Family
in its constitution and
authority, as the
necessary basis of
social order and as
indispensable to the
welfare of the Nation
and the State.*

Article 42

5   *In exceptional cases,
where the parents for
physical or moral
reasons fail in their
duty towards their
children, the State as
guardian of the
common good, by
appropriate means
shall endeavour to
supply the place of the
parents, but always
with due regard for
the natural and
imprescriptible rights
of the child.*

Article 41 acknowledges the right of the family based on marriage to govern itself as a family. This right is based on the nature of the family as the basic unit of society. The Article proceeds from the view that the family is antecedent to the state and therefore the autonomy of the family in its own sphere cannot be interfered with by the state. The Article is a bulwark between the freedom of the people and any unwarranted intrusions by the state – Article 42.5 requires the state to act in the exceptional cases where the parents fail in their duty to their children.

Over time certain legal interpretations have filled out the meaning of the Article. Thus when the Constitution was enacted the common law understanding placed the father firmly at the head of the family. In the fifties the courts declared that the father and mother held parental rights jointly (*Re Tilson, infants* [1951] IR 1; (1952) 86 ILTR 49). The courts have also found that children are entitled to all of the personal rights enjoyed in Article 40 and that they enjoy as well a number of rights that belong to the category of unenumerated rights in the Constitution, such as the right to bodily integrity and the right to an opportunity to be reared with due regard to religious, moral, intellectual and physical welfare.

However the silence of Article 41 in relation to children means that the rights of the family are effectively exercised by the parents and that the rights of children may not be given due weight within the family.

It is probably true that Irish people have supported the movement since World War II to define and assert the rights of children (as well as other human rights) through the European Convention on Human Rights in Europe and through the UN Convention on Human Rights worldwide. It is also probably true that Irish society did not appreciate that Irish children stood in need of protection. This attitude has changed with the revelation of the institutional abuse of children outside the home as revealed in the media and the abuse of children within the home as revealed in the Kilkenny Incest Enquiry.

The traditional model

Some supporters of the traditional model of the family feel that the rights of the child are already sufficiently protected in the Constitution, for instance in Article 40.3 which guarantees the personal rights of the citizen. They fear that any further strengthening of the rights of children would interfere with the authority and autonomy of the family. While they would agree that the UN Convention on the Rights of the Child has many admirable features, they fear that it leaves open the possibility that its interpretation by UN monitoring committees could result in the reduction of the authority of parents. For example the Council for the Status of the Family had this to say in its submission:

> We have read the UN Convention on the Rights of the Child accept most of the Articles which we consider relevant to marriage and family life in this society. However, this Council is strongly of the view that the *primary* rights in families are and must remain those of the parents. Provision has already been made in the Irish Constitution (Article 42.5) for cases where parents are unable to provide adequate care.

The Family and Media Association stated:

> The child already has rights as a human being independent of the family. More emphasis on the rights of the child would mean more external intervention, not necessarily in the best interests of the child.

Citywise expressed reservations about the UN Convention, among them the following:

> Many of these UN articles do not reflect the considered opinions of Irish people, deriving as they do from a culture which has a poor understanding of the relationship of trust within families, relationships which should not be subject to the divisive rights-based language of the UN Convention.

Other supporters of the traditional model of the family would support measures to achieve a balance between the rights of the family and the rights of children in the Constitution. The Church of Ireland submission contained the following statement:

> Save in relation to the courts' divorce jurisdiction, there is no specific reference to the rights of the child in Article 41. The courts have however interpreted the Constitution as conferring unenumerated constitutional rights on children, arising particularly under Article 40.3. For the sake of clarity, and in line with the Constitution Review Group's report, we recommend the express guaranteeing of the rights of the child in Article 41. Furthermore … there should be included in the Constitution an express requirement, such as is already contained in legislation, that in all actions concerning children paramount consideration should be given to the best interests of the child.

The joint submission from Irish Catholic Bishops' Conference stated:

> The Constitution Review Group, as has been noted, recommended that all the unenumerated rights conferred by Article 40.3 should be expressly enumerated and this recommendation was extended to the unenumerated rights of children. This is a question of jurisprudential and constitutional theory. It is a matter of prudential judgment for the appropriate experts as to whether the protection of children's rights is best effected through express constitutional enumeration or through entrusting to the courts the task of specifying said rights in particular circumstances.
>
> Particular issues arise when tensions emerge between families and outside agencies as to the determination of the best interests of children. The question may arise as to whether the family or the state is best positioned to safeguard the rights of children. Not all families are good environments for rearing children. They may be affected by the personal moral weaknesses and limitations of parents. Children may be exposed to sexual abuse, violence or neglect. In these and similar circumstances, the state may clearly intervene. Thus, for example, the Childcare Act 1991 and the Adoption Act 1988 enable children to be protected from the effects of the failures of their parents. The Supreme Court made it clear in *In re Article 26 and the Adoption (No. 2) Bill 1987* that Article 41 is no barrier to the compulsory adoption of children on the basis of continuing parental failure.
>
> …. It is clear that the Constitution must afford legal protection for measures which are necessary to protect the rights of children. However the family unit must be allowed to retain its appropriate authority and autonomy. Whether this balance is best achieved by express constitutional provision or by judicial interpretation of the existing constitutional parameters remains to be seen. The authors of *J M Kelly: The Irish Constitution* draw attention to the following statement from a judgment of Mr Justice Ellis: 'In my opinion, the inalienable and imprescriptible rights of the family under Article 41 of the Constitution attach to each member of the family including the children. Therefore in my view the only way the "inalienable and imprescriptible" and "natural and imprescriptible" rights of the child can be protected is by the courts treating the welfare of the child as the paramount consideration in all disputes as to its custody, including disputes between a parent and a stranger. I take the view also that the child has the personal right to have its welfare regarded as the paramount consideration in any such dispute as to its custody under Article 40.3 and that this right of the infant can additionally arise from "the Christian and

democratic nature of the State".' On the basis of their analysis of that judgment, they conclude that 'it indicates how a more balanced approach to the complex area of custody disputes ... can be achieved by re-arguing the constitutional principles involved and without the necessity of a constitutional amendment'. This view would seem to be re-enforced by the recent judgment of Mrs Justice Finlay Geoghegan in the case *FN v CO*.

The equality model

Supporters of the equality model strongly support express provision for the rights of children in the Constitution and many of them referred to the recommendation of the Constitution Review Group in relation to Article 41.

The Law Society stated the following:

> Children are a voiceless and vulnerable minority group in society. Indeed, the Constitutional position of children has proven to be far from secure. It hardly needs to be stated that the measure of a democracy is the manner in which the needs of the most vulnerable are considered and met. That said, one notable feature of the Irish family law system is the relative invisibility of children. For example, children are caught in the crossfire of relationship breakdown. Currently, with no way of exercising their rights, children are in a uniquely vulnerable position in that they cannot exercise their rights during childhood. It should be stated that childhood is only for a defined period of time and does not stand still. The Constitution should be amended to contain a specific declaration on the rights of children.

Barnardos made the following statement:

> The current position is that under the Irish Constitution, children's rights are not adequately protected .... The Constitution creates an environment where the rights of the family take precedence over the rights of individual children. This impacts on the culture of child protection work and policy-making. Also the decision-making flows from assumptions that plans for children are created around the rights of parents .... The question must be asked as to how the whole childcare system in Ireland could be strengthened if the Irish Constitution were to include an explicit children's rights provision. Barnardos is of the view that this would strengthen the effectiveness of child and family services in terms of child protection.

The Ombudsman for Children described the position of children in the Irish Constitution as 'a matter of concern':

> The Ombudsman for Children recommends an amendment to the Constitution to grant express rights to children. In defining these express rights the Ombudsman for Children recommends that the committee should consider the rights enumerated in the 1989 United Nations Convention on the Rights of the Child. In particular, the Ombudsman recommends that the Constitution should be amended to ensure that the right of children to have their welfare protected is given the paramountcy it deserves.

The Green Party described the UN Convention on the Rights of the Child as the most widely ratified human rights treaty, entitling it to be regarded as 'setting out the international community's norms on the rights of the child'. The Green Party submission went on:

> The Convention, similar to the Irish Constitution, recognises the family as 'the fundamental group of society' while, unlike the Irish Constitution, it more fully recognises the rights (and duties) of individuals within the family unit. We are particularly guided by the Preamble to the Convention: 'Convinced that the family, as the fundamental group of society and the natural environment for the growth and well-being of all its members and particularly children, should be afforded the necessary protection and assistance so that it can fully assume its responsibilities within the community...' The fact that Ireland has been cited in the European Commission's 2004 Report on Social Inclusion as having the highest rate of poverty for women and second highest for children in the EU markedly shows why reform is urgently required in this area.

The Labour Party in its submission proposed the insertion of a new subsection in relation to the rights of the child in Article 41:

> 1. The state guarantees in its laws to respect, and, as far as practicable, by its laws to defend and vindicate the rights of the child, having due regard to international legal standards and in particular to the United Nations Convention on the Rights of the Child, which rights include –
>
> > i. the right to have his or her best interests regarded as the first and paramount consideration in any decision concerning the child;
> >
> > ii. the right to know the identity of his or her parents and as far as practicable to be reared by his or her parents and each of them, subject to such limitations as may be prescribed by the law in the interests of the child; and

iii. the right to have due regard given to his or her views in any decision concerning the child.

2. In exceptional cases, where parents fail in their duty towards their children, where the interests of a child require intervention, the state as guardian of the common good, by appropriate means, must endeavour to supply the place of the parents but always with due regard for the rights of the child.

Treoir, the Federation of Services for Unmarried Parents and their Children, focused particularly in its submission on the status of children born outside of marriage:

Although parents who are not married do not benefit from the rights enunciated in articles 41 and 42 of the Constitution, it has been held that children born outside wedlock have the same 'natural and imprescriptible rights' as children born within marriage. However, the courts have held that in a number of instances it is permissible to treat children born outside of marriage differently to those born to a married couple. The non-marital family is effectively outside of constitutional protection and an unmarried cohabiting couple cannot, no matter how stable or continuous, bring themselves within the confines of Article 41.1.2.

The Irish Society for the Prevention of Cruelty to Children emphasised the same issue:

Articles 41 and 42 should be amended to grant equal status and rights to all natural parents and their children irrespective of the marital status of the parents. This would better reflect the social reality and ensure that parental decisions about marriage or non-marriage in no way disadvantage children of unmarried parents or deny either children or parents their constitutional rights.

Achieving a balance

In his submission to the Constitution Review Group Professor William Duncan provided a subtle analysis of how the rights of the parents might be retained while securing the appropriate protection for children. In the course of his analysis he made the following statements:

The Irish experience has shown that constitutional recognition of parental rights and duties may influence the legal system in a number of different ways. It has affected the interpretation of legislation and the status of common law principles relating to the parent-child relationship. It has resulted in judicial decisions declaring legislation unconstitutional and therefore invalid. It has had a sometimes remarkable influence on the drafting of legislation, especially relating to adoption. The constitutional provisions are frequently invoked in parliamentary debates during the passage of legislation. And on a broader front, the constitutional emphasis on parental rights and family autonomy (Article 41) has undoubtedly contributed to a social work tradition which places more emphasis on family support than family intervention. Whether the present constitutional provisions have on balance acted as a beneficial break on excessive state interference in family life, or rather as a straitjacket preventing the passage of legislation which would promote the interests of children, has been hotly debated for many years.

In the author's opinion the provisions of the Irish Constitution have on balance played a valuable role in curbing excessive state intervention in the name of child protection. At the very least the constitutional protection of parental rights and family autonomy has prompted the legislature and the courts towards explicit justifications for state action. The dangers, however, should not be underestimated. Strong constitutional support for family autonomy can provide an excuse for the underfunding of child-protection (and sometimes even family-support) services. It is important that respect for parental rights should not be allowed to degenerate into lack of vigilance on behalf of children who are genuinely in need of protection.

In its report the Constitution Review Group recommended that its proposed reconstituted Article 41 would include:

an express guarantee of certain rights of the child, which fall to be interpreted by the courts from the concept of 'family life', which might include:

a) the right of every child to be registered immediately after birth and to have from birth a name
b) the right of every child, as far as practicable, to know his or her parents, subject to the proviso that such right should be subject to regulation by law in the interests of the child
c) the right of every child, as far as practicable, to be cared for by his or her parents
d) the right to be reared with due regard to his or her welfare

an express requirement that in all actions concerning children, whether by legislative, judicial or administrative authorities, the best interests of the child shall be the paramount consideration.

The committee is aware that although Ireland has ratified the UN Convention on the Rights of the Child the provisions of that instrument do not form part of Irish law. It notes that in 1998 the United Nations Committee on the Rights of the Child, in its Concluding Observations, emphasised that the recommendations of the *Report of the Constitution Review Group* would reinforce 'the status of the child as a full subject of rights'. The committee is also aware that the European Convention on Human Rights and Fundamental Freedoms is now part of domestic law but it notes that its incorporation is at sub-constitutional level and children's rights therefore remain inferior and subordinate to parental rights.

Conclusion

Some people feel that children's rights are adequately secured by the existing constitutional provisions and therefore no amendment of the Constitution is necessary. Others believe that experience requires us to secure the rights of the child explicitly and forcefully in the Constitution. This might be secured by a complete re-write of Article 41 or by the addition of a new section in Article 41.

Chapter 6

The natural or birth father

Under Article 41 of the Constitution married parents have express rights (inalienable and imprescriptible) in the Constitution in relation to their children.

Unmarried parents do not have any rights in relation to their children under Article 41. However the courts have recognised that the unmarried mother has a natural right to the custody of her child. This right springs from Article 40.3 and not from Article 41. It is not therefore inalienable and imprescriptible and can be taken away in certain circumstances as adjudged by the courts.

The natural father has no rights in relation to his children under the Constitution. This applies to natural fathers who enjoy long-term stable relationships with their families as well as to natural fathers whose children have been born as a result of casual sex, rape, incest or sperm donation.

The Supreme Court in *The State (Nicolaou) v An Bord Uchtála* ([1966] IR 567) presented the position in relation to natural fathers as follows:

> i   a natural father is not a member of a family within Article 41
> ii   a natural father is not a 'parent' within Article 42
> iii a natural father has no personal right in relation to his child which the State is bound to protect under Article 40.3.

In its 1996 report the Constitution Review Group (CRG) stated:

> There has been much criticism of the continued constitutional ostracism of natural fathers. This can be readily understood in relation to those natural fathers who either live in a stable relationship with the natural mother, or have established a relationship with the child.

It went on to say:

> The Review Group considers that the solution appears to lie in following the approach of Article 8 of the ECHR in guaranteeing to every person respect for 'family life' which has been interpreted to include non-marital family life but yet requiring the existence of family ties between the mother and the father. This may be a way of granting constitutional rights to those fathers who have, or had, a stable relationship with

the mother prior to birth, or subsequent to birth with the child, while excluding persons from having such rights who are only biological fathers without any such relationship. In the context of the Irish Constitution it would have to be made clear that the reference to family life included family life not based on marriage.

In its submission to the committee the Adoption Board endorsed the position taken by the CRG and recommended that a new section should be inserted in Article 41 giving to everyone a right, in accordance with Article 8 of the European Convention on Human Rights, to respect for their family life. The Adoption Board pointed out that this would include rights of a natural/birth father in relation to his child. The Comhairle submission to the committee similarly recommended that provision be made in the Constitution for the rights of non-marital fathers in line with the views of the Constitution Review Group:

> The Constitution Review Group took the view that there did not appear to be justification for giving constitutional rights to every natural father simply by reason of biological links. The solution proposed by the Review Group was to grant constitutional rights to those fathers who have, or had, a stable relationship with the mother prior to birth, or subsequent to birth, with the child. This would be achieved by guaranteeing to every person a respect for family life, including non-marital family life but requiring family ties between the father and mother.

Treoir, the Federation of Services for Unmarried Parents and their Children, also endorsed the position taken by the CRG and went on:

> It is Treoir's position that children should have rights to both parents regardless of the family form but dependant on the nature and quality of the family tie which, as we have seen with the jurisprudence of the European Court of Human Rights [see the full text of this submission in Appendix 3], allows the court to employ necessary interpretive aids such as that of proportionality and within the context of the principle that children's rights are paramount.

> The current family law system is destructive of the family, of citizens' lives and of society in general. It is undoubtedly the greatest evil inflicted on the citizens of this State, by the State since the foundation of the State.

There is acknowledgement in the submissions of the legislative improvements in the position of the natural father since the Nicolaou case, for example the Status of Children Act 1987 provides that an unmarried father may apply to the court to be appointed guardian of his child. Some of the improvements have proceeded from human rights developments internationally. For example under the terms of Article 8 of the European Convention on Human Rights Ireland is now obliged in certain circumstances to give natural fathers a legal opportunity to establish a relationship with their children (*Keegan v Ireland* ((1994) 18 EHRR 342).

The Adoption Board listed the following legal rights relevant to adoption practice which natural/birth fathers currently have:

- the right to be appointed a guardian if both parents agree and if the natural/birth father's name is on the birth cert (Section 12:3(a, b) Status of Children Act 1987). If a natural/birth father is a guardian, adoption could not take place without his consent
- the right to apply to be appointed a guardian (Section 6 of the Guardianship of Infants Act 1964 as amended by Section 12 of the Status of Children Act 1987)
- the right to apply to adopt his child (Adoption Act 1952, Section 11:1 b as amended by Adoption Act 1991 Section 10:1 b)
- subject to four exceptions (as outlined in Section 4, 7E:2,3,4 and 5, Adoption Act 1998), the right to be consulted prior to the placement of his child for adoption
- the right to notify the Adoption Board that he wants to be consulted in relation to any proposal to have a child of his adopted (Section 4, 7D:1, Adoption Act 1998).

Further rights included in the proposals for adoption legislation change would give a natural/birth father:

- preferential adoption rights
- access to his child following adoption as conditions of access could be added to adoption orders.

Currently where the parents are not married the consent of a natural/birth father is not required for the adoption of the child. The European Court of Human Rights (*Keegan v Ireland*, 1994) found that Ireland was in breach of Article 8 of the ECHR. The Adoption Act 1998 was subsequently passed which gave natural/birth fathers a legal entitlement to be consulted before a child is placed for adoption. Natural/birth fathers are entitled to be heard regarding their views on the application and they have the right to apply to the Court for guardianship and custody; however, unless the natural/birth father's application to the Court is successful their consent to the adoption is *not* required.

The submissions highlighted the following areas as of concern to natural fathers: custody, guardianship, access and the lack of transparency in family law courts. The lack of any constitutional rights means that legislative remedies are partial and qualified because they are subordinate to the mother's constitutional rights. The advice and advocacy group Amen had this to say in its submission:

> The State's response to marriage breakdown is to set up a system that exacerbates hostility, encourages parents to abdicate their responsibilities and drives parents into an expensive legal system, which plunders scarce family resources. Invariably men emerge as the supreme losers in these cases. As one member of Amen said 'the State's response to the problem of marriage breakdown can be summed up in three words "wipe men out"'. The Family Mediation Service is ineffective and inadequate and is totally undermined by the legislation, standards and practices of the family law system.

The Men's Council of Ireland reiterated the point in its submission to the committee:

> It is well known (no thanks to any official reporting from our Family Law courts) that men are treated less favourably than women in Family Law courts. This discriminatory practice, which has been going on for years in secret, has effectively undermined the work of the mediation service. Women expect that they will get everything in court, so why negotiate any agreement in mediation? It's as ineffective as negotiating with someone 'who has a gun under the table'. This fact has already been recognised by the Family Mediation Service.

Providing rights for the natural father

The Constitution Review Group recommended that 'All family rights, including those of unmarried mothers or fathers and children born of unmarried parents, should now be placed in Article 41'. This should take the form of, in the words of the Constitution Review Group, 'a guarantee to all individuals of respect for their family life whether based on marriage or not'. This proposal would require a constitutional amendment involving an expanded definition of the family. If such an amendment were not sought, any enhancement of the rights of the natural father would rely on legislation. Such legislation could be given a broader and, of course, more secure base if there were a new Article on children's rights.

Conclusion

Some of the submissions support the giving of the same rights to the natural father as the natural mother possesses under Article 40.3. Many of the submissions, while in favour of giving rights to the natural father, point out that rights cannot be extended in absolute terms to natural fathers because, for instance, some children are born as a result of rape or casual sex. Constitutional provision for the rights of natural fathers could be made either specifically (through qualified and technical expression) or derivatively from another provision.

Chapter 7

Lone parents

Lone-parent families consist of a widow or widower and children, a separated or divorced man or woman and children, a single mother and children, or a single father and children. The concern with the rights of lone-parent families in the submissions centred largely on the single mother and her children.

OPEN (One Parent Exchange and Network), founded in 1994, is a national anti-poverty network which represents lone-parent self-help groups in Ireland. OPEN says:

> Lone parents are not a homogenous group. While the majority of lone parents are lone mothers, 15% of those identified by the Census are lone fathers. The routes into lone parenthood, a condition that can affect any of us, are many – separation, divorce, desertion, death, imprisonment of a partner or an unplanned pregnancy. Irish society is becoming more varied with a growth in non-national communities and a diversity of religious beliefs, all of which have lone parents in their midst. Statistics from the Department of Social and Family Affairs (2004) show that lone parenthood is experienced across the age spectrum. For example, while 57% of lone parents are aged between 25 and 35 years, 19% are over 40 years and 23% are aged less than 24 years. Lone parents are also present amongst other groups such as those with disabilities, those from the travelling community and within the gay, lesbian, bisexual and transgender community.

> While each family will have its own unique experiences, one-parent families have one thing in common: a high risk of living in poverty. In 1994, data from the Living in Ireland Survey (LIS) documented that 1 in 20 households in consistent poverty were headed by a lone parent. The most recent data from the LIS (2001) shows that 1 in 5 households in consistent poverty are headed by lone parents. While most groups have moved out of poverty, lone parents' experience of poverty has increased four-fold.

One Family, progressing the work of Cherish, established in 1972, provides voice, support and action for one-parent families through membership, professional services and campaigning, and aims to achieve equality and social inclusion for all one-parent families in Ireland. One Family says:

Modern family life in Ireland is remarkably different now compared with the period in which our Constitution was first developed. With declining marriage and birth rates, higher rates of extra marital cohabitation and birth and a growing diversification of the structure of families, the typical Irish family is no longer typical.

Census 2002 indicates that there are over 153,900 one-parent families in Ireland, representing almost 12% of all households. At One Family we believe that this number, although significant, is likely to be an underestimation given the lack of accurate and adequate collection methods which might take account of the many diverse situations within which one-parent families live, including a growing level of shared parenting arrangements and continuing patterns of inter-generational households.

During the period 1996–2002 there was a 25% increase in the number of households headed by a solo parent. One-parent families are increasing for a variety of reasons and forming a significant minority of families in modern Irish society. In 1937, at the introduction of Bunreacht na hÉireann, the significant majority of one-parent families would have been headed by a widowed person, predominantly female. A dramatic increase in the extra marital birth rates together with reductions in the numbers of single women placing children for adoption, increases in marital and relationship breakdown and the introduction of divorce have changed the profile of one-parent families. Census 2002 indicates that 85% are headed by females, 15% by males, 40% by widowed persons, 32% by separated or divorced persons and 24% by a single parent (CSO, 2004; Kennedy, F. (2004), *Cottage to Crèche: Family Change in Ireland*, Dublin: IPA).

However, although the profile of the family in Ireland is remarkably different, with an estimated 12% alone headed by a solo parent, 100% of the protection currently afforded to the family in Bunreacht na hÉireann is applicable only to the family based in marriage. Therefore a growing number of families are not considered equal in the eyes of Ireland's most superior domestic source of law.

F. Ryan, in a paper presented to the One Family biennial conference in 2004, 'Children of Our Times: a Child's Place in Family Law and Family Policy', says:

The family rights provisions of the Constitution borrow heavily from Roman Catholic theology on the family. The centrepiece of such theology is the concern for family autonomy, the main purpose being to limit state intervention in the family, and in particular to prevent the State from dictating how children be reared, in possible contravention of the religious values of the parents.

OPEN points to some of the practical difficulties for the lone-parent family that flow from the constitutional definition of the family:

> The piecemeal way in which the social welfare system in Ireland was developed can be reflected in the Constitution's definition of the family based on marriage. They [social welfare payments] were predicated on the notion that a mother should work full-time in the home raising children, and should not be obliged to engage in paid employment. The payments were largely restricted to women – until 1989 there was no deserted husband or widower's payment – and also reflected a societal distinction between 'deservedness' of different categories of mothers: those who were parenting alone 'through no fault of their own', i.e. as a result of widowhood or desertion, were covered for that contingency in the social insurance system; unmarried mothers however had to rely solely on a means tested payment.

> In the late 1990s the One-Parent Family Payment, a more unified payment, was introduced for all parents raising children on their own. Nonetheless, this type of family remains outside the mainstream, an exception to the rule, and social policy continues to reflect society's ambivalence towards this family type, on the one hand asserting that they are different, and on the other, insisting they abide by the same rules 'as everybody else', i.e. fit in with the same employment and housing policies which are formulated around the Constitution's definition of the family. The inadequacy of this payment, in terms of its earning disregard and its weekly rate, and the stigmatisation, which still exists towards one-parent families, means that these family types feel that they are anomalous within the society.

One Family draws attention to the tension between individual rights and family rights in the Constitution:

> Currently, the Constitution affords protection only to the family unit and not to the individual members. As noted above [see full text of this submission in Appendix 3] in relation to Article 40.3, personal rights are often deemed applicable to members of the family unit. It is however a considered view (Constitution Review Group: 1996; Ryan: 2002, 2004; Shannon: 2005) that the focus of Articles 41 and 42 overemphasise the rights of the family unit, which could possibly be detrimental to the rights of individual members. This is found within the reference to rights of the family as

'inalienable' and 'imprescriptible' which may place overemphasis on the importance of the rights of the family as a unit over the rights of the individuals within it.

A case in point is the overall lack of access to adoption of children born within marriage. Except in limited circumstances, due to being born within what is considered a family unit (with inalienable rights and duties) children born within marriage cannot be adopted. Therefore, their rights to family life, which could be provided in an adoptive family, are curtailed by the inalienable right of the family unit to be protected.

In relation to other European jurisdictions, Ireland would be unique, with the exception of Luxembourg, in that none of the other constitutions expressly guarantee the rights of the family unit in this way. Although they may, as Bunreacht na hÉireann does, recognise that the family unit is the fundamental unit of society and afford it certain protections, they also guarantee rights deriving from family membership to apply directly to the individual members.

Both OPEN and One Family favour a constitutional amendment which would afford equal rights to all families. The Irish Catholic Bishops' Conference, however, points out:

The Constitution Review Group, for example, drew attention to an increase from 3% to 20% in the proportion of births outside marriages. The Constitution Review Group did not, however, give attention to the implications of this change and no account is taken of the evidence which, although it needs careful and sensitive evaluation, would seem to suggest that the children of one-parent families, notwithstanding the best and commendable efforts of their parents, may be at a disadvantage when compared to those of traditional families. If the Constitution Review Group had attended to such issues then its laudable desire to offer support to those living in non-traditional family arrangements might well have been tempered by a more obvious concern to offer such a support in a manner which did not erode support for the family based on marriage or undermine its indispensability to the welfare of the nation and the state.

Conclusion

One-parent families are in a particularly vulnerable position and need special support from the state.

A constitutional change which would extend the definition of the family would embrace one-parent families, enhance the esteem in which they themselves and others hold their family life and provide a secure basis upon which state agencies could extend their services to them. If a constitutional extension of the definition of the family were not sought, an Article enhancing the position of children would enhance the position of all families, including one-parent families, in which children find themselves.

Chapter 8

Woman in the home

Article 41

41.2.1° In particular, the State recognises that by her life within the home, woman gives to the State a support without which the common good cannot be achieved.

41.2.2° The State shall, therefore, endeavour to ensure that mothers shall not be obliged by economic necessity to engage in labour to the neglect of their duties in the home.

Article 41.2.1° reinforces the position of the traditional family incorporated in the Constitution in Article 41.1 by asserting the particular value of the contribution of the woman in the home. Article 41.2.2° adds further support by committing the state to an effort to ensure that mothers will not be forced by economic need to seek paid employment outside the home that forced them to neglect their duties in the home. Articles 41.2.1° and 41.2.2° have been attacked by supporters of the equality model of the family as being outdated, stereotypical, biologically deterministic, and even insulting to women. The import of the attack is that the Articles should be deleted or at least amended so that they are gender neutral.

The case for retention

In general those who support the traditional model of the family embrace it as perennially relevant: it provides stable and loving support for children, and stability to family life – and thereby promotes the common good. They do not want any changes to be made in the Articles relating to it. They point out that it was not the intention of the constitution-makers to cabin and confine women in the home: for example Article 45 recognises the right of men and women equally to make a living and does not envisage that the only role for women lies in homemaking. DeValera's draft papers show that he never intended that the clause would confine women to the home; his intention was rather that the state should provide economic support if the mother needed to stay at home. The papers of John Hearne, who prepared the original draft heads of the Constitution, also make clear that there was no intention at the time to limit the rights of women. Moreover Denham J in *Sinnott v Ireland* has recently stated that Article 41.2 was 'not to be construed as representing a norm of a society long changed utterly' but rather was to be construed 'in the Ireland of the Celtic Tiger'. She continued:

> Article 41.2 does not assign women to a domestic role. Article 41.2 recognises the significant role played by wives and mothers in the home. This recognition and acknowledgement does not exclude women and mothers from other roles and activities. It is a recognition of the work performed by women in the home. The work is recognised because it has immense benefit for society. This recognition must be construed harmoniously with other Articles of the

Constitution when a combination of Articles fall to be analysed.

Supporters of the traditional model of the family point out further that judicial interpretation has effectively made the Article gender neutral. Thus in *DT v CT* Murray J in an *obiter* commented:

> The Constitution … is to be interpreted as a contemporary document. The duties and obligations of spouses are mutual and, without elaborating further since nothing turns on the point in this case, it seems to me that [the Constitution] implicitly recognises similarly the value of a man's contribution in the home as a parent.

Some of these supporters would accept a gender-neutral presentation of Article 41.2.1° through the use of the form 'carers' instead of 'woman'. Most of them are insistent on retaining Article 41.2.2° because it gives constitutional purchase on the possibility of attaining practical financial recognition for caring in the home, at present unremunerated. Many point out that the directive in Article 41.2.2° has been feebly pursued by the state.

WITH/Cúram, the Irish national parent and carer NGO, stated in its detailed submission to the committee that 'constitutional protection for unremunerated workers, especially those in the role of parent or carer, should be strengthened and that the wording should be gender-neutral'.

> WITH members, unremunerated parents and carers, want Constitutional recognition for their role, their work, and their contribution to the economy and society. WITH aims to ensure that family-based care be recognised and financially viable. Article 41.2 represents a key instrument for recognising unremunerated work in a variety of domains and situations and it forms the basis for legal, tax and social welfare provisions of benefit to parents and carers on a full-time or part-time basis.
>
> ......
>
> The UN's Commission for the Status of Women will undertake in March 2005 a ten-year review of the Beijing Platform for Action, which calls for the recognition of unremunerated work as a central aspect of ensuring equality for women. WITH will be participating in this process as representative of our EU umbrella group FEFAF (la Fédération Européenne des Femmes Actives au Foyer). FEFAF has submitted a statement requesting UN bodies and national governments to implement Strategic Objective H3, on the collection of data on unremunerated work. It is not only in Ireland that this is an important question: the process of changing Article 41.2 will be tracked with interest in other

countries by parents, carers and their representative organisations as well.

......

Unremunerated work in Ireland refers to many activities which benefit the economy and society, and more specifically local communities, families and individuals. It is estimated that the total value of this work equals between 30% and 50% of Gross Domestic Product, or between €40,435,800,000 and €67,393,000,000 (source: calculated on the basis of the CSO GDP figure for 2003, €134,786m, available on http://www.cso.ie/principalstats/pristat5.html). Unremunerated work includes:

- parenting and other childcare
- caring for dependent elderly and/or disabled relatives
- farming and farm support
- voluntary work in the community
- housework and domiciliary upkeep.

Ireland collects statistics on some of this unpaid work and those who carry it out.

The submission provides a summary of these statistics and other relevant research data, and continues:

Although unremunerated workers clearly create value-added goods and services, they lack the protections of other workers and are therefore more reliant on constitutional recognition for their role. Protections other workers enjoy include:

- the structured access to income based on their work
- pension and social welfare contributions and entitlements
- the protection of employment legislation and the Equality Act
- inclusion of the value of their work in the GDP and other statistics.

If the protection afforded to unremunerated workers is weakened through this process, how will they be able to vindicate their rights? How will families access choice in the area of care?

NEART (Coalition of Pro-Women's Rights, Pro-Family and Pro-Life Groups) states:

The Constitutional reference to a woman's 'life within the home' is a very important and relevant one, and must remain in the Constitution. The trouble is that the right of women to work within the home has been sadly and deliberately neglected by successive governments over the years, and has resulted in the break-up of families and the deprivation of children's basic right to the essential love and care of their mother in their formative years. The increase in the incidence of suicide, particularly in the case of teenagers and young adults; the breakdown of discipline in the schools; the increase in teenage pregnancy (often, sadly and tragically, resulting in the abortion of unborn children); alcohol abuse on the part of young people – all of these situations flow from the decline in official government support for the family based on marriage. Why can the government of the day not acknowledge that government policies that do not support the traditional family lead to chaos and are calculated to undermine society still further?

Comhar Críostaí states:

We do not agree that the Constitution's reference to the woman's life within the home should be deleted. Mothers should not be forced through economic necessity to take up paid employment outside the home. Had the state over the years fulfilled its obligation to protect the mother working in the home then the majority of mothers would have opted to remain at home and rear their children. Mothers working in the home exercise a tremendous influence for good, with consequent major benefit to society. This Article in the Constitution does not prevent any mother from engaging, if she so desires, in outside paid employment so there is no question of the rights of any person being limited by this provision. Article 41.2, in fact, could be strengthened by stating that the mothers working full-time in the home should have the same social welfare and tax benefits as a person working outside the home.

European Life Network states:

This is a very important provision and one which reflects the desire of the majority of Irish women, as shown in many surveys, to stay at home and rear their children. The Constitution demands that the government should ensure that women are not driven out to work by economic necessity. The choice of mothers to stay at home and their constitutional right to do so has never been vindicated by the State. Article 41.2 of the Constitution should not be changed but should instead be taken seriously by the State.

Family & Life states:

There is increasing evidence in western countries that many working women would prefer to be at home with their young children but are forced to take full-time work for financial reasons.

There is evidence that even high quality (and expensive) childcare cannot have the same value as a mother's undivided care for her young children. Does paid childcare answer the needs of small children? Or those of working parents?

There is evidence that, rather than juggle a career with children, women are postponing having children, having fewer children, and then often experiencing serious fertility problems.

The Irish Constitution calls on the government to 'endeavour to ensure that mothers shall not be obliged by economic necessity' to work outside the home. Is this so out of date? Or does it offend feminist theory? We suggest that many mothers in Ireland regret the government's neglect of this constitutional exhortation, and the Supreme Court's refusal to support it. Today, there is every need to retain it in the Constitution.

Muintir na hÉireann states:

[I]t is an important provision as recent statistics show that the majority of women work part-time outside the home. Indeed a survey done a few years ago revealed that most women, if given a choice, would prefer to stay at home. Economic conditions and the need of governments, due to falling birth rates, to force more women into the work-force to keep economic growth has proved in other countries as well as here to be very short-sighted. When both partners work the size of the family decreases – hence the falling population in Europe and Ireland. It has recently been estimated that Europe, in the next twenty years despite huge immigration, will still not have enough people for its economies. France has taken action and introduced measures to try to reverse this trend and increase its population. One of the things it has done is to allow the mother to stay at home until her child is of school age. A lot of social problems are due to the absence of mothers in the home.

Right Nation states:

In presenting the case for changing the Constitution to remove the recognition given to women working in the home, no one has even attempted to present a case of imperative necessity, nor even any single benefit that would accrue to society from doing so. That women who do work in the home perform an enormous and unpaid service to society is obvious, that the emotional wellbeing of children is vastly improved by them is a given. Why should it not be recognised? Surely in fact that recognition should involve a more practical acknowledgement, in the form of financial support? And that is what is clearly indicated by the provision that they not be forced out of the home by 'economic necessity'. Thus society would benefit and women would benefit. In fact the only group in society which could possibly uphold a grievance are men, and until such time as they are willing, in any appreciable numbers, to take on the role of homemaker, their case is weak.

In reality of course each and every government since the foundation of the State has reneged on its responsibilities outlined in Article 41 of the Constitution. In the early years the measures enacted were designed to force women into the home with punitive measures rather than the incentives which were clearly indicated, and in the later years they have sought to force women out of the home by 'economic necessity'.

It is an example of how public policy in this country is dictated by middle-class political mores, without regard to how the majority of ordinary people actually live, that the debate on this Article has largely concerned the issue of women with 'careers'. In fact very few women or men have 'careers', rather they have jobs, and the primary motivation in getting and keeping a job is financial necessity, not some notion of personal fulfilment. For ordinary people, which is to say the real working people of Ireland, personal fulfilment is derived from many sources, very rarely their job, and usually in one sense or another, their family.

The Mother & Child Campaign states:

This is a vital constitutional provision and one that reflects the desire of the majority of Irish women, as shown in many surveys, to have the right to stay at home and rear their children. Mothers who make many sacrifices to rear their children at home do the State an inestimable and unrewarded service, and that the emotional well-being of children is vastly improved by their sacrifices is now universally accepted. Most recently, research undertaken by Professor Jay Belsky, Director of the Institute for Studies of Children at Birbeck College, London, has found that there is no substitute for a child's parents, and especially for a mother in the early years of a child's life. He also says that children who spend more than twenty hours a week away from their parents, in childcare, from an early age are likely to be problem children, more aggressive and less well-behaved. The debate regarding childcare has shifted, in that we now discuss how damaging it may be – that it is damaging is widely accepted.

Mothers at Home states:

> MAH believes that the Family's needs are not being attended to by policies that force mothers to work outside the home. If parents are to be enabled to 'together assume responsibility for the care and maintenance of … and the socialisation of children', one parent – usually the mother – must be free to choose to be a full-time carer, a stay-at-home mum. Article 41.2.1° and Article 41.2.2° of the Irish Constitution enshrines this principle.

> MAH also endorses the view held by a number of international and European women's movements (Mouvement Mondiel des Meres – MMM International, to which MAH is affiliated, and also FEFAF – Federation Européene des Femmes Actives au Foyer, and others) that if a study was carried out of the social and economic value of the work done in the home, it would be apparent to all but the most blinkered of policy makers that the cost of replacing home care by state care would be enormous and not cost effective.

A notable presentation of the need to recognise the practical value of workers in the home was made by Global Women's Strike, Ireland, part of a network reaching to over sixty countries:

> Some have called for abolition of Article 41.2 on the ground that it is sexist. While it is obviously sexist to refer to work in the home as a woman's 'life' and as her 'duty', it would be even more sexist to obliterate the only constitutional recognition of unwaged caring work, done at great personal cost by generations of women and up to the present day, and its vital contribution to society's survival and welfare. Article 41.2 must be re-worded to reflect accurately the value of this work, the skill of the workers who do it and the entitlements it should earn them, and thus help end the gross discrimination women have suffered both as workers in the home and workers outside.

The submission goes on to point out that unremunerated work entered the international agenda in 1975, at the opening conference of the UN Decade for Women in Mexico City. The mid-decade conference in 1980 in Copenhagen, Denmark, gave it additional legitimacy with the International Labour Office (ILO) figure that women do two-thirds of the world's work, yet receive only 5% of its income. A campaign continues to have national accounts measure and value unwaged work, that is to say how much of their lifetime women (and to a lesser extent men) spend doing unwaged work and how much value this work creates. Trinidad & Tobago was the first country to put this into law in 1996. Spain followed in 1998. The Bolivarian Republic of Venezuela enshrined in its 1999 Constitution the social and economic recognition of unwaged work in the context of equality and equity between the sexes.

Global Women's Strike, Ireland continues:

> To enshrine in the Irish Constitution the principle that caring work in the home – which extends to caring for the whole community and in rural areas to caring for and protecting the land and the environment – is valued socially and economically, would ensure that women, particularly mothers, are not penalised with the lowest pay when they go out to work or discriminated against in areas such as pensions, healthcare, childcare, and social welfare.

Comhairle states:

> The role of the family as a caring unit has been the subject of much discussion and debate in recent years due mainly to changes in work patterns and in the role of women in society. Care in the home, whether for small children, dependent older people or people with disabilities of whatever age, is more and more becoming an issue of concern.
>
> Increasingly, potential carers are, either by necessity or choice, working outside the home. Contributory factors are career choice, spiralling housing costs, and a social welfare and tax system that does not provide adequate incentives and supports to people to stay at home to care for children or other dependants. Increased women's participation in the labour market has resulted in greater attention being given to the phenomenon of caring in the home and its associated costs and the urgent need to reconsider how work and familial organisation can be harmonised.

The Association of Irish Evangelical Churches addresses the question of datedness:

> If the reference to a 'woman's life within the home' sounds dated or old fashioned it is important to ask why. Ideas and social theories about the place of women in society go in and out of fashion and it can be difficult to get a properly objective view on one's own culture since it is as close to us as the air we breathe. How can we know that we are not being unduly influenced by an idea that is merely tremendously fashionable? What are the human consequences

of applying social theories through the laws of the land? In the twentieth century there were many examples in many different nations of ideas that were enacted as laws and which failed as they did not match up to what is true about people, human nature or society. One could refer to the kibbutz experiment in Israel, where all expectations were confounded when women who were free to choose high status jobs and day care for their children, repeatedly and insistently turned these things down so that they could nurture their own children and attend to their own living space. In other countries where legislation of social ideals has been brought in more forcefully, such as in the former USSR and China, the cost of failure has been very high. Untold misery and suffering resulted where social ideals did not match with reality, and what is true about human nature.

… Many women in Ireland today work outside the home not because they are ideologically committed to a career but out of economic necessity – specifically the cost of financing a mortgage in most cases … Interestingly, the Constitution expressly states that having to work outside the home from economic necessity should not happen. While the factors involved are undeniably complex, it can be seen that the cost to society of taking the mother out of the home has been very high. Society is now more fragmented than it has ever been, and the trend seems to be for families to become ever more fragmented.

… Let us make sure that the women of Ireland can give the greater share and the best part of their time to the people that need it most, and whom they most love: their families. Uireasa a mhéadaíonn cumha (Absence increases sorrow).

The case for abolition or change

In general, adherents of the equality model embrace that model because it seems to offer greater freedom and choice to both men and women in their lives both within the family and outside of it. They would like to see the Article removed or at least made gender neutral because they perceive it as a threat to their freedom and choice. This group, again in general, acknowledges the contribution to the common good made by parents and carers in the home. They would see the equity of practical recognition being given provided that such a measure was expressed in gender-neutral terms.

The Family Support Agency points out that:

Article 41.2.1° provides that the State shall recognise that by her life within the home a woman gives to the State a support without which the common good cannot be achieved. This concept is now outdated. Increasingly fathers share this role within the family. Often both a father and a mother may do so at different times for different lengths of time. The Family Support Agency also considers that joint parenting, of which this is a form, should be encouraged. The State should actively support families who both work outside the home with appropriate facilities and services.

AIM – Family Services states:

> This definition is patriarchal and sexist and reflects social thinking of the 1937 period. Thankfully, this has altered somewhat. It is also at odds with equality legislation that our membership of the EU has required from us. However, we feel that it is important to give practical recognition and value to the caring function in the family, a function which has had mainly lip service only paid to it to date. Apart from the provisions in the Separation and Divorce legislation of 1989, 1995 and 1996, the provisions of Article 41 have done little to improve the economic lot of women, whether wives or mothers; for those who remain married, their economic lot is tied to their ability to earn it for themselves, or dependent on the goodwill of their spouses. (We do recognise that social welfare provision has improved, but intra-family – there is no community of property regime, for example).

AMEN states:

> Article 41.2.1° recognises the contribution given to the State by women in the home. This provision is discriminatory in that it gives no recognition to the contribution made by women outside the home or to the contribution made by men either in the home or outside the home. It is wrong to give recognition to the contribution made by one sex within one domain and ignore the contribution made by others. There does not appear to be any reason why women in the home should be given such exclusive recognition. There may have been some justifiable reason for inserting this Article in 1937 but, given the changes in society in the intervening period, it appears to be somewhat redundant at this stage. Article 41.2. 1° should either be removed or similar recognition should be given to the contribution of men in the home and both men and women outside the home.
>
> Following on from this Article, 41.2.2° imposes an obligation on the State to endeavour to ensure that mothers shall not be obliged by economic necessity to engage in labour to the neglect of their duties in the home. Even though this Article does not contain an absolute guarantee it imposes a very

strong obligation on the State. It is surprising that no mother has taken a case against the State because of its abject failure to ensure that mothers are not obliged, through economic necessity to work outside the home. What is equally surprising is the manner in which this amazing commitment to mothers, to the exclusion of fathers, has been portrayed as discrimination against women rather than men. The points made in relation to 41.2.1° above apply to this Article also. There is no reason why a similar obligation should not apply in relation to fathers in the home. As with other Articles it is doubtful if the State could be said to be fulfilling its obligations under this Article given the number of mothers who feel obliged to go out to work because of economic pressures. Article 41.2.2° should either be removed or amended to impose a similar obligation on the State to endeavour to ensure that fathers shall not be obliged by economic necessity to engage in labour to the neglect of their duties in the home.

The Council on Social Responsibility of the Methodist Church in Ireland states:

[W]e note that Art 41.2 again includes a very specific and detailed issue of social policy (which should not be there at all), but also expressing a viewpoint that is totally contrary to current opinions (and indeed legislation) on equality and anti-discrimination based on gender or marital status. This existing Article should be removed, in our opinion, and replaced with a new Article which

- confirms a basic right to marry, in accordance with law
- states that the State respects and supports the important role, in support of of the common good, which families undertake in the care and nurturing of dependents, especially children.

The Law Society states:

[T]he Society feels that Article 41.2.1° should be removed from the Constitution or altered. One way of dealing with this matter would be simply to amend this Article to read as follows 'In particular, the State recognises that by his/her life within the home, a parent gives to the State a support without which the common good cannot be achieved'. The alternative, and the Society's preferred approach, is that Article 41.2.1° should be removed. The Society does not see any reason why 'life within the home' should have a greater value than life outside the home.

The National Women's Council of Ireland states:

> The Constitution should not ascribe gendered roles to either women or men, therefore it is the view of the NWCI that this reference should be removed.

> > Despite amendment over the years, the Constitution has not kept pace with social change and still bears the imprint of the period at which it was originally drafted. One of the ways in which this manifests itself is in its reference to women in certain roles, and its correlative lack of reference to men in these roles. Specific mention is made of the role of women in the home and as mothers (Article 40.3.3° and 41.2.1° and 2°). Nowhere in the Constitution is the word 'father' to be found; nor is the role of men in the domestic sphere specifically addressed. Furthermore, it is clear from the tenor of the relevant constitutional provisions that it is in their role as wives and mothers that women are especially valued.[39]

> It is abundantly clear that society should value the care work which predominantly women perform. The Irish Government has signed up to commitments under the Convention on the Elimination of Discrimination Against Women and under the 10 critical areas of the Beijing Platform for Action. The patriarchal assignment of women to perform certain roles within family and within society has not been to the advantage of women and has undermined the progression of equality for women.

The ICCL states:

> The role of carers in society, particularly within the home is essential. This function may be carried out by a parent, grandparent, sibling or other relative or *de facto* guardian. Carers in the home not only provide security, care and respect for those in need of care, but make an invaluable contribution to society – and the economy. Yet according to the Carers Association, fewer than twenty per cent of all those devoted to caring full time for others in the home in Ireland receive any financial assistance from the state. The ICCL submits that this reflects the complete undervaluation of carers in government and public policy.

> The ICCL therefore believes that the role which carers play in the home should be explicitly recognised in a gender-neutral provision.

---

39 From Connelly, A. (1993), 'The Constitution', in Connelly, A. (ed.), *Gender and the Law in Ireland,* Dublin: Oak Tree Press.

Another factor for change is Ireland's ratification of the UN Convention on the Elimination of Discrimination Against Women (CEDAW).

The Irish Human Rights Commission states:

> In accordance with Article 2(a) of CEDAW Ireland is required to embody the principle of equality of men and women in its national Constitution or other appropriate legislation. Article 5 of CEDAW also requires states to take all appropriate measures to modify the social and cultural patterns of conduct of men and women in order to promote gender equality. These measures should aim to eliminate prejudices and customary and all other practices which are based on the idea of the inferiority or the superiority of either of the sexes, or on stereotyped roles for men and women. One of the appropriate measures in this context would be the amendment of Article 41.2 of the Irish Constitution which is based on a stereotyped view of the role of women in Irish society.

> … This provision has been described as reflecting a sexual division of labour which is 'based on a biological determinism that assumes that one's social destiny is dependent on whether one is female or male, thereby closing off the options for both women and men, but particularly for women.'[40] In their Concluding Observations on Ireland's second and third periodic reports, the Committee expressed concern about the continuing existence in Article 41.2 of concepts that reflect a stereotypical view of the role of women in the home and as mothers.

The state is under continuous international political pressure so long as it fails to respond to the requirements of CEDAW. In July 2005 the CEDAW Committee on Ireland's implementation of the provisions of the Convention, following a presentation by an Irish delegation led by Minister of State Frank Fahey TD, stated in its concluding comments:

> The Committee recommends that the state party take additional measures to eliminate traditional stereotypical attitudes, including through sensitization and training of all educational actors and sustained awareness-raising campaigns directed at both women and men. It recommends that the All-Party Oireachtas Committee on the Constitution take the Convention fully into account in considering any amendments to Article 41.2 of the Constitution as well as

---

40 Connelly A. (1999), 'Women and the Constitution of Ireland', in Galligan, Y., Ward, E. and Wilford, R., *Contesting Politics: Women in Ireland, North and South*, p. 24, Oxford: Westview Press.

including a provision to underline the obligation of the state to actively pursue the achievement of substantive equality between women and men. The Committee also suggests that the state party consider replacing male-oriented language with gender-sensitive language in the Constitution to convey the concept of gender equality more clearly. Considering the important role of the media in regard to cultural change, the Committee furthermore recommends that the state party encourage the media to project a positive image of women and of the equal status and responsibilities of women and men in the private and public spheres.

The Constitution Review Group (CRG) took the view that Article 41.2 was indeed outdated:

> Article 41.2 assigns to women a domestic role as wives and mothers. It is a dated provision much criticised in recent years.

The CRG however considered it important that there should continue to be constitutional recognition of the significant contribution made to society by the large number of people who provide a caring function within their homes for children, elderly relatives and others. It favoured the retention of the Article in a revised form as follows:

> The State recognises that home and family life gives to society a support without which the common good cannot be achieved. The State shall endeavour to support persons caring for others within the home.

Focus on the Family states:

> Where one or other spouse chooses to remain at home, to raise children particularly, they should not in any way be discriminated against, as in making this choice they serve to strengthen the bedrock of family life and society, based upon the family, which has been a tremendous strength in this Nation for the past generations. Should there be any proposed changes, we would recommend something expressing a similar sentiment but in a gender neutral fashion, as per the wording suggested in the *Report of the Constitution Review Group* (1996).

The Irish Catholic Bishops' Conference states:

> The reference is frequently dismissed as dated and this would seem just if it were read to suggest that women only have a contribution to make in the home or that work in the home were to be the exclusive duty of women. The provision may, however, be seen as a 'pedestal rather than a cage'.

… A revision of this Article in more gender neutral form as suggested by the Review Group might be appropriate but perhaps unnecessary.

Conclusion

A great number of people strongly support the retention of Article 41.2.1° and Article 41.2.2°. The courts are disposed to interpret Article 41.2.1° as applying to either fathers or mothers caring in the home. The need to change the Article to make it gender neutral is therefore not a legal necessity. There is general support for recognition of the value of the work done by those who care for others in the home, and therefore for whatever practical support for them that the Houses of the Oireachtas, relying upon Article 41.2.2°, can provide.

Many people – they include people from supporters of both models of the family – believe that the language in which the Articles are expressed is outdated and even sexist. They feel the Articles should be rendered in a gender-neutral form. In addition the UN Convention on the Elimination of Discrimination Against Women (CEDAW), which Ireland has ratified, regards the employment of sexist language as a practical obstacle to women's drive for equality with men. They regard the language of the Articles as sexist and require change in them. Change, therefore, in the Articles is at least desirable.

Chapter 9

The committee's conclusions

Definition of the family

The strategic decision that faces the committee is whether or not to seek a change in the definition of the family so as to extend constitutional protection to all forms of family life.

The installation of the traditional family based on marriage in the Constitution in 1937 suited the demography and the ethos of the day. The considerable change in demography that has occurred since then and which has seen the appearance of a growing range of families other than the traditional one, means that the Constitution now serves our society less well than it formerly did. It is true that the ethos is changing. There is a general acceptance of the situation of cohabiting heterosexual couples and other non-marital family forms. State and voluntary organisations, who must deal with the problems and issues facing non-marital families, seek pragmatic solutions within the existing constitutional framework.

Despite the considerable change in demography and ethos the committee does not find a consensus that the definition of the family in the Constitution should be extended. Indeed, in the submissions the committee was faced with a sharp division. Many wish the Articles related to the family to remain unchanged. They fear that any change would threaten the position of the family based on marriage. It would undermine the stability of the traditional family and all the enhancement of the common good that flows from it.

Those who wish the definition of the family in the Constitution to be broadened are largely people who feel that the basic democratic value of equality should extend to all forms of family life. However, they appreciate and respect the contribution made by the traditional family to the common good. While they would like to see the Constitution changed they would wish at the same time to maintain support for the traditional family.

The Constitution Review Group sought to meet the needs of the situation by proposing a comprehensive reworking of Article 41 which would provide constitutional protection for all forms of family life while preserving the special character of the family based on marriage. However comprehensive, well-articulated and apt this proposal may be, it encounters the strong belief of many people that it is not practicable to provide constitutional recognition for all family types while at the same time maintaining the uniqueness of one.

Irish experience of constitutional amendments shows that they may be extremely divisive and that however well-intentioned they may be they can have unexpected outcomes.

Conclusion

In the case of the family, the committee takes the view that an amendment to extend the definition of the family would cause deep and long-lasting division in our society and would not necessarily be passed by a majority. Instead of inviting such anguish and uncertainty, the committee proposes to seek through a number of other constitutional changes and legislative proposals to deal in an optimal way with the problems presented to it in the submissions.

Cohabiting heterosexual couples

The committee's decision not to seek an extended definition of the family means that cohabiting heterosexual couples will not have constitutional protection for their family life. By definition such couples, for reasons of their own, have opted out of the traditional marriage. Nonetheless, they can face the same kinds of problem that sometimes face married couples, for instance through disagreement, unacceptable behaviour on the part of one of the partners, sickness, separation or death. Solutions must be sought at a legislative level.

The prepronderance of the Article 41 case law would seem to suggest (although this is admittedly far from certain) that the Oireachtas may legislate to provide 'marriage-like' privileges to cohabiting heterosexual couples provided they do not exceed in any respect those of the family based on marriage. This provision might be made by way of civil partnership legislation or a presumptive scheme such as the Law Reform Commission suggests in its Consultation Paper entitled *Rights and Duties of Cohabitees*.

Conclusion

The committee recommends legislation to provide for cohabiting heterosexual couples by either a civil partnership or a presumptive scheme.

Same-sex couples

The committee's decision not to seek an extended definition of the family means that same-sex couples will not have constitutional protection for their family life, assuming, of course, that the courts rule that the word 'marriage' in Article 41 (which word, incidentally, is not defined by the Constitution) is confined to the traditional understanding of marriage and does not extend to same-sex unions. It must be recognised that such a development, although perhaps unlikely, remains at least a distinct possibility and cannot be excluded from this particular debate. If, as Murray J pointed out in the *DT* case *(DT v CT* [2003] 1 ILRM 321*)*, Article 41 must be given a contemporary interpretation, the way is therefore open for the courts to say the traditional requirement that the couple be of the opposite sex is not of the essence of the marital relationship. On this reading of Article 41, common law and legislative stipulations that the couple be of the opposite sex would be found to be unconstitutional.

Nevertheless, the committee is of the view that the principal developments here should come at a legislative level. As we have already noted, the balance of the case law appears to suggest that the Oireachtas may legislate to provide 'marriage-like' privileges to cohabiting same-sex couples provided they do not exceed in any respect those of the family based on marriage. Since a presumptive scheme would not be appropriate, this provision might be made by way of civil partnership legislation.

Conclusion

The committee recommends that civil partnership legislation should be provided for same-sex couples.

The committee would recommend similar legislation to meet the needs of other long-term cohabiting couples.

Children

The committee found that now more than ever previously there is a sharp public concern to ensure that all children in the state are treated equally and protected closely and that the state should extend all the supports that it reasonably can to ensure that the best interests of the child are paramount in matters affecting the child's welfare.

Although it is frequently stated that the Constitution makes no reference to the rights of the child, this is not quite accurate. Thus, Article 42.5 refers to the 'natural and imprescriptible rights' of the child, albeit in a context where the state is obliged to have regard for these rights where it is endeavouring to supply the place of the parents.

The committee is nevertheless firmly of the view that there is a need to improve the constitutional rights of the child, while at the same time preserving appropriate parental authority. There is also a necessity to ensure in express and unambiguous constitutional terms that all children, irrespective of birth, have equal rights to family life. Given that so many children are born outside marriage, it is necessary to ensure in express constitutional terms that they have exactly the same constitutional rights and entitlements as all other children.

Conclusion

A new section should be inserted in Article 41 dealing with the rights of children as follows:

> All children, irrespective of birth, gender, race or religion, are equal before the law. In all cases where the welfare of the child so requires, regard shall be had to the best interests of that child.

The natural or birth father

The committee's decision not to seek an extended definition of the family means that the natural or birth father will not have constitutional rights *as such* vis-à-vis his child. The committee nevertheless believes that its proposed amendment in respect of the rights of children will indirectly improve the status of the natural or birth father. Thus, for example, if no child could henceforth be discriminated against on grounds of birth, this would surely oblige the courts to re-fashion a line of (highly controversial) jurisprudence since the Supreme Court's decision in *The State (Nicolaou) v An Bord Uchtala* [1966] IR 567 in which it was held that the natural mother (and not the natural father) had a constitutional right to custody of the child. If the Constitution were to contain an express guarantee of non-discrimination on grounds of birth and to have regard to the best interests of the child, this would mean that some of the *Nicolaou* rationale would disappear. The child under those circumstances would have the same right to the company and care of his or her father as would a child born within marriage. In any event, the welfare and best interests of the child (which considerations would, if the committee's proposals were to be accepted, now be elevated to constitutional status) would generally mean that the child had a constitutional right to have the company and care of his or her father and to ensure that the father played a part in decision-making concerning his or her welfare.

The committee was affected by instances presented to it of how society seems to be disposed to treat the natural or birth father heartlessly. Conciliatory systems seem to be under-funded and cases often become rapidly processed in legal and therefore adversarial terms. The operation of the in camera rule means, moreover, that the family courts system is too secretive and is insufficiently open to scrutiny. The committee suggests that judicial specialisms in the area should be developed. The operation of the legislatively-imposed 'in camera' rule, while obviously a well-intentioned measure designed to protect the privacy of families, has the effect of shielding from the public the manner in which the legal system functions in family law cases.

The absence of such public scrutiny has had unfortunate effects. It means, for example, that the performance of judges, lawyers and witnesses cannot be evaluated. But it also means that members of the public are often left in ignorance about the way the family law system operates, so that they may be unaware of the need for change and reform. While the committee notes that the 'in camera' rule has been relaxed somewhat by the Courts and Courts Officers Act 2004, it considers that there may be a necessity for further legislation which would modify the rule even further.

Conclusions

1   Legal procedures should be put in place to allow for the appropriate expression of the rights of the natural or birth father under the new section on children in Article 41.

2   While welcoming the modifications of the 'in camera' rule by the Courts and Civil Liability Act 2004, the strict operation of the 'in camera' rule should be further relaxed.

Lone parents

The committee's decision not to seek an extended definition of the family means that lone-parent families will not have specific constitutional protection for their family life. Lone parents are a group who are striving to bring up children as best they can while particularly subject to harsh economic conditions. The committee could not but be drawn to view their situation sympathetically. It believes its proposed new Article on children will have the effect of enhancing their position generally and in focusing on the needs of children it should give a more positive character to the attitudes of those working in state agencies that are concerned with family matters

Conclusion

Legislation to promote the welfare of children should have a special concern to secure adequate resources for lone-parent families.

Woman in the home

The committee's analysis has shown that while the language of the Article can be criticised for stereotyping a mother's role, there are hints by the courts that in the relatively few cases where Article 41.2 has been judicially considered the references in respect of the caring role within the family might permit of a possible gender-neutral interpretation.

One external pressure for change is derived from the State's ratification of the Convention for the Elimination of All Forms of Discrimination Against Women (CEDAW). CEDAW is charged to seek the removal from legislation, including constitutions, of sexist stereotyping. The committee proposes an amendment which would render Article 41.2.1° gender-neutral. That objective is, perhaps, not quite as simple as it might seem.

There are at present two elements to this Article. First, Article 41.2.1° recognises the importance of *women's* contribution within the home and, secondly, Article 41.2.2° provides that the state shall, therefore, endeavour to ensure that 'mothers shall not be obliged by economic necessity to engage in labour to the neglect of their duties in the home'. The first element can readily be rendered gender-neutral. The second element is more problematic, since the state can scarcely guarantee that neither mothers nor fathers should be obliged to work outside the home!

The CRG recommended a gender-neutral version thus:

> The State recognises that home and family life gives to society a support without which the common good cannot be achieved. The State shall endeavour to support persons caring for others within the home.

It may be noted that the CRG felt that the 'retention of Article 41.2.2° may not be appropriate to a gender-neutral form of the Article'. In other words, the CRG did not think (and this committee agrees) that the Constitution could give a guarantee (or even a quasi-guarantee) that neither parent would be obliged by economic necessity to work outside the home.

Advantages of the CRG version
The CRG version is simple and captures the essence of the idea – the value of family life – in a gender-neutral fashion. While the wording does not impose any strict obligation ('shall endeavour'), it seeks to ensure that the value of carers (including, of course, parents) is recognised.

Disadvantages of the CRG version
By deleting Article 41.2.2° the CRG version undermines whatever concrete guarantee exists at present. The second sentence is,

moreover, ambiguous. Childminders and au pairs come within this sentence, yet it is unlikely that it was intended that they should have this sort of special constitutional protection in an Article dealing with the family.

Against this background, the committee suggests an alternative wording.

Alternative version

1. The State recognises that by reason of family life within the home, a parent gives to the State a support without which the common good cannot be achieved.

2. The State shall, therefore, endeavour to ensure that both parents shall not be obliged by economic necessity to work outside the home to the neglect of their parental duties.

Advantage

This version re-instates the essence of Article 41.2.1° and Article 41.2.2° (albeit in a gender-neutral fashion), resonates with the language in which they are expressed, and does not import new values.

Disadvantage

Article 41.2.2° only makes sense when understood against the background of the traditional pattern of male breadwinner and mother staying at home to rear children. Would not the new version of it invite adverse comment as carrying some vestigial stereotyping?

Conclusion

Constitutional

The committee is satisfied that its alternative version of Article 41.2.1° and Article 41.2.2° meets the objective of rendering the Articles gender neutral. It therefore recommends the following amendments to Article 41.2:

Amend Article 41.2.1° to read

The State recognises that by reason of family life within the home, a parent gives to the State a support without which the common good cannot be achieved.

Amend Article 41.2.2° to read

The State shall, therefore, endeavour to ensure that both parents shall not be obliged by economic necessity to work outside the home to the neglect of their parental duties.

Legislative

The committee believes the capacity of the Department of Social and Family Affairs to support the work of carers in the home should be progressively increased. In its exploration of the issue the committee found that there is a growth of individualism in our society which creates a demand for institutional solutions by the state to meet the needs of the young, the disabled and the aged. These are increasingly expensive to provide; it is also difficult to ensure quality control within them. However, one of the great contributions made by the traditional family is social solidarity. Within the extended family the young, the disabled and the aged were cared for. State services were called upon only when specialised needs could not be provided by the family. The committee believes that an endorsement by the state of the traditional family should be accompanied by a scheme of practical support for its primary social role. In order to allow the state to invest in such a scheme with confidence the following steps should be taken:

- a solid research base should be established
- a rigorous cost/benefit analysis should be carried out to establish the value to the state of care within the home as opposed to institutional care
- reliable output measures should be established to allow the development of an accountable system.

Minority conclusions

While a majority of members of the committee endorsed the above changes, some members did not consider that they went far enough.

General right to family life

The minority members were of the view that the Constitution should expressly provide that all persons had a right to family life, irrespective of their marital status. This would not only ensure that the Constitution was not out of step with Article 8 of the European Convention on Human Rights (where this right is not confined to the traditional family based on marriage), but it would further ensure that *all* members of non-marital families enjoyed constitutional protection. While marriage would still retain special status, the significance of this change would be to extend fundamental constitutional guarantees in respect of family life to the non-marital family.

Such a change would also reverse the *Nicolaou* jurisprudence, grounded as it is on traditional understanding of the family based on marriage and stereotypical views of the role of the mother as opposed to the father. This line of authority – which concludes that natural mothers (but not natural fathers) have constitutional rights to the custody of the child – simply re-inforces sexist stereotyping of the role of fathers, often to the disadvantage of the child. This line of reasoning would be regarded as objectionable by many today and is, in any event, out of step with contemporary demographic realities.

To be relevant, the Constitution must keep pace with these contemporary realities. If more than one quarter of births are outside of marriage, the Constitution must accommodate itself to these facts and ensure that all persons (irrespective of marriage) have a right to family life.

Minority proposal

Insert at the end of Article 41

> The state also recognises and respects family life not based on marriage. All persons, irrespective of their marital status, have a right to family life. The Oireachtas is entitled to legislate for the benefit of such families and of their individual members.

APPENDICES

APPENDIX 1

APPENDIX 1

Letter from Frank Fahey TD, Minister of State, Department of Health and Children, to the Chairman of the All-Party Oireachtas Committee on the Constitution

Office of the Minister of State

20 June 1999

Mr Brian Lenihan TD
Dáil Éireann
Dublin 2

Dear Brian

I am writing to you in your capacity as Chairman of the All-Party Committee on the Constitution.

As you are aware, there is a commitment in the Programme for Government, *An Action Programme for the Millennium*, that the All-Party Committee will be asked to give consideration to a Constitutional amendment to underpin the individual rights of children.

Since I wrote to you last in January 1998 the UN Committee on the Rights of the Child has examined Ireland's First Report under the UN Convention on the Rights of the Child and has issued its concluding observations – one of which was that *the State should take all appropriate measures to accelerate the recommendations of the Constitution Review Group.*

Ireland will be submitting its Second Report under the UN Convention in 2000 and it would be of considerable benefit to the outcome of the UN Committee's next examination process if we are able to show progress in responding to their observations.

Against this background, I would be grateful if the Committee could prioritise its consideration of this matter.

Yours sincerely,

Frank Fahey TD
Minister of State

APPENDIX 2

APPENDIX 2

Notice inviting submissions

THE ALL-PARTY OIREACHTAS COMMITTEE ON THE CONSTITUTION

THE FAMILY

The Committee invites written submissions.

Bunreacht na hÉireann (the Constitution of Ireland) contains its main provisions in relation to the family in Articles 41, 42 and 40.3.

Following the enactment of the Constitution, legislation relating to the family has been developed in line with those Articles and elucidated by the courts in a substantial body of case law.

The All-Party Oireachtas Committee on the Constitution, which is charged with reviewing the Constitution in its entirety, is now examining these Articles to ascertain the extent to which they are serving the good of individuals and the community, with a view to deciding whether changes in them would bring about a greater balance between the two.

The Committee wishes to invite individuals and groups to make written submissions to it, whether in general terms or in terms of specific issues such as:

– **how should the family be defined?**
– **how should one strike the balance between the rights of the family as a unit and the rights of individual members?**
– **is it possible to give constitutional protection to families other than those based on marriage?**
– **should gay couples be allowed to marry?**
– **is the Constitution's reference to woman's 'life within the home' a dated one that should be changed?**
– **should the rights of a natural mother have express constitutional protection?**
– **what rights should a natural father have, and how should they be protected?**
– **should the rights of the child be given an expanded constitutional protection?**
– **does the Constitution need to be changed in view of the UN Convention on the Rights of the Child?**

Submissions should reach the Committee at the address below before 31 January 2005.

THE ALL-PARTY OIREACHTAS COMMITTEE ON THE CONSTITUTION
Fourth Floor, Phoenix House
7-9 South Leinster Street, Dublin 2
Fax: 01 662 5581 Email: info@apocc.irlgov.ie

APPENDIX 3

Submissions

Contents

APPENDIX 3

Submissions

This appendix reproduces a broad selection of the written submissions made to the committee. The selection is made on the basis of the intrinsic reference value of the submissions. Care has been taken to ensure that the range of views presented to the committee is widely represented.

THE ADOPTION BOARD

This submission addresses the specific questions raised by the Oireachtas Committee on Family Rights in the Constitution, as they pertain to adoption. Adoption was a feature of family formation in Ireland on an informal basis prior to 1952 and since that year has been incorporated in law under the Adoption Acts 1952–1998. Our comments take into account proposals for change in adoption legislation recently published by the Department of Health and Children (Jan 2005).

1 HOW SHOULD THE FAMILY BE DEFINED?

Current and proposed definitions of the family:

a) The Irish Constitution recognises the family as the natural primary and fundamental unit group of society, and as a moral institution possessing inalienable and imprescriptible rights antecedent and superior to all positive law. The Constitution also pledges the State to guard with special care the institution of marriage on which the family is founded and to protect it against attack.

b) The UN defines the family as 'any combination of two or more persons who are bound together by ties of mutual consent, birth and/or adoption or placement and who, together, assume responsibility for, *inter alia,* the care and maintenance of group members, the addition of new members through procreation or adoption, the socialisation of children and the social control of members.

The Adoption Act, 1952 and subsequent Acts provide for adoption by married couples and, in certain circumstances, by sole applicants. In the formation of such family units, one of the principal criteria is the *parenting capacity* of the applicants as defined by international best practice, research and standards in

adoption. The changing nature of Irish society is evident in the growth of individualism; the changing role of women; the changing social climate (marital breakdown and divorce); recent social legislation (on homosexuality, equality); the changing economic and demographic climate (including greater labour mobility and immigration); the changing attitudes to religion and the changing nature and composition of families.

In the light of these developments the Adoption Board recommends that the Oireachtas Committee give consideration to broadening the constitutional definition of the family in line with the UN definition of the family set out above, so as to more fully reflect the changing nature of Irish society in general and of adoption practice in particular.

2 THE BALANCE BETWEEN THE RIGHTS OF THE FAMILY AS A UNIT AND THE RIGHTS OF INDIVIDUAL MEMBERS

Modern adoption practice recognises that the welfare of the child must always be accorded primary consideration. The rights of the child are enshrined in International Conventions and in domestic law and practice including the European Convention on Human Rights (1950); the United Nations Convention on the Rights of the Child (1989); the 1991 Child Care Act; and the National Guidelines for the Protection and Welfare of Children (*Children First* published by the Department of Health and Children, 2000).

Article 8 of the United Nations Convention states that:

a) parties to the Convention undertake to respect the right of the child to preserve his or her identity, including nationality, name and family relations as recognised by law without unlawful interference, and

b) where a child is illegally deprived of some or all of the elements of his or her identity, parties shall provide appropriate assistance and protection, with a view to re-establishing speedily his or her identity.

The principal European Convention protections for children are Article 6 (fair hearing and trial), Article 8 (right to respect of family life) and Article 14 (prohibition of discrimination). Article 8 states, in regard to children, that everyone has the right to respect for his private and family life, his home and his correspondence. While the Constitution emphasises the rights of the family as a unit, the provisions of the UN and European

Conventions explicitly enshrine the rights of all children – adopted or otherwise. Professor William Duncan has identified the problem that currently exists as follows: 'the problem seems to be essentially that of achieving a legal balance which will offer security and a measure of equality to individual family members in a manner which does not devalue or endanger the family as an institution'.

Due to the Constitution's protection of the family unit based on marriage, children of marriage are not eligible to be adopted other than in very exceptional circumstances. Under the restrictive provisions of the Adoption Act, 1988 where parents, for physical or moral reasons, have failed in their duty and have been deemed by the Courts to have abandoned and neglected their children, such children are eligible for adoption. The Child Care Act, 1991 charges local Health Boards with promoting the welfare of children who are not receiving adequate care and protection and with the provision of adoption services in accordance with the Adoption Acts 1952–1988.

Recently published proposals (January, 2005) for new adoption legislation *that do not require constitutional change* will enable widowed parents to adopt children into their new marriage, and foster-parents will be entitled to apply for special Guardianship Orders in respect of children in their care for more than five years – these children will be eligible to apply to be adopted in their own right, when they reach adulthood. There is, however, no proposal to allow for the adoption of children of marriage who are long term (say, over five years) in foster care, despite international research demonstrating the benefits that the permanency of adoption can provide for such children. With the best interests of the child at the core of their policies, both the United Kingdom and the United States specifically target 'looked-after' children within their child-care and foster-care systems who need the legal, emotional and psychological security provided by adoption.

The Adoption Board recommends that the best interest and welfare of the child be a primary consideration underpinning any Constitutional change in this area. To this end, all children regardless of the marital status of their parents should be eligible for adoption in certain circumstances.

This is in keeping with Article 20 of the UNCRC which recognises the right to alternative care for children who, for any reason, cannot remain with their natural family, and the need to provide such children with special protection and assistance. Article 20 requires states to provide alternative care such as in the form of adoption for these children.

3 IS IT POSSIBLE TO GIVE CONSTITUTIONAL PROTECTION TO FAMILIES OTHER THAN THOSE BASED ON MARRIAGE?

While the Constitution recognises the family as the primary unit of society and entitled to special protection, the rights or duties deriving from marriage, family, parenthood, or as a child need to be upheld and guaranteed for each individual within the family. This is consistent with the UN definition of the family set out at 1 b) above, and in areas of conflicting rights, because of children's greater vulnerability, the rights of the child need to be particularly protected, having due regard to the rights and duties of parents in respect of the welfare of their children (see also Section 3(2) b in the Child Care Act, 1991).

Were the UN definition of the family to be incorporated into the Irish Constitution, the family so defined would be recognised as a primary and fundamental unit of society and entitled to special protection. The Adoption Board considers that the family unit should be so defined and constitutionally protected.

A child's development is nurtured positively if s/he grows up within a family where there is a good relationship between a couple and this relationship has a degree of permanency and security. Equally, if the family unit comprises the child(ren) and just one adult, that adult person can provide the child(ren) with the security and permanency required. Family units could include heterosexual couples married or unmarried, single persons or gay couples, if they have a relationship that is permanent and stable. The Board considers that each type of family unit should be included in, and protected and cherished by the Constitution.

Within each family unit it is the adult's capacity to parent the child (and, in an adoption context, matching the parenting capacities of prospective adoptive parents to the particular needs of the child) that is of key importance. Parenting capacities are not defined by marital status and in adoption practice parenting capacities are the issue of paramount concern in meeting children's needs. 'Parenting capacities' are outlined in standardised frameworks for intercountry adoption assessment and are being addressed and defined in the domestic adoption assessment framework currently being prepared by the Adoption Board.

4 SHOULD GAY COUPLES BE ALLOWED TO MARRY?

In relation to adoption, parenting capacities (as defined by international best practice, research and standards) are what is required, irrespective of whether couples are married or not. 'Parenting capacities' are outlined in standardised frameworks for intercountry adoption assessment and are being addressed and defined also in the domestic adoption assessment framework currently being developed by the Adoption Board. See also reply to question 3 above.

5 IS THE CONSTITUTION'S REFERENCE TO A WOMAN'S 'LIFE WITHIN THE HOME' A DATED ONE THAT SHOULD BE CHANGED?

As the role of caregiver can be interchanged between mother and/or father, the Adoption Board considers that the word 'woman' should be replaced by 'parent' or 'primary caregiver'.

Consistency of care, particularly in the early stages of placement and period of attachment formation, would usually be provided by one of the parents and it is recommended that every support should be given to adoptive parents to enable them to be available to their adoptive child (i.e. adoptive parent leave, unpaid leave and parental leave) during the critical periods of the early life cycle, i.e. the first year of placement.

6 CONSTITUTIONAL PROTECTION FOR THE RIGHTS OF A NATURAL MOTHER

In adoption, the language and terminology used can be open to different interpretation and can cause disagreement and hurt to relevant representative groups. To this end the internationally recognised terms 'birth parents' and 'birth families' are used alongside the terms 'natural parents' and 'natural families' throughout this submission.

It is recommended that a new section should be inserted in Article 41 giving everyone a right, in accordance with Article 8 of the European Convention on Human Rights, to respect for their family life, and this includes the rights of a natural/birth mother in relation to her child. Natural/birth mothers have unenumerated and personal rights including the right to privacy, which is of particular significance in adoption; the Adoption Board is charged with balancing this right with the right of the person who has been adopted to have information about his/her natural/birth parents.

A natural/birth mother currently has the following legal rights relevant to adoption:

- she is 'guardian of the infant' (Section 6:4, Guardianship of Infants Act, 1964)
- she has the right to apply to adopt her child (Adoption Act, 1952, Section 11:1 b as amended by Adoption Act, 1991 Section 10:1 b), usually accessed in stepfamily situations
- she must be enabled to make her decision about her consent to the adoption of her child in a free and informed manner and must 'understand the nature and effect of the consent and of the adoption order' (Section 15:3, Adoption Act, 1952)
- except in circumstances of incapacity, she must legally consent to the adoption of her child (Section 14, Adoption Act, 1952).

The Adoption Board supports the introduction of the following additional adoption rights, which are provided for in the recently published proposals for adoption legislation change:

- that a natural/birth mother would no longer be required to adopt her own child jointly with her husband in order for both of them to acquire parenting rights in a stepfamily situation;
- that a natural/birth mother would be able to avail of access to her child following adoption as conditions of access could be added to adoption orders.

Some limitations on the natural/birth mother's rights is also included in the proposed new adoption legislation which would place an emphasis on the quality of service offered to the natural/birth mother prior to placing her child for adoption and would not allow her to withhold her final consent to the process beyond nine months after her initial decision to place the child for adoption.

Openness and contact are now features of Irish domestic adoption, whereby natural/birth parents can meet the prospective adopters and can keep some contact with the adoptive family if that is agreed between all parties – the level of contact can range from an annual exchange of progress letters and photographs to a number of meetings during the year. Openness, contact and the proposed legal right to attach conditions of access to adoption orders support the right to family life and knowledge of identity of all natural/birth parents and their children, in adoption.

Further to the above, the Adoption Board recommends that natural/birth parents who place their children for adoption should be informed in the event of a breakdown in the adoption placement and should be consulted about future care arrangements for the child.

All children regardless of the marital status of their parents are included under Article 8 of the UNCRC and Article 8 of the ECHR, allowing them the right to identity and family life. All parents are included in Article 8 of the ECHR and in adoption this necessarily includes the rights of birth/natural parents and adoptive parents.

The Adoption Board would, therefore, recommend that the state grant natural/birth mothers recognition and protection in the Constitution, and for any limitations on such rights to be defined legally.

7 WHAT RIGHTS SHOULD A NATURAL FATHER HAVE, AND HOW SHOULD THEY BE PROTECTED?

The Adoption Board recommends that a new section should be inserted in Article 41 giving to everyone a right in accordance with Article 8 of the European Convention on Human Rights, to respect of their family life and this includes the rights of a natural/birth father in relation to his child.

Natural/birth fathers currently have the following legal rights relevant in adoption practice:

- the right to be appointed a guardian if both parents agree [and if the natural/birth father's name is on the birth cert (Section 12:3(a, b) Status of Children

Act, 1987). If a natural/birth father is a guardian, adoption could not take place without his consent;

- the right to apply to be appointed a guardian (Section 6 of the Guardianship of Infants Act, 1964 as amended by Section 12 of the Status of Children Act, 1987)
- the right to apply to adopt his child (Adoption Act, 1952, Section 11:1 b as amended by Adoption Act, 1991 Section 10:1 b)
- subject to four exceptions (as outlined in Section 4, 7E:2,3,4 and 5, Adoption Act, 1998), the right to be consulted prior to the placement of his child for adoption
- the right to notify the Adoption Board that he wants to be consulted in relation to any proposal to have a child of his adopted (Section 4, 7D:1, Adoption Act, 1998).

Further rights included in the proposals for adoption legislation change would give a natural/birth father:

- preferential adoption rights
- access to his child following adoption as conditions of access could be added to adoption orders.

Currently, the consent of a natural/birth father, who is not married to the child's mother, is not required for the adoption of the child. The European Court of Human Rights (*Keegan v Ireland*, 1994) found that Ireland was in breach of Article 8 of the ECHR and the Adoption Act, 1998 was subsequently passed which gave natural/birth fathers a legal entitlement to be consulted before a child is placed for adoption. Natural/birth fathers are entitled to be heard regarding their views on the application and they have the right to apply to the Court for guardianship and custody; however, unless the natural/birth father's application to the Court is successful his consent to the adoption is *not* required.

Where the existence of a family unit has been established, the state must act in a manner calculated to enable that unit to be developed and legal safeguards must be created that render possible, from the moment of birth, the child's integration in his family. As suggested by the Constitution Review Group in 1996 a reasonable solution appears to lie in following the approach of Article 8 of the ECHR in guaranteeing to every person respect for 'family life' which has been interpreted to include non-marital family life between the natural/birth mother and natural/birth father. However, it would seem appropriate if the UN definition of family and proposals for individual rights within the family are accepted, that all types of family unit should be cherished in the Constitution and limitations on the rights of any person to family life should then be defined legally.

Openness and contact are now features of Irish domestic adoption, whereby natural/birth parents can meet the prospective adopters and can keep some contact with the adoptive family if that is agreed between all parties – the level of contact can range

from an annual exchange of progress letters and photographs to a number of meetings during the year. Openness, contact and the proposed legal right to attach conditions of access to adoption orders support the right to family life and knowledge of identity of all natural/birth parents and their children, in adoption.

Further to the above, the Adoption Board considers that natural/birth parents who consent to place their children for adoption should be informed in the event of a breakdown in the adoption placement and should be consulted about future care arrangements for the child.

All children regardless of the marital status of their parents are included under Article 8 of the UNCRC and Article 8 of the ECHR, allowing them the right to identity and family life. All parents are included in Article 8 of the ECHR and in adoption practice this necessarily means the rights of natural/birth parents and adoptive parents.

The Board also recommends that the state allow natural/birth fathers recognition and protection in the Constitution and for any limitations on such rights to be defined legally (such as the exemptions provided for by the Adoption Act,1998).

8 SHOULD THE CHILD BE GIVEN EXPANDED CONSTITUTIONAL PROTECTION?

Children, because of their immaturity, dependency and vulnerability, have special rights that should be afforded constitutional protection. The Adoption Acts 1952–1998 place the welfare of children as the paramount consideration in any decision for adoption, as does Section 3 of the Guardianship of Infants Act, 1964. Adoption law includes the necessity of taking into account the child's view of his family situation from when the child is aged 7 years (Section 3: 1 and 3:2 Adoption Act, 1964) as does Section 3:2 b(ii) of the Child Care Act, 1991 which states that the health services should, 'in so far as is practicable, give due consideration, having regard to his age and understanding, to the wishes of the child'.

Article 41 should expressly guarantee those rights of the child that are not guaranteed elsewhere and are peculiar to children, and should guarantee similar rights to all children regardless of their parents' marital status.

The Board also supports the Review Group's recommendation that it is desirable to put into the Constitution an express obligation to treat the best interests of the child as of primary importance, in line with Section 3 of the Child Care Act, 1991 which regards 'the welfare of the child as the first and paramount consideration' in the health services' promotion of the welfare of those children 'who are not receiving adequate care and protection'.

See also reply to question 2 above.

9 DOES THE CONSTITUTION NEED TO BE CHANGED IN VIEW OF THE UN CONVENTION ON THE RIGHTS OF THE CHILD?

The Constitution should, as outlined above, enshrine 'the welfare of the child as the first and paramount consideration' in all decisions relating to the promotion of the welfare of children who do not receive adequate care and protection (Section 3, Child Care Act, 1991).

In enumerating a child's rights in this regard, we believe the UNCRC articles relating to the child's knowledge of his/her identity and rights to information about parents and family should be included in the Constitution, as this has particular relevance for children who are adopted. Also, the registration of all natural/birth fathers on children's original birth certificates would have far-reaching and positive effects in adoption, particularly in the areas of identity and future tracing, and is in line with the UNCRC recommendations as outlined in Articles 7.1, 8.1, 9.1 and 9.3.

Throughout this submission we state that in the area of adoption (which is a UN-validated form of child protection and care for some children who cannot be cared for within their natural/birth families) children should have guaranteed rights that allow them to be treated with safety, dignity, respect and inclusion regardless of the marital status of their parents. In relation to adoption, children should have equal rights in the state whether they are children of a marriage or not, in line with specific Articles as outlined at the United Nations Convention on the Rights of the Child and the European Convention on Human Rights, and this necessitates constitutional change.

AGE ACTION IRELAND

THE RIGHTS OF GRANDPARENTS TO HAVE ACCESS TO THEIR GRANDCHILDREN

There are a number of instances where grandparents can have difficulty accessing their grandchildren and there are no provisions in the Constitution setting out their rights.

1 The courts, in interpreting the family, have said that it means the family based on marriage, but the question of the extended family has not been raised. The constitutional provisions give parents rights to make all the major decisions about their children and the state can only intervene if the parents fail in their duties towards the children. So, if parents (or a parent) decide that grandparents should not have access, there is a significant problem. It can be argued that access is a right of the child rather than the parent. Under Article 8 of the European Convention, family life can include the relationship between grandparent and grandchild.

2 In the case of marriage breakdown, it is not clear what rights grandparents have to access their grandchildren. While the best interests of the child are paramount, there can be a presumption that ties with grandparents are important because of the special relationship between grandparents and grandchildren. In Ireland, this special relationship is recognised in that one can claim citizenship through one's grandparents. The grandparent/child relationship is also a special category for various tax provisions.

3 A third area that causes problems is when grandparents live in a country from which it is difficult to get a visa to visit Ireland. If an Irish woman is married to, say, a Congolese man and living in Ireland and they want his parents to come to visit, there is no guarantee they will be issued with visas. However, if a French woman is married to a Congolese man and they are living and working in Ireland, they are entitled to have their parents come to live in Ireland under the EU freedom of movement rules.

References

Mangan, Ita (2004) 'Access for Grandparents', paper presented at a conference on grandparenting, October, Chester Beatty Library, see www.ageaction.ie.

AIM FAMILY SERVICES

HOW SHOULD FAMILY BE DEFINED?

AIM propose the adoption of the UN definition of the family which states that the family is technically defined as 'any combination of two or more persons who are bound together by ties of mutual consent, birth and/or adoption or placement and who, together, assume responsibility for, *inter alia*, the care and maintenance of group members, the addition of new members through procreation or adoption, the socialisation of children and the social control of members." 'It is an all embracing, non-exclusive definition and any family form (regardless of the sexual leaning of its members) whose function and values conform to the above definition would be included.'

Article 41 as currently constituted gives special recognition to the family based on marriage only. Diversity of family life should also be included.

HOW SHOULD ONE STRIKE THE BALANCE BETWEEN THE RIGHTS OF THE FAMILY AS A UNIT AND THE RIGHTS OF INDIVIDUAL MEMBERS?

As currently interpreted, the rights protected are those of the *unit*, against external forces, not of the individual members within that unit. This can leave individuals unprotected, where their detriment comes from within the unit, e.g. where domestic violence is in issue, the vulnerable person(s) can be largely unprotected; similarly in cases of child neglect or abuse within the family.

IS IT POSSIBLE TO GIVE CONSTITUTIONAL PROTECTION TO FAMILIES OTHER THAN THOSE BASED ON MARRIAGE?

Yes, it should be. The rights of individual family members must be guaranteed within the family, as well as against external threats; this would include a guarantee of respect for their individual rights and a guarantee that children's welfare should be paramount. We note that the unborn child appears to have a stronger constitutional position than that of the born child. Currently the Constitution assumes that parents/guardians are the guarantor of children's rights. This may involve specific responsibilities, as well as rights, of parents/guardians being enumerated.

To be more specific, we believe that children's rights, as well as those of their parents in families not based on marriage, should be individually guaranteed (for reasons outlined in question two).

SHOULD GAY COUPLES BE ALLOWED TO MARRY?

At present, there is little legal protection for cohabitees who are not married to each other and their children, notably, in the tax/social welfare codes and in inheritance rules in particular. Domestic violence remedies are restricted. This affects both gay and heterosexual couples. However, in the short term, the relevant legislation should be reformed, so as not to discriminate against cohabitees of whatever sexual orientation. See AIM booklet 'A Comparative View on the Rights of Cohabitees).'

There is need for greater debate in this area. Firstly we should ascertain the wishes of the majority of Irish gay people and devise a system of registration of domestic partnerships that would confer the rights currently unavailable to same-sex and heterosexual cohabiting couples in the area of tax, social welfare and inheritance.

Other European countries allow gay couples to marry. In *The Irish Times* of 31 December 2004, we read where another predominantly Roman Catholic country, Spain, took a major step in becoming another country to legalise gay marriage when its Socialist Government approved a draft law to give gay couples rights to marry, divorce and adopt children. Despite strong criticism from the Roman Catholic Church, the Spanish Cabinet approved a draft text that would give gay couples the same rights as their heterosexual counterparts, including inheritance and pension benefits.

IS THE CONSTITUTION'S REFERENCE TO WOMEN'S 'LIFE WITHIN THE HOME' A DATED ONE THAT SHOULD BE CHANGED?

Yes. This definition is patriarchal and sexist and reflects social thinking of the 1937 period. Thankfully, this has altered somewhat. It is also at odds with equality legislation that our membership of the EU has required from us. However, we feel that it is important to give practical recognition and value to the caring function in the family, a function which has had mainly lip service only paid to it to date. Apart from the provisions in the Separation and Divorce legislation of 1989, 1995 and 1996, the provisions of Article 41 have done little to improve the economic lot of women, whether wives or mothers; for those who remain married, their economic lot is tied to their ability to earn for themselves, or remain dependent on the goodwill of their spouses. (We do recognise that social welfare provision has improved but, intra-family, there is no community of property regime, for example.)

SHOULD THE RIGHTS OF A NATURAL MOTHER HAVE EXPRESS CONSTITUTIONAL PROTECTION?

O'Higgins CJ as quoted, infers that a mother's natural right to custody of her child is protected by Article 40.3 subsection 1 of the Constitution. The mother's right to guardianship should be guaranteed subject to the conditions proposed for natural fathers.

What should be of prime concern is that the child is reared in a secure, safe and loving environment. The day-to-day care and maintenance of the child should receive priority.

WHAT RIGHTS SHOULD A NATURAL FATHER HAVE, AND HOW SHOULD THEY BE PROTECTED?

A natural father should in equity have automatic right to guardianship of his child. The thrust of the law on equality points in this direction and is underpinned by the decision of the Court of Human Rights of 26 May 1994 in the Keegan Case when it held that the father's rights under Articles 6 and 8 of the European Convention on Human Rights were violated when his child was put up for adoption without his knowledge or consent.

However, the right to guardianship should be capable of being rescinded where the father refuses to be actively involved in caring for his child, refuses to contribute materially to the welfare of his child or where the child is the result of rape. As a child has the right to the society of both its parents, removal of guardianship rights should not preclude rights to access being granted by the courts where such a course is in the child's best interest.

There is already a precedent in Irish law for the alienation of the parental rights of unmarried mothers.

(*G v An Bord Uchtála*) Supreme Court 1978. (1980 I.R.32) O'Higgins CJ ruled that 'the plaintiff as a mother has a natural right to the custody of her child ... this natural right of hers is protected by Article 40.3 subsection 1 of the Constitution ... these rights of the mother in relation to her child are neither inalienable nor imprescriptible as the rights of the family are under Article 41 ... they can be lost by the mother if her conduct towards the child amounts to an abandonment or an abdication of her rights or duties (Binchy, 1984 pp 130). Also, it is now possible for the High Court to grant an adoption order for a child of married parents who has been abandoned where this is deemed to be in the child's best interest.

It must be said there is a long history of lack of involvement of fathers providing materially for their children. (See research of Paul Ward into District Court maintenance orders defaults 1990/1993.) Our prime concern should be that of the child.

SHOULD THE RIGHTS OF THE CHILD BE GIVEN AN EXPANDED CONSTITUTIONAL PROTECTION?

Yes. See reply to previous questions. There have been a number of abuse cases where our Constitution has been found lacking in protecting the rights of the child.

DOES THE CONSTITUTION NEED TO BE CHANGED IN VIEW OF THE UN CONVENTION ON THE RIGHTS OF THE CHILD?

Yes. Refer to second question above. Serious issues require to be addressed here. These include the right of the child to representation and to be heard in legal proceedings affecting her/him, including matrimonial disputes between parents. However, this might require a rethink of the adversarial process in our legal system. Involvement in an adversarial dispute, or a 'tug of love' would not be an enhancement of the child's needs or welfare.

Another issue would involve the removal of the words 'inalienable and imprescriptible' from Article 41.1.1 of the Constitution. These words endorse the primacy of the unit as a whole, sometimes to the detriment of individuals within the family. Where there are problems within the family, they have militated against the best interests of the child, e.g. have prevented the acquisition of rights by long-term foster carers as against married parents with no ties save blood to the child; a parent virtually unknown to the child has the right to remove her/him from their long-standing foster home. It also has prevented the adoption of children by their foster families even where this would greatly enhance the child's life.

Bibliography

Binchy William (1982). *Casebook on Irish Family Law.* Oxon. Professional Books.

AMEN

The invitation for submissions refers to the main provisions on the family as articles 40.3, 41 and 42. It also poses nine specific questions.

ARTICLES 40.3, 41 AND 42

Our comments on the articles identified as pertaining to the family are as follows:

1 *Article 40.3*

Under article 40.3 (1) the state guarantees to respect, defend and vindicate the personal rights of the citizen. As this is one of the primary reasons for, and fundamental purposes of, having a Constitution, this provision should remain as it is.

40.3(2) specifies certain rights which must be protected and vindicated in particular, viz. the life, person, good name and property rights of every citizen. These are very important rights and should continue to receive prominent recognition in the Constitution. However, there is a serious question as to whether or not this article is sufficiently strong as it is quite clear that the state is failing abysmally to protect the citizen's right to a good name and also the citizen's property rights. At present any citizen can indulge in any form of character assassination and make any form of false accusation against another citizen, with impunity, safe in the knowledge that he/she will suffer no penalty. An attack on a citizen's good name should be regarded with the same seriousness as a physical assault and should be likewise criminalised. It may be that *the constitutional protection of a citizen's right to a good name needs to be strengthened by criminalising all forms of character assassination including slander, libel and false accusations and the state should be obliged by its laws and otherwise to facilitate the vindication of a person's good name.* The state is, at present, in breach of its constitutional obligations to its citizens by its failure to adequately protect their good names.

In addition to article 40.3(2), article 43 also recognises the citizen's right to own private property. These provisions deal with property in a general way. The family home should be recognised as unique and distinct from other property. *A citizen's right to live in his/her family home should be expressly stated in the Constitution, except in extreme circumstances, viz. failure to pay rent or mortgage or proven criminal conduct which endangers the safety and rights of other family members.* Neither the state nor any other citizen should have the power to remove any citizen from his/her family home except in the circumstances outlined above. Also, the rights of all family members to live in their family homes should be constitutionally protected against debts incurred by any member of the family.

40.3(3) acknowledges the right to life of the unborn and the equal right to life of the mother. This has proven to be the most flawed wording of any article in the Constitution. At the time of the abortion debate in 1983, both sides, pro-abortion and anti-abortion, were of the view that this wording provided absolute protection for the unborn child. The judgment in the X case interpreted it in a way that neither the protagonists nor the many 'experts' had foreseen. Despite two further attempts to clarify the situation by means of referenda the constitutional position is still confused. *The current confusion surrounding article 40.3(3) should be cleared up, by means of another referendum, if necessary.* The wording of any provision relating to this issue will have to be more precise than the present wording.

2 Article 41

Article 41.1(1) and (2) recognises the family as the natural and fundamental unit group of society possessing inalienable and imprescriptible rights, and guarantees to protect the family in its constitution and authority. Given the increase in marriage breakdown in recent years, and the nature of the State's response to this phenomenon, it is doubtful if one could argue that the state is fulfilling its obligations under this article. Indeed the damaging nature and extent of the state's intrusion into family life would, at the very least, appear to be in breach of the spirit, if not the letter, of the Constitution. *The Constitution should set clear limits on the extent to which the state can interfere in family life, evict spouses from their family homes and usurp parental rights and obligations.* At present it appears to be able to do so with impunity and as a matter of routine.

Article 41.2(1) recognises the contribution given to the state by women in the home. This provision is discriminatory in that it gives no recognition to the contribution made by women outside the home or to the contribution made by men either in the home or outside the home. It is wrong to give recognition to the contribution made by one sex within one domain and ignore the contribution made by others. There does not appear to be any reason why women in the home should be given such exclusive recognition. There may have been some justifiable reason for inserting this article in 1937 but, given the changes in society in the intervening period, it appears to be somewhat redundant at this stage. *Article 41.2(1) should either be removed or similar recognition should be given to the contribution of men in the home and both men and women outside the home.*

Following on from this article, 41.2(2) imposes an obligation on the state to endeavour to ensure that mothers shall not be obliged by economic necessity to engage in labour to the neglect of their duties in the home. Even though this article does not contain an absolute guarantee it imposes a very strong obligation on the state. It is surprising that no mother has taken a case against the state because of its abject failure to ensure that mothers are not obliged, through economic necessity, to work outside the home. What is equally surprising is the manner in which this amazing commitment to mothers, to the exclusion of fathers, has been portrayed as discrimination against women rather than men. The points made in relation to 41.2(1) above apply to this article also. There is no reason why a similar obligation should not apply in relation to fathers in the home. As with other articles it is doubtful if the state could be said to be fulfilling its obligations under this article, given the number of mothers who feel obliged to go out to work because of economic pressures. *Article 41.2(2) should either be removed or amended to impose a similar obligation on the state to endeavour to ensure that fathers shall not be obliged by economic necessity to engage in labour to the neglect of their duties in the home.*

Under article 41.3(1) the state pledges to guard with special care the institution of marriage, on which the family is founded, and to protect it against attack. The comments above in relation to articles 42.1(1) and 41.1(2) are also applicable here. It would appear that there is a conflict between the new article, 41.3 (2), inserted following the referendum in 1995, and 41.3(1). The destructive nature of the family law system and the enticement of spouses into separation and divorce proceedings as a first resort, rather than any real encouragement to resolve their difficulties, is a breach of article 41.3(1). The state's commitment to encouraging damaging adversarial legal proceedings (to the benefit of the legal profession) rather than resolving issues amicably is evidenced by the respective budgets for the Legal Aid Board on the one hand and the Family Mediation Service and the Marriage and Bereavement Counselling Services on the other hand. These are:

	Legal Aid Board	Family Mediation Service	Marriage and Bereavement Counselling
	million €	million €	million €
2004	18.3	2.4	7.6
2005	21.3	3.4	8.4

Given the fact that fewer people are prepared to commit to marriage, it is obvious that the state has failed in its obligations under article 41.3(1). *It is no exaggeration to say that the civil marriage contract is now the most lethal contract that a man can enter into. By entering into civil marriage a man is effectively signing a contract containing an unseen termination clause, written in various Acts of the*

Oireachtas, which provides that the other party can at any time, and for no specified reason, unilaterally break the contract, force him to continue to fulfil his obligations while freeing her from her obligations, confiscate his property, choose to live off him for the rest of her life, take his children, destroy his fatherhood, banish him to a life of emotional and financial poverty, usually living in sub-standard accommodation, and dictate the nature and extent (if any) of his contact with his children. Indeed if more men were fully informed of the terms of this termination clause then they simply would not get married. Creating such a family law system is clearly an attack on, rather than a defence of, civil marriage. Those who govern our society must decide whether they wish to promote civil marriage or discourage it.

In the Constitution as enacted in 1937 article 41.3 contained an absolute ban on divorce. This remained in place until 1995 when a new article 41.3(2) was inserted which provided that a court may grant a dissolution of marriage subject to certain conditions. The referendum on the new provision was carried by the slimmest of margins. One of the conditions included, and which was used as a strong selling point, is that 'at the date of the institution of the proceedings, the spouses have lived apart from one another for a period of, or periods amounting to, at least four years during the previous five years'. The courts now accept that spouses can be deemed to be living apart under the same roof, i.e. in the same house. At the time of the referendum it is doubtful if people were aware that it would be interpreted in this way and, given the slim majority in favour, there is a doubt as to whether or not it would have been carried if they had been so aware.

Divorce is practically available on demand despite assurances to the contrary at the time of the referendum. The same applies to judicial separation. This is compounded by the fact that a spouse can make a *unilateral* application for divorce/separation and all the ancillary orders, regardless of the wishes of the other party. The result is that innocent parents, especially fathers, are being left homeless and having their parenthood destroyed simply to satisfy a misguided aspiration on the part of some people to be seen as a 'modern progressive' society. There is nothing either modern or progressive in the institutions of state permitting and facilitating the hostility and destruction inherent in the current family law system and the eviction of spouses from their homes with impunity. The only real beneficiaries are the lawyers. If the state was serious about protecting families it would impede, rather than facilitate, the legal profession in pursuing their vested interest in pushing people into divorce and separation. *Article 41.3(2) should be amended to clearly provide that a divorce can only be granted*

1 *where both spouses agree to the granting of the divorce subject to 2 below or*

2 *where one spouse has been in desertion for a period of more than four years and cannot be contacted and*

3 *where the spouses have been living in separate houses for at least four years and*

4 *where both spouses have attended and completed a Families in Transition programme approved by the Minister for Social and Family Affairs and*

5 *where the parties can show to the satisfaction of the court that they have a legally binding agreement which makes adequate provision for:*

   a) *the religious and moral, intellectual, physical, and social welfare of any dependent children*

   b) *the ongoing parental rights and obligations of both parents as joint equal guardians and joint equal custodians of their children*

   c) *the housing needs of both spouses taking account of the fact that, where there are dependent children, both parents will have to be in a position to provide suitable accommodation for themselves and their children*

   d) *the ongoing financial needs of both spouses, taking account of the fact that, where there are dependent children, both parents will have to be in a position to provide adequately and directly for their children while in their care.*

6 *In the absence of the agreement of both spouses to the granting of a decree of divorce and in the absence of an agreement as outlined at 5 above, a court should not be entitled to grant a decree or make ancillary orders except in the circumstances outlined in 2 above.*

The article should also provide that no law shall be enacted providing for any form of marital separation unless it complies with the requirements set out at 1 to 5 above.

The current family law system is destructive of the family, of citizens' lives and of society in general. It is undoubtedly the greatest evil inflicted on the citizens of this state, by the state, since the foundation of the state. The state's response to marriage breakdown is to set up a system that exacerbates hostility, encourages parents to abdicate their responsibilities and drives parents into an expensive legal system which plunders scarce family resources. Invariably men emerge as the supreme losers in these cases. As one member of Amen said, 'The state's response to the problem of marriage breakdown can be summed up in three words: *"wipe men out".'* The Family Mediation Service is ineffective and inadequate and is totally undermined by the legislation, standards and practices of the family law system. A new article 41.3(2) on lines set out above should be included in the Constitution.

3 *Article 42*

Article 42.1 acknowledges that the family is the primary and natural educator of the child and guarantees to respect the inalienable right and duty of parents to provide, according to their means, for the religious and moral, intellectual, physical and social education of their children. It is clear that this provision goes way beyond formal education in recognising the primacy of parents in the upbringing of their children. This is as it should be. It is not clear whether or not the guarantee 'to respect the inalienable right and duty of parents' extends to unmarried fathers and unmarried mothers. Given that article 41.3(1) appears to define the family as the family based on marriage it could be interpreted as referring to married parents only. This guarantee should expressly cover all parents, married and unmarried, fathers and mothers. It is significant that the English translation states that 'the State ... guarantees to respect the inalienable right and duty of parents ...' while the Irish wording is much stronger in stating 'admhaíonn an Stát ... agus rathaíonn gan cur isteach ar cheart doshannta ná ar dhualgas doshannta tuisti ...' The English version merely obliges the state to respect the right and duty of parents while the Irish version prohibits the state from interfering (... rathaíonn gan cur isteach ...) with the right and duty of parents. Where there is conflict between the Irish and English versions the Irish version takes precedence as Irish is the first official language (article 8.1 Bunreacht na hÉireann). *Article 42.1 should be amended so that the State will be prohibited from interfering with the inalienable right and duty of all parents, fathers and mothers whether married or unmarried. The English version of article 42.1 should be amended to provide a correct translation of the official Irish wording.* There is no doubt that the State is in breach of this article as it interferes with the right and duty of parents to an inordinate degree.

Article 42.2 appears to be satisfactory and should remain as is.

Article 42.3(1) also appears to be satisfactory and should be left as is.

Article 42.3(2) gives the state a monitoring role to ensure that children 'receive a certain minimum education, moral, intellectual and social'. It is noteworthy that this article does not mention religious or physical education, which are referred to in article 42.1. It may be that giving the state a similar function in relation to religious education would conflict with article 44, which guarantees freedom of conscience and the free profession and practice of religion. In any event it is right that the state should not be entitled to encroach on the rights of parents in relation to the religious education of their children. The reason for the omission of physical education is not so obvious. The Review Group should give consideration to the reasons for the omission of physical education and its possible inclusion. There is a question as to how article 42.3(2) can be reconciled with, and balanced against, article 42.1. *Article 42.3(2) should be reworded so as to be more specific as to how it can be reconciled with, and balanced against, article 42.1.*

Article 42.4 appears to be satisfactory and should remain as is.

Article 42.5 enables the state to '... supply the place of the parents ...' in exceptional circumstances '... where the parents for physical or moral reasons fail in their duty towards their children ...'. This article gives the state a much greater power than article 42.3(2) in that it effectively gives the state the power to remove the parents from their parenting role. The primacy of the parents and the constraints on the state's interference should be strengthened in this article. *Article 42.5 should be amended to expressly provide that the burden of proof that the parents, for physical or moral reasons, have failed in their duty, shall fall on the state.*

SPECIFIC QUESTIONS

It would be interesting to know the basis on which these specific questions were selected and why it was deemed necessary to highlight them.

Our comments on the nine specific questions are as follows:

1 *How should the family be defined?*

The closest thing we have to a definition of the family in the current Constitution is article 41.3(1), which refers to the institution of marriage on which the family is founded. This would appear to exclude any unit which is not based on marriage from the definition of family. Given the changes in society since 1937, particularly the fact that the marriage contract has been so corrupted by family law, and the fact that fewer people, particularly men, are prepared to commit to marriage nowadays, there is a need to redefine the term 'family'. Most people can be regarded as part of some family. In some cases they could be said to be members of a number of families. *The family should be defined on the basis of blood relationships, as well as marriage, and should enjoy constitutional protection.* For example all children should be regarded as part of their parents' families, regardless of whether the parents are married, or living together, or not.

2 *How should one strike the balance between the rights of the family as a unit and the rights of individual members?*

The circumstances in which there could be conflict between the rights of the family as a unit and the rights of individual members are so many and varied that it would be impossible to deal with them in a Constitution. *The best way to strike a balance would be to provide that the personal rights of the individual, as set out in the Constitution, take precedence over the rights of the family as a unit.*

3 *Is it possible to give constitutional protection to families other than those based on marriage?*

Yes, if the family is defined on the basis of blood relationships as well as marriage (see answer to question 1 above).

4 *Should gay couples be allowed to marry?*

In addressing this question we must look at the purpose of marriage and why the institution of marriage was created. Essentially civil marriage exists for the protection of the next generation and to deal with succession rights, etc. At present Irish law requires that one party to a marriage must be male and the other must be female. This position has been clarified by a number of court decisions. Lord Penzance in *Hyde v Hyde* (140 years ago) defined marriage as 'voluntary union for life of one man and one woman to the exclusion of all others'. In *T.F. v Ireland* (1995) the Supreme Court approved the Costello J. definition of marriage in *Murray v Ireland* (1985) which is: 'the constitution makes clear that the concept and nature of marriage, which it enshrines, are derived from the christian notion of a partnership based on an irrevocable personal consent, given by both spouses which establishes a unique and very special life-long relationship'. The position was further clarified in *Foy v An tArd-Chláraitheoir* when McKenchie J. stated that 'marriage as understood by the Constitution, by statute and by case law refers to the union of a biological man with a biological woman'. The Inter-Departmental Committee on the Reform of Marriage Law proposed that the definition of marriage should be that approved by the Supreme Court, i.e. 'the voluntary and permanent union of one man and one woman to the exclusion of all others for life'.

Amen supports the continuation of the definition as outlined above, i.e. the voluntary union for life of one man and one woman to the exclusion of all others.

Perhaps the best way to deal with the position of gay couples is that outlined by Archbishop Diarmuid Martin on a recent radio programme:

'Church teaching stresses that marriage is exclusively between a man and a woman, because this is part of the basic structure of the complementarity of the sexes, something rooted in creation, and not simply a social or cultural construct. It may, in certain circumstances, be in the public interest to provide legal protection to the social, fiscal and inheritance entitlements of persons who support caring relationships which generate dependency, provided always that these relationships are recognised as being qualitatively different from marriage and that their acceptance does not dilute the uniqueness of marriage.' (Archbishop Diarmuid Martin on RTÉ radio)

5 *Is the Constitution's reference to woman's life within the home a dated one that should be changed?*

See response above re. Article 41.2(1).

6 *Should the rights of a natural mother have express constitutional protection?*
and

7 *What rights should a natural father have and how should they be protected?*

These questions should be dealt with together. *The rights of all parents should have express constitutional protection regardless of sex or marital status.* This is particularly important at a time when over one-third of children are born outside of marriage. At present unmarried fathers have no constitutional protection and can only establish their rights at the gift of the mother or the courts. This is an intolerable situation and should be amended urgently. Indeed, the current position is probably in breach of the UN Convention on the Rights of the Child which states that 'State parties shall use their best efforts to ensure recognition of the principle that both parents have common responsibilities for the upbringing and development of the child' and 'the child shall be registered immediately after birth and shall have the right from birth to a name, the right to acquire a nationality and, as far as possible, the right to know and be cared for by his or her parents'.

The following excerpts from articles by journalist John Waters are very relevant to these questions:

The Irish Constitution renders family rights 'inalienable and imprescriptible' because the proper nurturing of children requires profound forms of protection. The problem facing the actually existing Irish family has to do with our failure, in a changing society, to understand the point of this unique formulation of rights. Regardless of marital situation, each child has a father and a mother, but the legal and cultural practice has been such as to transfer virtually the entire protection of the Constitution to the mother. As a result, one-third of children born in this state this very Monday will fall outside the protection of the Constitution, which in practice means they will, to a greater or lesser extent, be deprived of the love and care of their fathers. Add the child casualties of broken marriages, and it becomes clear this crisis has implications for over fifty per cent of children. (John Waters, *Irish Times* 'The liberal destruction of marriage' 22/11/04)

One-third of Irish children are now born out of wedlock, and most of these will have little or no relationships with their fathers. Divorce has caused an exponential growth in the numbers of children from broken marriages being similarly disenfranchised due to the dearth of legal protection for father-child relationships. Roughly half the children growing up now will experience negligible fathering in their formative years. That is the crisis. There is no other.

Yet, whenever a discussion is initiated about redefining the family, the media, legal and political establishments say: 'Oh yeah – gay marriage'. Recently, when the all-party venture was announced, this newspaper ran a front-page story focusing exclusively on gay marriage. It has yet to run a front-page account of the daily abuses of the human rights of fathers and children by family courts. (John Waters, *Irish Times* 'The absurdity of cultural liberalism' 8/11/04)

8 *Should the rights of the child be given an expanded constitutional protection?*

In the vast majority of cases the best way to protect the rights of the child is to protect the rights of the parents. The recommendations above and the response to question 9 below would give an expanded constitutional protection to the rights of the child.

9 *Does the Constitution need to be changed in view of the UN Convention on the Rights of the Child?*

Articles 3, 5, 6, 7, 8, 9, 18, 19 and 20 from the UN Convention on the Rights of the Child should be incorporated, in some form, in the Constitution.

Other articles are adequately dealt with by the other changes recommended above or are more appropriately dealt with by legislation.

SUMMARY OF RECOMMENDATIONS

Article 40.3

1 The constitutional protection of a citizen's right to a good name needs to be strengthened by criminalising all forms of character assassination including slander, libel and false accusations and the state should be obliged by its laws and otherwise to facilitate the vindication of a person's good name.

2 A citizen's right to live in his/her family home should be expressly stated in the Constitution, except in extreme circumstances, viz. failure to pay rent or mortgage or proven criminal conduct which endangers the safety and rights of other family members.

3 The current confusion surrounding article 40.3(3) should be cleared up, by means of another referendum, if necessary.

Article 41

1 The Constitution should set clear limits on the extent to which the state can interfere in family life, evict spouses from their family homes and usurp parental rights and obligations.

2 Article 41.2(1) should either be removed or similar recognition should be given to the contribution of men in the home and both men and women outside the home.

3 Article 41.2(2) should either be removed or amended to impose a similar obligation on the State to endeavour to ensure that fathers shall not be obliged by economic necessity to engage in labour to the neglect of their duties in the home.

4 Article 41.3(2) should be amended to clearly provide that a divorce can only be granted

   1 where *both* spouses agree to the granting of the divorce subject to 2 below or

   2 where one spouse has been in desertion for a period of more than four years and cannot be contacted and

   3 where the spouses have been living in separate *houses* for at least four years and

4 where both spouses have attended and completed a Families in Transition programme approved by the Minister for Social and Family Affairs and

5 where the parties can show to the satisfaction of the court that they have a legally binding agreement which makes adequate provision for:

   a) the religious and moral, intellectual, physical, and social welfare of any dependent children

   b) the ongoing parental rights and obligations of both parents as joint equal guardians and joint equal custodians of their children

   c) the housing needs of both spouses taking account of the fact that, where there are dependent children, both parents will have to be in a position to provide suitable accommodation for themselves and their children

   d) the ongoing financial needs of both spouses, taking account of the fact that, where there are dependent children, both parents will have to be in a position to provide adequately and directly for their children while in their care.

6 In the absence of the agreement of both spouses to the granting of a decree of divorce and in the absence of an agreement as outlined at 5 above, a court should not be entitled to grant a decree or make ancillary orders except in the circumstances outlined in 2 above.

The article should also provide that no law shall be enacted providing for any form of marital separation unless it complies with the requirements set out at 1 to 5 above.

Article 42

1 Article 42.1 should be amended so that the state will be prohibited from interfering with the inalienable right and duty of all parents, fathers and mothers whether married or unmarried. The English version of article 42.1 should be amended to provide a correct translation of the official Irish wording.

2 Article 42.2 appears to be satisfactory and should remain as is.

3 Article 42.3(1) also appears to be satisfactory and should be left as is.

4 Article 42.3(2) should be reworded so as to be more specific as to how it can be reconciled with, and balanced against, article 42.1.

5 Article 42.4 appears to be satisfactory and should remain as is.

6 Article 42.5 should be amended to expressly provide that the burden of proof, that the parents, for physical or moral reasons, have failed in their duty, shall fall on the state.

RESPONSE TO QUESTIONS

1 *How should the family be defined?*

The family should be defined on the basis of blood relationships as well as marriage and should enjoy constitutional protection.

2 *How should one strike the balance between the rights of the family as a unit and the rights of individual members?*

The best way to strike a balance would be to provide that the personal rights of the individual, as set out in the Constitution, take precedence over the rights of the family as a unit.

3 *Is it possible to give constitutional protection to families other than those based on marriage?*

Yes, if the family is defined on the basis of blood relationships as well as marriage (see answer to question 1 above).

4 *Should gay couples be allowed to marry?*

Amen supports the continuation of the definition of marriage as outlined above, i.e. the voluntary union for life of one man and one woman to the exclusion of all others.

5 *Is the Constitution's reference to woman's life within the home a dated one that should be changed?*

See response above re. Article 41.2(1).

6 *Should the rights of a natural mother have express constitutional protection?*

and

7 *What rights should a natural father have and how should they be protected?*

The rights of all parents should have express constitutional protection regardless of sex or marital status.

8 *Should the rights of the child be given an expanded constitutional protection?*

In the vast majority of cases the best way to protect the rights of the child is to protect the rights of the parents. The recommendations above and the response to question 9 below would give an expanded constitutional protection to the rights of the child.

9 *Does the Constitution need to be changed in view of the UN Convention on the Rights of the Child?*

Articles 3, 5, 6, 7, 8, 9, 18, 19 and 20 from the UN Convention on the Rights of the Child should be incorporated, in some form, in the Constitution. Other articles are adequately dealt with by the other changes recommended above or are more appropriately dealt with by legislation.

THE ASSOCIATION OF BAPTIST CHURCHES IN IRELAND[1]

HOW SHOULD THE FAMILY BE DEFINED?

As one man and one woman committed in marriage to each other for life, together with any children of their marriage or adopted into it. This is the God-given building block of every society. The future stability of Irish society depends on a secure foundation. Healthy families are that secure foundation. To tamper with the definition of the family is to attack the foundations of the state.

HOW SHOULD ONE STRIKE THE BALANCE BETWEEN THE RIGHTS OF THE FAMILY AS A UNIT AND THE RIGHTS OF INDIVIDUAL MEMBERS?

Since the family unit is the bedrock of society for the protection and the provision of our children, then the rights of the family must be protected as a first priority. In principle the rights of the family outweigh the rights of the individual. However, it is recognised that the state should protect the rights of those who have experienced family breakdown and who continue to work for the good of family life and the provision of care to the remaining family members. But this should not lead to a change in the constitutional definition of a family. It should be possible to draft legislation which gives adequate protection to these rights without weakening the constitutional position and definition of the family.

IS IT POSSIBLE TO GIVE CONSTITUTIONAL PROTECTION TO FAMILIES OTHER THAN THOSE BASED ON MARRIAGE?

Of course it is possible – but the real issue is whether it is desirable to give the same protection to other domestic arrangements as is given to marriage. What is absolutely essential is to give unique and maximum protection to the institution of marriage, since this is the foundational building block of society. In western culture generally, marriage is under attack and needs special protection. Outside marriage, the issue is how to protect the weak and vulnerable in society, e.g. the elderly, orphans and widows. Lone parents and their children come under this category of those in need of special protection. But this should be protected without undermining the two-parent family, e.g. by tax or social welfare provisions.

SHOULD GAY COUPLES BE ALLOWED TO MARRY?

No. One of the main purposes of marriage, if not the main one, is the birth and nurture of the next generation in an environment which provides both fatherhood and motherhood. By definition gay couples neither (a) produce children on their own, nor, (b) provide both male and female role models. If gay couples are to be given some special legal status short of marriage, or special privileges and/or exemptions, then in fairness this should open the door to similar provisions for the benefit of all kinds of other domestic arrangements and commitments. For example, if two people of the same sex live together in a settled but non-sexual relationship, why should they not have the right to register their domestic arrangement and obtain the same tax benefits (such as exemption from tax for gifts to each other) as a gay couple? Or if a child commits himself/herself to look after an elderly parent, why should he/she not have the right to gifts from that parent free of tax if that commitment lasts for a certain period, say, three years? In short, why should a sexual element to a non-marital relationship be the magic ingredient that opens up the right to all kinds of tax and other benefits?

IS THE CONSTITUTION'S REFERENCE TO WOMAN'S LIFE WITHIN THE HOME A DATED ONE THAT SHOULD BE CHANGED?

The reference is dated in the sense that our society today encourages both parents to take an active role in the upbringing of their children. However, it must be recognised that the mother plays a unique role in the nurture of her children. Perhaps the reference could be revised to read: 'The State recognises the role of both parents in the upbringing of their children and in particular the unique role of the mother in the nurture of the family.'

SHOULD THE RIGHTS OF THE NATURAL MOTHER HAVE EXPRESS CONSTITUTIONAL PROTECTION?

No. What is needed is the constitutional protection of marriage and the family. Natural mothers should be granted appropriate rights by legislation, but only where consistent with the best interests of the child.

WHAT RIGHTS SHOULD A NATURAL FATHER HAVE, AND HOW SHOULD THEY BE PROTECTED?

The real issue is what *duties* should be imposed on the natural father, and how should the exercise of those duties be enforced? Too many natural fathers are allowed to evade their responsibilities towards their children and the mother of their children. Natural fathers should be granted appropriate rights by legislation, but only where consistent with the best interests of the child.

SHOULD THE RIGHTS OF THE CHILD BE GIVEN AN EXPANDED CONSTITUTIONAL PROTECTION?

The constitution could be expanded to include 'the right to bodily integrity and the right to an opportunity to be reared with due regard to religious, moral, intellectual and physical welfare'. However, the real issue here is the responsibilities of parents towards their children. Perhaps parenting should be a major part of the national curriculum in secondary level education. Where parents fail to protect and provide for their own children, the state has a duty to do so. It would help if this right of children to state provision and protection were made explicit. Whether this needs to be in the constitution is a moot point. Perhaps legislation is sufficient.

DOES THE CONSTITUTION NEED TO BE CHANGED IN VIEW OF THE UN CONVENTION ON THE RIGHTS OF THE CHILD?

Not in our opinion.

Article 41.3.1 reads 'The State pledges itself to guard with special care the institution of *marriage, on which the family is founded* and to protect against attack.'

In our view the wording in Article 41.3.1 'on which the family is founded' should be retained. Changing this because of changing social structures among a minority would have the effect of eroding the high value which the state places on the institution of marriage.

Notes
1   The Association of Baptist Churches in Ireland comprises over 100 independent churches on both sides of the border.

ASSOCIATION OF IRISH EVANGELICAL CHURCHES

PAPER ONE: THE SOCIAL IMPLICATIONS OF REDEFINING MARRIAGE
prepared by James McMaster and Rev Michael J. Walsh

The Association of Irish Evangelical Churches (AIEC) would like to thank this committee for allowing us the opportunity to voice our perspective on the important matters that you are deliberating. We pray that God will grant you wisdom and discernment in your discussions. The AIEC is a group of 35 Evangelical Churches around Ireland. Our desire is to serve Jesus Christ by proclaiming the Gospel in word and deed. We care deeply for the people of this island and we welcome any attempt on the government's part to strengthen existing and future families. The AIEC recognises the Bible as the standard by which society should define marriage. In the pages of the Bible we find the origin, privileges, and responsibilities of marriage.

I CHRISTIAN DEFINITION OF MARRIAGE

Marriage has historically been defined as a life-long covenant union between a man and a woman that is witnessed by God and the community. This definition has enjoyed almost universal acceptance across time and cultures. Marriage is of such importance that it is uniquely protected in law and culture.

It predates the law and any constitution, and is an anthropological and sociological reality, not primarily a legal one. No civilisation can survive without it, and those societies that allowed it to become irrelevant have faded into history.

Christians believe that this definition of marriage originates with God. The first book of the Bible, Genesis, lays the foundation for the Christian and Jewish understanding of this covenant union between a man and a woman:

The Lord God made a woman from the rib he had taken out of the man, and he brought her to the man. The man said, 'This is now bone of my bones and flesh of my flesh; she shall be called "woman", for she was taken out of man.' For this reason a man will leave his father and mother and be united to his wife, and they will become one flesh.[1]

Jesus reiterated this understanding of marriage in the Gospel of Matthew. He said:

Have you not read that he who created them from the beginning made them male and female, and said, 'Therefore a man shall leave his father and his mother and hold fast to his wife, and they shall become one flesh'? So they are no longer two but one flesh. What therefore God has joined together, let not man separate.[2]

These clear statements have been a foundation for marriage in Irish culture stretching back to the time of Patrick. The strength of this Christian definition rests 'on a foundation of tradition, legal precedent, theology and the overwhelming support of the people.'[3] We feel there is no need to tamper with this definition. The government should rather seek to safeguard it and do what it can to help our society live up to the responsibilities that marriage entails.

2 NEGATIVE CONSEQUENCES OF REDEFINING MARRIAGE

Marriage is the union of the two sexes, not just the union of two people. It is the union of two families and the foundation for establishing kinship patterns and family names, passing on property and providing the optimal environment for raising children.

Robert Benne and Gerald McDermott make the following comment in their article 'Speaking Out': 'Scrambling the definition of marriage will be a shock to our fundamental understanding of human social relations and institutions.'[4] The AIEC would concur with this assessment. We feel that redefining marriage to include same-sex relationships, polygamy, or any other deviation from biblically defined marriage, will bring disastrous consequences to our society.

First, we feel there will be negative consequences on the institution of marriage itself. Family psychologist Dr James Dobson has some poignant words. Dr Dobson says when a state broadens its definition of marriage beyond the traditional understanding, 'marriage is reduced to something of a partnership that provides attractive benefits and sexual convenience, but cannot offer the intimacy described in Scripture. Cohabitation and short-term relationships are the inevitable result.'[5]

Second, Dr Dobson points out that there will be negative consequences for the ideal of sexual fidelity. He says, 'With marriage as we know it gone, everyone would enjoy all the legal benefits of marriage (custody rights, tax-free inheritance, joint ownership of property, health care and spousal citizenship, and much more) without limiting the number of partners or their gender. Nor would "couples" be bound to each other

in the eyes of the law. This is clearly where the movement is headed. Activists [homosexual lobby] have created a new word to replace the outmoded terms *infidelity, adultery, cheating* and *promiscuity*. The new concept is *polyamorous* (literally "many loves"). It means the same thing (infidelity) but with the agreement of the primary sexual partner. Why not? He or she is probably polyamorous, too.'

Third, there will be negative consequences for children. Dr Dobson says: if 'the State sanctions homosexual relationships and gives them its blessing, the younger generation becomes confused about sexual identity and quickly loses its understanding of lifelong commitments, emotional bonding, sexual purity, the role of children in a family, and from a spiritual perspective, the "sanctity" of marriage.'[6]

David Chambers wrote in the 1996 edition of the *Michigan Law Review* that he expects gay marriage will lead government to be 'more receptive to [marital] units of three or more'. We can only imagine the confusion and complexity of custody cases when these unions fall apart.

One danger in same-sex marriage is the tendency of homosexuals to have short-term relationships. Researchers in the Netherlands, where same-sex marriage is legal, did a study that found gay people have an average of 8 partners per year outside of their primary relationship.[7] John Edmiston of the Asian Bible Institute says that 5% of homosexuals have relationships that last 3 years or more. He goes on to say: 'children in those polyamorous [new word used in homosexual circles meaning "many loves"] situations are caught in a perpetual coming and going. It is devastating to kids, who by their nature are enormously conservative creatures. They like things to stay just the way they are, and they hate change.'[8]

Dr Dobson said that 'more than ten thousand studies have concluded that kids do best when they are raised by loving and committed mothers and fathers. They are less likely to be on illegal drugs, less likely to be retained in a grade, less likely to drop out of school, less likely to commit suicide, less likely to be in poverty, less likely to become juvenile delinquents, and for the girls, less likely to become teen mothers. They are healthier both emotionally and physically, even thirty years later, than those not so blessed by traditional parents.'[9] This is why the AIEC feels now is the time to reaffirm marriage, not redefine it.

We feel it is wrong to create fatherless or motherless families by design. The drive for same-sex 'marriage' leads to destruction of the gold standard for custody and adoption. The question should be, 'What is in the best interests of the child?' The answer is: 'Place children, whenever possible, in a married, mum-and-dad household.' If same-sex relationships gain status, marriage loses its place as the preferential adoption family option. This effort is being driven by the desires of adults, not the needs of children.

Finally, we feel there will be negative consequences for freedom of religion if marriage is redefined.

Christians must uphold the teaching of scripture. This includes the Bible's prohibition against homosexual behaviour. This teaching will come into conflict with government policy if the government decides to sanction same-sex marriage. Government sanction of same-sex marriage has been the basis of the 'hate-speech' laws in Canada and Sweden. In those countries it has become a crime to speak out against homosexual behaviour. One assistant state's attorney in the United States said that if same-sex marriage becomes the law of the land then churches could be sued for refusing to perform such unions.

Christians have enjoyed religious freedom in Ireland since the inception of the state. This right is in jeopardy if the government redefines marriage to include anti-Christian, Jewish and Islamic practices.

Redefining marriage will be like opening a Pandora's Box. Marriage as we know it today has at least a 5,000 year track record. When the traditional definition is upheld, and adhered to, there has been stability for families and society. Marriages are coming under pressure but the answer is to reaffirm the ideal as set out by our Creator.

3 THE IMPORTANCE OF STRONG MARRIAGES

No doubt the Irish government recognises the stability that strong marriages offer to our society. It must also see the damage caused when marriages begin to break down. Strong marriages teach all of us about the importance of self-sacrifice, commitment and love. The opposite is also true. Broken marriages destabilise a society. *Child Trends* magazine ran an article about the positive influences of marriage in general. The article states 'people who are married are healthier, are likely to live longer, are more satisfied with their jobs, have more social support, have more wealth and income, are less prone to mental disorders, and are involved in fewer unhealthy or risky behaviours than people who are not married or who are divorced.'[10]

Children have many needs but their most basic need is for the support, love and protection of their parents. The relationships that provide children with the most stable environment in which to be raised are good marriages. Children are often the ones who suffer most when a marriage is not strong. There is universal agreement among sociologists that the most stable environment for a child is a home with a traditional marriage in place. 'Specifically, considerable research indicates that children develop best when their biological parents marry and remain married.'[11]

Child Trends magazine lists the following problems that children, and eventually society, will have to face when marriages are not healthy.

> For example, children born to unmarried mothers are more likely to be poor themselves and achieve lower levels of education than other children.[12] Children of divorced parents have more academic and behaviour problems than other children.[13] On average children growing up with step-parents also have lower levels of

well-being than children growing up with biological parents.[14]

We understand that some couples find it difficult to maintain the commitment they made to one another on their wedding day but that is where churches, government, family and friends can lend support. If marriage is a covenant union witnessed by the community, then the community bears a responsibility to help couples maintain their commitment.

The churches in the AIEC are willing to do their part to ensure that the God-ordained institution of marriage remains a stabilising factor in Irish society. The Irish government can help by reaffirming these basis commitments:

1 We will view marriage as lifelong and heterosexual. It is a relationship based on vows of total commitment that are made publicly and entail a change in legal status. Although it must be recognised that many marriages fall short of this ideal it is crucial that the ideal not be tampered with. The state has the responsibility to provide a legal framework that discourages divorce and encourages reconciliation.

2 We will support marriage because it is the basis of a stable society. Marriage serves an important cohesive role in society, requiring men and women to take on public vows of life-long commitment to each other and to their children. Marriage also provides the most committed relationship within which to share the support and care for a wider group of people, such as the elderly or other members of the extended family, a commitment and responsibility that is less likely to be found in the looser ties of cohabitation.

3 We reaffirm that marriage is the best environment for children to be raised in. The institution of marriage is society's established and recognised framework for providing a stable, enduring and committed environment for raising children – tomorrow's breadwinners and citizens. Children have many needs but their most basic is the support, love and protection of their parents. Those relationships that provide children with the most stable environment in which to be raised are found in heterosexual marriage.

The following words by the Family Research Report remind us of the importance of marriage. 'Every time the mortar that holds society together is weakened, another step toward the destruction of society is made. Marriage is one of the most important elements in our societal mortar'.[15]

Notes
1 Genesis 2:22-24
2 Matthew 19:4-6
3 James Dobson, 'Eleven Arguments Against Same-Sex Marriage', http://www.family.org/cforum/extras/a0032427.cfm
4 http://www.christianitytoday.com/ct/2004/107/41.0.html
5 Dobson, James, 'Eleven Arguments Against Same-Sex Marriage'
6 ibid

[7] http://ipsapp003.lwwonline.com/content/getfile/13/1073/12/abstract.htm

[8] http://aibi.gospelcom.net/aibi/samesex.htm

[9] Dobson, James, 'Eleven Arguments Against Same-Sex Marriage'

[10] Lillard, L.A., Brien, M.J., & Waite, L.J. (1995). Premarital cohabitation and subsequent marital dissolution: A matter of self-selection? *Demography, 32,* 437-457; Waite. Does marriage matter?; Mirowsky, J., & Ross, C. E. (1989). *Social causes of psychological distress.* New York: Aldine de Gruyter; Waite, & Gallagher. The case for marriage: *Why married people are happier, healthier and better off financially.*

[11] Parental conflict, marital disruption and children's emotional well-being. *Social Forces,* 76(3), 905-936.

[12] McLanahan, S., & Sandefur, G., 1994/

[13] Peterson, P.E., & Zill, N., 1986; Amato, P.R., 2000.

[14] Coleman, M., Ganong, L., & Fine, M., 2000.

[15] Lutzer, Erwin W., *The Truth About Same-Sex Marriage,* Moody Press, 2004, p. 70

PAPER TWO: SHOULD THE CONSTITUTION'S REFERENCE TO WOMAN'S 'LIFE WITHIN THE HOME' BE CHANGED?

prepared by Mary Hamilton

The All-Party Oireachtas Committee on the Constitution in its advertisement inviting submissions has asked the question: 'is the Constitution's reference the woman's 'life within the home' a dated one that should be changed?

The specific reference is found in Article 41:2

> 1 In particular, the State recognises that by her life within the home, woman gives to the State a support without which the common good cannot be achieved.
>
> 2 The State shall therefore endeavour to ensure that mothers shall not be obliged by economic necessity to engage in labour to the neglect of their duties in the home.

We have come a long way since 1937! Coming as we do from the perspective of an increasingly egalitarian modern Ireland, where most women work outside the home, the phrases in article 41.2 seem quaint and old-fashioned. Surely no one today would consider these words seriously, any more than a young woman of 2005 would consider dressing herself in her grandmother's flowered pinafore and headscarf! However, these words were written with the serious intent of promoting the common good and giving support to the state. They should also be considered in the light of the preamble to the Constitution:

> In the Name of the Most Holy Trinity, from whom is all authority, and to whom as our final end, all actions both of men and States must be referred

These are solemn words indeed, for the nation's leaders and lawmakers. They are accountable not only to their people but also ultimately to God himself. Our 'obligations to our Divine Lord Jesus Christ' must be taken very seriously indeed.

In view of the fact that the making or changing of the laws of the nation is done before God, it would be important to ensure that laws are not changed on superficial grounds, or merely to reflect changes in fashion. If the reference to a 'woman's life within the home' sounds dated or old-fashioned it is important to ask why.

Ideas and social theories about the place of women in society go in and out of fashion and it can be difficult to get a properly objective view on one's own culture since it is as close to us as the air we breathe. How can we know that we are not being unduly influenced by an idea that is merely tremendously fashionable? What are the human consequences of applying social theories through the laws of the land?

In the twentieth century there were many examples in many different nations, of ideas that were enacted as laws and which failed, as they did not match up to what is true about people, human nature or society. One could refer to the kibbutz experiment in Israel, where all expectations were confounded, when women who were free to choose high status jobs and day care for their children, repeatedly and insistently turned these things down so that they could nurture their own children and attend to their own living space. In other countries where legislation of social ideals has been brought in more forcefully, such as in the former USSR and China, the cost of failure has been very high. Untold misery and suffering resulted where social ideals did not match with reality, and with what is true about human nature. Jung Chang's book *Wild Swans* illustrates this point graphically.

So is it really possible to actually get at the truth? Is it possible to go beyond fashions in social theory?

The good news is that there is a reliable objective standard, which is true for all people, from every cultural group in the world, and true for all time, regardless of changing fashions. It is a standard that gives hope and dignity to people. It is a standard that works because it is true to life and human nature. It is the word of God – the maker's instructions – that set out the beauty and purpose of God's design for people. Truly, womanhood is a 'designer' creation.

So what does this great standard have to say about the role of women, and is there any reference to their 'life within the home'? The answer is in the affirmative, and it is replete with references to the joy that a woman experiences in fulfilling the purposes for which she was designed. Psalm 113 in the Book of Psalms is a hymn of worship which celebrates God as being worthy of worship at all times 'both now and for evermore' and in all places 'from the rising of the sun to the place where it sets'. In the last verse God is praised for 'he settles the barren woman in her home as a happy mother of children'. Another important reference is found in Proverbs chapter 31, which is a description of the 'wife of noble character'. This Hebrew poem is about a woman whose 'value is greater than rubies'. Notably, whilst she engages in home-based tasks and work outside the home – 'she considers a field and buys it' – she does all so that she may 'watch over the affairs of her household'.

In Ireland today, despite the fact that full-time paid work and a career are given great status, the job of rearing the next generation (i.e. motherhood) is still a coveted task.

Over the last thirteen years, since I became a mother myself, I have heard much said on this subject by many women from many different backgrounds. Many women in Ireland today work outside the home, not because they are ideologically committed to a career but out of economic necessity – specifically the cost of financing a mortgage in most cases. At times I have been quite shocked by the vehemence with which women have expressed feelings on this subject. I could multiply anecdotes here, but for the sake of brevity two examples should serve to illustrate.

While my two oldest children were still very young, I had to attend hospital outpatients for minor surgery. The nurse in attendance asked in a conversational way, 'What do you work at?' When I replied that I did not work in paid employment but worked at home with my children, she suddenly became very annoyed and with a red face said, "It's well for some that they can afford the luxury of staying at home!" Her reaction left me dumbfounded, but I wished that I could have told her that our own circumstances were anything but luxurious and that we were always in a struggle to meet basic financial commitments (if she had seen our elderly furniture – mostly given to us – and our children in second-hand clothes she might not have spoken so quickly!)

Another instance occurred just before our third child was born, when I attended a breastfeeding support group meeting for the first time. There were several other mums there for the first time, too. The main concern for most of these women was – how to express breast milk. In other words, they were there to try and come to a compromise between giving their babies the best and the necessity of returning to work. One mother said that she would love to stay at home with her new baby but they had a mortgage on their house and how would they pay it? Interestingly, the Constitution expressly stated that having to work outside the home from economic necessity should not happen.

While the factors involved are undeniably complex, it can be seen that the cost to society of taking mother out of the home has been very high. Society is now more fragmented than it has ever been, and the trend seems to be for families to become ever more fragmented.

In conclusion, may I challenge the Irish government to live up to its written commitments in the Constitution, and to make more efforts to ensure that Irish women are free to choose to rear their own children and to nurture their husbands and marriages, not being forced to take up paid work outside the home in order to survive financially. Let us make sure that the women of Ireland can give the greater share and the best part of their time to the people who need it most, and whom they most love: their families.

Uireasa a mheadaíonn cumha. (Absence increases sorrow).

CONCLUSION

Again the AIEC would like to thank you for allowing us this opportunity to voice our concerns on these matters. Our desire is to see marriages and families strengthened and we pray that your conclusions will be a means to that end.

BARNARDOS

INTRODUCTION

Barnardos welcomes the initiative taken by the Oireachtas Committee on the Constitution in reviewing family rights in the Constitution. Barnardos recently launched an ambitious long-term strategy for children in Ireland which set out the following vision and mission statements:

> Barnardos' vision is an Ireland where childhood is valued and all children and young people are cherished equally.
>
> Barnardos' mission is to challenge and support families, communities, society and government to make Ireland the best place in the world to be a child, focusing specifically on children and young people whose well-being is under threat.

Barnardos works with over 12,000 children and families in Ireland each year. Our services are led by the needs of children, working with 'a whole child approach' involving families and the community. Barnardos is also committed to advocacy and has identified four priority areas for advocacy: child poverty, child protection, educational disadvantage and alcohol abuse.

The importance of this constitutional review and the opportunity to effect positive change in the lives of children, particularly the most vulnerable children, cannot be over-estimated. In spite of a range of legislative provisions, policies, systems and services designed to protect children and to promote their welfare and development, there are many children who still experience threats to their development and whose lives are shattered by conditions of abuse, neglect, discrimination, violence, exploitation, alcohol and drug misuse and homelessness.

The content of this submission focuses on two particular issues raised in the Committee's terms of reference as follows:

• Should the rights of the child be given an expanded constitutional protection?

- Does the Constitution need to be changed in view of the UN Convention on the Rights of the Child?

The structure of the submission is presented as follows:

- The case for constitutional reform
- Case studies
- The Constitution and the family
- The Constitution and the child
- International law
- Conclusions
- Recommendations

THE CASE FOR CONSTITUTIONAL REFORM

The case for the inclusion of children's rights in the constitution was highlighted in the report of the Kilkenny Incest Investigation (1993):

> We feel that the very high emphasis on the rights of the family in the Constitution may consciously or unconsciously be interpreted as giving a higher value to the rights of parents than to the rights of children. We believe that the Constitution should contain a specific and overt declaration to the rights of born children. We therefore recommend that consideration be given by the government to the amendment of Articles 41 and 42 of the Constitution so as to include a statement of the constitutional rights of children. (Ibid p.96)

In 1996, the Report of the Constitution Review Group indicated that 'it is desirable to put into the Constitution an express obligation to treat the best interests of the child as a paramount consideration on any actions relating to children'. Any such provision might be modelled with the appropriate changes to suit an Irish context, on Article 3.1 of the CRC (UN Convention on the Rights of the Child) which provides:

> In all actions concerning children, whether undertaken by public or private social welfare institutions, courts of law, administrative authorities or legislative bodies, the best interests of the child shall be of paramount consideration.

In 1998 the United Nations Committee on the Rights of the Child, in its concluding observations, emphasised that the recommendations of the reports of the Constitution Review Group would reinforce 'the status of the child as a full subject of rights'.

In his seminal work *Child Law* (2005) Geoffrey Shannon concludes that 'injustice, inequality, hypocrisy and the denial of human rights occur in many areas of child law'. In considering the current constitutional provision as it relates to children, Barnardos has drawn on *Child Law* as the most authoritative source of legal analysis. However, Barnardos is also drawing on the extensive experience we have had in working with children and families over many years.

The most central issue that arises is that of the relationship and balance between the rights of parents and the rights of children. It is Barnardos' view, informed by our experience in working with very vulnerable children, that the Constitution as it currently stands creates an environment where the rights of the family supersede the rights of individual children. In order to illustrate the impact of this problem on the lives of children, we have included a number of case-studies of real children, with names and identifying details changed to preserve confidentiality.

CASE STUDIES

The following case studies have been gathered from Barnardos staff. Many of the issues that arise are linked with long-term plans for children, their ongoing relationships with their families of origin, and the impact that this has on their foster families.

Examples of Child Protection cases

Case A: Tara is a three year old little girl who has been with same foster family since the age of three months. She has court ordered access to her mother twice weekly for three hours. Tara displays great distress at going to access and her distress is given little credit in court and there is no *guardian ad litem* involved. The quantity of access and the disruption to their lives is affecting the foster carers' ability to care for Tara.

Case B: A four year old girl, Mary has been with same family since the age of six months. She has court ordered weekly access to her mother who is giving Mary messages that she is getting her back. The case is under review in court every six months. Each time the case is coming up, rehabilitation is looked at seriously. Mary is showing great distress and insecurity.

Case C: Two siblings Shane and Tom aged five and three years are in foster care. The last four years have been spent trying to rehabilitate, thus social workers have been unable to identify a permanent family. The three year old is showing signs of attachment disorder. Social workers appear very confused and parental rights are placed before the needs of the children. Courts assume that children and parents have an attachment, as do the social workers, and thus planning and access is based on this. However, the mother disappears for long periods and then turns up seeking access which is automatically given. Family care workers who are strangers to the children bring them to access in cars. Which parent among us would place their two young children into a car with a total stranger each week? The children are showing signs of great disturbance. Tom, the three year old, has been in care since three weeks old.

Case D: A case referred to us was of a fifteen year old girl who was introduced to heroin by her twenty eight year old boyfriend, and who quickly progressed to IV use. The man's previous partner died after an overdose injected into her body by him. The health board would not become involved. The case was referred to the solicitor by gardaí who were utterly frustrated by the girl's situation. Her solicitor referred the case to us as she wanted to take High Court proceedings to secure services for the girl. But the girl's mother would not agree to this and therefore the case could not progress. We recently heard again of the girl, who was before the courts for criminal activity related to drug taking.

Case E: A boy aged six was in foster care. The mother had long-term mental health problems and was unlikely to ever regain care of him, but had regular access. The foster carers did not propose providing a long-term home for the boy and he would have to move within the next twelve months. No foster placements were available locally and the child would be likely to be admitted to residential care. An extended family member in the UK, who knew the child, was willing to adopt him and to allow post-adoption contact with the mother. This person was assessed and approved. However, the mother would not give permission either for the adoption or the child's removal from the jurisdiction. The case was heard in the High Court but no information was made available as to the outcome of the case.

Case F: John is five and in long-term foster care, having been removed from his mother's care at birth. After several moves in his first year, John was placed in foster care at fifteen months with Ann and Mark Kennedy and their adopted son, Peter. John has access with his father Kevin once a week. His mother died a few months after his younger sister Fiona was born. Fiona joined John at the Kennedy's when she was six weeks old. Fiona, who has no legal guardian, is in the process of being adopted by the Kennedys. Kevin is not Fiona's father. At age three, she is a happy, healthy, secure child.

Kevin suffers from depression. He has had regular and good quality access when he has been well. He does not agree that John should be in care, and openly criticises the Kennedys' care of John. John has shown progress in many areas and is benefiting from foster care. However, when John is unsettled his behaviour deteriorates. He can be aggressive and threatening to other children. The Kennedys are exhausted and wondering how much longer they can cope.

Kevin has a right to see John. John has a right to grow up with a relationship with his father. However, John also has a need to grow up with stability. He is particularly vulnerable to change and cannot manage the stress of belonging to two households that he perceives to be in conflict. His tenuous sense of security is being undermined by the frequency of access arrangements and the resultant behaviour is placing strain on the placement. If John's placement breaks down it will be a developmental catastrophe for him and will create long-term, potentially lifelong damage. When Fiona's adoption is completed, she will have a different legal status than John and will have no legal relationship with him, even though they are brother and sister being reared in the same household.

Case studies from private law

There are many cases where children attend access, regardless of their wishes and feelings about the non-resident parent. There is one case at the moment where the father is requiring access, and the children have made very clear and credible allegations of abuse against him.

An 'audit' of children with whom we work in the High Court came up with the following:

Twelve of the twenty eight children we represented were in care prior to age eight. Six of those were raised in care since their infancy. All but two had social workers for most of their lives. They have a lengthy history of attachment difficulties and placement disruption. Family and environmental risk factors include behavioural and mental health disorders, lack of social commitment, drug and alcohol use by the child and/or within the family, growing up in poor housing conditions, low income, poor school achievement, bullying, harsh and erratic discipline, family conflict, and parental offending.

It can be difficult to separate out the individual causal factors which disadvantage children who are not able to be raised with their families. Certainly the emphasis on the rights of the parents, the priority placed on repeated rehabilitation attempts and the high frequency of access appears to Barnardos to impede the capacity of children and their foster carers to make long-term commitments to each other. The child who has already lost his family of origin can be denied the right to belong to any family. In some cases as illustrated above, this can have a significant detrimental impact on the child's welfare and development.

By contrast, however, there are a number of cases where positive and protected contact between parents and children has meant that when a placement has not worked for a child, and where the parent has made significant recovery, the child has been able to be reunited with his/her birth family.

There is huge variation in access arrangements and practice between various health boards. Some have dedicated access facilities with regular staff conducting the access, providing continuity for children, parents and carers, all of whom are involved in the planning. Others take place to a 'formula' – typically once a month for long-term care, and rely on *ad hoc* arrangements, taking place in hotel rooms and shopping centres, supervised by a variety of people, and it is hard to see how this can be a meaningful experience for any of the participants.

THE CONSTITUTION AND THE FAMILY

According to Shannon (2005) the main source of fundamental rights in Irish family law is the Constitution, with the key articles being Articles 41 and 42. Article 41 of the Constitution of 1937 relates to the family and 'recognises the family as the natural and primary unit group of society' and also guarantees 'to protect the family in its constitution and authority'. These rights are bestowed on the family unit as a whole rather than individual family members. An individual on behalf of a family may invoke them but as Costello J. noted in *Murray v Ireland*,[1] they 'belong to the institution in itself as distinct from the personal rights which each individual member might enjoy by virtue of membership of the family'.

Article 41 of the Constitution fails to recognise the child as an individual in his/her own right. This derives from the principle of parental autonomy inherent in Article 41. This article establishes a level of privacy within family life, which the state can enter only in the exceptional circumstances detailed in Article 42.5 of the Constitution as follows:

> 1 The State acknowledges that the primary and natural educator of the child is the family and guarantees to respect the inalienable right and duty of parents to provide, according to their means, for religious and moral, intellectual, physical and social education of their children.
>
> 5 In exceptional cases, where the parents for physical or moral reasons fail in their duty towards their children, the State, as guardian of the common good, by appropriate means shall endeavour to supply the place of the parents, but always with due regard for the natural and imprescriptible rights of the child.

The subordination of children's rights to the precedence of the family unit has been reflected in many Supreme Court judgments. Article 42 deals with education, which includes child-rearing and holds it to be not only a right but a duty of parents. This article

reinforces the decision-making autonomy of the family. Article 42.5 addresses the complete inability of some parents to provide for their children's education.

> It has been interpreted as being confined not just to a failure by the parents of a child to provide education for him and her, but may in exceptional circumstances extend to failure in other duties necessary to satisfy the personal rights of the child. This interpretation supports the assertion that the right to education in Article 42 is a mere extension of the concepts of 'the family' in Article 41. Articles 41 and 42 of the Constitution together render the rights of married parents in relation to their children 'inalienable'. (Shannon 2005, page 4)

The implication of these articles is that the scope for the legal overturning of the rights of married parents is severely limited and the experience of Barnardos, as illustrated by the case studies above, means that child protection and child welfare can be compromised.

Shannon also refers to the importance of section 3 of the Guardianship of Infants Act, 1964 which makes it clear that in considering an application relating to the guardianship, custody or upbringing of a child, the court must have regard to the welfare of the child as the 'first and paramount consideration.' The Supreme Court, however, has determined that the welfare of a child must, unless there are exceptional circumstances, be considered to be best served by its remaining as part of the marital family. Shannon concludes that there is 'an uneasy tension between, on the one hand, the provisions of Articles 41 and 42 of the Constitution and on the other hand, the welfare principle outlined in Section 3 of the Guardianship of Infants Act, 1964.' (Ibid p. 4)

THE CONSTITUTION AND THE CHILD

Court judgments over the past number of years have accepted that children have certain personal, unenumerated rights under Articles 40 and 42 of the Constitution. In the case of *G v An Bord Uchtála*, Finlay P. held that the child 'has a constitutional right to bodily integrity and has an unenumerated right to an opportunity to be reared with due regard to his or her religious, moral, intellectual, physical and social welfare'. O'Higgins C.J. in the Supreme Court expanded upon Finlay P.'s statement when he stated:

> The child also has natural rights … [T]he child has the right to be fed and to live, to be reared and educated, to have the opportunity of working and of realising his or her full personality and dignity as a human being. The rights of the child (and others which I have not enumerated) must equally be protected and vindicated by the state. In exceptional cases the state, under the provisions of Article 42.5 of the Constitution, is given the duty as guardian of the common good, to provide for a child born into a family where the parents fail in their duty toward the child for physical or moral reasons. In the same way, in special circumstances the

State may have an equal obligation in relation to a child born outside the family, to protect that child, even against its mother, if her natural rights are used in such a way as to endanger the health or life of the child or to deprive him of his rights.[2]

In this same case, Walsh J. stated that: '[T]here is nothing in the Constitution to indicate that in cases of conflict the rights of the parents are always to be given primacy.'[3] He went further by analysing the rights of children in the following terms:

> Not only has the child born out of lawful wedlock the natural right to have its welfare and health guarded no less well than that of a child born in lawful wedlock, but *a fortiori* it has the right to life itself and the right to be guarded against all threats directed to its existence whether before or after birth. The child's natural rights spring primarily from the natural right of every individual to life, to be reared and educated, to liberty, to work, to rest and recreation, to practice of religion, and to follow his or her conscience … It lies not in the power of the parent who has the primary natural rights and duties in respect of the child to exercise them in such a way as intentionally or by neglect to endanger the health or life of the child or to terminate its existence. The child's natural right to life and all that flows from that right are independent of any right of the parent as such.[4]

In a more recent case of *D.G. v Eastern Health Board*, Denham J. held that the child had 'the right to be reared with due regard to his religious, moral, intellectual, physical and social welfare; to be fed, accommodated and educated; to suitable care and treatment; to have the opportunity of working and of realising his personality and dignity as a human being'.[5]

More recently it appears that the Supreme Court has moved away from enumerating children's rights by holding that the government was responsible for articulating the rights of children. According to Shannon, 'this approach can be gleaned from four landmark judgments of the Supreme Court in the past four years on children's rights. They concern the children in society who are most in need; children who are dependent on the state for their education, health, welfare and citizenship. Such children now inhabit a legal limbo.[6]

Barnardos' concern is that if the state fails to protect the lives of individual children, and if the Supreme Court refuses, except in exceptional circumstances, to uphold children's rights, then vulnerable children will not be adequately protected.

INTERNATIONAL LAW

Our dualist approach to international law generally makes international human rights treaties binding on the state, though not on the courts, as such treaties have traditionally not been incorporated into Irish law. Ireland has ratified two international instruments that have a significant bearing on children's rights. Ireland ratified the 1989 United Nations Convention on the Rights of the Child (CRC), without reservation on September 21, 1992. That said, the provisions of the CRC do not form part of Irish law. This convention, it should be stated, gives recognition to children's rights in the widest of terms.

Ireland has also ratified the European Convention on Human Rights and Fundamental Freedoms (ECHR) into domestic law. However, the incorporation of the ECHR has been at sub-constitutional level which has resulted in children's rights remaining subordinate to parental rights. Without an expressed statement on children's rights in the Constitution, children's rights will remain inferior to parental rights.

CONCLUSIONS

- The current position is that under the Irish Constitution, children's rights are not adequately protected. (See Kilkenny Incest Investigation Report)
- The Constitution creates an environment where the rights of the family take precedence over the rights of individual children. This impacts on the culture of child protection work and policy-making. Also the decision-making flows from assumptions that plans for children are created around the rights of parents.
- The report of the Victoria Climbié inquiry (2003) has made one hundred and eight recommendations concerning early intervention, inter-agency co-operation and the need for increased social work resources. These recommendations reinforce the report of the Cleveland Inquiry (1988). The question must be asked as to how the whole child care system in Ireland could be strengthened if the Irish Constitution were to include an explicit children's rights provision. Barnardos is of the view that this would strengthen the effectiveness of child and family services in terms of child protection.

RECOMMENDATIONS

- That the Irish Constitution be amended to include an article which expressly guarantees and secures the protection of children's rights.
- With regard to the UNCRC Barnardos recommends that the terms of this instrument should be reflected in the constitution.

Notes
1. [1985] ILRM 542 at 547.
2. Ibid at 69.
3. Ibid at 78.
4. Ibid at 69.
5. [1998] 1 ILRM 241 at 262.
6. Shannon p. 6.

References

Shannon, G. (2005), *Child Law*. Thompson Round Hall.

Kilkenny Incest Investigation (1993), Government Publications.

Report of the Inquiry into Child Abuse in Cleveland 1987 (1988), Her Majesty's Stationery Office.

The Victoria Climbié Inquiry Report (2003), TSO.

BRETHERN

This submission is made by members of the Christian fellowship known to the government as the Brethern. It has in mind the well-being and moral protection of every man, woman and child in Ireland.

THE CONSTITUTION

We believe God, in his goodness, has provided the Irish nation with a Constitution that upholds true Christian values, especially in its recognition and respect for 'the most Holy Trinity and our Divine Lord Jesus Christ', and also in the protection of the true family unit as instituted by God himself. We submit that the government has particular responsibility to uphold our Constitution and *resolutely reject* every influence that would undermine the moral integrity of the nation.

- We acknowledge the fact of increasing marital breakdown and are sympathetic with the government's concern to provide suitably for and protect its citizens.
- We see the increasing, unrelenting pressures to come into line with current popular thinking and give respectability to unchristian and immoral practices.
- The government has its responsibility, given to it by God, to uphold law and order and protect its citizens from physical danger and moral decline, 'for rulers are not a terror to a good work but to an evil one' (Romans 13:3)
- Every citizen has his/her responsibility, firstly to God, but also to be subject to the authority of government and the laws of the country based on the Constitution: 'let every soul be subject unto the higher powers. For there is no power but of God; the powers that be are ordained of God. Whosoever therefore resisteth the power, resisteth the ordinance of God; and they that resist shall receive to themselves damnation'. (Romans 13:1 and 2)
- The use of the word 'family' in Article 41.1, sections 1 and 2, is intended to convey *only* the unit based on marriage and any honest right thinking person would acknowledge this. There are two pillars on which the family is based – the sanctity of the marriage bond and the care of the children which carries its own dignity and status throughout the world.
- It is right to guarantee constitutional protection to every individual but not to recognise improper and immoral relationships. Outside of the family unit, based on marriage, constitutional protection for the citizen can only be on an individual basis.

SHOULD GAY COUPLES BE ALLOWED TO MARRY?

The Constitution recognises the social strength and protection afforded by the institution of marriage and pledges to protect it against attack. God, in his infinite wisdom, created male and female for each other and for balance in bringing up the family. To put unnatural and immoral relationships on the same level as marriage would be an affront to God and would undermine the whole moral foundation of society. Marriage means the union of a man and a woman voluntarily entered into for life, to the exclusion of all others. We therefore urgently appeal that *no change* be made to the Constitution to recognise such evil practices.

- It is of interest that in eleven US states the following wording is used. 'Marriage means the union of a man and a woman to the exclusion of all others, voluntarily entered into for life.'
- The following wording is used in Australia: 'Certain unions are not marriages. A union solemnised in a foreign country between;
  a) a man and another man, or
  b) a woman and another woman
  must not be recognised as a marriage in Australia.'

IS THE CONSTITUTION'S REFERENCE TO WOMAN'S 'LIFE WITHIN THE HOME' A DATED ONE THAT SHOULD BE CHANGED?

It is our belief and practice that the holding of families together are best served by the mother's life within the home. The neglect of duties within the home is the single main contributor to the widespread marriage breakdown and moral disorder throughout the world. The common good given to the state by the woman should not be overlooked or weakened and is certainly not a dated reference.

RIGHTS AFFECTING THE NATURAL FATHER, MOTHER AND CHILD

It is our deep concern that the interests, protection and emotional well-being of the child are safeguarded in the traumatic event of parental separation. It is right that both parents should continue to have contact with their child after separation, provided that it is safe. We believe that 'safe' should relate not only to physical well-being, but also to the child's own personal sense of security, the protection of its own moral and spiritual integrity and recognition of its conscience and heritage.

Where a child has been born into a particular culture, environment and way of life, it acquires stability and depth of background from that environment. If in the course of parents separating from each other, a child may be introduced to ideologies, associations, and a way of life that conflict with its conscience and upbringing, causing distress and trauma, this is to be deplored.

While the natural father and the natural mother are firstly responsible for the care of the child it is beyond the responsibility of government to give exclusive constitutional rights to either as this would conflict with the child's best interests.

The father and mother are the responsible controlling influence in a family and every member is placed in subjection to them. 'Honour thy father and mother, which is the first commandment with a promise'. (Eph 6:1)

A REVISED ARTICLE 41 SHOULD INCLUDE THE FOLLOWING ELEMENTS

1) Recognition by the state of the family based on marriage as the primary and fundamental unit of society.

2) A right for all persons to marry must respect the fact that marriage means the union of a man and a woman voluntarily entered into for life.

3) A pledge by the state to guard with special care the institution of marriage and protect it against attack and to prevent any future legislation that would undermine the sanctity of the marriage.

4) A pledge by the state to protect the family and family life based on marriage in its constitution and authority.

5) An express guarantee of certain rights of the child, which fall to be interpreted by the courts from the concept of 'family life', as based on marriage which might include;

   a) the right of every child to be registered immediately after birth and to have from birth a name

   b) the right of every child, as far as practicable, to know his or her parents, subject to the proviso that such right should be subject to regulation by law in the interest of the child

   c) the right of every child, as far as practicable, to be cared for by his or her parents.

   d) the right to be reared with due regard to his or her welfare including his or her religious and cultural heritage.

6) An express requirement that in all actions concerning children, whether by legislative, judicial or administrative authorities, the best interests of the child shall be the paramount consideration.

7) An amended form of Article 42.5 expressly permitting state intervention either where parents have failed in their duty or where the interests of the child require such intervention and a re-statement of the State's duty following such intervention.

8) An express statement of the circumstances in which the state may interfere with or restrict the exercise of family rights guaranteed by the Constitution loosely modelled on Article 8 (2) of ECHR.

9) Retention of the existing provisions in Article 41.3.3° relating to recognition for foreign divorces

---

CATHOLIC ACTION NETWORK

PREAMBLE TO OUR CONSTITUTION

In the Name of the Most Holy Trinity, from Whom is all authority and to Whom, as our final end, all actions both of men and State must be referred. We, the people of Éire, Humbly acknowledge all our obligations to our Divine Lord, Jesus Christ, Who sustained our fathers through centuries of trial, Gratefully remembering their heroic and unremitting struggle to regain the rightful independence of our Nation, And seeking to promote the common good, with due observance of Prudence, Justice and Charity, so that the dignity and freedom of the individual may be assured, true social order attained, the unity of our country restored, and concord established with other nations, Do hereby adopt, enact, and give to ourselves this Constitution.

Without question, Article 41.2.1 and Article 42.2.2 have been ignored by successive governments to the detriment of family life. The state has seriously neglected married women in the home and made it extremely difficult for them to rear their children in the family environment.

Currently the state subsidises child-minding facilities almost everywhere to the detriment of the mother's desire to fulfill her irreplaceable role with her children in the family home. The state should pay a mother in the home an allowance equivalent to that paid in the child-minding industry for each child in care.

The state has a duty to guard and uphold what is enshrined in Article 42 of our Constitution which protects the rights and duties of parents, without interference, to provide for the religious, moral, intellectual, physical and social education of their children. There should be no conflict between the rights of the child and the rights of the parents. The only grounds on which the state can interfere at present with the authority of the family are set out in and controlled by Article 42.5 and this must be maintained.

The family based on the marriage of one man and one woman forms the basis of our society and must be defended. An attack on the integrity of this august institution is an assault on society. Marriage has always been recognised as a natural relationship between a man and a woman with the potential to procreate new life and the responsibility to cherish, nourish and protect that life. This traditional definition of family must continue to be enshrined in our Constitution as the fundamental unit necessary for the natural development of the individual and the common good of society.

The state acknowledges the right to life of the unborn with due regard to the life of the mother in Article 43.3.3 and this must not be touched. Our Constitution should not be changed to accommodate the UN Convention on the Rights of the Child while that institution denies the unborn child the most basic of all rights, the right to life, and continues to promote 'the culture of death' throughout the world.

Our Constitution was adopted and enacted by the people of Ireland in the name of and under the patronage of the Most Holy Trinity in the interests of the common good.

In the mystery of creation, Almighty God gave man the free will to accept or reject him in this life and in the next. We have no right to attempt or aspire to incorporate in the name of or under the patronage of the Most Holy Trinity that which we know to be gravely immoral, the legitimisation of specific rights of cohabiting persons. What right have we to make lawful what God has decreed to be unlawful? Such proposals are not only preposterous but sacrilegious. How could proposals to legalise what is gravely immoral be for the common good of the Irish people?

On this issue the Holy Father has stated that 'the future of the world passes by way of the *family.* Those who would move from tolerance to the legitimisation of specific rights of cohabiting homosexual persons need to be reminded that the approval of legislation of evil is something far different from the tolerance of evil. *One must refrain from any kind of formal cooperation in the enactment of such gravely unjust laws and as far as possible from material cooperation in the level of their application.* **To vote in favour of a law so harmful to the common good is gravely immoral.'**

As always the decision to accept or reject God is personal but never private because of its consequences on others. 'What you do unto the least of my little ones you do unto me' and finally 'he who denies me on earth I will deny before My Father in heaven.' In the name of God and the common good of our people do not lead us down that road.

CATHOLIC NURSES GUILD OF IRELAND

In general terms the Catholic Nurses Guild approves the primacy of the current constitutional protection and safeguards afforded to the family as well as the legal safeguards and definitions expressed in case law consequent on the constitutional provision.

DEFINITION OF FAMILY

The basis of the family is marriage: one man and one woman entering freely a contract which protects both themselves and the children of their union. The family is the basic unit of society. It provides both security and stability with an ethos which supports a personal growth and a sense of belonging. This Family unit is the best environment for rearing and nurturing children.

RIGHTS OF FAMILY VERSUS RIGHTS OF INDIVIDUAL MEMBERS

It should be noted that in the matter of balance – personal v. community good – the 'greater good' takes precedence. In an ordered society the concept of 'greater good' is the best determinant for personal growth since it recognises the limits of permissible actions and behaviours as well as protecting the possibilities for personal advancement within agreed parameters.

CONSTITUTIONAL PROTECTION TO FAMILIES OTHER THAN THOSE BASED ON MARRIAGE

The primacy of marriage must be upheld. Actions which detract from this must be avoided at all costs.

SHOULD GAY COUPLES BE ALLOWED TO MARRY?

Most definitely they should not. Marriage is a contract between a man and a woman. The future of society depends for its growth and stability and the safeguarding of future generational development on its status.

THE CONSTITUTIONAL RIGHTS OF THE MOTHER, FATHER AND CHILD

The state should support the constitutional family and continue to give it its protection. The rights of the natural father should be judged on its merits by the courts if there is a conflict. The rights of the child are well protected in our Constitution as a human being, independent of the family and should not be expanded to allow external interventions, which may not be in the best interests of the child.

DOES THE CONSTITUTION NEED TO BE CHANGED IN VIEW OF THE UN CONVENTION ON THE RIGHTS OF THE CHILD?

Absolutely not. Interference with our Constitution just to satisfy a UN Convention on the Rights of the Child would be a grave mistake and no doubt would lead to all kinds of trouble in the future.

CHRISTIAN WOMEN'S FEDERATION

We, in the Christian Women's Federation, are disturbed to note that in the suggestions put forward by the All-Party Oireachtas Committee on the Constitution (APOCC) there does not appear to be any mention whatsoever of the necessity to highlight areas in which marriage and the family are being undermined. This undermining of marriage and the family contributes in no small way to the breakdown in society which is evident in so many areas of life in Ireland today. Over the years, there has been an increasing tendency in government policies to follow trends (and directives) from outside sources without first carefully examining the consequences of such trends. One example of this is the introduction of tax individualisation – designed to get married women out of the home and into the workplace. Another instance of damaging policies is the putting into place of so-called 'sex-education' programmes for our young people. Instead of curbing the detrimental effects of international cultural influences (media, advertising, and entertainment by way of films, etc.), the government is in fact failing to address such influences, which add to the problems outside the control of parents that they experience in rearing their children.

Members of the APOCC would do well to read a report published a few years ago by the Institute for the Study of Civil Society (London). The report, entitled *Experiments in Living – The Fatherless Family*, states: '... the weight of evidence indicates that the traditional family based on a married father and mother is still the best environment for raising children, and it forms the soundest basis for the wider society.' Attached to the report is a lengthy list of references that provides ample opportunity of studying the other side to that which appears to occupy the minds of those in power in government.

A news item in today's *Irish Times* (27 January 2005) has been brought to our attention. In it are given the comments of Dr. Edward Walsh, Professor Emeritus of the University of Limerick, which are contained in a script due to be delivered by him next week. He says:

> Clearly in ways we do much better in 2005 in looking after young lone females who become pregnant and have children than we did previously. Yet the support the state provides may have moved further than it should: very real financial incentives are now in place that may actively encourage the formation of lone-parent families.

He goes on to say that it had been widely suggested in research literature 'that many of the social ills we face in Ireland can be traced to the growth of lone-parent families, and especially to families where the father is absent.' Further, he says that in the U.S.

> ... much research has been conducted on the cause of social breakdown, and while it may be politically incorrect to highlight it, many studies associate high levels of substance abuse, rape, child abuse and other unpleasant social phenomena with the growth of lone-parent families.

We quote at length from the report on Dr. Walsh's statement because we consider that to hear the words of a person of his authority and standing might better influence those in government whose responsibility it is to put into place policies that will protect and uphold the constitutional rights of the family.

Although the title of our organisation is Christian Women's Federation, we do not maintain that the institution of marriage belongs solely to Christianity. The institution of marriage exists outside all or any particular faith or belief.

- The family, based on marriage, is the fundamental social unit. The Constitution of Ireland recognises the special position of the family, and gives it inalienable and imprescriptible rights, antecedent and superior to all positive law. The Constitution pledges the state to guard with special care the institution of marriage, on which the family is founded, and to protect it against attack. Marriage, in Irish law, is the union of one man and one woman, to the exclusion of all others, for life. International covenants and charters recognise this also, and have called for the protection on the part of states for marriage and the family. The family is the unit, unified in marriage, of one man and one woman, together with their children – whether the natural children of the married couple, or adopted or fostered children.

- The rights of the family as a unit and the rights of individual members of that family are complementary.

- Following what has been said above, it is not possible, and must not be made possible, to give constitutional protection to 'families other than those based on marriage'. However, every protection and right should be given to the members of such groupings in accordance with those rights already established and provided in the Constitution.

- The homosexual and lesbian lifestyles are totally at variance with the institution of marriage and the family, and as such cannot therefore be accorded the legal 'right' or recognition of those lifestyles.

- The constitutional recognition of the importance to society of woman's life within the home is essential to the welfare and well-being of the family and society as a whole, and this constitutional recognition must therefore be left intact.

- The rights of a natural mother are sufficiently protected in the Constitution.

- The rights of a natural father, as a human being, are sufficiently protected in the Constitution, but some recognition could be given to the rights of, say, a deserted father to maintain contact with his children.

- The rights of the child are sufficiently protected in the Constitution, but the government must recognise these rights at all times. A case in point is where total protection is not at present afforded to the child in the womb.

- The Constitution *does not* need to be changed in view of the UN Convention on the Rights of the Child. While the Convention contains some good principles, we do not require to be told by international bodies how to bring up children.

CHURCH OF IRELAND

INTRODUCTION

The Church of Ireland welcomes the opportunity to make a submission on the constitutional provisions relating to the family. In January 1999 we commented on a number of recommendations made in the report of the Constitution Review Group and this submission builds on our earlier comments. The Constitution Review Group's recommendations in relation to the family have been a very useful reference point in formulating our response. The issues set out by the All-Party Committee provide a good structure and we have thus based our submission on this format.

Firstly, as a general comment on Articles 41 and 42, we feel that the natural law language used, albeit long valued by certain traditions within our society, is unhelpful and outdated in today's constitutional context.

Secondly, we are of the view that there is a need for greater transparency in family law cases without the violation of privacy. Currently there is a difficulty in obtaining accurate statistics relating to the outcome of family law cases as these are held *in camera* and often anecdotal evidence is all that is available. We feel that in family law cases there should be greater availability of judgments and decisions given, whilst protecting the anonymity of the parties. If, because of a conflicting constitutional guarantee of privacy, this can only be done by constitutional amendment, then the Constitution ought to be amended. Indeed, we would urge the minister to proceed accordingly.

Thirdly, equality of access to the courts in family law cases is vital. This may mean that increased expenditure on the provision of civil legal aid is necessary.

HOW SHOULD THE FAMILY BE DEFINED?

The family protected by the Constitution is the family based on marriage. The present-day understanding of the family, however, is something much broader than the traditional marriage-based family. A clear distinction needs to be made between the definition of marriage and the definition of the family. We favour

the inclusion in the Constitution of a broad definition of the family which will not only continue to protect the institution of marriage but will also allow the state to recognise the numerous units which are generally regarded as family units but which are not marriage based. The Church of Ireland, of course, continues to stress marriage as the optimum context, particularly for the nurture of children, but at the same time we feel that other domestic situations should be accommodated and legislative provision made for them.

As a good working definition of the family we suggest considering the UN definition, namely:

> Any combination of two or more persons who are bound together by ties of mutual consent, birth and/or adoption or placement and who, together, assume responsibility for, *inter alia*, the care and maintenance of group members, the addition of new members through procreation or adoption, the socialisation of children and the social control of members.

HOW SHOULD ONE STRIKE THE BALANCE BETWEEN THE RIGHTS OF THE FAMILY AS A UNIT AND THE RIGHTS OF INDIVIDUAL MEMBERS?

The emphasis on the family as a unit under Article 41.1 has meant that at times the rights of the unit have overridden the rights of the individual members of the unit. This situation is unsatisfactory. In line with the Constitution Review Group's views, we feel that, while the family unit may be entitled to special protection from the state, the individual rights and duties deriving from marriage, family, parenthood or childhood should be guaranteed to, and imposed on, the individuals concerned.

IS IT POSSIBLE TO GIVE CONSTITUTIONAL PROTECTION TO FAMILIES OTHER THAN THOSE BASED ON MARRIAGE?

By amending the Constitution to provide a definition of the family wider than that based only on marriage, such constitutional protection can of course be given.

SHOULD GAY COUPLES BE ALLOWED TO MARRY?

Marriage for us is understood as the joining together of a man and a woman in lifelong and exclusive commitment, in a covenant which in its purpose is relational, unitative and where possible procreative. A same-sex couple does not have of itself the capacity or potential to procreate and as such cannot under any circumstances fulfil this complete definition. A same-sex union can and should be given constitutional protection under the broad definition of the family favoured above, but cannot in our view be considered a marriage, nor should the language and distinctive ceremonies of marriage be associated with it in civil law.

IS THE CONSTITUTION'S REFERENCE TO 'WOMAN'S LIFE WITHIN THE HOME' AN OUTDATED ONE THAT SHOULD BE CHANGED??

The Constitution should retain a recognition of the value of family life, but in gender neutral terms. Once again, in line with the Constitution Review Group's Report, we suggest that Article 41.2.1 and 41.2.2 should be replaced with the following:

> The state recognises that home and family life gives to society a support without which the common good cannot be achieved. The state undertakes to support persons caring for others within the home.

SHOULD THE RIGHTS OF THE NATURAL MOTHER HAVE EXPRESS CONSTITUTIONAL PROTECTION?

At present the natural mother does enjoy constitutional rights (as well as many statutory entitlements), albeit under Article 40.3 rather than Article 41. If, as recommended, the definition of the family in Article 41 is broadened then the natural mother's rights will be included under this article.

WHAT RIGHTS SHOULD A NATURAL FATHER HAVE AND HOW SHOULD THEY BE PROTECTED?

We feel that rights of a natural father should be established by his willingness to relate to the child or by his demonstrating that he has endeavoured to establish and maintain a relationship with his child. In the event of rape or incest, for example, such rights should not apply. While accepting in general terms that natural fathers need to establish rights, this is not to say that we lack sympathy with conscientious natural fathers frustrated by their present unequal legal position *vis a vis* natural mothers. At present by statutory provision a natural father can be appointed joint guardian of his child in which case he will have the right to be involved in decisions on the child's upbringing as well as having potential custody entitlements and rights in relation to adoption. We support this provision.

Although a natural father has no automatic constitutional right in relation to his child, we concur with the current position that on proof of paternity a child has a right to seek nurture and support from its natural father.

SHOULD THE RIGHTS OF THE CHILD BE GIVEN AN EXPANDED CONSTITUTIONAL PROTECTION?

Save in relation to the courts' divorce jurisdiction, there is no specific reference to the rights of the child in Article 41. The courts have however interpreted the Constitution as conferring unenumerated constitutional rights on children arising particularly under Article 40.3. For the sake of clarity, and in line with the Constitution Review Group's report, we recommend the express guaranteeing of the rights of the child in Article 41. Furthermore, and this ties in with our response to the final issue raised, there should be included in the Constitution an express requirement, such as is already contained in legislation, that in all actions concerning children paramount consideration should be given to the best interests of the child.

DOES THE CONSTITUTION NEED TO BE CHANGED IN VIEW OF THE UN CONVENTION ON THE RIGHTS OF THE CHILD?

We warmly endorse the Convention and strongly urge the inclusion in our Constitution of the list of children's rights contained therein as well as the principle that in all actions concerning children the best interest of the child should always take precedence.

CHURCH OF SCIENTOLOGY

The All-Party Oireachtas Committee recently invited submissions which dealt with the Constitution's status in relation to the family in general terms, or specifically:

1 How should the family be defined?

2 How should one strike the balance between the rights of the family as a unit and the rights of individual members?

3 Is it possible to give constitutional protection to families other than those based on marriage?

4 Should gay couples be allowed to marry?

5 Is the Constitution's reference to woman's 'life within the home' a dated one that should be changed?

6 Should the rights of a natural mother have express constitutional protection?

7 What rights should a natural father have, and how should they be protected?

8 Should the rights of the child be given an expanded constitutional protection?

9 Does the Constitution need to be changed in view of the UN Convention on the Rights of the Child?

The issue of the family and its role in society is a continual debate. We all agree that the *ideal* family unit is a mother, father and children. That is the format that, on balance, gives the best opportunity for success, for the individual, for the family and for society. That is not to say that other formats are not and would not be successful – many single parent families are successful – but the odds are more stacked against them, and such families sometimes impose a greater burden on society than the *ideal* format.

It is acknowledged that the so-called *ideal* family unit is also prey to failure, and indeed does fail. Contemporary society, with widespread immorality, criminality and incompetence, is almost designed to ensure family failure. Domestic violence, emotional torture, alcohol and drug abuse can all destroy any family, *ideal* or not. However, the bulwark of having two parents makes survival, without state intervention, more likely.

The state must protect the family, however it is defined but it also must protect society (and the taxpayer) from abuse through the destruction of the family or via massive state support/intervention to dysfunctional families.

The Constitution should include *responsibilities* as well as *rights*. The Constitution should preclude state intervention wherever possible unless demonstrably necessary (not just someone's opinion as to intervention).

1 HOW SHOULD THE FAMILY BE DEFINED?

The Oxford Dictionary defines the family as:

1   Set of relations, especially parents and children
2a   Members of a household.
2b   A person's children.
3   All the descendants of a common ancestor.

The above definition should cover most possible conditions, including cohabiting couples with children, single parents etc. Thus it is not necessary to redefine the word 'family' (and therefore amend the English language), but simply to use the word in its full, expansive definition.

2 HOW SHOULD ONE STRIKE THE BALANCE BETWEEN THE RIGHTS OF THE FAMILY AS A UNIT AND THE RIGHTS OF INDIVIDUAL MEMBERS?

The individual is the basic *unit* of society; the family is the basic *social unit* of society. No civilisation can survive that does not protect and support the family unit; similarly, where the rights of the individual become completely subsumed to the dictates of the family, disaster ensues. That the requirements of each sometimes clash is inevitable from time to time and is most readily seen in cultural conflict. For example an individual decides to marry a partner of whom his/her family disapproves – clearly the individual's rights take precedence. Another is that the family decides to emigrate, against the wishes of the individual – clearly the family's rights take precedence.

A family is after all a group (small or large) of individuals, all with rights and responsibilities, related by blood or 'affinity'. Those individual rights should not be infringed unless it can be shown that the exercise of those rights would utterly destroy the family unit in a way that is detrimental to society – in this regard incest is an example.

In order to 'strike a balance' of competing rights one could list the rights of the family, and separately, a list of the rights of the individual and examine if and where they might be in conflict.

3 IS IT POSSIBLE TO GIVE CONSTITUTIONAL PROTECTION TO FAMILIES OTHER THAN THOSE BASED ON MARRIAGE?

The short answer is yes, provided the family is appropriately defined per the dictionary. A single parent is, by any definition, the head of a family and must receive the protection and support of the Constitution. This should include rights *and* responsibilities.

To take a very 'unromantic' viewpoint, a marriage is a contract between two people – and there are many forms of contract, with an infinite variety of clauses/ provisions. It is not beyond the ability of our legislators to legislate for different types of 'marriage' contracts with perhaps different levels of constitutional protection. For example a 'contract' between same-sex individuals might not attract the same *level* of constitutional support or protection as that between a man and woman simply because society may decide that such a contract is not as beneficial to society as the 'ideal' scenario.

4 SHOULD GAY COUPLES BE ALLOWED TO MARRY?

The Oxford English dictionary defines marriage as *'a legal union of a man and a woman for cohabitation and often procreation'*. So to use the word 'marry' for the union of two citizens of the same sex would require a redefinition of the term. Another word could be chosen to describe such a union.

However, whatever about the religious sensibilities of many faiths, two citizens should be allowed to formalise a relationship (whatever that may be, so long as it is legal, and between consenting adults). This relationship should assume most of the rights and responsibilities accorded a 'traditional married couple' – so long as such does not involve massive state subvention (for example should the state be expected to pay for a 'gender change'?). The electorate can decide what level of rights and responsibilities can accrue.

The 'parity of esteem' issue in relation to same-sex unions is a difficult problem. It is clear that same-sex unions may often financially support society to a greater extent than the *ideal* family unit, given the circumstances of twin incomes and no children. At the same time society requires a surfeit of *ideal* family units to continue and to support the population necessary for a civilisation to persist.

5 IS THE CONSTITUTION'S REFERENCE TO WOMAN'S 'LIFE WITHIN THE HOME' A DATED ONE THAT SHOULD BE CHANGED?

Yes. Given the rapid changes in our culture, from 'home' husbands, to double-income families, the entire sub-article should be removed from the Constitution completely, or made gender free.

6 SHOULD THE RIGHTS OF A NATURAL MOTHER HAVE EXPRESS CONSTITUTIONAL PROTECTION?

Yes, unless the mother is physically abusing her child, by:

a unnecessary corporal punishment
b non-nourishing food
c drugging the child
d refusing affection to the child
e refusing the child social interaction with his/her peers

Or damaging her child by refusing to educate, or allowing the child to be educated, in the basics of reading, writing and arithmetic commensurate with the child's age. Or permitting her child to become a criminal without taking all humane and legal steps to prevent it.

Such rights and responsibilities should also apply to natural fathers.

7 WHAT RIGHTS SHOULD A NATURAL FATHER HAVE, AND HOW SHOULD THEY BE PROTECTED?

See 6 above, Simply, the father must have the rights and responsibilities (including the financial responsibilities) of a parent, whether or not he is in a legal union with the mother. A father who defaults on his responsibilities must pay the costs of some other entity/individual to assume that responsibility – unless a mutual agreement is arrived at otherwise (via adoption, guardianship etc.)

There is anecdotal evidence that significant numbers of unmarried mothers are in fact in relationships of some sort, sometimes with the natural fathers of their child/children, sometimes not. It is an empirical observation that single parent families, in proportion greater than that of the *ideal* family unit, are a heavy burden to society, both via support payments required and the increase in familial dysfunction with the concomitant state intervention. That these family units, particularly unmarried mothers, are often housed in 'social sinks', not in proximity to expanded family support networks, can exacerbate problems. This is not politically correct but readily observable to anyone who lives in or adjacent to such environments.

8 SHOULD THE RIGHTS OF THE CHILD BE GIVEN AN EXPANDED CONSTITUTIONAL PROTECTION?

See 6 above.

9 DOES THE CONSTITUTION NEED TO BE CHANGED IN VIEW OF THE UN CONVENTION ON THE RIGHTS OF THE CHILD?

One could have some argument with the definition of 'child'. It is common sense that a seventeen-year-old, a sixteen-year-old or even a fifteen-year-old person is hardly a 'child' and can hardly be treated the same as an infant. It must be arranged that there is an intermediate designation, such as 'adolescent' for example,

between 'adult' and 'child'. Such a person would have more responsibilities than a child but less than an adult. In particular such a person would have much greater personal responsibilities for his/her behaviour than an infant. All such designations are arbitrary of course (some sixteen-year-olds are 'immature', some are not, some thirty-year-olds are immature) but a line has to be drawn somewhere, and perhaps fourteen is an appropriate age to separate childhood from adolescence.

Apart from the above issues the issue of a 'guardian' should be addressed in the Constitution. Clearly not all natural parents are responsible/competent enough to raise children, and thus as a *very last resort*, where the physical and emotional well-being of a child is in demonstrable danger, a guardian can take the place of the natural parent. In such a scenario the person who raises the child, gives the love, accepts the heartache and joy, and the hard work attached to such a responsibility, should be classed as the parent, with all the rights and responsibilities of a 'natural' parent. The original 'natural' parent's rights and responsibilities could be amended accordingly.

There is a case to be made that, on balance, a child is better off being raised in a calm, competent, loving, tolerant environment, away from his/her natural parents, if they have proven themselves to be incompetent/abusive parents. In this regard the laws of adoption must be looked at.

CITYWISE–MARK HAMILTON

As an educator I have worked with children and young people for many years. Our charitable work brings us into contact mainly with young people from disadvantaged backgrounds and we see at first hand the many problems faced by young people suffering poverty, family breakdown and other social problems.

Almost invariably those children who are worst off in our society are those living in dysfunctional family circumstances. Poverty leaves its mark, but family dysfunctionality leaves a much more enduring mark on young people. Absent fathers, uncaring parents, difficult step-parent situations are key indicators to the education, health and social problems of young people.

A wise state would do whatever is within its power to encourage stability within family life and thus mitigate in some small way the problems faced today by children growing up. It is not enough for the state to say that 'society is changing' and that it has to change along with it. Such a facile argument would not be accepted by a family or by a business where those involved saw damage resulting from change. They would seek to understand the change, redirect it or seek to remedy the cause in some way.

Nor is it enough for the state to say that 'change happens'. Sure it does, but it is also brought about through policy decisions. For example, if this state were to elevate the status of cohabitation within society, then it would directly cause more people in the future to choose that circumstance over marriage, because cohabitation makes less claims on people. In short, as the easier option it will, over time, become the norm. Naturally, children would be the losers as there would then be a greater likelihood of more family break-up and more disfunctionality in the future.

All this is common sense. We are well aware of the positive coercive effect of laws banning smoking or speeding, or laws controlling alcohol intake. We are also now aware of the devastating effect divorce is having on the stability of family life. It would be wrong to undermine marriage commitment further by elevating personal arrangements to an equivalent status to marriage. Some people wish to fool themselves and others by claiming in some way that we Irish have a special understanding of family, which will ensure that legal or social change will have less impact on us that elsewhere. This is nonsense. Perhaps our religious commitment as a people has served to some degree as a bulwark to reduce the negative impact of social change. But if it has, flying in the face of traditional/religious/Christian mores through the legal promotion of those of a secularist/individualist culture will soon undermine that defence.

As for homosexual unions, these contribute nothing to society over any other friendship bonds that might exist, so there is no reason why the state should promote such unions, in the way it promotes marriage. It would be a travesty of common sense to reward a relationship based on sexual relations which makes no special contribution to society (and indeed if a current case were to succeed, would receive taxation benefits!), while many other loose affiliations of two or more friends or living-together relatives or carer-cared relations are not likewise entitled to such benefits. The reality is that marriage gives society what it badly needs: stable relationships for the upbringing of children, who then in turn *pay back* the benefit received in the next generation, and that is why marriage is promoted by way of certain privileges.

Nor is there any issue of equality at stake here. All citizens are equal before the law, and no citizens are allowed to enter into a privileged relationship with another unless (a) they are of opposite sex; (b) neither are in an existing privileged relationship; (c) they are of age. Indeed to recognise homosexual unions would be to introduce real inequality by elevating these same-sex partnerships above father-son relationships, sister-sister relationships, carer-cared relationships, close friendships etc, for no just reason.

If one were to ask the simple question, what is best for children, then the answer is stable family relationships. This is the basis of marriage. So why undermine it through change, which has little to do with justice and a lot to do with the shifting sands of equality,

which can be made mean whatever one wants it to mean?

Finally, I would be extremely wary of any plan to introduce a number of the articles of the UN Convention on the Rights of the Child into our Constitution. I am well aware of the many children who suffer neglect by parents within our society. But it is equally true that the state is criminally neglectful as well with many children, despite the range of powers and resources it currently has. Further empowering the state in such circumstances will do nothing to help such children. Also on the downside, many of these UN articles do not reflect the considered opinions of Irish people, deriving as they do from a culture which has a poor understanding of the relationship of trust within families, relationships which should be subject to the divisive rights-based language of the UN Convention.

COMHAIRLE

1 INTRODUCTION

This Comhairle submission builds on feedback from citizens information centres (CICs). Queries to CICs and the citizens information phone service (CIPS), are an important source of information which is used by Comhairle to advise government on aspects of social policy and the development of social services. During 2004, CICs throughout the country dealt with over 600,000 queries. The most recent CIC survey (Nua 2004), showed that 7 per cent of CIC queries related to specific family matters – separation/divorce, joint parenting, custody/access/guardianship, maintenance, the family home and domestic violence. Also, many social welfare related queries refer directly or indirectly to family matters, e.g. welfare/work traps, family income supplement and supports for one parent families.

Comhairle recognises the complexity of family-related issues and the difficulty in making adequate constitutional and legal provision for all eventualities. We, therefore, very much welcome the fact that the All-Party Oireachtas Committee on the Constitution is now focusing its attention on family-related provisions. We suggest that in considering the constitutional matters relating to the family, full cognisance needs to be taken of both recent trends in family formation and the evolution of family policy, nationally and internationally.

2 UNDERLYING PRINCIPLES

In considering family policy Comhairle is mindful of the following:

i)   The principles and objectives which underpin family policy should be enunciated with as much clarity as possible.

ii) The basic and essential activities of care and belonging can take place in a variety of family forms and this diversity in family formation should be recognised.

iii) Continuity and stability in family relationships have major importance for the well-being of children.

iv) There is a need to give priority in legal and policy discourse to children's needs as distinct from parents' rights and to operate on the basis that children's needs and rights are paramount, particularly in the context of marriage and relationship breakdown when children may be particularly vulnerable.

v) Joint parenting is centrally important for the well-being of children and should be an integral part of policy development.

vi) The role of the State should be to support families and promote their general well-being and ensure access to appropriate services and supports.

vii) State interference in family life should be permitted where necessary to safeguard vulnerable members such as children, the elderly and people with disabilities.

viii) Family care should be promoted and supported with particular reference to vulnerable members within families – children, people with disabilities and dependent older persons.

ix) Social services and supports for families and on-going changes in family law should be planned and developed in tandem with constitutional reform.

3 FAMILY POLICY IN IRELAND

Legislation introduced during the 1980s and 1990s has endeavoured to provide increased protection for marital and non-marital families in Ireland. Legislation on judicial separation and divorce has widened the conditions under which couples may legally separate and has also set down additional provisions in respect of the family home, children and maintenance. The provision for the dissolution of marriage in certain specified circumstances included in the Fifteenth Amendment of the Constitution Act, 1995 marked a very significant departure from the provisions in the 1937 Constitution.

Social welfare legislation has broadly kept pace with the changing trends in family formation. Entitlements for deserted spouses, single mothers and lone parents were introduced in the 1970s and 1980s. The numbers of families in receipt of these benefits has increased substantially in recent years. More recent integration between social welfare and training/education has enabled lone parents to avail of further education and training without any loss of entitlement.

It has also become widely accepted that public policies and public services should be more accommodating of the growing diversity of partnership arrangements and family types which now characterise western societies while at the same time recognising the importance to children of having a stable and positive relationship with both parents, even where both parents do not live together. Many governments within the EU, including Ireland, have chosen a family policy which combines the twin approaches of accommodating family diversity while at the same time promoting key family relationships. In recent years, various legislative changes and social welfare provisions have been introduced in Ireland to reflect a broader understanding of family.

4 DIVERSIFICATION OF FAMILY STRUCTURES

The 2002 census of population shows that the fastest growing family types in Ireland are lone parents and cohabiting couples. However, the largest family type, 489,500, continues to be two first-time married parents with children. There are also more families from different ethnic and cultural backgrounds and a growing number of mixed race families.

Between 1996 and 2002 the number of separated persons (including divorced) increased by over 50 per cent. Within the overall separated category the number of persons recorded as divorced more than trebled, from 9,800 to 35,100, between 1996 and 2002, reflecting to a large extent the legalisation of divorce in the state in 1997. An indication of the relative extent of marital breakdown is provided by expressing the number of separated and divorced persons as a percentage of the total number of ever-married persons. In 2002 this proportion stood at 7.5 per cent compared with 5.4 per cent six years earlier (Central Statistics Office 2003).

The role of marriage in family formation has also changed. A rapid increase in the share of fertility occurring outside marriage began in the 1980s and continued unabated during the 1990s. However, it has been noted (Fahey and Russell 2001) that it appears that large proportions of those who begin childbearing outside of marriage subsequently enter marriage, though the exact proportion has not been fully quantified. Also, relatively little is known about the patterns of exit from lone parenthood through the formation of new unions.

Between 1996 and 2002, households comprising childless couples (whether married or not) represented the fastest growing category – up 38.7 per cent in six years. The number of households consisting solely of couples (married and cohabiting) with children increased by 11.1 per cent in the same period. Households consisting of lone parents with children increased by 25,800 (24.5 per cent) between 1996 and 2002.

5 THE CONCEPT OF 'FAMILY'

The family is regarded by the Irish Constitution as 'the natural, primary and fundamental group of society' (Article 41.1.1) and the state guarantees to protect it in its constitution and authority (Article 41.1.2). While the state pledges itself 'to guard with special care the institution of marriage, on which the family is founded and to protect it against attack' (Article 41.3.1), it is now widely accepted that the concept of 'family' encompasses various sets of relationships and living arrangements. In addition to the family based on marriage (with or without children), there are a number of other family types, e.g. lone mothers or fathers (widowed, separated or divorced) and children, cohabiting couples with children, single parents (usually a mother with one or more children), families brought up by grandparents and separated families who may live in two different households but who are still families. The United Nations (1990) referred to the family as a basic social group composed of a married or unmarried couple and children, including adopted ones. The International Year of the Family, 1994, used the term 'family' as an embracing, all-inclusive one, covering a wide range of structures and functions and had as one of its aims to recognise, support and empower diverse family forms. The European Court of Human Rights (1994) referred to ties and bonds 'amounting to family life' such as those that exist between some couples who are neither married nor cohabiting. The *Report of the Department of Social and Family Affairs Consultative Fora* (Daly 2004) suggests that a definition of family should be capable of embracing diverse family forms, including grandparents and children, foster parents and children, lone parents, unmarried partners and children and same-sex parents and children.

The Constitution Review Group (1996) favoured the retention in the Constitution of a pledge by the state to protect the family based on marriage but also to guarantee to all individuals a right to respect for their family life whether that family is, or is not, based on marriage. The Review Group also considered that a revised Article 41 should retain a pledge by the state to guard with special care the institution of marriage and to protect it against attack but that a further amendment should be made so as to make it clear that this pledge by the state should not prevent the Oireachtas from providing protection for the benefit of family units based on a relationship other than marriage. The Commission on the Family (1998) supported this view.

Comhairle recommends that the understanding of family, which underpins legislation, needs to be revised in the context of current family trends. In addition to the family based on marriage, there is a need to recognise and encompass other family ties and bonds which amount to family life.

6 COHABITING COUPLES

The increasing prevalence of extra-marital cohabitation in Ireland has resulted in calls for its legal recognition and regulation.

In 2002 there were 77,600 family units consisting of cohabiting couples, up from 31,300 six years earlier. Almost two-thirds of these were childless couples. Of the remaining 29,700 family units, over half had just one child. Overall, cohabiting couples accounted for

8.4 per cent of all family units in 2002 compared with 3.9 per cent in 1996. The number of children living with cohabiting parents increased from 23,000 in 1996 to 51,700 in 2002.

People in cohabiting relationships have relatively little protection under Irish law at present. This comes into sharper focus in situations of relationship breakdown (where there is no legal right to financial support) and in situations where one partner dies (where there is no right to the estate). Unmarried partners cannot adopt children as a couple, even the child of one of the partners. Cohabitees are treated as single persons for taxation purposes and are not entitled to married persons' tax credits or bands, the one parent family tax credit or the home carer's tax credit.

The Law Reform Commission in its consultation paper[1] on the rights and duties of cohabitees, proposes a scheme which would impose legal rights and duties on cohabitees who satisfy certain criteria. Such cohabitees are described as 'qualified cohabitees', i.e. 'persons who, although they are not married to one another, live together in a "marriage like" relationship for a continuous period of three years or two years where there is a child of the relationship' (Law Reform Commission 2004) (p. 4). The Commission acknowledges that 'marriage like' relationships exist between same-sex couples as well as opposite-sex couples. In order to qualify, a cohabitee must not be a party to an existing marriage. The Commission points out that this latter exclusion is necessitated by Article 41.3.1 of the Constitution which states that 'the state pledges itself to guard with special care the institution of marriage on which the family is founded, and to protect it against attack'. In determining whether the parties have been living together in a 'marriage like' relationship, it is suggested that the court would consider a wide range of factors.

The Commission also proposes that in exceptional circumstances qualified cohabitees should be entitled to apply for property adjustment orders on the breakup of the relationship. The Commission also examines succession rights and proposes that qualified cohabitees be given the right to apply for relief where they feel that proper provision has not been made for them in the will of the deceased or under the intestacy rules.

The Law Reform Commission (2004) proposal for a scheme which would impose legal rights and duties on cohabitees who satisfy certain criteria, appears worthwhile and balanced and should be explored further.

7 FAMILY CARE

The role of the family as a caring unit has been the subject of much discussion and debate in recent years due mainly to changes in work patterns and in the role of women in society. Care in the home, whether for small children, dependent older people or people with disabilities of whatever age, is more and more becoming an issue of concern.

Increasingly, potential carers are, either by necessity or choice, working outside the home. Contributory factors are career choice, spiralling housing costs, and a social welfare and tax system that does not provide adequate incentives and supports to people to stay at home to care for children or other dependants. Increased women's participation in the labour market has resulted in greater attention being given to the phenomenon of caring in the home and its associated costs and the urgent need to reconsider how work and familial organisation can be harmonised.

The Constitution Review Group recognised the importance of the caring function of the family and stated that it was important that there is constitutional recognition for the significant contribution to society made by the large number of people who provide a caring function within their homes for children, elderly relatives and others. The group suggested a revised form of Article 41.2 to provide for a gender-neutral constitutional recognition of this which would read:

> The state recognises that home and family life gives to society a support without which the common good cannot be achieved. The state shall endeavour to support persons caring for others within the home.

The Commission on the Family supported the Review Group's recommendation for constitutional recognition in a gender-neutral form of the caring function in the home as exercised by both men and women.

Comhairle supports the view that the Constitution should include a strong and gender-neutral recognition of people providing care in the home for children, people with disabilities and dependent older people.

8 RIGHTS AND OBLIGATIONS OF NON-MARITAL FATHERS

There has been ongoing criticism of the fact that the Constitution offers no protection for the rights of natural fathers. This issue takes on particular significance in the case of natural fathers who either live in a stable relationship with the natural mother, or have established a relationship with the child. It should be noted that the natural mother's rights are personal rights protected by Article 40.3 of the Constitution which states that 'the state guarantees in its laws to respect, and, as far as practicable, by its laws to defend and vindicate the personal rights of the citizen'.

A natural father is considered not to have any constitutionally-protected rights to his child. This arises from the decision of the Supreme Court in *The state (Nicolaou) v An Bord Uchtála*. In that case the child of a natural father had been adopted pursuant to the Adoption Act, 1952 without his consent. He challenged the provisions of the Adoption Act, which permitted that to be done. The Supreme Court held:

i) a natural father is not a member of a family within Article 41

ii) a natural father is not a 'parent' within Article 42

iii) a natural father has no personal right in relation to his child which the state is bound to protect under Article 40.3.

The question of the rights of natural (non-marital) fathers was addressed by the Law Reform Commission Report on Illegitimacy, which had among its recommendations that 'both parents of a child should be the joint guardians, whether the child is born within or outside marriage'. (Law Reform Commission 1982, p. 178)

Family law changed considerably with the enactment of the Status of Children Act, 1987. This went a long way to establishing the rights of all children to legitimacy and protect their right to a share in the estate of their natural parents. However, the Act did not advance the rights of natural non-marital fathers to automatic guardianship of their children. The provision in the Act for non-marital fathers to go to the court to obtain access to their child(ren) may be less than satisfactory in that the onus is on the father to demonstrate a genuine and proper interest in the child. However, it should be noted that the issue of guardianship is a highly complex one, which requires careful and sensitive consideration. For example, the concept of automatic guardianship would raise major difficulties in situations where a father demanded guardianship rights after having been absent for a long period of time without any involvement with the child, or in instances of children conceived through rape.

Child custody and guardianship and the rights of non-marital fathers are ongoing issues for many lone parents. Some fathers are clearly dissatisfied with custody arrangements. Some single mothers are concerned about registering a father's name on the child's birth certificate and, specifically, whether this would affect their entitlement to the one parent family payment. Also, some are concerned that registering the father's name might give him access rights to the child.

The Constitution Review Group took the view that there did not appear to be justification for giving constitutional rights to every natural father simply by reason of biological links. The solution proposed by the Review Group was to grant constitutional rights to those fathers who have, or had, a stable relationship with the mother prior to birth, or subsequent to birth, with the child. This would be achieved by guaranteeing to every person a respect for family life, including non-marital family life but requiring family ties between the father and mother.

Comhairle recommends that provision be made in the Constitution for the rights of non-marital fathers in accordance with the views of the Constitution Review Group.

9 CONSTITUTIONAL CHANGE

The Constitution Review Group made a number of recommendations in regard to constitutional provisions for families: recommendations refer to the family based on marriage and the family not based on marriage and specific recommendations refer to the rights of children.

Comhairle broadly supports these recommendations as a balanced and reasonable approach to addressing many of the problems arising from the diversification of family types and changing gender roles. The constitutional changes proposed would facilitate the development of a coherent family policy and legislative framework.

10 SUMMARY OF RECOMMENDATIONS

Comhairle recommends that the understanding of family which underpins legislation needs to be revised in the context of current family trends. In addition to the concept of the family based on marriage, there is also a need to recognise and encompass other family ties and bonds.

The Law Reform Commission (2004) proposal for a scheme which would impose legal rights and duties on cohabitees who satisfy certain criteria, appears worthwhile and balanced and should be explored further.

Comhairle supports the view that the Constitution should include a strong and gender-neutral recognition of people providing care in the home for children, people with disabilities and dependent older people.

Comhairle recommends that provision be made in the Constitution for the rights of non-marital fathers in accordance with the views of the Constitution Review Group.

Comhairle broadly supports the recommendations of the Constitution Review Group in regard to constitutional provisions for families as a balanced and reasonable approach to addressing many of the problems arising from the diversification of family types and changing gender roles.

Notes
[1] This consultation paper is intended to form the basis for discussion and accordingly the recommendations, conclusions and suggestions are provisional. The Commission will make its final recommendations following further consideration of the issues and consultation.

COMHAR CRÍOSTAÍ – THE CHRISTIAN SOLIDARITY PARTY

1 At the outset the Christian Solidarity Party reminds the committee that the Irish Constitution commences with an invocation to the most Holy Trinity and acknowledges all our obligations to Our Divine Lord, Jesus Christ. It is clear, therefore, that the Irish Constitution is intended to express the deep Christian faith of the Irish people. The Irish Constitution, in particular, expresses very strong support for the Christian understanding of both marriage and the family.

2 The Christian understanding of the family is a family based on marriage, a voluntary union of one man and one woman to the exclusion of all others. The family is a community of persons: of husband and wide, of parents and children, of relatives. Such an understanding of the family is essential for the promotion of the common good. Because of the indispensable role of the family for society, constitutional protection of the family, as already exists in our Constitution, must be maintained. As an outside observer of Irish society once remarked: 'Wherever you are in Ireland you have the family – and it counts for a great deal.'

Even in a secular society the family is essential for that society's well-being and is necessary for the material prosperity of the nation. The family must be protected in its natural structure which is and must necessarily be that of a union between a man and a woman founded on marriage.

A constitution reflects permanent values and should not be amended, from time to time, to accommodate the ever-changing 'spirit of the age'.

3 The Constitution Review Group, in its report, states that it considers that Articles 41 and 42 in the Constitution, which deal with the family, emphasise the rights of the family as a unit to the possible detriment of individual members. We do not share that view nor, do we suggest, would the Irish people. Individual rights of any citizen are already protected under Article 40.3.1 which states that 'the state guarantees in its laws to respect, and, as far as practicable, by its laws to defend and vindicate the personal rights of the individual.'

The consequence arising from amending this article, along lines which seem to be envisaged, would be to seriously disrupt the cohesion of the family and this Party would, consequently, be opposed to any change.

4 The Constitution Review Group asks if it would be possible to give constitutional protection to families other than those based on marriage As the family based on marriage gives stability to society it would not serve society to grant constitutional recognition to other unions. Such constitutional recognition in fact would be a step in the undermining of marriage. We repeat again that personal rights of citizens, including those in cohabiting unions, are protected under Article 40.3.1. This party would have no objection to the enactment of legislation, where required, to give legal protection to people in cohabiting unions to cover matters such as the particular rights of children arising from such unions, or, say, the distribution of property. We would like to emphasise that cohabiting heterosexual couples have the right to marry.

5 The question is posed by the Constitution Review Group as to whether homosexual couples should be allowed to marry. Our emphatic answer is no.

Marriage must be restricted to one man and one woman. There are no grounds for considering homosexual unions to be in any way similar or even remotely analogous to God's plan for marriage and family. We recognise that there are people with a homosexual orientation, and we would condemn any unjust discrimination in their regard. However, to give legal recognition to homosexual unions would be to radically redefine marriage and would become, in its legal status, an institution devoid of essential reference to factors linked to heterosexuality: for example, procreation and raising children. Were the state to put homosexual unions on a legal basis analogous to that of marriage and the family, then the state would be acting in contradiction to its duties.

6 Individual rights cannot be invoked for the purpose of supporting homosexual 'marriages'. Every citizen is free to engage in those activities that interest him or her and this falls within the common civil right to freedom; it is something quite different to hold that activities which do not represent a significant or positive contribution to society can receive specific and categorical legal recognition by the state. As marriages between men and women ensure the succession of generations and are therefore in the public interest, civil law grants them institutional recognition. Homosexual unions, on the other hand, do not need specific attention from the legal standpoint since they do not exercise this function for the common good. Provisions of law, as it applies to all citizens, can be availed of by all people in homosexual unions to protect their rights in matters of common interest.

7 Given that we are opposed to homosexual 'marriage' the Christian Solidarity Party would strongly oppose the granting of rights to people in homosexual unions to adopt children. Children require that the environment in which they are reared is a secure and loving one which is best provided in a family home headed by husband and wife.

8 We do not agree that the Constitution's reference to the woman's life within the home should be deleted. Mothers should not be forced through economic necessity to take up paid employment outside the home. Had the state over the years fulfilled its obligations to protect the mother working in the home then the majority of mothers would have opted to remain at home and rear their children. Mothers working in the home exercise a tremendous influence for good with consequent major benefit to society. This article in the Constitution does not prevent any mother from engaging, if she so desires, in outside paid employment so there is no question of the rights of any person being limited by this provision. Article 41.2, in fact, could be strengthened by stating that mothers working full-time in the home

should have the same social welfare and tax benefits as a person working outside the home.

9 The legitimate rights of natural mothers and natural fathers of children outside of marriage should be protected by legislation. Constitutional recognition, however, in order to deal with this situation would be an attempt to cater for every departure from the traditional family and we would not support such and amendment. If, at the present time, legislation protecting the legitimate rights of natural fathers is seen to be inadequate then new legislation can be introduced to correct this situation.

10 The UN Convention on the Rights of the Child and other extra-territorial conventions do not necessarily reflect Irish people's understanding of 'rights'. Neither can it be assumed that they are in any way influenced by Christian considerations. One has only to see former Christian Europe refusing to mention Almighty God in its present draft Constitution to be wary of being influenced by outside conventions. As the Irish child has constitutional protection at the moment there is no need to amend our Irish Constitution to reflect the UN Convention on the Rights of the Child.

11 To delete, as suggested, words such as 'inalienable' and 'imprescriptible' (two words which appear in Article 41.1.1 dealing with the family) could only be seen as another attempt to weaken the rights of the family and to increase the power of the state in this area. These words should not be removed from the Constitution.

CONCLUSION

The Christian Solidarity Party considers that the suggested amendments to the Constitution in so far as they relate to the family would have serious consequences for Irish society. We have been served well to date by our Constitution and we cannot understand why the radical changes being suggested are being put forward. Our Constitution expresses values which the Irish people hold dear and should not be changed. The amendments proposed would result in a less Christian Constitution and could be seen as a first step towards a secular Constitution. In such a secular Constitution the state would take more power on to itself whilst, at the same time, paradoxically, exalting freedom for the individual to the extent that it would be seen as an absolute and would make such freedom the source of values. We repeat that we strongly oppose the amendments proposed.

CORI – CONFERENCE OF RELIGIOUS OF IRELAND

These are some comments in response to the document of the All-Party Oireachtas Committee on the Constitution, with regard to the family.

DEFINITION OF FAMILY

We recommend that the understanding of family be left as it is, and that the constitutional protection given to marriage is to be reserved for heterosexual unions.

RIGHTS OF THE CHILD

Once the rights of the family as a unit are cherished, they become part and parcel of the vindication of rights of the individual members of the family. The real problems of society are not solved by constitutional drafting. The way of dealing with the problems of society is by giving the necessary resources to support the family structure, be it in relation to health, social or educational matters. These include the following:

- Provision of assistance to aid people who are full-time or part-time carers in the family, whether of aged parents or other family members who are in need
- Childcare facilities
- Appropriate health care provision for all members of the family
- Public health education
- Adequate provision of social assistance to families in difficulty
- Social and community development projects within new neighbourhoods where there is no traditional neighbour/family support network.

THE WOMAN AND LIFE WITHIN THE HOME

With the changed role of parents in the family, and both parents usually working, it is difficult to provide legislation or constitutional protection to a really unified family home life. The question is more in the realm of how support may be offered that supports the family structure.

RIGHTS OF THE NATURAL MOTHER AND NATURAL FATHER

A balance has to be struck. All rights should be in the context of obligations that go with these rights. Any rights that are granted to the father (or to the mother) should be subject to, and conditional upon, complying with those obligations.

COUNCIL FOR THE STATUS OF THE FAMILY

DEFINITION OF FAMILY

As recently submitted to the Inter-Departmental Committee on the Reform of Marriage Law, discussion paper No. 5 (September 2004), this Council fully supports the definition of marriage in *Murray v Ireland* (1985) IR 532 as 'a unique and very special life-long relationship'. We further agree with the Inter-Departmental Committee that future marriage law should be based solely on that definition approved by the Supreme Court, viz. 'the voluntary and permanent union of one man and one woman to the exclusion of all others for life' (see page 5 of discussion paper No. 5).

From another source, the definition of family in the *The Cambridge Encyclopedia* is one which this Council would fully support: 'the group formed by a co-resident husband, wife and children (which sociologists term the nuclear family)'.

We would further refer the All-Party Committee to the *Charter of the Rights of the Family,* issued by the Holy See on 22 October 1983:

> *Preamble B*: The family is based on marriage, that intimate union of life in complementarity between a man and a woman which is constituted in the freely contracted and publicly expressed indissoluble bond of matrimony, and is open to the transmission of life
>
> *Preamble C*: Marriage is the natural institution to which the mission of transmitting life is exclusively entrusted
>
> *Article 1, c*: The institutional value of marriage should be upheld by the public authorities; the situation of non-married couples must not be placed on the same level as marriage duly contracted.

FORMS OF FAMILY

The census of 2002 provides the most recent breakdown of families living in this state:

- 462,283 family units comprising husbands, wives and at least one child
- 27,188 family units comprising cohabiting couples (of one man and one woman), and at least one child
- 111,878 family units comprising a lone woman parent and at least one child
- 19,313 family units comprising a lone man parent and at least one child

Comment: Far from the nuclear family being 'dead', as a number of commentators appear to believe, the above statistics confirm clearly that the nuclear family is alive in our society in far greater numbers than some sociologists care to acknowledge.

This Council believes that, while family forms which include children should be fully supported, not all family forms are equal. The evidence from history suggests that the form of family based on marriage between one man and one woman has given the optimum results throughout the ages.

The *2003 Annual Report* of the US National Marriage Project at Rutgers University, New Jersey, states: 'A robust body of social science evidence indicates that children do best when they grow up with both married biological parents who are in a low-conflict relationship'. This finding will come as no surprise to any person with common sense.

This Council is fully aware that other forms of family exist and while these deserve the acknowledgment and support of our society, especially where there are children involved, we consider that the model of family which has a proven track record deserves the fullest encouragement and enthusiastic backing of the state, in other words, the family resulting from the marriage of a man and a woman

'GAY' MARRIAGE

We believe that legal recognition of homosexual unions would obscure certain basic values and cause devaluation of the institution of marriage as it is at present understood and universally accepted. It is difficult to see how such a major development in our society could be justified in terms of the government's moral and civil duty to defend marriage (Article 41.3.1 of *Bunreacht na hÉireann*). The anecdotal evidence from elsewhere (e.g. since the beginnings of the AIDS crisis in the 1980s) confirms that long-term relationships between men are uncommon and that much of the male homosexual culture is more concerned with promiscuity, rivalry and conquest than with lifelong fidelity. Statistics from that era reveal that, in San Francisco, 25% of male homosexuals had had over 1,000 sexual partners, another 25% more than 500 partners, while the remainder had had somewhat less. Lifetime relationships were very much the exception rather than the rule.

This Council considers that the use of vague abstract terms such as *growing recognition, popular support, new awareness, greater tolerance, diversity in family life* are not helpful in identifying the needs of *real families based on marriage which are the bedrock of every civilised society*.

CONSTITUTIONAL PROTECTION FOR FAMILIES OTHER THAN THOSE BASED ON MARRIAGE

This Council is firmly of the view that unless the All-Party Oireachtas Committtee on the Constitution comes out strongly in favour of the family based on the marriage of a man and a woman (as defined by the Supreme Court), rather than trying to broaden the definition to include other forms of relationship, its final report will have little impact and will, inevitably be left on the shelf as unworkable.

RIGHTS OF THE CHILD

We have read the UN Convention on the Rights of the Child and accept most of the Articles which we consider relevant to marriage and family life in this society. However, this Council is strongly of the view that the *primary* rights in families are and must remain those of the parents. Provision has already been made in the Irish Constitution (Article 42.5) for cases where parents are unable to provide adequate care.

CONCLUSION

It is our view that elastoplast (or *ad hoc*) solutions do not work in the long term. Why are the USA and the UK desperately trying to get back to basic definitions? It is certainly not for idealistic or religious reasons; no, it is for clear-headed, pragmatic, economic reasons. Why have eleven US states recently voted overwhelmingly against the possibility of 'gay' marriages being legalised? If a similar referendum were to be put to the Irish people at the present time, the result would undoubtedly be similar. There is a strong 'gay' agenda being actively promoted at present and it is finding a ready ear in the media of western societies – and even among people who should know better.

By all means, support – both from the state and through voluntary organisations – should be given where needed to *all* family forms, especially those who live in disadvantaged situations (such as single-parent households which struggle in so many aspects of their lives – finances, emotions, stress, relationships). Indeed, members of this Council who work in caring organisations such as the SVP are fully aware of the difficult circumstances in which many such families live.

Nevertheless, this Council firmly holds that *No Constitutional recognition* should be accorded to those forms of family. We believe that Article 41 of *Bunreacht na hÉireann,* which has protected the traditional model of family for over sixty years, should remain intact.

The yearning for a stable family life based on a lasting and happy marriage is what men and women in every society and of every age aspire to and it is this Council's view that our Constitution should, as well as having achievable aims, be at the very least aspirational.

The members of the All-Party Committee must surely be aware that in Ireland, as in other parts of the world, the family is like a window on a society suffering the pains of a rapid transition from a more traditional way of life to greater fragmentation and individualism. In this transition, moral and religious truths have been forgotten or rejected, while in their place certain models of freedom and behaviour are proposed as models, with little or no regard for the consequences.

It is our view that there are no sufficiently good reasons for recommending permanent Constitutional changes.

DADS AGAINST DISCRIMINATION

We feel that Article 41.2.1 should be non-gender specific and that the word 'woman' should be amended to 'parent' or 'guardian' or both. This amendment would place equal importance on both parents and would reflect the role twenty-first century fathers play in their families today.

Additionally we feel that any gender specific references in the Constitution discriminate against the gender that is omitted.

**DEPARTMENT OF SOCIAL AND FAMILY AFFAIRS –
FAMILY AFFAIRS UNIT**

CHANGING SOCIETY

1 Families and family life have been subject to profound changes, especially in more recent decades. These have included the following:

- The increasing participation of women in the workforce, especially in the case of married women, is now reaching the stage that it is the norm for both parents to work outside the home. Increased female participation in the workforce is now actively encouraged, for economic and social reasons and in the interests of gender equality, at both national and EU levels.
- Fertility levels have been falling and, while the birth rate in Ireland is still high by EU standards, it is low compared to fertility levels nationally in the past.
- There is an increasing incidence of non-marital births, cohabitation outside marriage, marital and family breakdown and reconstituted families after separation and divorce.
- There is a growing diversity of values and lifestyles.

2 These changes are helping to make a positive contribution to greater economic prosperity and the resulting higher standards of living for families and family members generally. State policy has been responding to these changes. These responses have included the Constitutional amendment permitting the dissolution of marriage, major changes to family law and in the whole area of equal treatment and non-discrimination across the various grounds, and in greater state provision being made to support families and family life.

3 A number of social welfare schemes which were introduced in recent decades specifically in response to such changes include the schemes providing weekly payments for parents caring alone for their children, mainly the one parent family payment, and caring for elderly relatives or those with incapacities, mainly the carers' allowance and benefit. The greatly increased child benefit and the family income supplement are specifically designed to provide income support that is neutral as between parents in employment and on social welfare to avoid such support becoming a disincentive to either or both parents taking up employment. Research abroad has shown that participation in employment of mothers from either two parent or lone parent families is a significant factor in combating poverty and social exclusion among families with children. The OECD has found that less than four per cent of two-income families are at risk of poverty, while lone-parent families with children are among the groups at highest risk.

4 Inevitably it is more difficult for one parent to rear and provide for his/her children than if this can be shared with the other parent. A main objective of the Family Support Agency (FSA), which operates under the aegis of the Department, is to strengthen parental relationships through the provision of counselling services, family mediation, family resource centres at community level and ongoing research into family related matters.

CONSULTATION

5 A nationwide consultation on families and family life was undertaken in 2004, the findings of which are published in the booklet *Families and Family Life in Ireland: Challenges for the Future*. Constitutional issues were raised particularly in relation to the definition of the family in the Constitution. The report on the fora (already with the Committee) may be of use in gaining insights into the views held by a cross-section of members of the public who participated in the consultation process.

RIGHTS OF THE CHILD

6. The UN Convention on the Rights of the Child, which Ireland has ratified, provides comprehensively for the rights of the child, and it is noted that the Committee will be taking this convention fully into account in its deliberations. The Committee may also wish to take into account the fact that the UN Convention on the Rights of the Child can also be seen as a convention on the rights of parents. An analysis of the provisions of the convention from this perspective is contained in a note by Mr Jaap Doek, Chairperson of the UN Committee on the Rights of the Child, presented to the Expert Committee of the Council of Europe on Families and Children in December 2004. A copy is enclosed with this submission for the information of the Committee.

CONSTITUTIONAL PROTECTION FOR THE FAMILY

7 The recognition by the state of the family as the primary and fundamental unit of society is reflected in Ireland's ratification of international instruments affording similar protection such as the European Convention on Human Rights (Article 8), the European

Social Charter (Article 16 – social, legal and economic protection), the European Union Charter of Fundamental Rights (Article II-7). The family, as defined in the Constitution, is the family based on marriage. Despite the changes to families referred to in this document, this form of family formation still predominates. It is encouraged, e.g. through the type of services provided by the Family Support Agency, given the continuity and stability in family life which it promotes, a fact that was recognised by the Commission on the Family in its report.

MARRIAGE

8 It is generally recognised that marriage makes a major contribution to promoting stability and continuity in family life, but that there have also been major changes affecting marriage in recent decades. These include:

- a growing proportion of couples in recent years cohabiting outside of marriage, although many marry if they have, or decide to have, children
- married couples not having children or deciding not to have children
- couples having fewer children which, together with increasing longevity, means that the period of childrearing represents a much shorter period of a couple's life together than in the past
- greater equality between men and women, with women, as a result of growing female participation in the workforce, not being as economically dependent on their husbands as in the past, reinforced by couples having fewer children
- same-sex couples seeking the right to marry and obtain the legal protection and social recognition for their relationship which marriage affords. Such couples are generally childless, but some may have children from previous relationships.

In the course of the consultation through the family fora, support was expressed for clearer legal recognition and protection of other partnerships, apart from marriage. There was also concern expressed from another perspective, however, that recognition of other partnerships could have the effect of reducing the status of marriage, and thereby weakening it as a key source of stability and continuity in family life.

Bibliography

Background reports/documents on family issues:

Strengthening Families for Life – report of the Commission on the Family (1998)
Marital Breakdown Research Project, Dr Colm O'Connor (Families Research Programme 2001)
Family Formation in Ireland: trends, data needs and implications, Prof Tony Fahey, ESRI (Families Research Programme 2002)
Contemporary Family Policy, Prof Mary Daly, Sara Clavero (Families Research Programme 2002)
Children's Experience of Parental Separation in Ireland, Diane Hogan et al (Families Research Programme 2002)
Unhappy Marriages: does counselling help? Kieran McKeon et al (Families Research Programme 2002)
Family Wellbeing: What makes a difference, Kieran McKeown et al (Families Research Programme 2003)
Strengthening Families Through Fathers, Harry Ferguson & Fergus Hogan (Families Research Programme 2004)
Grandparenthood in Modern Ireland, Francesca Lundstrom (Families Research Programme 2001)
Babies and Bosses: reconciling work and family life, OECD 2003
Families and Family Life in Ireland: Challenges for the Future (2004)

Appendix 1

Council of Europe
Committee of Experts on Children and Families (CS-EF)
Strasbourg, Dec. 8 and 9, 2004

Parents and the Rights of the Child

Jaap E. Doek
Chairperson, UN Committee on the Rights of the Child

1 INTRODUCTION

The UN Convention on the Rights of the Child (hereafter the CRC) is a unique document of international law. For instance: it is the most comprehensive single treaty in the human rights field and is ratified almost universally; that is by 192 states out of the existing 194.

It is also the only human rights treaty that explicitly requires state parties to respect the responsibilities, rights and duties of parents (Article 5 CRC) and contains various provisions in which the role of parents is further elaborated.

In this contribution I shall present an elaborated description and interpretation of the provisions relevant for the work of the Council of Europe's Committee of Experts on Children and Families (CS-EF).

2 THE CRC, PARENTS AND THE STATE PARTY

2a Some general observations

The most important effect of the CRC is that it explicitly acknowledges the child as a subject of rights, as a rights holder. Some people are afraid that this will result in the undermining of parental rights and that children are abandoned to their autonomy.[1]

I would like to underscore that the CRC does not see the child as a stand-alone individual and does not intend to serve only the self-interest of that stand-alone person.

The preamble of the CRC clearly states that one of the most important conditions for the realisation of the rights of the child is that the child grows up in a family environment and in an atmosphere of happiness, love and understanding, because that condition is crucial for the full and harmonious development of the child's personality. Given this important role of the family, it should be afforded the necessary assistance so that it can fully assume its responsibilities within the community. An important feature of these responsibilities is that it provides the natural environment for the growth and well-being of all its members and particularly children.

These guiding principles are reflected not only in articles concerning the role of parents (more about those in para 2b), but also in other articles. Just some examples:

Requests for family reunification shall be dealt with by state parties in a positive, humane and expeditious manner (Article 11, para 1 CRC).

A child who is temporarily or permanently deprived of his or her family environment shall be entitled to *special* protection and care provided by the state (Article 20, para 1 CRC). It is also clear from Article 20 that in case alternative care is needed, priority should be given to the provision of family-type care (foster care, kafalah, adoption (Article 21)).

That the CRC is not only about the self-interest of the child as a stand-alone rights holder is reflected in various articles. Just some examples:

> Article 23: State parties shall take measures to facilitate the active participation in the community of the child with disabilities and (para 3) measures conducive for the disabled child's fullest possible social integration;

> Article 29: Education should be aimed at – *inter alia* – the preparation of the child for responsible life in a free society;

> Article 39: Measures have to be taken to promote the social reintegration of a child victim of neglect or violence;

> Article 40: Treatment of children in conflict with the law should be such that the child can assume a constructive role in society.

In short, the CRC is not only a 'child friendly' human rights document, but also parent friendly, family friendly and community/society friendly.

With these observations I also like to illustrate that provisions of the CRC should not be seen in isolation, but as part of the wider context of that convention and its overall purpose and objectives. This means *inter alia* that state parties recognise and *ensure* all the rights discussed hereafter to each child within their jurisdiction, including, e.g. children of illegal immigrants (Article 2), and that in all decisions regarding children their best interest has to be a primary consideration.

The role and/or position of parents (or other care-takers or persons legally responsible)[2] can be found in quite a number of articles, e.g. Article 9 and 37, both mentioning the right of the child to maintain contact with the parents/family; Article 7, the right to know and to be cared for by her/his parents and Article 30 (+ Beijing Rules) about the role of parents in the penal law procedures.

I shall focus on the responsibilities of parents in the context of the CRC and discuss in particular Articles 5,18 and 27.

2b The CRC and parental responsibilities

Articles 5, 18 and 27 of the CRC are the ones in which parental responsibilities are explicitly mentioned. The core message of these provisions is that state parties to the CRC shall respect and/or recognise these responsibilities, a recognition that should have consequences for the state parties in terms of positive and concrete actions.

At the same time, these articles (and some others like Articles 23 and 24) contain some information on the nature/content of these responsibilities.

The central provision is Article 18, para 1 whereas Articles 5 and 27 can be considered as elaborations of this provision. The following provisions of the CRC are particularly relevant for the nature and content of parental responsibilities:

Article 18, para 1

State parties shall use their best efforts to ensure recognition of the principles that both parents have common responsibilities for the upbringing and development of the child. Parents or, as the case may be, legal guardians have the primary responsibility for the upbringing and development of the child. The best interests of the child will be their basic concern.

Article 5

State parties shall respect the responsibilities, rights and duties of parents or, where applicable, the members of the extended family or community as provided for by local custom, legal guardians or other persons legally responsible for the child, to provide, in a manner consistent with the evolving capacities of the child, appropriate directions and guidance in the exercise by the child of the rights recognised in the present convention.

Article 27, para 1 and 2

State parties recognise the right of every child to a standard of living adequate for the child's physical, mental, spiritual, moral and social development.

The parent(s) or others responsible for the child have the primary responsibility to secure, within their abilities and financial capacities, the conditions of living necessary for the child's development.

Some comment on each of these provisions:

Article 18, para 1

The drafting history does not give the meaning of 'common' but the same phrase 'common responsibility' (of men and women) can be found in Article 5 under b of the CEDAW Convention and likewise in Article 18 CRC in relation to the 'upbringing and development of their children'. A suggestion to replace 'common' by 'equal' did not result in a change of the text.

It seems fair to assume that 'common' means 'shared' responsibility. It is also in line with Article 16, para 1 under d) CEDAW to assume that men and women (fathers and mothers) do have the same rights and responsibilities as parents. But this equality does not concern the daily, routine parental responsibilities. During the drafting it was observed that families allocate parental responsibilities differently and that it was of no concern to the state how this was done, except in child support or other extreme cases. It is not clear what was meant with 'other extreme cases'. But it should be noted that Article 18, para 1 does not mention divorce or separation of parents as a reason for the termination of the common/shared responsibilities. This also applies for the equality of men and women in this regard. Article 16, para 1 under d) states that men and women do have 'the same rights as parents, *irrespective of their marital status*'.

The best efforts to ensure the recognition of this principle means that all members of the Council of Europe (all being state parties to the CRC) have to take legislative and other appropriate measures necessary to make common and equal rights and responsibilities a reality. Various measures can be mentioned, e.g.:

> awareness raising campaigns to underscore that fathers and mothers should share their parental responsibilities[3] and this may be strengthened with financial and/or other measures to facilitate not only maternity, but also paternity leave;

> divorce or separation of parents should not automatically result in assigning parental rights and responsibilities exclusively to one of the parents (e.g. the parent charged with the daily care). Joint legal custody by parents should in principle be maintained despite divorce/separation. In principle this means except in cases where the best interests of the child *require* sole parental custody. 'Evidence' to that effect should be presented by the requesting parent and the decision should be taken by a court;

> legislative and other measures to encourage/facilitate the change of single parent custody to shared and equal responsibilities and rights of both parents of the child.

Para 1 of Article 18 also clearly states that *parents* do have the *primary* responsibility. Sometimes the extended family or the tribe or community takes over. The CRC Committee has expressed concern, e.g. at the fact that community leaders assume parental responsibilities and are replacing parents which has a negative impact on the children (Congo Concluding Observations CRC/C15 Add. 143, para 36) or recommended a state party to place greater emphasis in its policies on the primary responsibilities of parents (....) reducing the role of the state to a subsidiary and not a primary one (Concl. Observations Democratic People's Republic of Korea, CRC/C/15/Add. 239, para 45 and 44).

This provision (Article 18 para 1) is not only meant to protect parents against excessive intervention by the state (even if that intervention takes place with the best intentions), but also to indicate that parents cannot expect the state to always intervene if a problem occurs. Upbringing and development of children is *primarily* the responsibility of their parents. 'The best

interests of the child will be their basic concern'. It may be somewhat 'strange' to find such a parental obligation in a human rights treaty that is addressed to states. But it at least implicitly requires state parties to the CRC to take legislative, social and other measures that can encourage and facilitate parents to act in accordance with this principle.

Parents may have different views of the best interests of the child depending on the circumstances, the nature of decisions to be made for the child. But the suggestion that 'the best interest' is a completely subjective concept is an exaggeration and in the light of the CRC not correct. There are some provisions in the CRC which clearly indicate what parents should do in the best interest of the child, in particular Articles 5 and 27.

Some remarks about these articles:

Article 5

Although the start of this article is rather broad: 'shall respect the responsibilities, rights and duties of parents ... etc.', it is not a comprehensive recognition of all the rights, duties and responsibilities (....etc.) *per se*. The second part gives a further qualification by stating that it is about the provision to the child of 'appropriate direction and guidance in the exercise by the child of the rights recognised in the present convention'. Despite this qualification ('limitation' if you will) the article is very important.

First: it is based on the assumption that children should be given the opportunity to exercise their rights by themselves.

Secondly: state parties shall respect the role of parents (and if they are not available the extended family or the community) in this exercise by the child of her/his rights.

Thirdly: the word 'appropriate' indicates that the parents (and others if applicable) do not have a *carte blanche* to provide any kind of direction or guidance. More importantly: guidance and direction should be provided 'in a manner consistent with the *evolving capacities* of the child'. What this means is clear from e.g. a proposal by the delegation of Denmark in relation to Article 12 (respect for the views of the child). 'As the child gets older, the parents or the guardian should give him more and more responsibility for personal matters with the aim of preparing the child for the life of a grown-up.'

It should be noted that a similar provision can be found in Article 13, para 2 regarding the exercise by the child of her/his right to freedom of thought, conscience and religion.

Fourthly: the article assumes that parents should allow the child to exercise her/his rights in a rather independent way if he/she has the capacities to do so. But it can be argued that it also implies that the state parties should take appropriate measures to facilitate this transition from childhood to adulthood. This could be done, e.g. by explicitly providing the child with a growing degree of autonomy linked e.g. to minimum ages for decision in the areas of education, medical treatment, membership of associations etc.

Article 27 is another article that provides indications of what is in the best interests of the child and should therefore be a basic concern of parents. Some comments:

Article 27, para 1 and 2
Every child has the right to a standard of living adequate for the child's physical, mental, spiritual, moral and social development. Or in the terminology of the preamble: the full and harmonious development of her or his personality. Parents have the primary responsibility to secure the conditions of living necessary for the child's development. The drafting history does not explain the different wording in para 2. I assume that 'conditions of living necessary' is the same as the 'standard of living adequate for the child's development' as mentioned in para 1.[4] But the responsibility of parents (or others responsible for the child) is limited to their abilities and financial capacities. This implies – as does the word 'primary' – that the state has the secondary responsibility to assist parents where necessary. This is elaborated in para 3 of article 27 (to be discussed in more details in para 2c hereafter).

In conclusion: the CRC requires that state parties recognise the responsibilities of parents for the upbringing and development of their children. These responsibilities should be shared by both parents in an equal manner, and they include more specifically the provision of guidance and directions to their children in their exercise of the rights enshrined in the CRC in a manner consistent with their evolving capacities and the responsibility to secure within the parents' abilities and financial capacities a standard of living for their children adequate for their healthy development.

2c The CRC and the responsibilities of state parties
But the CRC does not limit the state parties' obligation to just the recognition of the primary responsibility of parents. It is not enough that state parties do not interfere in this responsibility. They have to take various positive measures to support parents in the performance of their responsibility as is clear from in particular Article 18 and 27. The relevant paragraphs are:

Article 18
2 For the purpose of guaranteeing and promoting the rights set forth in the present convention, state parties shall render appropriate assistance to parents and legal guardians in the performance of their child-rearing responsibilities and shall ensure the development of institutions, facilities and services for the care of children.

3 State parties shall take all appropriate measures to ensure that children of working parents have the right to benefit from childcare services and facilities for which they are eligible.

Article 27
3 State parties, in accordance with national conditions and within their means, shall take appropriate measures to assist parents and others responsible for the child to implement this right and shall in case of need provide material assistance and support programmes, particularly with regard to nutrition, clothing and housing.

Some comments:

Article 18 para 2
It is important to note that the appropriate assistance state parties are obliged to provide ('shall render') has a special purpose: guaranteeing and promoting the rights of the child as enshrined in the CRC.

This indicates that the parents' performance of their child-rearing responsibilities is not limited to e.g. Articles 5 and 27 discussed above.

The responsibilities are covering the wide scope of all the articles of the CRC, and the assistance provided by the state should therefore help parents in all their activities concerning the implementation of the rights of their child, e.g. in the areas of birth registration (Article 7), of maintaining the contacts between child-parent (Article 9 and 10), of upbringing a child with disabilities (Article 23), of social security and insurance (Article 26), of protecting the child against all forms of violence and exploitation (Articles 19, 32-36 CRC).

In quite a number of these articles specific actions are required from state parties in terms of support for parents (provide them with information, Article 9, para 4; support programmes for parents to prevent abuse Article 19, para 2; special care and assistance for parents of a disabled child Article 23, para 2 + 3 etc.) and Article 18 para. 2 can be seen as the umbrella provision.

The appropriate assistance is made concrete in the last part of para 2. The obligation to ensure the development of institutions, facilities and services[5] for the care of children does not mean that a state has to establish these services. Private organisations can establish and run these services but the state is under obligation to provide financial and other support. At the same time, the state has to ensure that these services conform with standards set by the competent authority, particularly in the areas of safety, health, the number and suitability of the staff and competent supervision (Article 3, para 3 CRC).

Article 18 para 3
This paragraph focuses on care services for children of working parents and was the result of some lengthy debates and different proposals.[6] For instance, limiting the services to day care facilities for children till they reach school age; or limiting it to children until they have completed their schooling and to public day care facilities for which they are eligible.

The final text is quite general; the state has to do everything appropriate to *ensure* that children of working parents (both working or a sole provider) have the right to benefit from care services and facilities. The qualification 'for which they are eligible' allows a state party to develop a policy and practice that responds to the needs of these children. It provides them with some discretionary power in terms of determining which children (pre-school age and/or primary school age) can qualify for which kind of services. There is no obligation to provide the services for free, but the state has to prevent any kind of discrimination (Article 2 CRC) and use their available resources to the maximum extent possible (Article 4 CRC). Compare in this regard Article 23 about the special care for the eligible child with disabilities which shall be provided free of charge whenever possible and taking into account the financial resources of the parents.

Article 27, para 3

This paragraph is another and important recognition of the state's subsidiary or secondary responsibility for the implementation of the right of the child to an adequate standard of living. The assistance for parents (and others responsible) shall be, in case of need, very concrete: material assistance and support programmes, particularly with regard to nutrition, clothing and housing. In this regard it should be noted that Article 11 ICESCR deals with the right of everyone to an adequate standard of living, which includes the right to adequate food, clothing and housing.

In addition to what Articles 18 and 27 tell us about the (secondary) responsibility of the state to support parents in the performance of their child-raising responsibilities I can refer not only to Article 23 (see above), but also to Article 24 (health) and 28 (education).

Article 24

For the full implementation of the right of the child to the enjoyment of the highest attainable standard of health the state parties shall take *inter alia* the appropriate measures

– to ensure that (....) in particular *parents* and children are informed, have access to education and are supported in the use of basic knowledge of child health and nutrition, the advantage of breast feeding, hygiene and environmental sanitation and the prevention of accidents;

– to develop preventive health care, guidance for *parents* and family planning and services.

Article 28

Primary education has to be compulsory and free of charge. But in accordance with Article 28 state parties shall encourage the development of different forms of secondary education and vocational training, make it accessible, free of charge (if possible) but offer at least in case of need, financial assistance (to parents). It should finally be noted that all 192 states agree that education of the child should be directed *inter alia* at the development of respect for the child's parents (Article 29).

3 SOME CONCLUDING OBSERVATIONS

The Convention on the Rights of the Child is the human rights treaty with the most elaborated set of rules for the responsibilities, rights and duties of parents (and where applicable of others responsible for the child, including members of the extended family and the community if provided for by local custom).

It is also clear that the parental responsibility is not a goal in itself, but a function – and the primary one – in the full and harmonious development of the child (e.g. Article 27). The exercise of this function means that parents shall act with the best interests of their child as their basic concern (Article 18) and shall take into account the child's evolving capacities (Article 5) or the child's age and maturity (Article 12).

Furthermore, it is clear that parents in the performance of their responsibilities are not left to their own devices.

First and as I just said, the CRC provides some guiding principles and the overall purpose of the parental actions should be guaranteeing and promoting the rights of the child set forth in the CRC (Article 18, para 2).

Secondly, 192 state parties have taken upon themselves the obligation to support the parents, a support which is spelled out in various articles of the CRC. Some of them are rather concrete (Article 27, para 3), but the variety and accessibility of child care services and other support programmes for parents most likely will depend on the state party human and financial resources. But they have committed themselves to using the available resources to the maximum extent possible (Article 4 CRC). The CRC Committee is aware that quite a number of state parties struggle with a lack of resources that hampers the implementation of the CRC. But at the same time, state parties need to be able to demonstrate that they have implemented the CRC 'to the maximum extent of the available resources'. The Committee has expressed its concern that almost no state party can provide a fully accurate picture of the amount of money (% of national budget) that is spent on activities (by the state, NGOs etc.) directed at/meant for the implementation of the CRC.

The CRC Committee, joining the Committee on Economic, Social and Cultural Rights, is of the opinion that 'even where the available resources are demonstrably inadequate, the obligation remains for a state party to strive to ensure the widest possible enjoyment of the relevant rights under the prevailing circumstances ...'[7]

In this respect it is important to mention the fact that the CRC is the only convention (again) in which state parties are required to encourage and promote international cooperation and to take account of in particular the needs of developing countries in general (Article 4) and in particular in the areas of health care and of assistance and care for disabled children (Article 23, 24) and education (Article 28). This feature of the CRC is important not only for actions within the Council of Europe, but also for active support by members of this Council for, in particular, developing countries.

It is my sincere hope and wish that the results of the work of this Committee of experts will be inspired by and contribute to the progressive and full implementation of the CRC.

Notes

1 See in particular the concerns in the USA which (partly) explains why they have not ratified the CRC, for instance: Bruce C. and Jonathan O. Hagen, *Abandoning Children to their Autonomy: the United Nations Convention on the Rights of the Child,* 37 Harvard International law Journal, p. 449 (1996) and Richard G. Wilkins (ed.) *Why the United States should not ratify the Convention on the Rights of the Child*, Saint Louis University Public Law Review Vol. XXII, no. 2 (2003), p. 411.

2 I shall for pragmatic reasons focus on parents and not repeat that most of the articles relevant for them are also applicable to others legally responsible, like guardians or other caretakers.

3 The CRC Committee has regularly recommended to state parties to promote the principle of equal/shared responsibilities of both parents and to pay special attention to the role of fathers. See e.g. the Concluding Observations of the Committee regarding Denmark, Norway, Germany, New Zealand and South Africa (UN Doc. CRC/C/15 Add. 33, para 26; Add. 23, para 18; Add. 43, para 31; Add. 71, para 27 and Add. 122, para 22 respectively).

4 The right to an adequate standard of living is also recognised in Article 25, para 1 UDHR and in Article 11 ICESCR.

5 Facilities and services were added to the text at the proposal of Finland because 'in situations' was too narrow. Detrick (1992), p. 269.

6 See Detrick (1992) p. 266, 267.

7 See the CRC Committee's General Comment nr. 5 (2003). *General Measures of Implementation of the Convention on the Rights of the Child*, para 9 and see also General Comment nr. 3 (1990) of the Committee on Economic, Social and Cultural Rights: *The nature of states parties' obligations* (Article 2 para 1 of the Covenant) and nr. 9 (1998) *The domestic application of the Covenant*.

Resources

Sharon Detrick (1992), *The United Nations Convention on the Rights of the Child. A Guide to the Travaux Préparatoires* (Martinus Nijhoff Publishers, Dordrecht 1992).

Sharon Detrick (1999), *A Commentary on the United Nations Convention on the Rights of the Child* (Kluwer Law International, The Hague 1999).

Implementation Handbook for the Convention on the Rights of the Child, prepared for UNICEF by Rachel Hodgkin and Peter Newell (Fully revised edition 2002, UNICEF New York).

DONEGAL CITIZENS' INFORMATION CENTRE – LIZ STEELE

I believe that the definition of 'family' needs to be changed. It is fundamental to the Irish Constitution and I believe that the current definition is outdated. In particular, couples who cohabit need to come within the definition of a family and to have equal rights with those of married couples. Although unmarried partners are treated as a 'family' unit for the purposes of social welfare entitlement, they are not treated in the same way for the purposes of tax entitlements. Because of this they lose out on entitlements and there is a huge anomaly in operation. For example, an unmarried woman working full-time is unable to benefit from her unemployed partner's tax credits, even though the medical card will be lost for them both on the basis of a joint 'family' income. This is an equality issue and needs to be addressed by the government.

Couples who are cohabiting are usually in stable 'family' relationships and this is becoming the norm for many people. Legislation is required to bring the law within the country into line with the social situation.

The 'family' can take many forms and the current definition is an outdated and narrowly based one. It takes no account of the fact that women are employed within the workforce and can often be the main breadwinners in the 'family' unit. It pays no attention to the extended family or to the broadening unit based upon parents who have children together, from previous relationships or both.

In addition, the tax implications of the broadening family unit are complex. Lone parents with responsibility for at least one child are entitled to a one-parent family tax credit. But how is that 'responsibility' defined and what is the position of the so-called 'absent' parent who has joint responsibility for and access to those children on a weekly basis? I would argue that both parents have equal responsibility for their children whether they live together or apart and this should be reflected in the legislation. Moreover, the position of children needs to be protected with account taken of the changing nature of the extended 'family' unit.

We are living in changing times. The fact that there is a review of the definition of the 'family' is proof of this change. I hope that the panel will look at the social situation within Irish society and apply the structural situation sensitively and flexibly to the definition of the family within Ireland today.

EUROPEAN LIFE NETWORK

Following the public advertisement of the All-Party Committee seeking submissions in respect of the family, ELN (European Life Network) wishes to place on record the views of our members with regard to the changes that the APOCC proposes to make to the Irish Constitution.

First the very fact that Ireland is considering these 'changes' at this time shows the patent falsity of the assertion that the proposed new European Constitution 'doesn't change anything,' won't create a 'superstate,' and leaves important domestic matters (like family law) to each nation.

STATEMENT OF KEY ISSUES REQUIRING GOVERNMENT ACTION TO FULFIL ITS CONSTITUTIONAL OBLIGATIONS TO THE FAMILY

The family and society

The natural family based on marriage, i.e. the union of one man and one woman, is the fundamental social unit, inscribed in human nature, and centred on the union of a man and a woman in the lifelong covenant of marriage. Articles 41.1.1: 41.21.2: 41.3.1 and other clauses of the Irish Constitution lay down that it is incumbent on the state to recognise and uphold the family based on marriage.

The family and marriage

Marriage, the cornerstone of healthy family life, brings security, contentment, meaning, joy and spiritual maturity to the man and woman who enter this lifelong covenant with unselfish commitment.

The family and children

The natural family based on marriage provides the optimal environment for the healthy development of children.

The family and sexuality

Sexuality exists for the expression of love between husband and wife and for the procreation of children within the covenant of marriage.

The family, life and bioethical issues

Every human person has intrinsic value throughout the continuum of life from fertilisation until natural death. Any action therefore which would in any way interfere in that continuum is wrong.

The family and population

Procreation is the key to the survival of the human race, and must therefore be protected.

The family and education

Parents possess the primary authority and responsibility to direct the upbringing and education of their children, except in clear cases of abuse and neglect.

The family, economy and development

The natural family is the fundamental unit of society for economic growth and development.

The family and government

Good government protects and supports the family and does not usurp the vital roles it plays in society.

The family and religion

As the primary educators, parents have the right to teach their religious and moral beliefs to their children and raise them according to their own religious precepts.

Call to respect the family

We exhort all persons, families, social entities, the government and national and international organisations in Ireland to adopt a family perspective, to respect and uphold the institution of the natural human family for the good of present and future generations.

UNITED NATIONS RESOLUTION FOR THE YEAR OF THE FAMILY

We wish to draw the attention of the Committee to the most recent United Nations resolution on the family (A/Res/59/111), which was accepted without a vote on December 6 2004. [For copy of documents relating to this resolution (Doha), please see Appendix 4.]

Draft Resolution A/59L.29 and the Doha declaration and report obtained widespread support (only a few nations withdrew from consensus). Moreover, the entire process quite clearly reaffirms global commitments to marriage in the substantive provisions of these documents (such as the reference to husband and wife in the 'reaffirmation' section and the call for action to strengthen and protect marriage).

The Doha Declaration therefore represents an affirmation by the great majority of nations on earth about the meaning and understanding of marriage. The Doha Declaration, as an outcome of the Doha Conference, was noted by the UN General Assembly in GA Resolution A/59/I.29 (December 6, 2004).

IS THE CONSTITUTION'S REFERENCE TO A WOMAN'S LIFE WITHIN THE HOME A DATED ONE THAT SHOULD BE CHANGED?

This is a very important provision and one which reflects the desire of the majority of Irish women as shown in many surveys: to stay at home and rear their children. The Constitution demands that the government should ensure that women are not driven out to work by economic necessity. The choice of mothers to stay at home and their constitutional right to do so has never been vindicated by the state. Article 41.2 of the constitution should not be changed but should instead be taken seriously by the state.

SHOULD THE RIGHTS OF A NATURAL MOTHER HAVE EXPRESS CONSTITUTIONAL PROTECTION?

The rights of the natural mother are already protected under Article 40 of the Constitution. The natural fathers' rights should have equal recognition to those of the natural mother.

CURRENT SOCIAL SCIENTIFIC RESEARCH

Current social scientific research in the United States also confirms the importance of marriage and the family. We attach a pamphlet that summarises much of the current research from America: 'Why marriage matters'. [For a copy of this document, please contact European Life Network.] The twenty-one findings set out in this paper demonstrate beyond serious argument that there is a pressing need to encourage and support stable marriage between a man and a woman. And, while the studies (and the pamphlet) do not directly assert a 'definition' of marriage, *every single one of the findings is based on the outcomes that flow from a man and a woman learning to live together.* There is *no evidence* that you can obtain these positive outcomes from any other relationship.

SEXUAL ORIENTATION

We also attach a report issued by United Families International setting out family guidelines to the issue of sexual orientation, *Guide to Family Issues: Sexual Orientation*. [For a copy of this document, please contact European Life Network.] The 'reason' there is a debate about 'definitions' is that homosexual activists want to be clearly included in the definition of family. This is unacceptable – as it will further 'water down' the 'norm' of marriage, children, and intergenerational ties. Right now, homosexuals aren't 'excluded' from the definition of family – perforce they belong to *some* family somewhere – and the current 'lack' of a definition is not creating any terrible difficulties.

We wish to emphasise the importance of marriage, sound relationships between parents and children, and the need for intergenerational transmission of values.

SHOULD 'GAY' COUPLES BE ALLOWED TO MARRY?

Giving 'gay' relationships marital status will destroy marriage. Homosexual and lesbian pairings are not marriage and never can be. It is futile therefore to pretend that they can or should be given a special status or treatment equivalent to that of marriage.

Marriage is not just the union of two people, it is the union of two sexes. It is the union of two families, and the foundation for establishing kinship patterns and family names, passing on property and providing the optimal environment for raising children.

Marriage is of such importance that it is, and must remain, uniquely protected in Irish law and culture. No civilisation can survive without marriage, and those societies that allowed it to become irrelevant have faded into history.

Marriage laws are not discriminatory. Marriage is open to all adults, subject to age and blood relation parameters. As with any acquired status, the applicant must meet minimal requirements, which in terms of marriage means finding an opposite-sex spouse. Same-sex partners do not qualify.

Giving non-marital relationships the same status as marriage does not expand the definition of marriage; it destroys it. For example, if you declare that, because it has similar properties, grape juice must be labelled identically to wine, you have destroyed the definitions of both 'grape juice' and 'wine'. The term 'marriage' refers specifically to the joining of two people of the opposite sex. When that is lost, the term 'marriage' becomes meaningless. You cannot leave an entire sex out of marriage and call it 'marriage'. It becomes something else.

Requiring citizens to sanction or subsidise homosexual relationships violates the freedom of conscience of Christians, Jews, Muslims and all people who believe marriage is the union of the two sexes.

Civil marriage is a public act. Homosexuals, however much they may wish it, should not be placed in a position to impose counterfeit 'marriage' on their fellow citizens via the law.

Although marriage is especially important as the fountainhead of natural family life and the well-being of children, even childless marriages are a social anchor for children. It is wrong to create fatherless or motherless families by design. This has more to do with the desires of adults than the needs of children. Human experience and a vast body of social science research show that children do best in married, mother-father households. Marriage encourages the sexes to complement each other's strengths and weaknesses.

The drive for homosexual 'marriage' leads to destruction of the appropriate standards for custody and adoption. The question should be: 'What is in the best interests of the child?' The answer is: 'Place children, whenever possible, in a marriage, mother-and-father household.'

It is wrong to encourage people to remain trapped in homosexuality. As society rewards homosexual desires, more young people will be encouraged to experiment with homosexuality, and more will be discouraged from overcoming unnatural homosexual desires. If 'gay marriage' is legalised, children in schools will be taught that this is the moral equivalent of true marriage and that one day perhaps some might 'marry' a member of their own sex.

Unlike race or ethnicity, homosexuality is in no way immutable or genetically determined. It is a chosen behaviour. People need not embrace unnatural feelings, and many homosexuals have overcome 'gay' desires and gone on to lead heterosexual lives, including getting married and having children. Science has produced no credible evidence of innate homosexuality. The most famous 'born gay' study, by Dean Hamer, a homosexual activist researcher, could not be replicated. Thus, comparisons to inter-racial marriage cases, such as *Loving v. Virginia (US Supreme Court, 1967)*, are irrelevant and misleading. The very soul of marriage – the joining of the two sexes – was never at issue in the *Loving v. Virginia* case.

LEGAL AND SOCIAL FALLOUT

When same-sex relationships acquire marital type status in the law, several things occur:

- Businesses that decline to recognise non-marital relationships are punished through loss of contracts and even legal action. This is already occurring in parts of the United States and in Canada.
- Children are taught in school that homosexuality is a normal, healthy, safe alternative to actual marriage.
- 'Hate Crime' laws are employed against people who reasonably insist that marriage is the union of a man and a woman. An example of this occurred in Sweden last year when a Protestant parson (Parson Greene) was imprisoned for giving a sermon which was based on the biblical teaching on homosexuality.
- Corporate employee 'diversity' programmes step up their attack on traditional morality as a form of 'big-otry'.
- Traditional groups such as the boy scouts, already harassed and de-funded in the United States, come under even harsher attacks over their moral stance.
- Religious leaders eventually will be told by government authorities to recognise 'gay marriages' or lose their tax-exempt status. Enforced 'equality' trumps religious freedom. For example, in 1997, a Washington DC court overrode the religion-based objections of Georgetown University, a Catholic school, to sponsoring a homosexual activist group on campus.
- Other groups, such as bisexuals and bigamists, will demand the right to redefine marriage to suit their own proclivities. Once the standard of one-man, one-woman marriage is broken, there is no logical stopping point.

CONCLUSION

'Civil unions', 'domestic partnerships' and 'gay marriage' are being promoted as an extension of tolerance and civil rights. But they are really wedges designed to overturn traditional sexual morality and to construct a system to punish dissenting views.

For our children's well-being, and to protect the fragile freedoms of religion, speech and association, we must not allow the creation of government-imposed counterfeit 'marriage' under any guise whatsoever.

Marriage is civilisation's primary institution, and we tamper with it at our own peril.

THE UN CONVENTION ON THE RIGHTS OF THE CHILD IS A FLAWED CONVENTION AND THE CONSTITUTION SHOULD NOT BE ALTERED TO ACCOMMODATE IT

The rights of the child are not, and should not be seen as being opposed to the rights of parents. This only happened in a small minority of cases, and is already covered in the Constitution and by appropriate legislation. It is not necessary to create any new legislation or alter the Constitution to provide any additional rights under the CRC. In fact the position is quite the reverse and the government must seek changes in the Convention on the Rights of the Child in order to

redress the balance. There are many good aspects of the Convention, but these however are outweighed by many deeply flawed articles. The positive aspects of the Convention and the problem aspects are set out below.

Positive aspects

The Convention's *preamble* recognises the family as '*the fundamental group of society* and the natural environment for the growth and well-being of all its members and particularly of children'.

The preamble also says: 'the child, for the full and harmonious development of his or her personality, should grow up in a family environment.' Perhaps most encouraging for pro-family advocates is the preambular line that asserts the child 'needs special safeguards and care, including appropriate legal protection, *before as well as after birth'.*

The body of the Convention offers even more protection for children. Article Six recognises that '*every child has the inherent right to life'*. When this is read in conjunction with the preamble it clearly protects the child from before birth.

The Convention also protects the *rights of parents to direct the lives* of their children in a broad array of concerns. Article 14 insists: 'States parties shall respect the rights and duties of the parents ... to provide direction to the child in the exercise of his of her right to freedom of thought, conscience and religion ...'. Article 18 says: 'Parents ... have the *primary responsibility* for the upbringing and development of the child.'

Problem aspects

The Convention has many problems.

Article 13 guarantees the child's 'freedom to seek, *receive and impart information* and ideas of all kinds, regardless of frontiers [...] through any other media of the child's choice'. This is made without any provision for parental supervision.

Article 15 guarantees, nearly unhindered, *'freedom of association'*

Article 16 guarantees that 'No child shall be subjected to arbitrary or unlawful interference with his or her ... *privacy ...'*

Article 19 calls for the protection of the child from 'all forms of physical or mental violence, injury, or abuse, neglect or negligent treatment, maltreatment or exploitation ... while in the care of parents ...,' *On the face of it this paragraph appears quite sensible,* yet rulings by UN committees show a marked tendency to consider traditional religious belief and practice as forms of abuse.

Article 24 urges states parties to 'ensure that no child is deprived of his or *her right of access to ... health care services ...'* This would seem to be positive but, in UN parlance, it would include access to *'reproductive health care' which includes abortion.*

Autonomy rights were introduced in the Convention. These particular rights are considered by many of those aware of their application to have the potential to undermine the family. See Lynette Burrows, *The Fight for the The Family – the Adults behind Children's Rights* Family Education Trust, 322, Woodstock Rd. Oxford OX2 7NS. This book deals with experience in the UK, and calls our attention to the *interpretation* that is capable of being put on many apparently innocuous provisions. These provisions, as well as the more obvious 'autonomy' provisions, she says, sustain a lobby whose exclusive interest in 'rights' is confined to two: *a 'right' to behave badly*, and *a 'right' to enter into sexual relationships* at any age, without the knowledge and consent of their parents.

The Convention in its present form has the potential to:

1 prohibit any physical restraint or correction of children by parents, no matter how mild
2 forbid home schooling of children by parents
3 make children's rights independent of their parents.
4 give children the 'legal' right to all forms of information, however immoral or inappropriate
5 give children the 'right' to contraceptives and abortion irrespective of their parents' wishes and without their parents' knowledge
6 prohibit the teaching of religion by parents to 'unreceptive' children or from taking them to church or religious services
7 give children a 'right to privacy', which in practice gives children the legal right to tell parents not to interfere in their lives (and even make certain areas of their home off-limits to parents)
8 subject parental activity to undue and intrusive external scrutiny by government and social service agencies
9 remove children from parents to state care without parents' consent and against the parents' wishes and rights
10 corrupt good and well-behaved children who otherwise would never think of rebelling against their parents.

UNITED NATIONS UNIVERSAL DECLARATION AND IMPLEMENTING TREATIES

The Universal Declaration of Human Rights explicitly protects the prior right of parents to choose the kind of education that is given to their children, and gives the right of parents in that regard priority over all other rights.

The implementing treaties of the Universal Declaration – The International Covenant on Economic, Social and Cultural Rights and the International Covenant on Civil and Political Rights– are even more specific in protecting the liberty of parents to ensure the religious and moral education of their children in conformity with their own convictions.

THE DEVELOPMENT OF THE HUMAN PERSON

The development of the human person is a continuous process from the moment of conception through birth to natural death. The development of children before and after birth, just as the development of every person, has various stages. These stages are recognisable although not always amenable to precise differentiation.

The inability precisely to demarcate transition points follows upon the fact that development in the individual person is a continuum, but precisely because of that individuality, varies from person to person. There are no real grounds, on this basis, for argument against the continuous identity of the individual person throughout the various stages or against the existence of the various stages themselves. If anything it presupposes both the continuity in the personal development and the discontinuity in the stages of development of the person. This understanding of the development of persons is wholly in accord with the 'life-cycle' approach to development recognised by various UN bodies and documents and by bodies and organisations affiliated with the UN or its activities.

THE MORAL UNACCEPTABILITY OF THE CONVENTION ON THE RIGHTS OF THE CHILD

The Convention on the Rights of the Child lacks moral credibility, and its claim to be an instrument for the protection of the rights of children and their total well-being is without moral foundation. Nowhere is this more obvious than in the discontinuity between the preamble to the Convention and its content in regard to the status of the child in the womb. The preamble recognises the status of the child in the womb as that it has a right to life. Yet the Convention itself provides no protection to this right to life of the child in the womb. On its own terms of reference, then, the Convention disregards the most basic and fundamental rights of some children, indeed all children, at a particular stage of their life. As this is the most vulnerable stage of a child's life it is clear that the Convention, whatever its stated intent, is not consistent in its willingness to protect vulnerable children nor in protecting the rights of all children equally.

To recognise the right to life of children in the womb and yet allow abortion to be practised by those nations who are bound by the Convention is an inconsistency so fundamental that its destroys any claim to moral authority or credibility it may make. To fail to protect explicitly the recognised rights of those children who are most vulnerable and weak limits the exercise of the rights of the weak in order to extend the 'rights' of the strong, This extension of the rights of some at the expense of the most fundamental rights of those most incapable of defending themselves is unacceptable. In the case of the child in the womb it is not so much even as a clash of the exercise of the rights of some with the exercise of the rights of others but a denial of the most basic rights of some so that others can act without responsibility or obligation. (They are not acting on a right as there can be no right to violate the rights of another if a theory of rights is to make any sense at all. And as the right to life of the child in the womb is recognised in the preamble of the Convention this entails a responsibility and obligation on others to respect and defend this right. To ignore or violate this right is unacceptable.) Responsibility for the exercise of rights and the consideration of the totality of relationships has nothing to do with the selective picking and choosing of children's rights allowed by the Convention.

In this there is also a blatant contradiction of the stated intention of the Convention and the Children's Committee that the best interest of the child must be the primary consideration. Clearly this is not the case. If the 'priority to the child' doctrine is sincere then the Committee and a large number of states that have bound themselves to the Convention are breaking the Convention and should suffer the penalties due to such (human rights) violations. To make the laws but be above the laws is either hypocrisy or tyranny. A Convention that recognises the right to life of the child in the womb but allows abortion is in the same measure hypocritical and tyrannical.

EVANGELICAL ALLIANCE IRELAND

PREFACE

Evangelical Alliance Ireland is a national movement of churches, individuals and organisations representing evangelical Christians in Irish society. There are several hundred churches in the Republic of Ireland which claim an evangelical identity and more than thirty organisations involved in different aspects of Irish life, many of them linked to family issues. EAI is committed to the Christian gospel as a principle for living and believes that following this gospel is a way of life that must be freely chosen, not coerced. However, it is also convinced that there are many Christian principles that can be applied with benefit to wider society irrespective of people's religious beliefs. One of the most basic of these is the principle that marriage is a lifelong commitment between one man and one woman.

HOW SHOULD THE FAMILY BE DEFINED?

The family should continue to be seen as a man and a woman in a legally recognised marriage together with their children. There is no other solid, tried legal basis on which to define 'family'. The institution of a legally recognised marriage covenant between a man and a woman has provided the basic unit for almost every society for millennia. This does not mean that there cannot be families that deviate from the norm. There are. But accepting the traditional family unit as the norm enables society to look at how to respond to situations that differ from the norm and ensure that people in those situations are treated fairly.

On the other hand, trying to alter the norm means tampering with the unit that forms the basis of society. The nuclear family may be less popular than it used to be in Ireland but there is no other definition of family that has been tried and shown to be effective in providing stability to a society. Attempting to redefine the family will not serve society well and will not lead to greater protection for those who live outside a traditional family unit. It will instead weaken society and therefore weaken its ability to provide protection for its members.

HOW SHOULD ONE STRIKE THE BALANCE BETWEEN THE RIGHTS OF THE FAMILY AS A UNIT AND THE RIGHTS OF INDIVIDUAL MEMBERS?

Individuals cannot exist apart from community. As John Donne put it, 'No man (person) is an island, entire of itself.' Therefore the rights of individuals cannot take precedence over the rights of society as a whole or the rights of the family unit that provides the basic unit of society. Legislation and policy should address the need to protect individuals who are not part of a family unit and therefore do not benefit from the legal protection extended to a family. Those who choose not to be part of a family should not be penalised for that choice. Those who are in a vulnerable position because they are not part of a family need the protection of the state and the support of society. But this should not be at the expense of the protection and support of families. Support and protection of those living outside nuclear family units does not require a re-defining of 'family' in the Constitution.

IS IT POSSIBLE TO GIVE CONSTITUTIONAL PROTECTION TO FAMILIES OTHER THAN THOSE BASED ON MARRIAGE?

There are many kinds of domestic relationships outside the basic family unit operating in society. They vary from lodgers sharing a house to a stable long-term man + woman + children relationship that is not a legally recognised marriage. There are legal and policy protections that already apply to some of these arrangements. Lawmakers should regularly examine whether this legal protection is adequate. Particular attention should be given to arrangements where children are involved to ensure adequate protection for them. Special consideration should also be given to those who are vulnerable or less able to fight for their own rights such as widows, lone parents, the disabled and the elderly. However, given the variety of domestic arrangements that can and do exist, it is difficult to use the Constitution for this purpose. What protection is provided should not be at the expense of the constitutional protection given to the family formed through marriage. A family formed through a legally constituted marriage should be seen under the Constitution as unlike any other domestic relationship and therefore deserving of specific protection because all society benefits from that protection.

Under law it should be possible to recognise long-term established relationships and provide adequate protection for the parties involved. It could be possible for participants in such relationships to register their relationship as a long-term partnership and avail of legal protection for issues such as inheritance. However, the law should clearly recognise that such relationships are different to the family unit established through a legal marriage and maintain particular rights for marriage as a unique institution.

SHOULD GAY COUPLES BE ALLOWED TO MARRY?

No. Heterosexual marriage has played a unique historic role in the formation and development of most societies. It has faced many stresses and challenges but has remained the basis on which families are developed and the future of succeeding generations. It is because of this role that marriage has been given protection under the Constitution – that protection is a recognition that society needs marriage.

Granting homosexual partnerships the status of marriage is effectively a redefinition of marriage. If this redefining were to take place it would be done without any historical or sociological proof that homosexual relationships can provide the same benefit to society that marriage has done. It would also be without clear evidence that most gay couples would avail of the right were it granted.

The introduction of gay marriage would effectively discriminate against other domestic relationships that are often as permanent and stable as a gay relationship, such as siblings living together or an unmarried child living with an elderly parent. There are issues of legal and financial protection requiring attention in many such relationships. These issues can and should be dealt with under law without undermining the uniqueness of marriage.

IS THE CONSTITUTION'S REFERENCE TO WOMAN'S LIFE WITHIN THE HOME A DATED ONE THAT SHOULD BE CHANGED?

It is dated in that it does not reflect the situation that now exists which is very different from that envisaged in the Constitution. It would be appropriate to replace it with a reference to the need for adequate protection and support for either or both parents in their role as the primary carers and educators of their children.

SHOULD THE RIGHTS OF THE NATURAL MOTHER HAVE EXPRESS CONSTITUTIONAL PROTECTION?

The rights of the natural mother are better protected under legislation rather than through the Constitution, given the complexity of the issues. Legislation should balance the rights of the natural mother with the responsibility she has towards her children. Granting rights to the natural mother should not be at the expense of the rights of her children who are more vulnerable than she is.

WHAT RIGHTS SHOULD A NATURAL FATHER HAVE AND HOW SHOULD THEY BE PROTECTED?

The rights of natural fathers should be defined in law rather than in the Constitution and should be contingent on a father accepting his responsibilities for his children and his playing an active role in their lives. As with the mother, the natural father's rights should not be at the expense of the rights of the children who are unable to assert their own rights and therefore require a greater level of protection.

SHOULD THE RIGHTS OF THE CHILD BE GIVEN AN EXPANDED CONSTITUTIONAL PROTECTION? DOES THE CONSTITUTION NEED TO BE CHANGED IN VIEW OF THE UN CONVENTION ON THE RIGHTS OF THE CHILD?

Given that the state has already ratified the UN Convention on the Rights of the Child it would seem better to ensure adequate provision for children through legislation. In our view the present Article 42 of the Irish Constitution provides adequate constitutional basis for such legislation.

CONCLUSION

These are times of extraordinary social change in Ireland. Changes are taking place that will affect the shape of society for generations to come. Structures and institutions such as the family that have served society well should not be reshaped without a clear understanding of the long-term consequences of such actions. The protection that the Constitution affords to the nuclear family formed on the basis of a legally constituted marriage should not be removed.

THE FAMILY FIRST ASSOCIATION (IRELAND)

PREAMBLE

The Family First Association (Ireland) – FFAI – was established by a group of five persons who, either directly or indirectly, had experienced the emotional and psychological trauma of having been alienated from children within their families because of the disingenuous and malicious intent of others. The particular focus experienced by the group was recognised as being the psychological programming of children resulting in their alienation from once-loved parents within dissolution (divorce, separation), custody and parenting time (contact) situations.

The inducement (perpetration) of parental alienation syndrome – PAS – which is a form of child abuse, is a growing phenomenon within the complex scenarios of modern lifestyles, but most especially within scenarios of divorce and custody matters. It is a matter that urgently needs to be recognised and addressed by the child and family protection systems, including the family law court system.

Currently, there is no recognition of PAS in Ireland. Unscrupulous parents are psychologically battering their own children and using them as 'tools' within the adversarial family law court system for the purpose of alienating and humiliating *target* parents. Within the process such malicious persons are successfully 'using' an inadequate and a prejudiced family law court system (court and its agents) as third party support to 'approve' the alienation of children from once-loved parents.

The means by which the family law court system deals with child and family matters can only be described as stereotypical, derisive and destructive. People who have not had the misfortune to experience such crude and barbaric processes may well envisage a system that is fair and comprehensive. The reality is far from that! The system is based on conflict; is reliant upon stereotyped professional reports; is overtly prejudiced against fathers; is unnecessarily elongated and expensive; and is managed by people who are trained to cause division rather than build links to arbitration and conciliation.

The FFAI opines that the failure of the state to adopt family law and family law court (including its agents) processes in keeping with the protectorate aims of the Constitution has led to a deterioration of Irish civil society. The traditional family unit, which has been the recognised backbone of Irish survival and resurgence through the ages, has thus been attacked by the state itself, contrary to its own resolution as set out in Article 41.1 of the Constitution.

In essence, the purpose of the Constitution has been eroded by the state. It no longer serves as a protectorate to decent Irish people. It is now imperative that reform takes place. The Constitution must not be compromised to give further license to corrupt legislators. It must be amended in such a way that it will begin to give confidence back to the people and reflect a commitment by the state that it is willing to make radical changes to better protect the family, family members and family relationships.

ARTICLE 41.1

Article 41.1 states:

1 1° The State recognises the Family as the natural primary and fundamental unit group of Society, and as a moral institution possessing inalienable and imprescriptible rights, antecedent and superior to all positive law.

2° The State, therefore, guarantees to protect the Family in its constitution and authority, as the necessary basis of social order and as indispensable to the welfare of the Nation and the State.

Given the deterioration in the moral, civil and obedient society in modern Ireland it would be viewed as negligent to dismantle the essence and poignancy by which the family is recognised and protected by Article 41.1 of the Constitution. Families are central to society. Families are the resource, human capital and wealth of society, and hence they are the medium and motor that is the key to attain true social and sustainable development.

It is imperative that the general purposes of Article 41, as set out at 41.1.1 and 41.1.2, are maintained. The essence of the Family 'as the natural primary and fundamental unit group of society' must be enhanced and never fragmented.

The adjectives 'inalienable' and 'imprescriptible' must be maintained as a means to give the people of Ireland some form of security against further attacks by the state upon their Constitution.

ARTICLE 41.2

Article 41.2 states:

2 1° In particular, the State recognises that by her life within the home, woman gives to the State a support without which the common good cannot be achieved.

2° The State shall, therefore, endeavour to ensure that mothers shall not be obliged by economic necessity to engage in labour to the neglect of their duties in the home.

It is more essential that parenthood, being the biological role of two people, be determined and protected by the Constitution. Recognising one party, the woman, as the primary home maker and care giver, clearly undermines the equitable rights of fathers that should automatically be provided through biological, social and moral means.

Article 41.2 as it currently exists is potentially divisive and discriminatory. It therefore should be annulled in its present form – and be replaced with a reference to the protection of parenthood.

It is essential that all biological parents, whether they are married or not, are presumed equal under the law and shall have the right to be treated equally by the state and its agents.

Children have the fundamental right to the direct care and interaction of both biological and adoptive parents, and parents have the fundamental right of parenthood. It is imperative, therefore, that the state and the Constitution of Ireland serve to protect the family as set out in Article 41.1.

ARTICLE 41.3 (1 AND 2)

Article 41.3 (1 & 2) states:

3 1° The State pledges itself to guard with special care the institution of Marriage, on which the Family is founded, and to protect it against attack.

2° A Court designated by law may grant a dissolution of marriage where, but only where, it is satisfied that –

i at the date of the institution of the proceedings, the spouses have lived apart from one another for a period of, or periods amounting to, at least four years during the previous five years,

ii there is no reasonable prospect of reconciliation between the spouses,

iii such provision as the Court considers proper having regard to the circumstances exists or will be made for the spouses, any children of either or both of them and any other person prescribed by law, and

iv any further conditions prescribed by law are complied with.

The adoption of the England and Wales adversarial family law court module as a means of intervention in family matters in Ireland has seen the state allow a deliberate and concentrated attack upon the family and parenthood. Consequently, the main purpose of the Constitution relating to family matters has been seriously undermined. This is, admittedly, a very controversial and sensitive subject, but it is one that must be fully debated, understood – and, eventually, rectified.

The sad reality is that many of the vulnerable families that have faced a crisis period have been obliterated by a barbaric state system. The system is auto-confrontational, discriminatory, and stereotypical in outcomes on the basis of convoluted reasoning – and because of the in-camera rule, it is completely devoid of any form of public scrutiny.

The problems caused are across a spectrum of issues: the separation of innocent fathers from their children; the overburden of responsibility placed upon mothers; serious financial burdens; the prohibitive costs of ongoing legal action; the effects of deep-seated injustices; and the lack of support for parenthood, marriage and for well-behaved individuals who are dedicated spouses and parents.

The current state of the law regarding divorce and custody of minor children is in fact implemented in a fashion that leads to constitutionally-prohibited violations of the rights of both children and parents within Ireland in the aggregate, as the current mode:

- removes children from parents' direct care and control
- impermissibly denies children the right to the direct care, custody, and love of their natural parents in most cases without finding of predicate harm
- impermissibly denies parents the right to make decisions about expenditures that further the interests of their children and transfers that control to another through the enactment and enforcement of the current 'child support' laws
- operates in a manner that is biased against men as a gender in violation of the constitutional requirement for equal protection under the law
- impermissibly violates a citizen's rights to due process by assuming that allegations of criminal conduct such as physical and sexual abuse are proven prior to trial, and exacts punishment for alleged offences which have not been proven.

Why is family law system flawed and degenerate?

1 It is adversarial, based on worst-case scenarios and is often reliant upon exaggerated or unproven allegations.

2 It exacerbates hostility, causes unwarranted anxiety and depression and stigmatises emotional trauma.

3 It is a field area for covertly manipulative and disingenuous persons to gain material and monetary possession through the 'third party' support offered by the state systems.

4 The system is based on outcomes whereby the 'winner takes all' and the 'loser' faces isolation, alienation, ridicule and financial hardship, etc., irrespective of the fault basis or the moral/psychological maturity of the concerned parties.

5 The system is procedurally inadequate, in that it:

a lacks proper investigation of social and psychological factors;

b fails to carry out an assessment of causation

c places little emphasis on communication and counselling for the concerned personnel

d places no intent or interest in attaining best practical solutions.

Problems emanating from the family law court system include:

e elongated, stereotypical and contra-friendly procedures

f 'children's interests paramount' applied without restraint, so that the state effectively takes control of children from capable parents

g mother-priority without good reason

h children often placed in the sole care of parents who are personality disordered or psychologically manipulative

i child maintenance principles that never consider fault or need, and without any accountability that the money is actually spent on the children

j legal aid provision which supports ongoing legal activity, stripping of family assets, and supports the party with most to gain from the legal process.

6 The adversarial and elongated elements of the family law court system often cause children to become emotionally and psychologically programmed by one parent for the purpose of rejecting, denigrating and making false allegations against the target parent. Thus, the system exacerbates a form of child abuse, which has been defined as parental alienation syndrome. There exists a deliberate agenda to reject the existence of this form of child abuse, yet the state has not undertaken any form of research into the dynamics and ratios of PAS perpetration and PAS induced children.

7 The agents and professionals who run the system are not qualified or orientated to create a harmony of interests between the relevant parties.

8 The system is without any form of accountability. It is literally a law unto itself! Can the state categorically prove that the decisions made in the family law court are justifiable, equitable and serving in the paramount interests of the children and parents involved? Without a proper research and scrutiny of the system the state cannot give a definitive answer. But the answer is 'no'.

9 There has been no study done in Ireland to reveal the social, moral, economical, etc. effects caused by

the devastation of legally held adversarial divorce and separation. Issues such as homelessness, financial hardships, mental health problems, loss of parenthood, suicide, etc. have not been examined by the state for the purpose of identifying the consequences of such a barbaric state system.

10 Studies carried out in other countries have revealed an array of problems in children that have been separated from a parent, including crime and juvenile delinquency, premature sexuality and out-of-wedlock births to teenagers, academic under-achievement, depression, substance abuse, alienation among adolescent, and suicides.

Thus, it must be concluded that the state has not kept its pledge to 'guard with special care the institution of marriage, on which the family is founded, and to protect it against attack'. Instead, the state has systematically allowed the institution of the family, and worse still, the sanctuary of parenthood, to be attacked, ridiculed and fragmented.

The FFAI would urge that Article 41.3.1 is maintained, but that Article 41.3.2 is amended so as to embed a proactive commitment on the part of the state to take all reasonable and practical steps to (1) support the family unit and maximise its stability and (2) promote good behaviour in the family and in partnerships bonded through parenthood. It is ultimately acceded that 'a court designated by law may grant a dissolution of marriage', but only as a last resort.

ARTICLE 41.3 (3)

Article 41.3 states:

3° No person whose marriage has been dissolved under the civil law of any other State but is a subsisting valid marriage under the law for the time being in force within the jurisdiction of the Government and Parliament established by this Constitution shall be capable of contracting a valid marriage within that jurisdiction during the lifetime of the other party to the marriage so dissolved.

The FFAI agrees to the retention of the existing provisions relating to the recognition of foreign divorces.

ARTICLE 42

Article 42 states:

1 The State acknowledges that the primary and natural educator of the child is the Family and guarantees to respect the inalienable right and duty of parents to provide, according to their means, for the religious and moral, intellectual, physical and social education of their children.

2 Parents shall be free to provide this education in their homes or in private schools or in schools recognised or established by the State.

3 1° The State shall not oblige parents in violation of their conscience and lawful preference to send their children to schools established by the State, or to any particular type of school designated by the State.

2° The State shall, however, as guardian of the common good, require in view of actual conditions that the children receive a certain minimum education, moral, intellectual and social.

4 The State shall provide for free primary education and shall endeavour to supplement and give reasonable aid to private and corporate educational initiative, and, when the public good requires it, provide other educational facilities or institutions with due regard, however, for the rights of parents, especially in the matter of religious and moral formation.

5 In exceptional cases, where the parents for physical or moral reasons fail in their duty towards their children, the State as guardian of the common good, by appropriate means shall endeavour to supply the place of the parents, but always with due regard for the natural and imprescriptible rights of the child.

There are a couple of serious issues with regards to Article 42.5. Firstly, there have been instances where children have been removed from perfectly normal loving parents by the state on the basis of false allegations of abuse and neglect, and/or where children have been induced to the serious form of parental alienation syndrome causing overt rejections and the making of unwarranted allegations against *target* parents. The onus of proof, in such circumstances, must be upon the state.

Secondly, Article 42.5 does not have a clause indicating a commitment on the part of the state to endeavour to reunite family relationships.

It is recommended that Article 42.5 be amended to read: 'In exceptional cases, where it is proven that parents for physical or moral reasons ...'

In line with the rights of the child to natural parenthood an additional paragraph should state: 'That the State shall make all positive steps to maintain or reunite family relationships ....' Such a commitment would be in line with Article 8 of the UN Convention on the Rights of the Child

ARTICLE 40

Article 40 (1 & selected 3) states:

1 All citizens shall, as human persons, be held equal before the law.
This shall not be held to mean that the State shall not in its enactments have due regard to differences of capacity, physical and moral, and of social function.

3 1° The State guarantees in its laws to respect, and, as far as practicable, by its laws to defend and vindicate the personal rights of the citizen.
2° The State shall, in particular, by its laws protect as best it may from unjust attack and, in the case of injustice done, vindicate the life, person, good name, and property rights of every citizen.
3° The State acknowledges the right to life of the unborn and, with due regard to the equal right to life of the mother, guarantees in its laws to respect, and, as far as practicable, by its laws to defend and vindicate that right.

In pursuance of the arguments relating to the afore-mentioned Article 41.3 (1 and 2) it has to be concluded that the state has neither defended nor vindicated the personal rights of some of its citizens as set out in Article 40.3.1, especially in matters relating to the family.

This is seen as a violation of Article 8 (right to respect for private and family life) taken together with Article 6 (entitlement to a fair hearing) of the European Convention on Human Rights as per the cases of *Elsholz v. Germany* (European Court of Human Rights 2000 – App. No. 25735/94) and *Sommerfeld v. Germany* (ECHR 2003 – App. No. 31871/96).

In league with the big brother England and Wales family law court module, the shroud of secrecy and the institutional acceptance of unfair decisions eventually denies individuals the right to pursue claims to a higher level. Thus, family law court case grievances are deemed as having been 'concluded' within the party state of Ireland and, as such, they are not eligible for application to the ECHR in Strasbourg.

The practices of the family law court to purposefully exclude family relationships without proper investigation or reason are wholly contrary to Article 40.3.2 of the Constitution. The Constitution, as the primary proclamation of guardianship of Irish citizens, has been severely diluted as a result of the family law court system.

In conclusion, the oath and essence of the Constitution in relation to its protection of Irish citizens, as set out at various parts of Article 40 has been abused by the state.

HOW SHOULD THE FAMILY BE DEFINED?

The FFAI supports the UN broad definition of the family, as 'any combination of two or more persons who are bound together by ties of mutual consent, birth and/or adoption or placement and who, together, assume responsibility for, *inter alia*, the care and maintenance of group members, the addition of new members through procreation or adoption, the sociali-sation of children and the social control of members'.

As marriage is seen as the key component of 'the family' and parenthood the essential component of child welfare, then the value of marriage and parenthood must be distinctly recognised and protected within the Constitution.

The state would, therefore, be compelled to change the law and processes by which the state deals with families experiencing problematic situations. Instead of subjecting the family and its members to the barbaric experience of the Family Law Court process, it would actively arbitrate and support the respective roles of the various family members.

The guiding principle would be that in serving the best interests of the family, and in particular parent-hood, the state would be serving the superior interests of children.

HOW SHOULD ONE STRIKE A BALANCE BETWEEN THE RIGHTS OF THE FAMILY AS A UNIT AND THE RIGHTS OF INDIVIDUAL MEMBERS?

The present family law court system often rewards individuals who are intent on 'breaking' family units for their own disingenuous purposes. Indeed, the system can act as a catalyst for such immoral persons, with 'willing' players (professionals) fulfilling the role of third party support.

Thus, the Constitution must set out the guiding principle that the family as a unit has precedence over the rights of individual members. However, the rights of individual members must also be held as distinctive in terms of their spousal, parenting and contributing roles.

IS IT POSSIBLE TO GIVE CONSTITUTIONAL PROTECTION TO FAMILIES OTHER THAN THOSE BASED ON MARRIAGE?

Yes. The adoption of the UN definition of the family, coupled with a paragraph that recognises and protects the rights of parenthood, would embrace the rights of parents who are not bound by marriage.

SHOULD GAY COUPLES BE ALLOWED TO MARRY?

No. As gay couples do not have the biological means to 'create' a natural 'household' family then it would not be ethical to allow gay couples to marry.

It would be seen as contradictory if the state allowed for gay couples to marry, whilst it continues to 'attack' the present institution of marriage among heterosexual couples.

Furthermore, the high level of promiscuity amongst the gay community has the potential to create a new-wave style of divorce. Of course, it can be argued that gay marriage may bring about a greater loyalty factor.

Gay couples who are willing to make a lifetime commitment to each other should be allowed make a legal declaration/statement by way of an 'oath of fidelity', which would be state approved.

IS THE CONSTITUTION'S REFERENCE TO WOMAN'S 'LIFE WITHIN THE HOME' A DATED ONE THAT SHOULD BE CHANGED?
and
SHOULD THE RIGHTS OF A NATURAL MOTHER HAVE EXPRESS CONSTITUTIONAL PROTECTION?
and
WHAT RIGHTS SHOULD A NATURAL FATHER HAVE, AND HOW SHOULD THEY BE PROTECTED?

Social studies have proved that the decline of father-hood is a major force behind many of the most disturbing social problems that plague the modern west-world society. Modern governing structures (i.e. family law court and its agents) have acted to destroy the operational framework that sustains the civil society by undermining the traditional stability of the family unit and family relationships.

God, from the time of Adam and Eve, created social and cultural norms by which children were reared in the midst of two unique parents – a mother and a father. The network of rights and obligations that is naturally entrusted within parents is the mainstay of social stability. Parenthood by its very nature offers the care, guidance and developmental support to children that are necessary to ensure the moral and social foundation of future generations.

The gift of parenthood is the most poignant, spiritual, responsible and important role that most people experience – and it is the force of its social obligations and protections that ensures the most congenial climate for the development and fulfilment of human personality. Does the state, with its propensity to relegate the role of fatherhood, seriously believe that motherhood alone can sustain the stability and fruition of mankind? The forces of biology, tradition, culture, social ethics and the doctrines of all main religions recognise the importance of the respective roles of both parents.

The Constitution must, therefore, promote the well-being of the traditional two-parent family. Further, it must establish equal rights and responsibilities for both men and women, in matrimonial and family law, and in the social security provisions for families. The state must also recognise the interdependence of men and women, the balance of their roles, and their need for mutual respect.

SHOULD THE RIGHTS OF THE CHILD BE GIVEN EXPANDED CONSTITUTIONAL PROTECTION?
and
DOES THE CONSTITUTION NEED TO BE CHANGED IN VIEW OF THE UN CONVENTION ON THE RIGHTS OF THE CHILD?

The family, marriage, parenthood and children should each have defined, but coherent, provisions within the revised Constitution.

An article governing the constitutional rights of children must be very carefully considered. The Review Group recommendation to include 'an express requirement that in all actions concerning children, whether by legislative, judicial or administrative authorities, the best interests of the child shall be the paramount consideration' would not on its own be substantiated to the welfare of children. The principle, which is prevalent in the family law court, only ensures that the interests of the parties to a case, i.e. the father and mother, are secondary to the interests of others – i.e. of the children's interests. We do not know of any other area of civil law in which the interests of others come before the parties to a case.

The application of the principle ensures that the rights of capable parents over their own children are assumed by a judge against the wishes of these parents. It should be noted that this principle was introduced without public approval or knowledge.

The principle has allowed judges to subvert the written law, and to ensure that many parents are cut off from involvement in their children's lives for no good reason. The reason that they are cut off in reality is that the mother, most often, wanted this and judges will not bring sanctions against the mother. This has resulted in the disenfranchisement of decent fathers from their children by the law and its agents who disingenuously claim to be acting in the best interests of the children.

This is a very, very serious matter. The best interests of the children principle cannot be realised unless the best interests of the family and parenthood are fully protected. It cannot be the case that the state is citing the best interests of the Children principle in one hand, whilst it is fragmenting the family relationships of the same children on the other hand.

The US publication *Family Law Quarterly* noted, as far back as 1984, that the majority view of the psychiatric and pediatric profession is that mothers and fathers are equal as parents. There has been an abundance of studies since then indicating fathers as equally qualified parents.

The legal system uses an indeterminate criteria, pseudo-named a 'standard' called the 'best interests of the child standard'. If the courts were honest in their use of the 'best interests of the child' then so much social science information and information that 'the primary negative aspect of divorce reported by children in numerous studies was loss of contact with a parent' could not be ignored so easily.

The other banana skin concerning the rights of the child relates to 'the expressed wishes of the child'. Article 12 of the UN Convention on the Rights of the Child states: 'State parties shall assure to the child who is capable of forming his or her own views the right to express those views freely in all matters affecting the child …' The real problem here is that the overt views of the child may be fear induced on the part of one parent, whilst the covert wishes of the child to have a normal relationship with the other parent is hidden. This also jeopardises Article 9 of the Convention which states: 'State parties shall ensure that a child shall not be separated from his or her parents against their will.'

Children placed in such a scenario, whereby they have been programmed to make false statements, have been emotionally and psychologically abused. The state and its agents may further traumatise such children by placing them into very untenable and sensitive situations, whereby they become active players in the destruction of their own families.

The only way to overcome this is for the appropriate competent authorities to undertake causation investigations (the present trend is to do consequential investigations) and parental assessments (the present trend is for psychiatric reports) that would include PAS perpetration evaluations (alienating intentions and behaviours). Contrary to the Rad-Fem argument, the existence of PAS in children and alienating behaviours in parents are easily identifiable. The FFAI have developed programmes on this.

Any reference to eliciting the 'expressed wishes of children' must be preceded by reference to the fact that all preparatory and environmental factors are considered so as to ensure that the wishes of the children are, indeed, their own and have been carefully considered through their own logical thought processes.

An article or paragraph pertaining to the rights of children should embody the general purpose of the UN Convention on the Rights of the Child, but further, it must embrace the 'umbrella' principle that children have the right to identity, parenthood and their natural family.

The FFAI adopts the principle that the *paramount interests of the family and family relationships* are a prerequisite to *'serving the best interests of the child'*.

THE FAMILY FIRST ASSOCIATION RECOMMENDATIONS IN BRIEF

Article 40.1
Add
Include reference to family law

Article 41.1
No change
Remain without alteration

Article 41.2
Delete and replace
Rewrite paragraph so as to provide recognition and protection to 'parenthood' (i.e. all biological and adoptive parents).

Article 41.3.1
No change
Remain without alteration

Article 41.3.2
Delete sub-paras. ii-iv and replace
Embrace proactive commitment on part of state to take all reasonable and practical steps to: (1) support the family unit and maximise its stability and (2) promote good behaviour in the family and in partnerships bonded through parenthood. Ultimately 'a Court designated by law may grant a dissolution of marriage', but only as a last resort.

Article 41.3.3
No change
Remain without alteration

Article 42.1- 4
No change
Remain without alteration

Article 42.5
Amend to read
'In exceptional cases, where *it is proven that* parents for physical or moral reason ...'

Add as Article 42.6
'The state shall make all positive steps to reunite and/or maintain family relationships in circumstances where it has acted as guardian ....'

Definition of family
Yes
As per the UN broad definition

Balance between rights of the family and rights of individual members
Yes, but with sensitivity/provision to prevent further abuse of family and familial relationships
Family unit/relationships to have precedence with rights of individual members distinctive/interdependent in terms of spousal, parenting and contributory roles.

Provision of constitutional protection to families not based on marriage
Yes
Achieve through: (1) adoption of UN broad definition of family and (2) recognition and protection of 'parenthood' (as 41.2 above).

Should gay couples be allowed to marry?
No, but some public provision/acceptance to be allowed
No to gay marriage, but a legal statement (oath of fidelity) would be state introduced and publicly approved.

Constitution references to woman's life, natural mothers and natural fathers, etc
Yes. Emphasis on equality and parenthood
Rights of men and women, mothers and fathers to have an equitable basis. Constitution to embrace and protect the role of parenthood.

Expanded constitutional protection for the Rights of the Child /UN Convention on the Rights of the Child
Yes, but with sensitivity/provision to prevent further emotional and psychological abuse of children
Agree to adoption of constitution rights of the child, but: (1) paramount interests of the family and family relationships to have precedence and (2) better safeguards and detection of emotionally and psychologically programmed/traumatised children.

The Family First Association would welcome improvements to the Constitution, particularly in relation to the rights and recognition of parenthood and the family, they being the fundamental prerequisites to serving the best interests of children and the general society.

The FFAI fears that there exists an unwritten agenda among legislators that: (a) accepts that the family law court system is above, or peripheral, to the ethos of the Constitution and (b) the paragraphs of the Constitution relating to the family will be diluted to appease the adversarial and elongated (profit based) practices of the family law court system.

Ultimately, the FFAI urges that a complete overhaul of the family law court system be undertaken so as to comply with the ethos of a more proclaimed Constitution.

FAMILY AND LIFE

PART 1 INTRODUCTION TO THE QUESTION

1 Why the question?

Should Irish law change its definition of the family? Why is this question being asked in the first place? Family and Life is well aware of the changed social and economic conditions over the past half century, all of which have affected the family and family life in Ireland. We are also aware that certain lobby groups want changes in this area. But there is more. Over the past half century the very concept of the family has been subject to adverse criticism, especially by influential writers in the social sciences. Today, the family's negative image has filtered into mainstream opinion, especially in academic, professional and media circles. Before deciding that the constitutional definition of the family should change (be deleted, expanded or replaced?), the legislators should be aware of what has happened to the family in our western culture over the past fifty years.

2 Two competing definitions

What is the family? There are two *competing* definitions today. One defines the family as based on the marriage of a man and woman for life. Let's call this the *traditional* or *normative* family. The second definition is vague and general, and includes any grouping of individuals, any domestic arrangement that claims the name of 'family'. This allows for a *variety of families*, all of which have an equal claim to be 'family'. Let's call this the pluralist family.

A new definition, often touted as 'the United Nations definition', but not found in any UN human rights document, goes thus: 'Any combination of two or more persons who are bound together by ties of mutual consent, birth and/or adoption or placement and who, together, assume responsibility for, *inter alia*, the care and maintenance of group members, the addition of new members through procreation or adoption, the socialisation of children and the social control of members'.

This definition is minimal, allowing two or more people to combine (whatever that means) by 'mutual consent' and so form a family. According to this definition, there is no normative family, only various combinations. One obvious consequence would be the privatisation of 'family' since no legislation could adequately cover such a polymorphous social reality.

The above definition dispenses with marriage and gender, lifelong commitment and exclusivity. The minimum is 'the ties of mutual consent' which covers about every 'combination' of humans. If the government were to redefine the family in the name of 'inclusiveness', then where would it stop? Polygamy, multi-partner unions, child-adult unions?

3 The deconstruction of the family

In the 1970s fashionable academics predicted the end of the traditional family. They claimed to have discovered that it was a repressive and toxic institution. Making use of the ideology of deconstruction and critical theory, they described the family as a 'social construct', one of society's norms that has mistakenly been understood as rooted in nature but in reality was a creation of society. Some feminists applied Marxist analysis to condemn the family as an instrument of 'patriarchal oppression of women', and called for its abolition. Sexual liberationists objected to the family because it disapproved of sexual activity outside of marriage. 'Gays' and lesbian theorists attacked the family for excluding sexual minorities.

These and other theorists called for the abolition of the family or its radical redefinition to include all and any form of domestic arrangements or 'family forms'. According to this view, it is erroneous to think that there is one, unchanging family form; the family should be understood as a social reality in constant flux, in perpetual evolution.

Feminist groups, following a Neo-Marxist hermeneutic, defined the normative family as an instrument of patriarchal oppression. If motherhood is an essential part of women's nature, then women's role in society is defined as being a wife and mother, staying at home and rearing children.

4 Two incompatible theories of the family

The first view may be called constructivist. According to this, gender is a social construct that has varied in different times and places. The roles of father, mother and children are socially constructed by the culture we grow up in. Unlike our parents, we can choose – in the light of this discovery – from a spectrum of behaviours rather than be forced into one of two clear and separate roles.

For example, in the nineteenth century the nuclear family with its clearly differentiated roles for men and women was dominant but today it is in terminal decline. A variety of family forms exist, and should be encouraged by governments. Our enlightened generation understands that it is pointless to seek for a definition of the family, because, like other human constructs, there is no absolute family-reality but a constantly shifting process with no final conclusion.

The second view may be called realist. It points to the existence of the family as a constant in every culture in the history of the human race. Human beings are male or female and the family based on marriage is a natural and constant social reality in society. Motherhood and fatherhood are based on human nature, although there are various ways in which these gender roles express themselves in different cultures. To that extent there is a degree of social construction.

For the constructivist 'all is politics'. This bears on the meaning of law (positivist), human rights (relative) and politics – the on-going process of change, power and reconstruction. There are no absolutes, no limits to change, and no unchanging norms of behaviour, gender roles and families. Human rights accepted today may be changed tomorrow (the rulers of China would be happy with that).

For the realist one must look beyond the apparent diversity of place and people to the unchanging nature of human existence. Philosophers discover this nature, legislators recognise and respect it. Universal rights flow from the innate dignity of human beings, and governments do not grant such rights because these rights are independent of politics (apolitical and pre-political). The family whose essential value lies in child rearing is one such constant.

Behind these competing views of law and human rights, there is a set of philosophical assumptions. The Marxist/socialist thinking held that the institutions of capitalism were socially constructed and would wither away. In 1917 in Russia the state abolished marriage and the family, as well as gender roles. Within a few years, appalled at the social chaos, the government revived marriage and the family. Although communism now belongs to the past, some of its ideas remain popular in western academic circles, especially in the social sciences.

This is the context of the battle over the meaning of marriage and the family.

5 The disestablishment of the family

Responding to these theories of the social sciences, many western governments instituted policies and laws that were unfriendly to the family, despite the lip service that all political parties pay. Increasingly they treated the family based on marriage as an out-of-date institution and at best regarded as a private and individual choice, similar to a religious belief. More recently, feminist and gay groups have gained legal recognition for 'civil unions' and have initiated legal moves to redefine marriage as gender blind, as in Canada.

Government policies introduced easy divorce, accepted cohabitation, abolished the family wage and favoured both parents in full-time work, reduced/abolished tax allowances for wives and children, and gave generous financial support to one-parent households. The loss of family vigour has led to a huge rise in maladjusted young people.

6 The cost of family experiments

Few people would deny that these social changes have resulted in a major weakening of family life, and have come at a huge financial cost to society. The administration of divorce, and the support of single-parent families require major allocation of resources. More serious, if harder to measure, are the social problems arising – the devaluation of the marriage commitment, the psychological damage of family breakdown to adults and children, the long-term effects of broken families in terms of sickness and criminality, and the huge rise in maladjusted children and young people.

After half a century of easy divorce more marriages are likely to end in divorce than remain intact, increasing

numbers of younger people choose cohabitation rather than marriage, large numbers of children are born out of wedlock and grow up without fathers, and the number of units headed by a single parent with children has steadily increased.

Without doubt, Ireland has been influenced by these trends. Yet, there is no iron law that its legislators should follow the example of countries like Britain. 'Progressive' social experiments should be examined pragmatically, and if they don't work, should be rejected.

7 A definition of the family

The Irish Constitution's concept of the family is clear. It is the social unit based on the marriage of one man and one woman. The members of the unit belong to it through marriage, birth, blood ties or adoption. This for the Constitution is the 'normative' family, and it belongs to universal law, human nature, and is therefore prior to the state.

PART II ARGUMENT AND RECOMMENDATIONS

1 The normative family is part of universal human rights

In 1948 the United Nations proclaimed the authoritative 'Universal Declaration of Human Rights' (UDHR). This declaration is the foundation of all subsequent international instruments for human rights.

The UDHR was the world's response to the horrific violations of human rights in World War II, made public in the Nuremburg war crimes trials. Universal human rights are not dependent on positive law, political majorities or social fashions. They supercede national laws and are universal. After the Nuremburg trials at the end of World War II, the United Nations solemnly stated that there is a higher law than the laws of individual states, to which all owe respect and acceptance. The preamble to UDHR affirms unambiguously that the rights enumerated are 'inherent' and 'inalienable', and not dependent on political acceptance but arise from our human dignity.

Since the call for the redefinition of the family is made in the name of human rights, it may come as a surprise to some that the United Nations and the Council of Europe placed the normative family in the context of human rights that are universal, fundamental and inalienable, and an institution that all states have a duty to respect and protect.

2 The basic unit of society

The UDHR speaks of the normative family in Article 16. In 16.1 it speaks of the basic right to marry and found a family. Then, in Article 16.3, it states, 'The family is the natural and fundamental group unit of society and is entitled to protection by society and the state.' This is very similar to what was written about the family in the Irish Constitution in 1937.

Later, in Article 25 it speaks further about the breadwinner of the family that 'has the right to a standard of living adequate for the health and well-being of himself and of his family, including food, clothing, housing and medical care and necessary social services, and the right to security in the event of unemployment, sickness, disability, widowhood, old age or other lack of livelihood in circumstances beyond his control.'

Article 25.2 states, 'Motherhood and childhood are entitled to special care and assistance. All children, whether born in or out of wedlock, shall enjoy the same social protection.'

A series of legally binding instruments followed the authoritative UN Declaration of Human Rights (1948), which defined the family as the basic cell of society (Article 16, §§1,2,3). The European Convention on Human Rights, arts. 8 and 12, the Convention of Civil and Political Rights (1966), Article 23, and the American Convention of Human Rights (1978), Article 17 repeat and reinforce the UDHR.

Once again, as in the Irish Constitution, these basic human rights documents understand the family as the normative family.

If the normative family is 'the fundamental unit of society', and if it is part of the basic human right of men and women, how can governments follow policies that weaken the family, or even abolish it? In Nordic countries where governments have neglected the family for decades, the normative family is a minority among the various forms of 'families'. From the United Nations UDHR, the state is bound to support the normative family, and to do the opposite is to violate basic human rights.

Children, according to the UN Convention on the Rights of the Child (1989), have a right to know and be raised with and by their biological parents – a mother and a father – and, if that is not possible, with adoptive parents that are similar, that is, a mother and a father (Article 7).

It is an injustice to intend to bring a child into the world to raise him or her alone or in a homosexual household.

3 Ireland's Constitution

What does the Irish Constitution say about the family? Article 41 states, *inter alia* that:

'The State recognises the Family as the natural primary and fundamental unit group of Society,'

'... guarantees to protect the Family...'

'... shall endeavour to ensure that mothers shall not be obliged by economic necessity ...' to work outside the home,

'... guard with special care the institution of Marriage ...'.

The importance of the family is recognised by our own Constitution when it describes the family 'as the necessary basis of social order and as indispensable to the welfare of the Nation and the State' (Article 41.1.2.). The Greek Constitution expresses the same conviction when it describes the family as 'the foundation of the conservation and the progress of the nation'. Article 16

of the Social Charter of Europe (1961), Article 23 of the International Treaty on Civil Rights, Article 10 of the International Charter on Economic, Social and Cultural Rights as well as many other national and international instruments both affirm and develop this basic insight that the family is the nucleus of society, and for that reason is deserving of special status, development and care. Ireland's Constitution is not a symbolic document nor a set of hazy ideals that have little connection with legislation and judicial decisions. It is the supreme law of the state against which all judicial and legislative acts must be measured.

PART III SPECIAL QUESTIONS

1 Cohabitation or *de facto* unions

It is a fact that cohabitation has increased greatly over the past generation. Its very existence side by side with married couples weakens people's perception of marriage as a permanent commitment. That would be greatly increased, were cohabiting couples to be given legal recognition.

There was a time when it would have been difficult in Ireland to get married without an expensive religious ceremony. This was the reason for the refusal of some cohabiting couples to get married. Today a man and a woman can get married with the minimum of expense at a registry office that offers a purely secular marriage ceremony.

When people choose cohabitation in place of the married state they do so from an unwillingness to commit themselves to a permanent union. They wish to give each other the freedom to end the relationship when they choose. This is the essence of cohabitation just as permanence is the essence of marriage.

It seems illogical, on one hand, for the government to want to give cohabitees legal recognition and, on the other, for cohabitees to seek for the legal benefits of married couples. As the *Report of the Constitution Review Group* noted [p. 319f], it would be a legal nightmare to work out what a 'permanent' cohabitation is.

While recognising that some cohabitations last many years, offer stable homes for children and have the appearances of a family based on marriage, cohabitation of its nature is not a permanent or secure arrangement. Even where divorce is easily available, cohabitations fail three times more frequently than marriages. 'The evidence is irrefutable. Unmarried parents are five times more likely to break up than married parents.' (Frontpage report, *The Times*, February 5, 2005)

A family based on marriage offers children the best hope of a stable home-life. The law and government policy should encourage those who have children – or intend to – to be married. This remains in the 'best interests of the child'.

2 Single-parent families

Over the past twenty years the number of single-parent families has increased, largely due to the break-up of cohabiting couples rather than divorce or legal separation. Most of these families are headed by a woman (and even where the father wants to share the upbringing of his children, the family courts often prevent this happening) and few are the result of the woman's first choice. Although such women are slow to enter into a second relationship, having had a 'bad experience' with men, most realise that being a single-parent does no favours to either mother or child[ren].

This does not negate the fact that single mothers often bring up children successfully, whether the absence of the father is due to death or, as now is common, to an unwillingness of the man to accept the role of fatherhood.

While the government should support one-parent families, it is flying in the face of the evidence to say that 'all families are equal'.

3 Gender-neutral marriage

In Scandinavia, Canada and other countries there is a campaign to redefine marriage as gender neutral, that is, open to same-sex couples. This is a stage in a long development to weaken marriage and the family.

Why does the gay lobby seek the status of an institution that many have written off as outdated and bourgeois, and has been largely abandoned in certain countries? Why do gays want to change their legally-supported partnerships for the status of marriage? One, for the respect that marriage gives, and two, for all the family rights to which marriage is the door, the main one being the right to adoption. If the law defined marriage as gender neutral, gays and lesbians would have all the rights of married people. Further, the state's educational presentation would have to include the gay dimension, and all institutions, especially churches, would be required to accept this dimension.

Same-sex family couples would be a social experiment of huge social consequence. Can legislators experiment with children when all that we know tells us that girls and boys need both a father and a mother?

4 Unmarried fathers and mothers

We take note that unmarried fathers and mothers only have personal rights, since they do not form a family as defined by the Constitution. This is not unjustified discrimination since the essential element of a family is missing, namely the stability of the parents as a couple. The non-recognition of an unmarried couple should be no hindrance to the state's efforts to support the child.

5 Mothers at home

Apropos of Article 41.2.1-2, we repudiate the theory that women's equality with men will only be achieved when all women work outside the home, and share statistically fifty-fifty with men in every area of employment. This theory refuses to acknowledge the differences between men and women, and take note of the actual desires of women who want to stay home, even at the price of a loss of income.

There is increasing evidence in western countries that many working women would prefer to be at home with their young children but are forced to take full-time work for financial reasons.

There is evidence that even high quality (and expensive) childcare cannot have the same value as a mother's undivided care for her young children. Does paid childcare answer the needs of small children? Or those of working parents?

There is evidence that, rather than juggle a career with children, women are postponing having children, having fewer children, and then often experiencing serious fertility problems.

The Irish Constitution calls on the government to 'endeavour to ensure that mothers shall not be obliged by economic necessity' to work outside the home. Is this so out of date? Or does it offend feminist theory? We suggest that many mothers in Ireland regret the government's neglect of this constitutional exhortation and the Supreme Court's refusal to support it. Today, there is every need to retain it in the Constitution.

CONCLUSION

The Committee must consider two things, the common good of the community and, closely related, the best interests of children.

It should be obvious that the common good of the people of Ireland will benefit from stable families that rear healthy children. They are the future of the country, and their health – mental and physical – is essential to that future. On the contrary, if families are unstable – by divorce, desertion, serial marriage, domestic violence, poverty – then the common good is weakened now and in the future.

Are the best interests of children likely to be served by adopting a loose definition of the family, and giving equal status to all forms of family? The social sciences have done much research on the family, especially in those countries where the consequences of the social changes of the 1960s were obvious. Researchers have a much better understanding of the problems children face as they become adults, and they have found that not all 'family forms' are equally good places to bring up children.

Children are not happier and do not thrive equally in all families. Divorce, single-parent households, absent fathers or mothers have produced a generation of unhappy children, some who fare badly at school, and become unstable adults with a high risk of criminal behaviour. In contrast, the children of stable families tend to have a more settled home life, do better at school and, in the main, become productive citizens.

The Government cannot and should not apologise for insisting that other forms of relationship are not of the same nature and status as that of marriage and the family.

RECOMMENDATIONS

Family and Life offers the following recommendations to the Committee:

1 The decision of a man and a woman to marry, thereby forming a family, is not only a private choice but a public act of social importance. Therefore the state has a very real interest in safeguarding marriage and the family.

2 It should be recognised that the legal and financial benefits given to the family based on marriage are not privileges or inequalities, but arise from the recognition by the state that the family has a vital role in society, and the benefits are in recognition of the obligations undertaken.

3 The family is directed to the production and rearing of children and, however challenged this may be by contemporary culture, it is the reason why the family remains the basic unit of society.

4 Children are most likely to thrive in families with fathers and mothers in a permanent relationship. Thriving children will do well at school, learn to work with other people, and as adults make a positive contribution to the health of society.

5 Government policies and legislation should not be neutral about the normative family. They should support the normative family as enshrined in the Constitution.

6 In the 'best interests of the child', public policy should continue to support the normative family.

7 The laws of the country should encourage citizens to choose to form a family based on marriage.

8 The Committee should ignore political correctness, and give serious thought to the possibility that by their work within the home women give to the state a support without which the common good cannot be achieved.

9 The government should reform the family court procedures and policy to ensure that separated or divorced fathers are able to continue the shared rearing of their children as far as circumstances allow.

FAMILY AND MEDIA ASSOCIATION

1 HOW SHOULD THE FAMILY BE DEFINED?

Article 41.1.1 of the Irish Constitution recognises the importance of the family for the good of society. It states: 'The State recognises the Family as the natural primary and fundamental unit group of Society, as a moral institution possessing inalienable and imprescriptible rights, antecedent and superior to all positive law.'

Those who framed the Irish Constitution which was passed in a referendum by the people, understood that the family comprise one man and one woman, who have officially married, and the children of their union. Experience has shown that this is the best arrangement for the rearing of children. The family does not need to, nor should, be redefined.

2 HOW SHOULD ONE STRIKE THE BALANCE BETWEEN THE RIGHTS OF THE FAMILY AS A UNIT AND THE RIGHTS OF THE INDIVIDUAL MEMBERS?

This balance is struck naturally in every functional family. The issue of personal rights is dealt with in Article 40.3.1 of the Constitution. If a situation should arise where personal rights are being denied, the individual(s) may have recourse to counselling and to the courts.

3 IS IT POSSIBLE TO GIVE CONSTITUTIONAL PROTECTION TO FAMILIES OTHER THAN THOSE BASED ON MARRIAGE?

The best arrangement, as briefly stated in our answer to 1, has constitutional protection. In the case of heterosexual cohabiting couples, they are free to marry if they wish. Otherwise they are free to make legal contracts in relation to inheritance etc. in the long term or, for the circumstances of the break up of their relationships, in the short term.

In the Supreme Court judgment in the case of the *Government v An Bord Uchtála* (1980) the late Judge Brian Walsh said that '... orphaned children who are members of a family whose parents died continue to be a family for the purposes of the Constitution. The family is recognised as the fundamental unit group of society founded on marriage and the fact that the married parents of the children have died does not alter the character of the unit.'

4 SHOULD GAY COUPLES BE ALLOWED TO MARRY?

One of the main purposes of marriage is the having and/or rearing of children. Homosexual coupling is a sterile arrangement. Experience, backed by research, shows that only marriage provides the stable environment which children need for healthy psychological and emotional development. It is important to recognise this for the sake of the welfare of the state and the common good. Homosexual marriages would be inimical to this. Our answer to the question therefore is no.

5 IS THE CONSTITUTION'S REFERENCE TO WOMAN'S 'LIFE WITHIN THE HOME' A DATED ONE THAT SHOULD BE CHANGED?

Surveys have shown that, while most women would prefer to remain at home rearing their children, many cannot do so because of economic necessity. Article 41.2.1 of the Constitution recognises the contribution that women in the home give to the state 'without which the common good cannot be achieved.' And in Article 2.2.2 the state is committed to 'ensure that mothers shall not be obliged by economic necessity to engage in labour [outside the home] to the neglect of their duties in the home.'

The state has not lived up to its responsibilities in this matter. Its policies have reduced support for children: tax individualisation – which discriminated against single-income families – high costs of crèches and home help, money which would be better spent by the state in supporting mothers in the home. Our answer to the question is no.

6 SHOULD THE RIGHTS OF THE NATURAL MOTHER HAVE EXPRESS CONSTITUTIONAL PROTECTION?

No. The mother already has the support of the Constitution and deviations from it should not be accepted. Presumably, reference is being made in the question to mothers bearing children outside wedlock or to mothers separated from their husbands. Such mothers already have rights to their children and can avail of social welfare support and taxation rights.

7 WHAT RIGHTS SHOULD NATURAL FATHERS HAVE, AND HOW SHOULD THEY BE PROTECTED?

Such rights would be difficult to define, as natural fatherhood may result, and range, from casual, once-off intercourse to more committed relationships. It would be difficult to generalise in this area. The courts should judge each case on its own merits.

8 SHOULD THE RIGHTS OF THE CHILD BE GIVEN AN EXPANDED CONSTITUTIONAL PROTECTION?

The child already has rights as a human being independent of the family. More emphasis on the rights of the child would mean more external intervention, not necessarily in the best interests of the child.

9 DOES THE CONSTITUTION NEED TO BE CHANGED IN VIEW OF THE UN CONVENTION ON THE RIGHT OF THE CHILD?

See the answer to 8. Like most UN conventions, it reads quite blandly. UN conventions are often perversely interpreted by monitoring committees outside the parameters that member states originally signed. Our answer to the question is no.

CONCLUSION

Most of the population of this country are Christian and there is a strong Christian influence in our Constitution in terms of human rights. Not everybody believes in Christ but most reasonable people would accept that as a man, he was a wise humanist with a particular love of the poor, for families and children.

A written Constitution represents what a people are, their values, their aspirations and so forth. We should be very reluctant to change ours and particularly so in relation to the family.

FAMILY SOLIDARITY – BALLYROAN BRANCH

The above Branch wishes to reply to your invitation to make a submission regarding the current definition of the family within the Constitution and the need to make any alteration to the rights and privileges thereby given to both the family and the institution of marriage.

This Branch is very concerned that notwithstanding the erosion that has already been allowed to occur to the constitutional pledges regarding the family, further undermining of the concept of the family is now being contemplated.

1 The family as already stated in Article 41.1.1. and 41.3.1 should be left intact. It is the duty of the state to protect the institution of the family based on marriage of male and female for the procreation of new life, which is the life blood for the existence of the nation.

2 The personal rights common to all citizens is guaranteed by Article 41.3.1. The rights of family and individuals are complementary. Every person is directly or indirectly part of a family unit.

3 Trying to cater in the Constitution for cohabiting couples would damage the status of the traditional family. Siblings or other members living together need to have legislation introduced to regulate the distribution of property etc.

4 The legal rights to marriage, the union of man and woman, must be protected as it creates a secure environment for the protection of children. Adopting parents and the children they adopt must be given the same protection as natural parents. Homosexual and lesbian relationships are sterile and must not be given the status of family. Under no circumstances should homosexual or lesbian couples be allowed to adopt children. It is by its very nature an unhealthy environment in which to rear children. Most parents would suffer great distress if they thought that in the event of their death or other circumstances, the state would sanction the right of homosexuals or lesbians to adopt their children.

5 Under no circumstances should Article 41.2 be altered. It is well established that children reared in families where the mother stays at home are less likely to go astray. Many of the ills now rampant in our society can be attributed to the state introducing legislation that has undermined traditional family values, i.e. contraception and divorce to mention two. It is sad that mothers have been pressurised to leave the home by successive governments in the past, cutting down on the support for children and the introduction of tax individualisation measures which discriminate against single income facilities.

6 The rights of the natural mother are already adequately protected within the constitutional family under Articles 40 and 41.

7 Catering for the rights of the natural father outside the context of the constitutional family and marriage should be a matter for the courts.

8 The rights of children are already adequately protected within the Constitution and should be upheld by the state.

9 The Constitution should not be changed to cater for the Convention on the Rights of the Child as this has been seen to give rise to outrageous interpretations which would seriously damage the concept of the family and could interfere with parental duties in the rearing of their children.

In line with the above observations this Branch contends that to proceed with any of the constitutional changes outlined would substantially lessen the protection enjoyed by the family and thereby give rise to serious damage to the fabric of society.

FAMILY SUPPORT AGENCY

The Family Support Agency was formally established on 6 May 2003. The strategic plan of the agency was submitted to Minister Coughlan, November 2003. The agency hosted a conference in October 2004 and published its first annual report in November 2004. The Committee is referred to the plan, report and conference material. [For copies of these documents, please see the Family Support Agency.] The Family Support Agency is one of the main government agencies responsible for supporting families.

The board is made up of a number of members with wide-ranging experience and interests, and whose focus is on the support and welfare of families.

The Family Support Agency Act, 2001 does not define the family. In preparing the strategic plan, the board acknowledged the diversity of family life in Ireland today. The plan did not limit its scope to the family based on marriage in the strategic plan. The various agencies, services or centres do not restrict their work to such families.

The Committee is charged with the task of reviewing the Constitution in its entirety and examining in particular Articles 41, 42 and 40.3 to ascertain the extent to which they are serving the good of individuals and the community, with a view to deciding whether changes in them would bring about a greater balance between the two.

The board is making its submission in general terms based on the experience of its members, the work of the agencies and services and its responsibility and experience in family-related matters and to give voice to the conflicts of rights that can arise in reality. It is understood that a separate submission is being made by the Family Affairs Unit of the Department of Social and Family Affairs.

At the outset the board would like to make a number of general observations. The 1937 Constitution links marriage and the family. Article 41.3.1 states: 'the State pledges itself to guard with special care the institution of marriage, on which the family is founded and to protect it against attack.'

The board acknowledges that the family based on marriage (even with the availability of divorce) provides a stable framework for spouses and their children, and that society as a whole and the state benefit from the support spouses give to each other. The recognition and support that the unit receives from the extended family and friends is also important. Family life based on the commitment of marriage is an ideal which should be fostered and encouraged as it provides a solid foundation for society as a whole. It also ensures that the state adheres to the various commitments given in international conventions such as the European Convention on Human Rights, the European Social Charter, and the European Social Charter on Fundamental Rights.

However, the reality now is that many families are not based on marriage and many marriages do not give rise to children. With the advent of divorce, many people marry at an age when children are unlikely or not intended and therefore there will be no children of that marriage relationship, although both or either spouses in the marriage may have children of a previous marriage or other relationship. Increasingly statistics show there are a large number of children born to parents who are not married to each other and this figure is increasing.

Whether the present situation of the special place of the married family should be maintained in the Constitution is a matter for the Committee. If the right of the married family to constitutional protection is extended to provide constitutional protection for the rights of children, then a careful balancing approach needs to be taken to these different rights. Consideration could be given by the Committee to using the term 'family life'. The European Convention on Human Rights protects family life. Family life includes a broad range of relationships and focuses on the relationship between the people involved in creating family life rather than the legal structure from which that family life emanates. ECHR (European Court of Human Rights) is more concerned with substance than form and will look at the reality. It is a question of fact and degree.

There have been huge changes in family life since 1937. The reality of modern Irish life is that a growing number of adults and children are living in family relationships which are not based on marriage. The appendix attached to this memorandum shows a wide spectrum of such relationships.

The main objective of the Family Support Agency is to strengthen families, including parenting relationships for children, through the provision of family resource centres at community level, marriage, child and bereavement counselling services, a nationwide family mediation service as well as ongoing research into family related matters. (Further details are provided in the Strategic Plan and Annual report of the Agency which accompany the submission). [For copies of these documents, please see the Family Support Agency.]

RIGHTS OF CHILDREN

An increasing number of children are born into and are growing up in non-traditional family units. The present definition of the family in the Constitution (as based on marriage) excludes constitutional recognition of family life of an increasing proportion but still a minority, of people, including and especially children, in different family formations. The Constitution refers specifically to the importance of marriage, the family and the inalienable rights of parents, which cannot be undermined except if parents fail in their moral duty towards their children. The Constitution makes very little reference to the rights of the child save for the general principles contained in Article 42.5 that due regard shall be had to the natural and imprescriptible rights of the child. These rights are however not defined.

While society may benefit from stable family relationships based on marriage, children should not be disadvantaged by virtue of the fact that their parents are not married to each other or that the children are living in non-traditional family units.

Over the past two decades there has been much reforming legislation to reduce discrimination, for example the abolition of illegitimacy in the Status of Children Act, 1987, and the provision of joint custody of children in the Children Act, 1997.

This progress is piecemeal and fragmented. A major issue at the present time is the sense of alienation non-marital fathers feel towards their children. They do not have an automatic right of guardianship to their children as a married father does and they have no constitutional recognition for their role at present.

The board therefore feels that the Committee should focus on the rights and needs of the child. The Guardianship of Infants Act, 1964, which is the primary statutory framework for children, requires all decisions made in relation to the children to be in the best interests of the child and that those interests must be of the first and paramount consideration. It is now time to facilitate a broader and more inclusive definition of the family in a manner that will promote and foster the best interests principle.

LIFE WITHIN THE HOME

Article 41.2.1 provides that the state shall recognise that while her life is in the home a woman gives to the state a support without which the common good cannot be achieved. This concept is now outdated. Increasingly fathers share this role within the family. Often both a father and a mother may do so at different times for different lengths of time. The Family Support Agency also considers that joint parenting, of which this is a form, should be encouraged. The state should actively support families (and certainly should not discriminate) where a parent is providing full-time support to the other parent and children within the home. The state should also support parents who both work outside the home with appropriate facilities and services.

Appendix

DIFFERENT TYPES OF FAMILY LIFE

1 Mother and father married to each other and their biological children.
2 Mother and father married to each other and their adopted children.
3 The above parents separated or divorced.
4 The above parents as either widow or widower.
5 Parents who went through a ceremony of marriage with each other which was subsequently annulled by order of the Court.
6 Unmarried mother and her biological child.
7 Single parent with adopted child.
8 People who believe that they are validly married to each other on foot of a foreign divorce but the foreign divorce is not in fact capable of recognition and therefore the marriage will not be recognised under Irish law.
9 Mother from IVF, live sperm donation etc.
10 Mother and father not married to each other (but living together) with their biological children only.
11 Mother and father not married to each other (but living together) and child of mother and father from previous relationship, with or without their own children.
12 Mother and father not married to each other and not living together.
13 Persons standing *in loco parentis,* i.e. those people who assume a parental role over the child/children not their own.
14 Step parents.
15 Grandparents and grandchildren where the natural parents either or both are dead or not capable of rearing their own children.
16 Unmarried father and his child.
17 Partners of unmarried parent with child.
18 Partner of a married/separated/divorced parent or in a gay relationship with children of the marriage.
19 Siblings taking care of younger siblings.
20 Aunts/uncles/nieces/nephews acting *in loco parentis.*
21 Other difficult categories, surrogacy, families from polygamous marriages.

The legal definition is fixed and inflexible because of the constitutional definition and the rights of parents as primary educators and carers of their children.

FINE GAEL: MICHAEL COLLINS BRANCH, CORK SOUTH CENTRAL CONSTITUENCY

DEFINITION OF THE FAMILY

It would be better if the Constitution did not define the family; we feel that, where required, the general law of the state can be used to define the family.

RIGHTS OF FAMILY VERSUS RIGHTS OF THE INDIVIDUAL

The rights of the individual citizen are well defined in Article 40. We recommend no change.

GAY COUPLES BEING ALLOWED TO MARRY

The Constitution should not be changed: general law should give legal rights in the case of serious illness, succession etc. These should apply to any couple living together including gay couples of either sex and also siblings.

WOMAN'S ROLE

Outdated and should be omitted.

RIGHTS OF NATURAL MOTHER

When child is adopted natural mother's rights to child are conceded; right to privacy re adoption should be protected by general law rather than the Constitution

RIGHTS OF THE NATURAL FATHER

These rights should be relative to responsibilities accepted; where necessary the rights should be protected by general law rather than Constitution

EXPANDED CONSTITUTIONAL PROTECTION FOR RIGHTS OF THE CHILD

No. Should be defined in general law.

CHANGED IN VIEW OF UN CONVENTION ON RIGHTS OF CHILD

No. We do not recommend change.

FOCUS ON THE FAMILY IRELAND

INTRODUCTION

Focus on the Family Ireland is pleased to respond to the invitation for written submissions from the All-Party Oireachtas Committee on the Constitution, with regard to family rights in the Constitution.

Focus on the Family Ireland is a charitable organisation (CHY 14665), which supports, encourages and strengthens the family through education and resources.

Focus on the Family was founded in the US in 1977 by psychologist and best-selling author Dr James Dobson. With the experience gained by offices in eighteen countries around the world Focus on the Family is well placed to reach Irish families with support, encouragement and help.

Our services:

- Marriage and parenting seminars and conferences
- Family camps, giving parents and children time together, one-to-one.
- 'Take a Break' holiday weeks for single parent families
- Equipping families to pass on their faith and heritage – heritage builders
- Distributing quality resources, books, videos and magazines.

Focus on the Family Ireland is a wholly Irish owned organisation run and staffed by Irish people, with the backup and support of Focus on the Family's offices around the world. We aim to reach people at every stage of life from young children, through teens and young adults to parents and grandparents with timely advice, resources and programmes. Focus on the Family Ireland is founded on, and guided by, Christian principles and values.

CONSTITUTIONAL DEFINITION OF THE FAMILY

Bunreacht na hÉireann (the Constitution of Ireland) sets out its main provisions in relation to the family in Article 41 reproduced below.

The Family

Article 41

1 1° The State recognises the Family as the natural primary and fundamental unit group of Society, and as a moral institution possessing inalienable and imprescriptible rights, antecedent and superior to all positive law.

2° The State, therefore, guarantees to protect the Family in its constitution and authority, as the necessary basis of social order and as indispensable to the welfare of the Nation and the State.

2 1° In particular, the State recognises that by her life within the home, woman gives to the State a support without which the common good cannot be achieved.

2° The State shall, therefore, endeavour to ensure that mothers shall not be obliged by economic necessity to engage in labour to the neglect of their duties in the home.

3 1° The State pledges itself to guard with special care the institution of Marriage, on which the Family is founded, and to protect it against attack.

2° A Court designated by law may grant a dissolution of marriage where, but only where, it is satisfied that

i   at the date of the institution of the proceedings, the spouses have lived apart from one another for a period of, or periods amounting to, at least four years during the five years,

ii there is no reasonable prospect of a reconciliation between the spouses,

iii such provision as the Court considers proper having regard to the circumstances exists or will be made for the spouses, any children of either or both of them and any other person prescribed by law, and

iv any further conditions prescribed by law are complied with.

3° No person whose marriage has been dissolved under the civil law of any other State but is a subsisting valid marriage under the law for the time being in force within the jurisdiction of the Government and Parliament established by this Constitution shall be capable of contracting a valid marriage within that jurisdiction during the lifetime of the other party to the marriage so dissolved.

As can be seen above 'family' is never specifically defined in the constitution; nevertheless it is clear the intention of the authors was to so define the 'family' as one based on marriage (3.1). The Supreme Court judgement in *The State (Nicolaou) v An Bord Uchtála* interprets Article 41 as meaning the family based on the institution of marriage.

In the Ireland of 2005 there are now many 'families' which do not fit into the neat 'family based on marriage' definition. These families are often treated differently for social welfare purposes than for revenue and tax purposes, in one case as a 'family' and in another as individuals sharing a common address.

Focus on the Family Ireland agrees with the Report of the Constitution Review Group (1996) when it states that: '… the constitutional protection of the rights of any family unit other than a family based on marriage presents significant difficulties' for the many reasons stated therein, and for the additional reasons which we will argue in this submission.

There is little doubt that 'Family' is the fundamental building block of all human civilisations. If that is so then 'marriage' is the glue that holds it together (discussed further in next section). Focus on the Family Ireland believes that the health of our culture, its citizens and their children is intimately linked to the health and well-being of marriage. We therefore would not wish to see any change in the 'family based on marriage' constitutional definition of 'family'.

MARRIAGE

Marriage is the first human institution. Sociologically, marriage is the glue that holds communities together, regulates sexuality, civilises the home and provides for the proper development of the next generation.

Anthropologists tell us marriage, a permanent linking of men and women, is found in every civilised and uncivilised society throughout human history. However, the idea of marriage as an institution has lost favour with western society. In the past three decades we have seen a dramatic increase in rates of cohabitation, divorce, and single-parenting by choice. At the same time, marriage rates have significantly declined over this same period.

Over the past few decades huge amounts of research have been published on how family breakdown affects people. Scholars are finding that marriage has a far more important effect on society that was previously thought. Linda Waite and Maggie Gallagher, two leading sociologists in this area are quoted as saying, 'The evidence from four decades of research is surprisingly clear: a good marriage is both men's and women's best bet for a long and healthy life.'[1]

This powerful body of scientific inquiry reveals that *men and women who are in their first marriages, on average, enjoy significantly better qualities of physical and mental health than their peers in any other relational category.* As leading social scientist James Q. Wilson explains:

> Married people are happier than unmarried ones of the same age, not only in the United States, but in at least seventeen other countries where similar studies have been made. And there seems to be good reasons for that happiness. People who are married not only have higher incomes and enjoy greater emotional support, they tend to be healthier. Married people live longer than unmarried ones, not only in the United States but abroad.[2]

Dr Robert Coombs of UCLA reviewed more than 130 empirical studies on how marriage affects well-being. He found these studies indicate 'an intimate link between marital status and personal well being'.[3]

Professor George Akerlof, the 2001 Nobel Laureate in Economics, has highlighted compelling research that indicates the socialising influence of marriage for men. He explained, 'married men are more attached to the labour force, they have less substance abuse, they commit less crime, and are less likely to become victims of crime, have better health, and are less accident prone.' He found that cohabitation was incapable of providing these benefits because 'men settle down when they get married; if they fail to get married they fail to settle down.'[4]

There are many more studies and experts we could quote to support the benefits of marriage to society, but in the interests of being concise we will move on to look at *the impact of marriage on children.*

The relevant studies once again show the positive impact marriage has on children. *Children with married parents consistently do better in every measure of well-being than their peers in any other type of family arrangement.* And this is a stronger indicator of well-being than the race, economic or educational status of the parents. The US-based Centre for Law and Social

Policy recently reported: 'Most researchers now agree that ... studies support the notion that, on average, children do best when raised by their two married biological parents.'[5]

Sara McLanahan of Princeton University, a leading scholar on how family formation affects child well-being, finds in numerous studies that children raised with only one biological parent are about twice as likely to drop out of school than children being raised with two biological parents.[6] Children from married, two-parent families, on average have higher test scores, do better in exams, miss fewer days from school and have greater expectations of attending university than children living with one parent.

So all of the research is pointing to *one conclusion: marriage is good for society, good for parents and good for children*.

It is the function of government to enact social policy for the good of society as a whole. From the research it is clear that marriage, as between a man and a woman, needs to be encouraged, supported and defended for the good of individuals, families, children and society. We therefore would strongly support the current constitutional support for families based on marriage and would argue that if possible those supports should be increased rather than removed or reduced.

There have been calls from some quarters to grant 'equality of rights' as between married couples and those couples who are in cohabiting relationships. We do not see that as a valid option. As we have clearly argued, from the available research, marriage and cohabitation are *not* the equivalent relationships some would purport them to be; they have a different impact on individuals, their respective families and different impacts on society as a whole. For the good of society, parents and children, we support the retention of a distinction between married families and family units which are not based on marriage.

It is also our view that there does need to be a better balance between the constitutional protection of 'family based on marriage' and protection of individuals within family units which may not necessarily be based on marriage. We therefore would concur with the recommendation of the Report of the Constitution Review Group (1996) that while retaining the pledge by the state to protect the family based on marriage to also guarantee all individuals a *right to respect for their family life* whether that family is, or is not, based on marriage.

SAME-SEX MARRIAGE

The writers of the 1937 Constitution would never in their wildest dreams have contemplated allowing two people of the same sex to marry. Ireland, and the world, has changed out of all recognition in one generation. Marriage has always, for thousands of years, in every culture, been about bringing men and women together in a usually exclusive, domestic and sexual relationship. No human society, not one, has ever embraced homosexual marriage. It is not a part of the tradition of any human culture. Only in the last few 'nanoseconds' of history and experience have societies contemplated it. Homosexual unions, married or otherwise, have never been regarded as a *normal, morally equal* part of any society. Nonmarital same-sex unions have been tolerated in some places at some times, but have never been taken to be *morally equivalent* to marriage.

Marriage has always brought male and female together into committed sexual and domestic relationships in order to regulate sexuality and provide for the needs of daily life. Marriage ensures that children have the benefits of both their mother and their father, each in their distinctive and unique ways.

Together, these two aspects of marriage have been the means by which we build strong communities, generation after generation. As anthropologists tell us, these primary needs shape the family and social norms for all known societies.[7]

James Q. Wilson, professor emeritus in government at Harvard University, and one of the world's most emenient political scientists and social thinkers, brings clarity to what all societies need marriage to do:

> The purpose of marriage ... has always been to make the family secure, not to redefine what constitutes a family. The family is a more fundamental social reality than a marriage, and so pretending that anything we call a marriage can create a family is misleading ... By family, I mean a lasting, socially enforced obligation between a man and a woman that authorises sexual congress and the supervision of children .... There is no society where women alone care for each other and their children; there is none where fathers are not obliged to support their children and the mothers to whom they were born. Not only do men need women, women need men.[8]

This is what marriage is and needs to be; redefining marriage from this to something else is like putting a glass of water on the table beside a glass of clear, odourless and tasteless poison and saying that because they look, smell and taste the same they are the same. They are not: water is a unique joining of hydrogen and oxygen molecules in a particular combination which is necessary for life to exist; the other, while at first look seems to be the same thing, is poisonous, and leads to death.

The homosexual lobby argues that same-sex marriage is an issue of equality between homosexuals and heterosexuals, between two different orientations, on the surface a very persuasive argument; everyone is in favour of equality, aren't they? But we must look deeper into the issue to see the truth of the matter.

Homosexuals do have the right to marry, in the same way as everyone else; there are certain conditions that have been laid down, for good reasons, to regulate marriage:

• They are not already married.
• The other person is an adult and free to marry.

- The other person is not a close family member.
- The other person is someone of the opposite sex.

If these criteria are met then they can marry; no one is going to prevent them from marrying because they are gay. Current regulations don't prevent gays from marrying; they prevent gays from *redefining marriage* to something totally different by marrying a person of the same sex.

What about the issue of sexual orientation? Marriage has never been defined or regulated according to sexual orientation; in fact, the idea of sexual orientation has never previously been an issue in stable society. It has only come about because of the political activity of the homosexual lobby in gaining legitimacy for their opinions. No scientific institution in the world has ever established the immutability of homosexuality. Many scientists have tried, but none has ever succeeded. Homosexuality cannot be compared to genealogy or ethnic heritage which cannot be changed. In fact, Columbia University researchers William Byrne and Bruce Parsons carefully analysed all the major biological studies on homosexuality. Finding no studies that supported a purely biological cause for homosexuality they found the origins of homosexual identification rooted in a 'complex mosaic of biologic, psychological and social/cultural factors.'[9] Only two years ago, Professors Richard Friedman and Jennifer Downey, writing on the nature of sexual orientation, state:

> At clinical conferences one often hears that homosexual orientation is fixed and unmodifiable. Neither assertion is true .... [T]he assertion that homosexuality is genetic is so reductionistic that it must be dismissed out of hand as a general principle of psychology.[10]

Therefore it is wrong to assert that heterosexual and homosexual orientations are essentially the same and should therefore be treated equally. One is firmly rooted in nature and as a result is manifest as the foundation of all human civilisations. The other is far less common and the result of influences that are little understood and not intrinsic to human nature.

Focus on the Family Ireland would have grave difficulty with any attempt to redefine marriage beyond that of between a man and a woman. As we have shown, marriage is a unique pairing of male and female and to change that unique pairing would mean the death of marriage in the long term, by making it so generally ill defined that (ridiculous as it might seem) marriage could be possible between a mother and a daughter, and/or between a father and a son, in that event (currently illegal).

We would, however, like to see changes to the situation where people who are sharing a domestic arrangement, whether sexual or not (two unmarried brothers for example), are discriminated against in the matter of inheritance matters, hospital visits by 'next of kin' etc. This would not, in our view, require any constitutional change.

THE CONSTITUTIONAL REFERENCE TO WOMEN IN THE HOME

As we have stated previously Ireland has changed much since 1937 and the constitutional reference to women in the home has become somewhat of an anachronism. It is an important statement of principle for those parents who choose to remain in the home, in the interest of their families, and the value of this should not be underestimated.

The sentiment of Article 41.2 should be retained, as the undeniable benefits for both marriage and parenting of children specifically referred to above, goes to strengthen the family and family life. Where one or other spouse chooses to remain at home, to raise children particularly, he/she should not in any way be discriminated against, as this choice serves to strengthen the bedrock of family life and society based upon the family, which has been a tremendous strength in this nation for the past generations.

Should there be any proposed changes, we would recommend something expressing a similar sentiment but in a gender neutral fashion, as per the wording suggested in the Report of the Constitution Review Group (1996).

SUMMARY OF RECOMMENDATIONS

- We strongly hold that marriage is the glue that holds society together. Focus on the Family Ireland believes that the health of our culture, its citizens and their children is intimately linked to the health and well-being of marriage. We therefore would not wish to see any change in the 'family based on marriage' constitutional definition of 'family'.
- Marriage and cohabitation are not equal relationships, as is recognised in the commitments given to spouses, to one another when getting married, and engaging in a contract of marriage (and in the reverse, when seeking a dissolution of that marriage, as set out in Article 41.3.2 of the Constitution). Marriage and cohabitation have a different impact on individuals and their respective families, and different impacts on society as a whole. For the good of society, parents and children, we support the retention of a distinction between married families and family units which are not based on marriage.
- We would concur with the recommendation of the Report of the Constitution Review Group (1996) that while retaining the pledge by the state to protect the family based on marriage, to also guarantee all individuals a *right to respect for their family life* whether that family is, or is not, based on marriage.
- Focus on the Family Ireland would have grave difficulty with any attempt to redefine marriage beyond that of between a man and a woman. To quote Prof. James Q. Wilson again, 'The family is a more fundamental social reality than a marriage, and so pretending that anything we call a marriage

can create a family is misleading … By family, I mean a lasting, socially enforced obligation between a man and a woman that authorises sexual congress and the supervision of children ….' Redefining marriage would destroy it.

- If Article 41.2 is to be changed, it should be in a gender neutral fashion, as per the wording suggested in the Report of the Constitution Review Group (1996).

Notes

1 Linda J. Waite and Maggie Gallagher, *The Case For Marriage: Why Married People Are Happier, Healthier And Better Off Financially* (New York: Doubleday, 2000), p. 64.

2 James Q. Wilson, *The Marriage Problem: How Our Culture Has Weakened Families* (New York: Harper Collins 2002), p 16.

3 Robert Coombs, *Marital Status and Personal Well-Being: A Literature Review*, Family relations 40 (1991), 97-102.

4 George A. Akerlof, *Men Without Children*, The Economic Journal 108 (1998), 287-309.

5 Mary Parke, *Are Married Parents Really Better For Children?* Centre for law and Social Policy, Policy Brief, May 2003, p 1.

6 Sara McLanahan and Gary Sandefur, *Growing Up With A Single Parent: What Hurts, What Helps* (Cambridge, Mass.: Harvard University Press 1994), p 19.

7 Suzanne G. Frayser, *Varieties Of Sexual Experience: An Anthropological Perspective On Human Sexuality* (New Haven, Conn: Human Relations Area Files Press, 1985); Edward Westermarck, *The History of Human Marriage*, vols. 1-3 (New York: Allerton 1922); Helen E. Fisher, *Anatomy of Love: The Natural History of Monogamy, Adultery and Divorce* (New York: W.W. Norton, 1922) George P. Murdock, *Social Structure* (New York: Macmillan 1949).

8 James Q. Wilson, *The Marriage Problem: How Our Culture Has Weakened Families* (New York: Harper Collins, 2002), pp. 24, 29.

9 William Byrne and Bruce Parsons, *Human Sexual Orientation: The Biologic Theories Reappraised*, Archives of General Psychiatry 50 (1993), 228-39.

10 Richard C. Friedman and Jennifer I. Downey, *Sexual Orientation and Psychoanalysis: Sexual Science And Clinical Practice* (New York: Columbia University Press, 2002), p. 39.

FORÓIGE

Foróige, the National Youth Development organisation engaged in youth development and education, has been in operation since 1952. A principal objective of Foróige as stated in its constitution is to 'foster the development by its young people of essential knowledge, attitudes and skills necessary for effective living, especially in areas such as family life …'. Foróige believes it can play a significant role in family life by helping to ensure that relationships in families are beneficial and growth promoting.

FORÓIGE'S PURPOSE

The purpose of Foróige is to enable young people to involve themselves consciously and actively in their own development and in the development of society. This purpose challenges and supports young people to involve themselves in:

- Developing their character and talents
- Thinking for themselves, reflecting on their actions and taking responsibility
- Having fun and making friends
- Building positive and helpful relationships
- Acquiring knowledge and skills for life
- Improving the community.

FORÓIGE'S WORK

The organisation provides a comprehensive range of youth work services in the following ways:

- Foróige clubs enable young people to experience democracy at first hand through the election of their own club committee and the management and operation of the club in co-operation with their adult leaders.
- Local youth services enable communities to foster youth development, provide general youth work services to the various voluntary youth organisations and provide specialised services to young people with particular needs.
- Local youth development projects concentrate on the provision of specialised services directly to specifically targeted young people.
- Foróige youth information centres provide a free, confidential information service to young people and adults on a wide range of youth related topics.

Approximately 40,000 young people are involved with Foróige who employ 150 staff and have over 1,400 volunteers with the organisation.

Some of the benefits for young people include the following:

- Helps young people negotiate their way successfully through adolescence
- Provides a setting where young people can socialise in a safe and caring environment
- Makes it easy for young people, through suitable group structures, to express their opinions and exercise influence
- Involves young people in real life learning experiences using a 'learning by doing' approach
- Fosters participation, collective action and voluntary activity by youth and adults
- Involves local communities in the development of their young people
- Gives practical expression to the idea of the dignity, uniqueness, creativity and value of each individual person.

FORÓIGE SERVICE USERS

Services provided by Foróige are used by a wide variety of clients/groups including:

- Young people
- Voluntary youth leaders and organisations
- Parents and local communities
- Statutory youth-serving agencies
- Specific target groups such as early school leavers, potential early school leavers, young mothers, young Travellers, young people at risk from drugs/crime/homelessness, vulnerable young people and their families.

The work of Foróige is underpinned by a philosophy based on the dignity and creativity of each individual, its volunteers and staff driven by a belief in human growth and potential.

ROLE OF FORÓIGE IN FAMILY LIFE

Foróige commissioned a report to be done by the Centre for the Study of Human Development, St. Patrick's College, Dublin. The report called *Youth in a Changing Ireland* was completed in 2003. In this report it was stated that 'the key to Foróige's enduring relevance has, to a large extent, been its anticipation of and responses to social change and the problems that have flowed from it'. The report discussed the challenges facing youth and their families and it identified that interventions and educational supports need to take into account a variety of family and socio-economic circumstances.

Changes to Irish family life and adolescents have meant that Foróige must work creatively when responding to needs. Rooted in a strong philosophy and ethos Foróige's services continue to grow and strive to meet the needs of young people and their families. Foróige's approach to youth work embraces the young person as an individual with talents who should be enabled and empowered to grow and develop to their full potential.

Through youth work young people can be educated outside the life of academia and learn skills for life. They can develop confidence and a sense of self that will assist them in their relationships. These skills enable young people to take an active role in their own family life and that of their community. Families are also supported through youth work both formally and informally, in crisis and on a daily basis by Foróige staff. They are listened to, enabled to face issues, deal with them and learn future coping mechanisms.

RECOMMENDATION

All families experience difficulties. However, these are more pronounced when a family lives in poverty or with other risk factors that make them more vulnerable to breakdown, or crisis. It is in times of crisis and difficulty that the government needs to support young people and their families. To promote good family life there should be more support by the government to voluntary organisations who work with families in a non-stigmatising way. The support enables young people and parents to develop coping life skills and resilience in order to deal with issues in family life.

BRIEF DESCRIPTION OF FOUR SERVICES PROVIDING SUPPORT TO FAMILIES

Neighbourhood Youth Projects (NYP)

These are community based family support services delivered in partnership with the Health Service Executive. They provide direct intervention and on-going support on a non-residential basis for young people who are identified as 'at risk'. This 'at risk' category includes young people experiencing personal, family, educational or social problems. Foróige manage eleven Neighbourhood Youth Projects nationally and work with all young people aged 10-18 years and their families. There is a referral system whereby young people or parents requiring extra support or education on issues, for example – self-esteem, parenting, social skills, drugs/alcohol, in-care/foster care, mental health or bullying to name a few – are worked with in a planned and professional way.

Case Study

A young person from a lone-parent family where alcohol is an issue for her mother attended one to one and group work in a project as part of the overall family support plan. The young woman had been in foster care and moved back to the area. Individual work was carried out with the young person around self-esteem and relationships by project staff. Through her participation in the work she was enabled to realise and work within boundaries. Monthly plans and reviews were carried out between the young person and staff in order to keep the needs of the individual in focus. The NYP provided support and the young woman had an opportunity to discuss issues that are affecting her and develop a more positive self-image.

FORÓIGE CLUBS

There are 415 Foróige clubs nationally that are run by adult volunteers. These clubs provide young people with the opportunity to actively involve themselves in their own development and the development of society. Enabling young people to be proactive members in their communities, building friendships, learning new skills and developing their talents is happening every day all over Ireland in clubs. Foróige clubs are open to all young people aged 12-18 years of age.

BIG BROTHER BIG SISTER (BBBS)

This programme is based on the idea of creating a relationship between two persons – one older than the other. The rationale is that the relationship will act to prevent future difficulties or be a support to a young person facing adversity in his or her life. Having a caring adult friend can help build those positive assets for young people to enable them to have a commitment to learning, a positive sense of self and the future, positive values of caring, social justice, honesty and responsibility and social competencies of making friends, planning, making decisions, and resisting negative behaviour. BBBS uses a case management approach by which the professional worker screens the applicants.

Between 1992 and 1995, BBBS in the United States engaged in a major nationwide research and evaluation study focusing on various aspects of the programme, for example programme practices, volunteer recruitment and screening, building relationships and on the programme's impact. The study of programme practices identified critical aspects of BBBS, such as its intensive screening procedures for volunteers, its matching system, which emphasises the desires of parents and young people, and its rigorous supervision system. The research suggested that these and other BBBS characteristics appeared to improve the chances of the successful development and operation of mentoring relationships between adults and young people (Furano et al., *Public/Private Ventures*, 1993).

The most important findings came as part of the impact study (Tiernay et al., *Public/Private Ventures*, 1995). Based on a sample of almost 1,000 young people across eight US cities, the study demonstrated that young people who participated in BBBS were:

- 46% less likely to engage in drug use
- 27% less likely to initiate alcohol use
- One third less likely to hit someone.

In addition, young people who participated in the programme were likely to have better school attendance, more positive attitudes towards school and slightly better academic performance. Finally, they had better relationships with their parents and their peers at the end of the study. Thus, the evidence shows that the BBBS programme can play a critical role in promoting positive behaviours in key areas of young people's development.

THE CRIB YOUTH PROJECT & HEALTH CAFÉ

The CRIB Youth Project & Health Café provides a range of developmental programmes and activities for young people, including those at risk of isolation and homelessness, which will enable them to involve themselves in personal and community development. In essence, the centre is a safe place for young people to be themselves, meet friends, share concerns with each other and/or staff, and access appropriate information and services to enable them to lead happy, healthy and connected lives.

The CRIB is for all young people aged 12-18 years in Sligo town and its environs. It is a conjoint project funded by the Health Service Executive, North Western Area. The building is owned by the Diocese of Elphin and managed by Foróige. This innovative project delivers services through its youth project and café in a combined way to meet the needs of young people and their parents. This service promotes health in its broadest sense in order to support young people and their families.

Case Study

- A young person (15 years) came to the project seeking assistance as she wanted to leave home. After a home visit on that same day it emerged there was conflict at home between siblings and their mother who is parenting alone, separated from father of children due to his abuse of alcohol. It appeared the mother was feeling extremely stressed and very angry towards her children. As the project was open late that night the young people were able to attend giving their mother some space and time to herself. Family therapy was pursued and her children attend the project. She herself maintains contact with the project, discussing what is going well and what challenges she faces.
- A young woman informed staff during a discussion that she was self-harming. She was supported in talking to her parents regarding what was troubling her, she did not know her biological father and was having major difficulty raising the issue as she did not want to upset her step-father, mother or younger step-siblings. Ongoing support has been given to this family and especially the young person by choice.

Foróige as a national voluntary youth development organisation works with young people between the ages of 10 and 18 years. These young people, regardless of what class, culture, religion or 'family' they come from, are embraced as unique and special individuals. Our role is not to judge where they come from but to take them for where they are at and enable them to develop to their full potential.

Families are breaking down due to issues such as abuse, alcohol, mental health issues and domestic violence combined with poverty and the lack of parenting skills. Foróige are involved in preventative and supportive work to many of these families all over Ireland.

GAY CATHOLIC CAUCUS

INTRODUCTION

Sex between men and women can result in the transmission of new life and thus ensures the continuation of the species. Homosexual union cannot claim this purpose. For this reason, it has been treated as evil, unnatural, irrational, degenerate, criminal, and as flowing from some defect in genetics, or in psychological/personal development.

Courageous science and research, as well as the dawning of gay consciousness across the globe, mean that, for an ever wider number of the world's population, homosexual relationships and homosexual sex are now seen as falling within the 'normal' range of human sexuality.

We stand on a threshold. In most jurisdictions in 'the West' homosexual sex is no longer a criminal offence. Now, we face the choice of whether to accord equal dignity and respect to homosexual love as we do to heterosexual love. In many countries and on several continents, the issue of gay civil partnerships and gay civil marriage is now on the agenda. In the face of this, the rear-guard anti-gay-marriage stance is also ever more forcefully advanced, both in argument and in political action – from George W. Bush to the Vatican.

Our point of departure is something rooted in our experience – for some of us, it is the shock of our gayness. Unlike straight people, we do not live in a world which is structured around our sexual orientation. For straight people, everything around them says they are straight. By contrast, even when we have come out, we continually face moments in which we confront the risk of prejudice and even hate. We must speak who we are; we have to ask for the social space to be ourselves. In the past, gay people have suffered long in silence, and drunk deeply from the cup of rejection that our heterosexually structured society placed at our lips from adolescence onwards, and for some from even earlier. Every ten, or twelve, or fourteen-year old gay girl or boy, experiences this rejection in all its freshness when they realise they fall short of the accepted norm.

We contend that gay marriage is about more than just tax bands and pension rights. It is about the recognition of the value of gay love and about support for this love. Most profoundly, it is about visibility and normality. During every gay marriage ceremony, two gay people will kiss each other in public, in front of family and friends. They will exchange the rings, cut the cake, and celebrate their love as of central value in their lives and the lives of their community – no longer marginal, suspect, degenerate, but visible, central, and generative.

We write as a group of gay men who are also Catholics. We believe that Christianity and Catholicism provide powerful arguments in favour of gay marriage. These resources remain buried, however, unless one starts from the conviction that gay love is good love. As Catholics, we stand in disagreement with our Church's teaching on homosexuality, but we do so on the basis of common ground with most heterosexual Catholics, namely our disagreement with *Humanae Vitae*, the papal encyclical that 'disallowed' artificial contraception for Catholics.

We address overlapping audiences in what follows. Most widely, we speak to the straight community in Ireland. Our argument is that the gay marriage issue is not just a gay issue, but is an issue for all Irish people. Gay people are your sons, daughters, sisters, brothers, cousins, nephews, nieces, uncles, aunts, and even spouses; they are your co-workers, friends, neighbours, and co-citizens. 'Blithely' to deprive these people, your relatives and friends, of the right to marry, says something profound about what kind of society you choose, and also deprives you of the

resource that the full expression of gay love could be for Irish families and communities.

There is also a debate in the gay community itself and not all agree with us. We make the case that Christianity and Catholicism are not in essence homophobic, and that marriage is not in essence patriarchal or deadening. We believe that both Christianity and marriage offer rich resources for gay people.

Throughout, our touchstone is gay experience. We write from our own hearts as well as our heads. Our plea is that you, and all of Irish society, will support gay love by affording it the framework of law, custom and social visibility that is given in and through marriage.

PART ONE: THE STATE

SECTION A: SECULAR LANDSCAPES

A1 *The Global Picture*

Gay marriage/same-sex union seems to be an idea whose time has come. We are living in an exciting era of change in this regard. The growing list of countries which has passed legislation in this area has followed one of three broad approaches.

The 'registered partnership' approach was pioneered by Denmark in 1989. Couples who chose to register their partnership were guaranteed essentially the same rights and signed up to the same obligations as married heterosexual couples – except in the important area of the adoption of children. Countries which have broadly followed the Danish example include Norway, Sweden, Finland, Germany, France, some American states and, most recently, Britain.

Some countries (e.g. Austria, Hungary, Portugal, Australia) have chosen to tackle the issue in a less formal way. In these countries, same-sex couples are dealt with under legislation designed for non-married cohabiting couples, whether straight or gay. The mere fact of cohabitation over a more or less extended period is presumed to confer a certain weight on the relationship. The rights and duties attaching to such a 'presumed' partnership can hardly, in justice, approximate to the rights and duties attaching to a marriage or formally registered partnership.

The simplest – and boldest – solution is to extend the right to marry to same-sex couples. The Netherlands was the first country to take this step, in 2001. Belgium followed suit two years later. Six of Canada's eleven provinces have passed same-sex marriage legislation and the adoption of similar legislation at federal level is imminent. Spain is set to become the third European country to allow gay marriage. In May 2004, Massachusetts became the first American state to do so.

A2 *An Irish Answer?*

Ireland was the last European country, apart from Cyprus, to retain a complete legal prohibition on all sexual acts between males. However, given that Ireland is a much more open and socially progressive place now than it was in the 1970s and 1980s, it is reasonable to hope that, on the question of same-sex partnerships/marriage, Ireland will not again be content with the position of 'Paddy Last'.

In this section, we review the debate in Ireland on this issue as it has developed over the last two or three years. We begin with an examination of the Equality Authority's treatment of the issue of partnership rights in its report of 2002, *Implementing Equality for Lesbians, Gays and Bisexuals*. We go on to analyse the discouraging responses of various government departments to the Equality Authority's recommendations, as outlined in the NESF report of the following year, *Equality Policies for Lesbian, Gay and Bisexual People: Implementation Issues*.

The Law Reform Commission's *Consultation Paper on the Rights and Duties of Cohabitees*, published last year, is another useful pointer to developing thinking on this matter. It is welcome that the Commission, acknowledging 'that "marriage-like" relationships exist between same-sex couples', includes such couples within its definition of cohabitees. However, because any consideration of same-sex marriage is outside the remit of the consultation paper, it would be wrong to look to it for a comprehensive solution. Indeed, the Commission's favouring of the 'presumptive' over the 'registration' approach to cohabiting couples means that its recommendations cannot possibly be said to fully address the concerns of citizens who are denied the right to marry.

In tackling the issue of cohabitees, the Commission is mindful of the provisions within the Constitution safeguarding the family. The Minister for Justice, Equality and Law Reform, Michael McDowell has also spoken of constitutional difficulties in this regard. The forthcoming hearing of the Zappone/Gilligan case in the High Court should throw further light on this. If there is a problem, the work of the Constitution Review Group should point the way forward.

We include, in this section, a look at the debate on the issue within the gay community itself, as articulated in the pages of *Gay Community News*. We identify both fundamental differences in philosophy and also important differences in relation to tactics.

In December 2004, Senator David Norris published his proposed private member's bill, the *Civil Partnership Bill 2004*. In it, he endeavours to steer clear of making changes to the concept of marriage itself but, following the example of some of the foreign jurisdictions cited above, proposes to institute a parallel system of civil partnership, open to both different-sex and same-sex couples. Such civil partnerships would, in terms of rights and entitlements, be equivalent to marriages, although the bill's proposals relating to their dissolution seem to differ somewhat from the options of separation and divorce available to married people. The question of the eligibility of such couples to be considered as adoptive parents is not explicitly addressed.

It is only in the last year, largely on the back of headline-grabbing developments in America and elsewhere, that the issue has punctured the mainstream media and political consciousness in Ireland. In June 2004, Fine Gael became the first of the political parties to publish a comprehensive policy document on the issue of same-sex unions. Like Senator Norris, they propose a system of registered partnerships, open to both straight and gay couples. Under the Fine Gael proposals, however, such partnerships would be definitely inferior in status to heterosexual marriage. The stance of the government, as voiced by the Taoiseach, Bertie Ahern, and by Minister McDowell, is more cautious.

As of now, the consensus emerging in Ireland, even in progressive liberal circles, seems to be that this question will eventually be satisfactorily answered by the institution of some form of civil union or domestic partnership (either 'presumptive' or 'registered') which will either be subsidiary to, or run in parallel with, full civil marriage as currently defined. There is no strong voice arguing that part of the solution may involve the reform of the marriage law itself so as to allow same-sex couples to marry.

A3 The Rights Conferred by Marriage

Law can seem cold and abstract, but it has consequences for real flesh and blood people. For gay people who would like to marry, but are precluded from doing so by the Irish state, the law means that:

- They pay higher income tax.
- They pay higher capital gains tax.
- They pay higher stamp duty.
- They pay higher inheritance and gift tax if they make any gifts or bequests to each other.
- Their non-Irish spouse cannot easily work and live in Ireland.
- They may face discrimination in pension benefits.
- In cases of domestic violence, they are less protected by the law because they cannot claim barring orders under the Domestic Violence Act, 1996.
- They may not be recognised as next of kin if their partner is hospitalised.
- The partner of a deceased gay person will have no entitlement equivalent to that of a spouse, to a share of the estate of the deceased.
- In case of pregnancy, the partner of the pregnant person will not be entitled to parental leave.
- They can adopt, but only as single people.
- The child of a gay couple is disadvantaged because he or she cannot legally be recognised as a child of both parents. The disadvantages relate to gifts, inheritance and custody.

Is this fair? We think not. We illustrate these injustices against gay people by citing stories of individual cases. Some of these are real, some are composites of real stories that are known to us, and some are easily imagined cases.

'Full' equality is what gay people deserve. They do not deserve to be given only the sop of a presumptive cohabitation – especially a presumptive cohabitation that is extended so widely that the degree of equality it gives will be small, in order to minimise the cost to the exchequer. Gay people should be allowed get married in the eyes of the state.

A4 The Numbers Game

What percentage of the population is gay? The answer is not at all straightforward for a number of reasons.

For a start, what is at issue is not a simple physical characteristic nor (so far, at least) a genetic imprint nor even, strictly speaking, a pattern of behaviour, but rather merely an 'orientation'. It is important to realise that most studies in this area base their findings on questions relating to experience/practice rather than orientation/desire. There is no reason to assume, however, that the numbers of people whose homosexual desires are not acted out as sexual experience are so tiny as to be statistically insignificant.

Secondly, it is a question of degree. Human sexual orientation, so far as we can be sure, seems to range across a spectrum from an exclusive lifelong heterosexual orientation at one extreme to an exclusive lifelong homosexual orientation at the other. Some people have great difficulty in answering their *own* questions about their orientation, not to mention the questions of social researchers.

Thirdly, and crucially, is the issue of visibility. It is probable that the question on a Chinese census form: 'Are you a member of the Falun Gong?' would elicit a response unreliable for statistical purposes. We are unlikely to get a truthful answer to the sociological question 'What percentage of the population is gay?' until such time as the answer to the personal question 'Are you gay?' inspires neither fear nor shame.

Lastly, the question has been, so far, at least as much political as sociological. The results of opposing surveys have, down through the years, been trumpeted by the rival factions in the debate. The 10% figure, gleaned from Alfred Kinsey's surveys in post-war America, has traditionally been cited by those arguing for gay rights. Research indicating a lower figure (in some cases as low as 1%) is pushed by those antagonistic to gay rights. It is possible that some research has been coloured by political considerations.

Surveying the research of the last fifteen years in this area and subject to the *caveat*s above, we feel a figure of around 5% is more credible than the traditional 10% figure. In the Irish context, this would translate into 200,000 people – roughly equivalent to the number of Protestants in the Republic, or, put another way, to the population of Cork city.

SECTION B: DIGGING

B1 The Invisible Minority

In a society which was truly comfortable with its gay members, the question 'Do you mind me asking, are you gay?' would be no more outrageous than questions like 'Do you mind me asking, are you married?' 'Do you have children?' or 'Are your parents still living?' – personal certainly, slightly intrusive, but in no way taboo.

In this section, we examine the phenomenon of 'the closet'. 'The closet' is a system which operates in Irish society as a whole, not just within the gay sub-section of it. It is wrong to see it as just some sort of internal barrier in the minds, or in the lives, of a few isolated individuals. The real 'closet' is bigger than this and stands as a wall winding its way through the whole community.

The continued existence of 'the closet' is a symptom that Irish society is denying something about itself. Living in denial is as damaging for a society as it is for an individual. We look at the malign effects of 'the closet' on individuals and on society and imagine an Ireland where it no longer operates. The piece includes the real-life example of a gay couple living an unremarkable life integrated into a community in sub-urban Dublin.

Same-sex marriage legislation would bring what is half-hidden out into the open. What before was merely tolerated would now be accepted and approved of. The nationwide 'macro-closet' would have had the door yanked off it. This is why such legislation poses so big a challenge to those who are not entirely comfortable with their gay co-citizens. It is also why the benefits of such legislation would extend far beyond those couples who choose to avail of it.

B2 The Happy Couple

For many people marriage is an ideal to be striven for. For some, it is a system of social control to be rejected. In public discourse, it is all too often held up as a sacred cow, an institution which, while extremely powerful, is also extremely vulnerable, and one which, in its essentials, should be regarded as immutable and therefore closed to examination. We question this view, attempting to understand the half-articulated fears which underpin it. We show how some of these fears are similar to the ones which gay people have to confront, in summoning up the courage to come out.

However, discussing marriage on this lofty societal plane can obscure the real social meaning of marriage to real people in their everyday lives. When people say that, yes, certainly, something must be done about partnership rights for same-sex couples, something must be done to clear up anomalies around inheritance and pensions, but that, of course, whatever legislation is required, it will just be a tidying-up, it won't, clearly, amount to anything like gay marriage ... what is it they're really saying? They're saying: Do you honestly think you're equal? Do you really think your 'relationship' measures up to my marriage? That it actually matters to any of the rest of us? That it has any real value beyond your own little ghetto?

In down-to-earth language, marriage connects people. Marriage is a public expression, at a very profound level, of the intimacy between two people. It is a publicly celebrated declaration on the part of the couple of their investment in each other's future happiness. By their attendance at the wedding, their relatives and friends participate in this investment. They contribute. They offer an affirmation and support which may work – perhaps invisibly – to smooth the couple's way through hardships or crises. And this support can work both ways. Marriages form networks of relationships. In an unspectacular everyday way they act as a 'social glue'.

We illustrate what is meant by this phrase using the story of 'Sue and Rob', a heterosexual couple. We show how Rob graduates from being Sue's 'hot date' to being her 'new man' and then her 'steady boyfriend' or 'partner'. If they become engaged, he becomes her 'fiancé' and, eventually, her 'husband.' As the relationship grows and his status in Sue's eyes changes, he becomes known and connected to a wider circle of her family and friends.

When we consider 'John and Rob', a homosexual couple, the path is not so clear. In this case, often people close to John may never even get to hear of 'Rob'. Unknowingly, they forfeit the chance of connection and whatever riches it might have brought. At every stage of John and Rob's relationship, they have to negotiate obstacles. And, of course, the obstacle in the way of marriage is the law. Many 'John and Robs' will never reach the 'steady boyfriend' or 'partner' stages – not because they don't want to but because the odds are stacked against them. And, no matter how strong and solid John and Rob's relationship may be, its standing in the world will remain precarious.

B3 What Makes Marriage Work?

To understand why gay people should be allowed marry, we need to understand marriage properly. If we think about it narrowly – marriage is for rearing children – then gay marriage might seem superfluous. Or, if we buy into our 'luv' culture that promises instant happiness, then marriage might seem secondary to sex and fun. We understand marriage to be founded on loving communication that respects difference and negotiates conflicts on the basis of equality. This foundation is also the best context for children to be born in – as mature adults and not just physically. If this communication is absent then differences are resolved through power-play, and even the most stereotypically sexually attractive couples fall out of love.

In Irish society, both implicitly and explicitly, we rank different types of relationships in a social hierarchy. Married couples with children are at the top of the social tree, with the highest status. Gay people,

whether in relationships or not, with or without children, are at the bottom. We argue that couples without children, gay couples, and single people whether straight or gay, are equally but differently capable of showing loving communication that respects difference, in their relationships. They should not be judged as defective or lacking, because they are not the same as married couples with children. Gay couples are capable of providing as much love for each other, and in society in general, as married couples. Society loses if committed relationships whether gay or straight are not supported. Therefore, gay people deserve to be given the option to marry.

We ask the question, 'would bringing in gay marriage be a very big change?' When compared to some of the major changes in marriage in Irish society, it seems quite minor – despite its importance for gay people. Marriage in Ireland has changed, as we have moved from a patriarchal and sexually repressive society to the present day. Using the most up-to-date statistics, we show how household composition has been changing recently in Ireland. Key milestones were the change in the legal position of children born outside of marriage, especially in relation to inheritance, and also the introduction of divorce. Gay marriage is only a modest change, in comparison to these, because it only directly affects a minority.

We suggest that the state should have a range of options for couples that grant progressively more substantial rights along with the degree of commitment. These would start with presumptive cohabitation, then a fixed-term renewable cohabitation contract, and finally marriage. This has an analogy in religious life where novices are presumptive members; then they take time-limited vows that can be renewed, and then take final vows. This would allow the state to support commitment in relationships through incentives, while allowing for a diversity of relationships.

B4 Can Marriage Work for Gays?

Not all gay people agree that gay marriage will be good for gay people. They argue that marriage is inherently patriarchal and that those gay people who strive for marriage are just aping the heterosexual community and abandoning the project of creating new, properly gay, forms of relationship. This argument is an inversion of the Vatican argument – marriage is good; gays are bad; gay marriage will corrupt straight marriage. The gay 'anti-gay marriage' argument runs: marriage is bad; gays are good; gay marriage will corrupt gay people.

We disagree with both polar opposites. Marriage, we believe, continues to be popular because of its enduring value, and not because people are like lemmings that dash over the cliff. On the other hand, we argue that marriage is not the be all and end all of human relating. To set it in context, we reflect on the manner in which three key ingredients interact in human relationships – sex, emotional intimacy, and commitment. All of us face the challenge to integrate these elements and marriage is one valuable form of integrating them. For example, we cannot continue to have sex with someone without some emotional intimacy, and when there is emotional intimacy, promises are made whether in words or deeds. When you love someone, you want to avoid losing that person; thus commitment arises.

A key criterion of successful integration of the three ingredients is joy. We do not want to evaluate gay relationships by making gay marriage the measuring stick. Instead, we argue that gay people should be allowed marry and that all relationships, whether married or not, should be evaluated against the criterion, 'Do they bring joy to *all* the parties affected?'

Gay marriage does challenge gay culture, because gay culture was itself constructed within the reality of the closet, and when the closet disappears, then gay culture will evolve. This should not make us fear lack of creativity, because marriage, if it is to be joyful, requires that creativity, and each marriage is unique. Moreover, other gay relationships can be of equal, or more, value, when compared to any individual gay marriage, if they are equally, or more, joyful.

When gay emotional intimacy is awakened, in speaking the language of touch (through gay affection and gay sex), then it is 'natural' that some should seek to live that emotional intimacy for as long as possible. Some, in turn, will want to express that commitment to each other by making a promise in public that is recognised publicly. Why should they be prevented from marrying?

B5 Gay Parenting

There is a general recognition that the nature of family life has changed in Ireland and that this change needs to be recognised in law. There are many people, both children and adults, who are unfairly disadvantaged by this lack of recognition in addition to its effects on gay people. We trace what some of these disadvantages are to the children of gay people. For example, although gay individuals can already adopt children, gay couples cannot. We argue for a level playing field for gay couples who want to adopt. They should be treated no differently in the adoption process than heterosexual couples.

There are many prejudices which suggest that gay people are unfit to be parents and that the children of lesbians and gay parents fail to develop properly as a result; prejudices that gays are prone to depression and suicide, that gays are promiscuous and the environment created as a result is unsuitable for raising children. We look at some of these prejudices and see what research has come up with.

What has emerged is that no significant differences exist between lesbian and gay parenting, on the one hand, and straight parenting, on the other. In our reading, certainly none of these differences are disadvantageous to children. Studies we look at here have

pointed out that differences do exist between gay and straight parenting, but these differences do not imply that gay and lesbian parenting is an inferior model. On the contrary, a high level of compatibility between lesbian couples who parent children has been shown to be advantageous to both children and parents.

The prevalent assumption that the heterosexual model of parenting is the only legitimate one for raising children has been questioned by research. Interestingly, while the question arises about the appropriateness of gay parents for straight children, a similar question rarely arises about the appropriateness of straight parents raising gay children. We see, in fact, that heterosexual parenting is not the only legitimate model for rearing children.

PART TWO: THE CHURCH

SECTION C: RELIGIOUS LANDSCAPE

C1 Vatican Line

We trace the Vatican line on homosexuality in the various documents issued by the Congregation of the Doctrine of the Faith in the past thirty years.

In 1975, the Vatican claimed homosexuality arises from either an absence of normal human development or because of a pathological, incurable condition.

In 1986, it stated that not alone are homosexual acts 'intrinsically disordered' but the inclination itself is a strong tendency towards an intrinsic moral evil. It bases this teaching on three principles it finds in the Book of Genesis: the complementarity of the sexes, the institution of marriage and the call to procreate.

In 1992 it stated that because of the immoral nature of homosexuality it is sometimes legitimate to discriminate against homosexuals, for example in the employment of teachers or the consignment of children for adoption. The Vatican suggests, in this document, that the problem of discrimination wouldn't arise if gay people remained invisible.

In 2003, it states its opposition to same-sex marriage. In this document, for the second time, the Vatican uses the word 'evil' in reference to gay relationships, suggesting that tolerating such homosexual behaviour is a toleration of evil. The Vatican opposes same-sex marriage for all of the same reasons it opposes homosexuality and for some others to do with, for example, the common good.

As countries across Europe have begun to re-evaluate their position on the legalisation of same-sex relationships, the Vatican has become increasingly strident in its opposition to such unions. This issue affects people across all strata of society because, despite a strong belief to the contrary, gay people do not live in communes on the fringes of society. They are lawyers and dentists and doctors and bricklayers and barmen and children and brothers and sisters and mothers and fathers and they are all citizens of the state.

The Vatican line is relevant to non-Catholics as well because it has chosen to intervene in the political debate on same-sex unions. The 2003 document is addressed not only to Catholics but 'to all others committed to promoting the common good of society'.

SECTION D: DIGGING

D1 Church and State

The Vatican, in its document of 2003, teaches that legal recognition of same-sex unions would undermine marriage and destabilise society. It requires Catholics, as a matter of conscience, to oppose same-sex unions and, if politicians, to vote against them. The Vatican agenda includes keeping gay people in the closet.

The 2003 document draws on a papal encyclical of 1995 in a manner which treats the legal recognition of same-sex unions as of the same order of danger to society as the wrongful taking of innocent life. The Vatican does not provide evidence for its teaching in the 2003 document. The 1995 encyclical calls on the civil authorities to examine the relevant sociological and other matters to work out how to get rid of the wrongs which lead to the devaluing of life. Similar principles of engaging with the relevant disciplines should be applied in considering whether or not same-sex unions should be legally recognised.

The Second Vatican Council, in particular in its teaching on religious freedom, challenges the 2003 document. Religious freedom is a right attaching to the dignity of the human person, and it must be curtailed only in so far as necessary for the common good. We argue that religious freedom includes freedom in moral matters, and we explain what the teaching says about freedom of conscience.

As gay Catholics, we are sympathetic to the role of Catholics and the Catholic Church in a pluralistic world. Regarding how to vote, for example, you may be a Catholic politician who believes same-sex unions are morally wrong. If, however, you do not believe they are bad for society, you may still vote in favour of their legal recognition. You may, for example, believe that this promotes the common good by catering for the legitimate rights of a minority of the community. While the Vatican does not recognise gay people as a minority group, with legitimate rights to be protected, this has already been recognised in Irish law.

D2 Catholic Church Teaching on Marriage and Sex

The Catholic Church has changed its teaching about marriage throughout history:

• It accepted divorce in the Eastern Church even beyond the Council of Trent in the 16th century, but no longer does so.
• It did not consider marriage to be a sacrament up until the 12th or 13th centuries.
• It was only in 1907 that the Church universally imposed the condition requiring Catholics to get married in a Catholic ceremony. Unless they had a dispensation to do otherwise, the marriage would be invalid.
• In Vatican Two, it changed its teaching about the priority of the ends or goods of marriage. Prior to that, the unitive relationship (love between the couples) had been secondary to the good of procreation. Now both ends are seen as being equal.

The progress in thinking about sexuality in the Catholic Church was halted by the encyclical *Humanae Vitae*. It teaches that no sex act can be moral if it occurs outside of marriage and artificially intervenes to block openness to procreation.

This has implications for many forms of sexual expression that affect both gay and straight people alike – masturbation, use of artificial contraception, straight-sex practices like oral sex and anal sex (that end in orgasm rather than just as foreplay), *coitus interruptus*, and also all gay sex and gay marriage. It also has very restrictive implications for assisted reproduction techniques.

Along with most artificial contraception-using heterosexual couples in Ireland, we believe that this teaching is erroneous. It condemns gay people to compulsory chastity. If we fall, we can of course confess and be forgiven. However, if we fall in love (and integrate our sexuality with emotional intimacy and commitment), we cannot be forgiven because, we won't 'give up our oul' sins' i.e. we won't stop living in a state of sin.

Following the direction of Vatican Two, we believe that the unitive aspect of relationships is primary. Procreation, child rearing, and all other generativity of a relationship, are based on this love which binds together. Gay couples are equally capable of this unitive love, and so they are capable of full marriage.

We look at why the Church is afraid of this issue. For one thing, it is in denial that it has so many gay clergy, some of whom have deep internalised homophobia. For another, if it is wrong on this issue, then its whole claim to know and teach the truth in moral issues will be challenged. This is an appalling vista. Yet, the pity is, that the Catholic Church has valuable resources in its tradition to help society integrate sexuality better. These resources remain untapped while the Vatican promotes its erroneous teaching on sexuality ever more desperately.

D3 Sex Crimes in a Catholic Theocracy

Here, we put forward a *reductio ad absurdem*. We imagine that Catholic teaching on sex was implemented in Ireland with the zeal of the Taliban. We then describe the kind of sanctions that would be enforced proportionate to the level of violation of our relationship with God that the Church ascribes to various sex acts, including gay sex.

What we describe is something of a satire, rather than a nuanced portrayal of the Catholic Church's position. This much is clear from what we say about the Catholic understanding of the distinction between law and morality (see Section D1). However, as a satire, it is intended to shed light on the question 'Is it true?'

D4 Yes, But Is It True?

We look at one response to the Vatican's 2003 document from gay theologian James Alison entitled 'Yes, But Is It True?' Alison acknowledges the right and indeed the duty of the Church authorities to speak out on important matters of faith and morals. He uses as an example the Nazi holocaust and suggests that the Church could have, in fact, spoken out more strongly on certain issues.

He appeals to the gay community not to be provoked by the strong language used by the Vatican in condemning same-sex unions. A better approach, Alison suggests, is to ask 'Is It True?' In this he underlines one point in the 2003 document where the phrase 'As experience has shown ...' appears, related to the apparent detrimental effects on children placed with gay parents. Alison notes that the Vatican provides no evidence to support this claim. His own conclusion, in line with our own, on the basis of evidence we look at elsewhere in this document is that experience has shown no such thing.

Alison makes a very helpful point for trying to understand the Vatican's approach to homosexuality. He posits that lesbians and gays as a class of people do not exist in the eyes of the Vatican. Homosexuals are defective heterosexuals whose path lies in returning to the heterosexual lifestyle. So the question of the rights of homosexual people simply does not arise. Alison argues that we are under the radar of the Vatican: because we are invisible for them we have an opportunity to develop as a community outside their gaze.

D5 God, Gays, the Bible and the Church

We consider some aspects of Christian spirituality, prayer and the Bible from a Catholic perspective. If you, the reader, are not Christian, or do not believe in God, you may still find this section helpful in understanding how same-sex unions can be justified from a Catholic perspective.

In this life, we do not meet God directly, but rather in and through our personal relationships. Openness and trust between people, and goodness and justice towards each other, are ways of learning to know and love God.

We explain that opening our minds and hearts to God in prayer can be understood by analogy with friendships between people. We try to be open and trusting with God in the way people can be open and trusting with their friends. Falseness and fear, which is often the experience of gay people who are in the closet, can not only hinder personal relationships, but can also be a barrier between the gay person and God.

The Bible helps us learn how to know God and love God. However, it contains texts that many find unhelpful or even quite wrong, for example, texts that approve of slavery. We explain how to engage with biblical texts in a way which is helpful for us today, and how God's self-revelation to us is part of a process of community learning. The Bible is often used to beat down gay people, but we find it an inspiring and liberating source.

We relate to each other and to God as individuals in community. That is how we learn Christ's values and how to live them. It involves the tradition and the teaching authority of the Catholic Church, and also the gifts of the individual members of the Church. The gifts of each member, including gay members, are important and necessary. In the words of the Second Vatican Council, the Church is its people, 'the people of God,' travelling together. We are a 'pilgrim church.' We will be learning our way to the truth until the end of time. The proper consideration of same-sex unions is a vital step on our pilgrimage to God.

D6 Life At The Margins

We trace how the Catholic tradition has always placed a special value on the lives of those who live on the margins of society. The emergence of the different liberation theologies in previous decades expresses the political implications of this emphasis. What is important is the exploration here of the life experience of being on the edge by the marginalised themselves. This exploration reveals to wider society its marginalising behaviour. The struggle to move from invisibility to visibility is shared by many groups from the economically poor, to ethnic minorities, disabled, women and also gays and lesbians. The struggle involves first finding your voice and then expressing where it needs to be heard.

We see how in the story of Jesus a similar emphasis is found. Jesus spent much time with the outcasts of his day: the lepers, the tax collectors, the blind and lame, the sinners. The question arises as to what exactly the marginalised have to offer.

We explore the story of the Gerasene Demoniac in the Gospels to try to answer this question. How Jesus challenges the people of the local town, after healing the demoniac, by sending him to the townspeople to show himself in full control of his faculties. He who was marginalised, who carried the townspeople's projections of evil, appears among them as one of them. They are slow to accept him.

Just as much work remains for the townspeople in the story to re-integrate the marginalised, so for ourselves too much work remains to be done in accepting those among us, like gays and lesbians, who for too long have been forced to remain on the outside.

CONCLUSION

Since the adoption of the Irish Constitution in 1937, the attempt to maintain an appropriate 'fit' between it and the lives of all Irish people in the ensuing decades has been a recurring challenge. The original document was heavily influenced by the Catholic ethos of the time. The intervening period, however, has seen changes that would have seemed inconceivable to the original framers of the document. That such a fit should be attempted, however, is testament to the importance of the relationship between where we are as a people and what we aspire to in our Constitution. As a Republic, the Constitution is our ultimate legal document and its power and authority is drawn from us, the people. The current process of renewal is one which seeks to clarify, on the one hand, who we are and how we identify ourselves as Irish people at this point in our history and, on the other hand, how this identity can be best reflected in the Constitution, so that the vital relationship between the people and the Constitution can be maintained.

The exploration and clarification of our identity as Irish people is a multi-faceted process in which all the strands of Irish life and culture have their part to play. For our own part, we are delighted to have this opportunity to make a contribution. We feel it is important that the voice of Irish gay people be heard also. This opportunity is something which is very precious to us. There is hardly a lesbian or gay person in Ireland who has not felt the fear around saying 'I am gay' in public at some time in his or her life. The opportunity to take our place with other groups at this review is a sign of the changes which have occurred in Irish society since 1937.

The experience of being included is precious partly because the experience of being excluded is so painful. That it is a painful experience is not difficult to establish. It is the pain of confronting social prejudice. It is the pain of hiding affection, where even the most casual touch of lovers must be concealed, for fear of a violent response. The prejudices surface in work, family, health, wealth – the very fabric of our lives.

What is perhaps not so clear is how damaging it is as a nation to base our identity on this exclusion – to see ourselves primarily in terms of 'who we are not', rather than 'who we are'. A most extreme example of this is Nazi Germany, where an Aryan identity was promoted by excluding Jews, gypsies and homosexuals as sub-human. The insanity of this philosophy is clear and yet the lesson remains pertinent. Any approach which marginalises a particular section of society does violence to the social fabric and ultimately affects everybody. To ban people from getting married because they are gay is such a violence.

The 1990s were momentous years for the gay community. With the legalisation of homosexuality in 1993, lesbians and gays began, for the first time in the history of the state, to emerge from the long dark tunnel of social prejudice and take their rightful place with their fellow citizens. The process of inclusion was begun, but only begun – much like Catholic emancipation in 1829 was a first step on the long road to full equality for Catholics. This gradual process of inclusion is one which, of course, deeply affects those previously excluded but, it should be stressed, it also affects everybody else. This can be illustrated by an example of 'coming out'.

> Peter is 17 and has known for some time that he is gay. After agonising over it for a few months he finally sits his parents down and tells them he's gay. They are shocked. Neither of them had the slightest idea. However, they recover sufficient composure to reassure him that he's still their son and they love him.

There are big changes here for everybody. Peter has finally identified himself as a gay man and is included in the family as such. His parents, who thought they had a straight son and no doubt looked forward to bouncing grand-children on their knees some day, now find out they will have to put those dreams to one side and grapple instead with the possibility of the boy-friend staying over. As a result of these struggles, a different family unity has emerged. This new family identity is a struggle not just for the gay son but also for the rest of the family.

As a society too, we are coming to terms with this new identity. For gay people, the task remains to confront prejudice which denies our full humanity and seeks to relegate us to second class citizenship. For many straight people, sincerely held religious convictions about the nature of homosexuality have to be reassessed in the light of scientific research and the new visibility of gay people. Each of these struggles is, in one sense, an intensely personal journey. Of course, it is only one struggle and journey amongst many others for different groups in our society. Woven together, these struggles constitute our identity as a people at this point in our history. Ultimately, national identity is not something that is written in stone but an ongoing process of discovery.

In our paper, we have sketched the landscape of the secular struggle of gay people for gay marriage both globally and in national politics. We have also shown the legal benefits of marriage that are denied to gay people and examined the debate about how many gay people there are. Digging in this landscape brought us to the real life experience of gay people as an invisible minority. We explored how the image of marriage functions socially to include straight people and exclude gay people. We also looked at the deeper ingredients which make marriages work and found that gay lovers share in these ingredients equally and so should be allowed marry. In the debate about gay marriage in the gay community, we argue that opening up the option of marriage will be good for the gay community. It is another kind of coming out. Finally, we touched on the issue of gay parenting and adoption and suggested that gay parenting is a different but not inferior kind of parenting.

Our second landscape is the currently advanced official Catholic anti-gay-marriage position. We have outlined the Catholic Church's recent teaching and then dug beneath it. We analysed the recent Catholic 'three-line whip' imposed (on Catholics) by the

Congregation for the Doctrine of the Faith and criticise it in terms of other Catholic sources from the Second Vatican Council. Then we show how the Catholic teaching on artificial contraception is actually at the foundation of the opposition to gay sex and gay marriage. If that lynchpin fails then the whole Catholic teaching on sexuality needs revision.

On the other hand, if gay love were truly evil, then the Vatican's intervention would surely be justified and, if that were the case, we would say 'yes'. But we ask 'is it true?' We believe it is not true. Gay love is a profound expression of gay people's spirituality – love touches on the divine. Indeed, both the Bible and the Christian tradition can be sources of affirmation for all love, including gay love. The experience of gay people at the margins suggests that gay experience has something profound to say to all of society and all of the Church. Were Jesus alive today we believe he would open his table to gay people, along with the other marginalised groups, just as he did in his own day. As gay Catholics, we ask that Irish society invite us as equal citizens to its table, which includes celebrating our love at the wedding banquet.

In its invitation for submissions to the Committee the question was posed 'Should gay couples be allowed to marry?' Our answer, on the basis of our experience and research in this matter, is 'yes'. 'Yes' because, from a secular point of view, it is the best thing for Irish society to do; and 'yes', because it is the most Christian thing to do.

GLEN – GAY AND LESBIAN EQUALITY NETWORK

GLEN CALLS FOR CIVIL MARRIAGE FOR LESBIANS AND GAY MEN

There is a widespread consensus that there is an urgent need to introduce legal reforms to address the significant problems created by the lack of legal recognition of the intimate relationships of lesbians and gay men. There are various ways in which this discrimination can be addressed:

- Civil marriage irrespective of the gender of the couple. This is the approach taken in a number of countries including most recently Spain.
- New partnership (non-marriage) legislation either restricted to same-sex couples (as in Britain and per Fine Gael policy) or open to all couples (as in the David Norris bill).
- Legal rights for cohabiting couples.

Based on the principle of equality of rights, duties and responsibilities, we are asking now that the law on civil marriage be amended so that it is open to any two people, irrespective of gender. It should be stressed that civil marriage is quite separate from a religious marriage and that what GLEN is calling for is marriage in the eyes of the state in a registry office as distinct from a religious marriage ceremony in a church. We make no comment or any request about the codes that apply to religious marriage ceremonies.

It has been suggested that gay, lesbian and bisexual people are somehow eager to have the rights accruing to the married state without accepting the responsibilities. The reverse is true. We currently accept our responsibilities and try to implement them, while being hampered by the lack of any legal frameworks that allow us to do so.

There are a number of reforms that could be introduced immediately that would significantly improve the circumstances for lesbian/gay couples, in some cases even without legislation. There is an encouraging precedent in the reform of the capital acquisition tax which now allows a person who has shared a house to inherit it without being then compelled to sell it to pay the tax. GLEN has also proposed successfully that the Domestic Violence Act and the Powers of Attorney Act make provision for couples who are not married. In addition there are, in particular, two important administrative changes that would greatly benefit people in our communities, as well as being of benefit to many others.

Where one person in a relationship is a parent, and wishes his or her partner to become the recognised co-parent of a child (or children), then it should be possible to sign a legal document that would implement this change. This would give added protection to children, whose rights must be protected in any new legal codes.

Currently the non-EU (unmarried) partner of an Irish person may be refused entry to the country; effectively the state can split couples up/keep partners apart. GLEN proposes that where a person can show that he/she is in a committed relationship with someone from outside the EU, then it should be legally possible to ensure that the partner can reside and work in Ireland. (Just such permissions were allowed in the UK many years before the full partnership laws for gays and lesbians were introduced in 2004.) We welcome the statement in the recent discussion document *Immigration and Residence in Ireland* (Department of Justice, Equality and Law Reform) that the issue of same-sex relationships will have to be considered.

Other administrative reforms would also help to reduce inequalities faced by all unable to marry. People should be able to nominate others as their 'next of kin', and have that choice fully recognised by hospitals and other agencies. People should be allowed to nominate their successors to pensions (both state and private), which they themselves have paid for.

The issue of cohabitation was considered in a recent Law Reform Commission *Consultation Paper on the Rights and Duties of Cohabitees*. The Commission recommended the imposition of certain limited legal rights and duties on cohabitees, including same-sex cohabitees, who satisfy certain criteria. The consultation paper included the statement that ' .... generally speaking, the law should not inhibit the formation of family relationships and should recognise as valid the relationships people choose for themselves'. GLEN supports this principle and necessary reforms so that all unmarried individuals can better order their lives and help those to whom they are committed.

While GLEN will continue to work towards equality in the marriage laws, we will also work alongside those who campaign instead for partnership laws, which could in the interim greatly improve the lives of people in our communities.

The widespread support for partnership rights for same-sex couples is evidenced in the recent National Economic and Social Forum Report No. 27 – Equality Policies for Lesbian, Gay and Bisexual People – and in the recommendations of the Equality Authority. Another important development is Fine Gael's policy, since June 2004, on civil partnership. The Taoiseach too has expressed support stating last November that gay couples are entitled to, and should have, the same tax and inheritance rights as married couples. Currently a lesbian couple is seeking a judicial review to have their foreign married relationship legally recognised in Ireland. GLEN contends, however, that legislation introduced in the Oireachtas – that would make a court case unnecessary – is a much more preferable way forward.

GLEN was founded in 1987 with a simple purpose, reflected in its name. In our campaigns and in our lobbying we asked that gay, lesbian and bisexual people be treated as equal citizens. In our involvement, sometimes very direct involvement, in the widely welcomed 1993 reform of the criminal law, in the amendments to the Employment Equality and Unfair Dismissals Acts, in the introduction of the Equal Status Act, and in other reforms we argued successfully for that principle of simple equality.

Background

Equality Authority Report
NESF Recommendations in Report No 27
Fine Gael Policy
David Norris Partnership Bill
High Court Case
Law Reform Commission Discussion Paper
Senate Debates
Statement of An Taoiseach
EA Research Report on Partnership Discrimination

GLOBAL WOMEN'S STRIKE, IRELAND

Regarding the forthcoming review of the Irish Constitution, the Global Women's Strike has two proposals:

1 that Article 41.2 in the Irish Constitution pertaining to the woman's life within the home be altered to give economic and social recognition to housework and all other caring work along the lines of Article 88 of the Constitution of the Bolivarian Republic of Venezuela (30 December 1999).
    Article 88 states:

> ... The State recognises work in the home as an economic activity that creates added value and produces social welfare and wealth. Housewives are entitled to Social Security in accordance with the law.

2 that building on the Irish Constitution, a specific clause be added to make explicit Ireland's historic neutrality.

BACKGROUND

The Global Women's Strike is a grassroots, non-party political network of women in over sixty countries, including Ireland. It began in the year 2000 on 8 March (International Women's Day) when women all around the world together demanded recognition and payment for all caring work in land, pensions, wages and other resources.

The idea came from women in Ireland who proposed a national strike. The International Wages for Housework Campaign (IWfHC), which, for several decades has campaigned for the economic and social recognition of all the unwaged work that women mostly do, took up the strike call and made it global. Every year since 2000 on 8 March and increasingly throughout the year, women have taken all kinds of grassroots actions to demand together that society Invest in Caring Not Killing – that military budgets are spent instead on what our communities need, coming first of all to women, the chief carers everywhere. The Strike's network and activities highlight the fact that two thirds of the world's work is done by women, the majority of which is unwaged work in the family, in the community and on the land.

Previous IWfHC organising included the co-ordination of over 1200 women's organisations and NGOs to win the decision by governments to measure and value this unwaged work in the *Beijing Platform for Action* in 1995. Although the Irish government implemented a pilot study to count this work in 1997, no further progress has been made.

Since 2002, the Global Women's Strike has been working with grassroots women and the Women's

Development Bank (Banmujer) in Venezuela. Among other measures, women in Venezuela won Article 88 of the Venezuelan Constitution, which recognises unwaged work in the home as economically productive and entitles housewives to social security.

The Global Women's Strike would be glad to provide detailed information and oral evidence to the Select Committee or any other constitutional review body on the issues raised in this submission.

PROPOSED WORDING FOR ARTICLE 41.2 ON THE RECOGNITION OF WORKERS IN THE HOME AND OF PAY EQUITY

Proposed wording for 41.2.1

The state recognises caring work done within the home, often extending to the community, as a social and economic activity that produces social welfare and economic wealth, and entitles carers, starting with mothers, to economic and other support.

The state also recognises that in rural areas caring work has included work on the land which has kept families and communities alive and strong despite poverty and emigration.

Proposed wording 41.2.2

The state shall therefore ensure that carers, starting with mothers, are not obliged by economic necessity to engage in waged work which would increase their workload, and shall provide workers in the home with independent remuneration and pensions.

Proposed wording for additional 41.2.3

The state shall also ensure that women, particularly mothers who do most of the vital work of caring for children and/or other dependents, do not suffer discrimination in wages, pensions, health care and social welfare when they go out to work, and that pay equity, that is, equal pay for work of equal value, is fully implemented.

Current wording of article 41.2.1

In particular, the state recognises that by her life within the home, woman gives to the state a support without which the common good cannot be achieved.

Current wording of article 41.2.2

The state shall, therefore, endeavour to ensure that mothers shall not be obliged by economic necessity to engage in labour to the neglect of their duties in the home.

WHY THE PROPOSED CHANGES

Some have called for abolition of Article 41.2 on the ground that it is sexist. While it is obviously sexist to refer to work in the home as a woman's 'life' and as her 'duty', it would be even more sexist to obliterate the only constitutional recognition of unwaged caring work, done at great personal cost by generations of women and up to the present day, and its vital contribution to society's survival and welfare. Article 41.2 must be reworded to reflect accurately the value of this work, the skill of the workers who do it and the entitlements it should earn them, and thus help end the gross discrimination women have suffered both as workers in the home and workers outside.

The Global Women's Strike (GWS) – a network with national co-ordinations in 11 countries, including Ireland, and participating organisations in over 60 countries – was formed to urge the economic and social recognition of unwaged caring work. As early as 1952 the GWS's international co-ordinator was speaking out to make visible this unwaged contribution of women.

Unremunerated work entered the international agenda in 1975, at the opening conference of the UN Decade for Women in Mexico City. The mid-decade conference in 1980 in Copenhagen, Denmark, gave it additional legitimacy with the International Labour Office (ILO) figure (conservative in our view) that women do two-thirds of the world's work, yet receive only 5% of its income. In 1985 at the final conference of the UN Decade in Nairobi, Kenya, we won Paragraph 120 which stated that the work women do in the home, on the land and in the community is to be included in national statistics. Finally in 1995, in Beijing, China, the International Women Count Network (co-ordinated by the International Wages for Housework Campaign which also co-ordinates the GWS), supported by more than 2,000 organisations worldwide (including from Ireland), won the decision that national accounts are to include measuring and valuing unwaged work: how much of their lifetime women (and to a lesser extent men) spend doing unwaged work and how much value this work creates. It was a turning point globally.

Trinidad & Tobago was the first country to put this into law in 1996. Spain followed in 1998. The Bolivarian Republic of Venezuela went further, enshrining in its 1999 Constitution the social and economic recognition of unwaged work in the context of equality and equity between the sexes. Article 88 states:

> The state guarantees equality and equity between men and women in the exercise of their right to work. The state recognises work in the home as an economic activity that creates added value and produces social welfare and wealth. Housewives are entitled to social security in accordance with the law.

In March 2005, the GWS organised a European speaking tour for Nora Castañeda, President of Venezuela's Women's Development Bank, and Angélica Alvarez, the Bank's promoter in Bolívar state. When speaking about the importance of Article 88, Ms Castañeda explained that, 'Women are the carers of the species, there is no work more important than that and society has a debt to women.'

In her weekly radio programme, Ms Castañeda quotes Selma James, GWS co-ordinator:

> Caring for others is accomplished by a dazzling array of skills in an endless variety of circumstances. As well as cooking, shopping, cleaning and laundering, planting, tending and harvesting for others, women comfort and guide, nurse and teach, arrange and advise, discipline and encourage, fight for and pacify. This skilled work, which requires judgement and above all self-discipline and selflessness, is most often performed within the family. Taxing and exhausting under any circumstances, this service work, this emotional housework, has an additional emotional cost when it is done for and on behalf of those whom the woman is emotionally involved with. But all this is expected of women by everyone: friends and neighbours, workmates, employers (why else is the secretary called the 'office wife'?), as well as family; this emotional work is done both outside and inside the home. The Global Kitchen, London. 1985

Soon after Ms James added:

> We women are the first to defend and protect those in our care. It goes unremarked that it is usually women – mothers, wives, partners, sisters, daughters, grannies and aunties – who are the driving force of justice campaigns, whether or not we are prominent or even visible in them.

Recognition of the work that women do in the new Venezuelan constitution and Venezuela's determination to deal with poverty, starting with women (70% of those living in poverty are women), have led to other anti-sexist measures such as Article 14 of the Land Act which prioritises woman-headed households for the redistribution of idle land to those ready to work it, and the creation of the Women's Development Bank, a state micro-credit institution which has distributed 51,000 credits so far.

Venezuela's Article 88 has set a new standard for the world, including for Article 41.2 of the Irish Constitution. We have adapted it to the Irish situation, in the wording we are proposing for Paragraphs 41.2.1 and 41.2.2, and for an additional Paragraph 41.2.3.

In rural Ireland caring work, done mainly by women, has traditionally included making the land fruitful – tending orchards, gardens and fields, rearing and tending animals, gathering berries, herbs, etc. For centuries this field and yard work has helped to keep families and communities alive and strong in the face of poverty and emigration. Although large numbers of people have now moved to live in urban areas, 40% of us still live in rural areas and many more have roots in the countryside, wherever we live – we are the product of the caring work our mothers, grannies, sisters, aunties and other women single or married, and their

mothers before them, bestowed on us in times of great hardship.

The Irish Constitution has never before recognised the vital contribution of rural women. It is too late for those who while they lived received no pension or other entitlements in their own right which their work should have earned them. But it is not too late to pay tribute to their work by recognising its continuing value to society and the economy, and by recognising the role women continue to play in rural life today – particularly as the livelihoods of small farmers and all who depend on them are increasingly under threat in the global market.

In response to the international grassroots movement of women for the recognition of unwaged caring work, which has the support of many men, many countries are carrying out time-use surveys. And increasingly, unwaged work, its quantity and economic value, is a consideration in court decisions and governments' policies.

Many women are forced by economic necessity to work the double or triple day, going out to one or more waged jobs while also carrying the responsibility of caring work at home. At the waged workplace women are discriminated against in wages and working conditions – paid less than their male colleagues even when both do the same job. Even more widespread is the segregation of women in service work which is much like the caring work most of us do at home. While many of these jobs are highly skilled, these skills are not recognised financially, and the status of the work is dragged down by the low status of unwaged caring work at home. To end the sexist pay gap between women and men, equal pay for work of equal value must be added to the Constitution.

Pay equity is already the agreed standard in a number of international policies and agreements which the Irish state has signed on to, e.g. the ILO Equal Remuneration Convention, the Convention on the Elimination of All Forms of Discrimination Against Women (CEDAW) and the Beijing *Platform for Action*.

Article 2.1 of the ILO Convention states:

> Each member shall, by means appropriate to the methods in operation for determining rates of remuneration, promote and, in so far as is consistent with such methods, ensure the application to all workers of the principle of equal remuneration for men and women workers for work of equal value.
>
> (Concerning Equal Remuneration for Men and Women Workers for Work of Equal Value, 1951)

To enshrine in the Irish Constitution the principle that caring work in the home – which extends to caring for the whole community and in rural areas to caring for and protecting the land and the environment – is valued socially and economically, would ensure that women, particularly mothers, are not penalised with the lowest pay when they go out to work or discriminated against in areas such as pensions, health care, childcare, and social welfare. It would be a major step towards raising all women's status and entitlements.

Last but not least, it is our experience that men are aware of their dependence on caring work, starting with the work of their mothers. Many also agree that not counting caring work maintains the traditional division of labour between the sexes. They agree that raising the status of the carer would put women in a stronger position to demand that men, who often miss out on children's upbringing, take their full share of responsibility and become carers too.

GLUE – GAY AND LESBIAN UNIONS EIRE

INTRODUCTION

GLUE is an independent group promoting equal partnership rights for LGBTQ partnerships through awareness and advocacy.

Formed in May 2004 by Mark Lacey, Mo Halpin, Adriano Avila and Dil Wickremasinghe, GLUE represents hundreds of same-sex couples that are struggling with the immigration issue. We have carefully selected a range of case studies so as to illustrate the human plight that these couples must endure on a daily basis.

Currently in Ireland, marriage does not include same-sex couples, so we, as same-sex couples, cannot be legally married. Also, there is no provision for the legal registration of same-sex partnerships as civil registration and religious ceremony practically go hand in hand. This means that same-sex partnerships neither have equal rights or opportunities to achieve equal rights as heterosexual married couples.

In some European countries, legal recognition to varying degrees has been given to same-sex partnerships. In the Netherlands, for example, the definition of marriage includes same-sex relationships so lesbians, gays and bisexuals have the same partnership rights as heterosexual married couples. In France, Denmark and Germany, same-sex couples cannot get married but can register their 'life partnership' to give it legal status.

GLUE's main recommendation is that the Irish Constitution should embrace a broader definition of marriage and become an anti-discriminatory reflection of the citizens of Ireland.

OBJECTIVES OF THIS PAPER

It is not the purpose of this document to argue for or against the family. The above only serves to highlight that Article 41 is long overdue for change. It is the purpose of this document to argue that if after a limited number of years the Constitution has failed to protect that for which it was created, then a more adaptable, unbiased and more tolerant approach is needed if it is not to need changing again in seventy years time. For this to happen it needs to be designed for all and be inclusive of all irrespective of gender, race, sexual orientation, religious beliefs, colour, social or financial standing. It should also have the foresight to accommodate changes in Irish society in the future. This is also necessary given the flexible nature of the European constitution.

It is impossible to cover all aspects of the article and their impact. This paper is to set out the impact of Article 41 in respect of same-sex relationships where one partner is a foreign national from outside the EU. We would hope, however, that comparisons would be drawn in respect of all relationships. Since divorce has been legalised, the incidence of the problems experienced by same-sex couples in this situation will increase within opposite-sex relationships given the five year period it takes for divorce to take effect.

ARTICLE 41.1.1

'The state recognises the family as the natural primary and fundamental unit of society, and as a moral institution possessing inalienable and imprescriptible rights, and antecedent and superior to all positive law.'

When the above article was written 1937, this may have been the case but according to the 2002 census results Article 41.1.1 does not reflect modern society. The article is loaded with biased, discriminatory statements and is in direct contravention of European law and the Equal Status Act, 2000.

According to the census 2002, there were 77,600 family units based on cohabiting couples in Ireland, a figure that had more than doubled since the previous census. In the same census 1,300 couples described themselves as same-sex cohabiting couples, of whom two-thirds were male.

1.2 'The state therefore guarantees to protect the family in its constitution and authority, as the necessary basis of social order and as indispensable to the welfare of the nation and the state.'

This point discriminates and presumes that anyone who is not of a family as defined by the Constitution will lack the basis of social order and will be dispensable to the welfare of the nation and the state. The vast majority of same-sex and heterosexual unmarried couples are discriminated against and it assumes a very antiquated view that anyone falling outside the considered norms of society is something to be feared and frowned upon.

2.1 'In particular the state recognises that by her life within the home, woman gives to the state as a support without which the common good cannot be achieved.'

There isn't a woman in Ireland who wouldn't find this offensive. This article is in direct violation of the Equal Status Act, 2000.

2.2 'The state shall therefore endeavour to ensure that mothers shall not be obliged by economic necessity to engage in labour to the neglect of their duties in their home.'

In 2005, Ireland considers itself as an advanced and modern society. In fact, approximately three years ago Fianna Fáil introduced in its budgets cut backs that were designed to get the female out of the home and into the work force, which is perfectly acceptable in 2005. However, this would mean that Fianna Fáil was in breach of the Constitution under this article. Furthermore, most households cannot survive on a single income where this may have been the case in 1937.

3.1 'The state pledges itself to guard with special care the institution of marriage, on which the family is founded and to protect it against attack.'

With reference to the census of 2002, approximately 70% of households in Ireland are blatantly discriminated against. Article 41 implies that the family is founded on the institution of marriage alone and quite clearly that is not the case in 2005. This article promotes social stigma to be attached to those who choose not to or who cannot marry. It also implies that the state only gives special care to those who are married. This is not only discriminatory, it also suggests that the state *will* discriminate against anything other than marriage.

GLUE recommends a change in the Constitution's provisions on the family. Article 41.3, states:

> to guard with special care the institution of marriage, on which the family is founded, and to protect it against attack.

This would be replaced by the UN definition of family:

> any combination of two or more persons who are bound together by ties of mutual consent, birth and/or adoption or placement and who, together, assume responsibility for, *inter alia,* the care and maintenance of group members, the addition of new members through procreation or adoption, the socialisation of children and the social control of members.

This broad definition – free of troublesome words like 'marriage,' 'father,' 'mother,' 'husband' or 'wife' – would certainly put cohabiting couples on equal footing as couples who can marry.

3.2 'A court designated by law may grant a dissolution of marriage where, but only where, it is satisfied that:

i   At the date of the institution of the proceedings the spouses have lived apart from one another for a period of, or periods amounting to, at least four years during the five years

ii   There is no reasonable prospect of reconciliation between the spouses

iii   Such provisions as the court considers proper having regard to the circumstances exist or will be made for the spouses, any children of either or both of them and any other person prescribed by law, and

iv   Any further conditions prescribed by law are complied with.

This obviously does not apply to people who cannot marry. However, it should not be assumed that people who cannot or choose not to get married in a religious sense want only the benefits of marriages but they are also willing to honour its responsibilities.

3.3 'No person whose marriage has been dissolved under the civil law of any other state but is a subsisting valid marriage under the law for the time being in force within the jurisdiction of the government and parliament established by this Constitution shall be capable of contracting a valid marriage within that jurisdiction during the lifetime of the other party to the marriage so dissolved.'

Obviously this no longer applies since divorce law has changed in this country and more obviously it doesn't apply to people who cannot marry.

ARTICLE 41 – IN GENERAL

Reading Article 41 one cannot fail to miss the implications identified above. More interestingly, as it stands, it seems that no one in today's modern Irish society could live up to the impossible standard as set out by this article. Whether a person can marry or not almost becomes irrelevant in terms of the article.

Not all families are based around marriage as defined by the Constitution. Furthermore the majority of families that are would also have grave difficulty living up to its definition. The majority of families in Ireland today are subsisted by an extra income that comes from the wife and/or mother being in employment also.

This is often not a choice. In fact as mentioned earlier, the present government encourages it. The Constitution then only serves to discriminate against these women also by putting them second to women who can afford not to work.

Indeed it puts her entire family second in terms of the Constitution. In this respect it could be argued that the Constitution doesn't even protect those families that are based on marriage but can be detrimental to those same families. It could also be argued that the Constitution now only serves a limited number of families, which are financially better off than others. It could then be argued that Article 41 discriminates on the basis of a family's income.

Further to this it states that no woman should have to work outside the home due to limited finances and will endeavour to protect them from such. Quite clearly the state fails in this respect when it encourages women to enter the workforce. If the state cannot or won't uphold the Constitution as it sees fit, then it should be assumed that the state is also in agreement that Article 41 is obsolete. If the state is to lead by example, its citizenry should not have to uphold Article 41 either.

PARTNERSHIP RIGHTS OF SAME-SEX COUPLES

In line with the 'Legal Series', The Equality Authority published a report on 'Partnership rights of same-sex couples'. The following paragraphs taken from that report highlight the current situation in Ireland today and in terms of immigration and the discrimination associated therewith.

Immigration, work permits, Irish nationality and citizenship

'Where an Irish national marries a non-EEA national, it is necessary for the non-EEA spouse of the Irish national to follow a number of procedures in order for him/her to settle and work in Ireland. The couple must present the following documents to the immigration officer at the point of entry: an entry visa (if the person is a citizen of a country which requires an entry visa), a certificate of marriage, birth certificate of the non-EEA national and the passports of both parties. The immigration officer can stamp the passport to allow the non-EEA national to remain in the state for a maximum period of three months. During this period the non-EEA national must report to either a local garda station or the immigration office in Dublin and present to them the same documentation as above including the birth certificate of the Irish national. On the basis of the same the non-national can apply for residency in the state. The passport of the non-national is endorsed for a further period of twelve months after which, save for exceptional circumstances, residency is granted.

This is in stark contrast to the situation of an unmarried, non-EEA partner of an Irish citizen, who wishes to reside in the state with her/his partner. Such a person must apply for an extension every three months in order to remain and prove that, in so doing, he or she can support himself or herself, without being a burden on the state.

Work permits, work visas and work authorisations

All non-EEA citizens require a work permit, a work visa or a work authorisation, depending on their country of origin to enable them to work in Ireland, with the exception of the non-EEA spouse of an Irish national who no longer requires a work permit, to enable him or her to work in Ireland. The employment sought must be in an area in which there is a shortage of skills among Irish nationals and EEA nationals.

A citizen of the EEA may bring his or her spouse and dependants to Ireland without the need of a work permit. Similarly, partners in a same-sex relationship who are both EEA nationals can travel and work in a member state including Ireland without requiring work permits.

A citizen of the EEA whose spouse is a non-EEA national may be accompanied by that spouse, providing the marriage is recognised by the state. 'Marriage' is understood to refer to heterosexual marriage and would not by definition extend to homosexual marriages.

Irish nationality and citizenship

Under the terms of the Irish Nationality and Citizenship Acts, 1956 and 1986, there are three ways in which a non-national can become an Irish citizen: by descent, through naturalisation and through post-nuptial citizenship. This exposes an area of discrimination in that non-national persons who are married to Irish citizens may be accorded citizenship on the basis of their marital status, subject to certain conditions. As marriage is denied to same-sex couples in Ireland, an alien, involved in a homosexual relationship with an Irish national, is not entitled to citizenship under the post-nuptial provisions. Furthermore, the marriage would have to be one recognised in Ireland, ruling out same-sex marriages that are conducted abroad. The non-national same-sex partner of an Irish citizen, who wishes to become an Irish citizen, must apply for naturalisation under the relevant provisions of the Irish Nationality and Citizen Acts.

SAME-SEX PARTNERSHIP RIGHTS AROUND THE WORLD: A SUMMARY

These countries allow homosexual couples to marry: Belgium, Canada (British Columbia, Manitoba, Nova Scotia, Ontario, Quebec and Yukon Territory only), Netherlands and United States (Massachusetts only).

The Netherlands allows same-sex couples to marry, granting gay couples 'complete parity with married heterosexual couples'.

The countries listed below give residency permits to foreign partners of its homosexual citizenry, as well as many other rights like inheritance, property, pension, hospital visitation, social security, income tax, housing and various benefits to same-sex couples. Quite possibly the next countries which will give total equality to same-sex couples as heterosexual married couples will come from this list: Australia, Belgium, Brazil, Canada, Denmark, Finland, France, Germany, Iceland, Israel, Netherlands, New Zealand, Norway, South Africa, Sweden and the United Kingdom.

Countries that give national domestic partner benefits to homosexual couples: Australia, Belgium, Brazil, Canada, Denmark, France, Germany, Greenland, Hungary, Iceland, Israel, Italy, New Zealand, Norway, Portugal, Spain and Sweden.

Countries that have a national gay rights law that bans some anti-gay discrimination: Brazil, Bulgaria, Canada, Denmark, Ecuador, Fiji, Finland, France, Iceland, Ireland, Israel, Lithuania, Luxembourg, Malta, Mexico, Namibia, Netherlands, New Zealand, Norway, Romania, Slovenia, South Africa, Spain, Sweden, Switzerland and the United Kingdom.

Taken from data published by the International Human Rights Council in 2005.

PARTNERSHIP RIGHTS IN BRITAIN

Britain has been chosen for observation due to close political ties and proximity with Ireland as opposed to France which operates under Napoleonic Law. Britain, as Ireland, operates under Common Law. Our legislation is very similar. In some instances it is the same as a consequence of Ireland being under British rule for several hundred years.

Several interesting facts have occurred in Britain over the last ten years both in terms of immigration and gay partnership rights.

In the mid-1990s, after trying all the usual ways of obtaining citizenship for their non-EU partners, i.e. work permits, unlawful marriage etc, many couples started making applications to the British government on the basis of their relationship. Following this, Labour made a pact with the Stonewall Immigration Group (now the UK Lesbian and Gay Immigration Group – UKLGIG), to sort out the partnership situation.

In 1997 Labour introduced the 'Unmarried Partners Concession'. If a couple could prove that they had lived together for four years or more in Britain, residency would be granted to the non-EU partner, after which three years he or she could apply for citizenship.

In 1999 the time period was dropped to two years after it was deemed next to impossible for couples to remain legally in Britain for four years.

Last year (2004), the 'Civil Partnership Bill' was passed. The Queen has just ratified it and it is due to come into force later this year. This bill will give same-sex couples the same rights and entitlements as married couples, i.e. tax, immigration, etc.

A criticism of the bill could be that heterosexual couples cannot avail of civil partnership. It was felt that to allow heterosexual couples to enter into a civil partnership would be to undermine the institution of marriage.

Implications for Ireland and Irish nationals

Under the Good Friday Agreement Ireland and Britain are expected to uphold the laws of both countries. By the end of this year, Ireland will be expected under the agreement to honour the 'Civil Partnership Bill 2004'.

Due to the close political and legal ties that exist between Britain and Ireland, an Irish national can now move to England with his/her foreign national non-EU partner and register their relationship. There is no time frame to register the relationship as there isn't one for a couple who can marry. A couple can register their relationship and remain there legally once they have done so. So, a couple who have lived in Ireland for two years and where one is an Irish national can move to the UK, register their relationship and obtain residency (providing of course that they can prove that they lived in Ireland for two years). After residing there for a further five years the non-EU national can then apply for a British passport.

The time frame isn't written in stone though, nor is where the couple live. If they are a same-sex couple where one is from Australia and the other is Irish and they have lived in South America for four years, they can then move to England and register their relationship. The difference is that in this situation they only have to wait three more years to obtain a British passport for the non-EU national.

Please note that the time frame doesn't apply in terms of registering the relationship (civil union). It applies in terms of applying for the passport. The same would also apply to heterosexual couples who can marry. Furthermore, the three years it takes to apply for the passport is standard for any such application and as such always has been.

Should one of the partners be illegally residing in a country with an Irish/EU partner, he/she cannot enter the UK from that country. The person would have to return to his/her own country and enter the UK from there. Again there is no time specified on this. Such persons can return to their own country for as little as it takes to get their affairs in order. This can be as little as one day and therefore is little more than a formality.

PARTNERSHIP RIGHTS IN FRANCE

The Pacs is an alternative legal union in France for both heterosexual and homosexual couples, which is called *Le Pacte civil de solidarité*, commonly known as *Le Pacs*. While it falls well short of conferring the legal rights which married spouses enjoy, it has a legal status which offers both official recognition of the union and a number of rights for both individuals. It does not have any legal bearing over questions such as the adoption of children.

The Pacs is established before a local magistrate's court for civil cases, called a *tribunal d'instance*. The parties can draw up a document specific to themselves which defines their engagement concerning financial matters, such as the equal share of household finances. The Pacs can be signed between two unmarried people, regardless of nationality or sex.

Mutual and material help of the two partners

You can define the terms of this 'help' in the contract. If this is not defined, the partners will have to share (50-50%) any debts contracted by one of them in everyday life's costs and costs linked to the shared accommodation.

Whatever each partner owns

- Furniture: if not mentioned otherwise in the contract, furniture bought together after the signature of the contract will be equally shared between the two partners (50-50%).
- Any other assets (building, placements, cars, etc): anything bought or concluded between the partners after signature of the contract will be divided 50-50 unless specified otherwise in the contract.

Note: signature of the Pacs doesn't influence goods bought before the signature of the contact.

Other consequences

- The partner can benefit from social cover of the French *securite sociale* (illness, maternity and life insurance) of his/her partner.
- In case of a visa request from the non-French partner, the Pacs is a positive element in the definition of 'personal links' in France.
- If one of the partners is a civil servant, the partners will be entitled to geographical reunion in case they live apart.
- Rented accommodation: in case the owner of the lease leaves the place or in case of a death, the lease will be passed over to the partner, till the end of the leasing contract.

CASE STUDIES

As opposed to married couples, unmarried and same-sex couples are treated as individuals and not jointly when it comes to their immigration applications. Legally, they are strangers in law.

The following case studies highlight the numerous situations that same-sex couples can find themselves in when one or both partners are from outside the EU. These have been kindly submitted by the members of GLUE. (Some names have been changed to protect their privacy.)

Couples with one partner who is non-EU

These couples do not have the security and stability that would be awarded to a heterosexual couple of the same standing who have the convenience of marriage to resolve their immigration difficulties. The pre-mentioned same-sex couples cannot plan their future as the non-EU national depends on obtaining a work permit. Work permits are stringent and time consuming to obtain, and also do not offer job security or mobility and leaves them open to control and abuse by their employers. A couple in this situation may apply for residency. Frequently this is rejected on the grounds that they have a work permit, hence they are living legally in the country, and therefore residency is not deemed necessary.

Case Study – Mo and Dil

Dil is Sri Lankan and Mo is an Irish national. They met whilst working in the Middle East they are now living in Ireland. They have been committed to each other for the past 5 years and this is reflected by the fact that they have bought a house, have joint bank accounts and both families have accepted them as their own. The only difference about their relationship is that it is a same-sex partnership.

Dil had to resort to acquiring a work permit on an annual basis through her employer to stay in Ireland.

This is hardly ideal as the work permit system is deeply flawed in many respects. If they were a heterosexual couple a trip to the registry office would have ended all their residency issues.

They decided to lodged an application on the basis of their relationship with the assistance of a solicitor; however, after a painstaking two-year wait, the application was rejected due to the fact that Dil already had a legal work permit. The Department of Justice advised them to cancel Dil's work permit and to reapply.

Dil and Mo decided that this would be too risky as without a work permit Dil would not be able to work and their household like most could not exist on one income. They were infuriated that the Department of Justice even suggested this and gave up their efforts to gain residency.

[For the full text of Dil and Mo's personal submission, please contact GLUE.]

Couples where both partners are non-EU

As above, but also these couples cannot apply for residency due to the fact that neither is Irish or from the EU.

Case Study – Leona and Bibti

Both women arrived in Ireland on a student visa. As both are of non-EU nationality it is not possible for either of them to work legally for more then twenty euro per week. This not only limits both of them financially while they are studying in the country but also forces them, perhaps, to work illegally for extra money to support and pay for their accommodation, living, student expenses etc. Both Leona and Bibti have been recognised in their own country of origin, Canada, as legal partners, but in Ireland they have no standing as a couple. Once their studies have been complete, they will be forced to leave the country and return to Canada unless they can secure a residency permit to reside in the state.

Couples where one partner is illegal

This is where one partner is EU and the other is non-EU. This situation is not by choice as in most cases the non-EU partner has endeavoured to secure a work permit or a valid visa to remain in the country and has failed. In this situation the couple is subjected to intense stress, feelings of insecurity and uncertainty of what the future may hold.

Case Study – Matthew and Stephan

Matthew is Irish, Stephan is Peruvian. Although Matthew can work, live and reside in Ireland as a citizen, his partner Stephan cannot. Stephan entered Ireland on a three-month visa, and still remains in the country. Although Stephan arrived in Ireland more then seven years ago, he is not entitled to apply for naturalisation as he does not currently have a residency or work permit. When Stephan arrived in Ireland, it was not necessary for him to have a work permit, and was granted a PPS number. He applied for work, and he was granted a job, which he still holds today. His employer did not realise that he was from a non-EU country, and to this day, the truth has not emerged. Stephan works a forty hour week, earns a salary, paying tax and PRSI. However, should Stephan wish to move jobs, he will have to apply for a work permit and start from scratch.

His employer may suffer the consequences of employing a non-EU employee, unbeknownst to him, and may be penalised. Stephan does not advise his employer of this as it is his wish to remain with his partner Matthew in Ireland.

Couples where both partners are illegal

As above, but also these couples cannot apply for residency due to the fact that neither is Irish or from the EU.

Attention should be given to the fact that both these strangers to the country selected this country as their choice of home. These people could also be here due to refugee or asylum reasons. An example of where this could occur is where a couple from a non-EU country are living in Ireland because their lives are in jeopardy as it is illegal to be homosexual in their country and have had no choice but to leave despite the fact that they would be illegal in this country. This may seem like a trade off but in some countries the death penalty still applies for homosexual offences. Some could come here under the belief that they can apply for asylum or refugee status, not aware that this is not necessarily the case.

Case Study – Flavio and Marius

This is a Romanian couple who came to Ireland on a holiday visa in 2002 and are currently living and working in Ireland illegally. They are economic migrants and chose Ireland as it is a much wealthier country than Romania. Also their relationship was not accepted in Romania and they felt unsafe to remain there. Having to work illegally they are unprotected by employment law.

Couples where one partner is out of the country

This is where an Irish or EU partner is resident in Ireland and his/her partner, who is not Irish or EU, resides outside Ireland or the EU. This could very well be the worst scenario out of these examples. Due to the nature of immigration policy at present, it is extremely difficult for persons who are from a non-EU country to enter Ireland, or the EU, particularly if they have lived here before and had to leave because of various situations. These individuals are particularly suspected once they try to re-enter the country and would more then likely be refused entry. Applying for residency or leave-to-remain from outside any country will not lead to a successful outcome.

Note: General advice given by lawyers both in this country and other countries, is that under no circumstances should somebody who is in a same-sex relationship, where one of them is non-EU, leave the country, as it is generally understood amongst the legal profession that once the partner leaves the country, there is very little chance of ever returning.

Case Study – Anita and Siobhán

Anita is Indian and Siobhán is Irish. Siobhán moved to India in 2000 to work in a software company and while she was there she met Anita. After six months they moved in together and Anita introduced Siobhán to her family. This came as a huge shock and Anita's family disowned her and completely cut her off. They both decided to leave India as their life style would not be accepted. Siobhán travelled to Ireland first to make arrangements for Anita to join her but realised once she arrived that obtaining a visa would be difficult. Anita has applied for a visa from the Irish Embassy in Delhi but it has been refused. They are considering moving to the UK as they would stand a better chance there.

Couples where both partners are out of the country

With both partners residing outside Ireland or the EU legally, and with one partner being non-EU and the other EU, it may be that person's wish to return (for any reason) such as an ill parent or family member, but cannot return because their relationship would be void, not recognised in this country. This is a perfect example of the impact it would have on the people outside the relationship, i.e. their loved ones. In effect such persons are forced into a situation where they have to compromise their relationship or their loved ones.

Case Study – Gerry and Imran

Gerry is Irish and Imran is Pakistani. They are living in London and have been in a committed relationship for the last three years. The UK immigration authorities have recognised their relationship and have awarded Imran right to remain in the UK so that he can be with his Irish partner. Gerry would love to return to Ireland but cannot as Imran would not be able to come with him due to the lack of immigration rights for same-sex couples. Gerry and Imran can only come to Ireland on holidays till Imran can apply for British citizenship.

Couples where both partners are EU nationals

When the same-sex couple is constituted of two EU nationals they are both able to reside and work in Ireland but still cannot avail of the same benefits that a heterosexual married couple would have. This is especially unfair when one of the EU nationals is from a country where civil unions are accessible to same-sex couples but these are not recognised in Ireland.

Case Study – Cathy and Dee

Dee is Irish, Cathy is French. Both parties have the right to reside and work in Ireland legally. However, as a couple, they are not recognised in Ireland legally, and to some degree, socially as a couple. Inheritance rights, next of kin, pensions, social welfare benefits do not apply to them as they are applied to a heterosexual married couple. Dee and Cathy have been legally recognised in France under the Pacs. If they moved to France they would be able to avail of all the benefits.

[For the full text of Cathy and Dee's personal submission, please contact GLUE.]

THE EFFECTS ON THE IRISH AND NON-IRISH PARTNER

Effects on the Irish partner

- Irish partner resents own country more and more for excluding partner
- Feelings of helpless, frustration and anger because of not being able to help partner.
- Feelings of guilt for keeping the non-EU partner here and have him/her subjected to taking menial jobs and being paid minimum wages.
- Cannot travel with partner.
- Must be conscious of supporting the non-EU partner and therefore limited job mobility.
- Causes family of Irish partner concern.

Effects on the non-Irish partner

- Insecure about future/can't make any plans.
- Foreign partner feels guilty about holding Irish partner back from travelling, buying a house and basically can't settle down.
- Both partners cannot be full active members of society.
- Foreign partner can't travel to visit family, even in the case of an emergency – feeling intense isolation, can't leave because unsure of being able to rejoin partner.
- As foreign partner cannot work legally, unemployment is likely and person might have to rely on Irish partner thereby putting pressure on the relationship. Foreign partner may enter into illegal employment, which may leave him/her exposed to abuse and exploitation.

Immigration Control Case Study – Ruairi and Ismail

After two years living abroad, Ruairi arrives into Dublin airport immigration control with his same-sex life partner Ismail. They have been together for four years and Ismail is not an EU citizen. Ismail, who does not need an entry visa, enters through the non-EU gate. Ruairi, having an Irish passport accompanied Ismail though the non-EU channel to assist him with any difficulties. This channel is different from the one that

Ruairi has entered through a hundred times and this gives them cause for concern (nobody they have spoken to about this knows or recognises the gate they are talking about).

The officer then proceeds to question Ismail in a very hostile manner and then at a point tries to trick and confuse him by rephrasing the same questions, which required a rephrasing of the same answer. When the answer was offered Ismail was accused of changing his story in an intimidating manner from the customs official. For Ismail, this was a very upsetting and frightening situation. Ruairi's case is not only frightening but also humiliating and infuriating. Ruairi tells us that despite the fear of Ismail being deported at this point, the gut reaction is one of total anger and bracing yourself and your partner for anything that is about to happen.

Their feelings are that this point of entry is designated to deal with the 'non desirables' and filter them out before they can enter Ireland legally. They deal with them in a disrespectful, inhumane way which violates basic international human dignity.

The way in which this is done is reprehensible. Firstly, as noticed by Ruairi and Ismail, the vast majority of people passing did not have English as their mother tongue, and therefore had difficulty understanding and expressing their situation. Secondly, there is only a limited selection of European languages on the immigration forms, totally useless as this channel is for non-EU residents and should not be left to immigration officers alone.

OTHER ARGUMENTS

The following are arguments put forward by different groups over the past couple of years. GLUE's position on these arguments is put forward.

Last year the Law Reform Commission said, 'persons who, although they are not married to one another, live together in a "marriage like" relationship for a continuous period of three years or where there is a child of the relationship for two years. The commission acknowledges that "marriage like" relationships exists between same-sex couples as well as opposite-sex couples' (LRC 2004:1).

The LRC and Fine Gael have drawn up proposals outlining rights that would be given to cohabiting couples. While GLUE finds this encouraging, it is completely opposed to cohabiting couples having to be in a relationship for a continuous period of three years or two where there may be a child. Care should always be taken not to replace one discrimination with another. People who can marry do not have time periods imposed on them in order for their relationship to be deemed valid. This was tried in Britain (see above). Initially a time frame of four years was introduced. Two years later this was reduced to two years. Last year, the time frame was abandoned in the 'Civil Partnership Bill'. The period of proof comes after the registration of the relationship, in the same way as it applies to heterosexual couples. GLUE expects full and equal treatment as accorded to others. Anything else is privileging certain people above others and is against the Equal Status Act, 2000.

Another point to note is that when it comes to immigration, the proposal differs substantially. Fine Gael recommends that 'the right to residency in Ireland will automatically be conferred on a foreign registered partner of an Irish citizen'. The LRC recommends that no changes be made to either immigration law or naturalisation laws. 'The Commission does not recommend any change to immigration law insofar as it applies to cohabitees at present' (LRC, 2004:4).

'The commission does not recommend any change to the Irish nationality or citizenship acts to allow for the extension of the arrangements for the naturalisation of married partners to cohabiting partners' (LRC, 2004:160).

The LRC's recommendations are loaded and discriminatory towards people who cannot marry. Further to this, as Irish immigration law is generally considered to be obsolete and in desperate need of complete revision, GLUE questions any body that recommends that changes to immigration or naturalisation laws as fundamental as this should not be implemented. These decisions are against the recommendations of the National Economic and Social Forum, which in 2003 advised that 'the Department of Justice, Equality and Law Reform, Department of Enterprise, Trade and Employment (and Department of Foreign Affairs) should establish appropriate mechanisms to accord equal rights of residency and work entitlements for foreign partners of Irish citizens who are same-sex couples, or unmarried heterosexual couples as are accorded to married heterosexual couples' (NESF, 2003:64).

Despite the fact that Ireland is one of only three countries not to recognise some form of partnership (Italy and Greece being the other two) the LRC also recommends that 'no changes be made to the law to allow the state to recognise foreign registered partnerships or cohabitations' (LRC 2004:159).

It could be construed under International and European law that Ireland is in breach, by not upholding the rights of these relationships as granted by their own countries.

Last but not least, it should be noted that in the original Constitution which was written in Irish, the word that we commonly assume to be marriage is 'Teaghlach'. This is not actually true; 'Teaghlach' translated into English means household. Therefore it could be argued that all committed co-habiting relationships irrespective of gender or marital status are binding under the Constitution.

CONCLUSION

GLUE's primary concern for making this submission to the Oireachtas is to ensure immigration rights be granted to committed same-sex partnerships. We have highlighted the injustices that same-sex couples must endure on a daily basis and we hope that this submission will assist in the creation of legislation to encompass our fast growing cosmopolitan community. We also hope that this will benefit heterosexual couples.

GRACE BIBLE FELLOWSHIP

HOW SHOULD THE FAMILY BE DEFINED?

The family should be defined as the Constitution's original authors assumed it should be defined, as people who are related to one another through marriage and parenthood. To change the wording in Article 41.3.1 which states that marriage is the foundation of the family would be to drastically undermine its role as 'the fundamental unit group of society' and 'the necessary basis of social order'. Therefore any attempt to redefine this fundamental unit would be potentially very damaging to society.

HOW SHOULD ONE STRIKE THE BALANCE BETWEEN THE RIGHTS OF THE FAMILY AS A UNIT AND THE RIGHTS OF INDIVIDUAL MEMBERS?

The rights of the individual and the family should not normally be seen as competing. The individual should be considered as an organic, rather than atomic, member of the family unit. However, the state should guarantee the rights of the individual and should be particularly sensitive to those rights when normal family relations have ceased to function.

IS IT POSSIBLE TO GIVE CONSTITUTIONAL PROTECTION TO FAMILIES OTHER THAN THOSE BASED ON MARRIAGE?

The question should relate more to the advisability than to the possibility. It would be inadvisable to extend constitutional rights to 'families' based on arrangements other than marriage. This would encourage a rise in less stable, more easily dissolved, family units, with consequent emotional risk to any children who may have been part of that 'family'. They have the option to marry thereby obtaining the welfare rights pertaining thereto.

SHOULD GAY COUPLES BE ALLOWED TO MARRY?

Homosexual marriage is opposed to the spirit of the Constitution which assumes the traditional form of heterosexual union. Gay couples should not therefore be allowed to marry. Legalisation of homosexual marriage would probably, although perhaps not immediately, also allow for adoption. This could not be in the best interests of any children (whose rights the state is obliged to guarantee) as a same-sex couple is, of necessity, unable to offer the balanced domestic environment that can be provided by a heterosexual couple. Registered domestic partnerships may be an alternative course, but for all types of domestic relationships, not just those based on a sexual relationship, to deal with inheritance and property issues. There is no need to amend the Constitution to enact registered partnerships.

IS THE CONSTITUTION'S REFERENCE TO WOMAN'S 'LIFE WITHIN THE HOME' A DATED ONE THAT SHOULD BE CHANGED?

The underlying purpose of Article 41.2 is to value the contribution to society of a parent who devotes her time to the rearing of her children. The principle is still important, but should be expressed in gender neutral terms. (Legislators should perhaps be giving greater consideration to their constitutional obligation in this regard in view of the fact that the cost of living and especially the cost of house purchase is making it impossible for many to survive on one salary.)

SHOULD THE RIGHTS OF A NATURAL MOTHER HAVE EXPRESS CONSTITUTIONAL PROTECTION?

It would be wrong to give express constitutional protection, based simply on gender, to the rights of either parent over and against the rights of the other. When in conflict, the rights and responsibilities of each parent should be determined by the courts with particular regard to the best interests of the children involved.

WHAT RIGHTS SHOULD A NATURAL FATHER HAVE AND HOW SHOULD THEY BE PROTECTED?

Again, rights should be determined on a case by case basis when in conflict.

SHOULD THE RIGHTS OF THE CHILD BE GIVEN AN EXPANDED CONSTITUTIONAL PROTECTION?

The rights of all citizens are already guaranteed in Article 40.3 and it should be unnecessary to express that this includes children. However, if this is deemed necessary, we would support it.

DOES THE CONSTITUTION NEED TO BE CHANGED IN VIEW OF THE UN CONVENTION ON THE RIGHTS OF THE CHILD?

We are not aware of any need for change in this regard.

GREEN PARTY

The following are suggested amendments from the Green Party/Comhaontas Glas to sections of Articles 40.3, 41, and 42 of the Constitution pertaining to the family. These amendments are directed toward expanding the definition of the family, enhancing individual rights within the family unit, and, in particular, guaranteeing fundamental rights to the child and enhancing the protection of children.

We have also suggested amendments to Article 40.1 although this particular subsection is not part of the Oireachtas Committee's original remit. We see these proposed changes to 40.1 as being complementary to the other proposals on the family we have put forward in this submission.

ARTICLE 40 PERSONAL RIGHTS

The Green Party agrees with proposals from the 1996 Constitution Review Group (CRG) that the wording in this Article must be amended to afford more protection to personal rights and to ensure against discriminatory practices. In particular, discrimination by the courts against unmarried persons has been justified by the second paragraph in Article 40.1. The first paragraph guarantees all citizens equality before the law but the second allows the state to make enactments which have 'due regard to differences of capacity, physical and moral, and of social function'. We would support the replacement of this second paragraph with 'This shall not be taken to mean that the state may not have due regard to relevant differences' and also support the CRG's proposal for a new paragraph within Article 40.1, drawing on the European Convention on Human Rights, stating 'No person shall be unfairly discriminated against, directly or indirectly, on any ground such as sex, race, age, disability, sexual orientation, colour, language, culture, religion, political or other opinion, national, social or ethnic origin, membership of the Travelling community, property, birth or other status.'

We would also support the CRG's arguments for a comprehensive list of fundamental rights to be enumerated in Article 40.3.1°, drawing in part on international human rights conventions and personal rights already identified by the Irish courts. The CRG has deemed the present Article 40.3.1° to be flawed because of its broad wording and its failure to thereby give sufficient guidance to the courts in the identification of personal rights, e.g. the refusal of the courts to recognise fundamental personal rights of unmarried fathers [*The state (Nicolaou) v An Bord Uchtála*]. We would be concerned however that such a listing of rights would not remove the scope of the courts to interpret new rights in novel situations: the listing should be indicative and not definitive.

It is also vital that the guarantees of equality in Article 40 are explicitly extended to non-citizens as a fundamental human right and that references to 'citizen' within the Article be amended to 'person' where appropriate (e.g. Articles 40.3.1, 40.4, 40.5, 40.6).

The Constitution Review Group Report, when arguing for a comprehensive listing of rights, also suggested that specific rights concerning the family would be best placed within Article 41. This is the course the Green Party is following in this submission.

ARTICLE 41 THE FAMILY

The Green Party is concerned that the paramount rights of children are not adequately provided for in the current Constitution. The UN Convention on the Rights of the Child is the most widely ratified human rights treaty (Ireland ratified in 1992) and could therefore be regarded as setting out the international community's norms on the rights of the child. The Convention, similar to the Irish Constitution, recognises the family as 'the fundamental group of society' while, unlike the Irish Constitution, more fully recognises the rights (and duties) of individuals within the family unit. We are particularly guided by the preamble to the Convention: 'convinced that the family, as the fundamental group of society and the natural environment for the growth and well-being of all its members and particularly children, should be afforded the necessary protection and assistance so that it can fully assume its responsibilities within the community …'. The fact that Ireland has been cited in the European Commission's 2004 Report on Social Inclusion as having the highest rate of poverty for women and second highest for children in the EU markedly shows why reform is urgently required in this area. CSO statistics show that lone parents are overwhelmingly women and that lone parent families live disproportionately in poverty.

The Green Party also believes that Article 41 should be amended so as to cater for a broader concept of the family and to give greater rights to other forms of family units. The Constitution now focuses on protection of families based on marriage. This needs to be expanded to cover other caring relationships, for example, other forms of cohabiting couples (regardless of sexual orientation), grandparents and grandchildren, foster parents and lone parents. (The 2002 Census data showed that cohabiting couples comprised 8.4% of families and that nearly 30,000 of these families had children.)

We suggest the following amendments to Article 41 as a means of addressing some of the rights issues referred to above, to broaden the concept of family beyond the nuclear family, and to in particular give broader protection to the child, incorporating the 'welfare principle' regarding children's rights, while at the same time recognising the vital role that families play in our society. While maintaining the recognition of marriage, these changes would also permit the Oireachtas to legislate as to the prerequisites of marriage, and also permit the Oireachtas to allow for the recognition of institutions or agreements with some of the characteristics of marriage without this being regarded as an attack on marriage as per the current Article 41.3.1.

1.1° The state recognises the family as the primary and fundamental unit group of Society.

2° The state, therefore, guarantees to protect the family in its constitution and authority, as the necessary basis of social order and as indispensable to the welfare of the nation and the state.

2.1° The state recognises that parents and children have the right to knowledge and company of each other, with the welfare of the child being the paramount consideration informing this right.

2° The state recognises that parents are the primary guardians of their children's welfare, with the welfare of the child being the paramount consideration informing this right.

3.1° The state recognises that home and family life give society a support without which the common good cannot be achieved.

2° The state shall, therefore, endeavour to support persons caring for others within the home and ensure that such persons are not obliged by economic necessity to engage in labour to the detriment of their caring role in the home.

4.1° The state pledges itself to guard with special care the institution of marriage and to protect it against attack.

2° The right to marry will be governed by laws surrounding the exercise of this right.

3° The Oireachtas may provide, by law, for institutions or agreements containing some of the benefits and responsibilities of marriage.

[Since Article 41.3 became 41.4 with our amendments, the present Article 41.3.2° becomes Article 41.4.3° and the rest of the Article, pertaining to the dissolution of marriage, follows on as 41.4.3° i, ii, iii, and iv, and 4°]

The Green Party would also be anxious to ensure that constitutional recognition of the family, as the primary and fundamental unit of society would be reflected in state policy towards families of immigrants. We would support Sister Stanislaus Kennedy of the Immigrant Council of Ireland when she calls for more state protection of immigrant families and for greater legal entitlements to family reunification.

ARTICLE 42 EDUCATION

The Green Party believes that terms such as 'inalienable or imprescriptible' applied to family rights in Articles 41 and 42 should be removed from the Constitution. It is important that rights of the individuals within the family unit be given greater recognition and legal support and that the state is allowed to intervene to protect those individuals, particularly the child. We have already deleted such wording in our amendments to Article 41.1.1° and would do likewise in Article 42.1.

Article 42.1 should also be amended to ensure that the rights and duties of parents towards their children's education are not narrowly confined to married parents and their children, as currently interpreted by the courts. Such responsibilities and rights should be broadened out to apply to non-marital parents provided – in the words of the CRG – 'they have appropriate family ties and connections with the child in question'.

The Green Party also believes that issues raised in the Sinnott case should be addressed. The Supreme Court held that children as mentioned in Article 42 were persons under the age of 18. This means that the 'duty' of parents to provide for their children as outlined under Article 42.1 only applies to children under 18. Thus, after 18, in theory, a parent no longer has an educational duty to its physically/mentally disabled child.

The Green Party would also support amending Article 42.4 to ensure as a right to the child free primary and secondary education. The 1922 Constitution of the Irish Free State stated (Article 10) that: 'All citizens of the Irish Free State (Saorstát Éireann) have the right to free elementary education'. That 'right' was deleted in the 1937 Constitution which only guarantees that the state 'shall provide' for free primary education. Article 42.4 should explicitly state this right to the child and extend it into secondary education.

HEALTH SERVICE EXECUTIVE – DEPARTMENT OF CHILD PSYCHIATRY

This letter is written as a team submission from a community clinic for Child and Adolescent Mental Health. The issues highlighted for review were considered by this team. However, the profoundly philosophical nature of many of the questions posed hindered a direct response to the question specifics.

In lieu of this we considered that out submission would, instead, make some specific suggestions related to practice issues which are influenced by constitutional law. In the interests of brevity we have chosen to make only four points of specific interest to us.

1 The manner in which the family is defined as being based on marriage causes practical difficulties for involving unmarried fathers when a child is referred to this service. This is particularly challenging when parental conflict is present. Addressing the parental rights of fathers may prove more fruitful in resolving these difficulties then a redefining of the family.

Our resistance to a redefining of the family is the difficulty which would be inherent in this task, particularly given the variations which exist in its composition. If a redefining of the family is considered essential by the review group, then this clinic considers that Cypriot definition would be a useful model to follow.

2 Involvement of the child in decision-making is now part of Irish law, tied to our ratification of the UN charter on the rights of the child. However, it is important that any constitutional confirmation of these rights should be linked to a child's capacity and developmental stage. Criteria should be detailed for assessing this capacity as is the case in Scottish law. It should also have due regard to the importance of parental roles in assisting children to make decisions.

3 We note that a child's capacity to give or withhold consent for treatment has never received the attention it warrants in this jurisdiction. This matter has been considered in Northern Ireland, Scotland and England and Wales. The notion of 'Gillick Competence' is alluded to in Ireland but has never been subject to informed debate. In light of the implementation of the Mental Health Act, 2001, which has controversial sections on the detention of minors, a public consultation of the matter is timely.

4 In relation to points 2 and 3 above, and to any constitutional change, this team considers that it is essential, when making 'rights' legislatively explicit, that the responsibilities which accompany those rights be made equally explicit and enforceable.

5 Due consideration should also be given to 'needs based' legislative approaches rather than being 'rights based'. Such an approach would afford some legal flexibility in responding to the needs of individuals, children and their families.

HEALTH SERVICE EXECUTIVE – MIDLAND AREA, CHILDCARE ADVISORY COMMITTEE

PREAMBLE

Childcare Advisory Committees are established under Section 7 of the Child Care Act, 1991 which states that 'a health board shall establish a child care advisory committee to advise the health board on the performance of its functions under this act and the health board shall consider and have regard to any advice so tendered to it'. It is appropriate for a Childcare Advisory Committee to take a view on matters pertaining to the safety and welfare of children and to communicate this view to the relevant authorities. The Child Care Act, 1991 stands out as the most significant piece of child care legislation in Ireland since the foundation of the state. Under the provisions of this act, for the first time, health boards are charged with the responsibility of promoting the welfare of children in their areas. The act is founded on the premise that it is generally best for children to grow up in their own families and favours a preventative approach that prioritises child welfare. In pursuance of its duties and responsibilities as a child care authority it is incumbent on the Health Service Executive to balance the rights of the child with the rights of parents in the context of the family. This is particularly important in circumstances where it is necessary to exercise those duties to take a child into the care of the Health Service Executive because he or she is requiring care or protection.

1 EXPANDED CONSTITUTIONAL GUARANTEE FOR THE RIGHTS OF THE CHILD

The social context of family life in Ireland has changed considerably, particularly in recent years. For a child-care authority it is essential that there is absolute clarity in regard to the law upon which that authority rests, in as much as that clarity can be established. The Childcare Advisory Committee is particularly concerned that, within any amendment to the Constitution, the rights of the child are protected to include 'a specific and overt declaration of the rights of born children' as stated by Judge Catherine McGuinness in the *Report on the Kilkenny Incest Investigation*

The Childcare Advisory Committee is also of the opinion that the rights of the child, as set out in the United Nations Convention on the Rights of the Child, as ratified by Ireland in 1992, should be expressly stated in the Constitution. In addition the Committee is of the opinion that it is desirable to put into the Constitution an express obligation to treat the best interests of the child as a paramount consideration in any actions relating to children.

2 THE RELATIVE BALANCE BETWEEN PARENTAL AND CHILDREN'S RIGHTS

With regard to the relative balance between parental and children's rights the Committee is of the view that if both sets of rights are to be expressly guaranteed in any amendment to the Constitution, then in circumstances where there is a potential conflict between these two sets of rights, consideration should be given to the best interests of the child in resolving that conflict.

In consideration of the eleven issues identified by the Report of the Constitution Review Group, the Childcare Advisory Committee is in agreement with all of the recommendations of the Review Group, having a particular interest in the recommendations in regards to:

- Expanded constitutional guarantee for the rights of the child
- The relative balance between parental and children's rights
- The description and qualification of family rights

as set out above.

In addition the Committee makes the following observations:

The constitutional definition of the 'family': the role of the extended family in child rearing is becoming increasingly important in modern Ireland particularly the role of grandparents as day carers for working parents and as full-time carers for grandchildren.

Constitutional protection for the rights of a natural father: the definition and interpretation of 'family ties' and 'stable relationship' is crucial to the strengthening of the rights of natural fathers while protecting the rights of natural mothers, in the best interests of the child.

Express rights to marry and found a family: the Committee questions the need to expressly state in the Constitution an unremunerated right which has already been guaranteed by Article 40.3.

The Hague Convention: the Committee raised the issue of the protection of the rights of children removed from the jurisdiction/at risk of removal from the jurisdiction. This issue is currently subject to the Hague Convention. Should this issue be considered in the context of constitutional reform?

IMMIGRANT COUNCIL OF IRELAND

INTRODUCTION

The Immigrant Council of Ireland (ICI) is a national independent non-governmental agency that seeks to address the emerging needs of immigrants in Ireland. The ICI calls for government to adopt a strategic and long-term approach to immigration and integration policies reflecting international best practice and an ethical rights-base. In particular, ICI urges government to codify a common set of core rights and entitlements for migrants and their families and to introduce statutory rights to family reunification/unity.[1]

The fundamental importance of the family in society has long been recognised as worthy of protection by Irish society.[2] Indeed, Ireland specifically recognises the family as 'the necessary basis of social order and as indispensable to the welfare of the nation and state'. Acknowledging the fundamental importance of family within all societies and having regard to the needs of persons accessing its information services, the Immigrant Council of Ireland wishes to make general submissions to the All-Party Oireachtas Committee on the Constitution on the following:

MIGRANTS AND FAMILY REUNIFICATION ENTITLEMENTS

The Immigrant Council of Ireland's annual figures were released in July 2004 and an analysis of the data revealed that family reunification was the issue of most pressing concern to non-EEA migrant workers and recognised refugees accessing the Council's information and advice service.[3]

Whilst it is well established in international and European law that a state has the right to control immigration, the rights of migrants to family reunification have also been established under certain conditions. Indeed, Ireland is a signatory to a number of international and European legal instruments that uphold family unity and protection.[4] However, notwithstanding the existence of these important legal provisions, no domestic law specifically provides for a right to enter and remain in Ireland for the purposes of family reunification. It is also noteworthy that Ireland has not ratified the International Convention on the Protection of the Rights of All Migrant Workers and Members of their Families 1990[5], which entered into force in 2003.

In general, persons who are legally resident in Ireland are permitted to apply for family reunification in respect of dependent family members. Whilst the family rights of EU migrant workers are provided for by the EU treaties and secondary legislation, in the case of all other migrants in Ireland (excluding refugees[6]) there are no legislative provisions governing administrative practice and procedures. The policy that applies in individual cases depends on the immigration status of applicants.[7] Moreover, the rights and entitlements of different workers are not uniform and may be significantly affected depending on whether they are subject to visa requirements or even the type of employment they carry out.

For example, in the case of persons on work authorisation schemes[8], a spouse and minor dependent children can immediately accompany them to Ireland. In contrast, an individual with a working visa[9] may apply for his/her spouse and/or minor dependent children to join him/her after three months. Both of these workers must show that they have sufficient means available to support their family members for the duration of their stay in Ireland.

In further contrast and more notably, in the case of work permit holders, an application can only be made for a spouse to join them as a dependent after twelve months. Applications made by this category of workers are frequently refused on the grounds that the worker is unable to provide evidence of sufficient funds or earnings to support the spouse, although administrative guidelines that pertain in this area are not published or available to the public.

It must also be noted that some immigrants, who may not have originally entered the state for work purposes but who have subsequently been granted residency in the state and who exercise their right to enter employment, are not permitted to apply for family reunification at all. In such cases, immigrants have simply been informed that government does not have a policy for approving visas in respect of such applications for any family members. Individuals who wish to apply for residency in the

state on the basis of their parentage of an Irish child under a recently introduced administrative scheme[10] are required to sign a statutory declaration accepting that there is no entitlement to family reunification.

In a recent major study commissioned by the ICI[11], immigrants outlined their experiences – both positive and negative – of living and working in Ireland. The study found that a number of the research participants were living without close family members because of the difficulties they had experienced when trying to get family members (including minor dependent children) to join them in Ireland. These workers spoke of loneliness and homesickness due to being separated from their families.

In February 2004, the Tánaiste appeared to acknowledge some of the difficulties faced by migrant workers separated from their families and, in a welcome move, announced that some spouses of people on working visas would be automatically entitled to work in Ireland.[12] This shift in policy was introduced to ensure that people such as nurses and other groups whose skills are in demand remain encouraged to come to Ireland for work purposes. However, such measures only go a short way to achieving respect for the rights of migrant workers and it also fails to recognise the contribution that is made by all migrant workers in the state.

The issue of immigration and family reunification has also received increased attention from the institutions of the European Union following the Tampere Council in 1999. In 2003, the European Union approved a draft *Directive on Family Reunification of Third-Country Nationals*.[13] The aim of the directive is to safeguard and protect the fundamental right to family life at a European level by providing for the right of family reunification for people legally residing within the European Union. Whilst the provisions of this directive have been the subject of much criticism,[14] its introduction nonetheless provides important recognition by member states that family reunification measures are not only a way of bringing families back together, but they are also essential to facilitate the integration of immigrants.[15] Ireland did not 'opt-in' to the directive and therefore advancing the respect for the family rights of migrant workers in Ireland continues to prove difficult.

Whilst state agencies actively promote Ireland as a work destination, there is a growing danger that migrant workers are too easily perceived as economic units rather than people with rights. As an essential part of Ireland's future, immigrants must be fully accepted as more that just workers; they are also husbands, wives, fathers and mothers. In encouraging people to work in Ireland, it is imperative to ensure that immigrant workers are provided with family unity protections. Current administrative practices lack consistency and are, indeed, arguably discriminatory *vis á vis* different classes of migrant workers. Government must be called on to adhere to its commitments under international and domestic human rights laws regarding the family. Family reunification ought to be placed on a statutory footing, in an effort to ensure equal and fair applications processes and, more particularly, meaningful family life for all within Irish society.

PARNERSHIP RIGHTS AND IMMIGRATION

The current administrative arrangements for considering family reunification or unity applications, as set out above, are based on the nuclear model of the family and have little regard to diverse cultural and societal norms or the rights and entitlements of individuals with unmarried partners.

The ICI through its direct service provision and work with the voluntary organisation GLUE[16] is aware of many individuals who face difficulties, and even insurmountable obstacles, in seeking to join their partner or to remain with their partner in Ireland legally.

Currently opposite sex non-married couples and same-sex couples are not legally recognised in Ireland and this has very serious consequences for their rights and entitlements in relation to, for example, pensions, property, adoption, taxation, social welfare and inheritance.[17] In addition, the lack of legal recognition of partnerships also poses considerable immigration difficulties for non-EEA partners of Irish citizens seeking to migrate to or remain in Ireland. Unlike other jurisdictions, for example the UK, there is no provision for permitting a person to enter Ireland as a fiancé(e) and there are no legal mechanisms for recognising civil unions entered into by unmarried persons overseas.

In light of present administrative arrangements, unmarried couples and particularly same-sex couples are required to consider other ways in which the foreign partner can enter Ireland legally, either for study or work purposes. If permission to enter Ireland legally is secured, the permission is temporary in nature and must be renewed on an annual basis. Alternatively, the foreign partner can make an application to change his/her status and to remain in Ireland on alternative grounds, namely that he/she is in a relationship with an Irish person or other legal resident. This latter application is made subject to the absolute discretion of the Minister for Justice, Equality and Law Reform and it can take anything from several months to years for any decision to be granted. The ICI is aware of two cases where a same-sex partner has been granted residency as the dependent partner of an Irish citizen. However, the ICI is aware of far more cases where the application has been declined on the grounds that the partner had an alternative legal basis for residing in Ireland (a work permit). More particularly, the ICI is aware of several cases where the partners of Irish citizens have been living in Ireland illegally for periods of up to nine years. Aware that their relationship is not legally recognised, couples are fearful of making an application that may be declined and the foreign partner may be required to leave Ireland.

The current Irish position is not in line with the laws or administrative arrangements adopted by many other countries. Indeed, in most western European countries legal recognition to varying degrees has been given to same-sex partnerships and in 2003 at EU policy level the European Parliament approved a proposal to extend free movement rights to same-sex partners. In the UK where same-sex or unmarried partnerships are not yet officially recognised by law, both heterosexual and same-sex partnerships have been recognised for immigration purposes since 1997 when the Unmarried Partners Concession was introduced. In 2000 this concession was upgraded to the status of an Immigration Rule. To date, similar significant steps towards recognising same-sex unions have been taken by governments as widely spread as Israel, New Zealand, Canada and South Africa.

In recent years, the question of whether partnerships should be recognised by Irish law has received considerable attention and various proposals for conferring rights, including immigration rights, on unmarried couples have been suggested.

A recently published report of the Equality Authority included recommendations for the recognition of same-sex partnerships with regard to immigration. Following on from this report, the National Economic and Social Forum (NESF) recommended that partnership rights should include the right of a non-EU partner of an Irish person to live and work in Ireland and that, in the absence of legislation, the relevant government departments should establish 'appropriate mechanisms' to accord equal rights of residency and work entitlements for foreign partners of Irish citizens, as are accorded to married heterosexual couples. NESF did not elaborate on what form the 'appropriate mechanisms' should take.

In contrast, the Law Reform Commission, whilst taking the view that unmarried couples should be entitled to certain rights, ultimately recommended that no changes should be made to immigration laws insofar as they apply to unmarried partners at present. This recommendation was based on what the Commission identified as a practical problem, namely the difficulties in proving that partners have cohabited. Regrettably the Law Reform Commission did not attempt to identify any solutions to this problem and failed to consider the possible solution provided by the UK immigration system to these matters. It seems remarkable that evidential considerations of this nature appeared to outweigh the considerable human rights considerations of the parties affected.

The issue will be the subject of political debate when the Civil Partnerships Bill 2004, introduced by David Norris, is brought before the Senate later this month [February 2005]. The Bill proposes that both opposite sex and same-sex couples will be able to enter a civil partnership, which will confer on the couple exactly the same rights and entitlements as married persons, which necessarily includes immigration rights.

Some of the proposals referred to above are to be welcomed as positive steps in the right direction. In particular, legal recognition of relationships other than those based on marriage would certainly alleviate many of the problems that are currently faced by both opposite and same-sex unmarried couples. Foreign partners would have equal entitlements to foreign spouses to apply for entry to Ireland and to remain in Ireland based on their relationships and, if the application was granted, to enter into employment without any further restrictions.

However, it would remain the case that applications would be processed under the same discretionary administrative arrangements that currently apply – which, as identified earlier, lack transparency and consistency. ICI believes that the Minister for Justice's discretion ought not to be unfettered and ought to be exercised in accordance with set criteria that are published, clear and transparent. In the long term, a more satisfactory solution would be to place family reunification entitlements for all persons on a statutory footing.

PERMISSION TO RESIDE IN IRELAND AS THE PARENT OF AN IRISH CITIZEN

In December 2004 the Irish government announced that it would introduce a scheme in January 2005, following the enactment of the Irish Nationality and Citizenship Act, 2004, to enable parents of Irish children to apply for residency in Ireland. On 15 January 2005 the Department of Justice, Equality and Law Reform announced the details of the administrative arrangements of the scheme, which applied to parents of Irish children, born before 1 January 2005. Each parent who wishes to apply to remain in Ireland on the basis of his or her parentage of an Irish child must complete Form IBC/05 and accompanying Statutory Declaration, which sets out certain conditions that the person making the declaration understands and agrees to accept. Notably, an applicant is required to accept that the granting of permission to remain in Ireland does not confer any entitlement or legitimate expectation on any other person to enter the state. The government has indicated that applications for family reunification made by family members of Irish children overseas or by persons granted permission to remain will not be entertained.

Scheme IBC/05 was introduced in response to extreme political pressure on government to address the situation of migrant parents of Irish children living in Ireland with uncertain legal status. Prior to early February 2003, the position in Ireland was that the family members of Irish citizen children were entitled to make an application to the Department of Justice, Equality and Law Reform for residency in the state. This entitlement arouse from administrative procedures put in place by the Department of Justice, Equality and Law Reform following the decision of the Supreme Court in the *Fajujonu*[18] case. This case made clear that the state was entitled to refuse residency in certain cir-

cumstances, for example where there were serious criminal convictions or the parents had not resided in Ireland for an appreciable length of time. However, it became ordinary custom and practice within the Department to grant residency to all applicants and, consequently, it was widely believed that parents had an automatic entitlement to residency.

In February 2003, the Supreme Court in the cases of *L and O*[19] re-iterated the principles enunciated in the *Fajujonu* case and re-affirmed that the right of non-national parents of Irish citizen children to remain in the state is not absolute. It was, however, acknowledged that the Minister of the state has no right to deport any Irish citizen, including minors. It also noted that as citizens the children had certain constitutional rights including the care and company of their parents and other family members. However, it was held that such rights were qualified and that such rights do not exist to such an extent that the parents themselves acquire a right to reside in the state in all circumstances. The Court held that a parent of an Irish child could be refused residency where there were *exceptional circumstances* for refusing to do so in individual cases.

It is must be noted that the holding of the Supreme Court in *L and O* did not fundamentally alter the legal position in Ireland. It did, however, have serious consequences for the custom and practice of the Department of Justice, Equality and Law Reform responsible for processing applications for residency.

As a result of that decision, the Department of Justice, Equality and Law Reform announced the following month that applications for leave to remain in the state on the basis of an Irish child would no longer be accepted. In addition, was the Department's policy not to accept any family reunification applications in respect of family members outside of the state (even in the case of minor children), regardless of whether residency has been granted to the parents of the Irish citizen child.

More particularly, government announced that it would not further process any applications for residency based on parentage of an Irish child that had been submitted *prior* to the decision of the Supreme Court but which had not yet been finalised. Individuals in these circumstances were informed by public announcement that the process had been abolished and that if the Minister for Justice, Equality and Law Reform proposed to deport them they would be allowed to make representations in accordance with the provisions of section 3, Immigration Act, 1999. Pursuant to these provisions, the Minister is obliged to have regard to certain matters, including the age, domestic circumstances, length of residence in the state, etc. However, the Minister retains full discretion whether or not to grant leave to remain in any case.

In respect of applications for leave to remain made by parents of Irish children, the ICI, as a member of CADIC[20], expressed serious concerns that the constitutional and human rights of Irish citizen children of migrant parents were not being fully respected or protected by the state. Such concerns were based on the lack of transparency in the decision-making process and the failure of the state to put in place a child impact assessment ensuring that paramount consideration be given to the welfare and best interests of a child in any matters affecting him/her.

The ICI welcomes the introduction of the Form IBC/05 scheme, on the grounds that it is likely to be a more efficient means of regularising the immigration status of many parents of Irish citizens. Every Irish citizen child has a right of residence in the state and cannot be forcibly removed. The ICI submits that, in order to protect the rights of our minor citizens, Irish law should allow responsible parents to reside in the state with their children and to facilitate the exercise of their children's rights. If a parent is to exercise a right of residence in Ireland on behalf of his/her child but the parent is denied the right to reside in the state, it is manifestly contrary to the interests of the child and contravenes the principle of respect for family unity. Parents must be able to invoke a right of residence deriving from their minor children, otherwise the rights of minor children are entirely deprived of effectiveness.[21]

However, the administrative scheme introduced by Form IBC/05 is open to several criticisms, including, that the Minister for Justice, Equality and Law Reform retains an absolute discretion, in the absence of publicly available guidelines, whether or not to grant residency to an individual under the scheme. The ICI acknowledges that the state ought necessarily be entitled to refuse to grant residency to parents of Irish children on the grounds of public policy or public security, in cases where there are exceptional reasons for doing so. It is submitted that the Minister for Justice's discretion ought not to be unfettered and ought to be exercised, at a minimum, in accordance with set criteria that are published, clear and transparent. The Minister's exercise of discretion ought also to be informed by the relevant constitutional/European legal principles of proportionality and non-discrimination. Refusal to grant residency to the parent of an Irish child should be based exclusively on the public conduct of the individual concerned and must also be proportionate to the aim of the objective to be achieved.

The Minister for Justice, Equality and Law Reform has repeatedly stated that migrant parents of Irish children who are refused residency in the state and who are deported will be expected to take their children with them. The deportation of a parent of an Irish child therefore could result in the *de facto* removal of an Irish child to the parent's country of origin. In conducting this review, the ICI would urge the All-Party Oireachtas Committee to consider the following questions:

1 What obstacles exist that might prevent an Irish child from vindicating their constitutional and human rights whilst residing in their parent's country of origin?

2 How will Ireland guarantee the Irish child's constitutional rights, including rights to education, access to adequate medical care, protection from abuse and all the other rights children enjoy under the Irish Constitution and the UN Convention of the Rights of the Child should the Irish child be removed from Ireland?

3 What protections and assistance will be available to the Irish child if the authorities in the parent's country of origin subsequently refuse the Irish child a right of residence?

4 What are the constitutional rights of Irish children in circumstances where a migrant parent is refused residency and opts, in the best interests of his/her Irish child, to leave the child behind?

The ICI also takes this opportunity to express reservations regarding the apparent intention of government not to entertain any applications for family reunification made by persons granted residency under the scheme or made by family members currently overseas, even where such applications may relate to spouses or minor children. It is submitted that if government were to adopt a 'blanket family reunification policy' that had the effect of the Minister declining to consider applications, such policy would be unlawful and in breach of the Irish Constitution.[22]

Notes

1 Labour Migration Into Ireland, *Study and Recommendations on Employment Permits, Working Conditions, Family Reunification and the Integration of Migrant Workers in Ireland* (2003, Immigrant Council of Ireland)

2 Article 41, Irish Constitution

3 See Press Release *The State Criticised for Anti-Family Policies* dated 18th July '04 available on http://www.immigrantcouncil.ie/prfam.htm

4 See, for example, the European Convention on Human Rights (Article 8) and the Charter of Fundamental Rights of the EU (Article 7). See also the declaratory statement of principle in the Universal Declaration of Human Rights (Article 16).

5 http://www.unhchr.ch/

6 Recognised refugees have statutory entitlements to apply for family reunification. See section 18, Refugee Act, 1996.

7 The relevant legal provisions are set out comprehensively elsewhere. See *Handbook on Immigrants' Rights and Entitlements in Ireland*, Immigrant Council of Ireland, 2003.

8 Work authorisations are issued to prospective employees who are nationals of states whose passport holders do not need a visa to travel to Ireland.

9 Working visas are issued to prospective employees who are nationals of states whose passport holders require a visa to travel to Ireland.

10 Form IBC/05. See further below.

11 Kelleher Associates, *Voices of Immigrants – the Challenges of Inclusion* (Immigrant Council of Ireland, 2004).

12 See Department of Enterprise, Trade and Employment Press Release dated 18th February 2004 '*Tanaiste introduces new arrangements for spouses of skilled non-EEA nationals*' available at http://www.entemp.ie/press/2004/20040218.htm

13 Council Directive 2003/86/EC of 22 September 2003 on the right to family reunification *Official Journal* L 251, 03/10/2003 P. 0012 – 0018.

14 See: Oliynik, N. *Recent Developments in EU Immigration Law – Family Reunification Directive: Achievement or*

Failure of the EU Immigration Policy?, available on http://www.eumap.org/journal/features/2004/movt/eu
Also: European Coordination for Foreigners' Right to Family Life *Appeal to annul the directive concerning family reunification* available on http://www.gisti.org/doc/actions/2003/regroupement/arg-eng.pdf

[15] http://europa.eu.int/comm/justice_home/fsj/immigration/family/printer/fsj_immigration_family_en.htm

[16] GLUE is an organisation that offers information and support to lesbian and gay couples experiencing immigration difficulties. GLUE is lodging its own submission to the All-Party Oireachtas Committee on the Constitution.

[17] For a comprehensive overview of these issues, see: *Implementing Equality for Lesbians, Gays and Bisexuals* (Equality Authority), *Unmarried Couples within Irish Law: Current Law and Proposals for Reform* (2004, ICCL), *Consultation Paper on the Rights and Duties of Cohabitees* (2004, Law Reform Commission).

[18] *Fajujonu v Minister for Justice* [1990] 2 IR 151

[19] *Lobe & ors v Minister for Justice, Equality and Law Reform, Osayande & anor v Minister for Justice, Equality and Law Reform & ors* [2003] IRSC 3

[20] CADIC (*Coalition Against the Deportation of Irish Children*) is a coalition of a wide range of individuals and non-governmental organisations, spanning human rights organisations, legal aid groups, children's rights organisations, migrant support coalitions and church-based migrant support organisations. CADIC was a response to a call by AkiDwA – the African Women's Network – to respond to the fear and confusion following the retrospective abolition of the procedure whereby migrant parents of Irish children could apply for residency in Ireland.

[21] In support of this submission, the ICI refers to the concept of derived rights identified and endorsed by the European Court of Justice in Case C-200/02 *Zhu and Chen v Secretary of State for the Home Department*, judgment delivered on the 19th May 2004.

[22] See also the provisions of the UN Convention on the Rights of the Child regarding a child's separation from parents (Article 9) and family reunification entitlements of children (Article 10).

IPPA, THE EARLY CHILDHOOD ORGANISATION

IPPA, the Early Childhood Organisation is a charitable NGO which works with practitioners, parents and policy makers to improve the everyday experience of young children in early childhood services, through the development and delivery of training and quality improvement programmes and through a range of member-based services.

IPPA is grounded in the ecological theory of Bronfenbrenner (1979), who views the child within the context of family, community and the wider society. Equally we endorse the views of Bruner (1996) who proposes a view of the agentive child and other social constructivists such as Dahlberg (1999) who situates the young child within a democratic, participative model. Our work, which reflects our beliefs, enlightens and broadens our understanding of family. Similarly our view of the child is one of a competent being, contributing to, participating in and influencing family and community life.

Consequently, we welcome this opportunity to contribute to the discourse.

HOW SHOULD THE FAMILY BE DEFINED?/THOUGHTS ON THE FAMILY

IPPA acknowledges that the term 'family' is a term of some complexity and ambiguity and one which is interpreted in a rich variety of contexts. The family is culturally, socially and politically constituted. There are many ways in which we understand the term family – household, nuclear family, extended family, etc. and that each view or paradigm shifts the focus we adopt.

We believe that the family transcends households, and that family relationships extend beyond and between households. The traditional notion of family is exclusive and one that, according to Daly (2004) reporting on the public consultation for 'Families and Family Life in Ireland,' does not receive such widespread support. The call, from this forum, was for 'a more inclusive definition of family which can encompass all types of families'. The changing nature and function of family must be acknowledged. While the traditional views or understandings of 'family' can be maintained, the reality is somewhat different. Elkind (2002) suggests that the family can be viewed as a social organism that must adapt to the demands of its social habitat – when society changes so too must the family.

The family has become the locus of change, with historical influences exerting pressure on the unit. The development of a relatively homogeneous life cycle has resulted in a growing role for the state in matters with direct or indirect consequence for the family. On the other hand, changing social patterns such as urbanisation have facilitated notions of 'privacy' within and in relation to family. A further change which impacts on 'family' is that of the relationship between man and woman within the home. These relationships have become more equal, egalitarian, and democratic. So in grappling with the concept of 'family,' the crucial variables appear to include household, family relationships across households, work and employment and gender relationships.

In defining concepts of family IPPA would welcome an open and inclusive approach which embraces and validates the rich diversity of family lives and structures that can and potentially exist. Stemming from a revision of the 'family' must emerge a commitment to addressing social and family policy, which must be multi-layered and multi-faceted. The challenge will be to balance a more open definition of 'family' with appropriate support structures, which respects espoused and lived values.

SHOULD THE RIGHTS OF THE CHILD BE GIVEN AN EXPANDED CONSTITUTIONAL PROTECTION?

Until the introduction of the Childcare Act, 1991, the child has remained cloaked within the family unit. In foregrounding the rights of the family, the rights of the child have been negated. This discrepancy has emerged and been made explicit through more than a decade of abuse scandals. Ferriter (2002) suggests that it is at least strongly tempting to conclude that the greatest blot on twentieth-century Irish society's copy-book was its treatment of children.

Childhood has previously been conceptualised in de Valera's terms as 'romping of sturdy children' around 'cosy homesteads'. While society has changed, this attitude is very much reflected in the present form of the Constitution, which idealises the concept of family at the expense of the individuals. Childhood is a social construct, which is presented and viewed from the adult perspective and constituted through its relationship with adulthood.

While there are conflicting societal and cultural views on children and childhood, they have become the source of intense political interest over the last ten years with the advent of the ratification of the UN Convention on the Rights of the Child, the Childcare Act, 1991, the reorganisation of the Department of Health to the Dept. of Health and Children, the publication of the National Children's Strategy, the establishment of an Ombudsman for Children and the convening of Dáil na n-Óg.

IPPA would welcome an expansion on children's rights being made explicit within the Constitution, not necessarily constitutional 'protection'. If children are viewed and treated as participating citizens, with a voice, it is constitutionally incumbent that their rights are made explicit, enshrined in law and supported through national policy. The focus of constitutional reform should be on the granting of rights rather than the more limiting 'protection' of rights. Rights become protected through policy development/weighting and implementation.

DOES THE CONSTITUTION NEED TO BE CHANGED IN VIEW OF THE UN CONVENTION ON THE RIGHTS OF THE CHILD?

In a phase of reform, the Irish Constitution must focus on human rights – rights for all citizens regardless of age. In ratifying the UNCRC and drawing on this as the basis for the National Children's Strategy there must be a correlation with the Irish Constitution. The challenge arises in committing to and implementing these rights.

References

Bronfenbrenner, U. (1979) *The Ecology of Human Development,* Cambridge: Cambridge University Press.

Bruner, J. (1996) *The Culture of Education,* Massachusetts: Harvard University Press.

Dahlberg, G., Moss, P. and Pence, A. (1999) *Beyond Quality in Early Childhood Education and Care,* London: Falmer Press.

IRISH CATHOLIC BISHOPS CONFERENCE – COMMITTEE ON THE FAMILY (IRISH EPISCOPAL CONFERENCE AND THE OFFICE FOR PUBLIC AFFAIRS OF THE ARCHDIOCESE OF DUBLIN)

INTRODUCTION

Articles 41 and 42 of the Constitution, as originally drafted, represent a most important protection of marriage and the family. In striking contrast to the United States Constitution, for example, the Irish Constitution recognises the family as the natural unit of society and as a moral institution possessing inalienable and imprescriptible rights, antecedent and superior to all positive law. Under Article 41.3.1, the state pledged itself to guard with special care the institution of marriage, on which the family is founded, and to protect it against attack.

In setting out this position, the Constitution is clearly recognising the importance of the family based on marriage and the vital contribution it makes to the well-being of society and the state. It is not the Constitution that creates the family or that defines it, rather it recognises an institution that is prior to it.

In doing so, the Constitution recognises that in discussing the relationship between the family and society; there is much at stake. Marriage and the family are primary sources of stability, life and love in any society, they constitute a 'primary vital cell' from which the rest of society derives so much of its cohesion and potential success. This fact is recognised by our own Constitution when it describes the family 'as the necessary basis of social order and as indispensable to the welfare of the nation and the state.' (Article 41.1.2 Irish Constitution). The Greek Constitution expresses the same conviction when it describes the family as 'the foundation of the conservation and the progress of the nation'. Such values are consistent in turn with Article 16 of the Universal Declaration of Human Rights when it states: 'The family is the natural and fundamental unit of society and is entitled to protection by society and the state.' Article 16 of the Social Charter of Europe (1961), Article 23 of the International Treaty on Civil Rights, Article 10 of the International Charter on Economic, Social and Cultural Rights as well as many other national and international instruments both affirm and develop this basic insight that the family is the nucleus of society, and for that reason is deserving of special status, development and care.

Prior to any consideration of the specific content of the constitutional provisions of the family, it would seem opportune to endorse the present jurisprudential framework that clearly understands the family as a natural institution rather than the creation of positive laws. The Constitution, in establishing this framework, sets the context for our more analytical consideration of the specific provisions. It might also be argued that in so doing it achieves its fundamental role as a Constitution to shape subsequent legal reflection. As was pointed out by Wheare, 'a constitution is something more than a selection of supreme legal rules. It is often, and sometimes first, a political manifesto or creed or testament. As such, it can be argued, it evokes the respect and affection and, indeed, obedience of the people in a way which no exhaustively legal document can hope to do'. In outlining certain key insights into the nature of the family, the Constitution could be said to meet the aspiration expressed in Statement No. 2 of the Interim Report of the Commission on the Family that 'family policy has a fundamental role in expressing and affirming society's values and ideals concerning family life, at the symbolic as well as the practical levels'.

HOW SHOULD THE FAMILY BE DEFINED?

This is an issue that received significant attention in the Report of the Constitution Review Group and this submission will respond to said Report in advancing the argument that it is appropriate that the Constitution would continue to define the family as being founded on marriage.

PRELIMINARY CONSIDERATIONS

In its introduction to its review of the provisions dealing with Family, the Review Group prefaced its consideration with a brief presentation of the changes which had affected family life in the years since the Constitution was enacted in 1937. The analysis was not particularly detailed, yet the Review Group concluded that these 'social changes call for amendments in the Constitution'. The Review Group's conclusion ought to be questioned. Is it not appropriate for a Constitution to seek to shape civil society rather than merely to follow sociological trends? Surely it would have been appropriate for the Review Group to consider the desirability or otherwise of the changes which had occurred before giving them constitutional endorsement or support?

The Review Group, for example, drew attention to an increase from 3% to 20% in the proportion of births outside marriages. The Review Group did not, however, give attention to the implications of this change and no account is taken of the evidence which, although it needs careful and sensitive evaluation, would seem to suggest that the children of one-parent families, notwithstanding the best and commendable efforts of their parents, may be at a disadvantage when compared to those of traditional families. If the Review Group had attended to such issues then its laudable desire to offer support to those living in non-traditional family arrangements might well have been tempered by a more obvious concern to offer such a support in a manner which did not erode support for the family based on marriage or undermine its indispensability to the welfare of the nation and the state.

It is arguable that, if the Review Group had seriously considered the impact of the social changes which it

notes, it might not have come to its apparent conclusion that what is, is what ought to be. The Review Group seems to consider it to be the role of law simply to regulate existing arrangements and no attention is given to the possible educative value of law. Surely, concerning an issue as fundamental as family life, the Constitution ought to continue to signal the unique position and value of the family based on marriage.

Moreover, the Review Group's analysis of the philosophical basis of Articles 41 and 42 of the Constitution is inadequate and unconvincing. These articles do not represent an arbitrary concept of the family; on the contrary, they are clearly based on a philosophical understanding of the nature of family life, of the responsibilities attaching to marriage and of the relationship between the family and the state. The Group's Report betrays no apparent interest in this philosophical dimension.

It need hardly be pointed out that in societies where religion may play no significant role, the philosophical question of the role of the state in relation to the family is an important and controversial issue. The Review Group appears to be unconcerned with this crucial issue, preferring to transform the question into one of church-state relations. In fact, much more is at stake.

DEFINITION

The first specific issue to receive the attention of the Review Group was the constitutional definition of 'family'. It acknowledged that the family recognised and protected in Articles 41 and 42 is the family based on marriage. Mr Justice Walsh in the Supreme Court case, *The State (Nicolaou) v An Bord Uchtála* said it was: 'quite clear ... that the family referred to in [Article 41] is the family which is founded on the institution of marriage and, in the context of the article, marriage means valid marriage under the law for the time being in force in the State ...'

This view is supported by Article 42.3.1: 'The state pledges itself to guard with special care the institution of marriage, on which the family is founded, and to protect it against attack.'

The Review Group noted the existence in Irish society of numerous units which are generally regarded as family units but which are not families based on marriage. Such non-marital families are not included by the definition of family as outlined above and do not, *per se*, enjoy the protection or guarantees of Article 41. The Review Group expressed its appreciation for the view that persons living in family units not based on marriage should have constitutional recognition but observed 'that the constitutional protection of the rights of any family unit other than a family based on marriage presents significant difficulties.' The Review Group recognised that, once one gets beyond the family based on marriage, definition becomes very difficult. It commented:

Thus the multiplicity of differing units which may be capable of being considered as families include:

- a cohabiting heterosexual couple with no children
- a cohabiting heterosexual couple looking after the children of either or both parents
- a cohabiting heterosexual couple, either of whom is already married
- a cohabiting heterosexual couple, either of whom is already married, whose children (all or some of them) are being looked after elsewhere
- unmarried lone parents and their children
- homosexual and lesbian couples.

It noted that questions will also arise as to what duration of cohabitation should qualify for treatment as a family and it raises the issue of whether it would be an interference with the personal rights of those who have chosen deliberately not to marry to accord in effect a legal status to their family unit. It reviewed the provisions relating to family and marriage in many European constitutions, the ECHR and CCPR and concluded that 'none attempts a definition of a "family" in terms other than one based on marriage.'

Yet, having adverted to these formidable difficulties of definition that follow inevitably once one has broken the connection between marriage and the family, the Review Group thereafter continues its discussion on the basis that the concept of family does not in fact need to be defined by the Constitution. The Review Group seems to want to have it both ways. It insists that the Constitution should continue to protect the family based on marriage (p.323, p.331, p.336) and yet it seems to strip that protection of any real value when it suggests that the words 'on which the family is founded' should be removed from Article 41.3.1. which pledges to guard the institution of marriage. The Review Group's criticism that these 'words have led to an exclusively marriage-based definition of the family' (p.332) is not easily harmonised with its own recognition of 'particular difficulties if the family unit is extended beyond the family based on marriage' (p.323). Inevitably the Review Group cannot have it both ways and it would seem that it is the family based on marriage that loses out.

The result is that the Review Group effectively endorses a proposal to extend the definition of the family. This may present the appearance of a liberalising proposal: in fact it would suppress the proper independence of the family. Deprived of inherent rights and absolved from responsibility other than such as the state might choose to impose, the family would be subjected to unlimited interference as a mere creature of the state. This would be a violation of fundamental social responsibilities and rights. Once the family has been disconnected from marriage, the state must decide, in the interest of the common good, how it should be structured, how it should function and how it should be regulated. But it is the common good that requires marriage as the basis of the family. This is because marriage is the source of the stability of the family through the responsibilities and rights it confers with a view to ensuring the welfare of the family community. It is the duty of the state to protect the family from the destruction that would follow from the Review Group's readiness to abstain from defining the family in accordance with its own proper nature. The state must respect and support the family based on marriage: it cannot replace the family without sacrificing its own interest in social cohesion and undertaking responsibilities it has neither the mandate nor the capacity to fulfil.

The significance of marriage as the foundation of the family was recognised in the final report of the Commission on the Family, notwithstanding its endorsement of the proposals of the Review Group. 'A man and woman in getting married make a clear and public commitment to live together and to support each other, with the intention of their union being for life. Marriage is a legal contract. It is afforded a clear legal status by the state and both parties have legally enforceable rights and duties. These features of marriage result in a majority of cases in the union being permanent or at least continuing for a relatively long period. They facilitate, in particular, joint parenting and a stable family life for the children of married couples, which is conducive to their overall development.'

RECOMMENDATION

It is submitted that the constitutional understanding of family as being the family based on marriage should be retained in order to indicate the value of marriage and its irreplaceable contribution to the good of society. This proposal is not intended as a penalty for those who have chosen or find themselves in different family forms or relationships. A diversity of family forms support the fundamental human activities of care, intimacy and belongingness to varying degrees, yet it is appropriate that the Constitution should guard with special care the institution of marriage. Such a commitment to special care of the family based on marriage ought not, nor does it, prevent the state from seeking to offer appropriate support to individuals in other forms of family units.

HOW SHOULD ONE STRIKE THE BALANCE BETWEEN THE RIGHTS OF THE FAMILY AS A UNIT AND THE RIGHTS OF INDIVIDUAL MEMBERS?

This question arises in the context of the judgement of the Constitution Review Group that the Constitution, as interpreted by the courts, emphasises the rights of the family as a unit to the possible detriment of individual members. It recommends the removal of the qualification of the rights of the family as being 'inalienable and imprescriptible' and suggests that all rights or duties which derive from marriage or family ought to be guaranteed or imposed on the individuals rather than the family unit. This recommendation in conjunction with the recommended deletion of Articles 41.1.1,

41.1.2 and 41.3.1 would have the effect of making the family a creation of positive law rather than viewing it as 'a moral institution .... antecedent and superior to all positive laws.' It is not clear that these recommendations succeed in 'achieving the balance which will offer security and a measure of equality to individual family members in a manner which does not devalue or endanger the family as an institution.' The desire that underlines these recommendations to protect vulnerable members within family units and to afford a constitutional protection to the right, or even the obligation, of the state to intervene in family units to protect the rights of individuals is thoroughly laudatory. It is arguable, however, that the same end has been achieved by the courts through the exercise of their jurisdiction under Article 40.3 to protect individual rights and, more particularly in this context, through their more robust application of Article 42.5. This issue will be considered in further detail under the heading of the rights of the child. Because the issue of protection of individual members is not confined to children, it is important that the Courts exercise equal vigilance in affording a legal basis for state interventions in family life, where necessary to safeguard the welfare of the elderly, those with disabilities and other family members who are vulnerable.

IS IT POSSIBLE TO GIVE CONSTITUTIONAL PROTECTION TO FAMILIES OTHER THAN THOSE BASED ON MARRIAGE?

In accordance with its observations on the question of a constitutional definition of the family, this submission will not engage with questions concerning the manner in which specific constitutional protection could be afforded to non-marital family units *per se*. It is important that such units, especially insofar as they include children, are offered appropriate social and financial support as is already provided for by various statutory and regulatory measures. It is clear that such support can be, and is, offered in ways that do not undermine the position of the family based on marriage. The precise achievement of such a balance is a matter of prudent social policy judgements and is best achieved without specific constitutional direction. It is not clear that the recommendation of the Review Group that the pledge by the state to guard with special care the institution of marriage be subject to the express proviso that the pledge should not prevent the Oireachtas from legislating for the benefit of families not based on marriage is necessary. It could, however, make the pledge merely rhetorical.

Questions concerning the rights of individual members of non-marital units are best considered as personal rights. If there were to be a guarantee to all individuals of respect for their family life whether based on marriage or not, as envisaged by the Review Group, it is arguable that said provision would effectively render meaningless any attempt to define the family in terms of marriage.

In this context, it is appropriate to attend, albeit perfunctorily, to the recent consultation paper on the Rights and Duties of Cohabitees issued by the Law Reform Commission. It is interesting to note that the Commission was of the view that Article 41 does not prevent the Oireachtas legislating in respect of cohabitees, so long as the legislation does not grant cohabitees more extensive rights than those enjoyed by married couples. Whatever view one may hold about the actual proposals of the Commission, it is clear that the existing constitutional support for the family based on marriage would not seem to exclude extensive measures being taken in support of non-marital units. In terms of the specific measures, the Commission expressed the view that unmarried cohabitees who live together in a 'marriage like' relationship should be entitled to certain rights and duties. The Commission is of the view these rights and duties should be extended to same-sex as well as opposite sex cohabitees. The Commission did not recommend that the scheme be extended beyond 'marriage like' relationships and excluded non-sexual domestic relationships. The Commission advocated that the status of qualified cohabitee should be presumptive; the very fact of cohabitation would, subject to certain requirements, create the legal relationship independent of the wishes of the cohabitees. In arguing for this presumptive scheme, the Commission said that it would be desirable in order to protect the interests of the more vulnerable cohabitee who might not be in a position to insist on voluntary registration or the making of legal provision to provide for the protection of his or her interests.

This 'protectionist' rationale would seem to be justified in order to protect vulnerable individuals irrespective of the type of relationships they may have formed. It may, in certain circumstances, be in the public interest to provide legal protection to the social, fiscal and inheritance entitlements of persons who support caring relationships which generate dependency, provided always that these relationships are recognised as being qualitatively different from marriage and that their acceptance does not dilute the uniqueness of marriage. However, it would seem discriminatory to confine this protection to those in sexual relationships and thereby exclude from protection the interests of siblings and other non-sexually involved cohabitees. Moreover, the creation of a category of 'marriage like' relationships which would enjoy particular protections would seem to contradict in spirit, if not in law, the pledge in Article 41.3.1 to guard with special care the institution of marriage. In the cases of those who would in any event be free to marry, the scheme, which confers many of the advantages of legal marriage, might be judged to be an incentive not to marry.

SHOULD GAY COUPLES BE ALLOWED TO MARRY?

In accordance with the argument of this submission that marriage is a natural institution rather than an institution created by positive law, it would seem that the question is not whether gay couples should be allowed to marry, rather whether they can marry. Until recently it would have been seen as obvious to say that marriage is a relationship that by its very nature requires a man and a woman. The complementarity that a man and woman bring to marriage and the procreative potential that is rooted in their different genders would have been seen as constitutive of the institution of marriage. Church teaching stresses that marriage is exclusively between a man and a woman, because this is part of the basic structure of the complementarity of the sexes, something rooted in creation, and not simply a social or cultural construct.

The Catholic Church remains committed to advocating and promoting the common good of everyone in our society. The Catholic Church teaches that homosexual people are to be 'accepted with respect, compassion and sensitivity.' The Church condemns all forms of violence, harassment or abuse directed against people who are homosexual.

In recent years there have been significant changes to the law to remove discrimination against people on the grounds of their sexuality. These changes have removed injustices, without of themselves creating any parallel legal institution to marriage.

However, it is essential when considering future legislation concerning marriage and the family, to acknowledge the vital distinction between private homosexual behaviour between consenting adults, and formalising that behaviour as 'a relationship in society, foreseen and approved by the law, to the point where it becomes an institution in the legal structure'. Legal developments must be considered not only in terms of their impact on individuals, but also in terms of their impact on the common good and on the fundamental institutions of society such as marriage and the family. Civil laws play a very important and sometimes decisive role in influencing patterns of thought and behaviour. Legal recognition of homosexual unions would obscure certain basic moral values and cause a devaluation of the institution of marriage.

The recognition of same-sex unions on the same terms as marriage would suggest to future generations and to society as a whole that marriage as husband and wife, and a same-sex relationship, are equally valid options, and an equally valid context for the bringing up of children. What is at stake here is the natural right of children to the presence normally of a mother and father in their lives. Given the legal changes that have already taken place and the fact that two people can make private legal provision covering many aspects of their lives together, including joint ownership of homes, living wills and powers of attorney, the argument that same-sex marriage is necessary to protect human rights becomes a redundant one. When it is balanced against the manner in which it will undermine such a fundamental institution as marriage and the family, it is difficult to see how such a development could be justified in terms of the government's duty to defend marriage and the common good.

IS THE CONSTITUTION'S REFERENCE TO WOMAN'S 'LIFE WITHIN THE HOME' A DATED ONE THAT SHOULD BE CHANGED?

The reference is frequently dismissed as dated and this would seem just if it were read to suggest that women only have a contribution to make in the home or that work in the home were to be the exclusive duty of women. The provision may, however, be seen as a 'pedestal rather than a cage.' As Mrs Justice Denham has pointed out in *Sinnott v Ireland*: 'Article 41.2 does not assign women to a domestic role. Article 41.2 recognises the significant role played by wives and mothers in the home. This recognition and acknowledgement does not exclude women and mothers from other roles and activities. It is a recognition of the work performed by women in the home. The work is recognised because it has immense benefit for society. This recognition must be construed harmoniously with other articles of the Constitution when a combination of articles fall to be analysed.'

A revision of this article in more gender neutral form as suggested by the Review Group might be appropriate but perhaps unnecessary. Mr Justice Murray, as he then was, in *DT v CT* noted that 'the Constitution … is to be interpreted as a contemporary document. The duties and obligations of spouses are mutual and, without elaborating further since nothing turns on the point in this case, it seems to me that [the Constitution] implicitly recognises similarly the value of a man's contribution in the home as a parent.'

SHOULD THE RIGHT OF THE NATURAL MOTHER HAVE EXPRESS CONSTITUTIONAL PROTECTION?

At present, although a natural mother has no rights under Articles 41 and 42, she does enjoy a constitutional right to the custody and care of her child pursuant to Article 40.3. The Review Group suggested that this right should be expressly enumerated but it did so in the context of its recommendation that all the unenumerated rights protected by Article 40.3 should be enumerated. It is not clear that the enumeration of all such rights is either necessary or appropriate but that judgement involves the evaluation of jurisprudential and constitutional theories that are not required in the context of this submission. In any event, it would seem consistent with the views expressed above on the definition of the family that any express rights of a natural mother would be seen as personal rather than family rights.

WHAT RIGHTS SHOULD A NATURAL FATHER HAVE, AND HOW SHOULD THEY BE PROTECTED?

It would seem that it is best to provide for the rights of natural fathers through statutory provision and judicial determination. This allows for the necessary distinctions that can exist among natural fathers. As Chief Justice Finlay observed in the case *Re SW an infant, K v W*, 'The extent and character of the rights which accrue arising from the relationship of a father to a child to whose mother he is not married must vary very greatly indeed, depending on the circumstances of each individual case. The range of variation would, I am satisfied, extend from the situation of the father of a child conceived as a result of a casual intercourse, where the rights might well be so minimal as practically to be non-existent, to the situation of a child born as the result of a stable and established relationship and nurtured at the commencement of his life by his father and mother in a situation bearing nearly all the characteristics of a constitutionally protected family, when the rights would be very extensive indeed.'

Equally it would seem inappropriate to exclude the idea of a natural father having natural rights. It is submitted that the statement of Mr Justice Murphy, in the same case that what 'are described as "natural rights" whether arising from the circumstances of mankind in a primitive but idyllic society postulated by some philosophers but unidentified by any archaeologist, or inferred by moral philosophers as the rules by which human beings may achieve the destiny for which they were created, are not recognised or enforced as such by the courts set up under the Constitution' is overly positivistic and unduly restrictive of the role of the courts in balancing rights.

The position enunciated by Mr Justice Barrington seems more appropriate: '[I]llegitimate children are not mentioned in the Constitution. Yet the case law acknowledges that they have the same rights as other children. These rights must include, where practicable, the right to the society and support of their parents. These rights are determined by analogy to Article 42 and captured by the general provisions of Article 40.3 which places justice above the law. Likewise a natural mother who has honoured her obligation to her child will normally have a right to its custody and to its care. No one doubts that a natural father has the duty to support his child and, I suggest, that a natural father who has observed his duties towards his child has, so far as practicable, some rights in relation to it, if only the right to carry out these duties. To say that the child has rights protected by Article 40.3 and that the mother, who has stood by the child, has rights under Article 40.3 but that the father, who has stood by the child, has no rights under Article 40.3 is illogical, denies the relationship of parent and child and may, upon occasion, work a cruel injustice.'

This submission would join with the authors of *JM Kelly: The Irish Constitution* in questioning 'whether the distinction drawn by the courts between natural mothers and natural fathers in the context of their rights in respect of their children is not too absolutist in its denial of constitutional rights to all natural fathers and specifically those who have made a commitment to their children. Barrington J's critique of the reasoning in *Nicolaou* which led to this result is compelling and the current constitutional position clearly reflects a

stereotypical image of the natural father that does not accord with the reality in a growing number of cases.' The determination of the content of such rights and their enforcement would be ultimately a matter for consideration on a case by case basis.

SHOULD THE RIGHTS OF THE CHILD BE GIVEN AN EXPANDED CONSTITUTIONAL PROTECTION?

The Review Group on the Constitution, as has been noted, recommended that all the unenumerated rights conferred by Article 40.3 should be expressly enumerated and this recommendation was extended to the unenumerated rights of children. This is a question of jurisprudential and constitutional theory. It is a matter of prudential judgement for the appropriate experts as to whether the protection of children's rights is best effected through express constitutional enumeration or through entrusting to the courts the task of specifying said rights in particular circumstances.

Particular issues arise when tensions emerge between families and outside agencies as to the determination of the best interests of children. The question may arise as to whether the family or the state is best positioned to safeguard the rights of children. Not all families are good environments for rearing children. They may be affected by the personal moral weaknesses and limitations of parents. Children may be exposed to sexual abuse, violence or neglect. In these and similar circumstances, the state may clearly intervene. Thus, for example, the Childcare Act, 1991 and the Adoption Act, 1988 enable children to be protected from the effects of the failures of their parents. The Supreme Court made it clear in *In re Article 26 and the Adoption (No. 2) Bill 1987*, that Article 41 is no barrier to the compulsory adoption of children on the basis of continuing parental failure.

In *re JH (an infant)*, the Supreme Court held that section 3 of the Guardianship of Infants Act, 1964, which requires the court to regard the welfare of the infant as the first and paramount consideration, should: 'be construed as involving a constitutional presumption that the welfare of such a child is to be found within the family unless the court is satisfied that there are compelling reasons why this cannot be achieved or the evidence establishes an exceptional case where the parents have, for moral or physical reasons, failed, and continue to fail, to provide education for the child.'

The Review Group took issue with this approach and proposed that Article 41 should be modified by the inclusion of the express obligation that, in all actions concerning children, whether by legislative, judicial or administrative authorities, the best interest of the child is to be 'the paramount consideration'. This is the expression used on page 337 of the report; it contrasts with the expression 'a paramount consideration' on page 329. The Review Group does not appear to have been aware of the significance of this distinction, although the courts have pronounced upon it. It is interesting to note that the Report of the Commission on the Family used the term 'a paramount consideration' in its proposals to the All-Party Committee on the Constitution.

It is clear that the Constitution must afford legal protection for measures which are necessary to protect the rights of children. However, the family unit must be allowed to retain its appropriate authority and autonomy. Whether this balance is best achieved by express constitutional provision or by judicial interpretation of the existing constitutional parameters remains to be seen. The authors of *JM Kelly: The Irish Constitution* draw attention to the following statement from a judgement of Mr Justice Ellis: 'In my opinion, the inalienable and imprescriptible rights of the family under Article 41 of the Constitution attach to each member of the family including the children. Therefore in my view the only way the "inalienable and imprescriptible" and "natural and imprescriptible" rights of the child can be protected is by the courts treating the welfare of the child as the paramount consideration in all disputes as to its custody, including disputes between a parent and a stranger. I take the view also that the child has the personal right to have its welfare regarded as the paramount consideration in any such dispute as to its custody under Article 40.3 and that this right of the infant can additionally arise from "the Christian and democratic nature of the state".' On the basis of their analysis of that judgement, they conclude that 'it indicates how a more balanced approach to the complex area of custody disputes … can be achieved by rearguing the constitutional principles involved and without the necessity of a constitutional amendment.' This view would seem to be re-enforced by the recent judgement of Mrs Justice Finlay Geoghegan in the case *FN v CO*.

DOES THE CONSTITUTION NEED TO BE CHANGED IN VIEW OF THE UN CONVENTION ON THE RIGHTS OF THE CHILD

The Review Group stated that many of the child-specific rights contained in the Convention have already been identified by the superior courts as unenumerated rights under the Constitution. As already indicated, the question as to whether such rights need to be expressly specified is one which is beyond the scope of this submission. It would seem, moreover, that the superior courts could have regard to the Convention in understanding their mandate under Article 40.3 to vindicate the personal rights of all citizens including children.

In the event that this judicial protection were to be judged inadequate, further consideration could be given to the proposal in the Review Group Report, endorsed by the final report of the Commission on the Family, that certain rights of the child be given express constitutional protection. These would include a) the right of every child to be registered immediately after

birth and to have from birth a name, b) the right of every child, as far as practicable, to know her or his parents, subject to the proviso that such right should be subject to regulation by law in the interests of the child, c) the right of every child, as far as practicable, to be cared for by her or his parents, and d) the right to be reared with due regard to her or his welfare. Such rights might be expressly included among the personal rights enunciated in Article 40.

IRISH COUNCIL FOR CIVIL LIBERTIES

1 INTRODUCTION

1.1 The ICCL welcomes the opportunity to make a submission to the All Party Oireachtas Committee on the Constitution (APOCC) in relation to family rights in the Constitution. The ICCL notes that this review by APOCC follows on the Report of the Constitution Review Group (CRG) from 1996, which made a series of recommendations, none of which have been implemented.

1.2 Addressing inequalities in family law and the legal recognition of partnership rights for non-married opposite-sex couples and same-sex couples is a strategic objective for the ICCL (2004-2009).[1] To this end, ICCL has a Partnership and Family Diversity working group which is conducting research and consultation on issues of family law and partnership rights among communities and families in Ireland who currently enjoy none or limited protection of their rights under the Irish Constitution and law. As part of their policy development, ICCL has held two days of consultation, one in Dublin and one in Cork, conducted interviews with individuals, and held an open public forum on partnership and family diversity to inform our policy development. The policy document from this research will be available at the end of the month [March 2005].

1.3 Based on that research initiative, the ICCL believes that current Irish law and practice relating to family life and marriage does not comply with Articles 8, 12 and 14 of the European Convention on Human Rights Act.[2] However, the ICCL is also of the opinion that much of the reform needed to ensure that all people's rights are respected is a matter of law reform and does not require constitutional amendment, i.e. there is no constitutional bar to legislative reform.

1.4 For example, the ICCL submits that it would be possible and desirable to provide for a civil union providing the same rights as marriage for same-sex partnerships, or a civil partnership scheme, similar to the *Pacte Civil de Solidarité* (PACS) which exists in France, without requiring constitutional amendment.[3] Law reform could also take place to address the lack of security and protection for families outside of marriage, particularly the rights of natural fathers. Nothing in the Constitution would prevent such reform taking place.

1.5 Nevertheless the ICCL believes that Articles 41 and 42 of the Constitution, and their existing interpretation, do not reflect effective or proper protection for the family unit, members of the family, or children that are needed or appropriate for Irish society today. It is, for example, not acceptable that there are differing standards of constitutional protection of the family, whether based on marriage or not, or that a natural mother's rights have constitutional protection, but those of a natural father do not. The current constitutional protection afforded to children, is also inadequate. The ICCL therefore believes that constitutional reform of Articles 41 and 42 are necessary and desirable but must not stand in the way of immediate law reform.

2 THE CURRENT CONTEXT

2.1 The ICCL recognises that family is the fundamental unit of society. However, the forms that families take are changing and for many of us those forms may also change over the span of a lifetime. Family support networks may include for example, parents, children, grandparents, step-parents, step-children, adopted children, same-sex partners, ex-partners, or ex-sons and daughters-in law. The increase in working mothers, in people living alone and an increasingly ageing society in Europe have all brought further societal changes. Today global migration means that family commitments continue across continents. Despite the lack of official recognition or rights for relationships based outside of marriage, the numbers of such relationships are rising. As with all committed relationships people when faced with dilemmas generally negotiate 'the proper thing to do'. The decisions they make will be based on what is best for children and how best to sustain the relationships that are important to them. The shape of family forms may be changing but there is no evidence of a lesser commitment within them than those of the traditional kind.[4]

2.2 The Irish Constitution only provides protection to families based on marriage. This means that modern and diverse family forms are not given without any specific protection. Currently in Ireland Lesbian, Gay, Bisexual and Transgendered (LGBT) persons are denied any legal recognition of their right to form stable, long-lasting, personal and committed relationships. Non-married opposite-sex couples are also denied specific legal recognition, which has particularly negative consequences for the position of fathers in an unmarried family, and in tax and social welfare law are subject to whichever conditions are least favourable to them.[5] As a result all non-married cohabiting couples experience serious inequalities and major difficulties because of the state's failure to recognise their chosen relationships and family forms.

2.3 As is the case in many other countries, domestic relationships in Ireland appear to have become even more diverse in the past 30 years. Cohabitation is a growing trend in Irish society, and in many cases, marks the beginning of a new family unit. Opposite-sex cohabitation – whether as an alternative to marriage, as a prelude to marriage, or as a sequel to marriage – is a growing phenomenon that now has widespread social acceptance. Marriage rates have fallen and much family formation takes place outside of marriage. In contrast to the experience of the 1960s and 1970s, a surge in births in the 1990s preceded rather than followed a surge in marriages in the 1990s.[6] In addition, there has been a significant increase in the number of step-families or reconstituted families.

2.4 According to the 2002 census there were 77,600 units consisting of cohabiting couples in 2002, an increase of 46,300 since 1996. The census also showed that the number of cohabiting same-sex couples increased from 150 to 1,300 over the same period. Hence there are more couples and families now falling into this category who urgently need protection.

2.5 The number of cohabiting couples with children is also growing. The census reveals that the number of children living with cohabiting parents more than doubled from 23,000 in 1996 to 51,700 in 2002.[7] This represented 5.5 per cent of all couples with children.

2.6 The ICCL notes that recent Irish government policy on family acknowledges many of these realities. For example, the 2004 publication of the Department of Social and Family Affairs, *Families and Family Life in Ireland: Challenges for the Future,*[8] acknowledges the need for the state to modernise its social systems and to take account of recent changes in family formation. This new thinking is fundamental to the future development of inclusive government policy for future policy development by the Government and is most welcome. It is therefore all the more important that the Constitution is updated .to ensure that the rights of all families are upheld and in particular that the Constitution ensures equal respect and esteem for all children.

3 INTERNATIONAL HUMAN RIGHTS LAW AND FAMILY AND MARRIAGE

3.1 Ireland is a party to numerous human rights treaties which provide guarantees and standards that protect an individual's family life, private life and guarantee the right to marry. Of specific relevance are the International Convention on Civil and Political Rights (ICCPR) 1976, and the European Convention on Human Rights (ECHR). Ireland is also party to the UN Convention on the Rights of the Child (UNCRC) which, as the Committee has noted, is directly relevant to this review of the Constitution.

3.2 In particular, the ECHR has also been given effect in domestic law via the European Convention on

Human Rights Act, 2003. The ICCL has noted at the outset that it considers Irish law to be at odds with the European Convention on Human Rights.

Family Life

3.3 Article 8 of the *European Convention on Human Rights (ECHR)* provides that:

> 1 Everyone has the right to respect for his private and family life, his home and his correspondence.

> 2 There shall be no interference by a public authority with the exercise of this right except such as is in accordance with the law and is necessary in a democratic society in the interests of national security, public safety or the economic well-being of the country, for the prevention of disorder or crime, for the protection of health or morals, or for the protection of the rights and freedoms of others.

3.4 Article 7 of the *Charter of Fundamental Rights* of the European Union, signed on 7 December 2000, provides almost identical protection:

> Everyone has the right to respect for his or her private and family life, home and communications.

3.5 Article 23 of the International Convention on Civil and Political Rights (ICCPR) specifically protects the family:

> 1 The family is the natural and fundamental group unit of society and is entitled to protection by society and the state.

3.6 'Family life' under the ECHR is not confined solely to marriage-based relationships and may encompass other *de facto* 'family' ties where the parties are living together outside of marriage.[9] The European Court of Human Rights has explicitly interpreted Article 8 to be flexible, and by examining the extent to which close personal ties exist within a relationship, focuses on the social and *de facto* reality of family life. Therefore cohabiting couples who are not married, but are in committed relationships akin to marriage, enjoy a family life which attracts the protection of the ECHR. Moreover any child, whether born within or outside of marriage, 'is *ipso iure* part of a "family" unit from the moment of his or her birth and by the very fact of it. There thus exists between the child and his parents a bond amounting to family life even if at the time of his or her birth the parents are no longer co-habiting or if their relationship has then ended.'[10]

3.7 Under the ECHR, there is also little doubt but that the rights of the father in relation to his child, particularly where the father is not married to the mother, attracts much greater protection than Irish law currently affords fathers.[11] In repeated cases, the European Court has upheld the right of contact between father and child, even where there is minimal existence of a relationship between the father and child[12] and under

ECHR law, the rights of a father in relation to his child are not determined by his marital status. Of particular relevance to Ireland is the case of *Keegan v Ireland*,[13] which led to the Act. In that case the then law in Ireland which allowed a child to be placed for adoption without the consultation of her father was challenged. The European Court of Human Rights found that

> 55 the essential problem in the present case is ... the fact that Irish law permitted the applicant's child to have been placed for adoption shortly after her birth without [the father's] knowledge or consent. ... The government have advanced no reasons relevant to the welfare of the applicant's daughter to justify such a departure from the principles that govern respect for family ties.[14]

The Court affirmed that the father's rights under Article 8 had been violated. The Adoption Act, 1998 was passed as a result.

3.8 Other aspects of Irish law, for example whereby a step parent must adopt a child to be treated as a parent, thereby severing the rights of the natural parent, whereby the name of the natural father is not entered on a birth certificate, or whereby a natural father is required to go to court to be appointed as a guardian, unless the mother agrees, does not appear to comply with Article 8. When examining the law in the Netherlands where the father of a child was not recognised in law where the mother was still married to another man, the Court set out the following principles:

> A solution which only allows a father to create a legal tie with a child with whom he has a bond amounting to family life if he marries the child's mother cannot be regarded as compatible with the notion of 'respect' for family life ... In the Court's opinion, 'respect' for 'family life' requires that biological and social reality prevail over a legal presumption which ... flies in the face of both established fact and the wishes of those concerned without actually benefiting anyone.[15]

3.9 The ECHR also prohibits the sexual orientation of a parent being as a legitimate factor on which to draw distinctions between parental rights. The European Court has upheld the rights of a father who had separated from his wife and entered a same-sex relationship but who was then denied the custody and contact rights with his daughter on the grounds of his sexual orientation.[16]

3.10 Whilst the ECHR is protective of the rights of natural parents, it does appear that in the case of adoption, the Court is willing to allow individual states greater latitude in regulating its adoption laws, even where they would appear to be discriminatory or fail to balance the rights of all involved appropriately. For example, the Court upheld a law which excludes a single gay male from eligibility to adopt on the grounds of his sexuality,[17] and has also upheld the right of a natural mother to confidentiality of her identification thereby prohibiting a child from knowing the identity of his/her natural parent.[18]

3.11 The interpretation of family under Article 8 has meant that the European Court is capable of accommodating the diversity of modern family arrangements and the implications of divorce and medical advance. The Court has for example, recognised family life can exist between:

- Children and their grandparents[19]
- Siblings, both as children and as adults[20]
- An uncle or aunt and his/her nephew[21]
- Parents and children born into second relationships, or those children born as a result of an extra-marital or adulterous affair[22]
- Adoptive parents and children[23]
- A child and his/her foster parents[24]
- A transsexual and his/her child born by artificial insemination by donor (AID).[25]

3.12 The Court has not yet definitively considered whether same-sex relationships constitute family life.[26] However in, *Karner v. Austria,*[27] the Court ruled that discrimination suffered by same-sex couples was illegal. The applicant was the surviving partner who lived in the apartment rented by his male partner. Although Austria's domestic legislation protected persons living as life partners to leave rental leases to each other, when his partner died, the Austrian Supreme Court held that the landlord could expel Mr Karner because the legislature had not intended to include persons in same-sex relationships. The ECtHR ruled there had been a breach of Article 8 together with Article 14. It found that the provision at issue protected persons who had been living together for a long time without being married against sudden homelessness and applied to heterosexuals as well as homosexuals. In its judgement, the Court stated that:

> ... (F)or the purposes of Article 14, a difference in treatment is discriminatory if it has no objective and reasonable justification, that is, if it does not pursue a legitimate aim or if there is not a reasonable relationship of proportionality between the means employed and the aim sought to be realised. Furthermore, very weighty reasons have to be put forward before the Court could regard a difference in treatment based exclusively on the ground of sex as compatible with the Convention. Just like differences based on sex, differences based on sexual orientation require particularly serious reasons by way of justification.

3.13 Also pending is *M.W. v. United Kingdom* (Application No. 11313/02) where the denial of bereavement benefits to surviving same-sex partner when married different-sex partner qualifies is being challenged. It is likely that the European Court will follow *Edward Young* v. *Australia*[28] decided by the UN Human Rights Committee under the ICCPR, which found that it was unlawful discrimination to deny

pensions to surviving same-sex partners of veterans, when unmarried different-sex partners of veterans qualify.

3.14 Under Article 8, when family life is established, the guarantee is not limited to a prohibition on arbitrary interference (the minimal protection). There is also a positive duty under Article 8 to take steps to ensure that family life is recognised in law and safeguarded. This creates procedural obligations under Article 8. The European Court of Human Rights has pointed out that Article 8 of the Convention also has a procedural aspect: when a decision over a child is made, the parents must be involved in the decision making process to a degree sufficient to provide them with the requisite protection of their interests. As the Court has often explicitly spelt out:

> Whilst Article 8 (Article 8) contains no explicit procedural requirements, the decision-making process leading to measures of interference must be fair and such as to afford due respect to the interests safeguarded by Article 8 (Article 8):

> [W]hat ... has to be determined is whether, having regard to the particular circumstances of the case and [the nature] of the decisions to be taken, the parents have been involved in the decision-making process, seen as a whole, to a degree sufficient to provide them with the requisite protection of their interests. If they have not, there will have been a failure to respect their family life and the interference resulting from the decision will not be capable of being regarded as 'necessary' within the meaning of Article 8 .....

> ... the procedural requirement inherent in Article 8 covers administrative procedures as well as judicial proceedings, [and] it is ancillary to the wider purpose of ensuring proper respect for, *inter alia*, family life.[29]

3.15 The jurisprudence of Article 23 of the ICCPR is less developed than that of Article 8, but the Human Rights Committee has made clear that 'family' under this provision is also to be interpreted broadly and necessarily embraces the relationship between parent and child, irrespective of the marital status of the parent.[30]

Marriage

3.16 The right to marry is protected under both Article 12 and Article 23 of the ECHR and the ICCPR respectively. Both articles refer to the right of man and woman to marry. To date, the UN Human Rights Committee has determined that the express reference to men and women in Article 23 means that the failure to provide for same-sex marriage will not lead to a violation of the prohibition on discrimination on grounds of sexual orientation under the Covenant.[31]

3.17 However, in *Goodwin v United Kingdom* and *I v United Kingdom*[32] the Court, in a unanimous decision, found that the UK was in breach of Articles 8 and 12 of the ECHR. The Court found that although the right to marry is subject to the national laws of the contracting states the limitations on it must not restrict or reduce the right in such a way or to such an extent that the very essence of the right is impaired. The Court found that the UK laws, in prohibiting a post operative transsexual from marrying a member of their former gender, impaired the very right to marry and was in violation of the Convention. The Court acknowledged that although the first sentence of Article 12 refers in express terms to the right of a man and woman to marry, in 2002 it could not be assumed that these terms must refer to a determination of gender by purely biological criteria, or required some pre-requisite capacity to procreate.

3.18 In the context of the submission to the Inter-Departmental Committee on Reform of Marriage the ICCL has already raised the fact that Irish law is in violation of the ECHR due to its denial of the right to marry to transsexuals,[33] except ironically where that marriage would be *de facto* between same-sex partners.

3.19 The EU Charter in Article 9 however refers only to the right to marry without any reference to sex or gender.[34] This undoubtedly reflects the fact that the Charter is a document drafted fifty years after the ECHR and thirty years after the ICCPR, and reflects contemporary standards of equality. It also reflects the fact that in some member states same-sex marriages have already been legislated for,[35] others are in planning[36] and still others provide legal status and protection to same-sex couples, akin to marriage.[37]

3.20 Article 23 (4) of the ICCPR requires the government to

> take appropriate steps to ensure equality of rights and responsibilities of spouses as to marriage, during marriage and at its dissolution. In the case of dissolution, provision shall be made for the necessary protection of any children.

3.21 In the case of *Johnston v Ireland*,[38] the European Court of Human Rights upheld the right of the Irish state to deny the right to divorce. However, in *F v Switzerland*,[39] the Court held that to impose time limits on the right of a person to re-marry in a jurisdiction where divorce was permitted, constituted a violation of Article 12.

Children's Rights

3.22 Core to reform in the area of family life is respect for the rights of the child external to and within the context of family life. Those rights can be found explicitly with the ICCPR and the UN Convention on the Rights of the Child.

International Convention on Civil and Political Rights (ICCPR)

Article 24 of the Convention provides:

1 Every child shall have, without any discrimination as to race, colour, sex, language, religion, national or social origin, property or birth, the right to such measures of protection as are required by his status as a minor, on the part of his family, society and the state.
2 Every child shall be registered immediately after birth and shall have a name.
3 Every child has the right to acquire a nationality.

United Nations Convention on the Rights of the Child (UNCRC)

3.23 The UNCRC provides a number of rights that are directly related to the position of the child within the family. Article 3 of the convention sets down what is the golden thread of the convention – that the best interest of the child must be paramount in all decisions taken that impact on the child. Beyond Article 3, there are a number of other articles of particular relevance – Articles 5, 7 9 and 18:

Article 5
States Parties shall respect the responsibilities, rights and duties of parents ... to provide ... appropriate direction and guidance in the exercise by the child of the rights recognised in the present convention.

Article 7
1 The child shall be registered immediately after birth and shall have the right from birth to a name, the right to acquire a nationality and, as far as possible, the right to know and be cared for by his or her parents.

Article 9
1 States parties shall ensure that a child shall not be separated from his or her parents against their will, except when competent authorities subject to judicial review determine, in accordance with applicable law and procedures, that such separation is necessary for the best interests of the child....

2 In any proceedings pursuant to paragraph 1 of the present article, all interested parties shall be given an opportunity to participate in the proceedings and make their views known.

3 States parties shall respect the right of the child who is separated from one or both parents to maintain personal relations and direct contact with both parents on a regular basis, except if it is contrary to the child's best interests.

Article 18
1 States parties shall use their best efforts to ensure recognition of the principle that both parents have common responsibilities for the upbringing and development of the child. ...

3.24 While there are no explicit rights of the child in the ECHR, its case law has for the main part been compatible with and re-enforcing of the rights set out in the

UNCRC. Nevertheless there are controversial issues which arise in relation to the right of a child to know the identity of his or her parents in the case of adoption and conception by a donor or AID, which remain unresolved in the case law of the European Court, and unclear from the UNCRC. For example, while the European Court has set out that the right of persons to know information about their childhood and their paternity is central to their right to private life,[40] nevertheless, the Court decided in *Odievre v France*[41] that an adoptive mother's right to privacy and confidentiality could be protected at the expense of the right of an adopted child to know who her natural mother was. What is important from the perspective of the ECHR, is that there is an independent mechanism to determine a person or child's entitlement of access to information about their childhood or parents, and that the principle of proportionality is the standard to be used in reaching decisions.

3.25 The Irish Government is also a party to the United Nations Convention on the Elimination of Discrimination Against Women (CEDAW). Article 16 of that Convention addresses issues relating to marriage and the family.

Article 16

1 Parties shall take all appropriate measures to eliminate discrimination against women in all matters relating to marriage and family relations and in particular shall ensure, on a basis of equality of men and women:

(a) the same right to enter into marriage;

(b) the same right freely to choose a spouse and to enter into marriage only with their free and full consent;

(c) the same rights and responsibilities during marriage and at its dissolution;

(d) the same rights and responsibilities as parents, irrespective of their marital status, in matters relating to their children; in all cases the interests of the children shall be paramount;

(e) the same rights to decide freely and responsibly on the number and spacing of their children and to have access to the information, education and means to enable them to exercise these rights;

(f) the same rights and responsibilities with regard to guardianship, wardship, trusteeship and adoption of children, or similar institutions where these concepts exist in national legislation; in all cases the interests of the children shall be paramount;

(g) the same personal rights as husband and wife, including the right to choose a family name, a profession or occupation;

(h) the same rights for both spouses in respect of the ownership, acquisition, management, administration, enjoyment and disposition of property, whether free of charge or for a valuable consideration.

2 The betrothal and the marriage of a child shall have no legal effect, and all necessary action including legislation shall be taken to specify a minimum age for marriage and to make the registration of marriages in an official registry compulsory.

3.26 However, the Irish government has also made a reservation to CEDAW which states that the government is *'of the view that the attainment in Ireland of the objectives of the convention does not necessitate the extension to men of rights identical to those accorded by law to women in respect of the guardianship, adoption and custody of children born out of wedlock …'*

3.27 The ICCL believes that this reservation should not be necessary, and that there is no justification to fail to recognise the rights of the father in Irish law as currently exists. In the determination of matters relating to a child, it is the best interest of the child that is paramount, and pursuant to that principle, the process of determination must ensure that the rights of both parents are adequately protected.

4 COMPATIBILITY BETWEEN IRISH CONSTITUTIONAL LAW AND HUMAN RIGHTS STANDARDS

4.1 The ICCL notes the questions outlined by the Committee:

- How should the family be defined?
- How should one strike the balance between the rights of the family as a unit and the rights of individual members?
- Is it possible to give constitutional protection to families other than those based on marriage?
- Should gay couples be allowed to marry?
- Is the Constitution's reference to woman's 'life within the home' a dated one that should be changed?
- Should the rights of a natural mother have express constitutional protection?
- What rights should a natural father have, and how should they be protected?
- Should the rights of the child be given an expanded constitutional protection?
- Does the Constitution need to be changed in view of the UN Convention on the Rights of the Child?

4.2 The ICCL notes that many of these questions are those posed by the CRG in 1996. The CRG responded to those questions by saying that no rights should be described as inalienable or imprescriptible, but recommending that the Constitution should contain an article which would:

a. recognise all family rights, including the rights of all members of unmarried families

b. recognise the family as the primary and fundamental unit of society

c. recognise the right for all persons to marry in accordance with law and found a family

d. contain a pledge by the state to guard with special care the institution of marriage and to protect it against attack

e. contain a pledge to protect the family based on marriage in its constitution and authority

f. contain a guarantee to all individuals of respect for their family life whether based on marriage or not

g. contain an express guarantee of certain rights of the child including the right

- to be registered and to have a name,
- to know their parents subject to the best interest of the child,
- to be cared by his/her parents,
- to be reared with due regard to his/her welfare

h. contain an express requirements that the best interest of the child shall be the paramount consideration in all decision making processes

i. contain gender-neutral provision recognising the life of carers in the home

j. contain a provision expressly allowing for state intervention in the event of neglect of children

k. contain an express statement of when and how the government can intervene modelled on 8(2)

l. retain the rules of foreign divorce recognition.

4.3   As is set out below that ICCL believes that many of those recommendations (except (e)) still stand and should be followed.

Family definition and constitutional protection

4.4   The ICCL would endorse the definition of UN definition of the family (for the purposes of the International Year of the Family in 1994) as:

> Any combination of two or more persons who are bound together by ties of mutual consent, birth and/or adoption or placement and who, together, assume responsibility for, *inter alia*, the care and maintenance of group members, the addition of new members through procreation or adoption, the socialisation of children, and the social control of members.

4.5   The current constitutional narrow definition of the family that is based on marriage[42] precludes the recognition of the rights of the family as defined by the UN.

4.6   The ICCL submits that it is essential that the current reference to the family based on marriage in Article 41.3.1 is removed. The ICCL submits that it is preferable that the Constitution should not seek *to define* the family because for the purposes of international human rights law, and Ireland's obligations there under, it is clear that the family is defined by reference to close personal ties which are established between individuals and not a formal designation under national law. To unnecessarily impose a narrow definition would run the risk of excluding and discriminating against some families, and members thereof, including children, in the recognition and protection of their rights. The ICCL submits that the approach of the European Court of Human Rights to defining what is family life is to be preferred.

4.7   The ICCL submits that not only can the Constitution recognise all families, whether based on marriage or not, but that it is imperative that it does. The ICCL recommends that the Constitution should include a commitment *to recognise the family in its various forms as the primary and fundamental unit in society.*

Balancing the rights of the family unit and its members

4.8   The ICCL submits that balancing rights which are sometimes in competition is an integral part of ensuring respect for human rights, and that this exercise is therefore far from a new challenge to the government or the courts. Striking the balance does depend on a case-by-case basis, so that what is at stake for each party is fully considered. In a situation where there appears to be a conflict between the rights of the family as a unit, and those of the members, the following should be considered:

- Is there a child involved? – then the best interest of the child must be paramount
- Is the goal being pursued in limiting one set of rights a legitimate social aim?
- Is there an identifiable (including empirically) *pressing social need*, which justifies the restrictions on one set of rights?
- How important is that social aim, and the extent of the social need, in relation to the limitation to be imposed on the rights of either the family unit or an individual member?
- Which rights of the family unit and/or the member will be restricted and how important are the rights being restricted (e.g. are they absolute rights)?
- Is there a balance between the extent that the right has to be restricted to pursue the social aim, and the importance of the aim?
- Is there a measure which achieves the same aim without limiting an impact on the rights of either the family unit or the individual?

4.9   The ICCL submits that *the Constitution should recognise the right of everyone to family life, and that the right should only be capable of being interfered with in accordance with the law when it is necessary in a democratic society in the interests of public safety, the protection of health, or for the protection of the rights and freedoms of others, in particular dependent children.*

Access to the institution of marriage by same-sex couples

4.10   The ICCL believes that marriage is an institution deserving of respect. It remains the desired relationship option for most couples, and stemming from a recognition of equality of esteem, we believe that the benefits and duties of marriage should be extended to those who cannot currently marry under law in Ireland because of their sexual orientation. The ICCL therefore submits that marriage should be open to all couples who are willing to enter into a voluntary, committed union for life to the exclusion of all others.

4.11   The Irish Constitution does not recognise marriage as an institution which is open to same-sex partners. The exclusion of same-sex couples from that institution is not based on any definition within the Constitution of marriage, but the result of interpretation of marriage by the courts, based on common law definitions. Marriage was defined by Murray J. in 2003 as

> A solemn contract of partnership entered into between man and woman with a special status recognised by the Constitution.[43]

4.12   However, section 2(4) of the Civil Registration Act 2004 explicitly defines marriage as being a union between a man and woman. Section 19 of the Social Welfare (Miscellaneous) Act, 2004 and Section 39 of the Residential Tenancies Act, 2004 also specifically discriminate against same-sex couples in terms of access to benefits and other entitlements.[44]

4.13   In contrast to the recent legislative provisions passed by the Irish government, the trend across legal systems is to recognise same-sex relationships either through marriage or a form of civil partnership or union.

4.14   Within Europe there are three countries that provide equal parity in marriage to same and opposite sex couples: Netherlands, Belgium and Spain (*pending*).[45] The Netherlands was the first to do so by passing legislation in 2001[46] to open up marriage to same-sex couples. Belgium followed suit in 2003.[47] The third country to move towards legislation for same-sex marriage is Spain. In December 2004, the cabinet approved and introduced to parliament a law to permit same-sex marriage. The expectation is that the law will be passed in the first half of 2005.

4.15   Other countries in Europe, in particular the Nordic countries of Denmark, Sweden, Finland, Norway and Iceland have registered partnerships akin to marriage. In the United Kingdom, the Civil Partnership Bill 2003 is before the Parliament. If passed this law will open up civil partnerships to same-sex partners in England, Wales, Scotland and Northern Ireland. France has the Pacte Civile de Solidarite (PACS) dating from 1999, and in Germany same-sex couples may avail of a *Lebenspartnerschaft* or Life Partnership in Germany, which became available in 2001.

4.16   As already noted, the EU Charter refers only to the right to marry without any reference to sex or gender.[48]

4.17   An increasing number of 'common law' jurisdictions have also judicially determined that the common law definition of marriage should be interpreted so as not to exclude same-sex couples. In Canada the right to same-sex common-law marriage has existed nationwide since 1999, when the Supreme Court of Canada found that same-sex couples should be included in the definition of common-law marriage.[49] In 2004, the Court also ruled that under the Constitution, the definition of marriage was open to permitting same-sex marriages.[50] Following that judgment, same-sex marriages are widely anticipated to be legalised across Canada by Bill C-38, introduced in the Federal Parliament on February 1, 2005.

4.18   In South Africa, the Supreme Court of Appeal recognised the right of same-sex couples to marry in the case of *Fourie and Bonthuys vs. Minister for Home Affairs and Director-General of Home Affairs*.[51] In that case, the court eloquently traces the gradual removal of discrimination faced by same-sex couples, as well as the injustice that discrimination has caused the LGBT community. In upholding the rights of gay men and women to marry, Cameron J set out:

> At issue is access to an institution that all agree is vital to society and central to social life and human relationships. More than this, marriage and the capacity to get married remain central to our self-definition as humans. As Madala J has pointed out, not everyone may choose to get married: but heterosexual couples have the choice. [Satchwell v President of the Republic of South Africa 2002 (6) SA 1 (CC) para 16.] The capacity to choose to get married enhances the liberty, the autonomy and the dignity of a couple committed for life to each other. It offers them the option of entering an honourable and profound estate that is adorned with legal and social recognition, rewarded with many privileges and secured by many automatic obligations. It offers a social and legal shrine for love and for commitment and for a future shared with another human being to the exclusion of all others.

> [15] The current common law definition of marriage deprives committed same-sex couples of this choice. In this our common law denies gays and lesbians who wish to solemnise their union a host of benefits, protections and duties. ... More deeply, the exclusionary definition of marriage injures gays and lesbians because it implies a judgment on them. It suggests not only that their relationships and commitments and loving bonds are inferior, but that they themselves can never be fully part of the community of moral equals that the Constitution promises to create for all.

4.19   The ICCL submits that for the reasons set out above the definition of marriage must be changed to recognise that same-sex couples can contract a lawful marriage and thereafter are spouses. This can be done by following the lead of the South African Supreme Court of Appeal and marriage should be recognised as the 'union of two persons for life to the exclusion of all others'. Marriage, which is open to all, should enjoy the same status and recognition as marriage currently has.

4.20   The ICCL also submits that Irish law which currently denies the right to transsexuals to marry, in violation of Ireland's obligations under the ECHR, must be remedied as a matter of urgency, In Europe, only Ireland and Andorra deny this basic civil right to transgender persons.

4.21 The ICCL submits that *the Constitution should recognise the right of all persons to marry in the same manner that the EU Charter does, and that marriage should be defined as the 'union of two persons for life to the exclusion of all others'.*

Life within the home

4.22 The role of carers in society, particularly within the home, is essential. This function may be carried out by a parent, grandparent, sibling or other relative or *de facto* guardian. Carers in the home not only provide security, care and respect for those in need of care, but make an invaluable contribution to society – and the economy. Yet according to the Carers Association, fewer than twenty per cent of all those devoted to caring full time for others in the home in Ireland receive any financial assistance from the state. The ICCL submits that this reflects the complete undervaluation of carers in government and public policy.

4.23 The ICCL therefore believes *that the role which carers play in the home should be explicitly recognised in a gender-neutral provision.*

Recognition of the rights of the mother and father

4.24 The ICCL submits that there is no justification for providing explicit recognition of one set of parental rights to the detriment of another. The ICCL therefore submits that a provision which recognises the right of each person to family life, adequately protects the rights of the mother and father. The rights of the father and mother should then be provided for in legislation in line with Ireland's international human rights obligations. In the event that circumstances give rise to a situation where those rights may be in conflict with the rights of others, then they will be balanced on the basis as set out in paragraph 4.8.

The rights of the child

4.25 The ICCL submits that the rights of the child are currently under-protected in the Constitution, and that weak constitutional position runs the risk of denying to children the basic protection which they are afforded under international human rights law.

4.26 As well as the protection of the UN Convention on the Rights of the Child, the ECHR also sets out positive obligations for states to protect children. The ICCL therefore believes the Constitution should contain *an express guarantee of certain rights of the child based on Article 28 of the South African Constitution:*

> 28 (1) Every child has the right: to a name and a nationality from birth; to family care or parental care, or to

appropriate alternative care when removed from the family environment; to basic nutrition, shelter, basic health care services and social services; to be protected from maltreatment, neglect, abuse or degradation; to be protected from exploitative labour practices; not to be required or permitted to perform work or provide services that are inappropriate for a person of that child's age; or place at risk the child's well-being, education, physical or mental health or spiritual, moral or social development; not to be detained except as a measure of last resort, in which case, in addition to the rights a child enjoys under sections 12 and 35, the child may be detained only for the shortest appropriate period of time, and has the right to be kept separately from detained persons over the age of 18 years; and treated in a manner, and kept in conditions, that take account of the child's age; to have a legal practitioner assigned to the child by the state, and at state expense, in civil proceedings affecting the child, if substantial injustice would otherwise result; and not to be used directly in armed conflict, and to be protected in times of armed conflict.

> (2) A child's best interests are of paramount importance in every matter concerning the child.

5 CONCLUSIONS

5.1 The ICCL submits that Articles 41 and 42 of the Irish Constitution do not provide an appropriate framework to effectively respect and protect the rights of all persons to family life and to marry. On the contrary to date many provisions have led to the exclusion of persons from protection and enjoyment of their rights as guaranteed under Ireland's international human rights obligations.

5.2 The ICCL submits that new constitutional provisions should be adopted which

- recognise the family in its various forms as the primary and fundamental unit in society
- recognise the right of everyone to family life
- provide that the right should only be capable of being interfered with in accordance with the law and when is necessary in a democratic society in the interests of public safety, the protection of health, or for the protection of the rights and freedoms of others, in particular dependent children
- recognise the right of all persons to marry where marriage is the union of two persons for life to the exclusion of all others
- recognise in a gender-neutral way the role which carers play in the home
- recognise the rights of the child similar to Article 28 of the South African Constitution.

Notes
[1] Refer to Appendix 1 for an overview of the ICCL initiative on partnership rights and family diversity.
[2] E.g. in light of *Goodwin and I v United Kingdom, Karner v Austria, and ECHR jurisprudence on the definition of family.*

[3] The ICCL has also made a submission to the Law Reform Consultation Paper on the Rights and Duties of Cohabitees, December 2004, which sets out its recommendation in this regard.

[4] See Williams. F. (2004) *Rethinking Families*, Calouste Gulbenkian Foundation.

[5] i.e. under social welfare provisions are cohabitees, are treated as a couple, and received lower levels of entitlements, yet under tax legislation are taxed as single individuals therefore able to avail of less benefits.

[6] See for example, Fahey & Russell (2001) *Family Formation in Ireland: Trends, Data Needs and Implications,* Report to the Family Affairs Unit, Department of Social, Community and Family Affairs, The Economic and Social Research Institute: Dublin.

[7] www.cso.ie

[8] http://www.welfare.ie/publications/index.html

[9] See in particular *Johnston and Others v. Ireland* judgment of 18 December 1986, Series A no. 112, p. 25, para. 55 and *Keegan v Ireland*, judgement of 19 April 1994, Series A. No. 290, para. 44.

[10] See *Keegan v Ireland, ibid. Berrehab v the Netherlands* judgment of 21 June 1988, Series A no. 138, p. 14, para. 21., *Gül v. Switzerland*, 19 February 1996, Reports 1996-I, pp. 173-74, para. 32

[11] The relation of children born out of wedlock with their natural father has been the subject of much case-law in Strasbourg. See Appendix 1. In relation to Article 8 and its compatibility with Irish law, see further Kilkelly, Ursula, *Child and Family Law* in *ECHR and Irish Law,* Kilkelly, Ursula (ed.), Jordan Publishing 2004.

[12] *Boughanemi v. France,* 26 February 1992, Reports 1996-II *Söderbäck v Sweden* Judgement of 28 October 1998, Reports 1998-VII.

[13] *Keegan v Ireland*, judgement of 19 April 1994, Series A. No. 290.

[14] Para. 55 *ibid.*

[15] *Kroon v Netherlands* Judgement of 21 October 1994 Series A297-C.

[16] *Salgueiro da Silva Mouta v Portugal*, Judgement of 21 December 1999 Reports 1999-IX.

[17] *Frette v France*, Judgement of 26 February 2002, Reports 2002-I.

[18] *Odivere v France* 13 February 2003, Reports 2003-III. The applicant complained that France had failed to ensure respect for her private life by its legal system, which totally precluded an action to establish maternity being brought if the natural mother had requested confidentiality and, above all, prohibited the Child Welfare Service or any other body that could give access to such information from communicating identifying data on the mother.

[19] *Marckx Belgium*, Judgment of 13 June 1979, Series A no. 31.

[20] *Olsson v Sweden*, Judgement of 24 March 1988, Series A no. 130.

[21] *Boyle v United Kingdom*, Application No. 16580/90, Commission Report, 19 February 1993.

[22] *Jolie and Lebrun v Belgium*, Application No. 11418/85, Decision 14 May 1986, DR 47, p. 243.

[23] Eg. *Soderback v Sweden* Judgement of 28th October 1998, Reports 1998-VII.

[24] Whether ties between them will amount to family life will depend on the facts of the case, in particular, whether the child has close personal ties with his/her natural parents and the length of time s/he has been in the care of the foster family. The longer the foster-care arrangement, the greater the likelihood that family ties will be found to exist.

[25] *X, Y & Z v the United Kingdom*, Judgement of 22 April 1997, Reports 1997-II. The Court emphasised that but for AID, the relationship of father and son was indistinguishable from that enjoyed by the traditional family and secondly, that the transsexual applicant had participated in the AID process as the child's father

[26] In *Kerkhoven v. the Netherlands*, the Commission failed to find that a stable relationship between two women and the child born to one of them by AID amounted to family life.

[27] *Karner v Austria*, July 2003.

[28] Communication No. 941/2000, 6 August 2003.

[29] *McMichael v United Kingdom*, Judgement 24 February 1995, Series A 307 – B paras. 87 and 91. See also E ur. Court judgments of 8 July 1987, *W. v the United Kingdom*, Series A no. 121, p. 29, para. 64; *B. v the United Kingdom*, Series A no. 121, p. 73, para. 64, and *R. v the United Kingdom*, Series A no. 121, p. 118, para. 68.

[30] See General Comments 16 and 19 and *Hendriks v Netherlands*, Decision 201/85.

[31] Communication No 902/1999: *Joslin v New Zealand* 30/07/2002. CCPR/C/75/D/902/1999.

[32] Judgments 11 July 2002.

[33] *Foy v Registrar of Births*, High Court, Irish Times Law Report, 10 July 2002.

[34] 'The right to marry and the right to found a family shall be guaranteed in accordance with the national laws governing the exercise of these rights.'

[35] Netherlands and Belgium.

[36] Spain.

[37] Denmark, Sweden, Finland, UK (Civil Partnership Bill), France and Germany.

[38] Case No. 6/1985/92/139, Judgement of 27 November 1986.

[39] Case No. 21/1986/119/168, Judgement of 18 December 1987.

[40] *Gaskin v UK*, no 10454/83, Series A no 160, 12 EHRR 36 and *Mikulic v Croatia* Judgement of 7 February 2002, Reports 2002-I. In *Mikuli_*, the applicant, a 5-year-old girl, complained of the length of a paternity suit which she had brought with her mother and the lack of procedural means available under Croatian law to enable the courts to compel the alleged father to comply with a court order for DNA tests to be carried out. The Court weighed the vital interest of a person in receiving the information necessary to uncover the truth about an important aspect of his or her personal identity against the interest of third parties in refusing to be compelled to make themselves available for medical testing. It found that the state had a duty to establish alternative means to enable an independent authority to determine the paternity claim speedily. It held that there had been a breach of the proportionality principle as regards the interests of the applicant, who had been left in a state of prolonged uncertainty as to her personal identity (§§ 64-66).

[41] *Odivere v France* 13 February 2003, Reports 2003-III. The applicant complained that France had failed to ensure respect for her private life by its legal system, which totally precluded an action to establish maternity being brought if the natural mother had requested confidentiality and, above all, prohibited the Child Welfare Service or any other body that could give access to such information from communicating identifying data on the mother.

[42] See in particular the Supreme Court in *The State (Nicolaou) v An Bord Uchtála* [1966] IR 567.

[43] *DT v CT* [2003] 1 ILRM 321

[44] In light of the ECHR case of *Karner* (see above), it is hard to see how either of the foregoing provisions can be compatible with the ECHR Act 2003. There is also the case of *M. W. v United Kingdom.*

[45] For a full description of the development of the law in Netherlands and Belgium see Kees Waaldijk, *The*

Introduction of Marriage, Quasi-Marriage, and Semi-Marriage for Same-Sex Couples in European Countries, New England Law Review, Vol. 38:3 p.569.

[46] De Wet Openstelling Huwelijk (*Act on the Opening Up of Marriage*) of December 21, 2000.

[47] Loi Ouvrant le Mariage a des Personnes de Même Sexe et Modifiant Certaines Dispositions du Code Civil (*Law opening up marriage to persons of the same sex and amending certain provisions of the Civil Code*) of February 13, 2003.

[48] Article 9 *op. cit.*

[49] *M.* v *H.* [1999] 2 S.C.R. 3.

[50] *Reference re Same-Sex Marriage,* 2004 SCC 79, December 9 2004.

[51] Case no: 232/2003. Judgement 30/11/04.

IRISH FOSTER CARE ASSOCIATION

We are asking that the Constitution be amended to give greater protection to the rights of children. Currently, the rights of children are not specifically protected. Foster children, who may live all of their childhood with their foster family and who may wish to be adopted by that family and whose foster family may wish to adopt them cannot be adopted if they are the child of a marriage even though their birth family may have abused or abandoned them. We are talking about children in foster care, where all those involved are agreed that such a move is in the child's best interests.

We are also asking that children be given a voice and are heard, as a matter of course, either themselves or, where more appropriate, through a guardian *ad litum,* in court proceedings that affect them. I refer to care proceedings amongst others.

IRISH HUMAN RIGHTS COMMISSION

This submission is an extract from the submission of the Irish Human Rights Commission to the Committee on the Eliminiation of Discrimination Against Women (CEDAW), January 2005.

2 REVIEW OF THE IRISH CONSTITUTION FROM A GENDER EQUALITY PERSPECTIVE

2.1 Article 41.2 – Stereotypical role of women as homemakers and mothers

In accordance with Article 2(a) of CEDAW Ireland is required to embody the principle of equality of men and women in its national Constitution or other appropriate legislation. Article 5 of CEDAW also requires states to take all appropriate measures to modify the social and cultural patterns of conduct of men and women in order to promote gender equality. These measures should aim to eliminate prejudices and customary and all other practices which are based on the idea of the inferiority or the superiority of either of the sexes, or on stereotyped roles for men and women. One of the appropriate measures in this context would be the amendment of Article 41.2 of the Irish Constitution which is based on a stereotyped view of the role of women in Irish society.

Article 41 of the Irish Constitution headed 'The Family' states that the family is the fundamental unit group of society and is a moral institution which possesses inalienable and imprescriptible rights that are antecedent and superior to all positive law. It continues with a state guarantee to protect the family as the necessary basis of social order and as indispensable to the welfare of the nation and the state. In this context Article 41.2 of the Constitution states that,

> In particular, the state recognises that by her life within the home, woman gives to the state a support without which the common good cannot be achieved … [and] shall therefore, endeavour to ensure that mothers shall not be obliged by economic necessity to engage in labour to the neglect of their duties in the home.

This provision of the Constitution has been described as reflecting a sexual division of labour which is 'based on a biological determinism that assumes that one's social destiny is dependent on whether one is female or male, thereby closing off the options for both women and men, but particularly for women.'[1] In their Concluding Observations on Ireland's second and third periodic reports, the Committee expressed concern about the continuing existence in Article 41.2 of concepts that reflect a stereotypical view of the role of women in the home and as mothers.[2] In July 2000, the Human Rights Committee, in their Concluding Observations on Ireland's second periodic report under the ICCPR, also expressed concern that the reference to women made in Article 41.2 of the Constitution could perpetuate traditional attitudes towards the role of women.[3]

Within Ireland recommendations for the amendment of Article 41.2 have been made for many years. In 1993 the report of the Second Commission on the Status of Women recommended that Article 41.2.2 should be deleted.[4] In 1996 the Constitution Review Group[5] stated that Article 41.2 assigns to women a domestic role as wives and mothers, and is a dated provision which has never been of any particular assistance to women working exclusively within the home.[6] The Constitution Review Group recommended that in recognition of the significant contribution made to society by the large number of people who provide a caring function within their homes, Article 41.2 should be revised to state that the state recognises the importance of home and family life and will endeavour to support persons caring for others within the home. The All-Party Oireachtas (i.e. Parliament) Committee on the Constitution has also recognised that Article 41.2 is a dated provision that has been widely criticised because it presumes that women, by reason of their gender, are pre-determined to play a particular role in life, thus seeming to deny them the same freedom of choice as that enjoyed by men.[7] The All-Party Oireachtas Committee has recommended that an amendment similar to that recommended by the Constitution Review Group should be made to Article 41.2.

In November 2004 the All-Party Oireachtas Committee on the Constitution announced that it is now going to undertake an overall examination of the provisions of the Constitution that relate to the family including Articles 41, 42 and 40.3.[8] Individuals and groups have been invited to make submissions on, amongst other issues, whether the Constitution's reference to woman's life within the home is a dated provision that is in need of change. While it is reasonable to expect that the Committee will refer to Article 8 of the European Convention for the Protection of Human Rights and Fundamental Freedoms in relation to the definition of 'family life', it is also imperative that the Committee should have full regard to the provisions of CEDAW in its review of these particular articles of the Constitution.

The low priority afforded to amending what has been consistently recognised as one of the most dated provisions of the Constitution is illustrated by the fact that since the Committee on the Elimination of Discrimination Against Women made its concluding comments on Ireland's second and third periodic reports in 1999, four referenda have been held proposing six different amendments to the Constitution. None of these referenda have included a proposal to amend Article 41.2.

2.2 Article 40.1 – Equality before the law

The Irish Constitution does not explicitly embody the principle of equality of men and women and does not contain an explicit prohibition against discrimination on the basis of sex. The equality provision in the Irish Constitution, Article 40.1, states as follows:

> All citizens shall, as human persons, be held equal before the law. This shall not be held to mean that the state shall not in its enactments have due regard to differences of capacity, physical and moral, and of social function.

In general, it has been observed that in contrast to comparative and international jurisprudence on the subject of equality before the law, the Irish Constitution jurisprudence on the guarantee of equality is remarkably underdeveloped.[9] For example, Irish judges have not yet authoritatively considered the concept of indirect discrimination.[10] In addition, in general, the judiciary have interpreted the phrase 'as human persons' contained in Article 40.1 in quite a restrictive manner to

mean that the guarantee of equality only applies in relation to the 'essential attributes of the human person'.[10] In the case of *Quinn's Supermarket v. Attorney General*, it was stated that the equality guarantee 'refers to human persons for what they are in themselves rather than any lawful activities, trades or pursuits which they may engage in or follow.'[12] This 'human personality doctrine' has been widely criticised as unduly restricting the concept of equality in the Irish Constitution and as undermining the effectiveness of the equality guarantee.[13] The Constitution Review Group recommended that the words 'as human persons' should be removed from Article 40.1 on the grounds that it is not found in other constitutional orders or in the international instruments to which Ireland is a party.[14]

In contrast, the international human rights treaties Ireland has ratified place the norms of non-discrimination and equality as 'core norms' and define the concepts of non-discrimination and equality quite broadly to include direct and indirect discrimination, and to encompass a wide number of grounds. Article 2 of CEDAW requires states to condemn discrimination against women in *all its forms* and to pursue a policy of eliminating *all forms* of discrimination against women. In particular, Article 2(a) of CEDAW provides that states agree 'to embody the principle of the equality of men and women in their national constitutions or other appropriate legislation if not yet incorporated therein and to ensure, through law and other means the practical realisation of this principle'. Moreover, Article 26 of the ICCPR is a free standing non-discrimination and equality standard which guarantees equality before the law to all persons. This provision requires states to prohibit all discrimination and guarantee to all persons equal and effective protection against discrimination on any ground such as race, colour, sex, language, religion, political or other opinion, national or social origin, property, birth or other status.

In its 1993 report, the Second Commission on the Status of Women recommended the amendment of the Constitution to prohibit all forms of discrimination, whether direct or indirect, based on sex.[15] In its 1996 report, a majority of the Constitution Review Group recommended that a provision should be added to Article 40.1 which should state that no person shall be unfairly discriminated against, directly or indirectly, on any ground including sex, race, language, religion, political or other opinion, national, social or ethnic origin, property, birth or other status.[16]

The principle of equality has been given greater effectiveness in Irish law through the enactment of the Employment Equality Act, 1998 and the Equal Status Act, 2000. These Acts prohibit discrimination within certain spheres, including employment, vocational training, advertising, collective agreements, and the provision of goods and services to which the public generally have access. Discrimination is prohibited on the basis of nine distinct grounds including gender, membership of the Traveller community, race, disability, age, marital status, family status, sexual orientation and religion. However, the prohibition against discrimination in this legislation is limited to certain spheres of human activity. While this legislation has an extremely important role to play in advancing the equality of women, the existence of this legislation does not diminish the importance of having an all-embracing effective equality guarantee in the Irish Constitution to bring the Constitution into line with international human rights law.

The Committee on the Elimination of Discrimination Against Women also noted in its Concluding Observations on Ireland's second and third periodic reports that the constitutional guarantee of non-discrimination does not extend to private, non-state actors.[17] The wording of Article 40.1 appears to envisage that the equality obligation applies primarily to the state rather than to private, non-state actors.[18] Jurisprudence on the question of whether the guarantee of equality contained in Article 40.1 is capable of 'horizontal application' is not very well developed in the Irish legal system.[19] In two cases the courts have imposed constitutional obligations on trade unions to respect the constitutional rights of others.[20] However, it is not clear from the existing jurisprudence whether or not the *equality guarantee* under Article 40.1 is capable of horizontal application.

In its most recent General Comment, the Committee on the Elimination of Discrimination Against Women stated that states should ensure that 'women are protected against discrimination – committed by public authorities, the judiciary, organisations, enterprises or private individuals – in the public as well as the private spheres by competent tribunals as well as sanctions and other remedies'.[21] The Human Rights Committee has also stated that state parties have positive obligations to protect persons against acts committed by private persons or entities that would impair the enjoyment of their rights under the ICCPR. A state party is in violation of this positive obligation where it permits a private person to violate the rights of another person or where it fails to take appropriate measures, or fails to exercise due diligence, to prevent, punish, investigate or redress the harm caused by private persons or entities.[22]

2.3 Temporary special measures under Irish law

In its most recent General Comment on temporary special measures, the Committee on the Elimination of Discrimination Against Women recommended that states should include a provision allowing for temporary special measures in their constitutions, or in their national legislation. The purpose of temporary special measures is to accelerate the improvement of the position of women to achieve their substantive equality with men, and to effect the structural, social and cultural changes necessary to correct past and current forms and effects of discrimination against women, as well as to provide them with compensation. In its

General Comment, the Committee makes it clear that the application of temporary special measures should not be regarded as an exception to the norm of non-discrimination, but rather should be viewed as being an integral part of a necessary strategy to achieve the substantive equality of women with men in the enjoyment of their fundamental human rights.

As the report submitted by the government points out, section 24 of the Employment Equality Act, 1998 allows for positive action measures to ensure equality in practice between men and women in employment and to allow for specific advantages to make it easier for an under-represented sex to pursue vocational activity, or to prevent or compensate for disadvantage in professional careers. However, there is no provision in the Irish Constitution that allows for the application of positive temporary special measures to promote the full development or advancement of women and other disadvantaged groups. In recognition of past discrimination against women, the Report of the Second Commission on the Status of Women 1993 recommended that, in addition to the prohibition of direct and indirect discrimination, a provision should be inserted into the Constitution allowing for positive discrimination measures. Such a provision would ensure that the equality guarantee does not prevent the state from putting in place positive measures designed to redress imbalances and achieve substantive equality for women with men.[23]

2.4 Sexist language of the Irish Constitution

With the exception of a small number of specific references to women in the Constitution, the language of the Constitution is predominantly sexist and male-oriented. The President is referred to throughout the Constitution as 'he', as are the Taoiseach (ie. prime minister), the attorney general and the judges. Moreover, notwithstanding the fact that under the Constitution every citizen 'without distinction of sex' is eligible for membership of Dáil Éireann, a member of either House of the Irish Parliament is referred to as 'he'. The specific references to women in the Irish Constitution are limited to the reference in Article 41.2 to a woman's duties in the home and to the reference in Article 40.3.3 to the right to life of the unborn and the equal right to life of the mother. In addition, under the directive principles of social policy which are intended to generally guide the legislature and which are not cognisable in the courts, Article 45.2(i) refers to the equal right of men and women to an adequate livelihood.

The All-Party Oireachtas Committee on the Constitution has described the text of the Constitution as a product of the patriarchal times in which it was written, as being insensitive on the issue of gender, and as invariably presuming that officeholders will be male. This Committee further stated that a consistent rephrasing of the Constitution so as to ensure that it is gender-inclusive is a common courtesy the state should pay to more than half its citizens.[24]

2.5 Article 40.3.3 – The right to life of the unborn and the equal right to life of the mother

In its Concluding Observations on Ireland's second and third periodic reports, the Committee on the Elimination of Discrimination Against Women expressed concern about the fact that abortion remains illegal in Ireland with very limited exceptions and that women who wish to terminate their pregnancies have to travel abroad to do so. In particular, the Committee stated that this can create hardship for vulnerable groups, such as female asylum seekers who cannot leave the territory of the state.[25]

The Human Rights Committee in its Concluding Observations on Ireland's second periodic report also expressed concern about the fact that abortion can only be legally carried out in very limited circumstances when the life of the mother is in danger and that these limited circumstances do not include situations where pregnancy is the result of rape. The Human Rights Committee stated that Ireland should ensure that women are not compelled to continue with pregnancies where that is incompatible with obligations arising under Article 7 of the ICCPR and General Comment 28.[26] In General Comment 28 the Human Rights Committee states that in order to assess compliance with Article 7 of the ICCPR the Committee needs to know whether the state party gives access to safe abortion to women who have become pregnant as a result of rape.[27]

The Committee on the Elimination of Discrimination Against Women, in its last examination of Ireland's periodic reports, urged the government to facilitate a national dialogue on women's reproductive rights, including on the restrictive abortion laws.

Since the Committee examined Ireland's reports in 1999, the legal situation in relation to abortion in Ireland remains the same. Abortion can be carried out in Ireland under limited circumstances. Article 40.3.3 of the Constitution acknowledges the right to life of the unborn and, with due regard to the right to the life of the mother, guarantees to defend the right to life of the unborn as far as practicable. In addition, sections 58 and 59 of the Offences Against the Person Act, 1861 make it a criminal offence to carry out an abortion at all stages of pregnancy. In the case of *Attorney General v. X*.[28], the Supreme Court held that a termination is permissible where continuance of the pregnancy constitutes a real and substantial risk to the life of the mother. For these purposes, a threat of suicide constitutes a real and substantial risk to the mother's life. A risk to the *health*, as opposed to the *life*, of the mother is insufficient to justify an abortion in Ireland.

There is no legislation specifically governing the limited circumstances in which a legal termination can be carried out in Ireland despite numerous recommendations that the Parliament should legislate in this area including recommendations from the judiciary[29] and the Constitution Review Group.[30] There is no definition of what is meant by the 'unborn' in Article 40.3.3 of the Constitution. In addition, there is no express protection for appropriate medical intervention where the life of the mother is at risk, and there are no criteria for the assessment of a 'real and substantial' risk to the life of the mother.

Since the Committee's examination of Ireland's second and third periodic reports, a constitutional referendum on the issue of abortion was held in March 2002. The Twenty-Fifth Amendment of the Constitution (Protection of Human Life in Pregnancy) Bill 2001 proposed to further restrict the availability of abortion in Ireland by removing the probability of suicide as a ground for lawful abortion. Moreover, the Bill proposed a penalty of up to twelve years imprisonment for carrying out an illegal abortion, or aiding, assisting, or counselling another person to carry out an illegal abortion. The referendum was rejected.

The report submitted by the government does not address the question of vulnerable groups of women who may wish to terminate their pregnancies. Female asylum seekers and non-EU nationals are particularly vulnerable because their right to leave and re-enter the country is restricted, and they may not be aware of the fact that they can obtain temporary visas to allow them to leave and re-enter Ireland. According to media reports, more than sixty asylum seekers living in Ireland have been given exit entry visas to travel to the UK for an abortion.[31] In addition, media reports have revealed that the police force is now investigating some cases of backstreet abortions amongst immigrant communities.[32] In general, organisations working with women in crisis pregnancy report that the number of women from immigrant communities using their services has increased substantially.

2.6 List of recommended questions for the CEDAW Committee

a In the light of Articles 2 and 5 of CEDAW and the concluding observations of the CEDAW Committee on Ireland's second and third periodic reports, what steps do the government intend to take to amend Article 41.2 of the Constitution and what priority will be afforded to this issue?

b Does the government regard temporary special measures as a necessary part of achieving substantive equality for women and, in light of General Comment 25, is the government in favour of allowing for temporary special measures in the Irish Constitution?

c In the light of the recommendations of the All-Party Oireachtas Committee on the Constitution, what priority is being afforded to replacing the sexist language and terminology of the Irish Constitution with gender-inclusive language?

2.7 Recommendations

a The IHRC recommends that the All-Party Oireachtas Committee should take full consideration of Ireland's legal obligations under CEDAW in considering the appropriate amendments to the Constitution relating to the family, in particular Article 41.2.

b The IHRC recommends that immediate consideration should be given to holding a referendum within a specific time-frame to amend Article 41.2 of the Constitution which, in the view of the IHRC, is in violation of Article 2 and Article 5 of CEDAW.

c The IHRC recommends that the proposal to amend Article 41.2 of the Constitution should recognise the equal role and responsibility of men and women for carrying out the caring function in society. In addition, the constitutional amendment should recognise the significant contribution made to society by those who engage in caring work and should contain a state guarantee to actively support such persons.

d The IHRC recommends that immediate consideration should be given to holding a referendum within a specific time-frame to amend Article 40.1 of the Constitution to prohibit direct and indirect discrimination on the basis of gender, race, colour, age, disability, sexual orientation, religious belief, membership of the Traveller community, language, political opinion, property, birth or other status.

e The IHRC recommends that an amendment of Article 40.1 should also prohibit discrimination by private actors and should require the state to take the appropriate measures to protect persons against such discrimination.

f The IHRC recommends that a specific provision should be inserted in Article 40.1 to allow the state the possibility to put in place temporary special measures in a targeted, time-bound manner to accelerate the equality of women and other disadvantaged groups in Irish society.

g The IHRC recommends that immediate priority should be afforded to replacing the sexist terminology of the Constitution with gender-inclusive language within a specific time-frame.

h The IHRC recommends that the government should introduce legislation to define the circumstances in which an abortion can currently be legally carried out in Ireland.

Notes

1 Connelly A., 'Women and the Constitution of Ireland', in Galligan Y., Ward E. and Wilford R., *Contesting Politics: Women in Ireland, North and South* (Westview Press, Oxford, 1999), p. 24.

2 Concluding observations of the Committee on the Elimination of Discrimination Against Women on Ireland's second and third periodic reports, A/54/38, para. 161-201, para. 193.

3 Concluding observations of the Human Rights Committee

on Ireland's second periodic report, A/55/40, paras. 422-451, para. 20.

4 *Report of the Second Commission on the Status of Women* (Government Publications 1993), p. 27. The second Commission on the Status of Women was established in 1990 to consider and make recommendations on the means, administrative and legislative, by which women will be able to participate on equal terms and conditions with men in economic, social, political and cultural life and, to this end, to consider the efficacy and feasibility of positive action measures.

5 The Constitution Review Group was established in 1995 to review the Constitution, and in the light of this review, to establish those areas where constitutional change may be desirable or necessary, with a view to assisting the All-Party Oireachtas Committee on the Constitution, in its work.

6 *Report of the Constitution Review Group*, (Government Publications, May 1996), p. 333. In the case of *L v. L* [1992] 2 IR 77 the Supreme Court rejected a claim by a married woman which was based specifically on Article 41.2. The Supreme Court held that even though she had worked exclusively within the home throughout her marriage she was not entitled to a 50% interest in the family home by virtue of Article 41.2.

7 *First and Second Progress Reports of the All-Party Oireachtas Committee on the Constitution* (Government Publications, 1997).

8 The All-Party Oireachtas Committee on the Constitution was established to complete a full review of the Constitution. The function of the Committee is to provide a focus on the place and relevance of the Constitution and to establish those areas where constitutional change may be desirable or necessary with reference to the Report of the Constitution Review Group.

9 Hogan and Whyte, *JM Kelly: The Irish Constitution* (4th ed., Butterworths, Dublin, 2003), p. 1324, para. 7.2.05.

10 *Ibid.*

11 *Ibid.*, para. 7.2.40-7.2.56.

12 *Quinn's Supermarket v Attorney General*, [1972] IR 1 at 14.

13 Mullally S., 'The Myth of Constitutionalism and the "Neutral" State', in Murphy T. and Twomey P. (eds.), *Ireland's Evolving Constitution 1937-1997 Collected Essays* (Hart Publishing, Oxford 1998), p. 154.

14 *Report of the Constitution Review Group*, p. 224.

15 *Report of the Second Commission on the Status of Women*, p. 27.

16 *Report of the Constitution Review Group*, p. 230.

17 Concluding observations of the Committee on the Elimination of Discrimination Against Women on Ireland's second and third periodic reports, A/54/38, para. 193.

18 Hogan and Whyte 2004, para. 7.2.24.

19 See further Mullally S., 1998.

20 *Murtagh Properties Ltd. v Cleary*, [1972] IR 330; *Meskell v CIE*, [1973] IR 121.

21 General Recommendation No. 25, Temporary Special Measures, CEDAW/C/2004/I/WP.1/Rev.1, para. 35.

22 Human Rights Committee, General Comment No. 31, Nature of the General Legal Obligation on States Parties to the Covenant, CCPR/C/21/Rev.1/Add.13(2004), para. 8.

23 *Report of the Second Commission on the Status of Women*, p. 27.

24 *First and Second Progress Reports of the All-Party Oireachtas Committee on the Constitution* (Government Publications, 1997).

25 Concluding observations of the Committee on the Elimination of Discrimination Against Women on Ireland's second and third periodic reports, A/54/38, para. 161-201, para. 185.

[26] Article 7 of the ICCPR prohibits torture or cruel, inhuman or degrading treatment or punishment.

[27] Human Rights Committee, General Comment 28, Equality of Rights between Men and Women, CCPR/C/21/Rev.1/Add.10, para. 11.

[28] *Attorney General v X* [1992] IR 1.

[29] *Attorney General v X* [1992] IR 1, McCarthy J., stated as follows: 'In the context of the eight years that have passed since the [1984] Amendment was adopted and the two years since *Grogan's* case the failure by the legislature to enact the appropriate legislation is no longer just unfortunate; it is inexcusable. What are pregnant women to do? What are the parents of a pregnant girl under age to do? What are the medical profession to do? They have no guidelines save what may be gleaned from the judgments in this case. What additional considerations are there? ... The [1984] Amendment, born of public disquiet, historically divisive of our people, guaranteeing in its laws to respect and by its laws to defend the right to life of the unborn, remains bare of legislative direction.'

[30] On this issue the Constitution Review Group stated that 'While in principle the major issues ... should be tackled by constitutional amendment, there is no consensus as to what that amendment should be and no certainty of success for any referendum proposal for substantive constitutional change in relation to this subsection. The Review Group, therefore, favours, as the only practical possibility at present, the introduction of legislation covering such matters as definitions, protection for the appropriate medical intervention, certification of "real and substantial risk to the life of the mother" and a time-limit on lawful termination of pregnancy'.

[31] *Irish Times*, 17 September 2004.

[32] *Irish Times*, 9 July 2004.

IRISH SENIOR CITIZENS PARLIAMENT

1 The Irish Senior Citizens Parliament is the largest older people's organisation in Ireland with 350 organisations affiliated, representing a membership of 90,000.

2 We welcome this opportunity of making a few points in relation to the Constitution and 'the family'. We would, however, point out that we are not experts in the Constitution and there are certain aspects of this issue that we do not feel confident in making statements on. However, dealing with a number of the issues that are raised in your briefing document, the view of the Irish Senior Citizens Parliament is that the definition of 'the family' as currently enshrined in our Constitution is too narrow and does not take into account many of the changes that have taken place in our society. We are particularly anxious that the status of one-parent families be recognised.

3 One-parent families undergo more difficulties than many other families. The parent, usually the mother, is unable to return to the workforce and therefore is disadvantaged in terms of personal development and also having the ability to make proper provisions for her child. The lack of crèche facilities and other supports does not help in this situation.

4 Also noteworthy is that in Article 41 of the Constitution it states that the state shall therefore endeavour to ensure that mothers shall not be obliged for economic necessity to engage in labour to the neglect of their duties in the home. However, this has been in the Constitution since 1937 and very little regard has been paid to it in terms of economic and social policy. The situation at present is that unless mothers go to work, their children will suffer from lack of basic necessities, and nowadays there is even greater difficulty where there is low income and this is the case where 'the family' is totally dependent on state support. This support will never be enough to give a reasonable standard of living to 'the family' and many mothers require to return to the workforce for the economic and social well-being of themselves and their families. It is impossible for many to return to the workforce because of the absence of crèche facilities or their cost.

5 Definition of the family. The traditional definition of 'the family' is mother, father and children. Families may be mother and child or father and child. The Irish Senior Citizens Parliament believes there is a wider definition of family now needed to also include grandparents. Grandparents play a vital and important role in many families with the assistance of child-minding and in some cases child-rearing. Many children live with their grandparents but grandparents have little of no rights in regards to the relationship with their grandchildren. This is an issue that needs to be addressed and if not in constitutional reform certainly in legislation. There are occasions when there are family difficulties and where grandparents and children fall out. The grandparents are denied any access to their grandchildren. We believe that this, in many cases, is not in the best interest of the grandparents and certainly not in the best interest of grandchildren.

6 Grandparents' love and affection when reciprocated by the grandchildren can play a very important part not only in the development of the grandchild but also in the quality of life of the grandparent, and we believe that this needs to be recognised as part of the modern family. Often in times of family crisis the only ones that the authorities can look to give support to children who are in separated families are grandparents. If the state wishes to have grandparents play a positive role in society in the furthering and protection of family and human values it needs to give recognition to this.

7 Regarding the individual rights of parents as against the rights of a family as a unit, the Parliament believes it is important that protection is given to the rights of both the father and the mother and of the child itself as these are not specifically mentioned in the Constitution. The right of a father to have access to his child is an important one that is not defined in law. For two parents to have access to the child and to help with its upbringing is an important support for the child. It is interesting that while the Constitution guarantees family rights it does not say what these rights are.

8 John Kelly in his book on the Irish Constitution says that this has led the courts to rely on their instincts, and he draws particular attention to the case of *Ryan versus the Attorney General*, a case about the use of fluoridation in water in which a Mrs Ryan claimed that this was a violation of family rights under Article 41. Justice Kenny said that not one of the counsel in this case had attempted to state what were the inalienable and imprescriptible rights of the family, and the Constitution gives very little help in this regard. It is therefore clear that any mention of rights in the Constitution needs to be clearly spelt out and expanded in primary law, and the role of the Constitution should be to support primary law in defending rights to ensure that rights cannot be set aside by a constitutional challenge.

9 There is an urgent need to amend the Constitution to facilitate the introduction into law of the United Nations Convention on the Rights of the Child. Ireland ratified the United Nations Convention in September 1992; it is binding on the state; however, until it is incorporated into Irish law it is not binding on the courts. The dignity and rights of children will be greatly enhanced if the necessary changes are made to the Constitution to enable the Convention on the Rights of the Child to be transposed into domestic legislation.

10 In conclusion, the Irish Senior Citizens Parliament wishes the Committee on family rights in the Constitution well in its difficult task, and hopes that the outcome of its work will enhance human dignity by a clear constitutional article on the family and its members and their rights; and that the status and protection of one-parent families will be advanced, and the role of grandparents will be recognised in any proposed changes to the Constitution.

IRISH SOCIETY FOR THE PREVENTION OF CRUELTY TO CHILDREN (ISPCC)

THE ISPCC

The Irish Society for the Prevention of Cruelty to Children (ISPCC) is Ireland's oldest charity and has worked for over one hundred years to prevent cruelty to children. The ISPCC has five action pillars:

1 The child as a citizen
2 Protecting the child, preventing child abuse and promoting child-centredness
3 The child in the family – supporting positive parenting
4 The child in the school and the community
5 Giving children a voice.

The society focuses on these five pillars through four key strands of activity:

1 Service delivery
2 Public and professional education
3 Campaigning and lobbying
4 Children's consultation mechanisms

The society has a proud history of service delivery dating back to its formation in 1889. Since its formation, the ISPCC has sought to develop and deliver innovative child-centred services that meet the needs of children and their families.

The ISPCC has a vision – a society in which all children are loved, valued and able to fulfil their potential. The ISPCC believes that this vision can be achieved through a child centred approach to parenting, social policy and service delivery.

The ISPCC define 'child-centred' as follows:

a) Seeing the child's welfare and development as the paramount concern
b) Ensuring the child is the primary focus of services provision, legislation and social policy
c) Ensuring the child's wishes and views are considered in systems and decisions affecting their lives
d) Ensuring the child is facilitated in expressing his/her views, beliefs and feelings within society
e) Ensuring the child has equal rights as a child citizen
f) Seeking to ensure that adults and society have a positive view and vision of children and childhood
g) Ensuring society understands the developmental capabilities, limitations and goals of the child and integrates this understanding into social policy, planning and communication systems with children
h) Ensuring the child is facilitated in accessing and utilising help and advice services directly and/or in conjunction with an adult.

INTRODUCTION

The child is a citizen of society and in this regard the challenges and opportunities facing the child will be reflective of the challenges and opportunities facing adults and society in general. The key challenges and opportunities facing young people and in turn adults include:

- The growing acknowledgement and awareness of children's rights, the welfare of children being paramount and the need to value and protect children
- The growing diversity of cultures, races and nationalities within Ireland
- The changes in parenting structures with day-care and childminding playing a more significant role in the lives of children and parents
- The growing affluence and the widening divide between rich and poor
- The growing problem of alcohol and drug abuse and usage amongst adults and children.

There is little doubt that as Irish society in the twenty-first century has evolved, it has placed many challenges on children, parents and service providers alike. This evolution demands a society in which all children are loved, valued and enabled to fulfil their potential.

Over the last six years child protection, children's rights and childcare have had a higher public and political profile than ever before. Over this time Irish society has changed significantly, particularly with regard to its attitude to the treatment of children

The ISPCC is cognisant that any amendments/ changes in the Irish Constitution need to be in line with current legislation and minimum standards that Ireland has either enacted or signed up to, so as to promote the welfare and protection of children. These include:

1 The Child Care Act, 1991
2 The UN Convention on the Rights of the Child
3 The Non Fatal Offences Against the Person Act, 1997
4 The Domestic Violence Act, 1996
5 The National Children's Strategy
6 Children First – the National Guidelines for the Protection and Welfare of Children
7 Our Duty to Care – The Principles of Good Practice for the Protection of Children and Young People
8 The EU Constitution

For the purposes of this submission I will elaborate on two of the above:

1) The UN Convention on the Rights of the Child

The United Nations Convention on the Rights of the Child, which sets standards for the treatment of children worldwide, was adopted by the General Assembly of the United Nations on 20 November 1989. The Irish government signed the convention on 30 September 1990 and subsequently ratified it on 21 September 1992.

The convention contains fifty-four articles outlining the rights which should apply equally to all children whatever their race, sex, religion, language, disability, opinion or family background. The convention stresses that adults or organisations must always think first about what would be best for the child when making decisions that affect children (Article 3) and that children have the right to say what they think about anything that affects them.

The Irish government has agreed to be bound by this convention and has made its first national progress report to the UN Monitoring Committee on Children's Rights regarding Ireland's implementation of the convention. The review report from the monitoring committee indicates that while Ireland has made much progress, much still needs to be done.

In considering the needs and rights of children in relation to the Irish Constitution, the following articles of the convention are particularly relevant.

Article 2   Enshrines the principle of non-discrimination and equality for all children and requires state parties to ensure that the child is protected from all forms of discrimination.

Article 3   Requires that the best interest of the child is the primary consideration in all actions concerning children, recognises the rights and duties of parents and others, and sets out the need for standards in services and facilities responsible for the care of children.

Article 5   States that dependent children have rights independent of their parents and stresses the need for partnership between children, parents and the state in any society serious about the vindication of children's rights.

Article 9   Upholds the rights of children to live with both parents (unless it is deemed incompatible with his/her best interests), and the right to maintain personal relations and direct contact with both parents.

Article 12   Upholds the rights of children to express an opinion and to have that opinion taken into account in matters affecting the child.

Article 17   Sets out the state's obligations to ensure that children have access to information and material from a diversity of national and international sources and to take measures to protect children from harmful materials

Article 18   Sets out the duty of the state to support parents with their child-rearing responsibilities

Article 19   Sets out the duty of the state to take all measures necessary to protect the child from all forms of abuse

Article 27   Recognises the right of every child to a standard of living adequate to the child's physical, mental, spiritual, moral and social development

Article 28 Upholds the right of every child to an education.

2) The National Children's Strategy

The National Children's Strategy 'Our Children Their Lives' sets out a vision to work towards: 'an Ireland where children are respected as young citizens with a valued contribution to make and a voice of their own; where all children are cherished and supported by family and the wider society; where they enjoy a fulfilling childhood and realise their potential'. This national strategy upholds the principles as laid out in the UN Convention on the Rights of the Child.

This strategy has identified 3 national goals.

a) Children will have a voice.
b) Children's lives will be better understood.
c) Children will receive quality supports and services.

THE IRISH CONSTITUTION

The Constitution of Ireland (Bunreacht na hÉireann) was written in 1937. The Constitution reflected what were societal norms of the time. In this context it was appropriate to define the concept of the family as a group based on marriage because this was the norm. There have been since this time major social changes and in particular in the last twenty years, the old traditional roles of men working outside the home and women rearing children has clearly changed in this society. Changes in society have comparable changes within the domestic sphere. We now have a greater involvement of women in the employment sector; there is no doubt that this change affects the traditional view of family and family life. The old community and family supports, which were there in the past in urban and rural Ireland, are diluted. There are now many single parent families and an even larger number of people living together outside the framework of marriage, with or without children. There is a need to reconcile family life and work opportunity, and the state has a duty to reconcile competing demands of work and family.

In expressing concern about the very high emphasis on the rights of the family in the Constitution and an interpretation which gives a higher value to the rights of parents than to the rights of children, the report of 'The Kilkenny Incest Inquiry' chaired by Judge Catherine McGuinness clearly recommends 'that consideration be given by the government to the amendment of Articles 41 and 42 of the Constitution so as to include a statement of the constitutional rights of children'.

Full acknowledgement of children's rights within Irish society still remains a great challenge. The basic principle underlying the rights of children is that society has an obligation to meet the fundamental needs of children and to provide assistance to aid the development of the child's personality, talents and abilities.

The ISPCC believes that this challenge can be met by providing quality child-centred services in line with the UN Convention on the Rights of the Child. A child-centred approach will not only empower children and have a strong possibility of achieving significant change for children but will also empower and enhance parents' parenting, childcare services, family structures, the community and society in general.

Children's Rights

The ISPCC supports constitutional change to ensure that the rights of children are fully protected and promoted in the Irish Constitution, in Irish statutes and regulations. The ISPCC recommend that the principles and provisions of the United Nations Convention on the Rights of the Child be fully integrated in the Irish Constitution.

Children have rights under the Constitution as human beings, and the state has a responsibility and a duty to uphold these rights.

The Irish Constitution grants all citizens, including children, certain fundamental rights that can be cited as the constitutional rights of children.

• The right to be held equal before the law (Article 40.1).
• The right to have their personal rights as citizens respected, defended and vindicated by the state (Article 40.3.1).
• The right to life, person and good name protected and vindicated in the case of unjust attack (Article 40.3.2).

(Other articles within the Constitution, which refer to children but are not applicable to this particular submission, are as follows: Article 40.4.1, Article 40.5, Article 40.6.1.i and Article 40.6.1.ii).

The rights of children in their own right are specifically mentioned in the Constitution only in Article 42.5 and then only in the context of exceptional circumstances where parents fail in their duty towards their children. This article is a strong statement that parental rights derive from a duty towards, rather than ownership of, children.

The UN Convention on the Rights of the Child, the provisions of which the Irish government has internationally agreed to be bound by, clearly recognises the rights of children as citizens independent of their parents. Article 5 of the convention is clear that dependent children have rights independent of their parents and stresses the need for partnership between children, parents and the state in any society serious about the vindication of children's rights.

The Family and Marriage

Article 41.1 of the Irish Constitution grants special recognition to the family 'as the natural primary and fundamental unit group of society, and as a moral institution possessing inalienable and imprescriptible rights, antecedent and superior to all positive law'.

Article 41.3.1 states that 'The state pledges itself to guard with special care the institution of marriage on which the family is founded and protect it against attack'. The balance of rights between members of the family is not defined. Little account is taken within the Irish Constitution of the possibility of child/parent relationships and units outside the traditional family based on marriage. Parents who are not married do not possess rights under Articles 41 and 42. In practice, however, the rights of the family have been interpreted as a statement of parental rights whether or not a marriage exists.

It could accurately be said that the Constitution provides no clear statement of women's rights other than in their role as wife and mother. Attitudinal and societal change have, however, given rise to the development of a substantial body of positive law and practice, which recognises the rights of adult women independent of their family of origin or marriage.

Role of Fathers

Children have a right to know and have a relationship with both parents. Under the law, it could be argued that children of single parents are not treated equally to those of married couples in their relationship with their father, the relationship having an inferior status in the eyes of the law.

The ISPCC feel that it is very important that children have the knowledge and the influence of both parents. If we continue to promote the principle that parentage is solely tied up with marriage, particularly in the case of the father, we are not recognising the needs of the child, those of the parents, or the manner in which society is reforming and being reshaped.

Children should have the automatic right of access to both parents. The state should establish the equality and dignity of both parents in the parenting of their children.

RECOMMENDATIONS

- That Articles 41 and 42 be amended to include a clear statement of children's equal rights as full citizens. Alternatively, new Articles 41 and 42 should clearly state the full and equal citizenship of all family members irrespective of gender or age.
- While supporting the constitutional emphasis on supporting the 'family', 'The definition of family needs to be developed and defined in line with current social reality and thinking. Such a definition should focus on family structure and more on family function which sees the family as a unit of nurturance for children and adults based on positive communication rather than a relationship based on patriarchal power, authority, property relationships or the institution of marriage.

- Articles 41 and 42 should be amended to grant equal status and rights to all natural parents and their children irrespective of the marital status of the parents. This would better reflect the social reality and ensure that parental decisions about marriage or non-marriage in no way disadvantage children of unmarried parents or deny either children or parents their constitutional rights.
- Article 41.2 no longer reflects social or economic reality. With an increasing and healthy emphasis on shared parenting the Irish Constitution should reflect and promote gender balance in child rearing. It should emphasise the importance of parenting and place a responsibility on the state to ensure that its social, economic and employment policies take account of and address the needs of children and parents. Specifically the Irish state needs to accord parenting the same social status as work.
- The rights of children to equality before the law enshrined in Article 40 of the Constitution can be hampered at several levels by Articles 41 and 42. Children may not receive appropriate access to information about their rights or have ways of accessing services because of an absence of parental consent. The Constitution should clearly state that children have a right to directly access therapeutic/helping services in their own right as citizens of the state.
- The ISPCC calls on the Irish government to proceed with legal reforms to make the physical punishment of children illegal. Almost all European countries are now taking steps to legally prohibit the physical punishment of children and many have already introduced a ban.

ISLAMIC CULTURAL CENTRE OF IRELAND

From an Islamic point of view, family is the cornerstone of society. The more coherent the family is the more coherent the society will be, and the stronger the family is the stronger the society will be. On this basis Islam perceives the marriage contract as a covenant and establishes the family on the basis of tranquillity and mercy. Islam sets an equal balance to the rights of bride and bridegroom. Both of them are responsible for the family. Prophet Muhammad described them as responsible for the family and Allah will hold each one accountable for his responsibility.

Parents are responsible for the upbringing of the next generation who will protect the nation and contribute to the progress thereof.

On this basis, enacting laws to shield families against disintegration and deterioration is the duty of the whole society. On this basis we submit the following:

FAMILY: (SUGGESTED DEFINITION)

The family is the natural primary and fundamental unit group of society and is a moral institution possessing inalienable and imprescriptible rights, antecedent and superior to all positive laws. It is formed of a male and female according to a contract of civil or religious nature.

Suggestions to the recommendations

[The recommendations referred to are the recommendations of the Constitution Review Group: see *Report of the Constitution Review Group*, 1996, Stationery Office, Dublin, pp. 464–465.

Recommendation 4 ii

Text: A right for all persons to marry in accordance with the requirements of law and to found a family.

Suggestion: A right for all persons to heterosexually marry in accordance with the requirements of law and to found a family.

Recommendation 4 vi – a

Text: The right of every child to be registered immediately after birth and to have from birth a name.

Suggestion: The right of every child to be registered immediately after birth and to be from birth named after his biological father. We strongly recommend that the right of adoption should not be given to homosexuals or lesbians.

Recommendation 4 – xi

Text: Retention of the existing provisions in Article 41.3.3 relating to the recognition for foreign divorces.

Suggestion: Retention of the existing provisions in Article 41.3.3 relating to the recognition for foreign divorces and shortening the period the spouses have to live apart from one another from four years to six months, and in case of having children to one year, so that the court may grant dissolution of marriage.

ISLAMIC FOUNDATION OF IRELAND

- *Definition of Family*. The provisions of the Irish Constitution in relation to family enshrined in Articles 41.1.1, 41.1.2, 41.3.1 and 42.1 should be maintained.
- Any departure from the concept of the union of man and woman as being essential to the definition of family is unacceptable and repugnant to the religious beliefs of the vast majority of the Irish state.

This would be the view of Jews, Muslims and Christians.

- There seems to be a contradiction between the suggestion made by the Constitution Review Group of the state pledging to guard with special care the institution of marriage and protect it against attack on one side, and on the other hand affording recognition to families not based on marriage. It can also be argued that in accordance with the universally accepted concept of the state being the guardian of the common good – which is stated in the Constitution – the state should be seen as promoting marriage (in the form of union of man and woman) and discouraging relationships outside marriage in this sense as much as possible.
- The position of homosexuals living as partners cannot be regarded as a marriage or as a family union in the strict sense. Such a union is repugnant to the religious beliefs of the majority.
- The right of adoption and rearing of children may not be given under the Constitution to persons of a same-sex union.
- A natural father who has not been solemnly committed in matrimonial union to the mother of his child cannot be considered as a member of the family. This provision in Article 41 should be maintained. The amended Constitution, should, however, recognise the right of the natural father to partake fully in the upbringing of his child.
- The current position of divorce (dissolution of marriage) and the period of four years which the spouses have to wait for before they can apply for divorce – is too long and needs to shorten. For example, in Northern Ireland the waiting period is two years, yet this has been found to be a lengthy period. We would recommend a period of six months. The fact that dissolution of marriage (which is not favoured in any law including Islamic law) is a costly and difficult procedure in Ireland might discourage some people from contracting marriage in the first place – with all the disadvantages of that for spouses and children. If the marriage does not work and there is no reasonable prospect of reconciliation between the spouses, the couple would be in an awful situation having to wait for four years for their broken marriage to be dissolved. People need to move on with their lives and perhaps remarry instead of living in limbo for a long period.
- Divorce granted in other jurisdictions and by religious authorities in this jurisdiction should be recognised in the amended Irish Constitution.
- With regard to the rights of the child we would be in favour of maintaining the status quo.

JOHNNY GAY PEER ACTION CHARITY GROUP

1 EXECUTIVE SUMMARY

This submission clearly outlines the current injustice and discrimination that lesbian, gay, bi-sexual and transgendered (LGBT) couples experience as a result of the state's prohibition of marriage for same-sex couples. The lack of recognition has led to grave inequality in accessing state services and other associated benefits of which only state-recognised married couples can avail. Consequently, we argue that the state does not recognise each member of our society as equal; fails to acknowledge the diverse nature of the family unit; does not provide for the protection and well-being of every child; and has policies that do not correspond to the progress made across Europe and the world to end this discrimination.

In order to bring about equality, we ask for the introduction of legislation that allows for a wider interpretation of the term 'marriage' as used in the Constitution, and thus recognises civil marriage for same-sex couples.

2 GROUP OVERVIEW

JOHNNY is the leading LGBT voluntary peer education charity group on the island of Ireland; its primary aim is to promote health and well-being, provide services and resources to gay and bi sexual men in Dublin and the greater Dublin area.

3 ORGANISATIONAL HISTORY

JOHNNY was established in 1999 under the auspices of the Gay Men's Health Network (GHN), Gay Men's Health Project (GMHP) and was initially funded by the Eastern Regional Health Authority (ERHA) with the primary aim of increasing the level of awareness of health and well-being amongst gay and bi-sexual men. The organisation developed into a self governing, democratic, autonomous charity; promoting health and well-being, lobbying, representation on behalf of the LGBT community, in addition to the creation and provision of unique and tailored services.

JOHNNY is recognised as being a highly active and vocal advocate of the gay and bi-sexual community and is an officially registered charity (CHY 15505).

4 INTRODUCTION

We welcome the All-Party Oireachtas Committee's review of Bunreacht na hÉireann and the contents of Articles 41, 42 and 40.3. Moreover, we feel that it is particularly encouraging that the issue of marriage for same-sex couples is specifically listed as a topic that necessitates debate in the process of ascertaining the extent to which the Constitution is serving the good of individuals and the community as a whole. As a result, this document dispels many myths and misconceptions associated with homosexuality and demonstrates that there is no rational or logical reason to deny same-sex couples the opportunity to marry.

It is our inherent belief that the interpretation of the Irish Constitution, as executed in current legislation, does not reflect the multiculturalism of modern Ireland, the diversity of family structures (size, parental roles, gender/sexual orientations), the current gender roles in Irish life, and the equal right of an individual to determine her/his own destiny within a community as sanctioned by the UN Universal Declaration of Human Rights, the EU Convention on Human Rights and the UN Convention on the Rights of the Child.

Although the Constitution does not define 'marriage', a term which, within the wider context of the Constitution, is traditionally interpreted as being between a man and woman, we ask that legislation be introduced to include recognition of same-sex marriages in Ireland and create a wider interpretation of the term in the context of the Constitution. As is detailed below, we are seeking the right to participate in state-recognised *civil* marriage, which must be distinguished from *religious* marriage. It is clear that the interpretation of the 1937 Constitution must be updated to cater for the needs and the common good of a diverse and plural Irish society of the 21st century, and must recognise that 'equality' must mean equality for *all members* of the community.

The current interpretation of the Constitution is clearly discriminatory and biased against LGBT people specifically by excluding and limiting official state recognition of marital status solely to heterosexual couples. This exclusion fails to recognise the stability that same-sex parented families can provide to spouses/partners, their children, and the wider community, and thus degrades and devalues the significant contributions that LGBT couples already make to a democratic society. This document highlights the discrimination that many men, women and children face in relation to current family structures, to parental and guardian rights, as well as to availing of opportunities that make positive contributions to Irish society.

5 PROTECTING THE EQUAL RIGHTS AND THE HUMAN RIGHTS OF THE INDIVIDUAL

Equality: There can be no levels to equality. Some cannot be 'more equal than others'.

The Equal Status Act prohibits discrimination on the grounds of sexual orientation in regard to employment and the provision of services. The existence of such an Act signifies that the government recognises that discrimination on the grounds of sexual orientation is inherently wrong. This policy should extend to all areas of a democratic society, including marriage. Discrimination should not be used selectively.

It is possible to interpret the failure of the Irish state to legally recognise the marriages of same-sex couples as contravening several declarations of human rights.

The UN Universal Declaration of Human Rights states that 'all are equal before the law and are entitled without any discrimination to equal protection of the law' (Article 7) and that 'men and women of full age, without any limitation due to race, nationality or religion, have the right to marry and to found a family. They are entitled to equal rights as to marriage, during marriage and at its dissolution' (Article 16.1). It is also of interest to note that Article 14 'Prohibition of discrimination' in the EU Convention on Human Rights notes that 'The enjoyment of the rights and freedoms set forth in this Convention shall be secured without discrimination on any ground such as sex, race, colour, language, religion, political or other opinion, national or social origin, association with a national minority, property, birth or other status' which emphasises the Irish state's active discrimination against a national minority, the LGBT community.

The Constitution states that every Irish citizen has the right to equal treatment (Article 40). Economically, legally and socially the LGBT community are treated as 'less equal' than their heterosexual peers in a relationship, as outlined by the Equality Authority's report on 'Partnership Rights of Same Sex Couples.[1]

Therefore, current legislation does not reflect the right to equality that is outlined in the Constitution. The Equality Authority's report notes that 'a wide range of legal privileges and obligations are triggered by the status of marriage'[2] and that 'they relate to the care of children, access to workplace benefits, ownership of property, taxation, social welfare, protection around domestic violence, emergency health care situations and immigration and access to work permits'.[3] There is no rationale as to why these privileges are denied to same-sex couples. LGBT couples are clearly discriminated against by the state, neither having their economic rights protected nor their relational commitments validated.

Article 45.4 of the Irish Constitution stipulates that 'the state pledges itself to safeguard with especial care the economic interests of the *weaker sections* of the community' (our emphasis). It is evident that the LGBT community is a marginalised section of society and that LGBT people face discrimination and barriers against them at many levels.[4] It is evident that by not recognising marriages of same-sex couples and subsequently not awarding the associated economic benefits, the state violates this constitutional mandate.

Economically, same-sex couples are placed in a position of disadvantage in relation to their heterosexual counterparts.

Even though members of the LGBT community contribute to the PAYE and PRSI system, it is only married

couples who are entitled to a married tax credit, to a home carer's tax credit, to be treated jointly for the purpose of income tax, and to a widowed parent tax credit. For the purposes of capital gains tax the advantages conferred on a married couple living together include: entitlement to be jointly assessed; capital losses available to one couple can be used by the other spouse; entitlement to dispose of assets to each other without being subject to capital gains tax; spouses are exempt from CAT in respect of all gifts and inheritances given by one spouse to another, and spouses are exempt from stamp duty in respect of transfer of assets.

Also, the Family Home Protection Act, 1976 gives a spouse the right to veto any sale or lease of the family home by the other spouse. In order to sell or lease the family home, the written consent of both spouses must first be obtained. This Act does apply to same-sex couples so if you are living with your partner in his/her house, there is no need for your partner to obtain your written consent before he or she can sell or lease the house. These are just a few examples of the state's discrimination in this area. A more detailed list can be found in the Equality Authority's report mentioned above.

6 THE IMPORTANCE OF MARRIAGE AND FAMILY TO OUR SOCIETY

The state's need to recognise the importance and status of same-sex unions in the creation of a family unit is part of a much larger necessity to acknowledge the diversity of family structures in Ireland.[5]

'The Census data for 2002 shows that cohabiting couples accounted for 8.4% of families and 29,700 of these families had children.'[6] The census also recorded that 1,300 same-sex couples were living together (although not all same-sex couples will describe themselves as such for official purposes).[7] Clearly it is no longer acceptable to deny such couples and children the family rights and status that is currently afforded to married families.

The Department of Social and Family Affairs has already recognised the need to address the diversity of family units by stating that

> in the context of increasing diversity in Irish society, we need an inclusive definition of family, one that can encompass all types of families. To be inclusive a definition should be capable of embracing such diverse family forms as those made up of grandparents and children, those consisting of foster parents and children, those of lone parent and children, those of unmarried partners and children *as well as same sex parents and children.*[8] (our emphasis)

Same-sex parent families can be established in several ways, such as fostering, IVF treatment, and procreation.

For many, the issue of procreation was a key argument in prohibiting same-sex unions. However, it is well established that many heterosexual couples with state recognised marriages are unable to conceive or have any intention of doing so, yet would consider themselves a 'family'. Procreation is but one means of establishing a family. Also, many same-sex couples become parents (individually) through a variety of ways such as having children from previous relationships, through adoption, and also IVF treatment. However, progress in combating anti-gay discrimination has resulted in a dramatic increase in the number of lesbian, gay and bisexual couples who are planning families and parenting children.[9] In a recent ruling by the Supreme Court of Appeal of South Africa, in the case of *Fourie and Bonthuys vs. Minister for Home Affairs and Director-General of Home Affairs*, to recognise same-sex marriage in the state,[10] Cameron JA stated that 'The suggestion that gays and lesbians cannot procreate has already been authoritatively rejected as a mistaken stereotype'.[11]

As marriage is one of the main building blocks used to create a family (Article 41), we believe that the state should encourage the formation of such units rather than actively prevent them.

The family, in all its forms, is one of the necessary units that contributes towards a democratic and stable society. It is also evident that marriage is one of the building blocks upon which to found a family. Although not everyone may choose to marry, we recognise the important role that such an institution can make to society and that prohibiting a large section of the population from making such a contribution does not benefit the community as a whole. A quotation from Martin Grachola, a board member of Dignity Chicago, may be useful to illustrate this point: 'It is time to deal with the reality that gays and lesbians can form long-term relationships. Society has a vested interest in extending to same-sex couples the same kind of legal benefits, responsibilities, safeguards and protections it extends to married persons'.[12]

Same-sex relationships are 'not immoral'.

The Taoiseach's recent statement that same-sex relationships are 'not illegal, they're not immoral, they're not improper'[13] validates the argument that in the context of the Constitution (Article 41.3), same-sex marriage cannot be an attack on the moral values of the family (as there is nothing immoral about same-sex relationships) but is a means of reinforcing the importance of the family as enshrined in the Constitution. Marriage is an institution that will encourage monogamy and long-term committed relationships. same-sex unions will enhance the importance of marriage in society as noted by Marshall CJ in the Massachusetts Supreme Court of Judicature: 'If anything, extending civil marriage to same-sex couples reinforces the importance of marriage to individuals and communities'.[14]

Heterosexuals have a choice whether they wish to marry or not. Same-sex couples do not. A 'Partnership Rights Bill' that does not recognise same-sex marriage will not end discrimination.

As noted by Cameron JA in the Supreme Court of Appeal in South Africa: 'The capacity to choose to get married enhances the liberty, the autonomy and the dignity of a couple committed for a life to each other.'[15] If partnership rights are introduced, heterosexual couples will have the choice of opting for marriage or cohabiting rights. Same-sex couples will not have that choice. Allowing same-sex couples to avail of Partnership Rights will only lessen discrimination in a few areas, but will not end discrimination. Inequality can only end when same-sex couples are offered the same opportunities and choices as heterosexual couples. 'The right to marry is a right for everyone, without distinction. It cannot be understood as a privilege', Deputy Prime Minister of Spain, Maria Teresa Fernandez de la Vega told a press conference after Spain's socialist government approved a bill to legalise same-sex marriages.[16] We are not seeking legislation that will grant more extensive rights, but ask for parity in recognition and reward.

It is also necessary to make a distinction between religious marriage and civil marriage. In this context, emphasis must be placed on civil marriage.

We do not propose that the Church and its clergy (religious), be forced to sanction same-sex marriages; however it is necessary for the state (civil) to recognise same-sex marriages. We respect the rights of individuals to choose what to believe in. However, this cannot be used to persecute and undermine another group in society. We ask for a separation of Church and state on this issue as contemporary Catholic teaching does not favour same-sex unions. It is important to remember that *religion is a choice; sexual orientation is not.*

Same-sex unions recognised by the state should be known as 'civil marriage'.

Cultural theorists, linguists and philosophers from Jacques Derrida to Roland Barthes to Michel Foucault have recognised the use of language as an ideological tool in discourses of power within society. The terms and conditions of 'civil union' are still not equal to those of 'civil marriage', as demonstrated by the labels themselves. Providing same-sex couples with a different label encourages a culture of difference and exclusion and continues to attach a stigma to homosexuality. If we are all equal, then there is no need create a new term.

There is no such thing as 'gay marriage' or 'straight marriage', only 'marriage'.

In this debate it is important to analyse the language being used. Rather than applying terms such as 'gay marriage' it may be useful to refer to 'marriage for same-sex couples' as it prioritises the institution of marriage over the sexual orientation of those involved in marrying. There is no such thing as 'straight marriage' or 'gay marriage'; there is only marriage. Realising the importance of reflecting the changes in cultural attitudes, *the Oxford English Dictionary includes acknowledgement of same-sex partnerships in its definition of 'marriage'.*[17]

Recognition of same-sex unions has existed for thousands of years. This is not a new concept.

Despite the use of Biblical readings and interpretations that some religions use to undermine the progression of equality, it is essential to note that same-sex unions were sanctioned by the Church up until the 18th century as documented by Jim Boswell in his book *The Marriage of Likeness: Same Sex Unions in Pre-Modern Europe.*[18] In reference to Boswell's research, Jim Duffy notes that 'for the Church to ignore the evidence in its own archives would be a cowardly cop-out. That evidence shows convincingly that what the modern church claims has been its constant unchanging attitude towards homosexuality is in fact nothing of the sort' and that 'it proves that for much of the last two millennia, in parish churches and cathedrals … from Ireland to Istanbul and in the heart of Rome itself, homosexual relationships were accepted as valid expressions of a God-given ability to love and commit to another person'.[19] This evidence undermines the argument for a 'Christian' reading of the Constitution. In fact, there is no record that Christ ever made any specific reference to homosexuality, and neither condemned nor condoned same-sex unions.

Gay-parent families already exist in huge numbers. The state must protect the members of these families.

It is not the case that legalising gay marriage will suddenly 'create' gay-parent families. These families already exist and will continue to exist. The government must protect the rights of individual members of the family, partners, parents and children by providing the opportunity to avail of the benefits that accompany heterosexual parent families.

The exclusion of gays and lesbians from the choice of marriage also suggests that their relationships and commitments to each other are inferior to those of heterosexual couples and that they can never be fully part of the community.

Same-sex couples are as capable as heterosexual couples of expressing and sharing love, of forming intimate, trusting, committed and monogamous relationships. They are capable of creating a family unit and of establishing, enjoying and benefiting from family life similar to that formed by heterosexual relationships. Thus the impact of current discrimination experienced

by gay couples in an open democracy that promotes freedom and equality affects the personal dignity and identity of the LGBT community. This in turn can affect the emotional well-being of members of the LGBT community.

7 THE STATE DISCRIMINATES AGAINST CHILDREN

State policy does not adhere to the UN Convention on the Rights of The Child *as all children are not treated equally, particularly in relation to Article 2.*[20]

Prohibiting marriage does not only discriminate against an adult group, but also against an entire community of children and teenagers which directly affects their mental health and well being as they are not provided with the same rights and dignities as other children.

Prohibiting same-sex marriage results in state policy discriminating against a large group of children, which can affect their emotional and psychological well-being, and in many cases can lead to attempted child suicides.[21]

A recent survey in Northern Ireland identified that on average people realised they were LGBT at age of twelve or thirteen, but they did not tell someone about their sexuality until they were seventeen or eighteen.[22] The survey also details international research including a report from the US that concluded that gay/lesbian youth were two or three times more likely to attempt suicide and may account for 30% of total youth suicides.[23]

Throughout adolescence and teenage years, young people attempt to create a sense of identity and belonging that places them within an environment of stability and security within a wider culture and society. Part of this process is visualising themselves as a future parent or partner within supporting systems of mutuality and trust, developing a positive self-concept, experiencing social acceptance among peers of the same and opposite sex, and developing positive approaches to sexuality and care in a loving relationship.[24] Marriage is one of the foundation stones for the creation of such a sense of belonging. However, such aspirations are denied to the gay child. He/she is not allowed to have the same hopes and dreams as every other child. This can affect the child's maturation process and psychological development.

The state fails to protect the rights of the child within a same-sex parent family and, in a legal sense, does not offer them the chance of a stable and secure environment that marriage aims to create.

By denying same-sex marriage, the state is acting contrary to the philosophies of the Irish Constitution by not protecting the status of the family in this context, as well as failing to uphold the rights of individual members.

8 MARRIAGE AND ADOPTION

Marriage for same-sex couples must be equal in status to that of heterosexual couples. This includes granting the opportunity to adopt children.

As same-sex couples are allowed to foster children, there is no rational explanation as to why a child should not have the opportunity to be adopted into a stable and supportive same-sex parent family. Under Irish law it is possible for same-sex couples to foster a child but not to adopt. A same-sex couple is also prevented from jointly adopting a child *'even where one of the parties is the biological or legal parent of the child'*.[25] Such legislation does not serve the best interests of the child as the state consequently denies the child the possibility of a stable, secure and loving family structure. As Deputy Prime Minister of Spain, Maria Teresa Fernandez de la Vega has confirmed, her government proposes that same-sex married couples be allowed adopt. 'There is no proof that homosexual parents educate their children any worse. In adoption, the well-being of the children comes first, independent of the sexual orientation of the parents'.[26] A child relates to his or her parents as individuals and not as some representative of a larger group. We should be focusing on the individual things a person can provide for his or her child, and not resort to stereotypes about the behaviour of men and women.

Studies indicate that a child is not disadvantaged as a result of having same-sex parents.

Social science research has confirmed that love, stability, patience, and time to spend with a child are far more critical factors in being a good parent than a person's gender or sexual orientation. Studies have found 'a remarkable absence of distinguishing features between the lifestyles, child-rearing practices, and general demographic data' of lesbian and gay parents and those who are not gay.[27]

The *American Academy of Pediatrics, Technical Report: Co parent or Second-Parent Adoption by Same-Sex Parents, 109 Pediatrics 341* (Feb. 2002) is quoted as saying:

> Not a single study has found children of gay and lesbian parents to be disadvantaged in any significant respect relative to children of heterosexual parents. Indeed, the evidence to date suggests that home environments provided by gay and lesbian parents are as likely as those of heterosexual parents to support and enable children's psychosocial growth.[28]

In lending support to this argument it is important to note that Deputy Prime Minister of Spain, Maria Teresa Fernandez de la Vega also said that 'There are already thousands of children in Spain who live with homosexual parents ... more than fifty studies agree that there are no differences among children who grow up in homes with homosexual parents'; while Carlos

Alberto Biendicho, president of the *Popular Gay Platform*, noted that 'A child adopted by a homosexual couple is a child who is wanted, a child who is loved and in no way worse off than a child adopted by a heterosexual couple'.[29]

Concerns clarified regarding adoption by gay and lesbian couples.

Many argue that children need a mother and a father to have proper male and female role models, a concept which undermines the diverse nature of families in modern Ireland such as single mothers and fathers, as well as grandparents and siblings that act as primary carers to children. Children who need adoption have neither a mother nor father as role models. Children can, and do, get their role models from many places besides their parents. These include grandparents, aunts and uncles, teachers, friends and neighbours.

Same-sex parents have no influence in creating the child's sexual orientation.

All of the available evidence demonstrates that the sexual orientation of parents has no impact on the sexual orientation of their children and that children of lesbian and gay parents are no more likely than any other child to grow up being gay.[30] Of course, some children of lesbians and gay men will grow up to be gay, as will some children of heterosexual parents. These children will have the added advantage of being raised by parents who are supportive and accepting. This argument also undermines the dignity of the LGBT community as it incorrectly suggests that there may be something wrong with being attracted to members of the same sex.

The bullying argument is insubstantial.

Children make fun of other children for all kinds of reasons like being too short, tall, thin, fat, different religion or different nationality. There is the worry that children will be teased and harassed if adopted by gay and lesbian couples. All children who have anything different about them, which most children have, are vulnerable to teasing. Children show remarkable resilience, especially if they are provided with a stable and loving environment that acknowledges diversity in society.

9 GENDER DISCRIMINATION AND THE CONSTITUTION

Status of the woman in the home

Article 41.1 of the Irish Constitution stipulates, in particular, that the state recognises that 'by her life within the home, woman gives to the state a support without which the common good cannot be achieved' while 41.2 states that the 'state shall, therefore, endeavour to ensure that mothers shall not be obliged by economic necessity to engage in labour to the neglect of their duties in the home'. We believe that this article must be amended to reflect the diverse needs of citizens in contemporary Ireland. Part of this amendment should use the phrase 'primary carer' instead of using the term 'woman', thus avoiding discriminating against men, grandparents, siblings, friends, children or relatives, who offer primary care and support for vulnerable members of society in the home. While it is important to value the primary carer, this recognition should not limit or confine the person to working solely in the home. Ireland's diverse family structures should be given recognition and the rights of individuals should be equally protected.

10 RECOGNITION OF SAME-SEX MARRIAGE IN OTHER STATES

The Netherlands and Belgium recognise civil marriage for same-sex couples while both the Spanish government and the Swedish government have recently passed legislation that allows for same-sex marriages. Last September, the European Parliament recommended that homosexuals in member states should be allowed to legally marry and adopt.[31]

The Supreme Judicial Court of Massachusetts has ruled that same-sex couples are allowed to marry under state law. In Canada, courts in five provinces allow same-sex marriage, while the Canadian Supreme Court is debating a bill that will allow same-sex marriage across the country.

Civil unions exist in many countries, allowing same-sex couples some of the benefits and privileges of marriage, but still discriminating by preventing equality in terms of marriage, such as in the US state of Vermont as well as across Europe in France, Norway, Denmark, Sweden, Switzerland, Germany, Iceland, Sweden and Finland and the UK. We believe that 'civil unions' still discriminate, as same-sex couples are still not protected to the same extent as their married heterosexual counterparts.[32]

South Africa, a country plagued by discrimination, is the best example to cite in its efforts to treat all citizens as equal. With such a young Constitution (1997), the state has included a Bill of Rights that prohibits discrimination on the grounds of sexual orientation, reflecting the needs and concerns of a contemporary society. This has resulted in a recent ruling by the Supreme Court of Appeal of South Africa, in the case of *Fourie and Bonthuys v Minister for Home Affairs and Director-General of Home Affairs*, to recognise same-sex marriage in the state.[33] The Irish state should follow the lead of a country that knows only too well the causes and effects of discrimination, and put an end to inequality. In giving judgement, Justice Cameron JA noted that 'the exclusionary definition of marriage injures gays and lesbians because it implies a judgment on them. It suggests not only that their relationships and commitments and loving bonds are

inferior, but that they themselves can never be fully part of the community of moral equals that the Constitution promises to create for all' (Para. 15) and that there was no rational explanation as to why same-sex couples should be excluded from the institution of marriage.

The recent Spanish legislation is also important to note, proving that a predominantly Catholic country recognises the need to respect and accept diversity for the common good of society, with Spain's Deputy Prime Minister, Maria Teresa Fernandez de la Vega telling a press conference that 'We are putting an end to centuries of discrimination'.[34] As noted above, this will see same-sex couples granted equal rights and status in all areas including adoption.

11 CONCLUSION

It is clear that the LGBT community are a permanent minority in society and suffer from patterns of disadvantage. Because they are a minority unable on their own to use political power to secure legislative advantages, they are exclusively reliant on the state legislation to protect them from discrimination in society.

We call upon the All-Party Oireachtas Committee to initiate procedures to amend the legislation accordingly, so that it no longer is a source of discrimination and that it becomes a contemporary framework for equality, justice and progress in a modern Ireland. From our detailed examination we cannot identify any reasonable justification for the state not to amend legislation, so as to permit the recognition of same-sex marriages and equal access for all couples to the benefits that state-recognised marriage affords.

It is useful to conclude our argument with a succinct paragraph from Marshall CJ in the Massachusetts Supreme Court of Judicature:

> Here, the plaintiffs seek only to be married, not to undermine the institution of civil marriage. They do not want marriage abolished. They do not attack the binary nature of marriage, the consanguinity provisions, or any of the other gate-keeping provisions of the marriage licensing law. Recognising the right of an individual to marry a person of the same sex will not diminish the validity or dignity of opposite-sex marriage, any more than recognising the right of an individual to marry a person of a different race devalues the marriage of a person who marries someone of her own race. If anything, extending civil marriage to same-sex couples reinforces the importance of marriage to individuals and communities. That same-sex couples are willing to embrace marriage's solemn obligations of exclusivity, mutual support, and commitment to one another is a testament to the enduring place of marriage in our laws and in the human spirit. (para 57)

Upon reflection on the above information we appeal to members of the committee to put an end to the culture of hate and intolerance in Irish society which is fuelled by myths, stereotypes, and propaganda that have no rational foundation in fact. Civil unions will not end discrimination, and can only act as a stepping-stone towards marriage and equality for all. The Oireachtas committee has the power to end discrimination right now, without delay, to save future generations of adults and children from unfounded bias and prejudice. Legislation for same-sex couples will protect a marginalised group and benefit Irish society as a whole. The opportunity to create an Ireland with inclusivity, dignity and equality for all now lies with this Oireachtas committee.

Notes
1 Dr John Mee and Ms Kaye Ronayne (the Equality Authority, June 2000).
2 *Partnership Rights of Same Sex Couples*, p. 5.
3 Niall Crowley, in Foreword of *Partnership Rights of Same Sex Couples*, p. 4.
4 See Gay and Lesbian Equality Network and Nexus Research Co-operative, Poverty – Lesbians and Gay Men: The Economic and Social Effects of Discrimination (Dublin: Combat Poverty Agency, 1995). The report notes that: A quarter of respondents had been punched, beaten, hit or kicked; four fifths (81%) said that the possibility of anti-gay harassment had affected their behaviour; almost a third (31%) have left home at some time in their lives with no certainty as to where they were going to live next; one in ten respondents reported experience of discrimination around accommodation including being refused a mortgage, refused tenancy and verbal harassment from landlords; two fifths(39%) of respondents reported experiencing at least one act of discrimination in services such as pubs, clubs, restaurants, hotels and B+B because they are lesbian or gay.
5 This diversity is analysed in a recent *Irish Times* series that documents the changing nature of Irish families in the 21st century. See Kitty Holland, 'Weekend Review', p. 3, in *The Irish Times*, 4/12/2004.
6 TREOIR Submission to the Law Reform Commission in response to the Consultation Paper on the Rights and Duties of Cohabitees, 2004.
7 See Kitty Holland, 'Weekend Review', p. 3, in *The Irish Times*, 4/12/2000.
8 Mary Daly, *Families and Family Life in Ireland; Challenges for the Future, Report of Public Consultation Fora*, (Department of Social and Family Affairs, 2004) http://iyf2004.welfare.ie/Family_Life_FINAL.pdf.
9 April Martin, *The Lesbian and Gay Parenting Handbook* (1993); Cheri Pies, *Considering Parenthood* (1985); Joy Schulenberg, *Gay Parenting Complete Guide for Gay Men and Lesbians with Children* (1985).
10 Case no: 232/2003. Judgement 30/11/04.
11 *National Coalition for Gay and Lesbian Equality v Minister of Home Affairs 2000* (2) SA 1 (CC) para 50.
12 (www.natcath.com/NCR_Online/archives2/2003c/081503/081503d.htm National Catholic Reporter by Robert J McClory – issued 15/08/03, accessed09/01/05.
13 'Ahern backs legal recognition for gays', *The Irish Times*, 15/11/04.
14 *Goodridge v Department of Public Health* 440 Mass 309, 798 NE 2d 941 para 63; and see *National Coalition for Gay and Lesbian Equality v Minister of Home Affairs* 2000 (2) SA 1 (CC) para 56 ('there is no rational connection between the exclusion of same-sex life partners … and the

government interest sought to be achieved thereby, namely the protection of families and the family life of heterosexual spouses').
15 Case no. 232/2003
16 Breaking News Top Stories Website, 'Spain's Government approves gay marriage bill' issued 30/12/04, www.breakingnews.ie/2004/12/30/story182559.html
17 Oxford English Dictionary; 'The term is now sometimes used with reference to long-term relationships between partners of the same sex.' www.oed.com accessed 12/01/05.
18 London: Harper Collins, 1995.
19 Jim Duffy, 'When marriage between gays was by rite', *The Irish Times*, 11/08/1998.
20 '1 States parties shall respect and ensure the rights set forth in the present Convention to each child within their jurisdiction without discrimination of any kind, irrespective of the child's or his or her parent's or legal guardian's race, colour, sex, language, religion, political or other opinion, national, ethnic or social origin, property, disability, birth or other status.
2 States parties shall take all appropriate measures to ensure that the child is protected against all forms of discrimination or punishment on the basis of the status, activities, expressed opinions, or beliefs of the child's parents, legal guardians, or family members.'
21 Young men and women of same-sex orientation have been identified as one of a number of high-risk groups for youth suicide in Ireland: See 'ShOUT: Research into the needs of young people in Northern Ireland who identify as lesbian, gay, bisexual and/or transgender (LGBT)' by Youth Net (Belfast: 2003, Commissioned by The Department of Education, NI). The document reports that 29% (n=105) of respondents indicated that they had attempted suicide (p. 32).
BeLonGTo Youth Project works with LGBT young people in Ireland. In the group's submission to National Strategy for Action on Suicide Prevention they report that 'In 2004 BeLonG To referred five young people to the counselling services of The Northern Area Health Board due specifically to these disclosures and due to the project's fear for their safety. The experience of BeLonG To Youth Project suggests a link between the specific issues affecting LGBT youth and suicidal ideation and behaviour.' (unpublished, 2004).
For a further analysis of these issues see:
Crowley, P., Kilroe, J. & Burke, S. (2004) *Youth Suicide Prevention: Evidence Briefing* (London & Dublin: Health Development Agency and The Institute of Public Health in Ireland)
International research evidence on suicide risk for GLB youth: Morrison, L. & L'Heureux, J. (2001) *Suicide and gay/lesbian/bisexual youth: implications for clinicians*, Journal of Adolescence, 24, 39-49.
YouthNet (2004) ShOut: Research into the Needs of Young People in Northern Ireland who Identify as Lesbian, Gay, Bisexual and/or Transgender (Belfast: YouthNet).
Evidence of Homophobic bullying:
Equality Authority (2002) *Implementing Equality for Lesbians, Gays and Bisexuals*, (Dublin: Equality Authority).
Davis, C., Foley, B., Sheenan, B., Quinlan, M. & Watters, E (eds.) (2001) *Vital Statistics 2000: An All Ireland Gay Men's Sex Survey* (Dublin: East Coast Area Health Board Publishing).
Nayak, A. & Kehily, M J. (1996) *Playing it Straight: Masculinities, Homophobias and Schooling*. Journal of Gender Studies, 5, 2, 211-229.
Norman, J. (2004) *A Survey of Teachers on Homophobic*

Bullying in Irish Second-Level Schools (Dublin: Dublin City University).

22 Youth Net 2003, see http://www.belongto.org/files/booklet.pdf, accessed 17/01/05.

23 'ShOUT', P. 81.

24 These complex needs of adolescents are discussed in detail in A. Hargreaves, L. Earl and A. Ryan, *Schooling for Change: Reinventing Education for Early Adolescents* (Great Britain: Falmer Press, 1996).

25 'Adoption and same-sex couples in Ireland', *Oasis, Information on Public Services, An Irish Government Resource*: http://www.oasis.gov.ie/relationships/same_sex _relationships/adoption_and_same_sex_couples.html, accessed 17/01/05. Emphasis in original.

26 BBC News Website, 'Spain Approves Gay Marriage Bill', www.breakingnews.ie/2004/12/30/story182559.html issued 01/10/04

27 Beverly Hoeffer, *Children's Acquisition of Sex-Role Behaviour in Lesbian-Mother Families*, 51, (Am. J. of Orthopsychiatry 536, 1981).

28 'Adoption by Lesbian, Gay and Bisexual Parents: An Overview of Current Law', National Center for Lesbian Rights Web Site, Updated January 2004, www.nclrights. org/publications/adptn0204.htm, accessed 13/01/05.

29 'Gay Law News,' www.gaylawnet.com/news/2004/ pa0410.htm – issued 07/10/04, site accessed 03/01/05.

30 For a further discussion of these issues, see Bailey, J.M., Bobrow, D., Wolfe, M. & Mikach, S. (1995), Sexual orientation of adult sons of gay fathers, *Developmental Psychology*, 31, 124-129; Bozett, F.W. (1987). Children of gay fathers, F.W. Bozett (Ed.), *Gay and Lesbian Parents* (pp. 39-57), New York: Praeger; Gottman, J.S. (1991), Children of gay and lesbian parents, F.W. Bozett & M.B. Sussman, (Eds.), *Homosexuality and Family Relations* (pp. 177-196), New York: Harrington Park Press; Golombok, S., Spencer, A., and Rutter, M. (1983), Children in lesbian and single-parent households: psychosexual and psychiatric appraisal, *Journal of Child Psychology and Psychiatry*, 24, 551-572; Green, R. (1978), Sexual identity of 37 children raised by homosexual or transsexual parents, *American Journal of Psychiatry*, 135, 692-697; Huggins, S.L., (1989). A comparative study of self-esteem of adolescent children of divorced lesbian mothers and divorced heterosexual mothers, F. W. Bozett (Ed.), *Homosexuality and the Family* (pp. 123-135), New York: Harrington Park Press; Miller, B. (1979), Gay fathers and their children, *The Family Coordinator*, 28, 544-52; Paul, J.P. (1986). Source: *10Percent website*: http://www.10percent.org/adoption.

31 Elizabeth Bryant, *San Francisco Chronicle*, www.sfgate.com/cgi-bin/article.cgi?f=/c/a/2004/03/15/ MNG275KMPE1.dtl – (Chronicle Foreign Service, issued 15/03/04, accessed 03/01/05.

32 For a further discussion and proposals for change see The Young Greens' Website at http://www.younggreens.ie/ main/papers.php?subaction=showfull&id=1100600110&arc hive=&start_from=&ucat=2&

33 Case no: 232/2003. Judgement 30/11/04.

34 'Gay Law News', www.gaylawnet.com/news/2004/ pa0410.htm issued 7/10/04, accessed 03/01/05.

KERRY LIFE AND FAMILY ASSOCIATION

Kerry Life and Family Association, a Kerry-based pro-life, pro-family group, having consulted all our members and members of the general public in Kerry, would like to make the following submission on the position of the family in Ireland under Bunreacht na hÉireann.

1 HOW SHOULD THE FAMILY BE DEFINED?

Despite the many pressures and challenges the family has faced down through the centuries it has stood the test of time and remains the cornerstone of societies worldwide. Most of the breakdown in Irish society today can be attributed to the breakdown of the family. Despite the very strong emphasis on the family in our Constitution, successive governments have consistently neglected the family by failing to adequately protect and support it. Our government is in fact acting unconstitutionally by penalising married couples in its tax code. The government is directly contributing to and facilitating the breakdown of the family in Ireland. These actions by our government make no sense, economic or social, because the breakdown of the family is costing the taxpayer millions of euros every year through the support of single parent families, and the cost to our court system in dealing with the resulting rise in crime and unsocial behaviour amongst our youth. All of this is resulting in untold heartache, pain and suffering.

We do not wish any changes to our Constitution in regard to the family and we support the Supreme Court's decision that in our Constitution the meaning of the 'family' is confined to a family based on marriage. We also assert that marriage can only take place between a consenting man and woman.

2 IS IT POSSIBLE TO GIVE CONSTITUTIONAL PROTECTION TO FAMILIES OTHER THAN THOSE BASED ON MARRIAGE?

No. As Pope John Paul II said on Wednesday, November 24 2004. 'Anyone who destroys the family causes profound harm to society.' This was the Pope's message to the plenary assembly of the Pontifical Council for the Family. 'Whoever destroys this fundamental fabric of human coexistence, by not respecting its identity and by upsetting its tasks, causes a profound wound in society and provokes harm that is often irreparable,' said the pontiff. In his Italian-language address, the Holy Father emphasised that the 'mission of spouses and of Christian families, in virtue of the grace received in the sacrament of marriage at the service of the building of the Church and of the construction of the kingdom of God in history … has lost nothing of its timeliness.' 'What is more, it has become exceptionally urgent,' he said.

3 SHOULD GAY COUPLES BE ALLOWED TO MARRY?

No. Marriage can only be contracted between one man and one woman; 'male and female he created them'. We are opposed to all laws which would do harm to the family, striking at its unity and its indissolubility, or which would give legal validity to a union between persons, including those of the same sex, who demand the same rights as the family founded upon marriage between a man and a woman.

There needs to be a proper investigation into the gay agenda, and a facing up to our responsibilities to ensuring a decent society for our children. It may be politically correct at present to be in favour of gay rights but we are not doing our children and future generations any favours by not facing up to our responsibilities and restricting marriage to a man and a woman.

Because your committee has taken on the serious responsibility of looking into this issue, you should first educate yourselves on all aspects of the subject. It should be obvious to any reasonable person on investigation who has the well-being of Irish society at heart that to implement the homosexual agenda or even part of it would be detrimental to the well-being both socially and morally of this once great nation. One of the main duties of all politicians is to implement laws that are designed to protect the weak and vulnerable in society, and to implement all or part of the homosexual agenda would be to place these people in great moral danger. Sacred scripture is very clear about homosexual activity and clearly states that all those who support and promote that way of life are equally as guilty as those taking part in those practices.

4 IS THE CONSTITUTION'S REFERENCE TO WOMAN'S LIFE WITHIN THE HOME A DATED ONE THAT SHOULD BE CHANGED?

No. Many surveys clearly demonstrate that this provision in our Constitution reflects the wishes of the vast majority of Irish women who choose to stay at home to rear their family. The Irish government must give proper support to families. The tax system should be changed to favour married couples. Tax individualisation and other measures introduced by the government are blatantly anti-family and should be changed. Give generous allowances to families where the mothers choose to remain at home until their families are reared. By doing this we will have a much healthier society and a more responsible and balanced youth, leading to a safer, happier and more prosperous society.

Another area that needs to be carefully examined is the whole area of lone parents. Over 11% of households in Ireland are headed by a lone parent – this is one of the highest proportions in the EU.

The social welfare system treats cohabiting couples (of the opposite sex) in the same way as married couples. The income tax system treats cohabiting couples as single people. Our tax and welfare systems need to be ordered to at least discourage the popularity of single parenthood. There is in reality no such thing as a lone parent (except where one parent is deceased), only an abandoned parent. Every child has a father and a mother. In Ireland we need to make the person who abandons his child (usually the man) responsible financially for the bringing up of their child until the age of eighteen as happens in many American states. Our educational system needs to be looked at, as it appears that most of our youth come out of our school system with no sense of responsibility. They need to be taught that all actions have consequences, and that if they become sexually active outside of marriage they must accept responsibility for any children conceived. The so-called sex education programmes in our schools are leading to an increase in sexual activity in our youth, which proves that these courses should be renamed 'education for sex'. We need to look closely at the success in the US of greatly reducing sexual activity in their youth, and the corresponding reduction in the number of lone parents, and all of this achieved by simply removing the sex education programmes (education for sex) and replacing them with abstinence programmes.

5 DOES THE CONSTITUTION NEED TO BE CHANGED IN VIEW OF THE UN CONVENTION ON THE RIGHTS OF THE CHILD?

No. The Constitution should not be changed to come in line with the UN Convention on the Rights of the Child. The child already enjoys constitutional protection, which must be upheld by the state; this protection must extend from the moment of conception. The practice of sending Irish children to England by health boards to be killed in their mothers' wombs in abortion mills must be highlighted and stopped, as it is the duty of all legislators and all those who promote children's rights to first of all ensure that all children receive the most basic right of all, the right to life.

To conclude, Kerry Life and Family wish to state that Articles 41, 42 and 40.3 should not be changed. We also wish to state that it is our experience that the vast majority of Irish people would oppose any attempt to redefine the family. Again we call on our government to protect, defend and support the traditional Irish family as required under Bunreacht na hÉireann.

KNIGHTS OF ST COLUMBANUS

Articles 41 and 42 of Bunreacht na hÉireann (The Constitution of Ireland) recognises the family as the most important social unit within the state. As such the state guarantees its protection and pledges itself to guard with special care the institution of marriage on which it states the family to be founded.

Since 1937 the family has been placed on a constitutional pedestal. The earlier Constitution of the Irish Free Sate (in force from 1922-1937) contained no corresponding provisions concerning the family.

In discussing the relationship between the family and society there is much at stake. Not only are marriage and family grounded in the will of God and revealed by the order of nature, they are also the primary source of stability, life and love in any society, that primary vital cell from which the rest of society derives so much of its own cohesion and potential success. This fact is recognised in the Constitution when it describes the family as 'the necessary basis of social order and indispensable to the well being of the nation'. The Greek Constitution expresses the same conviction when it describes the family as 'the foundation of the conservation and the progress of the nation'. Such values are consistent in turn with Article 16 of the Universal Declaration of Human Rights when it states, 'the family is a fundamental nucleus or cell of society and of the state and, as such, should be recognised and protected.' Article 16 of the Social Charter of Europe (1961), Article 23 of the International Treaty on Civil Rights, Article 10 of the International Charter on Economic, Social and Cultural Rights as well as many other national and international instruments both affirm and develop this basic insight that the family is the nucleus of society, and for that reason is deserving of special status, development and care.

The 'family' referred to in Articles 41 and 42, although not defined within the Constitution itself, has been held by the courts to be confined to the family that is based on marriage, that is a marriage which is a valid subsisting marriage under the law of the state. A couple whose marriage is not valid according to the civil law of the state cannot form a family unit in the constitutional sense but may do so if they subsequently enter into a valid and recognisable marriage or if an initially invalid marriage is retrospectively validated. A married couple either with or without children may comprise a 'family' within the meaning of the Constitution.

The rights and duties recognised and acknowledged by the state as being invested in the family and the states guarantees in relation to them do not extend to the natural family or the non-marital family.

We the Knights submit that the meaning of 'marriage' as found by Costello J in *Murray and Ireland* (1985) IR 532 (1985) ILRM 542 in which he derived it from the Christian notion of 'a partnership based on an irrevocable personal consent given by both spouses which established an unique and very special life-long relationship' should be enshrined in legislation.

The so-called *de facto* unions have been taking on special importance in recent years. The common element of such unions is that of being forms of co-habitation of a sexual kind, which are not marriage. Some recent initiatives proposed the institutional recognition of *de facto* unions and even their equivalence to families which have their origin in a marriage commitment. It is important to draw attention to the damage that such recognition and equivalence would represent for the identity of marriage as traditionally understood. The question of recognition of same-sex unions has also been raised. The Knights of St Columbanus remain committed to advocating and promoting the common good of everyone in our society and to giving practical expression to our pastoral concern for homosexual people. The Knights of St Columbanus accept that homosexual people are to be 'accepted with respect, compassion and sensitivity'. The Knights of St Columbanus condemn all forms of violence, harassment or abuse directed against people who are homosexual. In recent years there have been significant changes to the law to remove discrimination against people on the grounds of their sexuality. These changes have removed injustices, without of themselves creating any parallel legal institution to marriage.

However, it is essential when considering future legislation concerning marriage and the family, to acknowledge the vital distinction between private homosexual behaviour between consenting adults, and formalising that behaviour as 'a relationship in society, foreseen and approved by the law, to the point where it becomes an institution in the legal structure'. Legal developments must be considered not only in terms of their impact on individuals, but also in terms of their impact on the common good and on the fundamental institutions of society such as marriage in the family.

The Knights of St Columbanus submit that the recognition of same-sex unions on the same terms as marriage would suggest to future generations and to society as a whole that marriage as husband and wife, and as same-sex relationship, are equally valid options, and an equally valid context for the bringing up of children.

What is at stake here is the natural rights of children to the presence normally of a mother and father in their lives. Given the legal changes that have already taken place and the fact that two people can make private legal provision covering many aspects of their lives together including joint ownership of homes, living wills and powers of attorney, the argument that same-sex marriage is necessary to protect human rights becomes a redundant one. When it is balanced against the manner in which it will undermine such a fundamental institution as marriage in the family, it is difficult to see how such a development could be justified in terms of the government's duty to defend marriage and the common good.

If it is accepted that Article 41.2 can include men, and that it furthermore does not assign a domestic role to women, it is not then, in fact, necessary to update it. The Knights of St Coumbanus, however, would welcome the opportunity to strengthen constitutional protection for the role and work of parents and carers. Any proposed change should be gender-inclusive; should retain the specific provision of parental care; and changes to other articles should not adversely affect the express recognition afforded parents and carers in a reformulated 41.2.

The Knights of St Columbanus put forward the following suggested reformulation:

41.2.1

The state recognises that those who care for dependants within the family give to the state a support without which the common good cannot be achieved.

41.2.1

The state shall, therefore, ensure that those who care for dependants within the family shall not be obliged by economic necessity to engage in labour to the neglect of those duties.

LABOUR PARTY

The Labour Party wishes to supplement its original submission of July 1995, with particular reference to family rights, as follows.

First, we adopt and endorse the recommendations of the Constitution Review Group, for the reasons set out in its report.

Specifically, we would support the re-framing of the Articles on the family, education and the rights of the child along the lines attached.

Second, while a consideration of family rights inevitably overlaps into a consideration of the constitutional provisions relation to education, this in turn might lead one on to religion. We presume, however, that you are trying to keep matters relatively compartmentalised and that, in particular, religion is to be dealt with at a later date.

Third, the constitutional jurisprudence relating to the rights of persons with a disability has largely been dealt with in the context of childhood and education. We believe that the concept would more comfortably sit in the context of enhanced guarantees of equality before the law. Such a constitutional amendment should be designed, in particular, so as to overturn the Supreme Court judgement on the unconstitutionality of requiring 'reasonable accommodation' of the needs of persons with a disability. This has to some extent, but not entirely, been overtaken by developments at EU

level. It remains a significant issue, not least on symbolic grounds.

We would propose a text along the following lines:

Existing provision: Article 40.1

All citizens shall, as human persons, be held equal before the law.

This shall not be held to mean that the state shall not in its enactments have due regard to differences of capacity, physical and moral, and of social function.

Proposed replacement

All persons shall have the right to equality before the law.

No persons shall suffer invidious discrimination, direct or indirect, on any ground such as race, colour, language, nationality, national, social or ethnic origin, membership of the Traveller community, age, gender, disability, sexual orientation, culture, religion, political or other opinion, birth or marital, family or other status. Regard may, however, be had to relevant differences.

Nothing in this section prohibits measures of a limited and proportionate nature for the protection and advancement of persons unfairly disadvantaged by discrimination, economic or social exclusion or disability in order to enable, as far as practicable, the full and equal enjoyment by them of their rights and freedoms and their full participation to the best of their abilities in the life of the nation.

In particular, the state may impose an obligation on some or all sections of the community to take reasonable steps to accommodate the needs of such persons, notwithstanding that the provision for that purpose of such accommodation may give rise to a cost.

Existing provision: The Family: Article 41

1   1° The state recognises the family as the natural primary and fundamental unit group of society, and as a moral institution possessing inalienable and imprescriptible rights, antecedent and superior to all positive law.

2° The state, therefore, guarantees to protect the family in its constitution and authority, as the necessary basis of social order and as indispensable to the welfare of the nation and the state.

2   1° In particular, the state recognises that by her life within the home, woman gives to the state a support without which the common good cannot be achieved.

2° The state shall, therefore endeavour to ensure that mothers shall not be obliged by economic necessity to engage in labour to the neglect of their duties in the home.

3   1° The state pledges itself to guard with special care the institution of marriage, on which the family is founded, and to protect it against attack.

2° A court designated by law may grant a dissolution of marriage where, but only where, it is satisfied that –
i.   at the date of the institution of the proceedings, the spouses have lived apart from one another for a period of, or periods amounting to, at least four years during five years,

ii. there is no reasonable prospect of a reconciliation between the spouses,

iii. such provisions as the court considers proper, having regard to the circumstances, exist or will be made for the spouses, any children of either or both of them and any other person prescribed by law, and

iv. any further conditions prescribed by law are compiled with.

3° No person whose marriage has been dissolved under the civil law of any other state but is a subsisting valid marriage under the law for the time being in force within the jurisdiction of the government and parliament established by this Constitution shall be capable of contracting a valid marriage within that jurisdiction during the lifetime of the other party to the marriage so dissolved.

Proposed replacement

1 The state recognises the family as the natural primary and fundamental unit group of society and that home and family life give to society a support without which the common good cannot be achieved. The state shall accordingly endeavour to support persons maintaining or caring for others within the family home.

2 The state pledges itself to guard with special care the institution of marriage and to protect it against attack and to protect the family based on marriage in its constitution and authority. All persons have the right to marry, in accordance with the requirements of law, and to found a family.

3 The state also recognises and respects family life not based on marriage. The Oireachtas is entitled to legislate for the benefit of such families and of their individual members.

4 A court designated by law may grant dissolution of marriage where, but only where, it is satisfied that –

i at the date of the institution of the proceedings, the spouses have lived apart from one another for a period of, or periods amounting to, at least four years during the previous five years,

ii there is no reasonable prospect of a reconciliation between the spouses,

iii such provisions as the court considers proper, having regard to the circumstances, exist or will be made for the spouses, any children of either or both of them and any other person prescribed by law, and

iv any further conditions prescribed by law are complied with.

No person whose marriage has been dissolved under civil law of any other state but is a subsisting valid marriage under the law for the time being in force within the jurisdiction of the state is capable of contracting a valid marriage within that jurisdiction during the lifetime of the other party to the marriage so dissolved.

Existing provision: The Rights of the Child

No specific provision, other than Article 42.5.

Proposed replacement

1 The state guarantees in its laws to respect, and, as far as practicable, by its laws to defend and vindicate the rights of the child, having due regard to international legal standards and in particular to the United Nations Convention on the Rights of the Child, which rights include –

i the right to have his or her best interests regarded as the first and paramount consideration in any decision concerning the child;

ii the right to know the identity of his or her parents and as far as practicable to be reared by his or her parents and each of them, subject to such limitations as may be prescribed by law in the interests of the child; and

iii the right to have due regard given to his or her views in any decision concerning the child.

2 In exceptional cases, where parents fail in their duty towards their children where the interests of a child require intervention, the state as guardian of the common good, by appropriate means must endeavour to supply the place of the parents but always with due regard for the rights of the child.

Existing provision: Education: Article 42

1 The state acknowledges that the primary and natural educator of the child is the family and guarantees to respect the inalienable right and duty of parents to provide, according to their means, for the religious and moral, intellectual, physical and social education of their children.

2 Parents shall be free to provide this education in their homes or in private schools or in schools recognised or established by the state.

3 1° The state shall not oblige parents in violation of their conscience and lawful preference to send their children to schools established by the state, or to any particular type of school designated by the state.

2° The state shall, however, as guardian of the common good, require in view of actual conditions that the children receive a certain minimum education, moral, intellectual and social.

4 The state shall provide for free primary education and shall endeavour to supplement and give reasonable aid to private and corporate educational initiative, and, when the public good requires it, provide other educational facilities or institutions with due regard, however, for the rights of parents, especially in the matter of religious and moral formation.

5 In exceptional cases, where the parents for physical or moral reasons fail in their duty towards their children, the state as guardian of the common good, by appropriate means shall endeavour to supply the place of the parents, but always with due regard for the natural and imprescriptible rights of the child.

Proposed replacement

1 The state acknowledges that parents are the primary and natural educators of their children and accordingly guarantees to respect the right and duty of parents to provide, according to their means, for the education of their children.

2 Parents are free to provide this education in their homes or in private schools or in schools recognized or established by the state. The state may not oblige parents in violation of their conscience and lawful preference to send their children to schools established by the state, or to any particular type of school designated by the state.

3 The state must, however, as guardian of the common good, require that children receive such certain minimum education as may be determined by law, with due regard to the right of parents to make decisions concerning the religious and moral education of their children.

4 Subject to the foregoing, the state –

i   shall provide for free primary and secondary education and, where necessary, training and education for adults who by reason of disability have enduring needs, and

ii may provide other educational facilities or institutions, and

iii may supplement and give reasonable aid to private educational initiative,

with due regard both to the rights of parents and those receiving education and to the aims of promoting equality of access to and participation in education, meeting special educational needs and accommodating diversity in the provision of education.

LABOUR LGBT

WHO ARE LABOUR LGBT?

Labour LGBT is a group of members of the Irish Labour Party who identify as Lesbian, Gay, Bisexual or Transgendered. Our main aim is to campaign for equality for all people; specifically members of the LGBT community both in society and within the Labour Party.

EXECUTIVE SUMMARY

This submission is drawn up by Labour LGBT. It aims to clearly outline the current discrimination and inequality that same-sex couples face in relation to lack of state recognition of marriage as outlined in the Irish Constitution (and Irish case laws which have defined marriage). We examine the role of the family and men and women in the Irish Constitution and argue that these need to be updated to reflect modern society. We will also argue that same-sex marriage can be legislated for without the need to amend the Irish Constitution.

SUBMISSION BASIS

It is our belief that the Irish Constitution is not reflective of modern Ireland in terms of not recognising: the diversity of families (parental roles, gender/sexual orientations), current gender roles in Irish life and the right of an individual to determine her/his own destiny without the need for lifestyle roles/choices to be stipulated by the state.

Ireland's Constitution does not specifically define marriage as between a man and a woman but this has been done so by specific case law, e.g. *B v R* where marriage was described as 'the voluntary and permanent union of one man and one woman to the exclusion of all others for life'. In *Foy v An tArd-Chláiritheoir* McKechie J stated that 'marriage as understood by the Constitution, by statute and by case law refers to the union of a biological man with a biological woman'. This interpretation not only prevents same-sex couples from marrying but also means that transsexuals are unable to marry a person of their former gender.

Article 41 is the main constitutional provision dealing with the family. In *State (Nicolaou) v An Bord Uchtála*,12 Walsh J in the Supreme Court stated that it was quite clear 'that the family referred to in [Article 41] is the family which is founded on the institution of marriage.' In addition, Article 41.3.1° requires the State 'to guard with special care the institution of marriage, on which the family is founded, and to protect it against attack'. The effect of this is that neither a non-marital family nor its members are entitled to the constitutional protections contained in Article 41.

These definitions of marriage and the family are clearly discriminatory and biased against LGBT people specifically by excluding and limiting official state recognition of marital status solely to heterosexual couples. This exclusion degrades and devalues the benefits that LGBT couples offer to the state and the stability that such families clearly provide to both spouses/partners and their associated children. By solely defining the family as that based on marriage the state, through the Constitution, is not recognising many different types of families – e.g. single parents, same-sex couples with children etc

Labour LGBT believe that the role of the woman in the household as outlined by the Irish Constitution is only using outdated gender stereotypes which are not relevant in today's society.

GAY MARRIAGE

In Ireland, the legal definition of marriage has not been interpreted to include same-sex couples, so at present they cannot become legally married. There is also no provision for the legal registration of same-sex partnerships. This means that same-sex partners do not have equal rights to heterosexual married couples. This institutional bias clearly contradicts Article 40.1 of the Irish Constitution which states 'All citizens shall, as human persons, be held equal before the law.'

Labour LGBT sees the fact that same-sex couples are unable to marry as inequality – nothing less. Labour LGBT also believes that by allowing same-sex couples to marry this would in fact strengthen the institution of marriage. It is evident that if the family is one of the building blocks of society and marriage is the state's process of ensuring its continuity and/or development, the state should also recognise non-heterosexual marriages so as to foster the creation, continuation and development of all forms of family.

PRESENT INEQUALITIES

The failure of the state to recognise a right for same-sex couples to marry results in many worries, difficulties and inequalities for same-sex couples. (It was estimated in the USA that persons entering into marriage accrued over 1000 individual rights[1]) :

- *Death*: Under the Succession Act, 1965, the spouse of the deceased is entitled to a significant section of the deceased party's estate if the deceased dies without making a valid will. In the case of same-sex couples, the surviving partner can be left with nothing because their partnership is not recognised.
- *Maintenance*: When a married couple split, either by separation or divorce, there is legislation to allow for the division of the couple's assets, and provision for the payment of maintenance and child support. Such protection is not readily available to same-sex or non-marital couples, regardless of the length of their relationship. Indeed, it was held by the High Court that even if a non-marital couple had made an agreement concerning maintenance in the case of the relationship breaking down, such an agreement could not be enforced by the courts as it would undermine the special constitutional protection of marriage.
- *Taxation*: The tax system is strongly biased against non-marital couples. Inheritance tax is significantly higher because of an inability to marry. The exemptions granted to married couples in respect of capital acquisitions tax, capital gains tax and stamp duties do not apply to same-sex couples as they are not considered spouses.
- *Next of Kin*: In the event of surgery or a medical emergency, partners in a same-sex relationship cannot act as next of kin. This prevents a partner

from making many decisions that spouses in a marriage would take for granted. This may also mean that a partner may be barred from accessing his/her loved one on that person's death bed.
- *Children*: Under current Irish legislation there is no facility for couples, other than married couples, to adopt a child. A joint adoption by a couple is only possible where that couple is married and living together. This rule prevents a same-sex couple from jointly adopting a child, even where one of the parties is the biological or legal parent of the child.
- *Family Home*: The Family Home Protection Act, 1976 provides for the division of the marital family home in the case of marriage breakdown. Such protection is not available to those in same-sex relationships, where the partner who does not own the house must prove that he/she made a direct financial contribution to its purchase or he/she will receive no interest in the property.
- Those who are in same-sex relationships with non-nationals face many obstacles such as inability to gain citizenship from marriage, work permit difficulties etc.

INTERNATIONAL EXPERIENCE

Marriage between same-sex couples is legal in: the Netherlands and Belgium and also will shortly be introduced in Sweden and Spain. The example of Spain is interesting because of its similarity to Ireland in terms of high levels of Catholicism, yet the Spanish public supported this move.

Same-sex marriage is legal in the state of Massachusetts, USA and in seven provinces in Canada. There is currently a proposed bill that would permit same-sex marriage to be legalised across Canada.

Civil unions, which have many of the characteristics of marriage, are available to same-sex couples in many other countries. The UK recently introduced its civil partnership act which will give a range of property rights, the same exemption as married couples on inheritance tax, social security and pension benefits, and also the ability to get parental responsibility for a partner's children

The states of Vermont and New Jersey in the USA have legislated for civil unions for same-sex couples. Civil unions for same-sex couples are growing throughout Europe, being recognised in France, Norway, Denmark, Sweden, Switzerland, Finland, Iceland, the Netherlands and Germany.

They have also recently been introduced by New Zealand and parts of Australia and Argentina.

Labour LGBT firmly believes that civil unions do not create equality. They are welcome but only as a stepping stone to full equal rights. Labour LGBT calls for full gay marriage rights.

REASONS FOR NON-RECOGNITION IN IRELAND

To date there has been no reasonable justification as to why the state should sanction heterosexual marriages and refuse to do the same for non-heterosexual couples. For some, the issue of procreation was an argument in favour of providing limited support to the non-recognition of non-heterosexual couples by the state. However, it is well established that many heterosexual couples who have state-recognised marriages are unable to conceive or have no intention of doing so. For others it is religious reasons, yet the state now allows for divorce. Labour LGBT feels there should be a separation of church and state and that old religious tradition can no longer discriminate against the LGBT minority. Others have used economic arguments that to provide same-sex couples with the same benefits as married couples would cost the taxpayer money. Our response is gay men and lesbians pay PAYE and PRSI too, so why should we not be given these benefits?

THE FAMILY

The Constitution needs by its very nature to be extremely broad in how it recognises families and cognisant of the fact that there are many different family structures/social situations.

The Irish Constitution does not define the family but states:

> The state recognises the family as the natural primary and fundamental unit group of society, and as a moral institution possessing inalienable and imprescriptible rights, antecedent and superior to all positive law.

> The state, therefore, guarantees to protect the family in its constitution and authority, as the necessary basis of social order and as indispensable to the welfare of the nation and the state.

> The state pledges itself to guard with special care the institution of marriage, on which the Family is founded, and to protect it against attack.

The Supreme Court has held that the constitutional meaning of 'family' is confined to a family based on marriage. Labour LGBT believes that this is extremely discriminatory and unjust in not recognising other groups outside of marriage. This is creating a heavy institutional bias weighted against those in family structures outside of marriage and is not recognising other groups, e.g. a divorced parent with primary custody of children; foster parents with foster children; a couple with children from other relationships; grandparents with custody of grandchildren; a lesbian couple; a never married couple who have a child; a couple with no children; a gay couple who have adopted children; a teenager of alcoholic parent(s) who takes responsibility for his/her siblings; adult siblings living together; an adult child and an ageing parent who live together; grandparent(s) living with children and grandchildren; single parents.

In a 2004 report the Department of Social and Family Affairs has recognised that change needs to occur in how we define a family by stating:

in the context of increasing diversity in Irish society, we need an inclusive definition of family, one that can encompass all types of families. To be inclusive a definition should be capable of embracing such diverse family forms as those made up of grandparents and children, those consisting of foster parents and children, those of lone parent and children, those of unmarried partners and children as well as same-sex parents and children.

Keegan v Ireland in the European Court of Human Rights 1994 gave a broader definition of the family than that of one just based on marriage. The European Court of Human Rights has indeed given quite a broad interpretation of the family in other countries and we would welcome this.

Labour LGBT believes that to define the family based solely on marriage is essentially discriminatory, unreasonable and unjust.

We would recommend that a definition along the UN's definition of the family be used in the Irish Constitution

The UN definition of a family is 'any combination of two or more persons who are bound together by ties of mutual consent, birth and/or adoption or placement and who, together, assume responsibility for, *inter alia*, the care and maintenance of group members, the addition of new members through procreation or adoption, the socialisation of children and the social control of members'.

ROLE OF WOMEN AND MEN

Article 41.2.1 of the Irish Constitution states in particular, that 'the state recognises that by her life within the home, woman gives to the state a support without which the common good cannot be achieved'.

Labour LGBT believes this to be out of date and flawed. It is using outdated gender stereotypes from Ireland of the 1930s and 1940s.

It is our belief that by stating this, the constitution is biased towards men and women and the right of families to choose freely and equally their desired roles in their own home. The state should not attempt to enforce perceived or desired roles, rewards and/or responsibilities upon men or women. Householders should be free to choose their own internal family roles and the associated benefits that doing so may give to them.

Article 41.2.2° of the Irish Constitution states that 'the state shall, therefore, endeavour to ensure that mothers shall not be obliged by economic necessity to engage in labour to the neglect of their duties in the home'.

Article 41.2.2° discriminates clearly against fathers by not recognising their valued role in the family and negates the benefits that fathers bring to their children in their homes, and directly imposes assumed duties on women in their own homes and yet at the same time equally projects no such associated duties on men.

Labour LGBT believe that it is positive to recognise those who work in the home, but we feel that specifically outlining mothers is wrong; what about fathers, what about other caregivers?

Labour LGBT recommends removing all gender references from Article 41 and replacing this with the phrase 'primary carer'.

CONCLUSION AND RECOMMENDATION

The Irish Constitution is seriously out-dated and in need of immediate reform. It does not reflect the society in which we currently live, the level of multiculturalism, the diversity of families and our current lifestyle choices in modern Ireland.

The Constitution is insulting to both women and men and degrades their inherent ability to conduct their own private household roles and responsibilities as they collectively or singularly see fit. It also discriminates heavily against the right of a father to stay at home and take on the role and responsibilities of a mother as outlined in the current Constitution.

In its current form the constitution restricts our society's ability to grow, mature and develop, it directly creates high levels of discrimination and significant disparity amongst citizens of all sexual orientations and gender.

From our detailed examination, we cannot identify any reasonable justification for the state not to bring in legislation so as to permit the recognition of same-sex marriages and equal access for all couples to the benefits that state-recognised marriage affords. The Law Reform Commission have stated that legislation giving cohabitees full partnership rights which are equivalent to marriage would not be unconstitutional.

We believe that the Constitution should be amended to allow for a broader definition of the family beyond that of the current heteropatriarch model.

We call upon the All-Party Oireachtas Committee to initiate procedures to amend the Constitution accordingly, so that it no longer is a source for the aforementioned discrimination and that it becomes an up-to-date framework for equality, justice and progress in a modern Ireland.

Bibliography

Partnership Rights of Same-Sex Couples, Dr John Mee and Kate Ronanyne, Jan 2001, The Equality Authority.

Implementing Equality for Lesbians, Gays and Bisexuals, May 2002, The Equality Authority

Equality Policies for Lesbian, Gay and Bisexual People: Implementation Issues, 2003, NESF

(Oireachtas) Inter-Departmental Committee on Reform of Marriage Law, Discussion Paper No. 5, September 2004

Consultation Paper on the Rights and Duties of Cohabitees, April 2004,The Law Reform Commission,

Families and Family Life in Ireland – Challenges for the Future, Report of Public Consultation Fora, Mary Daly, February 2004, Department of Social and Family Affairs

http://www.lawyer.ie/nullity.html

http://www.groireland.ie/docs/marriagelaw_discussion_paper_no5.pdf

http://www.lawreform.ie/Cohabitees%20CP%20%20April%202004.pdf

http://www.oasis.gov.ie/relationships/same_sex_relationships/adoption_and_same_sex_couples.html

http://www.equality.ie/stored-files/RTF/Partnership_Rights_of_Same_Sex_Couples.rtf

http://www.cidb.ie/live.nsf/0/802567ca003e043d80256ea600366547?OpenDocument

http://www.iyf2004.welfare.ie/

http://en.wikipedia.org/wiki/Same-sex_marriage

http://www.coe.int/T/E/Legal_affairs/Legal_co-operation/Family_law_and_children's_rights/Judgments/Press%20release%20Keegan.asp

http://www.drummajorinstitute.org/plugin/template/dmi/55/1693

Notes

1 http://www.drummajorinstitute.org/plugin/template/dmi/55/1693 – A 1996 government study found that there are at least 1,049 such protections, rights, and responsibilities that come with marriage under federal law alone. These protections include access to health care and medical decision-making for a partner and children, parenting and immigration rights, inheritance, taxation, social security and other government benefits, rules for ending a relationship while protecting both parties and the ability to pool resources to buy or transfer property without adverse tax consequences.

LABOUR WOMEN

Labour Women make the following submissions in relation to the family provisions in the Constitution:

ARTICLE 41.1.1

We feel that the reference to positive law is out of step with our modern understanding of constitutional law and leaves a very large area of judicial discretion as to which elements of natural law are to take precedence over positive law. It is unsatisfactory that, notwithstanding any possible amendments to the definition of 'family' which would attempt to broaden it out, the provisions of Article 41.1.1 could still be used to reimpose the definition based on marriage from an Aquinian view of natural law. Further, this provision was relied upon in *North Western Health Board v HW* [2001] 3 IR 623, to justify giving the parents in the family rights which were greater than those of the child. We therefore feel that the words from 'antecedent …' should be deleted.

ARTICLE 41.1.2

The balance between the rights of the family as a unit as opposed to the individual members thereof is a matter of concern. In particular, the emphasis on the family as a unit and on the need to protect it in its constitution and authority gives rise to a potential conflict which was most apparent in *North Western Health*

Board v HW [2001] 3 IR 623 where the best interests of the child were not the determining factor but maintaining the family authority was paramount. We favour the retention of a provision protecting the family but only if a provision based on Article 3.1 of the CRC is inserted and if the definition of family as based on marriage is removed.

ARTICLE 41.2.1

The model of woman's life within the home is an outdated, stereotyped and insulting view of the role of women in modern society and should be deleted. We rely in particular on Article 5 of the United Nations Convention on the Elimination of All Forms of Discrimination Against Women (CEDAW) in this regard which provides:

Article 5

State parties shall take all appropriate measures:

a) To modify the social and cultural patterns of conduct of men and women, with a view to achieving the elimination of prejudices and customary and all other practices which are based on the idea of the inferiority or the superiority of either of the sexes or on stereotyped roles for men and women;

b) To ensure that family education includes a proper understanding of maternity as a social function and the recognition of the common responsibility of men and women in the upbringing and development of their children, it being understood that the interest of the children is the primordial consideration in all cases.

We nevertheless recognise that many people do work within the home and that the contribution made by carers and homemakers be recognised but the article should be amended to become gender neutral. It should be replaced by 'In particular, the state recognised that by their life within the home, homemakers give to the state a support without which the common good shall not be achieved.'

ARTICLE 41.2.2

This provision which speaks of the duties of mothers has proved a toothless article in that attempts to rely on it, notably in *L v L* [1992] 2 IR 77, have failed to produce any tangible benefit for mothers based upon it, and it perpetuates the stereotyping of the roles of parents. It is also out of line with CEDAW Article 5 (B) and the CRC which provides at Article 18.1 that both parents shall have common responsibilities for the upbringing and development of the child. We recommend that it be deleted in its entirety.

ARTICLE 41.3.1

We believe that a significant proportion of Irish families are no longer based upon marriage and that this article no longer reflects the society in which we live. Families other than those based upon marriage should be recognised and therefore we recommend the deletion of the phrase 'on which the family is founded' from this Article. We acknowledge that the Article has been relied upon successfully to justify preferential treatment for married couples but we feel that it is inappropriate to single out married couples over and above other forms of families and that it is the family which should be guarded with special care, not the institution of marriage. Further, it seems desirable in light of Article 8 of the ECHR that the possibility of recognising unions between persons which are not marriages as understood by the Supreme Court in *TF v Ireland* [1995] 2 IR 321 as the traditional Christian type marriage, should be left open to the legislature and it is at least arguable that this is not possible while the Constitution continues to provide for family based on marriage. We therefore recommend that this article be deleted and replaced with a provision along the lines of the ECHR guaranteeing respect for family life.

ARTICLE 41.3.3

Insofar as this provides a constitutional basis for legislative recognition of foreign divorces and subsequent remarriages, this is necessary but the wording of the article is unclear and consideration should be given to replacing it with a clearer provision.

ARTICLE 42

As submitted above, the balance between the family as a unit and the rights of the child within the family are a matter of concern to us. This article was also relied upon in *North Western Health Board v HW* [2001] 3 IR 623 but this difficulty would, we feel, be resolved by the insertion of an express provision that the best interest of the child should be paramount in order to facilitate intervention in cases even where there is no moral failure by the parents but the interests of the child are being overlooked.

The family should not be defined as based upon marriage but the existence of a family is a matter of fact which could be decided on a case by case basis as it is pursuant to the ECHR. Once the definition based on marriage is gone, the issue of natural fathers' rights is also resolved as they would now have the same constitutional rights as any other parent within a family, but fathers who have no stable relationship with the child or mother (i.e. where there has been rape or incest etc) would remain in a position where they have no constitutional protection. Providing for respect for family life and an express provision that the best interests of the child be the paramount consideration would enable a balance to be struck between the rights of the family as a unit and the rights of the individual members thereof where conflict arises. The ECHR model provides protection for family life without tying that to marriage-based families and there is no reason why our Constitution cannot do the same thing. We support the recognition of marriage for gay couples and submit that this may not be possible unless the constitutional definition of the family is amended so that it is no longer based on a Christian/Aquinian model of the family.

LAW SOCIETY

INTRODUCTION

1 By public advertisement the All-Party Oireachtas Committee on the Constitution ('the Oireachtas Committee') invited written submissions in connection with possible reforms of the Articles in Bunreacht na hÉireann that make provisions in relation to the family in Articles 41, 42 and 40.3.

2 The advertisement noted that '[f]ollowing the enactment of the Constitution, legislation relating to the family has been developed in line with those Articles and elucidated by the courts in a substantial body of case law'. The advertisement went on to say that '[t]he All-Party Oireachtas Committee on the Constitution, which is charged with reviewing the Constitution in its entirety, is now examining these Articles to ascertain the extent to which they are serving the good of individuals and the community, with a view to deciding whether changes in them would bring about a greater balance between the two.'

3 The advertisement indicated that the Oireachtas Committee wished to invite individuals and groups to make written submissions to it on such issues as whether the rights of the child should be given an expanded constitutional protection, whether it is possible to give constitutional protection to families other than those based on marriage and how one should strike the balance between the rights of the family as a unit and the rights of individual members.

4 The Law Society of Ireland (the Society) welcomes the proposal of the All-Party Oireachtas Committee to review the provisions in relation to the family contained within Articles 41, 42 and 40.3 of the Constitution. The Society feels that it has a valuable contribution to make to the deliberations of the All-Party Oireachtas Committee in this vitally important area.

5 A report on family life in Ireland launched by the former Minister for Social and Family Affairs, Mary Coughlan, highlighted the need to provide a broader definition of the family in light of modern societal changes. The report titled *Families and Family Life in Ireland: Challenges for the Future*, launched on 25th February 2004, identified the issues that arose during public consultation fora hosted by the Minister in 2003[1]. (Dublin: Department of Social and Family Affairs, 2004). Minister Coughlan held that state policy should not favour one family form over another. Alluding to the fora discussions the Minister stated:

Given the major social and demographic changes that have occurred in Ireland in recent years it is necessary now to bear in mind the different forms of family in developing policies to promote the well-being of individual members, and social cohesion, a point that came through from many participants at the fora.

6 The issues highlighted in the report on family life are also reflected in the recent census figures. These figures have highlighted the fact that new family forms are on the increase. It is to be noted in particular that the number of lone parent families is rising. The number of divorced people has risen from 9,800 in the 1996 census to 35,100 in the 2002 census while the number of separated (including divorced) people has increased from 87,800 in 1996 to 133,800 in 2002. There has also been a significant 35% increase in the number of cohabiting couples, which now make up one in twelve family units. In fact, the number of cohabiting couples has risen since 1996 from 169,300 to 228,600.

7 Of the 15,909 births registered in the third quarter of 2003, 4,981 (31.3%) of all births were outside marriage. In Limerick city for this period, births outside marriage accounted for 55% of all births. Throughout Europe, and beyond, similar trends emerge. In fact, in Iceland in 1998 two out of every three births were outside marriage. One of the enduring ironies is that the number of children born outside of marriage in Ireland is greater than the European average of 1 in 4 births.

8 The existing legislative framework does not however reflect the foregoing changes in family structures. The reluctance to legislate in this area must now be addressed as a matter of some urgency. Any such legislation need not prevent marriage being regarded as a standard setter representing durability, security and stability in a relationship.

9 In the face of a restrictive interpretation of the 'family', individuals have sought redress under international law through international human rights treaties. The most significant international human rights treaty from an Irish perspective is the European Convention on Human Rights (ECHR). Article 8 of the ECHR guarantees as a basic right, the right to respect for private and family life, home and correspondence. It is concerned more with the substance rather than the form of the relationship. The ECHR unlike the Irish Constitution makes no distinction between the family life of a marital and non-marital family. The law in Ireland on the other hand leans strongly against the non-marital family. *De facto* families are effectively outside the ambit of legal protection in Ireland. Cohabitation agreements, for example, are not generally recognised by Irish law as such contracts are viewed as contrary to public policy and are therefore unenforceable. The High Court has recently stated that unmarried persons are 'free agents' who owe no duty to each other.

10   Children are a voiceless and vulnerable minority group in society. Indeed, the Constitutional position of children has proven to be far from secure. It hardly needs to be stated that the measure of a democracy is the manner in which the needs of the most vulnerable are considered and met. That said, one notable feature of the Irish family law system is the relative invisibility of children. For example, children are caught in the crossfire of relationship breakdown. Currently, with no way of exercising their rights, children are in a uniquely vulnerable position in that they cannot exercise their rights during childhood. It should be stated that childhood is only for a defined period of time and does not stand still. The Constitution should be amended to contain a specific declaration on the rights of children.

11   The current government has taken steps towards improving the family law system. For example, the need for some form of national machinery to advance the development of support services has, in part, been met by the Family Support Agency. A more tangible link between the court system and support services should also be created, as in New Zealand.

12   Since the adoption of the Irish Constitution in 1937 the nature of the Irish family has changed dramatically. There is little doubt that the Irish family law system now requires nothing less than a major overhaul if it is to meet the increasing demands placed on it. The law must now root itself in reality and not emotive or traditional rhetoric.

13   The time is now ripe to consider changing the law to facilitate a broader and more inclusive definition of the 'family' in a manner that will promote and foster the best interests of children. We need to adopt a more 'functional' approach to the family, an approach based on the fact of the parties living together rather than the nature of the relationship between the parties.

14   We need to depart from a system of family law where legal status alone is the sole determinant of family rights and privileges.

The Society's principal recommendation is to amend the Constitution to insert express rights for children.

15   Constitutional reform is necessary to recognise and protect the child as a legal person with individual rights.[2]

16   One of the significant conclusions of the 1996 Constitution Review Group was that Article 41 of the Constitution be amended. In particular it recommended the inclusion of the 'judicially construed unenumerated rights of children in a coherent manner, particularly those rights which are not guaranteed elsewhere and are peculiar to children'.

17   In the Kilkenny Incest Investigation Report, the investigation team, chaired by Catherine McGuinness SC (now Mrs. Justice Catherine McGuinness of the Supreme Court), proposed that Article 41 of the

Constitution be amended to include a Charter of Children's Rights. It stated:

> While we accept that the courts have on many occasions stressed that children are possessed of constitutional rights, we are somewhat concerned that the 'natural and imprescriptible rights of the child' are specifically referred to in only one sub-article (Article 42.5) and then only in the context of the state supplying the place of parents who have failed in their duty. We feel that the very high emphasis on the rights of the family in the Constitution may consciously or unconsciously be interpreted as giving a higher value to the rights of parents than to the rights of children. We believe that the Constitution should contain a specific and overt declaration of the rights of born children. We therefore recommend that consideration be given by the government to the amendment of Articles 41 and 42 of the Constitution so as to include a statement of the constitutional rights of children. We do not ourselves feel confident to put forward a particular wording and we suggest that study might be made of international documents such as the United Nations Convention on the Rights of the Child.

18   The Commission on the Family agreed with the Constitution Review Group and recommended recognition for children as individuals within the family.

19   In 1998, the United Nations Committee on the Rights of the Child, in its concluding observations, emphasised that the recommendations of the Report of the Constitution Review Group would reinforce 'the status of the child as a full subject of rights'.

20   Ireland has ratified two international human rights instruments that have a bearing on children's rights. Ireland ratified the 1989 United Nations Convention on the Rights of the Child, without reservation on September 21, 1992. However, the provisions of the United Nations Convention on the Rights of the Child do not form part of our domestic law.

21   Ireland has also ratified the European Convention on Human Rights and Fundamental Freedoms (ECHR). Unlike the United Nations Convention on the Rights of the Child, the ECHR has been incorporated into Irish law by way of statute. The incorporation of the ECHR at sub-constitutional level will ensure that child rights remain subordinate to parental rights.

THE CONSTITUTION OF IRELAND

22   The principal source of fundamental rights in Irish family law has been the Constitution. Articles 41 and 42 of the Constitution have had a major impact on the manner in which family legislation has been enacted and family law judgments delivered in Ireland. Article 41 of the Irish Constitution of 1937 relates to the family and 'recognises the family as the natural and primary unit group of society' and also guarantees 'to protect the family in its constitution and authority'.

23 The rights guaranteed by Article 41 are recognised as belonging not to individual members of the family but rather to the family unit as a whole. An individual on behalf of the family may invoke them but, as Costello J. notes in *Murray v Ireland*[3] they 'belong to the institution in itself as distinct from the personal rights which each individual member might enjoy by virtue of membership of the family'.

24 Article 41 lacks child focus. It fails to recognise the child as a person with individual rights. This derives from the principle of parental autonomy created by Article 41 of the Constitution. This article establishes a level of privacy within family life, which the state can enter only in the exceptional circumstances detailed in Article 42.5 of the Constitution. Article 42 provides as follows:

> (1) The state acknowledges that the primary and natural educator of the child is the family and guarantees to respect the inalienable right and duty of parents to provide, according to their means, for religious and moral, intellectual, physical and social education of their children ...

> (5) In exceptional cases, where the parents for physical or moral reasons fail in their duty towards their children, the state, as guardian of the common good, by appropriate means shall endeavour to supply the place of the parents, but always with due regard for the natural and imprescriptible rights of the child.

25 This article clearly provides that only in exceptional cases, where parents, for physical or moral reasons, fail in their duty towards their children, can the state as guardian of the common good attempt to supply the place of the parents.

THE CONSTITUTION AND THE FAMILY

26 The Irish Constitution is unique in that the family unit in Ireland takes precedence over and above that of the individual members of the family. In fact, the individual rights of the members of the family are both directed and determined by the family as an entity in itself. Thus, membership of the constitutional family subordinates the rights of the individual members in Ireland. This is specifically true in relation to the rights of children and Supreme Court judgments on the issue have proven to support this interpretation.

27 When examining Article 42 of the Constitution, it is true to say that this in fact has more to do with the family than it does with the substantive right to education and is an accompaniment and subordinate to Article 41. It deals with education in a broader sense than scholastic education. In referring to education, it alludes to the upbringing of the child, which it holds not only to be a right but a duty of parents. This article reinforces the decision-making autonomy of the family. This can be observed by examining the structure of Article 42, which assigns a strong sense of priority to parental autonomy.

28 Article 42.5 of the Constitution is of particular importance in that it addresses the complete inability of some parents to provide for their children's education. It has been interpreted as not being confined to a failure by the parents of a child to provide education for him/her, but extends, in exceptional circumstances, to failure in other duties necessary to satisfy the personal rights of the child. This interpretation supports the assertion previously made that the right to education in Article 42 is a mere extension of the concept of 'the family' in Article 41.

29 Looking at Articles 41 and 42 of the Constitution together, it is clear that they render the rights of married parents in relation to their children 'inalienable'. Article 41 of the Constitution alludes to the inalienable and imprescriptible rights of the family and Article 42 refers to the rights and duties of married parents. Only if the circumstances allow the constitutional restriction on inalienability, contained in Article 42.5 of the Constitution, is there then scope for the legal overruling of the rights of married parents. The threshold for state intervention is set at a very high level. As a result children can be placed at risk.

THE STATUTORY POSITION

30 In spite of the precedence afforded to the welfare and best interests of the child in section 3 of the Guardianship of Infants Act, 1964, the Constitution prevails. Section 3 of the Guardianship of Infants Act, 1964 makes it clear that, in considering an application relating to the guardianship, custody or upbringing of a child, the court must have regard to the welfare of the child. This, the section states, is 'the first and paramount consideration'. The Supreme Court, however, has determined that the welfare of a child must, unless there are exceptional circumstances or other overriding factors, be considered to be best served by its remaining as part of its marital family. The court considered in a number of cases that this was dictated by the constitutional preference for the marital family exhibited in Article 41.3 of the Constitution and the requirement therein that it be protected from attack.[4] There is, therefore, an uneasy tension between, on one hand, the provisions of Articles 41 and 42 of the Constitution and, on the other, the welfare principle outlined in section 3 of the Guardianship of Infants Act, 1964.

31 The apparent contradiction between Articles 41 and 42 of the Constitution and the principle of the welfare of the child in section 3 of the Guardianship of Infants Act, 1964 has been correctly reconciled by the judiciary by holding that the welfare of the child is to be found within the confines of the Constitution.[5] This is a negative definition of welfare insofar as it impacts on the child. The focus is not on actively promoting the welfare interests of the child, but merely with ensuring

that these are not seriously impaired. This approach derives from the wording of Articles 41 and 42 of the Constitution. It could therefore be argued that the current constitutional position in Ireland embodies a 'seen but not heard' approach to the concept of 'children's rights'.

CURRENT STATE OBLIGATIONS

32 The United Nations Committee on the Rights of the Child in its concluding observations on Ireland's implementation of the UN Convention on the Rights of the Child 1989 was critical of this approach to children's rights. The Committee held that the implementation of the recommendations of the Report of the Constitution Review Group[6] be accelerated which, it stated, would reinforce 'the status of the child as a full subject of rights'. The report of the Constitution Review Group recommended, *inter alia*, in 1996 that an express statement of identified rights of children be incorporated into the Constitution. Further, the Kilkenny Incest Investigation Committee[7] stated:

> We feel that the very high emphasis on the rights of the family in the Constitution may consciously or unconsciously be interpreted as giving a higher value to the rights of the parents than to the rights of children.

In light of this, the Committee therefore recommended:

> ... that consideration be given by the government to the amendment of Articles 41 and 42 of the Constitution so as to include a statement of the constitutional rights of children.

RECENT DEVELOPMENTS

33 Recently, however, the Supreme Court has veered away from enumerating children's rights by holding that the government was responsible for articulating the rights of children. This approach can be seen in four landmark judgments of the Supreme Court in the past four years on children's rights: *North Western Health Board v H.W. and C.W;*[8] *Sinnott v Minister for Education and Others;*[9] *T.D. v Minister for Education and Others;*[10] *Lobe and Osayande v Minister for Justice, Equality and Law Reform.*[11]

34 They concern the children in society who are most in need; children who are dependent on the state for their education, health, welfare and citizenship. Such children now inhabit a legal limbo.

35 In summary, the foregoing judgments signpost a shift to conservatism by the Supreme Court both legally and in terms of social policy.[12] That said, the judgments could also indicate a desire on the part of the Supreme Court to respect the principle of the doctrine of the separation of powers. Whatever interpretation one affords to the recent approach of the Supreme Court regarding children's rights, there is a gap in the current legislative framework where children's rights are concerned. The Supreme Court has, as previously outlined, recognised that the Constitution protects children's rights. That said, if the state fails to protect the rights of individual children, and the Supreme Court refuses to step in as guardians of the Constitution (save in exceptional circumstances), to uphold such rights, on whom does this duty now fall?

UNITED NATIONS CONVENTION ON THE RIGHTS OF THE CHILD 1989

36 Ireland ratified the United Nations Convention on the Rights of the Child 1989 without reservation on September 21, 1992. By virtue of Ireland's dualist nature, the provisions do not form part of the domestic law. The Convention gives recognition to children's rights in its widest sense. Article 3 states, *inter alia*:

> (1) In all actions concerning children, whether undertaken by public or private social welfare institutions, courts of law, administrative authorities or legislative bodies, the best interest of the child shall be a primary consideration.

> (2) State parties undertake to ensure the child such protection and care as is necessary for his or her well being, taking into account the rights and duties of his or her parents, legal guardians, or other individuals legally responsible for him or her, and, to this end, shall take all appropriate legislative and administrative measures.

37 While this article requires only that the children's interests be a primary consideration, not the primary consideration, it must also be read alongside the series of explicit rights which the Convention protects.

REPRESENTATION OF CHILDREN

38 Article 12 of the UNCRC 1989 provides for the separate representation of children:

> (1) State parties shall assure to the child who is capable of forming his or her own views the right to express those views freely in all matters affecting the child, the views of the child being given due weight in accordance with the age and maturity of the child.

> (2) For this purpose, the child shall in particular be provided the opportunity to be heard in any judicial and administrative proceedings affecting the child, either directly, or through a representative or an appropriate body, in a manner consistent with the procedural rules of national law.

39 Article 9 of the UNCRC provides for participation by children in separation and divorce processes:

> (1) State parties shall ensure that a child shall not be separated from his or her parents against their will, except when competent authorities subject to judicial

review determine, in accordance with applicable law and procedures, that such separation in necessary for the best interests of the child. Such determination may be necessary in a particular case as such as one involving abuse or neglect of the child by the parents, or one where parents are living separately and a decision must be made as to the child's place of residence.

40 Taking cognisance of the foregoing rights, and in particular Article 12, it is clear that the UNCRC 1989 is soundly based on a defensible concept of children's rights. The law in Ireland, however, falls far short of such a concept.

EUROPEAN CONVENTION ON THE EXERCISE OF CHILDREN'S RIGHTS 1996

41 Ireland has signed but not ratified the European Convention on the Exercise of Children's Rights 1996.[13] Article 1(1) of the Convention provides that the object of the Convention is to:

> Promote [children's] rights, to grant them procedural rights and to facilitate the exercise of these rights by ensuring that children are themselves or through other persons or bodies, informed and allowed to participate in proceedings affecting them before a judicial authority.

42 In some respects, the 1996 Convention is of more limited application than its 1989 counterpart. It focuses predominantly on procedural rather than substantive rights, the emphasis being on such matters as the right of children to participate in, and access information about, cases that concern their welfare. For example, Article 5 of the 1996 Convention states:

> Parties shall consider granting children additional procedural rights in relation to proceedings before a judicial authority offering them, in particular:
> (a) the right to apply to be assisted by an appropriate person of their choice in order to help them express their views
> (b) the right to apply themselves, or through other persons or bodies, for the appointment of a separate representative, in appropriate cases a lawyer
> (c) the right to appoint their own representative
> (d) the right to exercise some or all of the rights of parties to such proceedings.

43 Clearly these provisions are aimed primarily at children of sufficient age and maturity to understand the matters under scrutiny. In appropriate cases, a child should have a person to help the expression of his or her views. Articles 4 and 9 of the European Convention on the Exercise of Children's Rights provide for the appointment of such a special representative. The absence of a facility for children in Ireland to support and articulate their views, particularly where a case is settled in advance of a hearing, is a serious problem.

EUROPEAN CONVENTION ON HUMAN RIGHTS AND FUNDAMENTAL FREEDOMS

44 In discussing our obligations towards children, the relevant provisions of the European Convention on Human Rights and Fundamental Freedoms (ECHR) should be noted. The civil and political rights enshrined in the ECHR emphasise individual and familial freedom and autonomy and protection from excessive state interference. The ECHR is not child focused as such in the same way as the United Nations Convention on the Rights of the Child 1989. It does not recognise children as a special group requiring particular protection, because of their inherent vulnerability in a world of adults. The rights contained in the ECHR are as available to children as to adults; however, there is increasing awareness that the ECHR has potential as an important resource in the promotion of child rights. Whilst only a small body of ECHR case law deals with cases from the perspective of the child, it has been utilised very effectively to protect children within their family life with their parents.

45 The incorporation of the ECHR into Irish law has been by way of statute. As a result it is now possible to take proceedings in the Irish courts alleging a breach of the ECHR. Previously, to assert any rights under the ECHR, an injured party had first to exhaust all domestic remedies before bringing the case to the European Court of Human Rights (ECt.HR) in Strasbourg with the costs and delays associated with that process.

46 There is little doubt that inconsistencies will arise between Irish child law and practice and the standards required by the ECHR. The indirect or interpretative mode of incorporation preserves the domestic primacy of the Constitution.[14] Consequently, Article 41 of the Constitution will continue to act as an impediment to the effective implementation of the legal entitlements of children under the ECHR. More specifically, incorporation of the ECHR at sub-constitutional level will ensure that child rights remain subordinate to parental rights.

The Law Society recommends an amendment to the Constitution to grant express rights to children.

NON-IMPLEMENTATION OF LEGISLATION

47 While the Society welcomes the review of the Constitution it would like to draw attention to the non-implementation of key statutory provisions in the family law area. In particular, the non-implementation of section 28 of the Guardianship of Infants Act, 1964 is to be noted. This section was introduced in the Children Act, 1997 but has not yet commenced. This is in clear breach of obligations under international instruments to which the state is a party and has led to a chaotic system for the representation of children in divorce and separation cases.

The Society does not believe that the paramountcy of the family in Article 41 should be compromised.

48 Marriage is an institution of great antiquity, an association of persons encountered in almost every society in almost every age. It presupposes a union unlike any other, a coming together of persons in a relationship of some considerable intimacy and profundity. In law, it is generally acknowledged that marriage is not merely a contract, but rather the inception of 'a unique and very special life-long relationship'[15] and thus an event that imparts an entirely new legal status on the parties thereto. From this status flows a whole host of legal rights, privileges and duties from which persons who are not married are generally precluded.

49 The enormous symbolic power of marriage cannot be overlooked, even in a strictly legal text. O'Donovan speaks evocatively of '... the sacred character of marriage [that] calls on a past, understood and shared tradition and on an eternal future, a perpetuity'. The Chief Justice of the Family Law Court of Australia remarks in a similar vein that 'the concept of 'marriage' carries a meaning powerfully infused with tradition, history and religion even more so than the concept of 'family''. Marriage imparts not just a legal, but also a social and cultural, status traditionally valued by most societies. Even in modern times, marriage is widely viewed as a social and cultural pinnacle to which all should aspire. As Herma Hill Kay notes, even those who 'resist the regimentation that marriage entails ... accept it as a sort of "gold standard" that signifies the desire for deep and permanent commitment'. It is for this reason that the Law Society has taken the view that the state should continue to reflect the special position of marriage in Article 41 of its fundamental law.

50 Despite its widespread currency, marriage as a universal concept defies easy definition. The essential features of marriage can vary widely from age to age and from culture to culture.

51 Even in the relative homogeneity of the modern western world, the boundaries of marriage are the subject of great ideological and political debate. In *Hyde v Hyde and Woodmansee*,[16] Lord Penzance defined marriage as understood in the Christian world as 'the voluntary union for life of one man and one woman to the exclusion of all others'.[17] It is clear, nonetheless, that civil marriage in this jurisdiction need no longer be 'for life'. Since the introduction of divorce in 1997, marriages may now be terminated in the lifetime of both parties (provided certain stipulated conditions are met).[18] Nor can it be taken for granted that marriage will be for all time a union of 'one man and one woman', a self-evidently heterosexual union. A growing number of European jurisdictions (and now some North American jurisdictions) allow two persons of the same sex to enter into 'registered partnerships' that in terms of their legal consequences differ little from marriage.

Having regard to the foregoing international approaches to providing rights for cohabitees, the Society recommends that changes in family structures should be reflected in legislation rather than in the Constitution.

52 Legislation for new family forms has evolved in the context of a gradual but significant shift away from marriage as an exclusive basis for family life. While marriage retains much popularity as a phenomenon, attitudes to marriage, at least in the industrialised world, have changed considerably over the past four decades.

53 Europe, in particular, has witnessed a proliferation of couples cohabiting outside wedlock and of children being born to such unions. The stigma formerly attached to such relationships is now largely a thing of the past and in some jurisdictions these living patterns are gradually being accorded full legal recognition, sometimes, as in Sweden, on a virtual par with marriage.[19] Family law in general has seen a corresponding shift in analytical emphasis from the relationship between husband and wife, to that between parent and child, itself indicative of the gradual dilution of the significance of marriage, a theme to which this submission will return.[20]

54 In the face of international developments, Irish law has remained remarkably steadfast. Marriage continues to enjoy a unique and privileged position. The growing ranks of family groupings existing outside the boundaries of marriage by contrast attract virtually no legal recognition for their existence. While children born outside marriage are now treated for most purposes as having the same rights and privileges as children born of married parents,[21] their unmarried parents for legal purposes are largely regarded as strangers in relation to each other. It remains to be seen how long Ireland can hold out against the argument that couples in like situations, married or unmarried, should be treated in a like manner. There are some signs of change, for example, in the Domestic Violence Act, 1996,[22] which extends the right to seek barring and safety orders to parties not married to each other. Even the latter-mentioned legislation, however, discriminates between married and unmarried persons, and it would seem between homosexual and heterosexual cohabitants.[23] In other areas reform has been more pronounced. For instance the Employment Equality Acts 1998 to 2004[24] render unlawful most forms of discrimination in the workplace on the grounds of marital status and parental status; the Equal Status Acts 2000 to 2004 do likewise in relation to the sale of goods and supply of services.[25]

55 For a long time Ireland remained almost unique in Europe in that, once validly married, the parties to a marriage could not dissolve their marriage by means of divorce. Before 1997, the Irish courts had no jurisdiction to grant a dissolution of marriage. Prior to 1922, a person who wished to divorce could petition the UK

parliament with a view to obtaining a private bill terminating the marriage. Even this cumbersome facility was abolished in 1922 when the new Irish Free State Oireachtas suspended this residual power to grant a divorce. This was copper-fastened in 1937 with the enactment of the Constitution of that year, Article 41.3.2° of which ordained that 'no law shall be enacted providing for the grant of a dissolution of marriage'. The Fifteenth Amendment of the Constitution Act, 1995 removed this impediment but it was not until January 1997 that the first divorce was actually granted and then only on the basis of the Constitution itself.[26] Legislation for divorce, which was passed in November 1996 came into force the following February.[27]

56 In the intervening years, parties wishing legally to escape the consequences of an unhappy marriage had to rely largely on the nullity jurisdiction of the Irish courts.

THE CONSTITUTIONAL RIGHT TO MARRY

57 It is well established in the US jurisdiction that the Constitution affords a right to marry.[28] In *Loving v Virginia*[29] a statute prohibiting the marriage of persons of different colour was struck down partly on the ground that it was repugnant to this principle. Similarly, in *Zablocki v Redhail*[30] the US Supreme Court declared invalid a Wisconsin law that restricted the right to marry in cases where one party to the marriage had not fulfilled his financial obligations towards any children he may have fathered prior to the contemplated marriage.

58 The possibility of a constitutional right to marry has received comparatively little attention in Ireland. The right to marry is an unenumerated constitutional right protected by Article 40.3 of the Constitution.[31] It seems to have been first invoked in *Donovan v Minister for Justice*[32] although the judgment is most unsatisfactory on the point. In that case, Kingsmill Moore J. expressed the opinion that there was nothing 'unconstitutional or improper'[33] in a provision that required members of the Garda Síochána to seek the permission of the Garda Commissioner before marrying. Where such permission was not forthcoming, the rules of the Gardaí required the officer in question to desist from marrying. As a matter of marriage law, there was nothing to stop an officer from marrying without permission. The High Court judge seems to have concluded as a result, that there was no bar to marriage. The provision 'could not be attacked as an absolute prohibition of marriage, for persons intending to join the force could make themselves aware of the section before joining, or they could resign if the provision became embarrassing or otherwise'.[34]

59 The only other situation in which the point appears to have arisen is noted in Hogan and Whyte, *Kelly: The Irish Constitution* referring to *The Irish Times*, January 25, 1978. It appears that proceedings were commenced in 1976 in respect of a male and female prisoner who, while incarcerated in separate prisons, wished to marry. The state initially opposed the request, but it appears eventually relented, allowing the parties to marry.

60 The question of a right to marry has arisen quite frequently in other jurisdictions specifically in relation to the present exclusion from marriage of couples of the same sex.

As previously stated the Society recommends no constitutional change in this area. It does, however, urge the government to introduce legislation granting rights to cohabitees without delay, in order to reflect in legislation the increasing existence of such units; the Society also recommends a greater emphasis on family support in the family law system.

THE SPECIAL POSITION OF MARRIAGE

61 As noted above, Article 41.3.1° requires the state to '... guard with special care the institution of marriage ... and to protect it against attack'. This special position has, on occasion, been successfully invoked to justify legislative discrimination against unmarried persons and their children. Prior to 1988 the latter were, in particular, excluded from the categories of persons entitled to succeed to the estate of a deceased parent who had died without making a will (intestate). In *O'B v S*[35] the defendant was the natural child of a man and woman who were not married to each other. In 1975, her father died without leaving a will. The defendant claimed that she was entitled as daughter of the deceased to a share of his estate. The Supreme Court ruled that the Succession Act, 1965[36] was, at that time, restricted in its application so that only children born to parents who were married to each other were entitled to succeed to a parent's estate on intestacy. While the Court did acknowledge that this was, at face value, a denial of the guarantee of equality contained in Article 40.1 of the Constitution, it nevertheless concluded that such unequal treatment was permitted by Article 41.1 and Article 41.3 thereof. The state's duty to protect the institution of marriage justified the decision of the Oireachtas to place the family based on marriage in ' a position superior to that of an unmarried union'.[37]

62 The courts have been correspondingly reluctant, even in recent years, to recognise cohabitation and separation agreements between parties who are unmarried. The most notable example was in *Ennis v Butterly*.[38] In that case, Kelly J. refused to award damages for what was alleged to have been a breach of an implied contract of cohabitation between the parties. At least part of the rationale for Kelly J.'s ruling rested on the special position of marriage in Article 41. Even assuming that there was a contract between the parties, Kelly J. effectively argued that the constitutional position of marriage would be undermined if such a cohabitation contract were to be enforced.

63 The comments of Kinlen J. in *EH v JM*[39] appear to support this perspective. In that case, an unmarried couple with two children had entered into a separation agreement in 1996. In the course of his judgment, however, Kinlen J. seemed to suggest that he would only consider the agreement insofar as it related to the upbringing of the children. As unmarried persons, he remarked, the parties were 'free agents' who owed no duty to each other. His deliberations, consequently, would be confined to considering the parties' duties *vis-à-vis* their children.

64 While the Status of Children Act, 1987[40] abolished for most legal purposes the distinction between legitimate and illegitimate children, it is evident that the outstanding difference of treatment as between married and unmarried couples is well within constitutional limits. It is interesting to consider whether the special position of marriage merely allows such divergent treatment or whether it, in fact, mandates it. Would Article 41 preclude the state from treating unmarried persons for certain purposes as if they were married? Would it be possible to eliminate all legal distinctions between married and unmarried persons without upsetting the privileged status of the marital union? The extension of such rights, arguably, would in no way diminish the rights accorded to married persons, although it is likely that a court may conclude that it would deny marriage its special status, and may thus amount to an unconstitutional conferral of legal rights.

65 What is certainly clear is that measures that actively penalise the marital state are unconstitutional. *Murphy v Attorney General*[41] concerned tax provisions (no longer in force) that placed married couples at a distinct fiscal disadvantage as compared to their unmarried counterparts. Married couples were treated for the purposes of tax law as if they were one person. Where two unmarried persons living together would receive separate allowances and benefits, two married persons were only entitled to one set of allowances and benefits between them. The effective result of this was that a married couple, where both husband and wife were working, would probably pay more in tax than a similarly situated unmarried couple. This, in the opinion of the Supreme Court, was a breach of the constitutional guarantee to guard with special care the institution of marriage, and thus the measures were deemed null and void. For fiscal reasons, however, the Court limited the application of the judgment to cases pending before the courts at the time of their judgment.[42] In *Muckely v Attorney General*[43] however, the court ruled that measures attempting to collect unpaid tax owing from the years prior to 1982 could not require late taxpayers to pay the full amount of tax that would have been payable on the basis of the legislation struck down in *Murphy*.

66 A similar conclusion was reached in *Greene v Minister for Agriculture*[44] where means-testing criteria for the allocation of agricultural aid were found to have imposed an unfair disadvantage on married couples. The provisions in question aggregated the income of both spouses for the purpose of determining eligibility for European Union farm aid. This was found to have imposed on married couples living together a burden substantially different from that placed on unmarried couples in like circumstances. Following *Murphy v Attorney General*[45] Murphy J. concluded that the impugned provisions amounted to a breach of the pledge contained in Article 41.3.1°. In a similar vein, Barrington J., in *Hyland v Minister for Social Welfare*[46] struck down provisions of the social welfare code making it less economically advantageous for a couple to be married than single. In the course of his decision Barrington J. observed that if a married couple 'is in fact receiving less by way of social welfare payments than a couple living together outside marriage', the enjoyment by married couples of other rights, not extended to unmarried couples, is no defence to a claim that the privileged position of marriage has been subverted. Nor is it relevant to show that no person was, in fact, induced by the provisions in question to remain unmarried.[47]

67 The state is entitled nonetheless to take into account the different living situations of different categories of parents in determining the financial aid to which persons with children are entitled. In particular, as the judgment of the Supreme Court in *MhicMhathúna v Ireland*[48] bears out, it is possible to distinguish 'between the needs and requirements of single parents and those of married parents living together and rearing a family together'. Thus, there is no attack on marriage where the state gives additional financial support to parents living alone. Far from being an attack on marriage, or an inducement to live outside the marital state, this was merely in recognition of the added difficulties and burdens placed on single parents.

68 Before leaving the present issue, it is worth noting the individualisation of taxation proposals contained in the budget for 2000-2001 (formally put to the Dáil in December 1999). It was effectively proposed therein that, where both parties to a marriage worked outside the home, a couple would be entitled to a higher joint tax-free allowance than where one spouse worked outside the home and the other spouse worked at home as a homemaker. These measures were possibly designed to encourage married homemakers to work outside the family home, thereby increasing the pool of available labour. Following considerable public controversy, steps were taken to dilute this proposal and restore some measure of equal treatment. It is suggested, indeed, that the original measures might well have amounted to an infringement of Article 41.2.2° of the Constitution whereby the state guarantees to 'endeavour to ensure that mothers shall not be obliged by economic necessity to engage in labour' outside the home. Arguably, the measure in question amounted to

an incentive rather than a situation of 'economic necessity' although, it might equally be said that the proposals infringe the spirit of Article 41.2.2° by encouraging and privileging double income families. As a matter of tax equity alone, it might be argued that the government confused its priorities, it being arguable that many single income families are more in need of such advantageous tax provisions, than their double income counterparts.

69 On balance, the Society is of the view that the special position of marriage recognised by the Constitution should be maintained.

70 However, the Society feels that Article 41.2.1 should be removed from the Constitution or altered. One way of dealing with this matter would be simply to amend this Article to read as follows 'In particular, the state recognises that by his/her life within the home, a parent gives to the state a support without which the common good cannot be achieved'. Alternatively, and the Society's preferred approach, is that Article 41.2.1 should be removed. The Society does not see any reason why 'life within the home' should have a greater value than life outside the home.

NULLITY

71 A report published by the Law Society of Ireland's Law Reform Committee in 2001 entitled *Nullity of Marriage: The case for reform* explored the anomalies and injustices arising from the current law of nullity of marriage, and made recommendations for reform. Two aspects of nullity law in particular give rise to difficulty and injustice. The first relates to the unavailability of ancillary relief on the granting of a nullity decree. This has the potential to give rise to great injustice in cases where a financially weaker spouse has no rights arising out of a relationship which may have lasted many years, have resulted in children, and into which the spouse may have entered with all good faith. The report recommended that limited ancillary relief on an equitable basis should be available as part of nullity decrees. It further proposed that the availability of discretionary ancillary relief remedies, similar to (though more limited than) those available on divorce or separation, would assist in resolving financial and other problems arising from past transactions entered into on the basis that there was a valid marriage.

72 The second major issue identified by the report concerned the grounds for nullity of marriage. Depending on the facts of a particular case, the uncertainty arising from the concept of a voidable marriage can make it impossible to advise people as to their status with any certainty. The ground of 'inability to enter and sustain a marital relationship' requires court adjudication to establish the existence or otherwise of a valid marriage, and the resulting judgment, that one party at least is inadequate, may be hurtful and stigmatising. This is also the case with impotence, the

other ground on which a marriage may be voidable. With the availability of the remedy of no-fault divorce, the circumstances which gave rise to these grounds have largely disappeared. The report recommended that the concept of a voidable marriage should be abolished and the grounds which make a marriage voidable, both impotence and the inability to enter and sustain a normal marital relationship, should be abolished. It recommended that cases which could be pleaded on those grounds should instead be pleaded under the divorce jurisdiction.

73 The Law Reform Committee report was preceded by a number of other studies, in which reform of the law was repeatedly advocated. Relevant reports include:

The Office of the Attorney General: *The Law of Nullity in Ireland*, The Stationery Office, 1976

The Law Reform Commission: *The law relating to the age of majority, the age for marriage and some connected subjects* – working paper 1977

The Law Reform Commission: *The age of majority*, no. 5, 1983

The Law Reform Commission: *The law of nullity*, no. 9, 1984

The Joint Oireachtas Committee on Marriage Breakdown: *Report*, 1985

The Department of Justice: *White paper on Marriage Breakdown, Review and Proposed Changes*, 1992

The Second Commission on the Status of Women: *Report*, 1993

The Constitution Review Group: *Report*, 1996

74 All of these reports were consistent in calling for statutory reform in this area. The courts also have called for reform and have very clearly pointed up the need for statutory reform in this difficult and complex area.[49] Thus far, however, the only aspects of legislative reform which have concentrated upon the formalities of marriage are: the Marriages Act, 1972; the Age of Majority Act, 1985; the Family Law Act, 1995; the Family Law (Miscellaneous Provisions) Act, 1997; and the Civil Registration Act, 2004.

The Constitution has been influential in relation to both of the above aspects of nullity law.

THE CONSTITUTIONAL CONTEXT

Ancillary relief

75 The Family Law Bill which was enacted as the Family Law Act, 1995 originally provided for discretionary ancillary relief for parties to annulled marriages. Under pressure to achieve enactment because of the forthcoming divorce referendum, those provisions were withdrawn by the government at report stage because of concerns about their constitutionality.

Article 41 is the main provision of the Constitution dealing with the family, and Article 41.3.1° requires the state 'to guard with special care the institution of marriage, on which the Family is founded, and to protect it against attack'. It was feared that by giving entitlements, similar to those available to married persons, to parties whose marriages had been annulled the state could be accused of equating unmarried (annulled) relationships with marriages, and thereby undermining the special position of marriage. The government of the time recognised the need for the provision of ancillary relief to nullity decrees, but stated its resolve to make this provision in separate legislation. To date, no such legislation has been published.

76 It is unclear whether the granting of discretionary relief in relation to nullity decrees would in fact be considered to be unconstitutional. In *Ennis v Butterly* [1997] 1 ILRM 28, Kelly J. stated that:

> Given the special place of marriage in the family under the Irish Constitution . . . the public policy of this state ordains that non-marital cohabitation does not amount and cannot have the same constitutional status as marriage.

77 The judge further held that cohabitation contracts or agreements will not be enforced under Irish law. It has been argued, however, that the ground for this decision – that it would be contrary to the pledge in the Constitution to guard the institution of marriage against attack – involves an unreasonably conservative interpretation of the Constitution and is inconsistent with the Supreme Court's more realistic attitude to unmarried cohabitation in *WO'R v EH* [1996] 2 IR 248.[50]

78 The Constitution Review Group in their 1996 Report recommended changes to Article 41 of the Constitution, to recognise that family formations also exist outside marriage. It recommended that the revised article should explicitly state that the protection of marriage in the article should not prevent the Oireachtas from legislating for the benefit of non-marital relationships and the parties thereto.

79 The caselaw of the European Court of Human Rights under the European Convention on Human Rights and Fundamental Freedoms (ECHR), now given effect in Irish law by the European Convention on Human Rights Act, 2003, gives much greater recognition to relationships outside marriage as 'family life'.[51] This is likely to influence the future interpretation of Irish law under section 2 of that Act, which requires legislation and rules of law to be interpreted in accordance with the Convention if possible.

80 In its consultation paper on the Rights and Duties of Cohabitees (April 2004), the Law Reform Commission stated as follows:

> The Commission is of the view that the law as it stands allows the Oireachtas to legislate in respect of the non-marital family insofar as it does not place such rela-

tionships in a more favourable position than the marital family. The Commission has reached this conclusion having considered a number of cases in which married couples have challenged some legal or administrative arrangement on the basis that it gives an advantage to cohabitees as compared with married couples.[52]

81 The Commission concluded that the line of authority (*Murphy v AG* [1982] IR 241, *Hyland v Minister for Social Welfare* [1989] IR 624, *Green v Minister for Agriculture* [1990] 2 IR 17 and *MacMathúna v Ireland* [1989] IR 504) 'would not prevent the legislature increasing the rights of cohabitees to bring them on a par with those of a married couple, as it only appears to prevent married couples being treated less favourably than cohabiting couples are'.

82 It therefore seems unlikely that legislative provision for ancillary relief related to nullity decrees would be unconstitutional, even without amendment to Article 41. The recommendation of the Law Society's Law Reform Committee was made on that basis. Clearly, however, the clarification of this point by constitutional amendment as recommended by the Constitution Review Group would remove any doubts on the matter.

VOIDABLE MARRIAGES

83 The unavailability of divorce prior to the divorce referendum in 1995 caused parties to broken marriages to look to the nullity jurisdiction for a remedy to regularise their status. This followed developments at the time in the Roman Catholic Church, which was granting annulments on the basis of mental and emotional incapacity to be a party to a marriage, and a greater understanding of the psychological element of impotence. In *RSJ v JSJ* [1982] ILRM 263 and *D v C* [1984] ILRM 173 the applicants argued for the extension of the ground of impotence to cover mental illness or disability, amounting to an inability to enter into and sustain a normal marital relationship. Initially limited to cases of recognised psychiatric illness or disability, in later cases wider grounds were accepted including lack of emotional maturity (*BD v MC (orse MD)* unrep, Barrington J., HC, 27 March 1987), personality disorder (*W (C) v C* [1989] IR 696) and sexual orientation (*UF (orse C) v JC* [1991] 2 IR 330).

84 It is likely that the extension of impotence as a ground for nullity of marriage to cover cases of psychological, mental and emotional incapacity by judicial activism would not have occurred in the period from 1982 if the remedy of divorce had been available at that time. Alan Shatter has written:

> Over the past twenty years the law of nullity has been radically developed and expanded by a creative and humane judiciary. The developments that have occurred have largely been attributed by the judiciary to a greater understanding of sexuality and human affairs and modern advances in psychiatry and psychology. It

is reasonable to also regard recent development of the law as a compassionate judicial response to the human consequences for couples of being constitutionality imprisoned for life by the divorce prohibition in failed marriages that from the outset had little chance of success.[53]

85 The amendment of the Constitution as a result of the divorce referendum and the introduction of divorce in the Family Law (Divorce) Act, 1996 have removed one major rationale for the preservation of the concept of voidable marriages, together with the traditional and newly developed grounds giving rise to voidability.

CLEAN BREAK DIVORCE

86 One consequence of abolishing the concept of voidable marriages and the grounds of impotence and inability to enter and sustain a marital relationship is that persons availing of the alternative divorce remedy will no longer be able to benefit from a 'clean break', that is, a final financial settlement.[54] It seems unjust that a potential lifelong obligation should survive a marriage, often brief, which obviously was doomed from the start.

The Society would therefore see the benefit of introducing amending legislation to allow for clean break divorce in appropriate circumstances, to be potentially available to all divorcing couples. There is no constitutional impediment to such a legislative amendment.

SAME-SEX PARTIES

87 Although there is as yet no Irish case or legislation directly on the point, it is generally understood that a valid marriage may only be contracted between parties who are respectively male and female. The definition of marriage referred to in *Hyde v. Hyde and Woodmansee*[55] alludes to the presence of 'one man and one woman' in marriage as understood in Christendom. In *Corbett v Corbett (otherwise Ashley)*[56] Ormrod J. observed that 'sex is clearly an essential determinant of the relationship called marriage because it is and always has been recognised as the union of man and woman. It is the institution on which the family is built, and in which the capacity for natural heterosexual intercourse is an essential element.' Arguably, such capacity is, in fact, not necessary.

88 In *Talbot (Poyntz) v Talbot*[57] the petitioner, a widow, had gone through a ceremony of marriage with a person whom she believed (honestly but incorrectly) to be male. In fact, the groom was, unbeknownst to the petitioner, a female. Ormrod J. granted a decree of nullity on the ground that there had 'plainly [been] no marriage'.

89 The Society notes that the prohibition on same-sex marriage is an issue of considerable social and political controversy. The constitutionality of the prohibition has been tested, usually without success, in several United States jurisdictions. The Supreme Court of Minnesota in *Baker v Nelson*[58] and the US Supreme Court at 409 US 810 (1971) refused to recognise the apparent marriage of two men, noting that 'the institution of marriage as a union of man and woman uniquely involving the procreation and rearing of children within a family is as old as the book of Genesis'. In fact, a marriage between persons of opposite sex will be valid notwithstanding the parties' inability to procreate. Subsequent challenges in Kentucky and Washington (*Singer v Hara*[59] and *Jones v Halahan*[60]) respectively met a similar fate.[61] On November 2 2004, eleven states (Arkansas, Georgia, Kentucky, Michigan, Mississippi, Montana, North Dakota, Ohio, Oklahoma, Oregon, Utah) passed constitutional amendments defining marriage as between one man and one woman, joining six states that have similar constitutional provisions (Alaska, Hawaii, Louisiana, Missouri, Nebraska, Nevada). In the meantime, seven Canadian jurisdictions (British Columbia, Ontario, Quebec, Manitoba, Nova Scotia, Yukon Territory, Saskatchewan) recognise same-sex marriage, creating questions of comity in the United States. New York State's public employees pension fund has indicated it will recognise Canadian same-sex marriages. The courts in Hawaii, however, have ruled in *Baehr v Lewin*[62] that the prohibition on same-sex marriage amounts to an impermissible discrimination based on suspect classification of sex.[63]

90 Several European and North American jurisdictions have introduced legislation that extends to couples of the same sex, upon registration of their relationships, the rights, privileges and duties normally reserved only to married couples. For most purposes such couples are treated as 'married', and rights and obligations attach to their relationship as if they were husband and wife. The first such legislation was passed in Denmark in 1989[64] but Belgium, Norway, Sweden, Finland, Iceland, British Columbia and Vermont have followed suit in quick succession.

91 In September 2000, the Dutch took one step further, eliminating entirely the bar on marriage between persons of the same sex in the Opening up of Marriage Act, 2000.[65] The key difference between this and the aforementioned changes is that whereas other jurisdictions allow the recognition of same-sex unions by means of 'marriage-like' institutions ('registered partnerships', 'civil unions' and so forth), the Netherlands simply dropped the requirement that persons who marry in that state be of opposite sex.

92 This ostensibly simple procedural step may yet have far-ranging implications for the recognition of Dutch marriages throughout the rest of the European Union. There is at least an argument that such marriages should not be recognised as they are not, to paraphrase Lord Penzance *in Hyde v. Hyde*[66], marriages 'as understood in Christendom'. The flip side of

this contention, however, is that the non-recognition of such unions might potentially offend the principle of free movement of persons contained in the European Union and Community treaties. Non-recognition may be seen as an effective barrier to the free movement of persons between EU member states, effectively deterring Dutch nationals in such unions from working beyond the Dutch border.

Consequently, the Society believes that legislation should be introduced facilitating registered partnership agreements, but does not see the need to change our fundamental law.[67] *In summary, the Law Society endorses the recommendations of the Law Reform Commission in its recent Consultation paper* Rights and Duties of Cohabitees.

SUMMARY OF RECOMMENDATIONS

1 The Society recommends an amendment to the Constitution to grant express rights to children.

2 The Society recommends that the rights of cohabitees should be reflected in legislation rather than in the Constitution. It believes that legislation should be introduced facilitating registered partnership agreements, but does not see the need to change our fundamental law. In summary, the Law Society endorses the recommendations of the Law Reform Commission in its recent Consultation paper *Rights and Duties of Cohabitees*.

3 The Society also recommends that the Government introduce legislation granting rights to cohabitees without delay, in order to reflect in legislation the increasing existence of cohabiting arrangements.

4 The Society recommends a greater emphasis on family support in the family law system. Steps have been taken towards improving the family law system. For example, the need for some form of national machinery to advance the development of support services has, in part, been met by the Family Support Agency. A more tangible link between the court system and support services should also be created, as in New Zealand.

5 The Society is of the view that the special position of marriage recognised by the Constitution should be maintained.

6 The Society believes that Article 41.2.1 should be removed from the Constitution or altered. One way of dealing with this matter would be simply to amend this article to read as follows: 'In particular, the state recognises that by his or her life within the home, a parent gives to the state a support without which the common good cannot be achieved.' Alternatively, and the Society's preferred approach, is that Article 41.2.1 should be removed. The Society does not see any reason why 'life within the home'

should have a greater value than life outside the home.

7 The Society would see the benefit of introducing amending legislation to allow for clean break divorce in appropriate circumstances, to be potentially available to all divorcing couples. There is no constitutional impediment to such a legislative amendment.

8 While the Society welcomes the review of the Constitution it would like to draw attention to the non-implementation of key statutory provisions in the family law area. In particular, the non-implementation of section 28 of the Guardianship of Infants Act, 1964 is to be noted. This section was introduced in the Children Act, 1997 but has not yet commenced. This is in clear breach of obligations under international instruments to which the State is a party and has led to a chaotic system for the representation of children in divorce and separation cases.

Notes

1 Daly, M., *Families and Family Life in Ireland: Challenges for the Future*
2 See generally Shannon, G., *Child Law* (Thomson Round Hall, 2004).
3 [1985] I.L.R.M. 542 at 547.
4 See, for example, ReJH (An Infant) [1985] I.R. 375 *and North Western Health Board v HW and CW* [2001] 3 I.R. 635.
5 *North Western Health Board v HW and CW* [2001] 3 I.R. 622. See, however, *Southern Health Board v CH* [1996] 1 IR. 231, where O'Flaherty J. observed, in a case concerning the admissibility of a video-taped interview containing allegations of parental abuse, that: 'it is easy to comprehend that the child's welfare must always be of far graver concern to the court. We must, as judges, always harken to the constitutional command which mandates, as prime consideration, the interests of the child in any legal proceedings'.
6 Constitution Review Group, Report of the Constitution Review Group (Stationery Office, 1996).
7 Kilkenny Incest Investigation Report presented to Mr Brendan Howlin TD, Minister for Health by South Eastern Health Board (Stationery Office, May 1993).
8 [2001] 3 I.R. 622.
9 [2001] 2 I.R. 598.
10 [2001] 4 I.R. 259.
11 [2003] 1 I.R. 1.
12 See, however, the recent judgment of Finlay-Geoghegan J. in *FN and EB v CD, HD and EH,* unreported, High Court, Finlay-Geoghegan J., March 26, 2004.
13 European Treaty Series No 160. The European Convention on the Exercise of Children's Rights was opened for signature at Strasbourg on January 25, 1996, and Ireland was one of the seven signatories to the Convention on that date. It came into force on July 1, 2000, following ratification by Greece (September 11, 1997), Poland (November 28, 1997) and Slovenia (March 28, 2000) in accordance with Article 21(3) of the 1996 Convention.
14 See s.2 of the European Convention on Human Rights Act 2003.
15 *Per* Costello J. in *Murray v Ireland* [1985] I.L.R.M. 542 at 545.

16 (1886) L.R. 1 P and D 130 at 133.
17 See also Costello J. in *B v R* [1995] 1 I.L.R.M. 491 (HC) at 4795.
18 See Article 41.3.2° of Bunreacht na hÉireann 1937 and the Family Law (Divorce) Act, 1996 (No. 33 of 1996).
19 See generally 'The Death of Marriage' in *Newsweek*, January 20, 1997.
20 See Dewar, 'Policy Issues in Law and the Family' in Wilson (ed.), *Frontiers of Legal Scholarship* (Chancery Law Publishing, Chichester, 1995), Chapter 5, in particular pp. 64-67.
21 Status of Children Act, 1987 (No. 26 of 1987).
22 No. 1 of 1996.
23 See Ryan, 'Queering' the Criminal Law' (1997) 7 I.C.L.J. 38.
24 No. 21 of 1998
25 See also the extensive definition of 'family member' used in section 1 of the Non-Fatal Offences against the Person Act, 1997 (No. 26 of 1997).
26 *RC v CC* [1997] 1 I.L.R.M 401.
27 Family Law (Divorce) Act, 1996 (No. 33 of 1996).
28 See *Meyer v Nebraska* 262 US 390 (1923).
29 388 US 1 (1967).
30 434 US 374 (1978).
31 See *Ryan v AG* [1965] I.R. 294 at 313, per Kenny J. (obiter).
32 (1951) 85 I.L.T.R. 134.
33 *ibid.* at 136, col. 2.
34 *ibid.*
35 (1984) I.R. 316.
36 No. 27 of 1965.
37 *ibid.* at 334, per Walsh J.
38 (1996) 1 I.R. 426.
39 Unreported, High Court, Kinlen J., April 4, 2000.
40 (No. 26 of 1987).
41 (1982) I.R. 241.
42 It is possible that the Court overestimated the extent of the state's liability in this case. Considering the low rates of female participation in the workforce prior to the 1980s, it was perhaps unlikely that many couples would have been owed significant amounts of illegally collected tax.
43 (1986) I.L.R.M. 364.
44 (1990) I.L.R.M. 364.
45 (1982) I.R. 241.
46 (1989) I.L.R.M. 196.
47 See also *Murphy v. Attorney General (loc. cit.)*.
48 (1995) I.L.R.M. 69 at 79.
49 *N (orse K) v K* [1985] IR 733, SC, Henchy J. and *F (P) v O'M (G)* [2001] 3 IR 1, SC, McGuinness J.
50 By John Mee, *The Property Rights of Cohabitees*, (1999, Oxford, Hart Publishing) at p. 31
51 For example, *Keegan v Ireland* (1994) 18 EHRR 342
52 At 1.14
53 Shatter, *Family Law*, (4th ed. 1997, Butterworths).
54 S. 22 of the Family Law (Divorce) Act 1996.
55 (1866) L.R. 1 P and D 130 to 133.
56 (1971) P. 83 at 105.
57 111 Sol. J. 213 (1967, HC).
58 291 Minn. 310, 191 NW2d 185 (1971).
59 11 Wash. App. 247, 522 P2d (1974).
60 501 SW2d 588 (Ky 1973).
61 See also *Frances B v Mark B* 78 Misc. 2d 112, 355 NYS2dg 712 (Sup. Ct 1974) and, *per* Handler J. A.D. in *MT v JT* 335 A. 2d. 204 (1974).
62 852 P. 2d. 44 (Haw., 1993).
63 (1996) 30 F.L.Rev. 727. See Pham, 'Let's Get Married in Hawaii'. For a good overview of the debate on same-sex marriage, see Sullivan (ed.), *Same Sex Marriage: Pro and Con; a Reader* (Vintage Books/Random House, New York, 1997.
64 Registered Partnership Act 1989 (Denmark) No. 372/1989.
65 Source: Canadian Broadcast Corporation news www.cbc.ca/news/indepth/background/gayrights2.html.
66 (1860) L.R. 1 P a nd D 130 at 166.
67 See Family Law Practitioner (Round Hall 2001) Division A.

LESBIAN, GAY, BISEXUAL AND TRANSGENDER CAMPAIGN – TCD

1 HOW SHOULD THE FAMILY BE DEFINED?

In these changing times is the word 'family' really what we should be interpreting? There are so many different types of families living in Ireland now that they contradict the definition of a traditional 'nuclear family', i.e mother, father and offspring. Today we have many different types of families such as single mothers, single fathers, unmarried couples with chidren, unmarried couples without children, divorced couples with children, homosexual couples with children, and those without.

In essence, we're talking about the union of adults with the purpose of spending their life and times with each other such that they are better for being together than being apart, and with the possibility, but not the purpose, of having and raising children if that is their wish.

Article 41 of Bunreacht na hÉireann only gives protection to this in what is defined as a 'nuclear family' but as was stated above, we are living in changing times and there are now differing social norms that to the everyday person would be accepted as family. Using the word 'household' would therefore seem to be much more acceptable in defining the rights of a group of people living under the one roof.

The term 'household' is the defining phrase within the Irish language version of the Constitution. This is a matter for interpretation, not necessitating a need to alter the Constitution.

2 HOW SHOULD ONE STRIKE THE BALANCE BETWEEN THE RIGHTS OF THE FAMILY AS A UNIT AND THE RIGHTS OF INDIVIDUAL MEMBERS?

The adults in the family unit should have equal responsibilities in both law and practice. Children in the family should have their rights protected if the adults fail in their responsibilities.

Senator Norris' bill on civil unions makes provision for adults within a home in a similar way to that of traditional marriage.

Ultimately, the ideal balance is to be struck in the understanding that the rights of the family unit as a whole should not be allowed to compromise the rights of the individual in such situations where they are in conflict. That being said, the rights of the family unit ought to allow protection and well-balanced rights between all members.

3 IS IT POSSIBLE TO GIVE CONSTITUTIONAL PROTECTION TO FAMILIES OTHER THAN THOSE BASED ON MARRIAGE?

This question should be a given. As we have previously detailed, in Ireland of the twenty-first century, there is no longer a clear line to be drawn to decide that the family is one thing and not another. As the Constitution stands, if a couple are married and one of them dies the remaining partner only has to pay a minimum amount of inheritance tax on the demise of the spouse and is entitled to claim the pension (or a portion of the pension) of the deceased.

The Constitution does not preclude the giving of protection under the law to families based on something other than marriage. Through the enacting of laws which give those families protection, which is equal, but not in excess of the rights and protection afforded to families founded on marriage, the Constitution would not need to be changed.

4 SHOULD GAY COUPLES BE ALLOWED TO MARRY?

Yes. Marriage in the civil sense of the word should be open to all adults, regardless of gender, while still respecting the laws regarding familial closeness, mental competence and age.

Marriage in the religious sense should be left to the individuals' consciences and the doctrine of the churches. While the concept of marriage is inextricably linked to the religious sacrament for many people in this country, it should be made very clear, in law if necessary, that such laws would not force churches to perform ceremonies they are not comfortable with. It is important to clarify, at this juncture, the separation of church and state.

Senator David Norris has recently published his bill on civil partnerships which should be looked at very closely. Under Part 1 Section 6 of this bill, all people who enter into civil union would be afforded all the rights of marriage under the Family Law Act, 1995 and the Civil Registration Act, 2004. The other fact to note about this bill is that it will not only give rights to same-sex couples, but also to those who are cohabiting and not in some other form of legal union, irrespective of gender.

To talk of 'marriage' is an uncomfortable situation for the LGBT community as a whole, because of the religious implications we have already stated. As for the civil union of people, we can see no justifiable or reasonable excuse to exclude people based on their sexuality.

5 IS THE CONSTITUTION'S REFERENCE TO WOMAN'S 'LIFE WITHIN THE HOME' A DATED ONE THAT SHOULD BE CHANGED?

Yes, but there are many pieces of language in the Constitution that reflect the time in which they were written, and although somewhat dated and in need of change, this particular phrase does not impact on the current considerations for the extension of partnership rights and marriage to non-classical family units. As we have already detailed above, the rights of the woman within the home would be as equal as those of a man, and ought to be protected as such.

6 SHOULD THE RIGHTS OF A NATURAL MOTHER HAVE EXPRESS CONSTITUTIONAL PROTECTION?

Yes, but in so far as they do not reduce the rights of the child or those of the father. If one person's sets of rights are listed and protected, then so should the rights of every person in the family unit. As we have already stated, the family unit should not come into conflict with the rights of the individual.

7 WHAT RIGHTS SHOULD A NATURAL FATHER HAVE, AND HOW SHOULD THEY BE PROTECTED?

The rights of a biological or adoptive father should be equal to that of the mother. The idea that the mother is automatically more capable of looking after a child is a dated, unfair concept. Rather, each case ought to be judged on a case-by-case basis, to appreciate the individual merits.

8 SHOULD THE RIGHTS OF THE CHILD BE GIVEN AN EXPANDED CONSTITUTIONAL PROTECTION?

Legislation should be the first tool to clarify and extend the rights of any individual. If the rights of individuals are being held back by the Constitution then it should be changed. Through acknowledgement of the fact that children are in no position to defend themselves, the Constitution and the state should provide support and explicit protection for those not in a position to support themselves.

9 DOES THE CONSTITUTION NEED TO BE CHANGED IN VIEW OF THE UN CONVENTION ON THE RIGHTS OF THE CHILD?

If it is deemed necessary to change the Constitution, the UN Convention on the Rights of the Child ought to be an important reference point. However, it is necessary to remember the fact that Ireland has already ratified this convention, and accepted it, and is therefore subject to monitoring by the Committee on the Rights of the Child.

The human rights of children, and the standards to which all governments must aspire in realising these rights for all children, are most concisely and fully articulated in one international human rights treaty, the UN Convention on the Rights of the Child. The convention is the most universally accepted human rights instrument in history.

LESBIAN, GAY, BISEXUAL AND TRANSGENDER CAMPAIGN–USI

1 HOW SHOULD THE FAMILY BE DEFINED?

In these changing times is the word 'family' really what we should be interpreting? There are so many different types of families living in Ireland now that they contradict the definition of a traditional 'nuclear family', i.e mother, father and offspring. Today we have many different types of families such as single mothers, single fathers, unmarried couples with children, unmarried couples without children, divorced couples with children, homosexual couples with children, and those without.

In essence, we're talking about the union of adults with the purpose of spending their life and times with each other such that they are better for being together than being apart, and with the possibility, but not the purpose, of having and raising children if that is their wish.

Article 41 of Bunreacht na hÉireann only gives protection to this in what is defined as a 'nuclear family' but as was stated above, we are living in changing times and there are now differing social norms that to the everyday person would be accepted as family. Using the word 'household' would therefore seem to be much more acceptable in defining the rights of a group of people living under the one roof. The term 'household' is the defining phrase within the Irish language version of the Constitution. This is a matter for interpretation, and necessitating a need to alter the Constitution.

2 HOW SHOULD ONE STRIKE THE BALANCE BETWEEN THE RIGHTS OF THE FAMILY AS A UNIT AND THE RIGHTS OF INDIVIDUAL MEMBERS?

The adults in the family unit should have equal responsibilities in both law and practice. Children in the family should have their rights protected if the adults fail in their responsibilities.

Senator Norris' bill on civil unions makes provision for adults within a home in a similar way to that of traditional marriage.

Ultimately, the ideal balance is to be struck in the understanding that the rights of the family unit as a whole should not be allowed to compromise the rights of the individual in such situations where they are in conflict. That being said, the rights of the family unit ought to allow protection and well-balanced rights between all members.

3 IS IT POSSIBLE TO GIVE CONSTITUTIONAL PROTECTION TO FAMILIES OTHER THAN THOSE BASED ON MARRIAGE?

This question should be a given. As we have previously detailed, in Ireland of the twenty-first century, there is no longer a clear line to be drawn to decide that the family is one thing and not another. As the Constitution stands, if a couple are married and one of them dies the remaining partner only has to pay a minimum amount of inheritance tax on the demise of the spouse and is entitled to claim the pension (or a portion of the pension) of the deceased.

The Constitution does not preclude the giving of protection under the law to families based on something other than marriage. Through the enacting of laws which give those families protection, which is equal, but not in excess of the rights and protection afforded to families founded on marriage, the Constitution would not need to be changed.

4 SHOULD GAY COUPLES BE ALLOWED TO MARRY?

Yes. Marriage in the civil sense of the word should be open to all adults, regardless of gender, while still respecting the laws regarding familial closeness, mental competence and age.

Marriage in the religious sense should be left to the individuals' consciences and the doctrine of the churches. While the concept of marriage is inextricably linked to the religious sacrament for many people in this country, it should be made very clear, in law if necessary, that such laws would not force churches to perform ceremonies they are not comfortable with. It is important to clarify, at this juncture, the separation of church and state.

Senator David Norris has recently published his bill on civil parnterships which should be looked at very closely. Under Part 1 Section 6 of this bill, all people who enter into civil union would be afforded all the rights of marriage under the Family Law Act, 1995 and the Civil Registration Act, 2004. The other fact to note about this bill is that it will not only give rights to same-sex couples, but also to those who are cohabiting and not in some other form of legal union, irrespective of gender. To talk of 'marriage' is an uncomfortable situation for the LGBT community as a whole, because of the religious implications we have already stated. As for the civil union of people, we can see no justifiable or reasonable excuse to exclude people based on their sexuality.

5 IS THE CONSTITUTION'S REFERENCE TO WOMAN'S 'LIFE WITHIN THE HOME' A DATED ONE THAT SHOULD BE CHANGED?

Yes, but there are many pieces of language in the Constitution that reflect the time in which they were written, and although somewhat dated and in need of change, this particular phrase does not impact on the current considerations for the extension of partnership rights and marriage to non-classical family units. As we have already detailed above, the rights of the woman within the home would be as equal as those of a man, and ought to be protected as such.

6 SHOULD THE RIGHTS OF A NATURAL MOTHER HAVE EXPRESS CONSTITUTIONAL PROTECTION?

Yes, but in so far as they do not reduce the rights of the child or those of the father. If one person's sets of rights are listed and protected, then so should the rights of every person in the family unit. As we have already stated, the family unit should not come into conflict with the rights of the individual.

7 WHAT RIGHTS SHOULD A NATURAL FATHER HAVE, AND HOW SHOULD THEY BE PROTECTED?

The rights of a biological or adoptive father should be equal to that of the mother. The idea that the mother is automatically more capable of looking after a child is a dated, unfair concept. Rather, each case ought to be judged on a case-by-case basis, to appreciate the individual merits.

8 SHOULD THE RIGHTS OF THE CHILD BE GIVEN AN EXPANDED CONSTITUTIONAL PROTECTION?

Legislation should be the first tool to clarify and extend the rights of any individual. If the rights of individuals are being held back by the Constitution then it should be changed. Through acknowledgement of the fact that children are in no position to defend themselves, the Constitution and the state should provide support and explicit protection for those not in a position to support themselves.

9 DOES THE CONSTITUTION NEED TO BE CHANGED IN VIEW OF THE UN CONVENTION ON THE RIGHTS OF THE CHILD?

If it is deemed necessary to change the Constitution, the UN Convention on the Rights of the Child ought to be an important reference point. However, it is necessary to remember the fact that Ireland has already ratified this convention, and accepted it, and is therefore subject to monitoring by the Committee on the Rights of the Child. The human rights of children, and the standards to which all governments must aspire in realising these rights for all children, are most concisely and fully articulated in one international human rights treaty, the UN Convention on the Rights of the Child. The convention is the most universally accepted human rights instrument in history.

L.INC (LESBIANS IN CORK)

AN OVERVIEW

L.inc (Lesbians in Cork) is a community based organisation in Cork which has as its stated overall aim:

> To provide a safe, accessible and secure resource unit through which Cork lesbians, bisexual women and transgendered/transitioning women who identify as lesbian or bisexual can develop networks for the benefit of both those individuals and the lesbian/bisexual community as a whole.

Since 1999, L.inc has developed to become an organisation rooted in community development practice and principle which provides services to lesbian and bisexual women in Cork city and country, and to lesbian and bisexual women in other parts of the country who do not have access to services. To date, L.inc has put in place, through its community focused programme, a series of supportive groups/networks for lesbian and bisexual women ranging from a twice weekly drop-in service, to groups focusing specifically on the needs of lesbian parents, young lesbians and lesbians over forty.[1] L.inc is the only lesbian and bisexual women's resource centre through the lesbian, gay and bisexual community in the Republic of Ireland.[2] Its partner organisation – the Gay Men's Community Development Project in Cork – caters specifically for men in the city.

HISTORICAL CONTEXT

L.inc has emerged from recognition, by the lesbian and bisexual community in Cork, of the need for such a resource and the organisation we see in practice throughout this report has a long history based upon the work of the community itself. L.inc was constituted out of a community based voluntary organisation, Cáirde Corcaigh, in 2000. L.inc, as an organisation, has benefited significantly from the experience of lesbian and bisexual community members in Cork who have been engaged in the process of developing supportive services for lesbian and bisexual women for over twenty years.

L.INC MEMBERSHIP

Membership of L.inc totals 731; this is made up of members most often in contact by e-mail (252), postal members – L.inc mailing list subscribers – (339) and drop-in/group membership (140). This membership has a diverse profile, based on the self selected sample of drop-in/group members, that is, direct service users, surveyed for this research. It comprises the following:

- 56% of L.inc's members are aged between 26 and 45 years;
- Just over half (54%) of members live in Cork city;
- 88% of members identify as lesbian and 12% identify as bisexual;
- Just under half (48%) are cohabiting with a partner;
- Just under half (48%) have a third level qualification;
- 56% of members are parents;
- 44% of members volunteer with the organisation, with almost one third of those taking on more than one voluntary role.

FUNDING

L.inc is dependent upon a number of funding sources, the primary one being the National Development Plan Equality for Women Measure, which accounts for 83% of the organisation's financial resourcing. Other funders include the Southern Health Board (11%), Department of Social and Family Affairs (3%), the Arts Council (2%) and Cork City Partnership (0.5%). In addition, FÁS Community Services provides resourcing for two part-time Community Employment Scheme participants.

Chart 1: L.inc Funding 2003

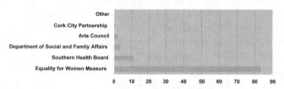

L.inc is a Munster-based community resource centre providing services/networks for women who identify as lesbian/bisexual. L.inc runs a resource centre in Cork city and has a membership of over seven hundred women and their families. L.inc is funded by the Health Service Executive and also receives funding under the Equality for Women Measure from the Department of Justice, Equality and Law Reform.

There are many issues of concern to the lesbian population that could be affected by constitutional change, among them being the recognition of partnerships, 'gay marriage', or civil unions. That a significant minority of the Irish population is prohibited from availing of the constitutional protection of marriage currently open only to heterosexual couples is unjust and indefensible. These issues, however, have been comprehensively addressed in numerous other submissions, notably those from the National Women's Council of Ireland, GLUE, GLEN, the Gay Catholic Caucus, and David Norris, all of which we support in principle, on the basis that they call for equality in law for heterosexual and homosexual couples.

Historically, and certainly since the writing of the 1937 Constitution, the only legitimate way to signal

intent to parent was through marriage (although since 1988, the natural father of a child may apply to the courts to be appointed a guardian of his child, subject to the principle of the best interests of the child[3]).

However, in 2005, with one third of births occurring outside of marriage, with separation, divorce and second unions resulting in the creation of 'blended families', and with ever-increasing use of assisted reproduction technologies, it can sometimes be difficult to establish just exactly who are the parents of any given child, and thus, who are its family? Are they those on the birth certificate? Are they those whose biological materials contributed to the child's conception? Are they those who give birth to the child? Those who are committed to parenting the child? Or are they those who actually care for and protect the child on a daily basis? These are very complex questions, and I probably cannot provide a simple answer. Although in the past marriage provided a clear-cut definition of family, it seems evident that any answer meriting serious consideration in contemporary society must position itself in the context of social and technological change, and place the welfare of the child at its heart.

L.inc is an community development organisation representing lesbian women in the south of Ireland. What L.inc wishes to communicate is the perspective of lesbian families themselves, in their own voices, talking about the issues they and their children must negotiate daily and at times of crisis.

I am researching a PhD in NUI Galway on the issues involved in lesbian family formation. My interest and commitment stems from deep personal involvement in this area. Part of the research involves interviewing lesbian couples who have or wish to have children born through assisted conception (donor insemination), or who have adopted or wish to adopt either their partner's biological child or an unrelated child. At the time of writing, the following stories describe the situations that the women I have spoken to have found themselves coping with.

I have two sons from my previous marriage who share their time between our house and their father's in a shared custody arrangement. My partner and I decided a few years ago that we would like to open up our lives to more children. We decided that we would like to foster children and after a lengthy training and assessment process, our second placement was a newborn baby boy. He will be three in June and he is still living with us. We are in the process of trying to adopt him.

As the law stands, were we to be successful in our attempts to adopt our young son, we will have to choose who is to be his 'mother'. He will have no claim on the other parent, and will not be legally related to his whole extended family on that side, grandparents, aunts, uncles and cousins, even perhaps including his two older brothers. In the meantime, we continue to foster and have so far fostered, as a couple, a total of twelve other children for the Health Board.

INTERVIEWS WITH LESBIAN COUPLES

One of the couples I have spoken to, who adopted their daughter in the UK while they were living there, were able at that time to protect her rights to the company and care of the non-adoptive parent by means of a 'residence order'. A law has now been passed making it possible for same-sex couples in the UK to adopt jointly. However, this particular couple no longer lives in the UK, the residence order is not valid in this jurisdiction, joint adoption is not permitted, so this little girl who in effect had two parents in her early life, now legally, in Ireland, has the protection of only one of them.

Gay and lesbian couples form stable and loving relationships in spite of the lack of social, legal and financial incentives to do so. They currently provide loving care and protection to children living with them from previous heterosexual relationships, children born through assisted reproduction within their own relationships, children whom they have adopted abroad, younger siblings whom they have inherited through bereavement, and foster children cared for through health boards around the country. However, their families do not receive the constitutional protection currently confined exclusively to marital families.

In families headed by lesbian couples, children's rights are not protected. A lesbian couple who, for example, decide to have a child, cannot put in place any protections in respect of the non-biological mother's rights and duties towards the child except in the eventuality of the death of the biological mother. They cannot jointly adopt the child, an option open to married heterosexual couples, nor can the biological mother appoint the co-parent as guardian during her lifetime. If the biological mother dies, the child, even if the co-parent has been named in a will as guardian, could be deprived of that parent if a close family member contests.

Although the biological mother can appoint her partner as guardian in the event of her death, this can be contested by other interested parties in court. Some of the women I have spoken to have talked about their worries for their children should anything happen to the biological mother. They express a real fear that grandparents, on the event of the death of their daughter, might, in their grief, renege on promises to respect her wishes for the child, and the child could end up in the middle of a custody battle:

> So it wouldn't matter what agreement they came to. I would still be left without Chloe. And that to me is absolutely and utterly appalling. I mean, we have raised Chloe together, Jenny is her biological mother, but I'm, I'm her mother. You know, I didn't carry her, I didn't give birth to her, but I'm her mother in every other way. Yet there is nothing in our laws that says that, you know, that I am that important to her, or that she's that important to me. So, I have no rights legally over Chloe, which I find, this is two thousand and five,

and it's appalling that there isn't legislation there that Jenny and I, we're not equal parents of Chloe. (Taped interview)

With constitutional protection currently afforded only to the marital family in Article 41.3, these concerns are not unfounded.

One couple I spoke to who are hoping to have children together, are planning to marry in Canada later this year. One partner is Canadian and they are getting married before they embark on any attempts to get pregnant, in order to protect their future children from the risks posed by possible custody disputes with relatives should the Canadian partner die. They are aware that this safeguard will only be enforceable in Canada, but they see it as affording their children the only protection they can under present circumstances. They lament that there is nothing in Irish law that would protect the integrity of their family in the event of such a tragedy.

In lesbian-headed families, if the non-biological mother dies, neither the child nor the biological mother has any claim on her estate, which means that unless a will has been made, the child is not provided for. If there is a will, both the mother and child will be liable to inheritance tax.

Even while the couple is alive and together, the non-biological co-parent has no legal duty or rights to take care of the needs of the child. She cannot make decisions regarding religious upbringing, education, health care or travel for the child, even in the absence of the biological mother.

Where couples separate after the birth of a child, there are no safeguards for the child to maintenance, access to or custody by the other parent, even if that child has known the partner as a parent all his/her life. One woman expressed her worries:

> Because we all like to think that we're going to be big people, and we all like to think that we're going to, you know, put our children first, but over and over again people haven't. So that's quite a risk to take. (Taped interview)

Because of a lack of legitimacy at policy level, there is a lack of legitimacy at societal level, which makes everyday encounters complicated and difficult. For example, the non-biological mother will constantly have to explain why 'her' child does not have her name, who she is if she is not the child's 'real mother', and whether she has any right to make decisions affecting the child. The child in turn faces difficulties explaining to teachers, health professionals, and all too frequently to complete strangers, what his or her relationship to the co-parent is.

> But if you have a child, you're hurtled, as a lesbian, out into the wider community in a way that you hadn't bargained for, and that's quite a lot to take on, as regards, you don't do that lightly because you know that you're going to now have to be out as a lesbian: to the schools; to the hospitals; to everywhere you go.

Because in order to ensure that your child knows that everything is good about the kind of family that he/she comes from, you have to be as much out there as possible, and be very positive about it as well. But it's worth doing because I want Aisling to get the strongest sense of, I want everybody in Ireland to feel very positively about, Aisling's family. Therefore I have to be a bit more upfront than I would normally be, you know, if I were heterosexual I would quite happily just blend into the background. (Taped interview)

The rights of the child should be given an expanded constitutional protection. They should be based on empirical evidence rather than on principles of contested legal and social legitimacy (such as 'natural law' or principles derived from religious beliefs) and should supersede all other interests where there is a conflict. These rights should inform legal, social and institutional practice. Where laws or practices seem to conflict with the best interests of the child, they should be challengeable under this constitutional protection.

ADOPTION

An example of an issue that has been legislated for on the basis of principles rather than evidence is the area of adoption, especially the issue of the adoption of the children of lesbian and gay parents. In other countries, second-parent adoption has been introduced, which allows the non-biological parent of a child to adopt that child while the biological parent retains his/her rights and duties towards the child.[4] Joint adoption rights for non-relative children have also been introduced in many countries giving children the right to be adopted by the family which is best suited to them, rather than by families which fit a prescribed ideal family form.[5] Adoption assessment procedures in these countries are deemed capable of deciding upon the merits of each family, regardless of its similarity to a particular ideal.

The recent consultation process on adoption legislation in Ireland posed the question as to who should be eligible to adopt. Of the 300 submissions received, 32 were from private individuals made solely to protest *against* same-sex couples' eligibility to adopt, not a single one of which produced *any* empirical evidence to support their view that such adoption would be detrimental to children. Among the nine submissions made solely *in favour* of same-sex and unmarried couples' eligibility to adopt, there was a heavy emphasis placed on international empirical research on the effects on children of living in non-traditional families.

More importantly, there was a notable absence of opposition to same-sex couples adopting from *those organisations working in the area of child protection and adoption,* with the vast majority arguing that *assessments* were the best way to determine suitability to adopt based on the welfare of the child. The Adoption Board (now being reconfigured as the Adoption Authority) makes a strong case for unmarried

couples' eligibility to adopt, and while it makes no mention of homosexuality *per se*, it argues that no family situation should be regarded *prima facie* suitable or unsuitable.

In the Department of Health and Children's 2005 report on the Adoption Consultation, there is a recommendation that there be *no changes* in the area of unmarried heterosexual or same-sex couples' eligibility to adopt, or rights to appoint a partner as guardian, in the absence of formalised rights for cohabiting couples. This is inconsistent with the standards laid out in the UNCRC, for the right to respect for family life (Article 8), and in that it would seem difficult to justify by appeal to the paramountcy of the interests of the child. So if Tristan Dowse's adoptive parents were to jointly apply for inter-country adoption in this country, as a married couple they would have the automatic right to be assessed. A lesbian couple similarly applying would automatically be refused assessment. Although neither couple might pass the assessment, there seems to be little evidence to support the continuation of this discriminatory practice.

CHILDREN'S RIGHTS WITHIN THEIR FAMILIES

The definition of the family as used by the United Nations is inclusive and promotes the well-being of all family members regardless of family form. The family is:

Any combination of two or more persons who are bound together by ties of mutual consent, birth and/or adoption or placement and who, together assume responsibility for, *inter alia*, the care and maintenance of group members through procreation or adoption, the socialisation of children and the social control of members.

The Ceifin Report 2004, *Family Well-Being: What Makes a Difference?* which studied various types of family in Ireland, found that the type of family in which one lives has virtually no impact on family well-being. This finding would be well supported in international research on children brought up in lesbian-headed families, for example in the study on heterosexual and lesbian families born through donor insemination conducted by Fulcher *et al* (2002) which found that 'family process variables such as parental adjustment and couple adjustment were more strongly related to children's outcomes than were family structural variables such as parental sexual orientation or relationship status. The family process variables showed the same pattern of associations in families headed by lesbian and heterosexual parents.'[6]

In spite of the recommendation by the 1998 Commission on the Family[7]

that the pledge by the state on marriage should not prevent the Oireachtas from legislating for the benefit of family units not based on marriage and that a clear constitutional basis for this should be provided in Article 41 (p.191) it is clear that adoption legislation as it now stands does not benefit family units not based on marriage. The children or potential children of those families do not receive the same protection available to those children whose parents do have the right to marry. The Commission also recommends that instead of giving recognition to the rights of the family unit based on marriage, as is the case at present in Article 41.3, provision should be made affording individuals the right to respect for their family life. 'Family unit' is taken to refer to adults with links by marriage, kinship or parenthood, and children with links by birth, adoption or placement. Furthermore, the Commission goes on to elaborate that

> family life within these units would be characterised by its members together assuming responsibility for the care and support of each other, particularly children and other dependent family members, and by the sharing of time and resources which promotes intimacy and belongingness. (p.625)

It follows from these considerations that children should be afforded respect for their family life, and possess rights within all types of families, even those which are not 'legitimated' by marriage (or some other kind of registration), where they have the expectation of the care and company of the adults in a parental role within that family.

The rights of children and those in positions of dependence because of age, infirmity or disability should be paramount in any consideration of conflicting rights. The rights of the family as a unit, while having due weight as a cornerstone of society, should be secondary to the rights of the members of that family, with due regard to the rights of anyone in society whose well-being will be significantly affected by the exercise of those rights. Giving primacy to the family over and above the welfare of individual members can lead to tragic lapses in the duty of care as demonstrated unequivocally by our history in this country of failure to deal with abuse and neglect within families. That notwithstanding, individuals should be afforded respect for their family life where that family is providing care, stability and continuity for its members.

The 1998 Commission on the family in chapter 2 of its interim report stresses the importance of joint parenting as follows:

> continuity and stability in family relationships should be recognised as having a major value for individual well-being and social stability especially as far as children are concerned. Joint parenting should be encouraged with a view to ensuring as far as possible that children have the opportunity of developing close relationships with both parents which is in the interests both of children and their parents. (p.627)

As is currently the case with unmarried heterosexual parents where the father can apply to the courts for guardianship, there should be this same provision for the second-parent in a lesbian relationship to signal

intent to parent. Although not based on blood-ties, other types of non-biological parent-child relationships based on *intent* to parent are currently legally recognised, such as in laws on adoption, or the practice of registration of birth following the use of donor gametes, and these same principles could be similarly applied in this instance.

Many of our laws remain inconsistent with the standards laid out in the UNCRC in that they do not take as paramount the interests of the child. One example of this are the laws on adoption which prevent children born to a same-sex couple (through anonymous donor insemination) from being legally adopted by the non-biological parent, thus denying them any of the rights they would have if their parents were heterosexual. When heterosexual couples have a child though donor insemination, the non-biological parent is allowed to register as the father on the birth certificate.[8] Since in the case of heterosexual parents, the social relationship of the non-biological father to the child appears to supersede the biological relationship of the donor to the child, it appears discriminatory that the non-biological mother should not be allowed to register as the second parent on the birth certificate of the child born to her and her partner. This would open up the possibility of registering as the guardian of that child (under the Guardianship of Children (Statutory Declaration) Regulations 1998 currently confined to heterosexual couples who have a child in common) who would then be legally recognised as having two parents and enjoy the protection that this affords.

Children born to same-sex couples, like heterosexual couples, should have the right to have both biological and social parents' names on their birth certificate, unless it is explicitly demonstrated that genetic parenthood is what is indicated in the laws on the registration of births. Currently, an unmarried woman and any man of her choosing who consents can register, albeit perhaps with dubious legality, as the parents of a child born to that woman. If biological parenthood is a legal requirement for birth registration, the issues of donor insemination, egg donation, surrogacy and other future developments in new reproductive technologies will have to be legislated for in all their complexity as they apply to heterosexual couples as well as lesbian and gay couples.[9]

Research from around the world on lesbian and gay families would appear to unequivocally support the inclusion of gay or lesbian families in the definition of family. The American Psychological Association, on reviewing the research, found that 'not a single study has found children of gay or lesbian parents to be disadvantaged in any significant respect relative to children of heterosexual parents' and in conclusion found that 'home environments provided by gay and lesbian parents are as likely as those provided by heterosexual parents to support and enable children's psychosocial growth'.[10]

However, there is still a lot of public hostility to

homosexuality especially as it relates to children. Marian Finucane recently featured a short programme on lesbian parenting with myself and Rita Wild, then director of L.inc as guests.[11] When I rang the researcher a few days after the show to enquire about public feedback to that and the following day's short follow-up programme, she sent me these quotes:

- One caller was 'Physically sick and full of revulsion and lesbianism is contrary to the laws of God and humanity.'
- Of lesbians 'It's not their fault, it's a disease.'
- 'No child should ever be brought into the world to satisfy the emotional needs of an adult.'
- 'I don't care what kinds of relationships adults are in. It's their choice but the baby has no choice.'
- 'I am a wife, mother and a normal family person. I have no problem with gay people, but I am sick and tired of listening to people "coming out". They should just get on with their lives and stop sticking it in people's faces.'

Legal change in this area has been slow due to reluctance on the part of political parties to introduce legislation that might be politically unpopular or constitutionally challengable. David Norris' recent Civil Partnerships Bill (2004) was one such thwarted attempt. Successive governments have instead often relied on the courts to legislate for them, through judgments in cases taken by individuals such as *McGee v AG, Norris v AG* and *Attorney General v X*. Judges' interpretations of the Constitution have, in the words of one commentator, been 'notably activist' in the last thirty years, and have reflected changing values and needs in the society in which they operate (Morgan, 2001). However, this same commentator points out that this making of policy choices by individual judges conflicts with their stated and perceived objectivity, i.e. that the judgments they make are based on fixed and clearly-declared principles of law, and relies instead on their own situatedness as individuals within a political society. If they can claim to reflect society's values and needs, it is their *personal* interpretation of those values and needs that is in danger of being represented.

The Commission on Assisted Human Reproduction has just sent its report to the government. One of the recommendations is that the partner of a recipient of donated sperm should give a legal commitment to be recognised as the child's parent, which could have major implications for the children of lesbian families if applied to them (Coulter, 9/5/05). Other recommendations are that assisted reproduction services be made available irrespective of sexual orientation or marital status. Whether these recommendations are translated into law remains to be seen, and will in all likelihood depend on the will of government to take on a potentially unpopular cause.

Perhaps all that is needed is time for public opinion to change in the direction it already seems to be moving in. But do we need to, and can we afford to wait for the tide of public opinion to change? The EOS Gallup Europe survey conducted in January 2003 to measure public opinion on marriage of homosexual couples and child adoption by homosexual couples, showed a range of responses across the thirty countries surveyed. Interestingly, in some of the countries, notably Sweden and the UK, which already have legislation in place that allows adoption by same-sex couples, public opinion was still more strongly weighted against than for this (EOS Gallup, 2003). In the area of human rights, public opinion sometimes has to be dragged along with the machinery of change. Our children cannot wait for the moral majority to embrace their cause. As well as the care and protection of their parents, they need the care and protection of our Constitution.

As one of the women I interviewed said:

> I think it's interesting when you look at what *is* a normal family. Because I think if you tease apart what are the good qualities that we value in families, because most people come from families, so most of us have an experience of growing up or spending some time with a family. And if we look back at the good times, it's like, fun, and laughter, or remembering the support that we got off our brothers or sisters or parents, if something terrible had happened and we were in bits, or the laughter we had when we went to the seaside. Like, they're the sort of things we remember. And those things aren't based on whether our parents were heterosexual or homosexual. They're based on feelings of love and being wanted, and feeling supported, and having good craic. And they're the things we should be looking at when we look at what sort of things, what sort of environments do we want for our children. (Taped interview)

[Submission prepared by Mary Hogan and Angela O'Connell. The appendix included by L.inc is taken from the Report of the Commission on Assisted Human Reproduction and is Appendix VII of that report entitled 'The Best Interests of the Child in Assisted Human Reproduction'. For further information, contact L.inc.]

References

American Psychological Association. *Lesbian and Gay Parenting: A Resource for Psychologists* (1995).

Barrett, H and Tasker, F. (2001) 'Growing up with a gay parent: Views of 101 gay fathers on their sons' and daughters' experiences' *Educational and Child Psychology*, 18, 62-77.

Campion, J.M. (1995). *Who's Fit to Be a Parent?* London: Routledge.

Coulter, Carol. 'Major Changes in Infertility Treatment Proposed.' *Irish Times*, 9/5/05.

Daly, Mary. *Families and Family Life in Ireland: Challenges for the Future*. Report of Public Consultation Fora. Dublin: Department of Social and Family Affairs, 2004.

Department of Health and Children. *Adoption Legislation: 2003 Consultation and Proposals for Change*. Dublin: Stationery Office, January 2005.

Equality Authority. *Implementing Equality for Lesbians, Gays and Bisexuals*. Dublin: Author, 2002.

Fahey, T. and Russell, H, 2001. *Family Formation in Ireland: Trends, Data Needs and Implications*. Policy Research

Series No 43, Dublin: The Economic and Social Research Institute.

Frith, Lucy. 'Gamete donation and anonymity: The ethical and legal debate.' *Human Reproduction*, Vol. 16, No. 5, 818-824, May 2001.

Fulcher, Megan; Sutfin, Erin L.; Chan, Raymond W.; Scheib, Joanna E.; Patterson, Charlotte J. 'Lesbian Mothers and Their Children: Findings from the Contemporary Families Study.' Chapter for A. Omoto and H. Kurtzman (Eds.), *Recent Research on Sexual Orientation, Mental Health and Substance Use*. Washington: APA, 2002.

Golombok S, Perry B, Burston A, Murray C, Mooney-Somers J, Stevens M, Golding J. 'Children with Lesbian Parents: a Community Study'. *Developmental Psychology* 2003 Jan; 39(1):20-33.

Golombok, S.L., Spencer, A. and Rutter, M. (1983). 'Children in lesbian and single-parent households: Psychosexual and psychiatric appraisal.' *Journal of Child Psychology and Psychiatry*, 24, 551-572.

Golombok, Susan.2000. *Parenting: What Really Counts?* London: Routledge.

Govt. of Ireland. *Strengthening Families for Life: The Final Report of the Commission on the Family to the Minister for Social, Community and Family Affairs*. Dublin: 1998.

Green, R., Mandel, J.B., Hotvedt, M.E., Gray, J. and Smith, L. (1986). 'Lesbian mothers and their children: a comparison with solo parent heterosexual mothers and their children.' *Archives of Sexual Behaviour*, 15, 167-184.

Halley and Associates. *Adoption Consultation: Oral Consultation*. Second Stage Feedback. Dublin: Halley, 2004.

Halman, L. *The European Values Study: A third Wave*. Source book of the 1999/2000 European Values Study Survey. The Netherlands: WORC Tilburg University, 2001: 43, in NESF (2003).

Herek, Gregory M. 'Assessing Heterosexuals' Attitudes Toward Lesbians and Gay Men: A Review of Empirical Research With the ATLG Scale.' Herek and Greene, 206–228.

Hoeffer, B. (1981). 'Children's acquisition of sex-role behaviour in lesbian-mother families.' *American Journal of Orthopsychiatry*, 5, 536-544.

Huggins, S.L. (1989). 'A comparative study of self-esteem of adolescent children of divorced lesbian mothers and divorced heterosexual mothers'. In F.W. Bozett (ed.), *Homosexuality and the family* (123-135). New York: Harrington Park.

Jenny, C. and Roesler, T.A. (1994). 'Are children at risk for sexual abuse by homosexuals?' *Pediatrics*, 94, 41-44.

Kennan, Siobhan. *Adoption Legislation Oral Consultation – 17 October 2003, Summary of Submissions*. Dublin: Department of Health and Children, 2003.

Kirkpatrick, M., Smith, C. and Roy, R. (1981). 'Lesbian mothers and their children: A comparative survey.' *American Journal of Orthopsychiatry*, 51, 545-551.

Lamb, M.E. (ed), (1999). *Parenting and Child Development in 'Nontraditional' Families*. London: Lawerence Erlbaum Associates.

Madden, Deirdre. *The Law Relating to Assisted Conception in the Republic of Ireland*. Cork: Unpublished PhD dissertation, 2000.

McKeown, K, Pratschke, J. and Haase, T. *Family Well-Being: What Makes a Difference?* Clare: Ceifin, 2003.

Mee, John and Ronayne, Kaye. *Partnership Rights of Same-Sex Couples*. Dublin: Equality Authority, 2000.

Mill, John Stuart. *On Liberty*. Oxford: Oxford University Press, 1991 (Originally published in London, 1859).

Miller, J.A., Jacobsen, R.B. and Bigner, J.J. (1981). 'The child's home environment for lesbian versus heterosexual mothers: A neglected area of research.' *Journal of Homosexuality*, 7, 49-56.

Morgan, David Gwynn. *A Judgement Too Far: Judicial Activism and the Constitution*. Undercurrents series, Cork: CUP, 2001.

Morgan, Derek, and Lee, Robert G. *Blackstone's Guide to the Human Fertilisation and Embryology Act 1990: Abortion & Embryo Research, the New Law*. London: Blackstone, 1991.

Mucklow, B.M. and Phelan, G.K. (1979). 'Lesbian and traditional mothers' responses to adult responses to child behaviour and self-concept.' *Psychological Reports*, 44, 880-882.

Patterson, C.J. (1994). 'Children of the lesbian baby boom: Behavioural adjustment, self-concepts and sex-role identity.' In B.Greene and G. Herek (eds.), *Psychological perspectives on lesbian and gay issues: Vol. 1. Lesbian and Gay Psychology: Theory, Research and Clinical Applications*. Thousand Oaks, CA: Sage.

Puryear, D. (1983). 'A comparison between the children of lesbian mothers and the children of heterosexual, single mothers.' *Unpublished doctoral dissertation*, California School of Professional Psychology, Berkeley.

Rumball, Anna and Adair, Vivienne. 'Telling the story: parents' scripts for donor offspring.' *Human Reproduction*, Vol. 14, No. 5, 1392-1399, May 1999.

Ryan, Fergus. 'Legal Rhetoric, Social Reality: Towards a New Legal Concept of Family for the 21st Century'. *Proceedings of Biennial Conference on Family Diversity: Exploring Issues, Reflecting Reality, Challenging Assumptions*. Dublin: Cherish: The National Association of Single Parent Families, 2002.

Shanahan, Suzanne. 'The Changing Meaning of Family: Individual Rights and Irish Adoption Policy, 1949-99'. *Journal of Family History*. Vol. 30 No. 1, January 2005, 86-108.

Shannon, Geoffrey. *Children and the Law*. Dublin: Round Hall Sweet and Maxwell, 2001.

Tasker, F.L. and Golombok, S. (1995). 'Adults raised as children in lesbian families.' *American Journal of Orthopsychiatry*, 65 (2), 203-215.

Tasker, F.L. and Golombok, S. (1997). *Growing up in a Lesbian Family: Effects on Child Development*. New York: Guilford.

Notes

1   For detailed information on L.Inc Groups, see Appendix 1.
2   LASI (Lesbian Advocacy Services Initiative) has recently received government funding in Northern Ireland.
3   Section 6A of the 1964 Act [as inserted by section 12 of the Status of Children Act 1987]. (Shannon, 2001).
4   Among these are South Africa, Spain, Iceland, Sweden, Netherlands, United Kingdom, United Sates, Australia, Norway, Israel, Germany, Finland, Denmark.
5   Among these are Australia, Canada, Iceland, South Africa, Spain, Sweden, Netherlands, United Kingdom.
6   See Golombok, Susan. *Parenting: What Really Counts?* London: Routledge, 2000, for an overview of the literature.
7   Strengthening Families for Life: The Final Report of the Commission on the Family to the Minister for Social, Community & Family Affairs. Govt of Ireland, Dublin, 1998.
8   This of course raises other issues, such as the right of the child to know its biological origins, but in the case of the same-sex parents, there is less opportunity (and research in Australia and the US shows, much less inclination) to lie about the child's circumstances than in a heterosexual couple (where the research shows a very high level of non-revelation of the child's origins), (Rumball, 1999).

[9] The Commission on Assisted Human Reproduction is due to publish its report shortly, which will presumably address these issues as did the Warnock Report (1987) in the UK.

[10] C.J. Patterson. *Lesbian and Gay Parenting: A Resource for Psychologists*. American Psychological Association (1995). See also bibliography of this paper for more references to research in the area.

[11] The Marian Finucane Show, RTE Radio 1, Thursday, 11/11/04.

LIFE PREGNANCY CARE SERVICE IRELAND

Life is a voluntary organisation and a registered charity (9172) caring for women with unplanned pregnancies. The services offered include pregnancy testing, one-to-one pregnancy counselling, telephone counselling every day from 9am to 9pm (1850 281 281), advice on medical, legal and social welfare aspects, short-term accommodation for single pregnant women and mothers with babies, support after birth and post-abortion counselling. All services are free and confidential.

Life Pregnancy Care Service makes the following submission:

- Every child has the right to be born.
- The rights of the child are paramount.
- All fathers should have rights as well as mothers.
- The reference to women within the home should be adjusted to 'parent' to take account of the fact that in some cases the primary carer is the father and not the mother.

MA IN WOMEN'S STUDIES CLASS, UNIVERSITY COLLEGE CORK

With regard to the provisions in relation to the family in the Constitution of Ireland Articles 41, 42 and 40.3:

1 IMPLICATIONS OF DEALING WITH FAMILY ISSUES IN THE CONSTITUTION

Given that social attitudes in Ireland have changed in recent years and that ongoing scientific developments – in the area of reproductive technologies, for example – may further alter our thinking, we suggest that it would be prudent to deal with a number of the questions raised by the Committee through legislation rather than by writing into the Constitution definitions that may become obsolete in the near future and that could only be changed by a further review of the Constitution and a referendum.

2 DEFINITIONS OF THE FAMILY

The UN definition of the family seems appropriate to Irish needs. Thus a family would be defined as:

> Any combination of two or more persons who are bound together by ties of mutual consent, birth and/or adoption or placement and who, together assume responsibility for, *inter alia,* the care and maintenance of group members through procreation or adoption, the socialisation of children and the social control of members.

3 STRIKING THE BALANCE BETWEEN THE RIGHTS OF THE FAMILY AS A UNIT AND THE RIGHTS OF INDIVIDUAL MEMBERS

a In Ireland the family can no longer be thought of as static or of comprising two birth-parents and their children. Dealing with the rights of individuals in changing social and personal circumstances is a complex issue that would be better dealt with in legislation that can be changed to take account of social, moral and other developments that may further affect our thinking on family forms and individual rights. [We could look to Scandinavian models for legislation.]

b The rights of dependent children and others who require care because of age, disability etc. should be protected, but these rights might be expressed in terms of the rights of individuals as citizens rather than in the context of a balance of rights within the 'family'.

4 GIVING CONSTITUTIONAL PROTECTION TO FAMILIES OTHER THAN THOSE BASED ON MARRIAGE

a Many Irish people live together in stable relationships outside marriage and many of them have children. In practice they form families. If we accept the UN definition of the family, we should extend to these families any constitutional rights and protections enjoyed by the married family.

b A legal mechanism should be established to allow partnerships not based on marriage to be registered, but non-registration should not undermine the rights of family members – particularly of children. [For further discussion of this issue see 5 c – on legal partnerships.]

5 GAY MARRIAGE

a Lesbian and gay couples form family units and care for natural, adopted, or foster children.

b Gay and lesbian couples should have the same civil marriage rights as heterosexual couples.

c All citizens, regardless of sexual identity, should have the right to enter into legal partnerships (as opposed to marriages), to own property in joint names, to name their partners as next of kin and to leave them their property on death on the terms enjoyed by married couples.

6 REFERENCE TO WOMAN'S 'LIFE WITHIN THE HOME'

a This is a dated reference and should be removed or changed so that a gender-neutral term is used – particularly since the state has signed up to European treaties (e.g. Lisbon) that require it to ensure that a higher percentage of women will be in the workplace.

b Article 41.2.2 states that 'the State shall ... endeavour to ensure that mothers shall not be obliged by economic necessity to engage in labour to the neglect of their duties in the home'. The state has failed in this endeavour. The wording of this section does a disservice to men and women. The section should be deleted as it is meaningless unless the state provides financial supports for carers in the home. If it is not deleted, the word *mother* should be replaced with *principal carer*.

c It would be more useful to require that the state will create adequate childcare places to meet the needs of Irish children.

d The role of carers in the home should be valued and they should be paid a carer's allowance regardless of the income of their partners.

e The rights of children, the disabled and the elderly to care, education and a basic standard of living should be constitutionally protected.

7 THE 'NATURAL' MOTHER

Articles using terms such as 'natural' mothers and 'birth-mothers' could quickly become outdated given developments in reproductive technologies. The rights of 'parents' and children could be established through legislation that can be changed to take account of new developments, rather than written into the Constitution.

8 RIGHTS OF FATHERS/MOTHERS/CHILDREN

a We would refer back to the UN definition of the family quoted in section 2 above and suggest that the rights of such families should be given constitutional protection and supported by appropriate legislation.

b The Committee should give particular consideration to whether the Constitution reflects International and European Human Rights Conventions.

c The rights of children have not been adequately protected in the past. While suggesting that special care should be taken (because the use of certain language and concepts may change with developments in reproductive technologies) children's rights, as expressed in the UN Convention on the Rights of the Child, for example, should be reflected in the Constitution.

METHODIST CHURCH IN IRELAND: COUNCIL ON SOCIAL RESPONSIBILITY

The Methodist Church has a strong tradition of involvement in social issues and in reflecting social concerns. We have always argued that faith must be seen as relevant to the issues of society. In this spirit, we are therefore happy to make this submission as a contribution to the work of the Committee.

1 GENERAL REMARKS

The Methodist Church has consistently articulated a number of perspectives which are relevant to the current matters being deliberated by the Committee. These are:

• We hold strongly to the view that the Constitution is not the place to determine detailed matters of social policy. Rather its role is to delineate general principles of public and social policy, which can then be instantiated in whatever detail is required through ordinary legislation, and revised from time to time as deemed necessary in the same manner. Thus for this reason we opposed proposals to insert specific regulations into the Constitution regarding abortion, divorce, etc quite apart from our views for or against those specific proposals. And so in the present case, we would argue that the Constitution should only state general principles relating to families and family rights. The existing text could therefore be streamlined and we would also oppose adding any new specific matters of detail.

• Secondly, we have consistently argued that it is not the role of the Constitution to uphold or enforce the specific viewpoint of any church (or other faith or philosophy) *per se*, no matter how much we might agree or not with such a viewpoint. The general framework for social policy in the Constitution should be framed so as to be, as far as is feasible, objectively intended to maximise the common good. Whether or not we agree with the viewpoint in such a Constitution, or indeed the legislation implementing it, is our concern, not that of the state. Of course, the religious tradition in Ireland will naturally influence the way these matters are considered, and that is right and proper, but a clear distinction needs to be made between that fact, and the actual endorsement of any specific religious perspective. Given the increasing multi-cultural nature of Irish society, this factor takes on an extra dimension and urgency at the current time. [These comments of course do not in any way negate the fact that it is appropriate for the Constitution to recognise and value the profession and practice of religion in all its forms, and to recognise the valuable role that religion, at its best, can play within society.]

- Thirdly, turning to the current topic, it must be recognised that in relation to some aspects of it, and in particular to laws and issues around marriage, religious requirements and the requirements of the state have become heavily intertwined over the years. In considering these topics, we feel it is useful, and indeed important, to recognise that these two aspects are logically separate, and to keep the distinction clear as we discuss this matter.

- And finally in these general comments, we note that while churches, or other faith communities, have in the past been seen as the primary determinants of moral values, that role has been increasingly taken up by the adoption within civil society of ethical and moral codes. The most prominent of these are of course the UN Convention on Human Rights (and the many conventions flowing from that) and the European Convention on Human Rights. We as a church respect and endorse this trend, believing that it represents a maturing of human society and civilisation. We would argue, however, that within this scenario, there is still a role for churches to articulate issues of morality and ethics on an ongoing basis, while accepting that we are just one voice among many and no longer have any privileged role in this regard (and which in our own case in the Methodist Church, we probably never had).

2 SPECIFIC COMMENTS

We now turn to address the specific questions posed in the request for submissions. We will consider groups of related questions together for convenience.

- Definition of the family; family not based on marriage?; gay marriage; reference to women's 'life within the home'; rights of the family versus rights of its members

Given the general comments made above, we believe that Article 41.1 is in general a positive feature in our Constitution, with its support for the concept of the family and its positive role within society. We would wish to see this retained (perhaps in a more up-to-date wording) or something very similar put in its place. However, the second part of Article 41.1.1° ('… and as a moral institution ….') is arguable and problematic, and should be removed.

With regard to Article 41.3.2 we accept that given the relatively recent referendum on divorce, it

would be difficult to argue, in practice, for any further change in this. We do not have a problem with its content, only that, as stated above, we do not believe the Constitution is the place for such detailed prescription.

However, when we look at the other parts of Article 41, we have serious concerns. Firstly, we note that Article 41.2 again includes a very specific and detailed issue of social policy (which should not be there at all), but also expresses a viewpoint that is totally contrary to current opinions (and indeed legislation) on equality and anti-discrimination based on gender or marital status. This existing article should be removed, in our opinion, and replaced with a new article which

- confirms a basic right to marry, in accordance with law
- states that the state respects and supports the important role, in support of the common good, which families undertake in the care and nurturing of dependants, especially children.

With regard to Article 41.3.1, we believe that this should be removed, for two reasons. Firstly because it has given rise to many complications since it was introduced. Secondly, the state's support for the family in Article 41.1.2 is sufficient, and does not need to be extended specifically to marriage as well.

With regard to Article 41.3.3, we fail to see what purpose it serves, and believe it should be removed. Its subject matter should be a matter for ordinary legislation as deemed necessary.

Given the changes as proposed, we believe that they also deal with a number of related questions:

- The Constitution would support the family, and its role in society, not the 'family based on marriage' per se.
- Except for the issue of divorce in Article 41.3.2, the topic of marriage is thus taken out of the Constitution and becomes a matter for ordinary legislation only.
- It is therefore a matter for the Oireachtas to legislate, if deemed appropriate, for civil unions, same-sex marriage and any other related matters. If and when proposals for such measures arise, we may well argue for or against them as we feel appropriate, but we still believe the Constitution is not the place for them.
- We believe it removes the current difficulties in regard to balancing the rights of the family with the rights of the members of a family.

The question remains as to whether the Constitution should define the concept of the 'family' in any further way. Our initial instinct would be to say that this does not need to be defined further, and can be left to legislation. The specific proposal for constitutional amendment as outlined below takes this approach. However, it might be considered necessary to define the family in order to ensure equity under tax, social welfare or other regulations and/or to ensure no unnecessary barrier to defining the rights of natural parents or children (see next section). In that case it would be important to define it in a way that does not bring any particular presupposition to bear. A definition, if so required, might thus include something to the effect that 'the circumstances which are deemed to constitute a family may be determined in accordance with law but shall include married couples, long-term relationships between two adults for mutual care and support, and/or one or more adults in a long-term relationship to provide care and support to dependants, especially children'. This definition is intended to include single parent families, 'traditional' marriages, any 'non-traditional' marriages which may be permitted by legislation, stable cohabiting partnerships, etc.

- Rights of natural mother; rights of natural father; expansion of rights of the child

We believe that the changes proposed above would remove any constitutional difficulties relating to the roles and rights of natural fathers and/or mothers. This comes as a consequence of shifting the emphasis towards family units and away from marriage *per se* in the constitutional protection, and including the care and support of children as one important component of a family unit. There is no barrier to making whatever legislative provision is deemed appropriate in relation to natural fathers, natural mothers and children.

- UN Convention on the Rights of the Child

We would support the proposal to amend the Constitution wherever necessary in order to ensure that it conforms to the Convention. We believe that some of the proposals made above will deal with a number of these issues. We further reiterate our view that, when considering this issue, the focus should be on general principles of social and public policy, not on specifics.

The net effect of the proposals we are making is that Article 41 be amended as shown below:

Article 41

1. 1° *The State recognises the family as the natural primary and fundamental unit group of society,*
   2° *The State, therefore, guarantees to protect the family in its constitution and authority, as the necessary basis of social order and as indispensable to the welfare of the nation and the State.*

2. 1° *The State guarantees the right to marry, in accordance with law, and shall support the institution of marriage. Marriage, and such other situations as may be determined by law, shall be deemed to constitute a family.*

2° *The State recognises the role of families as the primary carers for children and other dependants, and this gives society a support which contributes significantly to the common good. The State therefore pledges itself to respect and support this function.*

3. *A Court designated by law may grant a dissolution of marriage where, but only where, it is satisfied that*
   i. *at the date of the institution of the proceedings, the spouses have lived apart from one another for a period of, or periods amounting to, at least four years during the five years,*
   ii. *there is no reasonable prospect of a reconciliation between the spouses,*
   iii. *such provisions as the Court considers proper, having regard to the circumstances, exist or will be made for the spouses, any children of either or both of them and any other person prescribed by law, and*
   iv. *any further conditions prescribed by law are complied with.*

MEN'S COUNCIL OF IRELAND

The Men's Council of Ireland supports the views expressed and the recommendations contained in the submission by our member organisation AMEN. We would also like to add the following comments and recommendations.

CHILDREN AND PARENTS

Parenthood is more than just producing children. It's about 'living' with children. Being a parent is about nourishing a child's every need: physical, emotional, spiritual, moral needs along with social education. A parent's job is one of feeding, washing, clothing as well as providing. A parent is a child's protector, teacher, counsellor, carer, confidant and friend. A parent passes on skills, values and beliefs. A parent is a child's connection with the past and a child's role model for the future. A parent teaches a child life skills like communication and how to balance independence with inter-dependence; how to love oneself and how to love others. That's what a parent is. Parents are best placed to know what is in their children's best interest. Parents love their children. At present the state appears to be pushing all parents into the work place without any regard for the welfare of the children. This may be good for GNP but not for children. This policy of creating more so-called 'childcare' facilities is destroying the fabric of family life. It is in fact counterproductive as the 'second' income is absorbed in higher house prices and transport costs. The state should be encouraging and providing financial incentives (e.g. tax deductions etc.) to ensure that one parent looks after the children in their home.

As a society, we should be very careful about destroying this very special relationship that children have with their parents. As a democratic society, we have to carefully monitor the people to whom we give the power to remove parents from children's lives. All children have a right to know and have a meaningful relationship with both their parents. Parents have a right to the same relationship with their children, unfettered and without interference by the state, except in extraordinary and proven circumstances where such relationships are contrary to the well being of the child.

In recent years and with the advent of divorce in Ireland, family relationships have been breaking down at an alarming rate. Some of these relationship breakdowns between spouses or partners are inevitable and, sadly irreversible, particularly where children are involved. But there is a recent destructive force that has come into the picture, which has exacerbated (and even precipitated) relationship breakdown. This toxic and adversarial element is known as 'family law' and is held in secretive courts.

> As long as government is perceived as working for the benefit of children, the people happily will endure almost any curtailment of liberty
>
> Rabbi Daniel Lapin

FAMILY LAW

Family law operates on an old-fashioned, adversarial 'win-lose' basis (although *all* family members who fall foul of this process are losers eventually). The adversarial approach to 'solving disputes' (with its built-in financial incentive for all the associated professionals), between previously intimate partners, is patently counterproductive. (God help us if they ever got involved in solving disputes between friends.) It has become a lucrative industry and should not go unchallenged in its capitalising on human suffering. Instead of promoting inequality in family relationships, the state and vested 'experts' should be advocating joint responsibility, compassion, understanding, tolerance and respect between family members.

Many of the victims of this family law process have been so traumatised that they dare not ever risk entering marriage or intimate relationships again. Indeed there are many unmarried young men who are aware of the devastation caused by the family courts and consequently have understandably decided that they will never commit to marriage. An increasing number of men know that in the event of a marriage breakdown they will in all likelihood lose their homes, other property including savings, be impoverished by crippling maintenance payments to their former wives and worst of all, have their parenthood reduced to the point where it is almost meaningless. The state must take a clear position on marriage and either promote it (as per Article 41.3 of the Constitution) or abolish civil marriage altogether. The state's current approach to marriage is schizophrenic. While recognising and facilitating civil marriage on the one hand, it is also undermining marriage by its family legislation.

At present, people are entering into marriage contracts, not knowing what is involved from a legal perspective. The state should be obliged to honestly and comprehensively inform prospective marriage partners as to the terms of the contract and the likely or possible manner in which it can be terminated. Marriage is the only contract where the party in breach (if a woman) can legally renounce her obligations while forcing the other party to continue to fulfil his contractual obligations. In essence, what this means is that a man will be obliged to continue maintaining his former wife while she will be relieved of any obligation to make any contribution to his well-being.

The terms of the marriage contract are dictated by the state and the parties concerned cannot influence or amend these terms. Indeed the state can, at any time in the future, retrospectively amend the terms of the contract and have done so on numerous occasions in the past. People who got married years ago are now subjected to the provisions of divorce and judicial separation legislation, which did not exist at the time they got married. This legislation fundamentally altered the terms of the marriage contract they entered into. There is a question as to whether or not the retrospective effect of this legislation is unconstitutional. The All-Party Committee should investigate this matter and publish an opinion.

> Nobody (knowingly) commits to disadvantage –
>
> Dr Warren Farrell

IN CAMERA

Currently, there is no reporting on family law cases yet there has been a growing level of anecdotal evidence that can no longer be ignored. Both men and women complain of abuses experienced in the secretive courts by professionals whose malpractice is protected by the *in camera* rule. Parties are told they can 'never' speak of these experiences or proceedings outside of the secretive chambers. This would have been par for the course in the old Soviet regime, but it is shocking to think it goes on in Ireland today. Men and women who have experienced the family law process, have reported (in breach of the *in camera* rule) to the MCI and its member organisations that they felt like they have been psychologically violated and emotionally raped by judges, barristers, solicitors, psychiatrists, psychologists and social workers – all in secrecy. They have complained of gratuitous, intimate probing of their private and sexual lives – all in secret. These victims of institutional abuses will have long-term problems – who is responsible? How many people have been abused by this process? Denial is how wrongdoers usually respond – at least initially. Do administrators of the family law system deny the harm they have caused; the suffering they have imposed; the fear they have instilled; the sadness they have created; the hostility they have provoked and the lives they have destroyed? It has been suggested that a tribunal be set up to investigate these claims and to bring those responsible to justice. Many simply give up and become dysfunctional, social outcasts, unemployed and homeless ... they become no good to themselves and to their children and become a 'burden on the state' ... who is responsible? How does a society tackle such issues when their origins are shrouded in secrecy ... who is responsible?

RESPECT FOR THE LEGAL SYSTEM

It is important that the rule of law is respected for a democracy to function. We have created offices of power in law. These offices are entrusted to members of the legal profession. The Catholic Church in Ireland lost respect, authority (and power) as a result of 'mismanaging' sexual abuse claims. The Catholic Church did not have the *in camera* rule to hide behind. The media were not silenced and were able to investigate and expose the abuse. The legal profession (judges, barristers and solicitors) itself is in a very precarious position, as it cannot, due to the *in camera* rule, defend itself from accusations of corrupt practices. This has resulted in a public loss of respect and confidence in the secretive family law process and the people who profit from it (the 'family law industry'). It can no longer carry on under the pretence of protecting the privacy of family members and children. Such a loss of confidence in the legal process has very serious implications for democracy and the rule of law.

It is well known (no thanks to any official reporting from our Family Law courts) that men are treated less favourably than women in Family Law courts. This discriminatory practice, which has been going on for years in secret, has effectively undermined the work of the mediation service. Women expect that they will get everything in court, so why negotiate any agreement in mediation? It's as ineffective as negotiating with someone 'who has a gun under the table'. This fact has already been recognised by the Family Mediation Service. The Committee should view their training video shown at the Family Support Agency conference in the Royal Hospital, Kilmainham last October.

STATE INTRUSION IN FAMILY LIFE

Generally speaking, the public is not aware of how much the state intrudes in people's family lives. Current legislation allows excessive and gratuitous intrusion into people's lives. To what extent should the state have a right to meddle in the private and intimate lives of citizens? Should citizens who are simply 'separating' from each other have their private lives exposed and 'plundered' in the adversarial and intimidating atmosphere of a courtroom? These issues need public debate.

The state can assist therapeutically in the lives of citizens and families (when invited to) and treat all family members with respect and equality, instead of interfering destructively and adding to the problems faced in familial relationships. This can be done through relationship and communication training and parenting skills courses. Where relationships break down, helping professions such as psychotherapists, psychologists and social workers can help all family members with sustaining parent-child relationships in joint custody arrangements and help them to cope with change and with parental skills, financial management and back to work skills. Family Law interference should be greatly restricted as it is adversely affecting family life, marriage, parental rights and obligations and the welfare of children. Responsibility for Family Law should be transferred to the Department of Social and Family Affairs from the Department of Justice, Equality and Law Reform.

The state is failing in its current constitutional obligations to respect and protect

a) the family
b) the institution of marriage
c) the right of parents as primary and natural educators of their children.

RECOMMENDATIONS

The Men's Council of Ireland submit the following recommendations:

That the legislature amend laws to allow courts to operate effectively by imposing equal rights and equal responsibilities on fathers and mothers to include the following:

1   All parents of children, regardless of marital status, are automatic guardians with joint custody of children from birth (until proven, through due process, to be unfit parents).
2   All parents will be equally held responsible for the social, psychological, emotional, educational and financial upbringing of their children.
3   All newborn children should undergo a DNA test to conclusively establish paternity. (Children have a right to know who their biological parents are for medical and other reasons and this would probably promote responsible behaviour by sexually active people.)
4   All parties to divorce or separation should be entitled to expect joint custody and equal parenting time (other parents can agree mutually acceptable arrangements as suits).
5   All parents proposing to separate will be required to firstly draft a parenting plan.
6   All parents proposing to separate will be required to undergo separation counselling and a families-in-transition programme.
7   All parents proposing to separate will be required to first attend mediation and the mediator supply a report to any court or tribunal.

8 Separating parents will be required to do parenting courses/provider courses to upgrade skills for joint custody arrangements.

9 Abolish 'statements of claim' (the 'gimme list') in all family law cases and require parties to put forward written proposals on the reorganisation of the family unit which respect and provide for the on-going parenting of children by both parties, the housing requirements of both parties (having regard to the fact that both parties must be in a position to provide accommodation for the children) and the financial needs of both parties.

10 Any court removing a parent's custodial or guardianship rights and responsibilities should be obliged to take all steps necessary to rectify these circumstances so that the parent will be able to resume the parental role as soon as possible. The court should also be obliged to give that parent, in writing, the reason for removing such rights so that the parent may show this to his/her child, should the parent wish to do so, when the child is of an appropriate age.

11 All courts will keep full and accurate records of all family law proceedings for future records and appeals.

12 All courts will treat false allegations as a serious crime and apply severe penalties when such allegations are proven to be false.

13 Reporting of family law proceedings should be published, maintaining parties' anonymity, by *independent* reporters (not lawyers). This would enlighten consumers in their decisions around using family law services, assist social debate, law reform and case law.

14 Change the name 'in camera' to 'in secret' and stop misleading the general public (a number of whom think *in camera* means we have cameras in court).

15 Have end-user representatives on the Law Society Disciplinary Committee, and the Court Services Board, representing male interests and female interests respectively and equally.

MOTHER AND CHILD CAMPAIGN

INTRODUCTION

The Constitution of Ireland – Bunreacht na hÉireann – was enacted in 1937 and is one of the youngest existant constitutions. Other countries, with constitutions ranging in age from seventy-five to two hundred and seven years, are loath to change or replace them. Family law reform and social reform of marriage has never formed part of any political party's manifesto and this current review answers no public demand. Reviewing Articles 41, 42 and 40.3 may be within the remit of the All-Party Oireachtas Committee on the Constitution (APOCC), but the Mother and Child Campaign questions the statement of An Taoiseach, Bertie Ahern, who, in making public this review, said that the Constitution needed to be changed to give better rights to the family which, he says, has undergone a major transformation in the past sixty-seven years.

The fact remains that a majority of Irish people consider the life-long marriage of a man and woman to be the best environment in which to raise children and the best basis for a stable and healthy society. The Mother and Child Campaign agree, as does Bunreacht na hÉireann, and recognising that the family as so described constitutes best practice, does not invoke discrimination against other circumstances.

The APOCC, in the view of this organisation, did not make an appropriate attempt to ensure that their review of the constitutional provisions dealing with the family was widely known amongst the electorate. Tens of thousands of people were only informed and facilitated in making submissions by the efforts of the Mother and Child Campaign. The APOCC should consider then, that the majority of families in this country are healthy and happy, and should not attempt to invoke further social changes which will add to the number who are not.

THE CONSTITUTIONAL FAMILY

The family is the fundamental social unit. Article 43.1.1 of Bunreacht na hÉireann recognises the special position of the family and gives it inalienable and imprescriptible rights, antecedent and superior to all positive law. Article 41.3.1 pledges the state to guard with special care the institution of marriage, on which the family is founded, and to protect it from attack. The Committee should not attempy to change or broaden this constitutional definition of the family.

The Mother and Child Campaign does not accept the UN definition of family, which, if used as a basis for any attempted changes to our Constitution, would effectively remove the status of marriage (on which the family is based and which is constitutionally protected and generally recognised and accepted) as an institution and to reduce it to one of the number of options, including – among others – homosexual units. We wholly reject any attempt to change, in any way, those articles of our Constitution pertaining to the family based on marriage.

The state has a duty to ensure that, for the future well-being of society, families be given such support as is necessary to maintain their acknowledged role in that society with dignity. The *Constitution Review Group Report* 1996 admits that none of the constitutions of countries consulted by them appears to attempt a definition of a 'family' in terms other than one based on 'marriage' (p. 322 of the Report). Indeed, in that report it is admitted that once one goes beyond the family based on marriage, definition becomes very difficult.

HOW SHOULD ONE STRIKE A BALANCE BETWEEN THE RIGHTS OF THE FAMILY AS A UNIT AND THE RIGHTS OF INDIVIDUAL MEMBERS?

The Constitution already does this, firstly by Article 41 which contains the main provisions relating to family, and, secondly by Article 40.3.1 which deals with personal rights. The identification of personal rights under Article 40.3 assures such rights are common to all citizens. The rights of the family as a unit and the rights of the individual members are complementary.

IS IT POSSIBLE TO GIVE CONSTITUTIONAL PROTECTION TO FAMILIES OTHER THAN THOSE BASED ON MARRIAGE?

The family based on marriage is the world's most enduring institution, largely because it is held to be life-long and faithful and because it has provided the best environment for raising children. The Mother and Child Campaign recognises the superb efforts made by lone parents to raise their children as best they can, but it remains the case that the two-parent family is the ideal. Recognising that ideal does not discriminate against, nor make judgment on, individual circumstances.

Every individual, because of his/her inherent human dignity, must be protected by the state. The family based on marriage is guaranteed protection under the Constitution and this must remain. It is not possible to give constitutional protection to families other than those based on marriage because the family is a union of a man and a woman in the lifelong convenant of marriage. Unions not based on marriage already have protection by the personal rights identified under Article 40.3. Where siblings or other family members reside together, some legal protection with regard to say, distribution of property etc, can be provided. The Constitution currently recognises that the family based on marriage offers the stability and security needed by society. This must not be weakened by affording the same status to other unions.

The Mother and Child Campaign also note that successive governments have failed in their duty to the family based on marriage and have in fact enacted anti-family legislation which has contributed to the breakdown of families. A review of the family policies of the state should be undertaken without delay and anti-family measures addressed.

WHO HAS THE RIGHT TO MARRY?

The legal right to marry should be restricted to one man and one woman, in the best interest of the nation's children and our society. The primary purpose of marriage is to rear children in a loving and secure environment. Children have the right to a mother and a father, and children being adopted are entitled to an adoptive mother and an adoptive father, to fulfil the roles of a natural mother and father. Homosexual and lesbian unions should not be given the status of marriage.

If the advocates behind gay marriage are to make a valid case of discrimination, they have some further explaining to do. Discrimination is unjust only when we give unequal treatment to people or things that are essentially the same. Thus no discrimination arises when restricting the right to marry to a man and a woman. The institution of marriage is an ancient and venerable one, and its meaning and nature cannot be changed by the state, who only serve to recognise and register it.

WHO HAS THE RIGHT TO ADOPT CHILDREN?

Homosexual and lesbian unions should never have the right to adopt children. They cannot provide the secure and loving best environment that children require. Parents of Irish children would be horrified to think that their children could, in the event of their deaths, be adopted by homosexuals or lesbians. No public support exists to give homosexuals or lesbians the right to adopt Irish children.

IS THE CONSTITUTION'S REFERENCE TO 'WOMAN'S LIFE WITHIN THE HOME' A DATED ONE THAT SHOULD BE CHANGED?

Absolutely not. This is vital constitutional provision and one that reflects the desire of the majority of Irish women, as shown in many surveys, to have the right to stay at home and rear their children. Mothers who make many sacrifices to rear their children at home do the state an inestimable and unrewarded service, and that the emotional well-being of children is vastly improved by their sacrifices, is now universally accepted. Most recently, research undertaken by Professor Jay Belsky, Director of the Institute for Studies of Children at Birbeck College, London, has found that there is no substitute for a child's parents, and especially for a mother in the early years of a child's life. He also says that children who spend more than twenty hours a week away from their parents, in childcare, from an early age are likely to be problem children, more aggressive and less well-behaved. The debate regarding childcare has shifted, in that we now discuss how damaging it may be – that it is damaging is widely accepted. Article 41.2 should not be changed – instead the Committee should recommend to the State that it fulfils its obligations to protect the mother at home.

The state has failed the mother at home and its current tax policies penalise families who provide full-time parental care for their children. These policies are unjust, unconstitutional and, in view of the demographic nightmare facing an aging Europe, are economically short-sighted and dangerous.

The Mother and Child Campaign note that the manner in which this question was phrased, gives rise to concerns regarding the objectivity of the APOCC. Had the Committee already decided that the constitutional protection of mothers at home is 'outdated' or was the Committee trying to be provocative? In either case the APOCC should wake up to the reality of the wishes and needs of Irish mothers, who do not enjoy the privilege of political patronage or attend the well-heeled gatherings of feminist Ireland. The Mother and Child Campaign will meet any attempt to remove protection from mothers at home with determined and successful opposition.

SHOULD THE RIGHTS OF A NATURAL MOTHER HAVE EXPRESS CONSTITUTIONAL PROTECTION?

The rights of the natural mother are already protected under Article 40 of the Constitution. A natural father's rights should have the same recognition as those of a natural mother.

SHOULD THE RIGHTS OF THE CHILD BE GIVEN AN EXPANDED CONSTITUTIONAL PROTECION?

Articles 41 and 42 formulate first principles with power and clarity for religion, for marriage, for the family and the children. Children's rights particularly as regard to education are protected by Article 42. As a result of Article 42, the Islamic Community in Ireland were able to insist on having their own Muslim primary school funded by the state, something they have not been able to achieve to date in England and France.

Legislation regarding the welfare of children has been established in accordance with the Constitution and children's rights are adequately protected. The only amendment we would seek to the Constitution which would further protect the rights of the child, is an amendment to fully prohibit abortion and embryo research.

DOES THE CONSTITUTION NEED TO BE CHANGED IN VIEW OF THE UN CONVENTION ON THE RIGHTS OF THE CHILD?

The child already enjoys constitutional protection which must be upheld by the State and the Constitution should not be amended to reflect the UN Convention on the Rights of the Child, or any other extra-territorial conventions.

A government conference in November 2004 in Doha, Qatar, adopted a ground-breaking document that endorses the traditional family as the foundation of society. The Doha declaration reaffirms that the 'family is the natural and fundamental group unit of Society and is entitled to the widest possible protection and assistance by society and the state' and calls upon all nations to 'uphold, preserve and defend the institution of marriage'.

The Doha International Conference for the family was convened by the State and Qatar to commemorate the tenth anniversary of the UN's International Year of the family. The Doha Conference was the culmination of a series of preparatory events around the world, including a number of high-level regional conferences that started in March with the Third World Congress of Families in Mexico City, evidencing the strength of a new international effort to recognise and protect the traditional family as the basis of a stable society.

The Doha Conference attracted hundreds of participants from different countries and cultures, including members of parliaments, scholars and non-governmental organisations. Prominent religious speakers included Pope Shenonda III of the Egyptian Coptic Church, Orthodox Jewish Rabbi Daniel Lapping, and Alfonzo Cardinal Lopez Trujillo of the Catholic Church.

The wife of the Emir of Qatar opened the conference with a speech praising the family as a 'sacred institution' that forges a 'strong bond between males and females which conforms to human nature in bearing and raising new generations'. Sheikha Mozah Bint Nasser Al-Missned warned against current attempts 'under the guise of modernity' to redefine the traditional religious and cultural understanding of the family.

The Doha declaration calls on governments to 'reassess' their 'population policies, particularly in countries with below replacement birthrates' and to 'ensure that the inherent dignity of human beings is recognised and protected throughout all stages of life'.

The 59th General Assembly of the UN meeting in New York on 6 December 2004 agreed by consensus, a resolution entitled 'Celebrating the Tenth Anniversary of the International Year of the Family' and formally noted the outcomes of the Doha International Conference on the Family held in Qatar in November 2004 including the Doha declaration.

The aspirations of the Doha declaration are already contained in our Constitution which protects the family based on marriage and should not be interfered with.

THE STATE AND THE FAMILY

Despite the constitutional protection afforded to the family based on marriage, the state continues to fail in its duty to protect and support the family, and has introduced a blatantly anti-family tax measure – tax individualisation – which actively discriminates against single-income families. The Committee should urge the state to reverse that policy immediately.

BUNREACHT NA hÉIREANN

The rights of the family under the Constitution should not be interfered with. Articles 41, 42 and 40.3 reflect the opinions of the majority of Irish people and the best practice for our nation, our children and our society.

MOTHERS AT HOME

INTRODUCTION

Mothers at Home supports the Irish constitutional definition of the family based on marriage.

MAH supports the current legal definition of marriage as laid down by Lord Penzance in *Hyde v Hyde* as 'voluntary union for life of one man and one woman to the exclusion of all others', expanded on by the Irish courts in *Murray v Ireland [1985]* Costello J: 'the Constitution makes clear that the concept and nature of marriage, which it enshrines, are derived from the Christian notion of a partnership based on an irrevocable personal consent given by both spouses which establishes a unique and very special life-long relationship'.

MAH supports the Supreme Court definition of marriage (*B v R [1995]*), as 'the voluntary and permanent union of one man and one woman to the exclusion of all others for life.'

MAH understands that when the Minister for Social Welfare declared (launch of the International Year of the Family, Dublin Castle, 1994), that his Department had embraced the UN technical definition of the family, he did not intend the UN definition to be understood other than in accordance with the Irish constitutional definition of the family based on marriage (as defined by the Irish courts). The UN definition is: 'any combination of two or more persons who are bound together by ties of mutual consent, birth and/or adoption or placement and who together assume responsibility for, *inter alia*, the care and maintenance of group members, the addition of new members through pro-creation or adoption, the socialisation of children and the social control of its members'. MAH takes it that the 'ties of mutual consent' means 'marriage' as defined by the Irish courts (above).

There is ample proof worldwide that faithfulness in marriage is a bulwark against the legion of existing threats to our children's and society's future, including the threat of the deadly AIDS virus, and enlightened policy makers cannot, dare not, ignore this proven fact. MAH supports the view that society needs the family based on marriage. The marriage-based family (as defined above by the Irish courts) is the fundamental unit of society – the *only* unit that can offer security and stability to our children and to future generations. Cohabitation, which is not permanent, does *not* offer security and stability, and enlightened policy-makers who truly care about how society is organised could *not* support the legalisation of social insecurity and social instability.

MAH believes that the family's needs are not being attended to by policies that force mothers to work outside the home. If parents are to be enabled to 'together assume responsibility for the care and maintenance of … and the socialisation of children', one parent –

usually the mother – must be free to choose to be a full-time carer, a stay-at-home mum. Article 41.2.1 and Article 41.2.2 of the Irish Constitution enshrines this principle. MAH also endorses the view held by a number of international and European women's movements (Mouvement Mondiel des Meres – MMM International – to which MAH is affiliated and also FEFAF – Federation Europeene des Femmes Actives au Foyer – and others), that if a study was carried out of the social and economic value of the work done in the home, it would be apparent to all but the most blinkered of policy makers that the cost of replacing home care by state care would be enormous and *not cost effective*. MAH wants that study done, before any decision is taken by the All-Party Oireachtas Committee review on the family.

We wish to refer our policy makers to the preamble to the European Foundation for the Improvement of Living and Working Conditions, which insists that achieving the EU goal of improving living and working conditions will only be possible when policy makers have good quality information. There is a wealth of good quality information available to support the view that the future of society passes by way of the marriage-based family as defined by the Irish courts (above). MAH is prepared to make this information available to policy makers here. If Ireland and the EU are seriously concerned about improving living and working conditions, then they will undoubtedly choose to protect and promote the proven vehicle, the marriage-based family, and oppose policies and laws that weaken or undermine this social unit.

The invitation by the APOCC for submissions directs respondents under nine headings. Based on the above statement, we endeavour to respond under the nine headings, although we are at a loss to understand why some of these questions are even included:

1 The Irish constitutional definition of the family should be upheld – i.e. a man and a woman united in marriage, together with their children.

2 The vast majority of families are functional units. Their differences are resolved and a balance struck within the family. The state has no authority to interfere in the functional family. The Constitution obliges the state to respect the authority of the family. MAH wants this obligation to remain and to be strengthened in law and policy. Questions of personal rights have always been resolved and should continue to be so under Article 40.3.

3 It would be contrary to the common good to give recognition to unions other than those based on marriage as defined above. There is abundant proof to show that promoting any other form of unions other than those based on heterosexual marriage leads to instability in society and poses a serious threat to the rights and needs of the child. The common good is not served.

4 Our position on homosexual coupling is clear for reasons that must be obvious to anyone with a

scrap of common-sense. Homosexual coupling can never be marriage.

5 Again our answer to this is uncompromisingly *no*. The reasons are thoroughly explained in the introduction to this submission. Far from being outdated, Article 41.2.1 and Article 41.2.2 were never more necessary than they are at this point in time, for the sake of mothers, for the sake of fathers, for the sake of the children and in the interests of the common good.

6 The constitutional rights and duties of the stay-at-home mother (including natural, adoptive, foster mother) as expressed in Article 41.2.1 and in Article 41.2.2 should be upheld in law and policy. These rights, which imply rights and duties to the married father, cannot and should not be understood or interpreted other than in accordance with the natural law understanding of the family as defined at (1) above.

7 Refer to (6) above. MAH supports the current legal position that makes the married father (including natural, adoptive, foster-father) the custodian of his family.

8 MAH supports the true rights of all children, born and unborn. The right to kill a child, born or unborn, at home or abroad, should not be protected by the Constitution.

9 UNCRC should respect *an* Irish constitutional position in line with (8) above.

GAY MARRIAGE

We feel strongly that the term marriage should be reserved for the traditional concept of marriage, but consider that other domestic situations should have legislative provision made for them in the Constitution including civil unions, mutual wills, inheritance and property rights.

WOMAN'S PLACE IN THE HOME

The reference to this is outdated. The Constitution must recognise the value of family life and support persons (of both sexes) who care for others in the home. Mothers should not be obliged to work outside the home by economic necessity if they do not wish to do so.

THE NATURAL FATHER

The natural father should have rights equal to the mother where he provides materially for the child, and takes part in its upbringing. It should be obligatory for him to provide maintenance for the child, if necessary by deduction from his earnings or state benefits.

RIGHTS OF THE CHILD

The Constitution needs to be changed to include the provision of the UN Convention on the Rights of the Child. The best interest of the child must always take precedence in all cases concerning children.

MOTHERS UNION IN THE DIOCESE OF CASHEL AND OSSORY

The Mothers Union in the Diocese of Cashel and Ossory, endorsed by the Trustees of the All-Ireland Mothers Union, would like to make the following submission to the All-Party Oireachtas Committee on the Constitution.

The Mothers Union is a world-wide Anglican organisation promoting Christian marriage and family life. Two of its objects are to promote conditions in society favourable to stable family life and the protection of children, and to help those whose family life has met with adversity.

In view of these objects members of the Cashel and Ossory Mothers Union would like to make the following comments for consideration.

DEFINITION OF THE FAMILY

The family protected by the Constitution is the family based on marriage. At present there are many family units not based on marriage – cohabiting couples, lone parents, same-sex couples. We think the UN definition of the family is all-embracing and acceptable.

MUINTIR NA hÉIREANN

The Constitution of Ireland – Bunreacht na hÉireann, enacted in 1937, is one of the youngest extant constitutions. Other countries, with constitutions ranging in age from seventy-five to two hundred and seven years, respect their constitutions and are loath to change or replace them.

The following are some thoughts on a number of issues raised in the advertisement for submissions.

1 HOW SHOULD THE FAMILY BE DEFINED?

The Mother & Child organisation does not accept the UN definition of family which was adopted by the then Minister for Social Welfare on behalf of the Irish people. This definition, if used as a basis for the proposed changes to our Constitution, would effectively remove the status of marriage (on which the family is based and which is constitutionally protected and generally recognised and accepted) as an institution and to reduce it to one of a number of options, including – among others – homosexual units. We wholly reject any attempt to change, in any way, those articles of our Constitution pertaining to the family based on marriage. The state has a duty to ensure that, for the future wellbeing of society, families be given such support as is necessary to maintain their acknowledged role in that society with dignity. The relevance of religious and moral values for the economic vitality of families and communities is most important. In a report by the Constitution Review Group in 1996 it is admitted that none of the constitutions of countries consulted by them appears to attempt a definition of a 'family' in terms other than one based on marriage. Some clearly link family with marriage (p322 of the Report). Indeed in that report it is admitted that once one goes beyond the family based on marriage, definition becomes very difficult.

2 HOW SHOULD ONE STRIKE THE BALANCE BETWEEN THE RIGHTS OF THE FAMILY AS A UNIT AND THE RIGHTS OF INDIVIDUAL MEMBERS?

The Constitution already does this, firstly by Article 41 which contains the main provisions relating to family, and secondly by Article 40.3.1 which deals with personal rights. The identification of personal rights under Article 40.3 assures such rights are common to all citizens precisely because, whether or not they may wish to believe or accept it, the fact is that all persons' rights derive initially from God.

3 IS IT POSSIBLE TO GIVE CONSTITUTIONAL PROTECTION TO FAMILIES OTHER THAN THOSE BASED ON MARRIAGE?

It is not possible nor is it desirable to give constitutional protection to families which are not based on marriage. Every society should have a moral basis and an ideal for people to strive for and marriage between a man and a woman should be the moral ideal. Families which are not based on marriage already have protection by the personal rights identified under Article 40.3.

4 SHOULD GAY COUPLES BE ALLOWED TO MARRY?

Under no circumstances should gay couples be allowed to marry. Marriage is the unit most suited to raising children. Homosexuals by their relationship itself cannot produce children, therefore have no need of marriage. The preamble to the Constitution states: 'In the name of the most Holy Trinity, from whom is all authority and to whom, as our final end, all actions both of men and states must be referred.' To allow homosexual marriage would be to fly in the face of God. It would also give homosexual couples the right to adopt children up to 18 years of age. I do not think any parent surrendering their child for adoption in this or any other jurisdiction would give up their child for adoption if they believed they would be adopted by homosexuals. It would also mean that a sixteen year old, who could be homeless, could be adopted by a homosexual couple for perverted reasons. History should teach us that any society which condoned homosexuality ended up as decadent and collapsed, e.g. Roman and Greek empires.

If the advocates behind gay marriage are to make a valid case of discrimination, they have some further explaining to do. Discrimination is not inherently unjust. It is unjust only when we give unequal treatment to people or things that are essentially the same. So when someone cries 'discrimination' because the law does not recognise gay marriage, what he is really saying is that homosexual sex and marriage are essentially the same as heterosexual sex and marriage. Before the law is changed to allow gay marriage, the gay activists (and the judges who seek to empower them) should be required to explain this essential similarity.

Some gay activists try to meet that burden by claiming that marriage is, at its core, the legal recognition of a committed, loving relationship between adults, but that is incorrect. Marriage is not, and has never been, the mere recognition of committed and loving relationships between adults. Lots of adults love one another and are committed to one another (a grandmother and her adult grandchild; or war buddies, or close sisters, and the like), but these commitments have never been considered marriage. No one would argue that these relationships are essentially the same as a heterosexual marital relationship. So it remains an open question why two homosexuals should qualify for marriage merely because they claim to love one another dearly.

Gay activists might also argue that marriage is the formal recognition of a monogamous sexual relationship, and since the Supreme Court recently removed all legal barriers to homosexual sex, the government should likewise bestow formal recognition on monogamous sexual relationships between homosexuals. But let us not forget that two homosexual people are anatomically incapable of having sex with one another. The mutual stimulation engaged in by homosexuals is very different from sex, for which heterosexual couples are uniquely equipped.

Given these differences, the burden lies squarely on the homosexual activists to press the case further. To do so, they must delve into religion and morality. If they want government to redefine sex and marriage, they must be required to explain the very origins of sex and marriage and prove that human government has the authority to redefine them. Therefore, they will have to argue, first that heterosexual marriage is either merely a man-made social construct or else the result of blind social evolution, and secondly that the sexual organs of males and females were not designed to fit together for any special purpose beyond mere biological reproduction.

Looking at the debate in this light, it becomes clear that gay activists are engaged in that which they purport to hate. They are trying to force their world view (be it religious or irreligious) onto their fellow citizens.

Don't get me wrong. This is their prerogative. It is the very purpose of legislatures to debate the rightness or wrongness (read the 'morality') of the law and it is the very purpose of elections to try to force one's beliefs onto others by electing one's preferred candidate over the preferred candidate of one's neighbour.

Supporters of traditional marriage should not fear the struggle over the morality or immorality of gay marriage. Rather, they should fear that our lawmakers – or worse yet, our courts – might make a decision without addressing the real issues: are we certain that there is nothing supernatural about heterosexual sex and marriage? And are we certain that human government should claim the authority to redefine them?

The strongest defenders of traditional marriage defend it because they believe it was instituted by God. They believe that government merely recognises marriage and cannot redefine something it did not create. The strategy of the gay activists is to remove marriage from this vaunted status and bring it down to earth, where mankind can tinker with it. Their claim is that government – not God – has the sole authority to define sex and marriage. With the wind of some bizarre Supreme Court rulings at their backs (holding that the law may reflect irreligion but not religion), the gay activists have reason for optimism.

The supporters of traditional marriage should not underestimate what is at stake. Whether the gay activists know it or not, they are poised to destroy not just discrimination against homosexuals, but marriage itself. Outwardly, the advocates of gay marriage claim to admire marriage. But to claim that authority to redefine marriage they must first claim that marriage is a flawed man-made institution that needs to be reworked, or worse yet, that it is merely a result of an unguided evolutionary process. Do not miss what is happening here. In order to gain the right of gay marriage, its advocates must first strip it of all transcendence, destroying the very thing that makes marriage lovely.

Gay activists claim to believe marriage is so meaningful that it should be extended to gays, but their case rests on the belief that marriage is so meaningless that it can be claimed by anyone who wants it. They say they want to broaden marriage to extend its joys to more people, but if marriage is expanded to encompass all committed, affectionate relationships, it will lose all of its meaning and will vanish from the earth.

5 IS THE CONSTITUTION'S REFERENCE TO 'WOMAN'S LIFE WITHIN THE HOME' A DATED ONE THAT SHOULD BE CHANGED?

No. It is an important provision as recent statistics show that the majority of women work part-time outside the home. Indeed a survey done a few years ago revealed that most women, if given a choice, would prefer to stay at home. Economic conditions and the needs of governments, due to falling birth rates, force more women into the workforce. This has been proved

in other countries as well as here to be very short-sighted. When both partners work the size of the family decreases, hence the falling population in Europe and Ireland. It has recently been estimated that Europe, in the next twenty years, despite huge immigration, will still not have enough people for their economies. France has taken action and introduced measures to try to reverse this trend and increase its population. One of the things it has done is to allow the mother to stay at home until her child is of school age. A lot of social problems are due to the absence of mothers in the home. It is very important that a mother be there when her children come home from school so that they can tell what happened at school, because they will have forgotten by the time their mother comes in at six. I think that Article 41.2 enshrines the support mothers give to the state in the Constitution.

6 SHOULD THE RIGHTS OF A NATURAL MOTHER HAVE EXPRESS CONSTITUTIONAL PROTECTION?

These are already protected under Article 40 (particularly under Article 40.3) and Article 41. What is needed is legislation to back up what is already in the Constitution.

7 WHAT RIGHTS SHOULD A NATURAL FATHER HAVE AND HOW SHOULD THEY BE PROTECTED?

These similarly can be protected by legislation. Alan Shatter in his book *Family Law in the Republic of Ireland* says 'whereas the state pledges itself "to guard with special care the institution of marriage, on which the family is founded and to protect it against attack" there is nothing in the Constitution which of necessity withholds constitutional recognition from the family not based on marriage.' There should be no discrimination against fathers as is favoured by feminist groups and the UN. The Constitution at present protects natural fathers under personal rights but the legislature, because of feminist activists, does not safeguard these rights.

8 SHOULD THE RIGHTS OF THE CHILD BE GIVEN AN EXPANDED CONSTITUTIONAL PROTECTION?

Articles 41 and 42 formulate first principles with power and clarity for religion, for marriage, for the family and the children. Children's rights particularly as regard to education are protected by Article 42. As a result of Article 42 Muslims in Ireland were able to insist on having their own Muslim primary school funded by the state, something they have not been able to achieve to date in England and France and this is thanks to the Constitution. Legislation regarding the welfare of children has been established in accordance with the Constitution and children's rights are adequately protected. The only amendment we would seek to the Constitution which would further protect the rights of the child is that abortion should be prohibited. This was the intention of the people who voted for the amendment to the Constitution in 1981 but was interpreted differently by the courts.

9 DOES THE CONSTITUTION NEED TO BE CHANGED IN VIEW OF THE UN CONVENTION ON THE RIGHTS OF THE CHILD?

No. See in particular reply to No 1. I don't think any views of the UN should be entertained with regard to the rights of the child while it actively promotes abortion as a means of birth control in third world countries. If families based on marriage are actively supported in the Constitution the rights of the child have a better chance of being protected.

NATIONAL CONSULTATIVE COMMITTEE ON RACISM AND INTERCULTURALISM (NCCRI)

> Although there are a myriad of family types in Ireland not all have equal opportunities to do well, to access appropriate services, to flourish under positive state policies and services designed for them and to live up to their full potential.
>
> – Karen Kiernan, Family Diversity Initiative

A INTRODUCTION

The National Consultative Committee on Racism and Interculturalism (NCCRI) was established in 1998 as an independent expert body focusing on racism and interculturalism. The NCCRI is a partnership body which brings together government and non-government organisations, and is core funded by the Department of Justice, Equality and Law Reform.

The NCCRI hosted a major national conference on Minority Ethnic Families in December 2003. In the context of the tenth anniversary of International Year of the Family (2004), the NCCRI published an issue of *Spectrum* looking at this area. *Spectrum* is available on the NCCRI website, www.nccri.ie. One of the key recommendations coming out of the conference in December 2003 was that forthcoming review of the position of family in the Irish Constitution should seek to take into account all forms of diversity, including cultural diversity among families.

The launch of the National Action Plan against Racism (NPAR) on 27 January 2005 provides a framework for the development of intercultural policies in Ireland. Initiatives to promote the integration of minority ethnic families should be contextualised within this framework, consequently this submission will provide a brief overview of the NPAR, as a context for the discussion of racism and diversity in Ireland. Ethnic minority families face the same challenges as all families; however these can be exacerbated by their vulnerable

position in Irish society. The submission will conclude with a brief look at some of the key issues which are of concern to the NCCRI, and which cause particular hardship for minority ethnic families in Ireland. In particular:

1 The experience of the Traveller community
2 The impact of Direct Provision on asylum seekers
3 The experience of migrant families.

National Action Plan against Racism

On 27 January 2005 the government launched 'Planning for Diversity: The National Action Plan Against Racism'.

The NPAR originates from commitments given by governments at the United Nations World Conference Against Racism in South Africa in 2001. The decision to develop the NPAR was further reaffirmed in the Social Partnership Agreement for 2003-2005. The emphasis throughout the Plan is on developing reasonable and common sense measures to accommodate cultural diversity in Ireland. The Plan outlines an intercultural framework which will underpin the overall approach to its implementation. The framework consists of five key priorities: protection, inclusion, provision, recognition and participation. Accommodating diversity in service provision includes a focus on common outcomes in education, health, social services and childcare, and the administration of justice. Recognition and awareness of diversity, includes a focus on awareness raising, the media and the arts, sport and tourism. The framework is summarised in Table 1.

Table 1: Summary of the Intercultural Framework underpinning the NPAR

Protection	Effective protection and redress against racism
Inclusion	Economic inclusion and equality of opportunity
Provision	Accommodating diversity in service provision
Recognition	Recognition and awareness of diversity
Participation	Full participation in Irish society

The Plan will be monitored though a high-level strategic monitoring group and will be supported by the Department of Justice, Equality and Law reform.

B RACISM AND DIVERSITY IN IRELAND

There has always been cultural diversity in Ireland, despite the widely believed myth that Ireland has been and still is a homogeneous and mono-cultural society or encounters diversity solely along religious grounds (Protestant and Roman Catholic). In addition to the Traveller community there is a long established Jewish community and growing Islamic, Asian and Chinese communities in Ireland. However, there has been a significant broadening of cultural diversity in recent years, both in terms of numbers of people and national or ethnic origin.

There are now approximately 160 different nationalities living in Ireland.[1] According to the 2002 census there were 224,261 non-Irish people usually resident in Ireland, 133,436 of which are EU nationals, 23,105 are nationals of other European countries, 20,981 are African, 21,779 are Asian, and of the remainder the vast majority are from North America and Australia. 2,340 people indicated they were of multiple nationalities, while in 48,412 cases nationality was not stated. The 2002 Census of population indicates that non-nationals make up 5.8 percent of the population, of which almost half were UK nationals (2.7 percent).

The 2002 Census indicates that there are 23,681 Irish Travellers, representing approximately 0.65 percent of the population.

In the context of Ireland's growing economy the number of migrant workers has increased significantly in recent years. The Central Statistics Office published its Population and Labour Force Projections in December 2004. It estimated that Ireland will need 30,000 immigrants a year to the period to 2036 if economic growth is to be maintained. It forecasts that the economy will need 45,000 immigrant workers every year for the next 12 years to sustain economic growth. There were approximately 34,000 work permits issued in 2004.

Racism

> Any distinction, exclusion, restriction or preference based on race, colour, descent, or national or ethnic origin which has the purpose or effect of nullifying or impairing the recognition, enjoyment or exercise, on an equal footing, of human rights and fundamental freedoms in the political, economic, social, cultural or any other field of public life.[2]

Racism is a specific form of discrimination and exclusion based on the false belief that some 'races'[3] are inherently superior to others because of different skin colour, nationality, ethnic or cultural background. Racism deprives people of their basic human rights, dignity and respect. There are different forms of racism in Ireland including the racism experienced by:

- Travellers on the basis of their distinct ethnic identity and nomadic tradition
- migrant workers, refugees and asylum seekers
- minority ethnic groups, including black people on the basis of their skin colour and ethnic and/or national identity, regardless of their legal status.

It is also important to emphasise the connection between racism and other forms of
discrimination including gender, disability and sexual orientation.

The government's Know Racism campaign[4] published research findings on racism and attitudes to minority groups in February 2004. The study found that 18 per cent of respondents had personally witnessed racist behaviour. 48 per cent of respondents believe that Irish society is racist to some degree. 72 per cent agreed that the settled community is not willing to accept the Traveller community living among them.[5]

2003 was the first full year in which racially motivated incidents were clearly defined to members of An Garda Síochána, and recorded through PULSE. According to An Garda Síochána 81 incidents of racist motive were recorded in 2003. This compares to 102 in 2002, 43 in 2001, 65 in 2000, and 12 in 1999. The most common forms of incidents were criminal damage, assault and public order offences.

In May 2001 NCCRI established a system for recording incidents related to racism in Ireland. Incidents are analysed and compiled into six monthly reports.

Table 2: Summary of incidents reported to the NCCRI to August 2004

May 2001- October 2001	41
November 2001- April 2002	40
May 2002 - October 2002	67
November 2002 - April 2003	48
May 2003 - October 2003	46
November 2003 - April 2004	42
May 2004 – October2004	70

In its latest report, covering May 2004 to October 2004, the NCCRI recorded seventy racist incidents. Examples of racist incidents that involved assaults, abuse and harassment, include:

- A South African family experienced racist verbal abuse from a person in a blacked out car when out taking a walk by the beach in southern Ireland. The person kept stopping and starting the car in a very threatening and intimidating manner.
- A Pakistani woman and her child were at home in their rented apartment in a local housing complex when people tried to break into her apartment. She rang the guards and fled to the street. The two men who tried to gain entry to her apartment followed her, accompanied by a third person, and hurled racist comments and threats at her. One of the men struck her in the face. The woman fears for her life and the life of her child. She is desperate to be located in another area but she is afraid that she will face the same problem of racism there also. She intends to bring these men to court.
- A Filipino national and her child reported that they had been subjected to ongoing racist verbal abuse from their neighbour in Co Galway. The abuse was constant over a period of many months until the family were compelled to report it to the Garda.

C FAMILY DIVERSITY IN IRELAND: MINORITY ETHNIC GROUPS

Families of immigrants and ethnic minorities, of course, experience the same difficulties as other families in relation to parenting, relationship difficulties, reconciling work and family life, childcare and care of the elderly, with these being exacerbated by their situation of vulnerability.

Racism and discrimination can undermine the enjoyment of family life for minority ethnic groups. However the challenges for minority ethnic and multi-ethnic families are not limited to discrimination, they also experience a whole range of issues on a day-to-day level which are specific, including questions relating to international adoption, and parents from different backgrounds.

However the extent to which diversity has been reflected in social policy relating to the family is limited. As Mary Daly puts it:

> The extent to which the existence of difference and diversity has been absorbed by policy remains limited however. Diversity tends to be seen in terms of structure (the fact that Ireland now has families of different types) rather than in terms of culture (people having different values and practices around childrearing and other aspects of family life)... The main underlying point was that, in the context of increasing diversity in Irish society, we need a definition of family that encompasses all types of families.
>
> – Mary Daly (2004) *Families and Family Life in Ireland,* Challenges for the Future.

Failure to accommodate multiple-diversity may be the cause of additional levels of marginalisation, discrimination and disadvantage.

The range of experiences of minority ethnic families, and the specific difficulties they face through racism and discrimination must be targeted and addressed in Irish social policy. By recognising difference and providing a structure to accommodate it, the State will promote the rights and entitlements of all families in Ireland, including minority ethnic families.

D INTERCULTURAL APPROACHES TO SOCIAL INCLUSION

Interculturalism is essentially about interaction, understanding and respect. It is about ensuring that cultural diversity should be acknowledged and catered for. It is about inclusion for minority ethnic groups by design and planning, not as a default or add-on. It further acknowledges that people should have the freedom to keep alive, enhance and share their cultural heritage.

Interculturalism, as a term, has emerged as the dominant conceptualisation in the European context in terms of mediating policy strategies which seek to avoid the identified problems with earlier approaches to integration.

The concept of interculturalism can be distinguished from polices based on ideas of assimilation, or the absorption of minority ethnic groups into the dominant culture. Assimilation was in the past the dominant approach to integration. It has now largely recognised that this approach fails to respect the human rights of minority ethnic groups. The concept of multiculturalism emerged largely as a reaction to the assimilation

approach. However criticism of some conceptualisations of multiculturalism have focused on the fact that it constructs minority communities as homogenous entities with no internal divisions. It has also been criticised for failing to address state racism and strengthening systems of power relations within communities.

A key concept which has emerged in terms of the social inclusion of minority ethnic groups is integration. Integration has been defined as:

> Integration means the ability to participate to the extent that a person needs and wishes in all the major components of society, without having to relinquish his or her own cultural identity (Department of Justice, Equality and Law Reform, 1999).

Integration is generally regarded as a two-way process between minority ethnic groups and the majority populations.

The full enjoyment of family life is a key element of the integration process; without a focus on the family it will not be possible to secure the full social inclusion of minority ethnic groups. As Gerry Mangan of the Office of Social Inclusion, has put it:

> Strengthening families must be of even greater importance for the well-being of immigrants and ethnic minorities than for other residents, and for helping them achieve social inclusion. At the same time, family cohesion must also be at greater risk, especially from poverty and social exclusion.

Research at an international level has shown that ethnicity can be a major factor in determining access to, participation in, and outcomes from service provision, including those services that directly impact on minority ethnic families.

It is important that the full range of services which impact on family life in Ireland adopt an intercultural approach which facilitates the needs of minority ethnic groups. As Naina Patel has put it:

> A good practice approach which is sensitive to the needs of minority clients is to adopt an open-ended approach. Being receptive to situations rather than putting situations in a pre-designed framework is the good that we should strive for – Naina Patel (2004), *Spectrum*

In particular minority ethnic groups and the community and voluntary sector have identified a clear need for proactive targeting of minority ethnic families for accessible information on rights and entitlements.

F SPECIFIC ISSUES

1 Traveller community

Racism and discrimination in relation to the Traveller community in Ireland, has raised specific difficulties with regard to the enjoyment of family life. Specific issues which have been raised by the NCCRI in recent years include educational disadvantage and problems relating to the provision of Traveller accommodation.

Educational disadvantage

There are consistent problems of underachievement by members of the Traveller community at all levels of the educational system. Table 3 demonstrates the number of Travellers aged 15 and over, classified by the highest level of education completed at the last census.

Table 3: Irish Travellers aged 15 years and over, classified by highest level of education completed, 2002 (Source: CSO)

Total	13,680
Total whose full-time education has ceased	11,035
Primary	7,491
Lower secondary	1,444
Upper secondary	338
Third level – non-degree	81
Third level – degree or higher	116
Not stated	1,565
Education not ceased	2,645

Accommodation

January 2005 saw the launch of a report by the National Traveller Accommodation Consultative Committee (NTACC), which showed that there are 788 families on unauthorised sites, 408 on the roadside with 380 in private houses and on other sites. There have also been cases where members of the Traveller community were targeted for attack in residential contexts. For example at the end of November 2004 the national newspapers carried the story of a Traveller family whose caravan was burnt down and who were living in a tent after local residents stopped them moving into a short-term home.

In recent years the introduction of conflicting legislation has proved particularly controversial. For example The Housing (Miscellaneous Provisions) Act 2002 allows for gardaí to remove caravans, and to allow owners to be brought before the District Court charged with trespass. The owner can be fined €3,800. There is evidence which suggests that an increasing number of Travellers are being evicted.

2 Direct provision

Since April 2000 most asylum seekers have been housed through 'direct provision'. This means that newly arrived asylum seekers are directly allocated full-board hostel/hotel accommodation typically based outside Dublin, they receive a residual income maintenance payment of €19.05 per week for an adult and €9.52 for a child. Discretionary needs payments can also be provided in exceptional circumstances.

Research has identified that asylum seekers in direct provision accommodation are particularly vulnerable. In the context of reduced social welfare payments, some have suggested that asylum seekers cut down on food intake, which is having health implications. The reduced payment hinders contacts with the wider society and the lack of meaningful occupation and the resulting dependency is perceived as a real source of mental distress by asylum seekers. As Dibelus (2001) has concluded:

> Poor reception conditions, substandard housing, social isolation and long periods of inaction during the asylum determination procedure are all among the factors that can influence the capacity of refugees and asylum seekers to become independent and fully participate in the economic, social, political and cultural life of the host society.

There has been increased attention given to the position of *unaccompanied minors* in recent years. Unaccompanied minors who are aged between 12 and 18 live in hostel accommodation outside the direct provision system, younger children are placed in care. Particular media attention has been given to the number of unaccompanied minors who are currently missing in Ireland. According to an article in the *Village* (20 January-4 February 2005) 48 children went missing from the Eastern HSE region in 2004. In 2004 174 unaccompanied minor asylum seekers came into the care of the ECAHB.

3 Migrant families

> It is often said in relation to immigration policy that 'we looked for workers, but got people' and, for the fortunate ones, families.

Discrimination in the housing sector

There are significant concerns that minority ethnic groups face ongoing discrimination in the private rented sector in Ireland, this negatively impacts families in terms of their accommodation arrangements. A study by the Vincentian Refugee Centre found that refugees and asylum seekers face problems in finding and securing rented accommodation. twenty-six per cent of the Centre's clients experienced discrimination and racism while looking for accommodation.[6] Respondents often described bad-quality accommodation as the only type they could secure in the private sector.[7] A national housing agency has warned that foreigners are more likely to face illegal evictions by landlords. The agency stated that landlords are still carrying out illegal evictions and that foreigners are particularly vulnerable. These comments were made after a court case where a Sri-Lanka couple was awarded €25,000 after being thrown out on the street by their landlord.[8]

Family reunification

The question of family reunification is often the most pressing one facing minority ethnic families in Ireland. Organisations working with migrants and refugees have raised serious concerns about the implications of the current family reunification system in Ireland. According to Catherine Cosgrave of the Immigrant Council of Ireland 'no domestic law specifically provides for a right to enter and remain in Ireland for the purposes of family reunification'.

In the case of work permit holders an application can only be made for a spouse to join them as a dependent after twelve months. In a recent major study commissioned by the Immigrant Council of Ireland, immigrants outlined their experiences – both positive and negative – of living and working in Ireland. The study found that a number of the research participants were living without close family members because of the difficulties they had experienced when trying to get family members (including minor dependent children) to join them in Ireland.

There are also problems of family reunification of refugees. In particular the Irish Refugee Council has pointed out that 'unfortunately the process of family reunification can presently take in excess of two years from the date of application until the family member arrives in Ireland. This is due primarily to an increase in applications in recent years and a subsequent back log in processing applications...'

Organisations working with migrants and refugees have expressed concern regarding the restrictive family reunification rights, under the new provisions for residency for the parents of Irish born children.

Notes
[1] Unfortunately in the 2002 Census the ethnicity question was limited to the Traveller community; consequently we do not have a real sense of ethnic diversity in Ireland and are reliant on data relating to nationality.
[2] Article One of the UN International Convention on the Elimination of all Forms of Racial Discrimination (CERD). Ireland's combined first and second report under the Convention will be considered by the Committee on the Elimination of all Forms of Racial Discrimination on 2/3 March 2005.
[3] The term 'race' has been used in the past in an attempt to rank people according to physical and biological criteria. Nowadays, 'race' is often written in inverted commas to underline the difficulty in defining that term.
[4] The government's three-year Know Racism public awareness campaign came to an end in 2004, though the activities of the campaign will be continued through the implementation of the NPAR.
[5] Millward Brown IMS (2004) *Presentation of Research Finding on Opinions on Racism and Attitudes to Minority Groups,* 26 February 2004, Dublin: Know Racism.
[6] Melia, P (2004) 'Refugees face racism barrier in search for rented housing', in *Irish Independent,* (01.03.2004.
[7] Kenna, P and MacNeela, P (2004) *Housing and Refugees: The Real Picture,* Dublin: The Vincentian Refugee Centre.
[8] Brennan, M (2004) 'Foreigners more vulnerable to illegal evictions', in *Irish Examiner* (31.03.2004).

NATIONAL MEN'S COUNCIL OF IRELAND

CONSIDERING YOUR ADVERTISEMENT

Upon considering the matter and with the benefit of examining the briefing documents produced by the Committee but not made generally available to the citizens through your advertisement, we make the following observations.

1 Under the Constitution of Ireland, 1937 it is the responsibility of the elected representatives to submit their proposals for amendments to the Constitution to the people who are the sovereign power. Article 46.2:

> 1 Any provision of this Constitution may be amended, whether by way of variation, addition, or repeal, in the manner provided by this Article.
>
> 2 Every proposal for an amendment of this Constitution shall be initiated in Dáil Éireann as a Bill, and shall upon having been passed or deemed to have been passed by both Houses of the Oireachtas, be submitted by Referendum to the decision of the people in accordance with the law for the time being in force relating to the Referendum.

Your request for 'submissions' from the people, the sovereign power, to yourselves, an informal committee of Deputies that holds no statutory power, would appear to be a *usurpation of sovereignty.*

2 You appear to have failed to properly inform the citizens of Ireland of the true agenda of your committee. The advertisement placed in national newspapers omitted the following paragraph.

> The committee's concern will be to analyse the issues to determine whether or not legislative provision has been constrained by the Constitution so as to prevent a proper balance being achieved between the rights of the individual and the good of the community; and if it has, *to make recommendations for constitutional change.*

Of all the documentation that you have provided, only this paragraph describes precisely the whole purpose of your activities. *Therefore any group or individual who responded to your advertisement without knowledge of your purpose was deceived.*

It is plain from this paragraph that your committee intends to entirely disregard any public concerns that their constitutional protections should be retained, protected or strengthened and that your intention is simply to filter out material that does not support your own agenda and to only consider *change to the Constitution which would act, by definition, contrary to the current common good.*

This is not declared in the advertisement.

3 It would appear from the following paragraph that does appear in your advertisement

> The All-Party Oireachtas Committee on the Constitution, which is charged with reviewing the Constitution in its entirety, is now examining these Articles to ascertain the extent to which they are

serving the good of individuals and the community, with a view to deciding whether changes in them would bring about a greater balance between the two.

that you have failed to comprehend the purpose of these Articles [41,42].

The Preamble to the Constitution will assist you to a proper understanding:

> And seeking to promote the common good, with due observance of Prudence, Justice and Charity, so that the dignity and freedom of the individual may be assured, true social order attained, the unity of our country restored, and concord established with other nations …

The Articles of the Constitution, as you can see, and in particular the family articles exist to serve only 'the common good' from which the dignity and freedom of the individual will be assured. Your stated purpose therefore is obviously futile since the balance you seek to ascertain is neither intended nor given effect by these Articles.

4 The concern of your Committee, as you have stated in your briefing document No. 2, is to determine if a *proper balance* has been achieved between the *rights of the individual* and the *commond good,* and *if by your evaluation it has not, you intend to recommend change to the constitution.*

Your concerns appear to be almost identical to the agenda of the Irish Human Rights Commission stated to us in a letter dated 8 December 2004, where the Chairman Mr Manning wrote:

> Our job is to examine the law and practice to ensure that it does comply with all human rights law, both in the Constitution and international covenants and if we are not happy that it is so, to ask that the law be changed.

However, it would appear to us that your proper job in this instance of the matter of constitutional amendment is laid out for you in Article 46.2 which states:

1 Any provision of this Constitution may be amended, whether by way of variation, addition, or repeal, in the manner provided by this Article.

2 Every proposal for an amendment of this Constitution shall be initiated in Dáil Éireann as a Bill, and shall upon having been passed or deemed to have been passed by both Houses of the Oireachtas, be submitted by Referendum to the decision of the people in accordance with the law for the time being in force relating to the Referendum.

and Article 6:

1 All powers of government, legislative, executive and judicial, derive, under God, from the people, whose right it is to designate the rulers of the State and, in final appeal, to decide all questions of national policy, according to the requirements of the common good.

It is quite clear from this that your job as TDs is, if you feel it is necessary, to propose to the citizens by way of a Bill any amendment 'according to the requirements of the common good', and obviously you must present argument in favour of your own proposal to explain clearly to the people how this amendment will benefit the common good.

Your job is not to determine 'a proper balance' between individual rights and the common good. Your job is to co-ordinate these factors.

> President de Valera: 'The position of a legislature, … for the future as in the present must be that it will be free to co-ordinate the public good, the individual good and the individual right. That is its prime, main duty.
>
> {Debates on the Constitution, 4 June 1937}

It would appear, therefore:

i That you have attempted to usurp the sovereign power of the people.

ii That you have misinformed and deceived the people of your true purpose and in doing that have wasted the public's time and abused their genuine concern for the family and the well-being of the nation.

iii That you have misused public funding in that you are undertaking a job that the Constitution does not require you to do and which can serve no purpose.

DEVELOPMENT OF THE LEGISLATION

We are particularly concerned by the second paragraph of your advertisement and your claim that,

> Following the enactment of the Constitution, legislation relating to the family has been developed in line with those Articles [41, 42 and 40.3] and elucidated by the courts in a substantial body of case law.

Professor Delaney in his work *The Administration of Justice in Ireland* describes this process of 'elucidation' and the technique of statutory interpretation that has developed.

> The interpretation of a piece of enacted law requires not only a familiarity with the meaning of technical legal terms, but also with the whole branch of the law of which the statute forms a part; in particular, it requires a knowledge of the rules of interpretation which are themselves rules of law. Thus there is a rule against taking into account anything said or done while the statute is passing through parliament; and there are certain statutory rules with regard to the construction to be placed on words importing number and gender. If a question as to the meaning of a statute arises in an action at law, the judge will have to decide the meaning, and his decision will be binding for all future cases in which the same question arises.

If we compare the will of the legislature and the way that eminent judges have interpreted their legislation we can see immediately how the will of the people, the sovereign power in Ireland, can never be safely implemented through the courts.

In the lead up to the vote on Article 41 of the Constitution, on 4 June 1937, Éamon de Valera is asked to clarify the meaning of 'inalienable and imprescriptible rights' so that the legislators would understand clearly what they were voting for.

> Professor O'Sullivan: That is all I want to know. The court will then be in the position of deciding what 'inalienable and imprescriptible rights' are, ...

> President [Éamon de Valera]: ... The inalienable and imprescriptible rights are the rights [of parents] to look after the maintenance and control of the children. ... We want to stress the fact that these inalienable and imprescriptible rights cannot be invaded by the State.

> Article 41 put and agreed to.

Compare this with the interpretation of these 'inalienable and imprescriptible rights' by Barrington J in the Supreme Court in *O'R (W) v H (E) [1996]* IESC 4 (23rd July 1996)

> Article 42 of the Constitution is an extension of Article 41 and refers to parents and children within a family context. It refers to the inalienable rights and duties of parents and to the imprescriptible rights of the child.

It clearly does not according to the will of the legislature. Barrington then continues,

> In other words it refers to a relationship between three people which carries with it reciprocal rights and duties which the positive law is enjoined to respect. The rights of the child are clearly predominant. They alone are described as being imprescriptible ...

Again reference to the debates and the meaning specified and agreed to by the Oireachtas clearly shows that parents' rights are also imprescriptible and clearly predominate. Barrington's interpretation is fallacious. De Valera explained to the Oireachtas that the parents needed their inalienable and imprescriptible rights so they could look after and control their children.

Again Barrington opined,

> Article 42 is concerned primarily with the relative rights and duties of parents and children. Article 41, by contrast, is concerned with the family as a group or institution and with its rights vis-a-vis other groups or institutions in society.

As we have seen, this is plainly not true because de Valera explained to the Oireachtas that the inalienable and imprescriptible rights are the rights of parents to look after the maintenance and control of the children and the Article was passed on that basis.

If no account is taken by Judges, in the interpretation of the Constitution, of the debates where the true meaning of provisions are explained and the legislation passed on that basis then democracy is seriously at risk and the morals of the nation are prey to the sort

of judicial activism perpetrated by Barrington J in the example given.

We must note here that despite the accepted rules of interpretation, it appears judges are free to ignore them when it suits and even second guess so-called 'intentions of parliament'. As an example Murray J, currently Chief Justice and Chairman of the Courts Service, in the Supreme Court, *R v R* and the State, April 2 2004, 436SS., who apparently felt able to,

> know the clear *intention of parliament* that the courts should have a discretion to award custody to either separated parent according to what was in the best interests of the children.

THE CONSTITUTION PROTECTS THE PEOPLE

Fundamentally, the 1937 Constitution of Ireland recognises that the greatest possible danger to the freedom and well-being of its people lies in interference by the state in the family.

By observation of the breakdown of social structure by other nations, the people of Ireland were able to identify that the root cause of the problem was founded in the unfettered authority of the state.

It can come as no surprise, therefore, that Ireland's Constitution is incompatible with many of the international conventions at present in existence. This was the deliberate intention of the family provisions of the Constitution and their sole purpose is to protect the Irish people from descending into the pit of moral and social chaos that has engulfed many other nations.

Successive Irish governments over the past forty years have betrayed the Irish people through the introduction of legislation repugnant to the Constitution and through signing, ratifying and implementing international conventions which are in conflict with the fundamental rights of Irish people.

> First of all, the family stands as a bulwark against the state. It has been described as the greatest fortress of human liberty. All serious tyrannies have tried to undermine it.
> – Baroness Young, 'Standing Up For The Family'

FUNDAMENTAL PRINCIPLES RELATING TO THE FAMILY BROUGHT ABOUT BY THE ENACTMENT OF THE CONSTITUTION

1 The state no longer has the authority of the crown of England. The people are no longer subjects of the King and are *free persons and as citizens hold the sovereignty of the nation.*

2 The family is an institution with its own constitution and authority.
From the debates on the Constitution 2 June 1937:

> Mr. McDermot: There is one question I would like to put to the President: what is the meaning of subsection 2° of Section 1: 'The State, therefore, guarantees to protect the family in its constitution and authority...' What does 'authority' mean? Does it mean the authority

of the head of the family over the family? If it does not mean that, what alternative meaning is there?

President de Valera: It is the authority of the heads of the family over their children, their right to look after their education and not to be interfered with by another authority in the State except for reasons that would be mentioned; that is to say where there was failure or neglect on their part to provide for the children, or, from the social point of view, failure to see that the children received a proper education. The family have rights antecedent to and superior to all positive law, and any interference with the authority of the head of the family will have to be justified on certain grounds. That is the authority that is referred to there.

3 The only grounds on which the state can interfere with the authority of the family are stated in and controlled by Article 42.5.

42.5 In exceptional cases, where the parents for physical or moral reasons fail in their duty towards their children, the State as guardian of the common good, by appropriate means shall endeavour to supply the place of the parents, but always with due regard for the natural and imprescriptible rights of the child.

The family has inalienable and imprescriptible rights derived from God which cannot be invaded by the state.

From the debates on the Constitution 2 June 1937:

The President: ... The inalienable and imprescriptible rights are the rights to look after the maintenance and control of the children ... We want to stress the fact that these inalienable and imprescriptible rights cannot be invaded by the State.

Article 41 put and agreed to.

4 The family's constitution is hierarchical – this is essential for the protection of the family from external forces. It has by necessity, like all institutions, a hierarchical structure for its efficient management, its safety in emergencies and its general well-being.

In England in 1925 the Lord Chancellor made clear the opposition to the idea of joint equal guardianship, which the promoters of a bill had put forward, and the English parliament rejected the idea as being detrimental to married family harmony.

Objections to equal guardianship by parents were that the,

net result of the bill would be to substitute a legal for a domestic forum in every household ... that to put mothers on an equal footing with fathers in all matters concerning their children would simply produce deadlock; that although woman has almost the same status as man, she has not altogether the same status because it is necessary to preserve the family as a unit and if you have a unit you must have a head.

In 1937 the head of the family institution was acknowledged to be the father. His authority and position was recognised by the courts in the matter of N.P. an infant [1943] 78 I.L.T.R. 32[HE]:

the father is the head of the household and is liable to contribute to the cost of maintenance of his wife and family [and in the matter of custody] if the circumstances show that he has not disentitled himself I rather lean in favour of conceding to him a greater claim than to the mother.

The constitution of the family has not changed and can only be changed by referendum of the people. *At the present day the father is held to be head of the family.*

5 In exercising his authority in his position as head of the family he must respect his wife's rights and implement any agreement he makes with her regarding the children's education.

6 Authority within the family is transferred hierarchically, under certain circumstances (such as death or failure), from the father to the mother and so on through the available relatives.

7 Despite the father being recognised in the Constitution as head of the family and as having authority this is not made explicit in the Guardianship of Infants Act, 1964 so that it might assist him to exercise his duty to maintain and protect his family. Instead the courts use this position against him.

LEGISLATION UNDER THE ENGLISH CROWN

Prior to the enactment of the Constitution the Irish people were subjects of the English monarchs. Under English law the father's authority had become almost absolute over the centuries and mothers had very little, if any, rights with regard to their children. The father's position was such that even the Royal Courts of Chancery could not override his authority unless he had disentitled himself.

The equity jurisdiction of the Royal Courts of Chancery was derived from the prerogative of the crown to act as 'supreme parent' to all children. This position permitted the King's court to interfere with the father's authority to resolve family disputes. It evolved solely and only out of the absence of mothers' rights under English law.

Even under the equity jurisdiction the Royal Court could not supersede the father's authority without him first disentitling himself to his children and a set of grounds for disentitlement were established *(see discussion of these below)*.

Hence the equity jurisdiction in custody and guardianship matters has three requirements:

1 That the court has a crown prerogative as 'super parent' to its child subjects.

2 That the Mother has no rights in law.

3 That the court first find the father has disentitled himself to his absolute authority.

In 1937 this entire situation ended with the enactment of Bunreacht na hÉireann. The implications of the new situation were:

1 The state was released from its crown jurisdiction and could henceforth serve the people, the new sovereign power, in place of the monarchy and was obliged to promote the common good by vindicating the rights of its new Irish citizens.

2 Such was the authority of the new family as recognised in the Constitution that the state was henceforth made to pledge itself not to interfere with the family and to protect it from attack.

3 Only under exceptional circumstances as laid down in the Constitution would the state be called upon to endeavour to replace the position of the parents in a child's life.

4 Under the Constitution Irish mothers, in contrast with mothers in the past, are now entitled to extensive rights.

Under this new system of government and sovereignty it would be reasonable to expect that legislation relating to the law of the family would develop on the basis of provisions enabling the vindication of parental rights. For example it would be reasonable to assume that a mother's rights could be easily vindicated in a marital dispute by simply regulating the father's authority by way of injunction. It would very rarely appear to be necessary for the state to entirely supersede a father's authority in order to resolve a dispute.

Similarly a father's authority could be protected by injunctions where necessary against his wife.

A system such as this would ensure that justice prevailed and that the welfare of the children would continue to be found within the family and that the common good would be preserved and protected.

DEVELOPMENT OF THE LAW OF THE FAMILY
1937–1963

In dramatic contrast to the aforementioned position the published case law reveals that the Irish courts dealt with the new arrangement very tentatively, perhaps due to the precariousness and uncertainty of the prevailing political situation.

The courts appear to have been preoccupied with establishing the grounds on which parental authority could be superseded and case law slowly established the circumstances under which the state could interfere with the family. But the vindication of rights of parents to protect their children is extremely low on the agenda and is in fact, as a concept, almost absent.

The courts established the circumstances under which a father's authority ought be transferred to the mother, or in the case where there was only one parent living, where the state might supersede that parent's authority and place the children under the authority of a third party.

All these decisions had been grounded upon the exceptional circumstances laid down by article 42.5 of the Constitution.

> where special disturbing elements exist, which involve the risk of moral or material injury to the child, such as the disturbance of religious convictions or of settled affections, or the endurance of hardship or destitution with a parent, as contrasted with solid advantages offered elsewhere. *O'Hara, 1900 Fitzgibbon L.J.*

The *test* applied for intervention in all these cases was not, as has been claimed, that 'differences' between the father and mother had developed which jeopardised the child's welfare. This is just a statement of the facts.

The test applied was – whether or not the parent entitled to exercise authority over the child (that is the head of the family) had conducted themselves in such a manner so as to satisfy the court that this was an exceptional case that required the transfer of that authority to the other parent or a third party.

Such exceptional cases includes a violation of an agreement with the other parent regarding the religious education of the child – such a violation would be held to disturb the convictions of the child and would be judged to be a moral failure on behalf of the parents.

The law certainly did not develop on the basis of injunctions against parents who have violated the rights of the other spouse which accounts for almost all private family law cases today.

In our opinion, in custody cases involving parents and their minor children, the state's proper concern can only be – firstly to establish whether or not the case is an exceptional one that requires {for reasons of the child's welfare laid down in Article 42.5} the transfer of authority away from the parent entitled to exercise authority over the children.

Where those grounds are found not to exist, the state is not entitled to act in opposition to the parental right, so it must next consider if it is necessary to vindicate the rights of one of the parents if the other parent is violating those rights.

This appears to us to be the settled position prior to the enactment of the Guardianship of Infants Act, 1964.

THE GUARDIANSHIP OF INFANTS ACT

In 1963 something went terribly wrong.

Charles Haughey, then Minister for Justice, introduced a new bill called the Guardianship of Infants Bill.

The first and inexplicable feature of this bill is that it was introduced as a consolidation of the five British statutes that amended the English law of custody and guardianship that had developed under the English monarchy in the previous three hundred years prior to the creation of the Republic.

The English law had developed on the principle that mothers had no rights and on the principle that the people were subject to the authority of a reigning monarch. These principles are obviously redundant in the modern Republic of Ireland.

An analysis of the Act and debates reveals that it promotes itself by claiming to deal with two burning feminist issues of the time:

1 The demand from women for 'equality' with men in every aspect of life. In this case the framers of the Act sought to appease women by pretending to provide equality between husbands and wives. Minister Haughey claimed in introducing the Act that,

> the bill proposes to give statutory effect to the legal principle that the mother and father of a child shall have equal rights to guardianship and custody.

In fact it does not do this at all.

2 The problem of illegitimate children, their mothers and the scandal of children held in state-approved institutions or disposed of by those institutions.

The Act relieved the state of their own problem by placing these children in the sole unmonitored care of their unmarried mothers and provided a mechanism by which these women might reclaim their children from the institutions. These measures, which were intended at the time to get the state 'off the hook' of guilt, in fact, whether on purpose or not, established the female-headed household in Ireland and created the enormous problems we are faced with today.

Apart from these provisions to look after unmarried women this Act provides no mechanism for married parents to vindicate their rights no matter what their circumstances. Nor is there any reference to Article 42.5 that controls the state's jurisdiction in family matters whereas the Oireachtas had a clear expectation that the Act would not only be implemented in the High Court only, but that it would also be implemented according to constitutional law.

> Mr M.J. O'Higgins: 'The Minister has expressed the fear that this bill might be accused of being legislation for the abnormal situation or the broken home. That might be, but in some respects it is the kind of legislation which is possibly likely to give rise to family disputes rather than to settle them. This is a subject in respect of which the Minister and the House generally must step rather gingerly having regard to the constitutional provisions which are there. The Minister has referred to some of those constitutional provisions and I am glad he has, because it shows that the matter has been under examination in his Department.
>
> The difficulty I see with regard to this bill and with regard to any law on this subject, having regard to the provisions of the Constitution, is that it is difficult to see that we can unequivocally declare that the welfare of the child must be of first and paramount importance. I am not saying that that should not be the position, but what I have in mind is that there are very definite provisions in the Constitution which seem to me to provide that the family unit as a whole, not the individual component parts of that unit, must be regarded as of first and paramount importance.

The Minister has referred to Article 42 of the Constitution. He quoted Article 42.1 which states:

> 'The state acknowledges that the primary and natural educator of the child is the family and guarantees to respect the inalienable right and duty of parents to provide, according to their means, for the religious and moral, intellectual, physical and social education of their children.'

> In dealing with the bill and, it seems to me to be clear from the terms of the bill itself, the emphasis is laid rather on trying to secure in the case of children that the parents will do their duty but this Article of the Constitution which was quoted by the Minister refers not only to the duty of the parents but also to their inalienable right. I would suggest to the Minister that he must be very careful to see in relation to this bill whether or not it is open to challenge on the grounds of the very Article of the Constitution which he himself quoted ...

> I do, as I say, recognise that there is certain authority being vested in the courts under this bill but Article 42.5 of the Constitution does provide that only in exceptional cases can the state step in. It reads:

> 'In exceptional cases, where the parents for physical or moral reasons fail in their duty towards their children, the state as guardian of the common good, by appropriate means shall endeavour to supply the place of the parents, but always with due regard for the natural and imprescriptible rights of the child.'

> In other words, the degree of failure under that Article of the Constitution is clearly defined and very limited and restrictive in character. Where the parents for physical or moral reasons, and only for physical or moral reasons, fail in their duty towards their children, the state as guardian of the common good, by appropriate means shall endeavour to supply the place of the parents, but always with due regard to the natural and imprescriptible rights of the child. As I say, the class of cases in which the state can step in, as it is to some degree stepping in under this bill, is very limited and confined in character. *Debates of Guardianship of Infants Bill, 1963, 11 July, 1963*

The section of the Guardianship of Infants Act, 1964 that is used almost exclusively since its implementation has been Section 11. Inexplicably there is no record of any debate on the significance of this section in the Oireachtas records.

Combined with the rest of the Act this section re-enacts the equity law of England that was in existence before the Constitution superseded it. This unthinkable retrogressive step ignores the whole existence of mothers' rights, fathers' rights, the restrictions on state interference, the state's obligation to vindicate parental rights recognised in the Constitution and all of the established principles that had developed in case law over the previous quarter century!

Far from giving equal rights of custody to mothers, as claimed by Mr Haughey, *Section 11.2 is a provision solely for married mothers to apply for custody.*

This subsection from the 1886 Guardianship of Infants Act is founded on the principle that mothers have no rights of custody and that the state has a crown prerogative to grant and regulate custody rights to Irish married mothers.

It gives statutory effect to the legal principle that fathers hold the custody of the children of the marriage by re-enacting Section 5 of the 1886 Act which *also has the effect of enacting the entire rules of equity which require that the father be disentitled to his children before the state can resolve any family disputes.*

The equity rules of the Royal Courts of England enacted in this subsection of the Act were declared as marginal notes in the published bill and it is apparent from the explanatory memorandum that mothers and fathers do not have joint custody as is often claimed.

However, the published Act omits these marginal notes which are essential for any interpretation of the Act by the courts or court users. As a result the people have been kept in ignorance by this concealment of the true nature of this foundation stone of the so-called family law acts.

The whole legal system has become embroiled in Mr Haughey's deception and to this day family law textbooks, the Legal Aid Board's explanatory leaflets and the government information website continue to attempt to deceive the public even though everyone knows that there is something terribly wrong going on in the secret family law courts.

In an attempt to hide what would have by now become glaringly obvious as a fraud and a flagrant violation of constitutional rights if the Act was used in isolation, the Guardianship of Infants Act, 1964 has been incorporated into many other family law acts that deal with the welfare of children, such as Judicial Separation Act, Divorce Act and Domestic Violence Act.

Where custody issues arise under section 11, which accounts for almost every case, this dispute resolution mechanism is only available to married mothers.

Married fathers cannot use this provision and have no alternative process available to them.

Under section 11 the officers of the court set out to 'establish' the grounds that the judge requires to make a finding that the father is disentitled and so set in motion his crown jurisdiction (authorised by Mr Haughey's government in 1963) to regulate the whole family's affairs.

The Victorian grounds under equity that 'disentitle' a father appear to be as follows:

1 Unfitness in character or conduct.

2 Failure to provide support for his children. Fathers are advised to pay 'maintenance' even where their wives have deserted them and removed the children from the family home without his consent and this payment, by way of his continuation to perform his constitutional duty, is taken as a 'confession' by the court that the father has 'failed' to provide support.

3 Lack of means to support his children. Being unemployed disentitles a father or even having inadver-

tently 'failed' to provide a deserting wife with what she claims for herself and for the children.

4 By agreement between the father and third parties if the third parties have acted so that revocation would prejudice the child. This means that a deserted father asking for assistance risks permanently losing his children.

5 If the father intended to leave the jurisdiction with the child. Possession of a passport or passports for the children will be construed as intention to leave the jurisdiction.

THE SECRET EFFECT OF THE RULES OF EQUITY

A study of current family law legislation will reveal that it is enacted in apparently gender-neutral terms. For example the Non-fatal Offences Against the Person Act, 1997; The Domestic Violence Act, 1996; The Family Law (Maintenance of Spouses and Children Act), 1976; The Lone Parent Allowance Scheme.

Although these appear on the face of it to be equally applicable to men and women, when a married father becomes involved with any of these pieces of legislation, and they interact with the secret laws of equity used in the family courts, it will be seen that this automatically triggers the empowerment of the state to acquire jurisdiction and over-ride his authority.

The vast structure of Irish family law is based almost solely on Section 11 of the Guardianship of Infants Act, 1964.

We have noted that although the father is recognised in the Constitution as head of the family and as having authority this is not made explicit in the Guardianship of Infants Act, 1964 so that it might assist him to exercise his duty to maintain and protect his family.

Instead the courts use this position against him.

Thus the position of a married father vested with the authority to protect his family from the state puts him in the front line of attack from the very state that is pledged in the Constitution to not interfere with his family and protect his marriage from attack.

The result of these secret laws implemented in secret courts, which persecute good men and deprive honest women of their real rights, is that thousands upon thousands of families have been dismantled without any regard to their constitutional rights, thousands of children have been deprived of the love, protection and guidance of their fathers, who themselves have been stripped of their children, their homes, condemned to destitution, debt-bonded slavery and driven to desperate acts – many taking their own lives in utter despair.

This is an incalculable atrocity perpetrated upon the Irish nation.

THE PEOPLE MUST ACT

Whereas in the USA and most other republics where the state education system ensures that every child studies the Constitution and in fact can recite chunks of it off by heart, the state in Ireland has ensured its citizens have been kept in the dark about the content and purpose of the Constitution.

By this neglect of the state's duty, the people are unaware that they hold the sovereign power and that the Constitution is specifically in place to protect their freedom and to keep in check the otherwise unfettered tyranny of a totalitarian state.

Furthermore the state broadcasting station, Radio Telefís Éireann refuses to acknowledge its constitutional commitments to the common good and continues to spread its anti-family, anti-faith and anti-freedom propaganda unabated by the mounting complaints from the people.

Cloaked by the cover of the in-camera rule, parents are not being permitted in the courts to vindicate their constitutional rights and prevent interference by the state into their families and private lives.

On the basis of the overwhelming evidence, it can not be denied that the state machine detests the Constitution.

It hates the protections that it gives the people.

It vehemently resents the restrictions and obligations that the Constitution imposes upon it.

The conclusion that must be drawn from the evidence is that the state is hell-bent on destroying the very Constitution that created it.

The people must resist this by working together, by educating themselves as to the power that the Constitution gives them and by standing up against the state machine when their conscience guides them to do what is right.

In these harsh times we need to remind ourselves of and find solace in the preamble to the Constitution:

> In the Name of the Most Holy Trinity, from Whom is all authority and to Whom, as our final end, all actions both of men and states must be referred, We, the people of Éire, Humbly acknowledging all our obligations to our Divine Lord, Jesus Christ, Who sustained our fathers through centuries of trial, Gratefully remembering their heroic and unremitting struggle to regain the rightful independence of our Nation, And seeking to promote the common good, with due observance of Prudence, Justice and Charity, so that the dignity and freedom of the individual may be assured, true social order attained, the unity of our country restored, and concord established with other nations, Do hereby adopt, enact, and give to ourselves this Constitution.

Our rallying cry must be:

> We shall not permit our Constitution to be stolen from us!

[Four appendices entitled 'Parental Rights and Marriage in Ireland and the Constitutional Review', 'Open Letter to all TDs and Senators' 'The Family – Marriage and Children' and 'The Rights of Women and the Violation of their Marriage by the State' were included with this submission. For copies and further information, please contact the National Men's Council of Ireland.]

NATIONAL WOMEN'S COUNCIL OF IRELAND

WHAT IS THE NATIONAL WOMEN'S COUNCIL OF IRELAND?

The National Women's Council of Ireland – Comhairle Náisiúnta na mBan – is the national umbrella organisation for women's groups and organisations. Its membership is diverse and includes national, regional and local organisations, single issue groups and service providers, trade unions, community development organisations and women's groups.

The National Women's Council of Ireland, formerly known as the Council for the Status of Women, was founded in 1973 by seventeen women's organisations to monitor the implementation of the First Commission on the Status of Women. The Council now has one hundred and sixty member groups representing three hundred and fifty thousand women.

Working as the national representative organisation of women in Ireland, our mission is to achieve women's equality, empowering women to work together, while recognising and mobilising difference, in order to remove structural political, economic, social/cultural and effective inequalities.

HOW SHOULD THE FAMILY BE DEFINED?

The Concept of the Family in the Ireland of Today

The NWCI advocates using the definition of family as outlined by the United Nations. The technical definition of the family used by the UN is:

> Any combination of two or more persons who are bound together by ties of mutual consent, birth and/or adoption or placement and who, together, assume responsibility for, inter alia, the care and maintenance of group members, the addition of new members through procreation or adoption, the socialisation of children, and the social control of members.

The Family and the United Nations

Article 16.3 of the Universal Declaration of Human Rights states that:

> The family is the natural and fundamental group unit of society and is entitled to protection by society and the state.

The recognition of the family as the natural and fundamental group unit of society is also contained in the International Covenant on Economic, Social and Cultural Rights (Article 10) and in the International Covenant on Civil and Political Rights (Article 23). Ireland is a party to both of these International Treaties and thus under international law is bound to abide by them.

It is to be noted that these Conventions, although recognising the right to marry, do not expressly restrict the understanding of family to that of the family based upon marriage. The United Nations itself accepts that the concept of family is not restricted to that of the traditional family based upon marriage. One of the principles underlying the United Nations International Year of the Family 1994 was as follows:

> Families assume diverse forms and functions from one country to another, and within each national society. These express the diversity of individual preferences and societal conditions. Consequently, the International Year of the Family encompasses and addresses the needs of all families.

The Irish Constitution, on the other hand, through the provisions of Article 41, recognises the family as the natural, primary and fundamental unit of society only in so far as it is based upon marriage:

> ...that the family referred to in Article 41 is the family which is founded on the institution of marriage and, in the context of the Article, marriage means valid marriage under the law for the time being in force in the state.
>
> per Mr Justice Henchy in *The state (Nicolaou) v An Bord Uchtala* [1966] IR 567.

This restricted view of the family has already placed Ireland in breach of its international human rights obligations. In the case of *Johnston and Others v Ireland* (1987) 9 EHRR 203, the European Court of Human Rights found that the inferior position at law of the Applicant, who was a non-marital child, violated the guarantee under Article 8 of the European Convention of Human Rights to respect for family life. Many of the inequalities faced by a non-marital child were rectified by the Status of Children Act 1987. In the case of *Keegan v Ireland* (1994) 18 EHRR 342 the European Court of Human Rights held that the Applicant's right to respect for his family life had been violated when he, as a natural father, had no right to be appointed guardian and thus to have had a role in the adoption proceedings concerning his child.

In order to comply with international human rights requirements, and to reflect the reality of family diversity the Constitution must therefore have due regard to the rights and concerns of all families.

SHOULD GAY COUPLES BE ALLOWED TO MARRY?

The NWCI believes the Constitution should explicitly recognise gay and lesbian partnerships as family units and the subsequent recognition of the necessity to provide rights for gay and lesbian couples. Under Irish law same-sex couples, and indeed non-married heterosexual couples do not have the same rights as married couples. This has the potential for discrimination of same-sex couples, e.g. in the area of property rights, inheritance and the rights of partners in emergency situations (Equality Authority (2000): Partnership Rights of Same-Sex Couples).

Recognition has been forthcoming from many European countries through Domestic Partnership laws which allow gay and lesbian couples many of the rights which are enjoyed by married people. Examples of European countries which provide for domestic partnerships are Denmark, Norway, Sweden and the Netherlands. Debate on this issue has also taken place in the legislatures of the Czech Republic and Spain. In addition, Australia and New Zealand recognise lesbian and gay partnerships for the purpose of immigration. In the United states of America many cities and private companies also recognise lesbian and gay partnerships.

IS THE CONSTITUTION'S REFERENCE TO 'WOMAN'S LIFE WITHIN THE HOME' A DATED ONE THAT SHOULD BE CHANGED?

The Constitution should not ascribe gendered roles to either women or men. Therefore it is the view of the NWCI that this reference should removed.

> Despite amendment over the years, the Constitution has not kept pace with social change and still bears the imprint of the period at which it was originally drafted. One of the ways in which this manifests itself is in its reference to women in certain roles, and its correlative lack of reference to men in these roles. Specific mention is made of the role of women in the home and as mothers (Article 40.3.3 and 41.2.1 & 2). Nowhere in the Constitution is the word 'father' to be found; nor is the role of men in the domestic sphere specifically addressed. Furthermore, it is clear from the tenor of the relevant constitutional provisions that it is in their role as wives and mothers that women are especially valued.
>
> (from Connelly, Alpha in *Gender and the Law in Ireland*, ed. Connelly, Alpha. Oak Tree Press : Dublin 1993)

It is abundantly clear that society should value the care work which predominately women perform. The Irish government has signed up to commitments under the Convention on the Elimination of Discrimination Against Women and under the ten critical areas of the Beijing Platform for Action. The patriarchal assignment of women to perform certain roles within family and within society has not been to the advantage of women and has undermined the progression of equality for women.

Even the current Irish Constitution, which expressly recognises that *'by her life within the home, woman gives to the state a support without which the common good cannot be achieved'*, did not give any substantive rights to women. For example in the case of *L v L* [1992] 2IR 101 the Supreme Court held that only a married woman who made monetary contributions to the acquisition of the family home could have an intrinsic property right. It is only through breaking down stereotypes that the value of women and the work they do will be recognised by Irish society.

CONCLUSION

It should be recognised that the state has used its concept of the family primarily to mould the role of women into that which suits a patriarchal society. In addressing the future of the Constitution, there is a critical opportunity to reject gendered stereotypes and establish rights for men, women and children. It is also a critical opportunity to recognise family diversity in Ireland and provide rights for all family units.

THE NATIONAL YOUTH FEDERATION

INTRODUCTION

It is clear that the role of the family in Ireland is changing. Over 30% of all births are now to unmarried parents. Families are getting much smaller and the traditional extended family may be less prominent in the future. In more instances two parents work outside the home. The provision for divorce and remarriage will lead to first and second families. Increased immigration will lead to significant numbers of people living here who have a different cultural view of the family. Practical issues of tax and social welfare also need attention.

In our National Youth Poll young people told us that family was the second most important issue in their lives after health. We are currently doing qualitative follow up work on this to examine this finding in more detail.

The Report of the Constitution Review Group has commented on and analysed this change in depth. It is important at this juncture to inject some urgency into the process of proper legal recognition and rights for those who have heretofore fallen outside of the traditional definition of the family. There are literally thousands of parents and children who live in a legal and constitutional limbo which affects major parts of their everyday lives. Analysis and debate on constitutional reform has gone on for many years (the original Review Group reported in 1996!) now and it seems important that action replaces analysis as soon as possible, particularly given the criticism of precisely this inaction by the UN Committee on the Rights of the Child in its observations on the implementation of the UN Convention in Ireland.

OUR VALUES

The national Youth Federation works on a set of values as outlined in our Strategic Priorities.[1] Two of these values have direct relevance here. We seek to empower young people, that is give them influence and power in society; the Constitution as the basic law is of major importance in this. We also seek to promote equality amongst young people particularly on the nine grounds of equality legislation; the constitutional treatment of the family has significant bearing on the equality of young people.

PRINCIPALS

Protection of children

Modern legal thinking gives a greater emphasis to the protection of children than the protection of the family unit. The protection of children (those under eighteen) should be central to any constitutional changes in relation to the family regardless of where or with whom such children live.

Children's rights

Closely related to this is the concept of children having rights independent of their parents or guardians. The UN Convention on the Rights of the Child which Ireland signed in 1992 is the prime legal instrument in this area and any domestic changes necessary to give it full force should be made.

Express rights, not implied

Many family rights have arisen from an implied right to privacy in the Constitution and personal rights, these need to be expressed in a more definitive way. Such issues are too fundamental to be granted by interpretation by judges. Family rights and the individual's rights to family life should be given express recognition.

Societal cohesion

Clearly we need to respond to the changing nature of society. However, many people will be concerned about going too far in the other direction. The value placed on family is a positive thing that needs to be enhanced and improved, not removed.

Bearing this in mind we have sought to answer the questions posed by the committee

How should the family be defined?

Most other questions follow from this fundamental one. The inference the courts have drawn from the Constitution that the family that receives constitutional protection is the family based on marriage leads to a lot of problems. Indeed in certain geographic areas families based on marriage may be in the minority.

Given the changing nature of society this provision seems to be the one that is most in need of updating and would have knock-on effects on other areas. It is clearly important to value a widespread feeling that the family based on marriage is in need of protection and this is the view of most religions and many non-religious people.

Therefore a balance needs to be struck. The perverse situation whereby a couple can be treated jointly for social welfare purposes but not for tax or succession purposes is one major anomaly which can even disincentivise marriage and stable family formation.

The Review Group has set out six examples of non-marital families. The difficulty of the state adjudicating on different relationships and their bona fides is clear. What type and duration of relationship could qualify? Clearly the presence of children is important but married couples with no children currently receive rights and protection.

However the subject of these current considerations is the provision in the Constitution. It is possible to qualify provisions with the phrase 'as shall be provided for in law' thus giving the Oireachtas the power to regulate these matters or indeed to delegate such matters to tribunals of some sort.

The route favoured by the Review Group based upon rulings of the European Court Of Human Rights has distinct advantages. This essentially provides for protection of individuals family rights as opposed to the collective rights of the family unit. The question of what is or is not a family would be decided on a case-by-case basis; however an amendment to the Constitution would guarantee the respect for family life while maintaining the protection for the family based on marriage.

We are happy to endorse this approach as balancing the desire for the protection of the family based on marriage with the need for rights of people in non-marital situations, particularly children and young people.

HOW SHOULD ONE STRIKE A BALANCE BETWEEN THE RIGHTS OF THE FAMILY AS A UNIT AND THE RIGHTS OF INDIVIDUAL MEMBERS?

One of the major developments in this area over the last number of years has been that of children's rights (defined as all those under eighteen in the UN Convention). The rights of children are thus recognised in certain instances as being independent of their parents or guardians. The general trend is to work with families in all instances, however even with the strong constitutional position of the family in Ireland, outside involvement is often sanctioned in extreme circumstances.

The extent of independent children's rights will be controversial in certain areas for example access to medical treatment without the consent of a parent or in adoption.

However, in the round, allowing for the development of children's rights and the UN Convention it would seem necessary to give some rights to individuals within the family.

It is also important that adoption and fostering are valued by society and that parents and children in these situations can have clarity and certainty.

IS IT POSSIBLE TO GIVE CONSTITUTIONAL PROTECTION TO FAMILIES OTHER THAN THOSE BASED ON MARRIAGE?

This is covered in question one. The Review Group's comments on continuing the protection for marriage but removing the phrase 'upon which the family is founded' are consistent with this approach as is a greater role for the Oireachtas.

SHOULD GAY COUPLES BE ALLOWED TO MARRY?

We don't have a position on this issue. However we have an equality policy that emphasises equal treatment for people regardless of sexual orientation. It would seem easier to make some progress under the rubric suggested under the first question. The rights of the individuals are thus the defining issue as opposed to the unit formed.

IS THE CONSTITUTION'S REFERENCE TO WOMAN'S 'LIFE WITHIN THE HOME' A DATED ONE THAT SHOULD BE CHANGED?

In short yes, however some protection for the role of people who care for others in the home as suggested by the Review Group is welcome and should be gender neutral.

SHOULD THE RIGHTS OF THE NATURAL MOTHER HAVE EXPRESS CONSTITUTIONAL PROTECTION?

We favour the Review Groups approach to give constitutional status to rights which have previously been unenumerated in this area. It still seems open to debate whether the change envisaged under the first question should be gender or parent specific. On the face of it and in a spirit of equality it seems it should not be so.

WHAT RIGHTS SHOULD A NATURAL FATHER HAVE, AND HOW SHOULD THEY BE PROTECTED?

It seems quite incongruous in this day and age that the natural father of a child does not have constitutional rights or that they are seriously inferior to those of the mother; further that marriage confers rights on non-biological fathers that can be superior to those of natural fathers.

Such a legal order can discourage responsible attitudes amongst many fathers and hamper fathers who after lack of initial interest may want to be a part of their children's lives when at a more mature stage; this may be common amongst teen parents.

While lack of presence and lack of interest by fathers in their children should be discouraged it is important to always hold out the hope of both parents being actively involved in parenting. It should be borne in mind that the UN Convention on the Rights of the Child provides children with the right to know and have a relationship with both parents.

The fact that Ireland has been found to be in breach of the European Convention of Human Rights in this area is another cause for prompt action. Once more this situation may be open to remedy with the amendment envisaged under the first question, as appears to be envisaged by the Review Group.

SHOULD THE RIGHTS OF THE CHILD BE GIVEN AN EXPANDED CONSTITUTIONAL PROTECTION?

Yes. All international and domestic developments support this view. Once more the unenumerated rights should be expressly provided for. It will also be necessary to give some indication as to whose rights take precedence and at what stage, for example in terms of medical treatment. It might be best to allow this to be done by the Oireachtas outside of fundamental areas.

DOES THE CONSTITUTION NEED TO BE CHANGED IN VIEW OF THE UN CONVENTION ON THE RIGHTS OF THE CHILD?

Yes, as above. It also seems clear that the state has a good way to go to meet the provision that every child has the 'right to know and be cared for by his or her parents' whether this be fathers rights, adoption, succession or administrative procedures such as the granting of birth certs and passports.

The Review Group has also outlined the issues around putting the 'best interests of the child' first.

A full paragraph on the rights of the child consistent with the UN Convention should be inserted.

OTHER PROVISIONS, EDUCATION, HOUSING AND SOCIAL

It is important to recognise that other parts of the Constitution outside of the express provisions have effect on family life. Reference is made by the review group to provisions on education. There may be scope for improvement in these articles to provide for minimum levels of education. Social provisions such as a right to a home can also have major benefits to families and family life. One practical example here is the number of young parents who cannot return to education after having a child in their teenage years. A Constitutional guarantee in this situation would be a pro family measure. Constitutional change to ensure the equalisation of the treatment of nonmarried couples for tax and social welfare purposes should be introduced.

CONCLUSION

Overall we are supportive of the work of the Constitutional Review Group. Given the serious import of these matters on people and their everyday lives we believe that it's recommendations should be progressed speedily.

Notes
1   *Empowering Young People Networking Quality Youth Services, Strategic Priorities 2003-2007.*

NEART
(COALITION OF PRO-WOMEN'S RIGHTS, PRO-FAMILY AND PRO-LIFE GROUPS)

1

Article 41 of the Constitution of Ireland (Bunreacht na hÉireann) lays down that the state must recognise and uphold the family based on marriage.

The Inter-Departmental Committee on Reform of Marriage Law recognises marriage in its constitutional legal sense as the union between a man and a woman, and its acceptance traditionally as the giving of mutual consent to the public recognition of the union, in marriage, of one man and one woman to the exclusion of all others. The Supreme Court defines marriage as the voluntary and permanent union of one man and one woman to the exclusion of all others for life.

The International Convention on Economic, Social and Cultural Rights proclaims that: 'The widest possible protection and assistance should be accorded to the family, which is the natural and fundamental group unit of society'; and the International Covenant on Civil and Political Rights proclaims that: 'The family is the natural and fundamental group unit of society and is entitled to protection by society and the state'.

Experience worldwide, and research, shows that throughout history the need for society to uphold and defend the institution of the family – the married mother and father and any children they may have – is essential for the good of humanity.

In December 2004, the UN General Assembly observed the final event in the celebration of the International Year of the Family. Following on conferences held earlier in the year (Mexico, Doha, etc), national representatives affirmed foundational principles of human rights such as: marriage is the foundation of families, families are the foundation of societies, and the role of government is to protect and support families. It was noted that: 'The state's foremost obligation is to respect, defend, and protect the family.' The European Union, whose dissent from these principles sadly marred the proceedings, tried to use the occasion for the advancement of various anti-family measures, including the 'legalization' of homosexual and lesbian unions. Other world representatives, however, affirmed that marriage and the family form the case upon which every human society has always been built.

The definition of the family and laid down in the Constitution, and as recognised in law, must be retained.

2

The rights of the family as a unit and the rights of the individual members of the family are complementary. It is the duty and the obligation of the state, under the

Constitution, to ensure a harmonious interaction between members of the family by ensuring that adequate support such as by way of finance, housing, etc, is made available to the family. The Constitution provides for instances where such material means do not adequately provide for harmonious relations within the family, and all other appropriate avenues for the maintenance of such relations have been tried and failed.

3

Every individual, because of her/his inherent human dignity, must be protected by the state. The family based on marriage is guaranteed protection under the Constitution. It follows, therefore, that 'families other than those based on marriage', while meriting a degree of special protection where children are involved, are not the same as the family as defined in the Constitution. It is the duty and responsibility of the government to tend to the needs of the real family, which is the basis of every civilized society.

4

Homosexuals and lesbians must not be allowed to have any legal, or other recognised form of relationship. One of the reasons behind the move to achieve such 'rights', apart from the destruction of the institution of marriage (the union of one man and one woman) is the attempt to adopt and foster children. In the interests of children, in the interests of future generations, and in the interests of society as a whole, this must not be allowed to happen.

5

The constitutional reference to a woman's 'life within the home' is a very important and relevant one, and must remain in the Constitution. The trouble is that the right of women to work within the home has been sadly and deliberately neglected by successive governments over the years, and has resulted in the break-up of families and the deprivation of children's basic right to the essential love and care of their mother in their formative years. The increase in the incidence of suicide, particularly in the case of teenagers and young adults; the breakdown of discipline in the schools; the increase in teenage pregnancy (often, sadly and tragically, resulting in the abortion of unborn children); alcohol abuse on the part of young people - all of these situations flow from the decline in official government support for the family based on marriage. Why ca the government of the day not acknowledge that government policies that do not support the traditional family lead to chaos and are calculated to undermine society still further?

6 AND 7

The rights of the natural mother and of the natural father are already protected in the Constitution. If the reference here is to the situation where a married mother or father has died, or has left the marital home, or indeed where a man amrries a woman whose child is not his natural child, or a woman marries a man whose child is not her natural child, or in the case of an unmarried mother – then basic rights here are protected in the Constitution. In the case of an unmarried father, besides having rights under the Constitution he should also be obliged to recognise his duties towards his child and his child's mother.

8

No.It would be dangerous to give an expanded constitutional protection to he rights of the child, except insofar as to copper-fasten the right of the child to life before as well as after birth.

9

The Constitution does not need to be changed in view of the UN Convention on the Rights of the Child. There are many parts of the CRC which are contrary to the best interests of the child, and to the family and also, therefore, to society.

NEART considers that the suggestion on the part of the APOCC that the Articles of the Constitution relating to the family need to be examined is basically an attempt to undermine the institution of marriage, on which the family is founded. Some members of the All-Party Oireachtas Committee on the Constitution may consider this to be a difficult statement to accept, but the evidence is there for all to see. An obvious instance is the existence of committees set up and attached to various international conventions. These committees appear to spend their time urging countries to change their domestic laws and national constitutions in order to adopt policies that ultimately will adversely affect women and children.

A further example is the rejection by the UN in its Declaration on Youth, Lisbon, 1998, of the inclusion of a statement supporting the role and importance of marriage, of parents, and of families to the upbringing of youth.

OFFICE OF THE OMBUDSMAN

The Ombudsman's submission of 2 August 1995 drew attention to complaints received concerning anomalies in the respective treatment of separated persons and persons living together as man and wife, arising from legislative provisions which define a couple as a married couple. Complaints received in recent years continue to draw attention to the adverse effect on certain taxpayers of currently applicable legislative definitions of the family and of a couple. These complaints also highlight discrepancies between the treatment of couples for purposes of Revenue and of Social Welfare claims. While the following issues of concern have been raised in relation to couples living in heterosexual partnerships, they also have an impact on same sex couples or family units

DEFINITION OF COUPLE

Inheritance tax

Cohabitees are obliged to pay inheritance tax on property inherited from their partner, while married couples are exempt from this provision. The Ombudsman received a complaint from a woman who had cohabited with her partner for eighteen years. He left her the home in which they had lived together. On his death she found herself in difficulties concerning the payment of inheritance tax to Revenue and was faced with the prospect of having to sell the home in order to do this. While the Ombudsman advised the complainant to explore options for dealing with this dilemma with the Revenue, the law appeared to be correctly enforced in this case and there was no basis on which the Ombudsman could uphold the complaint.

Discrepancies between Revenue and Social Welfare arrangements

Tax allowances granted to married couples are not available to cohabiting couples, while payments available to them as single people/lone parents under social welfare legislation may be withdrawn if they cohabit.

Medical Expenses – a working partner is not entitled to claim medical expenses against income tax on behalf of the cohabiting partner. The Ombudsman has received a number of complaints on this issue which highlight the relative disadvantage of these couples in contrast with the allowances available to married couples

Income Tax allowances – the legislation provides for the transfer (under joint assessment) of allowances between married couples only. A cohabiting couple may not transfer allowances to each other.

Lone parent tax allowance – legislation provides for an allowance for widowed and single parents with qualifying children and specifically provides that the allowance is not due in the case of a man and woman living together as man and wife. (cohabiting)

DEFINITION OF FAMILIAL RELATIONSHIPS

Certain tax allowances – affecting inheritance and stamp duty in particular – are available in the context of transactions between members of a family who have a blood or legal relationship and is confined to those particular circumstances, including adoption as defined by law. The Ombudsman's attention has been drawn to circumstances in which individuals claim to have enjoyed the equivalent of a blood or legal relationships with others, and yet are denied the benefits for tax purposes. In a particular case the complainant had claimed

a reduced rate of stamp duty – the so-called consanguinity relief – which would normally apply in the case of transfer of land from father to son, on the basis that the relationship between himself and a couple had been that of parent and child, although he had never been adopted formally. In recognition of this the deed of transfer provided that the transferee undertook to provide for the transferor and his wife during their lifetime. He was denied the allowance, and given that the legislation was being applied correctly, there is no basis on which the Ombudsman could uphold his complaint.

THE OMBUDSMAN FOR CHILDREN AND GEOFFREY SHANNON

FOREWORD

The Office of the Ombudsman for Children is less than one year old. The Office is one of a growing number of international offices dedicated to the promotion and safeguarding of children's rights.

The Ombudsman for Children has two main functions: to investigate complaints made against public bodies, schools and voluntary hospitals and to promote the rights and welfare of children.

Dealing with individual complaints is of great importance to the complainants but it is also recognised that complaints can provoke sufficient analysis to recommend strategic policy and practice change to ensure that children's rights are fulfilled. We suggest that strategic actions should have wider impact on child rights than solving individual complaints.

In trying to influence or effect change at a strategic level, there could be no opportunity as great as that presented by a review of the Irish Constitution. We have taken this opportunity to make a submission which we hope will be heard and accepted by the All-Party Oireachtas Committee on the Constitution in its deliberations. We have considered the pertinent Articles of the Constitution and have proffered suggestions which we see as advancing the rights of the child in Ireland. In drawing up these recommendations, the Office has been greatly aided by the legal expertise of Geoffrey Shannon and we owe him a great debt of thanks.

Children are human beings and rights holders. Children's rights are human rights. International and European human rights instruments guarantee rights for everyone, for all members of the human family. In this submission, we seek express rights for children in the Irish Constitution.

We look forward to seeing changes in the Irish Constitution which recognise that children too are holders of rights, not possessions of parents or of the state.

Emily Logan
Ombudsman for Children

INTRODUCTION

The Ombudsman for Children is the first of its kind in this state. The Office was established under the Ombudsman for Children Act 2002. The Ombudsman for Children's Office is an independent, statutory body which came into force by Statutory Instrument on 25 April 2004.

The Office investigates complaints made against public bodies, schools and voluntary hospitals. The Office also has the responsibility for the promotion of the rights and welfare of children and young people under the age of eighteen in all aspects of public policy, practices, procedures and law. The Ombudsman for Children is one of a growing number of international offices dedicated to the promotion and safeguarding of children's rights.

This paper acknowledges the existence of three previous reports that recommended constitutional change to include an express statement of children's rights.

In 1993, the Kilkenny Incest Investigation Committee recommended to the government that an amendment be made to Articles 41 and 42 of the Constitution. The Committee recommended:

> ...that consideration be given by the Government to the amendment of Articles 41 and 42 of the Constitution so as to include a statement of the constitutional rights of children.

In 1996, the Report of the Constitution Review Group highlighted the need for a review of Articles 41 and 42 of the Constitution. The Review Group indicated the need to:

> ...put into the Constitution an express obligation to treat the best interests of the child as a paramount consideration in any actions relating to children.

In 1998, the United Nations Committee on the Rights of the Child, in its Concluding Observations, emphasised that the recommendations of the Report of the Constitution Review Group would reinforce 'the status of the child as a full subject of rights'.

Ireland has ratified two international human rights instruments that have a bearing on children's rights. Ireland ratified the 1989 United Nations Convention on the Rights of the Child, without reservation on 21 September, 1992. However the provisions of the United Nations Convention on the Rights of the Child do not form part of our domestic law.

Ireland has also ratified the European Convention on Human Rights and Fundamental Freedoms (ECHR). Unlike the United Nations Convention on the Rights of the Child, the ECHR has been incorporated into Irish Law by way of statute. The incorporation of the ECHR at sub-constitutional level will ensure that child rights remain subordinate to parental rights. Without an express statement on children's rights in the Constitution child rights will remain subordinate to parental rights.

THE CONSTITUTION OF IRELAND

The principal source of fundamental rights in Irish family law has been the Constitution. Articles 41 and 42 of the Constitution have had a major impact on the manner in which family legislation has been enacted and family law judgments delivered in Ireland. Article 41 of the Irish Constitution of 1937 relates to the family and 'recognises the family as the natural and primary unit group of society' and also guarantees 'to protect the family in its constitution and authority'.

The rights guaranteed by Article 41 are recognised as belonging not to individual members of the family but rather to the family unit as a whole. An individual on behalf of the family may invoke them but, as Costello J notes in *Murray v Ireland*[1] they 'belong to the institution in itself as distinct from the personal rights which each individual member might enjoy by virtue of membership of the family'.

Article 41 lacks child focus. It fails to recognise the child as a person with individual rights. This derives from the principle of parental autonomy created by Article 41 of the Constitution. This Article establishes a level of privacy within family life, which the state can enter only in the exceptional circumstances detailed in Article 42.5 of the Constitution. Article 42 provides as follows:

> (1) The state acknowledges that the primary and natural educator of the child is the family and guarantees to respect the inalienable right and duty of parents to provide, according to their means, for religious and moral, intellectual, physical and social education of their children...

> (5) In exceptional cases, where the parents for physical or moral reasons fail in their duty towards their children, the state, as guardian of the common good, by appropriate means shall endeavour to supply the place of the parents, but always with due regard for the natural and imprescriptible rights of the child.

This Article clearly provides that only in exceptional cases, where parents, for physical or moral reasons, fail in their duty towards their children, can the state as guardian of the common good attempt to supply the place of the parents.

THE CONSTITUTION AND THE FAMILY

The Irish Constitution is unique in that the family unit in Ireland takes precedence over and above that of the individual members of the family. In fact, the individual rights of the members of the family are both directed and determined by the family as an entity in itself. Thus, membership of the constitutional family subordinates the rights of the individual members in Ireland. This is specifically true in relation to the rights of children and Supreme Court judgments on the issue have proven to support this interpretation.

When examining Article 42 of the Constitution, it is true to say that this in fact has more to do with the family than it does with the substantive right to education and is an accompaniment and subordinate to Article 41. It deals with education in a broader sense than scholastic education. In referring to education, it alludes to the upbringing of the child, which it holds not only to be a right but a duty of parents. This Article reinforces the decision-making autonomy of the family. This can be observed by examining the structure of Article 42, which assigns a strong sense of priority to parental autonomy.

Article 42.5 of the Constitution is of particular importance in that it addresses the complete inability of some parents to provide for their children's education. It has been interpreted as not being confined to a failure by the parents of a child to provide education for him/her, but extends in exceptional circumstances, to failure in other duties necessary to satisfy the personal rights of the child. This interpretation supports the assertion previously made that the right to education in Article 42 is a mere extension of the concept of 'the family' in Article 41.

Looking at Articles 41 and 42 of the Constitution together, it is clear that they render the rights of married parents in relation to their children 'inalienable'. Article 41 of the Constitution alludes to the inalienable and imprescriptible rights of the family and Article 42 refers to the rights and duties of married parents. Only if the circumstances allow the constitutional restriction on inalienability, contained in Article 42.5 of the Constitution, is there then scope for the legal overruling of the rights of married parents. The threshold for state intervention is set at a very high level. As a result children can be placed at risk.

THE STATUTORY POSITION

In spite of the precedence afforded to the welfare of the child in section 3 of the Guardianship of Infants Act 1964, the Constitution prevails. Section 3 of the Guardianship of Infants Act 1964 makes it clear that in considering an application relating to the guardianship, custody or upbringing of a child, the Court must have regard to the welfare of the child. This, the section states, is 'the first and paramount consideration'. The Supreme Court, however, has determined that the welfare of a child must, unless there are exceptional circumstances or other overriding factors, be considered to be best served by its remaining as part of its marital family. The Court considered in a number of cases that this was dictated by the constitutional preference for the marital family exhibited in Article 41.3 of the Constitution and the requirement therein that it be protected from attack.[2] There is, therefore, an uneasy tension between, on one hand, the provisions of Articles 41 and 42 of the Constitution and, on the other, the welfare principle outlined in section 3 of the Guardianship of Infants Act 1964.

The apparent contradiction between Articles 41 and 42 of the Constitution and the principle of the welfare of the child in section 3 of the Guardianship of Infants Act 1964 has been correctly reconciled by the judiciary by holding that the welfare of the child is to be found within the confines of the Constitution.[3] This is a negative definition of welfare insofar as it impacts on the child. The focus is not on actively promoting the welfare interests of the child, but merely with ensuring that these are not seriously impaired. This approach derives from the wording of Articles 41 and 42 of the Constitution. It could therefore be argued that the current constitutional position in Ireland embodies a 'seen but not heard' approach to the concept of 'children's rights'.

CURRENT STATE OBLIGATIONS

The United Nations Committee on the Rights of the Child in its Concluding Observations on Ireland's implementation of the UN Convention on the Rights of the Child 1989 was critical of this approach to children's rights. The Committee held that the implementation of the recommendations of the Report of the Constitution Review Group[4] be accelerated which, it stated, would reinforce 'the status of the child as a full subject of rights'. The report of the Constitution Review Group recommended, inter alia, in 1996 that an express statement of identified rights of children be incorporated into the Constitution. Further, the Kilkenny Incest Investigation Committee[5] stated:

> We feel that the very high emphasis on the rights of the family in the Constitution may consciously or unconsciously be interpreted as giving a higher value to the rights of the parents than to the rights of children.

In light of this, the Committee therefore recommended:

> ... that consideration be given by the Government to the amendment of Articles 41 and 42 of the Constitution so as to include a statement of the constitutional rights of children.'

THE CONSTITUTION AND THE CHILD

The courts have, in the past, accepted that children have certain personal, unenumerated rights under Articles 40 and 42 of the Constitution. In the case of *G v An Bord Uchtála*, Finlay P. held that the child 'has a constitutional right to bodily integrity and has an unenumerated right to an opportunity to be reared with due regard to his or her religious, moral, intellectual, physical and social welfare'.[6] O'Higgins CJ in the Supreme Court expanded upon Finlay P's statement when he stated:

> The child also has natural rights... [T]he child has the right to be fed and to live, to be reared and educated, to have the opportunity of working and of realising his of her full personality and dignity as a human being. The rights of the child (and others which I have not enumerated) must equally be protected and vindicated by the state. In exceptional cases the state, under the provisions of Article 42.5 of the Constitution, is given the duty, as guardian of the common good, to provide for a child born into a family where the parents fail in their duty towards their child for physical or moral

reasons. In the same way, in special circumstances the state may have an equal obligation in relation to a child born outside the family, to protect that child, even against its mother, if her natural rights are used in such a way as to endanger the health or life of the child or to deprive him of his rights.[7]

In this same case, Walsh J stated that: '[T]here is nothing in the Constitution to indicate that in cases of conflict the rights of the parent are always to be given primacy.'[8] He went further by analysing the rights of children in the following terms:

> Not only has the child born out of lawful wedlock the natural right to have its welfare and health guarded no less well than that of a child born in lawful wedlock, but a fortiori it has the right to life itself and the right to be guarded against all threats directed to its existence whether before or after birth. The child's natural rights spring primarily from the natural right of every individual to life, to be reared and educated, to liberty, to work, to rest and recreation, to practice of religion, and to follow his or her conscience .... It lies not in the power of the parent who has the primary natural rights and duties in respect of the child to exercise them in such a way as intentionally or by neglect to endanger the health or life of the child or to terminate its existence. The child's natural right to life and all that flows from that right are independent of any right of the parent as such.[9]

In the case of *D.G. v Eastern Health Board*, Denham J, in a laudable judgement held that the child had 'the right to be reared with due regard to his religious, moral, intellectual, physical and social welfare; to be fed accommodated and educated; to suitable care and treatment; to have the opportunity of working and of realising his personality and dignity as a human being'.[10]

RECENT DEVELOPMENTS

Recently, however, the Supreme Court has veered away from enumerating children's rights by holding that the government was responsible for articulating the rights of children. This approach can be seen in four landmark judgments of the Supreme Court in the past four years on children's rights:

North Western Health Board v H.W. and C.W;[11]
Sinnott v Minister for Education and Other;[12]
T.D. v Minister for Education and Others;[13]
Lobe and Osayande v Minister for Justice, Equality and Law Reform.[14]

They concern the children in society who are most in need; children who are dependent on the state for their education, health, welfare and citizenship. Such children now inhabit a legal limbo.

In summary, the foregoing judgments signpost a shift to conservatism by the Supreme Court both legally and in terms of social policy.[15] That said, the judgments could also indicate a desire on the part of the

Supreme Court to respect the principle of the doctrine of the separation of powers. Whatever interpretation one affords to the recent approach of the Supreme Court regarding children's rights, there is a lacuna in the current legislative framework where children's rights are concerned. The Supreme Court has, as previously outlined, recognised that the Constitution protects children's rights. That said, if the state fails to protect the rights of individual children, and the Supreme Court refuses to step in as guardian of the Constitution (save in exceptional circumstances), to uphold such rights, on whom does this duty now fall?

INTERNATIONAL LAW

Internationally the traditional view of the family is changing. The designation of the family in Article 41 of the Irish Constitution is virtually impenetrable. The restrictive interpretation of the family has meant that Irish litigants have sought redress under international law through international human rights treaties. Our dualist approach to international law generally makes international human rights treaties binding on the state, though not on the courts, as such treaties have traditionally not been incorporated into Irish law.[16]

This has changed more recently with the inclusion of the European Convention on Human Rights and Fundamental Freedoms (ECHR) into domestic law. The European Convention on Human Rights Act 2003 came into force on 31 December, 2003 and section 1 of the Act provides that Articles 2 to 14 of the ECHR and Protocols1, 4, 6 and 7 be incorporated into Irish Law.

NATIONS CONVENTION ON THE RIGHTS OF THE CHILD 1989

Ireland ratified the United Nations Convention on the Rights of the Child 1989 (UNCRC) without reservation on 21 September, 1992. Again, by virtue of Ireland's dualist nature, the provisions do not form part of the domestic law. The Convention gives recognition to children's rights in its widest sense. Article 3 states, *inter alia*:

> (1) In all actions concerning children, whether undertaken by public or private social welfare institutions, courts of law, administrative authorities or legislative bodies, the best interest of the child shall be a primary consideration.

> (2) state parties undertake to ensure the child such protection and care as is necessary for his or her well being, taking into account the rights and duties of his or her parents, legal guardians, or other individuals legally responsible for him or her, and, to this end, shall take all appropriate legislative and administrative measures.

While this article requires only that the children's interests be a primary consideration, not the primary consideration, it must also be read alongside the series of explicit rights which the Convention protects. These include:

General Principles

'the inherent right to life' (Article 6)

'the right of the child who has the capacity to form his or her own views to express those views freely in all matters affecting the child, the views of the child being given due weight in accordance with the age and maturity of the child' (Article 12)

Civil Rights and Freedoms

'the right from birth to a name, the right to acquire a nationality and, as far as possible, the right to know and be cared for by his or her parents' (Article 7)

'the right of the child to preserve his or her identity, including nationality' (Article 8)

'the right to freedom of expression' (Article 13)

'the right of the child to freedom of thought, conscience and religion' (Article 14(1))

'the right of the child to freedom of association and to freedom of peaceful assembly' (Article 15)

'the right to the protection of the law against arbitrary or unlawful interference with the child's privacy, family home or correspondence and unlawful attacks on the child's honour and reputation' (Article 16)

Family Environment and Alternative Care

'the right of the child who is separated from one or both parents to maintain personal relations and direct contact with both parents on a regular basis, except if it contrary to the child's best interest' (Article 9 (3))

Basic Health and Welfare

'the right of every child to a standard of living adequate for the child's physical, mental, spiritual, moral and social development' (Article 27)

Education, Leisure and Cultural Activities

'the right of the child to education' (Article 28)

Special Protection Measures

'the right of every child alleged as, accused of, or recognised as having infringed the penal law to be treated in a manner consistent with the promotion of the child's sense of dignity and worth' (Article 40.)

Representation of Children

Article 12 of the United Nations Convention on the Rights of the Child, 1989 provides for the separate representation of children:

> (1) state parties shall assure to the child who is capable of forming his or her own views the right to express those views freely in all matters affecting the child, the views of the child being given due weight in accordance with the age and maturity of the child.
>
> (2) For this purpose, the child shall in particular be provided the opportunity to be heard in any judicial and administrative proceedings affecting the child, either

directly, or through a representative or an appropriate body, in a manner consistent with the procedural rules of national law.

Article 9 of the UNCRC provides for participation by children in separation and divorce processes:

> (1) state parties shall ensure that a child shall not be separated from his or her parents against their will, except when competent authorities subject to judicial review determine, in accordance with applicable law and procedures, that such separation is necessary for the best interests of the child. Such determination may be necessary in a particular case such as one involving abuse or neglect of the child by the parents, or one where parents are living separately and a decision must be made as to the child's place of residence.

Taking cognisance of the foregoing rights, and in particular Article 12, it is clear that the UNCRC 1989 is soundly based on a defensible concept of children's rights. The law in Ireland, however, falls far short of such a concept.

EUROPEAN CONVENTION ON THE EXERCISE OF CHILDREN'S RIGHTS 1996

Ireland has signed but not ratified the European Convention on the Exercise of Children's Rights 1996.[17] Article 1(1) of the Convention provides that the object of the Convention is to:

> Promote [children's] rights, to grant them procedural rights and to facilitate the exercise of these rights by ensuring that children are themselves or through other persons or bodies, informed and allowed to participate in proceedings affecting them before a judicial authority.

In some respects, the 1996 Convention is of more limited application than its 1989 counterpart. It focuses predominantly on procedural rather than substantive rights, the emphasis being on such matters as the right of children to participate in, and access information about, cases that concern their welfare. For example, Article 5 of the 1996 Convention states:

> Parties shall consider granting children additional procedural rights in relation to proceedings before a judicial authority offering them, in particular:
>
> (a) the right to apply to be assisted by an appropriate person of their choice in order to help them express their views;
>
> (b) the right to apply themselves, or through other persons or bodies, for the appointment of a separate representative, in appropriate cases a lawyer;
>
> (c) the right to appoint their own representative;
>
> (d) the right to exercise some or all of the rights of parties to such proceedings.

Clearly these provisions are aimed primarily at children of sufficient age and maturity to understand the matters under scrutiny. In appropriate cases, a child should have a person to help the expression of his or her views. Articles 4 and 9 of the European Convention on the Exercise of Children's Rights provide for the appointment of such a special representative. The absence of a facility for children in Ireland to support and articulate their views, particularly where a case is settled in advance of a hearing, is a serious problem.

EUROPEAN CONVENTION ON HUMAN RIGHTS AND FUNDAMENTAL FREEDOMS

In discussing our obligations towards children, the relevant provisions of the European Convention on Human Rights and Fundamental Freedoms (ECHR) should be noted. The civil and political rights enshrined in the ECHR emphasise individual and familial freedom and autonomy and protection from excessive state interference. The ECHR is not child focused as such in the same way as the United Nations Convention on the Rights of the Child 1989. It does not recognise children as a special group requiring particular protection, because of their inherent vulnerability in a world of adults. The rights contained in the ECHR are as available to children as to adults; however, there is increasing awareness that the ECHR has potential as an important resource in the promotion of child rights. Whilst only a small body of ECHR case law deals with cases from the perspective of the child, it has been utilised very effectively to protect children within their family life with their parents.

The incorporation of the ECHR into Irish law has been by way of statute. As a result it is now possible to take proceedings in the Irish courts alleging a breach of the ECHR. Previously to assert any rights under the ECHR, an injured party had first to exhaust all domestic remedies before bringing the case to the European Court of Human Rights in Strasbourg with the costs and delays associated with that process.

There is little doubt that inconsistencies will arise between Irish child law and practice and the standards required by the ECHR. The indirect or interpretative mode of incorporation preserves the domestic primacy of the Constitution.[18] Consequently, Article 41 of the Constitution will continue to act as an impediment to the effective implementation of the legal entitlements of children under the ECHR. More specifically, incorporation of the ECHR at sub-constitutional level will ensure that child rights remain subordinate to parental rights.

RECOMMENDATIONS

The current position of children in the Irish Constitution is a matter of concern. The Ombudsman for Children recommends an amendment to the Constitution to grant express rights to children. In defining these express rights the Ombudsman for Children recommends that the Committee should consider the rights enumerated in the 1989 United Nations Convention on the Rights of the Child. In particular, the Ombudsman recommends the Constitution should be amended to ensure that the right of children to have their welfare protected is given the paramountcy it deserves.

Notes
1 [1985] ILRM 542 at 547.
2 See, for example, *Re J.H. (An Infant)* [1985] IR 375 and *North Western Health Board v H.W. and C.W.* [2001] 3 IR 635.
3 *North Western Health Board v H.W. and C.W.* [2001] 3 IR 622. See, however, *Southern Health Board v C.H.* [1996] 1 IR 231, where O'Flaherty J observed, in a case concerning the admissibility of a video-taped interview containing allegations of parental abuse, that: 'it is easy to comprehend that the child's welfare must always be of far graver concern to the court. We must, as judges, always harken to the constitutional command which mandates, as prime consideration, the interests of the child in any legal proceedings'.
4 Constitution Review Group, *Report of the Constitution Review Group* (Stationary Office, 1996).
5 *Kilkenny Incest Investigation Report* presented to Brendan Howlin TD, Minister for Health, by South Eastern Health Board (Stationary Office, May 1993).
6 [1980] IR 32 at 44.
7 Ibid at 69.
8 Ibid at 78.
9 *Ibid* at 69.
10 [1998] 1 I.L.R.M 241 at 262.
11 [2001] 3 IR 622.
12 [2001] 2 IR 598.
13 [2001] 4 IR 259.
14 [2003] 1 IR 1.
15 See, however, the recent judgement of Finlay-Geoghegan J. in *F.N. and E.B. v C.D., H.O. and E.H.,* unreported, High Court, Finlay-Geoghegan J., March 26, 2004.
16 Most of the other Member states of the Council of Europe adopt a monist approach to international law, where international law is automatically applicable in domestic law without the need for any implementing legislation.
17 European Treaty Series No 160. The European Convention on the Exercise of Children's Rights was opened for signature at Strasbourg on 25 January, 1996, and Ireland was one of the seven signatories to the Convention on that date. It came into force on 1 July, 2000, following ratification by Greece (11 September, 1997), Poland (28 November, 1997) and Slovenia (28 March, 2000) in accordance with Article 21(3) of the 1996 Convention.
18 See s.2 of the European Convention on Human Rights Act 2003.

ONE FAMILY

POLICY POSITION PAPER NUMBER ONE – WORKING FOR A CONSTITUTION WHICH AFFORDS EQUAL RIGHTS TO ALL FAMILIES

Background

Progressing the work of Cherish, established in 1972, One Family provides voice, support and action for one-parent families through membership, professional services and campaigning. Our aim is to affect positive change and achieve equality and social inclusion for all one-parent families in Ireland.

We work to achieve our aims through

Voice   we are the national membership organisation of one-parent families, supporting organisations and others concerned with the issues facing one-parent families.

Support   we offer a comprehensive range of professional services to one-parent families, to those experiencing a crisis pregnancy and to those working with one-parent families.

Action   we campaign with and on behalf of our members to affect positive change for one-parent families.

One Family works with all types and all members of one-parent families, respecting the realities of family life in Ireland.

During the implementation period of the One Family *Strategic Plan 2004-2006*, the organisation's campaigning work will concentrate on 8 strategic goals:

1 Working for a constitution which affords equal rights to all families
2 Recognising the realities of the diversity of family life in Ireland
3 Ensuring equality of access and opportunity in education for one-parent families
4 Working for a positive work life balance for one-parent families
5 Striving for equality for one-parent families in all housing tenures
6 Championing quality childcare for children in one-parent families
7 Campaigning for access to an adequate income for all one-parent families
8 Working for equitable services in all pregnancies

THE CHANGING NATURE OF FAMILY LIFE IN IRELAND

Modern family life in Ireland is remarkably different now compared with the period in which our Constitution was first developed. With declining marriage and birth rates, higher rates of extra marital cohabitation and birth and a growing diversification of the structure of families, the typical Irish family is no longer typical.

Census 2002 indicates that there are over 153,900 one-parent families in Ireland, representing almost 12% of all households. At One Family we believe that this number, although significant, is likely to be an underestimation given the lack of accurate and adequate collection methods which may take account of the many diverse situations within which one-parent families live, including a growing level of shared parenting arrangements and continuing patterns of inter-generational households.

During the period 1996-2002 there was a 25% increase in the number of households headed by a solo parent. One-parent families are increasing for a variety of reasons and forming a significant minority of families in modern Irish society. In 1937, at the introduction of Bunreacht na hÉireann, the significant majority of one-parent families would have been headed by a widowed person, predominantly female. A dramatic increase in the extra marital birth rates together with reductions in the numbers of single women placing children for adoption, increases in marital and relationship breakdown and the introduction of divorce have changed the profile of one-parent families. Census 2002 indicates that 85% are headed by females, 15% by males, 40% by widowed persons, 32% by separated or divorced persons and 24% by a single parent (CSO, 2004; Kennedy, 2004).

However, although the profile of the family in Ireland is remarkably different, with an estimated 12% alone headed by a solo parent, 100% of the protection currently afforded to the family in Bunreacht na hÉireann is applicable only to the family based in marriage. Therefore a growing number of families are not considered equal in the eyes of Ireland's most superior domestic source of law.

BUNREACHT NA HÉIREANN – ISSUES OF CONCERN REGARDING CURRENT PROVISIONS FOR THE FAMILY

Historically, Bunreacht na hÉireann is regarded as a document which was largely influenced by dominant moral teachings of the time, particularly those of the Roman Catholic Church. As such it is no surprise that the provisions pertaining to the family in the Constitution, which are mainly to be found in Articles 41, 42 and 40.3, are heavily influenced by Catholic teaching regarding the role and function of the family as that based upon Catholic marriage. As Ryan (2004:2) notes 'The family rights provisions of the Constitution borrow heavily from Roman Catholic theology on the family. The centrepiece of such theology is the concern for family autonomy, the main purpose being to limit state intervention in the family, and in particular to prevent the state from dictating how children be reared, in possible contravention of the religious values of the parents'.

DEFINITION AND PROTECTION OF THE FAMILY

Bunreacht na hÉireann recognises the family as that based on marriage. Article 41.1.1 notes that 'The State recognises the Family as the natural primary and fundamental unit group of Society, and as a moral institution possessing inalienable and imprescriptible rights, antecedent and superior to all positive law'. Therefore, the Constitution includes recognition for the sphere of family life and states that the family as a unit should not be subject to undue interference by law or other state mechanism. It is important to note here that it is the family as a unit rather than the individuals within the family that is offered protection under the Constitution as it currently stands.

Article 41.3.1 specifically defines the type of family to which such protection will apply. 'The State pledges itself to guard with special care the institution of Marriage, *on which the Family is founded*, and to protect it against attack' (author's emphasis).

As a result, the family unit is found to have inalienable and imprescriptible rights and that unit is deemed to exist when within marriage. As such there is no protection afforded to families which are not deemed to be within marriage. Given the increasing diversity of the structure and form of families in Ireland and the tendency for families to form outside of marriage, there is therefore a gap between the constitutional and therefore legal protection of families based on marriage on the one hand and a significant minority of families not based on marriage, or to whom the protection of marriage no longer applies following dissolution. Included here are cohabiting heterosexual and gay, lesbian, bisexual and transgender families and a diverse range of one-parent families headed by a formerly or never married parent.

Although Article 41 has been interpreted as protecting the rights of the family as a unit (and not those of its individual members), Article 40.3 has been construed as conferring personal rights on selected members of a family unit resulting from a family relationship. Again, these may not be deemed to extend to some members of non-marital families, especially fathers, under the terms of Article 40.3 'The State guarantees in its laws to respect, and, as far as practicable, by its laws to defend and vindicate the personal rights of the citizen'. While non-marital mothers and their children have been deemed to benefit from this clause, non-marital fathers have to date been excluded from the remit of Article 40.3. Also, rights under Article 40.3 are not imprescriptible or inalienable and thus are weaker than family rights under Article 41.

It is evident therefore that it would be plausible to review the current definition of the family unit in the light of the radical changes in the pattern and trends of family formation and change since the enactment of the Constitution. Also of consideration here is whether or not to continue to give special protection to the institution of marriage within the Constitution. These will be considered further in discussing possible recommendations for change.

Individual rights versus family rights

Currently, the Constitution affords protection only to the family unit and not to the individual members. As noted above in relation to Article 40.3, personal rights are often deemed applicable to members of the family unit. It is however a considered view (Constitution Review Group: 1996; Ryan: 2002, 2004; Shannon: 2005) that the focus of Articles 41 and 42 overemphasise the rights of the family unit, which could possibly be detrimental to the rights of individual members. This is found within the reference to rights of the family as 'inalienable' and 'imprescriptible' which may place overemphasis on the importance of the rights of the

family as a unit over the rights of the individuals within it.

A case in point is the overall lack of access to adoption of children born within marriage. Except in limited circumstances, due to being born within what is considered a family unit (with inalienable rights and duties) children born within marriage cannot be adopted. Therefore, their rights to family life, which could be provided in an adoptive family, are curtailed by the inalienable right of the family unit to be protected.

In relation to other European jurisdictions, Ireland would be unique, with the exception of Luxembourg, in that none of the other constitutions expressly guarantee the rights of the family unit in this way. Although they may, as Bunreacht na hÉireann does, recognise that the family unit is the fundamental unit of society and afford it certain protections, they also guarantee rights deriving from family membership to apply directly to the individual members.

Rights of non-marital parents

Given the preceding discussion regarding the prescription of rights to marital rather than other family types and rights flowing to the family unit rather than individuals, it is also evident that in relation to non-marital parents there is a lack of protection of their relationship with their children under the Constitution as it currently stands. Although the law has been interpreted as recognising a relationship between a non-marital mother and her child there is no such recognition awarded to non-marital fathers.

One Family firmly believes that it is generally in the best interests of children to maintain a relationship with both parents and as such the current inequalities in the application of constitutional law to parents based on their marital status undermines children's access to relationships with their parents if they are unmarried.

Rights of the child within the Constitution

Bunreacht na hÉireann makes little reference currently to children. Children could be said to be invisible in the current Constitution and without prescribed and specific rights. Instead their rights are inferred from those of their family unit, if their family unit is constructed within the realm of marriage.

Given the increasing body of law and discourse relating to the need for the protection of the express rights of children, it is currently an anomaly that although we have a body of legislation and legal provision in Ireland for children's rights, albeit in limited form, our superior source of domestic law currently regards children as invisible. As Shannon (2005:4) states 'it could therefore be argued that the current constitutional position in Ireland embodies a 'seen but not heard' approach to children's rights'.

Not only are children regarded as invisible, but in relation to reference to their welfare, rights are deemed to flow to their parents as the guardians of that welfare. This parent-focused perspective would not be considered in keeping with the international body of law on the rights of the child. 'It is almost universally recognised, and copper-fastened in the United Nations Convention on the Rights of the Child 1989, that in any legal matter concerning children, it is the child's best interests that are of paramount weight' (Ryan, 2004:2). Judge Catherine McGuinness in the *Report of the Kilkenny Incest Investigation* noted that one could derive from the high emphasis on the rights of the family in the Constitution that parents' rights were of higher value than those of children.

Working for a Constitution which affords equal rights to all families – recommendations for change

Principally, One Family recommends a rank and file review of the constitutional provisions regarding the family in order to achieve the following objectives:

1. *To displace the privileged position of the marital family by the recognition of alternative family forms.*

The current constitutional position of the marital family can be argued to discriminate against alternative family forms. This is particularly true of the inclusion in Article 41.3 of the phrase *'on which the family is founded'.* Given the significant changes in family type and structure since the Constitution was enacted, this phrase now, rather than simply describing the majority of families, in fact acts to exclude a significant and increasing minority of valid family forms, including many one-parent families, from legal protection and recognition.

The question is whether to replace the current 'definition' of the family, as could be said to be intrinsic in that phrase in Article 41.3, with another definition, or to leave the Constitution without any definition as to what constitutes families. Although the latter may be preferable from an equality and diversity perspective it may be impractical in enabling the judiciary to interpret the extent to which constitutional protection applies to varying family forms. However, in proffering a definition of the family we also run the risk of recreating the past and allowing for the future exclusion of alternative family forms which may not currently be evident in Irish society.

The alternative may be to proffer a definition which focuses not on the structure of family but on the nature of the relationship between family members, to move from the position that family is viewed in terms of a prescribed form to one where family and family ties are evident in the substance of relationships between members. This alternative stance has been used in the interpretation of Article 8 of the European Convention on Human Rights and Fundamental Freedoms in determining where family life exists in the absence often of formal traditional family structures (Ryan:2004, Shannon:2005).

One Family would recommend that in order to fully allow for equality for all families before the law, the phrase 'on which the family is founded' be removed from the Constitution to end the preferential treatment of marital family forms over any other form (Constitution Review Group:1996). Instead the definition of family, if needed, could be drawn from the United Nations definition: 'any combination of two or more persons who are bound together by ties of mutual consent, birth and/or adoption or placement and who together assume responsibility for, *inter alia*, the care and maintenance of group members, the addition of new members through procreation or adoption, the socialisation of children and the social control of members'. (Daly,2004:23).

2. *To place the child and his or her \ at the heart of our family law policy and to make practical efforts to realise this aim.*

The current constitutional provision regarding the family has often been interpreted as giving greater protection to the family as a unit than to individual members. This has led to a policy framework, particularly evident in child placement and protection, of non-interference with certain family types which may not always be in keeping with the best interests of the child.

One Family recommends that the Constitution be reviewed to include express and specific rights for children. These rights could be derived from the UN Convention on the Rights of the Child (UNCRC) which Ireland has ratified. In doing so, not only would the position of individual family members' rights, in the case of children, be strengthened in position to those of the family unit but also the current difficulties regarding differing rights for marital and non-marital parents regarding their children could be circumvented by focusing on a children's rights perspective. Let us consider for example Article 9.3 of the UNCRC: 'States Parties shall respect the right of the child who is separated from one or both parents to maintain personal relations and direct contact with both parents on a regular basis, except if it is contrary to the child's best interests'. If this was expressly provided for in the Constitution as applicable to all children then the current difficulties and debate surrounding the best ways to provide for express rights for non-marital parents, particularly fathers, could be avoided using a 'best interests' principle, as rights would naturally flow from child to parent in this case.

In providing for the inclusion of express rights for children it is also essential that those rights reflect the best interests principle, in which case One Family would strongly recommend that express rights to be included in the Constitution reflect those in the UNCRC. As Ryan notes: 'While the temptation may be to increase the scope for the State to intervene in favour of children's rights, one should not too readily assume that the State is better equipped or inclined to promote the child's well-being. The State has often proved itself to be a particularly lousy parent, either in its own right or in respect of the sometimes ill-suited characters it chooses to act in place of the parents' (2004:5).

3. *To bring Irish law into line with the ECHR by placing an obligation on the state to respect and support family life in all its manifestations and to create laws which reflect the realities of the diversity of family life in modern Ireland.*

This point is linked also to point 1 above whereby it is essential that any review of the constitutional provisions regarding family life embraces an approach which respects the validity of the diversity of family forms, structures and relationships and treats all equally. In doing so it is also essential that any resultant or existing legislation be proofed to ensure that it does not discriminate against diverse or non-marital family forms, not currently enjoying privilege or protection in the Constitution. This may require a review of legislation, for example regarding adoption, guardianship of infants, child protection and indeed a substantial element of the body of family law.

Conclusion

In order to proffer a way forward in reforming the Constitution to take into consideration the variety and diversity of families and the needs for equality of treatment under the law and to increase the visibility of the protection of the rights of children, regardless of their family situation, One Family suggests the following addendum to Article 42:

Article 42A

1. Notwithstanding any other provision of this Constitution, the State guarantees to respect and shall endeavour to support all families in the State, regardless of the form that such families may take, and to protect and defend the rights of all individuals who are members of those families.

2. Notwithstanding any other provision of this Constitution, the State guarantees in particular, and as far as practicable, to assist and support all parents and guardians in promoting the best interests of the child. In so doing, the State shall promote the welfare of the child as the paramount consideration in all proceedings concerning the child's best interests.

3. The State shall in particular, endeavour to assist and support parents and guardians, as far as practicable, in securing for all children a basic quality of life and in particular food, clothing, education and accommodation sufficient to his or her needs.

It is hoped that these suggestions mark the beginning of a root and branch investigation of how we might frame laws that genuinely place the child at the heart of our family law, regardless of the form their family might take.

References

CSO (2004) *Census 2002, Volume 3: Household Composition and Family Status*, Dublin, Central Statistics Office.

Daly, M (12004) *Families and Family Life in Ireland, Challenges for the Future – Report of Public Consultation Fora*, Dublin, Department of Social and Family Affairs.

Duncan, W. (1993) *'The Constitutional Protection of Parental Rights'* in Eekelaar, J.M. and Saracevic, P. (eds) *Parenthood in Modern Society*, Klewer Academic Press, Dordrecht.

Fahey, T. & Russell, F. (2001), *Family Formation in Ireland – Trends, Data Need and Implications*, Policy Research Series Number 43, Dublin, Economic and Social Research Institute.

Government of Ireland (1937) *Bunreacht na hÉireann*, Dublin, Stationery Office.

Government of Ireland (1996) *Report of the Constitution Review Group*, Dublin, Stationery Office.

Kennedy, F. (2004) *Cottage to Crèche – Family Change in Ireland*, Dublin, Institute of Public Administration.

Shannon, G. (ed.) (2003) *Family Law* (2nd edn), Oxford, Oxford University Press/ Law Society of Ireland.

Shannon, G. (2005) *Child Law*, Dublin, Thomson Round Hall.

Ryan, F. (2002) *Legal Rhetoric Social Reality: Towards a New Legal Concept of Family for the 21st Century*. Paper presented to the Cherish Biennial conference 2002.

Ryan, F. (2004) *Child of our Times: The Child's Place in Family Law and Family Policy*, paper presented to the One Family biennial conference 2004.

POLICY POSITION PAPER NUMBER TWO – RECOGNISING THE REALITIES OF THE DIVERSITY OF FAMILY LIFE IN IRELAND

What is family diversity?

Family diversity can be understood to describe the range of varying family structures and types as well as the varying situations in which families live in modern society. The term is indicative of the changing nature of family structure and family life particularly in western economies and welfare states.

Most state's demographic profiles have been characterised by decreasing marriage rates and changes in the age profile of partners on marriage, increasing patterns of extra-marital cohabitation as well as increasing rates of extra marital births and increases in marital and relationship breakdown.

Family diversity is not an exclusive term and can describe the changing patterns of family formation as well as a range of situations in which families live, including families who live in intergenerational or solo parent headed households.

Family change in Ireland

Ireland is no different to a range of other western countries in the changing profile of family life and formation in recent years. Ireland's demographic profile has begun to mirror those of other countries. This is particularly evident in relation to increasing occurrences of extra-marital cohabitation and extra-martial births and increasing marital and relationship breakdown, reflected in the increasing number of one-parent families in Ireland in recent years.

Ireland's demographic and family change can be characterised by a move from traditional patterns of family formation and change to an increasing tendency towards diversity in both the formation and change of family forms. Traditionally, Irish families were regarded as homogenous, with low recorded levels of diversity. Families generally formed on marriage with little recorded levels of extra-marital birth or cohabitation. Changes in family life were traditionally isolated to instances of the death of a spouse and the widowhood of the remaining spouse and recorded levels of marital separation were low (Fahey and Russell: 2001, Kennedy:2004).

In the mid-1900s family life started to see its biggest changes, perhaps also correlated with changes in the demographic profile in general, particularly given patterns of outward migration which characterised this period. The younger age profile of emigrants often resulted in a reduction in marriages in those of the corresponding age group. Extra-marital cohabitation and particularly extra-martial births started to become evident in the mid to late 1900s and continued to increase towards the end of the century. In 1972, when Cherish was established, the extra-marital birth rate stood at 3%; today it represents over 30% of all births (CSO: 2004a).

Recent years have also seen a decrease in the overall marriage rate although this has peaked at particular times but seems to be slowing down in general. It could be argued that people are postponing marriage rather than choosing not to marry at all, using cohabitation as a precursor to marriage. However, comprehensive statistics on cohabitation would be needed to test this point accurately (Fahey and Russell: 2001, Kennedy: 2004, CSO:2004).

Marital and relationship separation rates have also continued to rise and are expected to continue to do so given the recent introduction of divorce into Irish legislation in 1995.

Family diversity and one-parent families

As seen above traditional patterns of family formation in Ireland have begun to change and nowhere is this more evident than in the analysis of the changing profile of one-parent families in Ireland.

Family diversity is a useful concept to bear in mind not only when looking at changes in traditional family types but also in identifying changes in the one-parent family. 'A child born in Ireland in 1900 was just as likely to spend some of his or her childhood in a household lacking a parent as a child born today – and the risk of such an experience for children was likely to have been much greater the further back in time one goes' (Fahey and Russell, 2001: 22). This point notes that one-parent families in Ireland are by no means a new family type. However, predominantly a widowed spouse, usually female, has headed the one-parent family given the traditional patterns of younger female

marital age and higher mortality among men in particular age categories. The point that Fahey and Russell are making is that we have traditionally always had one-parent families in Irish society, due to high incidences of widowhood. However, changes in marriage and extra-marital birth rates, particularly from the 1960s and changes in attitudes towards marital breakdown and single parenting have dramatically changed the profile of one-parent families.

The one-parent family is now a diverse family type and is also increasing as a proportion of Irish families. Between 1991 and 2002 alone there has been a 75% increase in the number of one-parent families enumerated in the Census. Census 2002 indicates that there are 153,900 solo parent headed households in Ireland, representing over 12% of households. These figures indicate that 11% of the population live in a one-parent family (CSO:2004b).

Routes into solo parenthood

As noted above, the traditional route into solo parenthood was predominantly and almost exclusively resultant of the death of a spouse, as traditional and widely held Roman Catholic values would not have been supportive of extra-marital or non-marital parenthood or marital separation. With dilution of these values and particularly with the liberation in moral and sexual values of the 1960s and 1970s in Western societies, both extra-marital birth rates and marital separation increased. Single women who became pregnant outside of marriage also started to consider keeping their child rather than the traditional routes of outward adoption or marriage which had been considered the only options until then.

Thus, one-parent families started to diversify and have continued to do so. As evident from Figure One, Census 2002 indicates that 40% of solo parent headed households are headed by widowed persons, 32% by separated or divorced persons and 24% by single (never-married) persons. There are also variations in these types of one-parent families when correlated with age, in that younger parents (particularly under 20) heading one-parent families are also more likely to be never-married, whereas widowed and divorced and separated persons tend to be in the older age groups (CSO:2004b).

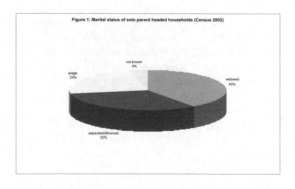

Figure 1: Marital status of solo parent headed households (Census 2002)

Size of one-parent family units

Diversity in the size of family units among one-parent families is also linked to the status of the head of household. Single parents tend to form smaller families and have a reduced fertility rate in comparison with other solo parents. As Fahey and Russell suggest : '...having a birth outside of marriage and entering lone parenthood leads to lower fertility than would be the case if the women involved had married or formed a long-term cohabiting relationship' (2001: 38).

Gender and one-parent families

Official statistics also lead us to believe that the gender differential in one-parent families is still significant although it may be decreasing. Given the changing entry routes into solo parenthood there is an increasing number of one-parent families now headed by males. Census 2002 figures show that 85% of one-parent families are headed by a female and 15% by a male. However, these figures may be a significant underestimation as official statistics do not measure the extent to which shared parenting in separate households is a feature of marital or relationship separation in Ireland today, which would greatly boost the numbers of males parenting in one-parent families. We will turn to this issue again.

Ethnic origin of solo parents

Recent years have also seen an increase in diversity of ethnic origin of solo parents with an increase in the number of one-parent families headed by a parent whose nationality is not Irish. However, there is a dearth of accurate information on the ethnic origin of one-parent families. Anecdotal evidence from services supports the view that there is an increasing number of female headed one-parent families which may have been created either by the asylum process and the separation of families or by the birth of an Irish-born child to a non-Irish single mother. Research conducted by One Family in 2004 gives further information on this aspect of diversity (One Family:2004).

Family policy and family support for one-parent families – issues to consider

We therefore know that there is an increasing number of one-parent families in Ireland today and that these families are diverse in their size, the age at which the parent formed the family, the route of entry into solo parenthood and the gender of solo parent head of the household.

We also know that one-parent families now make up at least 12% of Irish households. This is a very significant minority in modern Irish society. However, in a range of other statistics and indicators one-parent families make up a significant majority and unfortunately most of these figures are negative indicators relating to socio-economic difficulties challenging the full social inclusion of at least 11% of the Irish population.

One-parent families and poverty

One-parent families face a significantly higher risk and rate of poverty than their two-parent counterparts and the overall population. The EU Survey on Income and Living Conditions released in January 2005 indicates that 33% of one-parent families live in consistent poverty in comparison with 9% of the population overall. Moreover, 42% are at risk of poverty in comparison with 23% of the overall population. One-parent families also had the highest levels on each of the eight deprivation indicators used in the survey. These include the findings that 33% could not afford new clothes, 31% experienced debt from ordinary living expenses and 24% stated that they went without heating at some stage in the preceding 12 months.

Welfare dependency and poverty

There are a range of factors which contribute to the higher incidence and risk of poverty among one-parent families. These include high dependency rates on social assistance as the primary source of income. In 2003, One Family estimated that over 50% of the one-parent families in the state were in receipt of the One Parent Family Payment (OPFP). Conditions of the OPFP stipulate that any additional income will be assessed against entitlement to the payment in excess of €146.50 per week. This level has not increased since 1993, despite increases in the average industrial wage, the introduction of the minimum wage and significant increases in the cost of living, especially regarding housing costs. Of particular relevance in this case is the escalating cost of childcare for pre-school age children. It is therefore increasingly difficult for one-parent families in receipt of OPFP to make the transition fully from welfare to work due to the interaction of earned and benefit income.

One-parent families and the labour market

The employment participation rates of solo parents are therefore low, particularly among those with young children. Contributory factors not only include the aforementioned interaction of earned and benefit income but also relate to the inflexibility of traditional Irish working arrangements and the lack of availability of part-time or flexible employment which will provide sufficient income to offset high childcare costs and loss of benefits.

According to the 2002 Census there were 59,075 solo parents who described their principal economic status as being at work. Of these 11,522 (20%) were men and 47,553 (80%) were women.

Data from the 2001 Living in Ireland Survey suggests that households headed by a person who works full time in the home are at the greatest risk of poverty compared to households that are headed by a person that is in employment (including self employment), sick/disabled or unemployed.

Solo parents and access to education

Also related to high poverty and low employment rates are the low educational attainment rates of solo parents. Access to education and training for parents in a one-parent family varies depending on several factors. These include the age of the parent, how long they have been out of the education system and their current level of accredited education (NESF:2001).

According to the 2002 Census, of a total of 350,774 people over 15 who were students, only 0.5% (1,867) were solo parents in full-time education. The NESF (2001) found 38,642 solo parents in participation in mainstream education and training programmes, which included vocational and skills training provided by FÁS.

Solo parents are often characterised as having low educational attainment levels in comparison with married parents. The NESF (2001), drawing on the 1996 Labour Force Survey estimated that solo mothers in particular are 'more than twice as likely as their married counterparts to have no qualifications' (NESF, 2001: 65). As Figure 2 shows, 23% of solo mothers have no formal qualifications in comparison with 9% of married mothers. 38% of solo mothers attained only a junior certificate or equivalent level compared with 25% of married mothers. The highest educational level attained by 27% of solo mothers was a leaving certificate or equivalent compared with 42% of married mothers while only 12% of solo mothers attained a third-level qualification compared with 24% of married mothers.

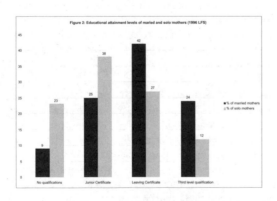

Figure 2: Educational attainment levels of married and solo mothers (1996 LFS)

Law, policy, services and the definition of the family

To date, family law, family policy and the design and delivery of family support services have all tended to focus on the family as a homogenous type, based on a single household unit of two, predominantly marital, parents and their children. The Constitution itself notes that the family is founded on marriage and so legal protection for other family forms is not currently available. Family law, as a consequence, tends to be biased towards what are considered to be the more stable relationships of two-parent families. Family law as a result often proves reactionary in its response to one-parent families or when one-parent families are forming through the dissolution of a previous union.

Family policy has tended to focus primarily on the marital family as the norm and has turned its attention to diverse forms, including one-parent families, as anomalies which require separate provision. What would be preferable would be to work from the principles of equality and family diversity, allowing for a diverse model and appreciation of family life to influence future policy.

Family support services also may be characterised as having a problematic and fixative approach to one-parent families in many cases. Many one-parent families interact with family support services due to the pressures of solo parenting without adequate supports. Due to the absence of greater supports to enhance solo parenting one-parent families are increasingly regarded as requiring the assistance of formal support services which may envisage two-parent families as the ideal type without any definitive research data to indicate the optimal family conditions for child well-being.

Recognising the realities of the diversity of family life in Ireland – recommendations for change

If we are to progress towards a society and its legal, administrative and service provision framework which respects all forms of family life as equal to one another and appreciates the validity of that diversity then there are a number of steps which must be taken. Moving from the current position to one which will accept diversity will require a mind and policy shift of a significant degree.

A position of acceptance of diversity will result in legal, administrative and service provision frameworks which will appreciate the differing levels of need of each diverse group and will focus on delivery of mechanisms and services which will endeavour to meet each need. A family diversity approach would fully recognise the inequality of the position of many one-parent families and would provide a framework for service, policy and legal provision which would seek to address that inequality in a way which respects the validity of the one-parent family and seeks to support it.

An inclusive definition of family life

Firstly, the current working definition of family in Irish law, policy and services must be changed from one based on a single family type exclusively to one which appreciates diversity. In order to do so, constitutional reform in relation to the provision for family in Bunreacht na hEireann is required. For further details please see One Family's policy position paper *'Working for a Constitution which affords equal rights to all families'*. As the superior source of domestic law, the Constitution embodies the rights and responsibilities of Irish citizens and also holds our aspirations as a nation. If it continues to include a preference for a single family type then a full appreciation of the value of diversity will not be possible.

A comprehensive understanding of diverse families and family life

In order to fully comprehend the nature of the changing profile of family life in Ireland it is essential to amend and perfect our methods of data collection on family life to fully assess not only the levels of diversity but also the needs of diverse families towards full equality.

Particularly in relation to one-parent families, data collection and data gaps hamper a full understanding of the level and diversity of one-parent families. Current methods such as the household enumeration models of the Census and other studies exclude an understanding of the extent to which relationship or marital separation can lead to the formation of two one-parent families and the extent to which non-resident parents continue to maintain a full parenting role with their children. Without this understanding we will not know how best to serve the needs of children in one-parent families in Ireland.

As recommended to the Central Statistics Office in relation to the next Census of Population, One Family proposes that the incidence of intergenerational households and the extent to which several families may inhabit a single household be explored fully and represented statistically. The forthcoming Longitudinal Study of Children must also involve a representative number of children from diverse families and must also look at the nature of the relationship between family structure, well-being and social inclusion.

One Family recommends that a comprehensive study of one-parent families be commissioned with the full weight of government support to fully understand the nature and needs of a significant number of families in Ireland today. This examination would be underpinned by the principles of equality and diversity and the results should be utilised towards supporting the full social inclusion of one-parent families as valid family forms.

A work-life balance for all families

The nature of participation in the labour market requires radical change if we are to support parenting and childhood in Ireland. In order to strike a balance between work and other areas of life, including family life, a shift is required in how we envisage the workplace and the role of workers within it. Work-life balance can only be achieved if parents are supported to fully participate to the best of their ability without constraint. This will lead us to move towards flexible work patterns and a less static definition of the workplace to include an emphasis on alternative working methods including such as home and teleworking as realistic options.

Respecting diversity in family life

Services require a shift from 'fixing' non-traditional family forms to one which recognises and celebrates their diversity and supports the full inclusion of the family, regardless of its structure. Changes in family support services will be central to this goal.

Family support should at all times be concerned with the needs and circumstances of a particular family and how best to meet those needs with respect for the family type and situation and the needs of individual members as well as the family as a unit. If we continue to have a policy, legal and service model which has a definitive ideal of the ways families 'should' look then all other family types will appear as an anomaly. It is therefore necessary that family diversity become a working principle in the fields of law, policy and service provision to ensure that all families are treated equally and derive equal benefit from their interactions with them.

References

CSO (2004a) *Vital Statistics*, Dublin, Central Statistics Office.

CSO (2004b) *Census 2002, Volume 3: Household Composition and Family Status*, Dublin, Central Statistics Office.

Daly, M. (2004) *Families and Family Life in Ireland, Challenges for the Future – Report of Public Consultation Fora*, Dublin, Department of Social and Family Affairs.

Fahey, T. and Russell, F. (2001) *Family Formation in Ireland – Trends, Data Need and Implications,* Policy Research Series Number 43, Dublin, Economic and Social Research Institute.

Kennedy, F. (2004) *Cottage to Crèche – Family Change in Ireland*, Dublin, Institute of Public Administration.

Mc Keown, K., Pratschke and Haase T. (2003) *Family Well-Being – What Makes A Difference*, Report to the Céifin Centre, Dublin, Department of Social & Family Affairs/Family Support Agency.

NESF (2001) *Lone Parents – report No. 20*, Dublin, National Economic and Social Forum.

One Family (2004) *Meeting the Needs of Asylum Seeking and Refugee One-Parent Families- One Family and the Effects of a Changing Clientele*, Dublin, One Family.

OPEN

THE ORGANISATION

OPEN is a national anti-poverty network which represents lone parent self help groups in Ireland. These groups have joined together to represent the interests of lone parents living in poverty and social exclusion. We support our member groups to strengthen their capacity to provide services for lone parents living in their communities and we campaign for policy change that recognises family diversity, supports economic independence and improves the quality of life for lone parents and their children.

OPEN (One Parent Exchange and Network) was founded in 1994. The need for a national network of lone parent self help groups was identified when, in the early 1990s, lone parents in many parts of the country began forming groups to provide mutual support, advice and information about issues relevant to their type of family.

The common bond of all groups in the network is self help – lone parents *themselves* recognising their own ability to deliver information and advice services, and to pool their experiences to campaign for more inclusive social and economic policies and structures. OPEN's groups are made up of all types of lone parents, men and women: never married; previously married and those with partners who are institutionalised or otherwise unavailable to fulfil their parenting role.

From a core number of eight groups, OPEN now has almost eighty member groups throughout the country. Our 'Group Kit' is available since 1999 to lone parent groups who are starting out and has been well received by other types of community groups. As well as supporting the ongoing work of our member groups, we also enable new lone parent groups to develop in rural and urban areas. In 2001, we established a small Policy Unit and we publish research about one-parent families and the issues which affect them; all of our research is 'proofed' by lone parent members of our groups. Members also receive a bi-monthly newsletter to which they contribute. In 2002, OPEN became formally regionalised and has seven regions, which are supported by our member groups on a voluntary basis and by dedicated staff members from the core national team. In 2003 we initiated the 'Your Vote, Your Voice' programme which aims to increase the numbers of lone parents who vote; it is entirely politically independent and has been rolled out throughout our regions by lone parent trainers. In 2004 we have secured funding support from the Department of Social and Family Affairs towards a national plan for one-parent families, which will be published in 2005.

In the past ten years, OPEN has emerged as a national voice of lone parents and has been involved in policy development at the highest level. OPEN is also the Irish member of the European Network of One-Parent Families.

OPEN welcomes the opportunity to make a submission to the All-Party Oireachtas Committee on the Constitution as it undertakes a review of the main provisions in relation to the family in Articles 41, 42 and 40.3. As the national representative of lone parent groups in Ireland, we are particularly concerned with the impact that the current provisions may be having on lone parent families.

1 LONE PARENTS IN IRELAND

A major data deficiency exists in relation to lone parents – we don't know how many there are. This difficulty stems from the constitutional definition of the family which focuses on one family unit. The 2002 census shows that there were 150,634 lone parent households in Ireland, the majority of which (85%) are lone mothers. The census counts the entire population, via self-recorded information. People are counted where they happen to be on census night, rather than at their usual residence. This means the absence of a parent on census night can artificially reduce a two-parent household to a one-parent one, which may overstate the number of one-parent households relative to two-parent ones. However, a more fundamental problem is that the census fails to identify lone parents who are living with their own parents. The nature of lone parenthood means that many lone parents live with their own parents, for example younger lone parents may not have the resources, financial and otherwise to set up an independent home. Statistics from the Department of Social and Family Affairs shows that there were 80,926 recipients of the one-parent family payment in March 2004 (Loftus, 2004).

Lone parents are not a homogenous group. While the majority of lone parents are lone mothers, 15% of those identified by the census are lone fathers. The routes into lone parenthood, a condition that can affect any of us, are many – separation, divorce, desertion, death, imprisonment of a partner or an unplanned pregnancy. Irish society is becoming more varied with a growth in non-national communities and a diversity of religious beliefs, all of which have lone parents in their midst. Statistics from the Department of Social and Family Affairs (2004) show that lone parenthood is experienced across the age spectrum. For example, while 57% of lone parents are aged between 25 and 35 years, 19% are over 40 years and 23% are aged less than 24 years of age. Lone parents are also present amongst other groups such as those with disabilities, those from the travelling community and within the gay, lesbian, bisexual and transgender community.

While each family will have its own unique experiences, one-parent families have one thing in common: a high risk of living in poverty. In 1994 data from the Living in Ireland Survey (LIS) documented that one in twenty households in consistent poverty were headed by a lone parent. The most recent data from the LIS (2001) show that one in five households in consistent poverty are headed by lone parents. While most groups have moved out of poverty, lone parents' experience of poverty has increased four-fold.

2 THE IMPACT OF THE CONSTITUTIONAL DEFINITION OF THE FAMILY ON LONE PARENTS

The constitutional definition of the family, that of the family based on marriage, has had a strong influence on legislative and institutional arrangements in Ireland. This in turn has had knock-on effects for other diverse family structures. For example, in terms of accessing public housing, the National Economic and Social Forum (NESF) report on *Lone Parents* (2001) notes that 43 per cent of those on local authority waiting lists are one-parent households; 67 per cent of these are lone parents with one child. Local authority housing lists tend to favour larger families, particularly those with more than one adult, over smaller family units.

Article 41.2.2, 'the state recognises that by her life within the home, woman gives to the state a support without which the common good cannot be achieved' is problematic. On the one hand this notion is outdated, as the last number of decades have seen a phenomenal increase in women's participation in the labour market. Between the period 1971 and 1996, women accounted for 90% of the increase in employment (O'Connor, 2000). In 1994 40.1% of women between the ages 15-64 years were in employment: this figure had increased to 55.8% in 2004 (CSO, 2004).

The welfare system in Ireland is strongly based on the male breadwinner model. This model of social welfare 'suggests that states built their wages' policy, tax and welfare systems around a prototype family of a fully employed male earning a family wage and supporting a dependent spouse and children in a lifelong stable marriage' (NWCI, 2003: 14). This definition of our social welfare system is similar to the provisions made in the Constitution.

The current political ideology of 'a job being the best route out of poverty' has meant that qualification for certain social welfare payments has been dependent on 'labour market attachment' (NWCI, 2003: 14). In this instance, it is difficult for those involved in caring duties within the home to be actively looking for work as in the Irish context 'a person has to prove that (s)he has immediate provision of childcare in the event of a job offer' (NWCI, 2003: 14). Women are defined in the social welfare system by the status of their relationship with their husband (e.g. widow's allowance, deserted wives benefit).

Social welfare payments for lone parents have historically been based on the deservedness and undeservedness of lone parenthood. In 1935 a means-tested and social insurance-based payment for widows was introduced. It was not until the 1970s that a means-tested payment for deserted wives was introduced. In 1973 a means-tested payment for unmarried mothers was created along with a social insurance payment for deserted wives.

The piecemeal way in which the social welfare system in Ireland was developed can be reflected in the Constitution's definition of the family based on marriage. They were predicated on the notion that a mother should work full-time in the home raising children, and should not be obliged to engage in paid employment. The payments were largely restricted to women – until 1989 there was no deserted husband or widower's payment – and also reflected a societal distinction between 'deservedness' of different categories of mothers: those who were parenting alone 'through no fault of their own', i.e. as a result of widowhood or desertion, were covered for that contingency in the social insurance system; unmarried mothers however had to rely solely on a means-tested payment.

In the late 1990s the one-parent family payment, a more unified payment, was introduced for all parents raising children on their own. Nonetheless, this type of family remains outside the mainstream, an exception to the rule, and social policy continues to reflect society's ambivalence towards this family type; on the one hand asserting that they are different, and on the other, insisting they abide by the same rules 'as everybody else', i.e. fit in with the same employment and housing policies which are formulated around the Constitution's definition of the family. The inadequacy of this payment, in terms of its earning disregard and its weekly rate, and the stigmatisation which still exists towards one-parent families, means that these family types feel that they are an anomaly within the society.

3 THE ROLE OF MOTHERS WITHIN THE HOME

Statistics from the CSO (2004) show that 87.2% of women without children were in employment. However, women are more and more frequently combining work and family responsibilities, with 52.4% of women with the youngest child aged 0-3 years in employment and 63.6% of women where the youngest child was aged 6 or over CSO (2004). While motherhood has a negative effect on employment (O'Connor, 2000) the same cannot be said about fatherhood. The employment rate for men varies very little across family status (94.4% for those with no children, 90.1% for men where the youngest child was under 3 years of age) (CSO, 2004). While mothers are increasingly moving into employment, men are still assuming the breadwinner role.

If we look at a gender breakdown of those engaged in home duties, less than 1% are men (CSO, 2004). For those who do remain in the home to look after their children, the way in which the social welfare system is structured means it is not viable if they do not have a partner to support them financially. For example, a recent study carried out by the Vincentian Partnership for Social Justice (2004) on low-cost budgets found that a household with a lone parent and two children dependent on social welfare incurred a weekly shortfall of €23.62. This meant that the family was falling into debt each week in order to try and live at a low-cost but acceptable standard of living on the one-parent family payment.

The lack of recognition for the caring work undertaken in the home is also highlighted by the findings of the study. A lone mother working full-time on the national minimum wage will have a shortfall of €61.18 per week. The high childcare costs incurred by this family is a contributory factor to the shortfall. In comparison to this, a two-parent household with one adult working full-time on the national minimum wage will have a discretionary income of €77.24. While an extra adult in the household increases the costs, this is offset by the provision of 'free' childcare, as one adult in the household does not go out to work.

4 CONCLUSION

There has been much progress in breaking down the stigma historically associated with one-parent families.

Nonetheless, this type of family remains an anomaly in Irish social policy: we can't count their number accurately; on the one hand, our policy goals are to increase participation in the workforce, while on the other, our childcare provision is scant and expensive, and the complex nature of the interaction between the one-parent family payment, welfare-to-work incentives and the tax system distorts lone parents' choices in relation to paid employment.

Our Constitution declares that no mother should be obliged by economic necessity to work outside the home, and yet almost a fifth of families reliant on the one parent family payment live in consistent poverty, unable to afford things that by definition 'nobody should have to do without'.

The current situation of one-parent families is testament to the fact that when it comes to social policy, one size does not fit all: one-parent families are expected to squeeze in to policy measures based on the constitutional definition of the family based on marriage. The result is an unacceptably high level of poverty for people parenting alone and their children.

MAIN RECOMMENDATIONS

OPEN makes the following recommendations to the All-Party Oireachtas Committee on the Constitution in relation to the provisions made for families in the constitution.

Article 41

- On considering the family and marriage provisions in many of the European constitutions and in the European Convention on Human Rights (ECHR) and International Covenant of Civil and Political Rights (CCPR), it appears that with the exception of Luxembourg, none guarantees expressly the rights of the family unit as such. Many recognise the family as a primary or fundamental unit in society and some state that it is entitled to the special protection of the state or society, but the rights or duties which derive from marriage, family, parenthood or as a child are guaranteed to or imposed on the individuals. This would be the better approach in any revised form of Article 41.
- The express inclusion of the unenumerated rights of the child. A child is, of course, a person, and therefore the general constitutional rights shared by adults, such as the right to bodily integrity, will be protected elsewhere in the Constitution. Article 41 should contain an express guarantee of those rights of a child which are not guaranteed elsewhere and are peculiar to children, such as the right to be reared with due regard for his or her welfare.
- A revised Article 41 should include a guarantee to all individuals of respect for their family life whether based on marriage or not.

Article 41.2

- The revision of Article 41.2 as follows:

  The state recognises that home and family life gives to society a support without which the common good cannot be achieved. The state shall endeavour to support persons caring for others within the home.

- In order to address the continuing poverty of one-parent families we agree with the National Women's Council of Ireland (NWCI) that the following changes take place in relation to 'Develop a Contingency for Parenting and Wage for Caring' (NWCI, 2003: 32):

1 Extension of maternity benefit to twenty-six weeks
2 Introduction of paid parental leave benefit for parents of young children
3 Introduction of part-time parental benefit for parents of children up to the age of eleven
4 Introduction of a means-tested parental allowance
5 Introduction of a means-tested part-time allowance
6 Development of a mechanism to value care of older people as paid work by turning carer's benefit and allowance into a wage.

Article 41.3.1

- Retain in the Constitution a pledge by the state to protect the family based on marriage but also to guarantee to all individuals a right to respect for their family life whether that family is, or is not, based on marriage.
- The favouring of an express pledge by the state to protect the family based on marriage. It does not favour the retention of the words 'upon which the family is founded' in Article 41.3.1°. These words have led to an exclusively marriage-based definition of the family which no longer accords with the social structure in Ireland.

In addition to this, OPEN recommends that the following is taken into consideration when revising the provisions in the Constitution in relation to families: Article 8(1) of the European Convention on Human Rights which provides:

  Everyone has the right to *respect* for his private and family life, his home and his correspondence. (emphasis added)

References

Central Statistics Office (2003) *Census 2002: Volume 3 Household Composition and Family Units,* Dublin: The Stationery Office

Central Statistics Office (2004) *Women and Men in Ireland 2004,* Dublin: The Stationery Office

Department of Social and Family Affairs (2004) *Statistical Information on Social Welfare Services,* Dublin: The Stationery Office

Loftus, C. (2004) *'One Size Fits All?' – Irish Governments' Failed Approach to One-Parent Families,* Dublin: OPEN

NESF (2001) *Lone Parents* Forum Report No. 20, Dublin: NESF

NWCI (2003) *A Woman's Model for Social Welfare Reform,* Dublin: NWCI

OPEN (2004) *'Living on the Book'* Dublin: OPEN

O'Connor, P. (2000) 'Ireland: A Man's World?' in *Economic and Social Review,* Vol. 31(1), January 2000, pp 81–102

Vincentian Partnership for Social Justice (2004) *Low Cost But Acceptable Budgets for Three Households,* Dublin: Vincentian Partnership for Social Justice

PARENTAL EQUALITY

This is a submission to the All-Party Oireachtas Committee on the Constitution on behalf of Parental Equality. Parental Equality is a voluntary group which has been raising public consciousness and supporting the concept of shared parenting since 1992. The mission statement for Parental Equality reads as follows: Our mission in Parental Equality is to seek both through our own activities and through our involvement with the education of our future generation of parents to play a proactive role in creating a culture of shared family responsibilities, enabling women and men equally to realise their optimum potential both in their family lives and careers.

In recognition of the UN Convention on the Rights of the Child, Parental Equality aims to achieve parity of esteem for all members of the family system. In furtherance of this goal, Parental Equality undertake to support, promote and encourage with due respect for the freedom of the individual, increased participation for men as carers of the family system and opportunities for women to open up their traditional domain as child carers.

This mission statement by Parental Equality fundamentally sets out the values which we would like to see enshrined in our Constitution. We believe that the object of having a Constitution is to lay out a framework which supports and protects the necessary elements to create and maintain a stable, sustainable, civilised society, particularly in areas affecting the family. We believe that it is quite clear that for more than a generation the Constitution, as it now stands, and particularly as it has been interpreted in the practice of the courts, is out of kilter with the reality of modern Irish society.

In the original Constitution, which was framed in 1937, the societal landscape which existed at the time consisted of fairly standard family models, where the normal expectation was marriage for life and that marriage encompassed the expectation of procreation and providing for the next generation of children in our society. The nature of work was such that men were the traditional breadwinners as husbands in the family and that women were traditionally the homemakers. The very concept of travel infrastructure and communication as we now know it, was unforeseen at the time of the establishment of the first Irish Constitution.

Over the past twenty years there has been a spiralling level of relationship breakdown within families, and an acknowledgement of thousands of abortions of potential Irish babies which while not permitted on the island of Ireland are actually undertaken by the pregnant women travelling abroad.

We have seen over the last twenty years the percentage of children born outside of marriage constantly increasing to the degree that at the end of December 2004, for example, the reported percentage of births outside of marriage in County Louth was almost 40 per cent. During the mid-1990s, repeated attempts to have a constitutional ban on divorce were finally successful and we now have a decade of experience of a divorce regime in Ireland. Whereas contraception was relatively unknown in the late 1930s, it is now statutory policy to recommend the use of condoms in order to practice safe sex for the reason of protecting people against sexually transmitted diseases, including the killer AIDS virus.

The issues of in vitro fertilisation, surrogate parenthood, homosexuals raising children etc, are now part of the reality of our everyday discussions. It is ironic that in the year 2005, and having failed to respond in a timely and appropriate manner to the needs of our society, the cumbersome process of reviewing the Constitution yet again looms as a possibility, but only that. We only have to look at the discussions that are ongoing in relation to genetic engineering, and to look at the massive rate of change that has occurred in our society over the last fifty years to envisage with any realism that cloned babies, genetically modified human beings will be issues facing our society within the next generation or two.

In recognition of the fact that the Constitution has already failed to keep pace with the changes in our society, it is questionable whether the topics suggested for discussion by the All-Party Oireachtas Committee on the Constitution reflected on these real and future possibilities. Whereas a lot of the debate and struggle has been around the issues of the rights of the child, the rights of unmarried fathers, whether gay couples should be allowed to marry and the Constitution's reference to the special place of the mother in the home, we should be designing a Constitution that can take into account the inevitable eventuality of, effectively, cyber children.

When one looks at Article 40.1 of our Constitution that deals with personal rights and which, on the surface, suggests that all citizens shall as human persons be held equal before the law, before then going on in the sub-clause to dilute that equality by stating that the state effectively can differentiate, and thus discriminate, on the basis of social function, we are left to wonder about what will happen in a society when genetically modified and generated children, who are potentially more efficient according to the values of a future state, might end up creating the possibility that the naturally generated humans might find themselves all as second class citizens to the cyborg generation.

Mindful of the insights of leaders of the American Indian tradition who stated that when changes were being introduced in a society, one should think of the impact of those changes seven generations hence, Parental Equality have struggled when considering this submission to find some lasting and universal values that could be inserted and established in our Constitution, which could support a stable, viable and co-operative society in the present time, and which could prove resilient and adaptable to the inevitable changes that will emerge over the coming generations.

Since the original Constitution was put in place in 1937, one of the fundamental changes to the expectation to marriage and the family has been in the area of pro-creation. Prior to the situation where contraception was readily available and was socially acceptable, and when abortion, and certainly the public awareness of it, was relatively unknown, it would be reasonable to submit that when a man and woman got married the normal expectation of that relationship was that it would be bearing of children. While it is true that some couples would have used various strategies to remain childless, or that in some percentages they may not have been capable of having children, the reality of the decision to get married fundamentally included an expectation that there would be children of that relationship.

In the present day, the decision to marry is a separate decision to the decision to have children. It is quite possible to marry and not to have children by choice, and it is quite possible to have children and not to marry by choice. It is also possible to marry and to parent by choice. In the event where people wish to live together as a couple and where there are no children involved, there are no trans-generational impacts and implications for society, and when those adults who are in a relationship die childless there is no follow through from them to the future generation. If people wish to cohabit and live together then the nature of their relationship, whether they are heterosexual or homosexual or whether they are ones based on friendship or caring without a sexual element, as long as there are no children involved then there are no implications or complications which follow through to the next generation through the children.

On the other hand the act of parenting and pro-creation creates the flow and supply for future generations. It is therefore in the area of parenting that Parental Equality would like to focus the minds of the All-Party Oireachtas Committee on the Constitution as the structures that support, regulate and protect the parenting function are ultimately the one vital element in ensuring continuity of the species in a sustainable society for future generations.

It appears from our reading of the report of the Constitution Review Group that their recommendation seemed to suggest a move away from the concentration of inalienable and imprescriptible rights to the family unit itself, towards the provision of rights to individuals within families.

The Review Group also seems to suggest the desire to invest specific constitutional rights to unmarried mothers while at the same time deliberately deciding not to give specific constitutional rights to unmarried fathers. The group then seems to go on to seek to provide specific rights to the child when suggesting that giving constitutional rights to the child through a relationship with its father in some way ensures that fathers, and their relationship with their children, will have their needs met.

The Review Group also seems to suggest that the terms 'inalienable' and 'imprescriptible' should be removed from the Constitution, and that the specific reference in Article 41 referring to a mother's specific role in the home should either be modified to be gender neutral, or broadened to include all carers in the home.

Parental Equality submit the following proposal for how we in society might address how we respond to pregnancy, birth or abortion and the raising of children following birth. Essentially, we believe that where a male and female have consensual sex which results in a pregnancy, that in terms of society evaluating or adjudicating either the behaviours that led towards this pregnancy or whether such pregnancies, for example outside of marriage, are to be supported and promoted by society, or whether there is an attempt to minimise them and to ensure that pregnancies occur within a legally committed framework, then the male and female concerned should both be held legally accountable.

At present we have developed a culture, often extrapolated from culturally manicured myths, of feckless fathers, of young men who are irresponsible in terms of their sexual behaviour, who effectively prey on and take advantage of women, while at the same time the women are unsuspecting victims who become unwillingly pregnant and then are left, too often, to face the task of going through with the pregnancy, having the child and raising the child alone.

Based on these myths in the year 2005, the Irish social welfare system is now weighed down by almost €800 million of lone parent payments. The Constitution Review Group, when looking at the rights of unmarried fathers, for example, yet again fell into the well-worn trap of concentrating unnecessarily on the fairly minuscule percentage of pregnancies that occurred from rape. Almost invariably, procreation is a result of consensual sex. It may be irresponsible sex; it may be as a result of too much alcohol; it may be as a result of extra-marital affairs but, almost invariably, it is consensual sex between males and females which lead to pregnancy.

By supporting or criticising both the male and female involved on an equal basis, there is a far greater probability that men and women might move from the model of blaming each other to concentrating on the job at hand in negotiating co-operative arrangements to provide for their offspring. Consequently, we feel that it is a constitutional imperative that while the state might choose to discriminate in a positive way to encourage a formation of a legal entity, as a couple, for parents of children, thus incentivising this legal coupling justified by the greater goal of creating continuity and a stable society, sustainable into the future, there should be no differentiating between parents on a gender basis. The family based on marriage in the tradition where a man and woman have a legally binding contract to maintain and look after each other, is part of a subset of a much larger community of extended family. It has served the civilisation well over the millennia. Married parents, their children, and their extended relations help form sustainable supportive communities. By entering these contractual relationships, it increases the probability of a stable and continuous environment for children during their formative years. Over the last decade or so, the emerging research continues to restate the fact that a stable cohabiting parental relationship is the best environment for children to be raised in. Therefore, it is reasonable that social policy should incentivise this structuring of parental relationships.

One of the questions asked by the All-Party Oireachtas Committee on the Constitution is how should one strike the balance between the rights of the family as a unit and the rights of individual members. It appears that the Constitution Review Group seeks to enumerate the rights of the individual members. However, in this case it seems to lean towards giving rights to mothers and to children, and in some way hoping that fathers will continue to have some identity, but only through their children's needs. It seems to us that the unit which is formed by biological parents and their children is a fundamental system, and that for the system to be functional and healthy it is necessary that every element of the system, in a balanced and holistic way, must also be healthy and functional. If any element of the family system, whether it be the mother, the father or children are out of balance or dysfunctional, then the whole system is out of balance and dysfunctional. There is a fundamental flaw in the reductionist thinking that if one separates out the individual rights from the system as a whole then the Constitution can protect an individual but not damage the family system.

Looking again at our belief that the object of the Constitution is to provide a framework to support and protect stable and sustainable societies into the future, and given the fact that the model of families and communities made up of extended families has been a fundamental element in sustaining society for thousands of years, Parental Equality would not like to see

a watering down of the emphasis placed on the family as a system, and do not see any contradiction between that and the enumeration of the rights of individual members within that family.

There is another element here which involves the relationship between rights and responsibilities. In some way the Constitution Review Group seems to suggest that, for example, unmarried fathers should have responsibilities to look after their children but should not be given the commensurate rights to a relationship with those children. It seems to us that the issue of rights and responsibilities are two sides of the one coin. If a society attaches responsibility, for example to fathers, without providing them with the commensurate authority and rights to carry out their responsibilities, then the outcome will be destructive. It seems to us that the only people who have responsibilities with no rights are second-class citizens and, effectively, slaves.

All rights go hand in hand with responsibilities. In fact, only children and individuals within families who, because of certain disabilities, are incapable of looking after themselves are the only group of people who should have rights without responsibilities for that period of time. Inevitably, as children grow up, they should gradually learn to take on responsibility so that as adults the issue of rights and responsibilities should again go hand in hand for them. It seems obvious to us that to provide for a sustainable society, men and women, fathers and mothers should be given rights and responsibilities in equal measure.

Article 42.1 of our Constitution, under the heading of education, states: 'The state acknowledges that the primary and natural educator of the child is the family and guarantees to respect the inalienable right and duty of parents to provide, according to their means, for the religious and moral, intellectual, physical and social education of their children'. In what we believe to be a much stronger version of the same sentiment the Irish version of the same Article states:

> Admhaíonn an Stát gurb é an Teaghlach is múinteoir príomha dúchasach don leanbh, agus ráthaíonn gan cur isteach ar cheart doshannta ná ar dhualgas doshannta tuistí chun oideachas de réir a n-acmhainne a chur ar fáil dá gclainn i gcúrsaí creidimh, moráltachta, intleachta, coirp agus comhdhaonnachta.

The use of the words 'gan cur isteach', as we understand them, actually means not to interfere with, and our interpretation of this is that the sentiment as expressed by the creators of our original Constitution was that the state should not interfere with the role of guardians in providing for the religious, moral, intellectual and physical and social education of their children.

It would seem that the Review Group felt that elements of this section could be extended to the welfare of children as beyond that of pure education. Parental Equality feel that this Article has universal and lasting value. The obvious normality is that the child is more likely to be loved and cared for by the same parents who created that child than by any other elements of society. In the minority of situations where parents, for whatever reason, fail to do their best for their children and to live up to the requirements of Article 42.1, then we can refer to Article 42.5 which states that 'in exceptional cases, where the parents for physical or moral reasons fail in their duty towards their children, the state, as guardian of the common good, by appropriate means shall endeavour to supply the place of the parents, but always with due regard for the natural and imprescriptible rights of the child'.

This protection, in the minority of situations where parents fail to do their duty, held together with Article 42.1, should make a very powerful core message in terms of the role of parenting. Instead of being distracted, as the Review Group seem to have been when considering the right of unmarried fathers, it is Parental Equality's firm view that fathers and mothers, married and unmarried, should by default, all be guardians of their children and all invested with equal guardianship rights.

Surely Article 42.5, which addresses the exceptional cases, could be extended to include providing for situations where pregnancy occurred as a result of rape, as mentioned earlier in relation to Article 40.1 which, on the face of it, purports to treat all citizens equally but in its sub-clause actually allows the state to discriminate against certain citizens based on their social function. Parental Equality has a major concern in relation to how this Article has been and could be utilised to discriminate against fathers.

As mentioned by the Constitution Review Group, in the case *Denneby v The Minister for Social Welfare* in 1984, Barron J. used Article 41.2 to support his conclusion that the failure of the state to treat deserted husbands in the same way as deserted wives for the purposes of social welfare was justified by the proviso of Article 40.1 in terms of the recognition of a difference in capacity and social function. Given the changes since the European Union Directive on Equality in 1975, on how the issue of gender equality has been mainstreamed and legislated for under Equal Status Acts, Parental Equality submit that Article 40.1 should be further modified to ensure that the state has no right to discriminate between men and women in terms of them playing their role as parents of their children.

Parental Equality since 1992 has been espousing and promoting the concept of shared parenting and joint custody where relationships break down. Almost every act of social policy over the last twenty years has promoted a culture, where relationships break down, of driving divisions between mothers and fathers, of promoting both culturally and statutorily through social welfare payments etc on a discriminatory basis for a model of sole custody to the mother and limited access to the father.

The irrefutable and consistently emerging evidence about the outcome of this model is moving towards the American and English experience of fifty per cent of children losing contact with their fathers within two years of relationship breakdown. In light of the ever-spiralling cost to the Exchequer of supporting one-parent families and the necessity for state resources in many other areas, whether through education, mental health, the criminal justice system etc, the fallout from the experience of children growing up in homes without fathers must surely challenge the total strategy, trajectory and direction of our social policies.

On the face of it, it would seem that Article 42.1, which recognised fathers as inalienable joint guardians of their children, would provide a safe environment for fathers and ensure that in the family courts their role as equal parents of their children would be respected. However, the reality of the experience of fathers in the family courts is invariably different.

Parental Equality do not feel that there is a requirement for anything other than the strengthening of Article 42.1, extending towards the area to cover welfare as well as education, and then ensuring that unmarried fathers are given the same rights as unmarried mothers.

However, all of these rights are meaningless within the context of the abuse of Article 34.1, namely in the area of the abuse of the *in camera* secret family law court system. Article 34.1 states that: 'Justice shall be administered in courts established by law by judges appointed in the manner provided by this Constitution and save in such special and limited cases as may be prescribed by law shall be administered in public.' When the Constitution was originally established in 1937 the level of marital breakdown in Ireland was almost non-existent. The level of activity in the family law courts was almost unheard of. Quite apart from anything else, the sums of money involved made it almost inaccessible to the vast majority of the population. From our understanding of the Denham review of the courts system a few years ago, it was then established that over twenty per cent of all civil law cases were made up of family law.

How anybody could continue to suggest that this massive amount of activity in the courts system constitutes 'special and limited cases' seems astounding.

Parental Equality for over a decade has campaigned for the revocation of the *in camera* rule as implemented in the Irish court system. While there are some elements of change coming into force at the end of March 2005 in relation to the supposed relaxation of the *in camera* court rules, a closer reading by interested lay litigants and members of the public actually show a completely different view. Far from creating a transparent accountable legal system, the modifications are carefully worded to ensure even greater protection for the professional classes who operate within the courts system.

We note that the modifications to the *in camera* rule were voted on by the Oireachtas, and we questioned the technical competence of the elected Dáil representatives to make informed decisions about any aspect of

A232

the family courts system given that, due to the *in camera* rule, even elected members of the Dáil and Seanad are not entitled to know anything about the details of what goes on within the family court system. So, all the modifications on which they were voting were being voted on with total ignorance, or else they were secretly breaking the *in camera* rule by discussing accounts of family law cases with participants in these cases. As a result of the black hole of information about what actually goes on in the regulation of family law in our courts, there is by definition no quality control system in place. The consistent discrimination against fathers in terms of child custody and access, whether they be married and separated fathers or unmarried fathers, is propagated and protected by secrecy.

It is Parental Equality's belief that if proper accountability and transparency of what goes on in the family courts were in place, then the rich and lasting values that are invested in Article 42.1 would inevitably win out, as the moral pressure from the public at large, who we believe are fundamentally fair minded, would bring about a holistic and natural balancing in terms of the treatment of fathers and mothers in the courts.

Therefore, it is imperative in order for any successful and sustainable regulation of family, marital and parenting matters that there is a fundamental shift in the wording and application of Article 34. A good starting position would be to write into the Constitution a clear and fundamental requirement that the contents, evidence and decisions of all courts and hearings are accurately and properly recorded; that all judgments are made public; that rationales for making such judgments must be recorded and stated on the public record; and that all such judgments are traceable back to the original evidence given in the courts. The technology for implementing this requirement is readily available and, with advances in technology, will become much easier and cheaper to implement at a very secure level.

For over a decade now the Irish Constitution has been modified so that courts can grant dissolutions of marriage through divorce. In Article 41.3.2 a divorce may only be granted where the court is satisfied that such provisions as the court considers proper, having regard to the circumstances, exist or will be made for the spouses, any children of either or both of them and any other person prescribed by law and that this requirement is met before a divorce is granted.

The existence of divorce fundamentally changes the very concept of marriage. From the period in 1937 when the first Constitution was enacted up to the introduction of divorce, a man and woman who were getting married were giving a lifelong undertaking, a contract which is indissoluble and would only terminate on the death of one or the other of the parties. Since the introduction of divorce, the marriage contract is fundamentally changed in that now when a man and woman get married they are only committing to remain married to the other person for, effectively, as long as

it suits both parties. If either one or both of the parties are unhappy with that relationship and wish to terminate the marriage through divorce they can do so providing they meet certain achievable criteria.

Whereas in the era of marriage before divorce there was much more security for both parents in terms of their expectation for a continued relationship with their children, even in a situation where they were separated, compared to a situation now where a couple who have been married for a few years and have had children, providing they have satisfied the four year requirement prior to divorce, can divorce and either or both members of that marriage can remarry other people.

It is perfectly possible that over a normally sexually productive life cycle, a man or a woman could be married three or four times and have a multiplicity of children in different situations. Under these circumstances, the security of the continuity of the relationship, particularly between fathers and their children in scenarios where the state continues to discriminate against shared parenting and provides statutory and welfare models which force parents down the sole custody/access route, is increasingly under threat. It is necessary to rebuild the sense of security and confidence which both mothers and fathers would have had in the pre-divorce era in terms of their expectation of both continuing to be involved with their children for their lifetime and expecting the other partner to also be continually involved with their children ....

PLUMBLINE NETWORK OF CHURCHES IN IRELAND

INTRODUCTION

The Plumbline Network of Churches is a family of contemporary churches with a strong family ethos, which are members of the Evangelical Alliance Ireland.

We would like to make the following comments in response to your invitation for submissions.

The family unit is the most fundamental unit of society. It has been under immense pressures in recent years due, in part, to relationship breakdowns between parents, more temporary arrangements such as cohabitation, which are even less durable than marriage, and to single motherhood.

All available research shows that children do best when brought up in a family with both a mother and father actively involved. Many of the social and psychological problems which children develop occur when the traditional family model is not in place or is not working properly. It is in the interests of the state and of society in general to foster and nurture the best possible framework for the healthy development of its children, who will constitute its future citizens. With this in view, we recommend the following:

1 We see no need to redefine the family in the Constitution. The health and well-being of our society is directly linked to the health and well-being of marriage. The concept of the family as one man and one woman legally married and nurturing the children of their marriage is still the best definition of the family and should be maintained as the norm.

2 If cohabiting couples want the protection of the Constitution for their family, they are free to marry legally, and thus also give to their children the emotional security which marriage affords. It is not desirable to lower the unique status of the traditional marriage.

3 Homosexual couples should not be afforded the status of marriage. They are not able to produce children through their union and should not be allowed to adopt the children of others. Children deserve the best possible environment to develop, and the Constitution should do nothing which would deny the rights of children to a father and a mother with the distinctives that each brings to the parenting role. We don't want 'political correctness' gone mad. Registered domestic partnerships may be an alternative course of action to deal with inheritance and property issues. There is no need to amend the Constitution to enact registered partnerships, which could also serve for all other sorts of domestic arrangements, which are not necessarily based on a sexual relationship.

4 There is no need to give the rights of the child any expanded constitutional protection. A child already has rights as a human being. More rights for the child could end up reducing the rights of parents to bring up their own children and lead to more undesirable intervention which would not be in the best interests of the child. We need to keep the right balance of rights. Special focus on any category in the Constitution would inevitably lead to the diminishing of the rights of others in the event of any conflict of rights.

5 No change in the Constitution is necessary to align with the UN Convention on the Rights of the Child.

POWER PARTNERSHIP PROGRAMME

POWER stands for Politically Organised Women Educating for Representation, and delivers a women's political education programme to politically active women from the twenty-six counties. Participants are drawn from various backgrounds, and include community activists, trade unionists and political activists, including some local politicians.

After a facilitated session, in response to your recent advertisement, the participants of one of the programmes devised the following list of suggestions in relation to the articles in the Constitution which relate to the family:

HOW SHOULD THE FAMILY BE DEFINED?

'A primary and fundamental social unit, not restricted to legal marriage, where the members take responsibility for the care and nurturing of each other.' It was also suggested that both the UN definition of the family and the definition of the family in the South African constitution should be referred to in coming up with a definition.

HOW SHOULD ONE STRIKE THE BALANCE BETWEEN THE RIGHTS OF THE FAMILY AS A UNIT AND THE RIGHTS OF INDIVIDUAL MEMBERS?

The rights of the family shall not supersede the rights of the individual family members.

SHOULD GAY COUPLES BE ALLOWED TO MARRY?

All individuals over the age of eighteen, regardless of gender and sexual orientation, should be allowed to legally marry.

THE RIGHTS OF THE NATURAL MOTHER AND FATHER

Both parents should equally share both the rights and responsibilities of parenthood. These rights and responsibilities include financial, emotional and caring.

THE RIGHTS OF THE CHILD

All children should be entitled to live in a secure, safe environment, free from all forms of violence (physical, sexual, verbal, emotional and psychological).

PRESBYTERIAN CHURCH OF IRELAND

The Presbyterian Church in Ireland supports and endorses Article 41 (1) of the Constitution on the status of the family. We believe that the health of any nation and state is based on the health of its family life.

We believe the Constitution is right to describe the family as 'a moral institution possessing inalienable and imprescriptible rights, antecedent and superior to all positive law'. Its weakness is in failing to define what is meant by 'family'.

While recognising that there is an increasing variety of living arrangements among the citizens of Ireland, we do not believe that the way for legislation to deal with this matter is by redefining the nature of the family in a way that is different from mainline Christian teaching as presented in Scripture.

We recognise the rights of those in our society who choose to live in a way which does not follow the Christian teaching we espouse. There may be, therefore, issues surrounding tax, inheritance, welfare benefits etc that could be re-examined by the government in relation to those who live in such relationships. However, especially at a time of increasing social disintegration, no legislation, still less a constitutional amendment should be allowed to undermine the traditional family unit.

We affirm that marriage between a man and a woman is the best context for human relationship and the nurture of children, as has been until now recognised as the universal teaching of the Christian Church based upon Scripture. All other forms of relationships, both heterosexual and homosexual are less than this, and should not be afforded the status and privilege of marriage.

PRO LIFE CAMPAIGN – NORTH TIPPERARY BRANCH

The North Tipperary branch of the Pro Life Campaign wish to make the following submissions and record our objection to any change(s) which would in any way diminish the special position of the family as enshrined in Article 41 of Bunreacht na hÉireann.

SUBMISSIONS

('The family' as referred to in this submission is at all times to be understood to be the family based on the marriage of one man and one woman.)

1   'The family is the fundamental social unit. Article 41.1.1° of Bunreacht na hÉireann recognises the special position of the family ' … as a moral institution possessing inalienable and imprescriptible rights, antecedent and superior to all positive law.'

   The family based on the marriage of a man and a woman is undoubtedly the type of family referred to in the Constitution and is unquestionably the best foundation for society, and our Constitution should *continue* to reflect that, and our laws to uphold it.

   The family does not need to be 're-defined'.

2   The issue of personal rights is dealt with in Article 40.3.1° of the Constitution. There is no need for change.

   If the personal rights of individual members of a family are being denied, it is open to them to seek counselling and/or have recourse to the courts.

3   The family based on marriage is guaranteed protection under the Constitution which currently recognises that the family based on marriage offers the best foundation for a stable society – Article 41.1.2° – 'The state, therefore, guarantees to protect the family in its constitution and authority, as the necessary basis of social order and as indispensable to the welfare of the nation and the state.'

   Affording the same status to other unions must not be tolerated and would be a most damaging and retrograde step. Whether or not it may be possible to give constitutional protection to various types of family units is not the point. Even if it were possible to afford 'protection' across the board, this would most certainly lower the unique status of traditional marriage and family. At a time when traditional marriage and family is suffering more than at any time in the past, and as a result society as a whole is suffering, the state, rather than countenance any demotion of the status of the traditional family, should defend the traditional family's position, should promote it and encourage it.

   We would like to point out that heterosexual cohabiting couples are free to marry if they wish.

4   Gay couples should not be given the right to marry or to adopt children. Theirs is an unnatural union which does not provide security for the raising of children and must be regarded as totally unacceptable, and an attack upon the family. The rights of a child to be raised by a father and a mother is infinitely superior to any so-called right of gay couples to adopt.

   The reason the state has an interest in marriage and family matters is because of the children produced. Homosexual unions *will never of themselves* produce children and cannot be regarded as marriages at all. The state needs children for the nation to survive, continue and prosper, therefore – Article 41.3.1° – 'The state pledges itself to guard with special care the institution of marriage, on which the family is founded, and to protect it against attack.'

5   The Constitution's reference to woman's life within the home is not a dated one and Article 41.2 should *not* be changed. As has been borne out in several surveys down through the years, the first choice of the majority of women is to stay at home to raise their children. And while Article 41.2 states that the state 'shall therefore, endeavour to ensure that mothers shall not be obliged by economic necessity to engage in labour to the neglect of their duties in the home', the Oireachtas has paid lip service to this in recent years, e.g. state policies cut down financial support for children, driving women out to work, most notably through changes in tax bands and allowances and the 'individualised' tax system introduced by the current government. Urgent changes need to be made to redress this situation and restore the support to women in the home, which is rightfully theirs.

6   The rights of a natural father would be difficult to define, as natural fathers range from casual one-

night stands to more committed relationships. It is hard to generalise in this area. The courts should judge each case on its own merits.

7 The child already has constitutional protection; therefore, our Constitution should not be amended.

8 The Constitution most certainly should not be amended to reflect the UN Convention's interpretation of a child's rights. Similar to most UN conventions its wording is quite bland, which leaves the door open for monitoring committees to perversely interpret it outside of the parameters that member states originally signed.

The family, as referred to in the Constitution, can only be understood to be that unit which is based on the marriage of a man and a woman. This is our belief, and is based on what we know would have been commonly understood to be, and regarded to be the family at the time the Constitution was drafted; it is also based on tradition and Christian teaching before God, before whom this Constitution was drafted –

> In the name of the Most Holy Trinity, from Whom is all authority and to Whom, as our final end, all actions both of men and States must be referred, We, the people of Éire, Humbly acknowledging all our obligations to our Divine Lord, Jesus Christ, Who sustained our fathers through centuries of trial … do hereby adopt, enact, and give to ourselves this Constitution.

Therefore, we ask God to guide this committee in its deliberations on these most important issues.

Under the Constitution, the people are entitled to a referendum on any changes in the Constitution. In view of this, the people expect a full discussion on any proposals to the government and Dáil Éireann.

PRO LIFE: CORK NORTH-WEST

The state pledges to guard with special care the institution of marriage on which the family is founded. Any alterations to the constitutional status of marriage would reduce the value of the family and its commitment to society. Individual rights are guaranteed in law, therefore it is unnecessary and inadvisable to give constitutional rights to families other than those based on marriage. The institution of marriage requires the extra commitment and permanence so necessary for family life, and therefore deserving of its constitutional status. We must also remember that cohabiting couples are free to marry if they so wish.

When the question of gay couples arise, why can't they make their own legal arrangements distinct from marriage? After all, heterosexual couples often make

their own arrangements. As regards the adoption of children by homosexual couples, they may be well cared for, but more than physical care is necessary for the rearing of children. A homosexual environment is incomplete. There are many studies which prove that the best environment for a child to grow up in is a stable relationship, with the loving care of a father and a mother.

The mother who stays at home to rear a family should not suffer an insult from the state by removing her constitutional recognition for her well-earned contribution to the common good.

The rights of the child are well guarded. The child as a human being has rights independent of the family. I would certainly disagree with any input from the United Nations conventions regarding rights for children. If the Irish state carried out the wishes of the Irish people as endorsed by them, in the Irish Constitution, there would be no need for any input by the United Nations.

REFORMED PRESBYTERIAN CHURCH OF IRELAND: WESTERN PRESBYTERY

Much of the current Constitution regarding the family is in line with what the scriptures teach. Therefore, we urge the Committee to retain much of the current content of the Constitution and to strengthen it where necessary.

For the sake of brevity we confine ourselves to some of the points highlighted in your advertisement:

1 HOW SHOULD THE FAMILY BE DEFINED?

A family in normal circumstances is comprised of a man and woman, who have entered into the legally binding agreement of marriage, and whatever offspring result from that union. This is the basic unit of society and has been designed by God for the greatest benefit to mankind and society.

Children need the influence of both male and female parents, and the stability that a marriage can bring, in order to give them a balanced upbringing.

Of course there will be situations where a parent dies, or leaves, but those are single-parent families by default rather than by design, and deserve the support of government.

There is a wealth of evidence to demonstrate the benefits to society of marriage. I strongly urge you to read 'Adoption Briefing 2' and especially the section 'Benefits of marriage for children' (Although the paper deals with adoption, it gives important figures on the benefits of marriage to society. Please contact Western Presbytery for copies.)

2 IS IT POSSIBLE TO GIVE CONSTITUTIONAL PROTECTION TO FAMILIES OTHER THAN THOSE BASED ON MARRIAGE?

God has instituted the family as described above for the good of the wife and the protection of the children, and also for the benefit of society, and the governing of society.

God's guidelines on marriage and family are to make it easier for governments to rule. When people disregard God's guidelines on marriage they place a burden on society, and on government. To provide constitutional protection for these families is to promote this additional burden, and to provide financial incentive to add to the government's burden.

3 SHOULD GAY COUPLES BE ALLOWED TO MARRY?

No. God has directed that families are comprised of male and female for good reason:

For teamwork – God has designed each sex with its own particular strengths; male and female working in complement are stronger than two of the same sex.

For reproduction – One of the purposes God gives to marriage is for the multiplication of the human race. He designed us to have children and for children to be raised within a loving secure environment, where the most vulnerable will find protection and care.

For the balanced upbringing of children – Men have their strengths and women theirs, and so God's word says that the best place for children to be raised is in the context where both are evident – a one man, one woman, family environment. God has designed the family in this way to give children the example of both parents to model their own lives on.

Also, in a survey of over two hundred studies carried out over the last fifteen to twenty years by reputable scientists and research facilities who were either positive or neutral towards homosexuality, it was found that the percentage of homosexual relationships that last beyond five years is so small as to be almost non-existent. Of those that last that long, virtually none is monogamous. The stereotype of the happy gay man and his lifelong loving partner is a myth. As a lifestyle, homosexuality is extraordinarily destructive and dysfunctional.

The homosexual lobby is vocal and manipulative of the facts. The government should not condone a lifestyle that defies God and causes further problems for its citizens.

4 IS THE CONSTITUTION'S REFERENCE TO WOMAN'S 'LIFE WITHIN THE HOME' A DATED ONE THAT SHOULD BE CHANGED?

We recognise that women make a great contribution to society in many roles. We feel that the current constitution is right to give status to the most important of their roles – her life within the home. It is right and necessary that this be protected.

Through childhood, the foundations of a child's life are being laid, and it is important that one parent should be able to be at home, to undertake this noble task. A government wishing to build a strong community will take seriously the role of the mother in the home.

[Two papers were attached to this submission, 'Sidelining Stability and Security' and 'Counterfeit Marriage'. For futher information and/or copies, please contact the Reformed Presbyterian Church of Ireland, Western Presbytery.]

THE RESPONSIBLE SOCIETY

HOW SHOULD THE FAMILY BE DEFINED?

There is no need to redefine it. It is almost universally agreed that the constitutional family is one man and one woman who have formally married and the children of their union. Most research indicates that this is the best arrangement for the rearing of children. The state needs children for the nation to survive and to pay the pensions of the present generation when they retire. In general, this millennia-old family unit is the best environment for rearing children.

HOW SHOULD ONE STRIKE THE BALANCE BETWEEN THE RIGHTS OF THE FAMILY AS A UNIT AND THE RIGHTS OF INDIVIDUAL MEMBERS?

In practice, this balance is struck all the time but generally only where a particular family unit itself is defective. Where there is crime or violence between family members, state agencies intervene.

IS IT POSSIBLE TO GIVE CONSTITUTIONAL PROTECTION TO FAMILIES OTHER THAN THOSE BASED ON MARRIAGE?

Whether it is possible or not, it is certainly inadvisable, as it dilutes the unique status of marriage. If one is talking about cohabiting heterosexual couples, a minority of whom have children, they are quite free to marry if they so desire.

SHOULD GAY COUPLES BE ALLOWED TO MARRY?

No. The reason for the state's interest in promoting marriage and the family is because of the children produced. Homosexual unions will never of themselves produce children and cannot be regarded as marriages at all. Some propose registered civil partnerships instead, and suggest that it is a far different thing from marriage. Certainly, any theoretical distinction there is would be blurred by the media and homosexual campaigners, and would be regarded as a stepping stone to full 'marriage'. The state has no legitimate interest in specifically registering homosexual relationships.

IS THE CONSTITUTION'S REFERENCES TO WOMAN'S LIFE WITHIN THE HOME A DATED ONE THAT SHOULD BE CHANGED?

No. It pays tribute to an ideal honoured in practice by past generations up to about thirty years ago. State policies cut down financial support for children, drove women out to work, affected the birthrate and with the high costs of crèches, made child bearing the privilege of the very rich or the very poor.

SHOULD THE RIGHTS OF THE NATURAL MOTHER HAVE EXPRESS CONSTITUTIONAL PROTECTION?

No. The state should support the ideal family, not every deviation from it. It is also hard to see how that would advantage the natural mother. As it is, she has rights to her child and can avail of all social welfare and taxation rights.

WHAT RIGHTS SHOULD A NATURAL FATHER HAVE AND HOW SHOULD THEY BE PROTECTED?

They would be difficult to define as natural fathers range from casual one-night stands to more committed relationships. It is hard to generalise. They are dependeant on the mother's goodwill. If they had married the mother it would be different.

SHOULD THE RIGHTS OF THE CHILD BE GIVEN AN EXPANDED CONSTITUTIONAL PROTECTION?

No. It has rights as a human being independent of the family already. More emphasis on the child's rights means more intervention by social workers and others, not in the child's interests.

DOES THE CONSTITUTION NEED TO BE CHANGED IN VIEW OF THE UN CONVENTION ON THE RIGHTS OF THE CHILD?

Most certainly not. Like most UN conventions, this one reads quite blandly. But they are often perversely interpreted by monitoring groups. Some groups claim that this convention should facilitate access to contraception and abortion for children.

RIGHT NATION

INTRODUCTION

The Constitution of the United States, as the Committee will no doubt be aware, was written in the late 1780s and broadly speaking was enacted to resolve the deficiencies in the Articles of Confederation, which had governed the relations of the various states since independence. These perceived deficiencies were noted empirically, which is to say, derived from practical experience. From that day to this there have been only twenty-seven amendments to the document, and since the first ten, otherwise known as the Bill of Rights, were authored by the initial framers it can be argued that they did not constitute amendments as such, but were rather a delayed portion of the original. In this light we have then just seventeen amendments, and this must further be reduced as one, prohibition of alcohol, had to be repealed as unworkable, amounting to two inoperative amendments, enacting it and then repealing it. Just fifteen are then currently in force, spanning a period of more than two centuries and almost unrecognisable transformation, in every other area of natural life.

Without arguing the merits or otherwise of the various amendments, one thing stands out immediately, namely the paucity of change in American constitutional law as written. Moreover, prior to the Supreme Court being presided over by Justice Earl Warren, and the advent of 'judicial activism', there was remarkably little change in the Court's interpretation of the Constitution. Previous Justices had applied the law according to the plain language meaning of the words, and in cases where some doubt arose by reference to statements and writings made contemporaneously.

The primary result was a degree of constitutional stability and legal certainty unprecedented in any political system starting from first principles. Few Americans, other than those to be found in the furthest recesses of the far-left, would suspect the Constitution as anything but a nearly unmitigated success, while in observable terms thirteen colonies on an Eastern seaboard, with a population considerably less than Ireland's today, grew, under its protection, to bestride first a continent and later the world. That there were other factors in play there can be no doubt; neither, however, can it be doubted that the Constitution was a decisive one.

The experience of other former colonies of Britain was more often markedly different, and with different results. In many areas of the third world, a significant factor in creating and maintaining economic, and other forms of dysfunction, has been perpetual constitutional revolution. Often the assumption of government by a political party, whether by force or otherwise, has been accompanied by the enactment of an entirely new Constitution. Consequently the Constitution, and by extension the whole of the law, has been brought into disrepute. Both are seen by political factions within these failed states as merely expressions of ideology, rather than the permanent framework for peace and stability. The result has been catastrophic.

In Ireland we have been fortunate enough to enjoy a fair degree of constitutional stability. Despite the origins of the Constitution in troubled times, its success can be best measured in the reluctance of the Oireachtas to propose amendments to it, and the reluctance of the Irish people to endorse a number of the suggested amendments put to them. We have not of course, prospered to super-power status, and are not likely to, but neither have we been plagued by repetitive civil war, revolution, coups etc, and have generally speaking maintained in the bulk of the populace a respect for the rule of law, even in instances where some might wish the law were different. Persons dissatisfied with current laws have, with only one major and a few minor exceptions (confined to the left), made recourse to the constitutionally provided means for enacting change.

Thus together with the United States and other former colonies of Britain, Ireland and its Constitution serve as testimony for the case that constitutional change is seldom a positive in the life of nations. Understood thus, the measure of evidence must be set at a very high bar for its contemplation, and in practical terms this means presenting a case of imperative necessity and nothing less.

Right Nation would wish to see the All-Party Committee make this principle of imperative necessity a guide in all their deliberations, though many of the recommendations found in previous progress reports have shown a deleterious tendency towards innovative experimentation, especially when directed by ideological whim and fancy. That the remit of the Committee lends itself to such musings does not of itself prevent its members individually and collectively from showing foresight beyond currently fashionable trends. In short, we would commend to you the merits of caution.

This is especially true of the current phase of work by the Committee. Unless we are very much mistaken, there is an *a priori* acceptance by all parties seriously engaged in the debates surrounding family issues of the crucial importance of the family in the maintenance of a sound society. It is then, perhaps, the most important phase of the Committee's work. We have therefore formulated a submission on foot of your invitation to do so which we earnestly hope will be given the due attention, and be of some help in your deliberations.

THE FAMILY DEFINED

Of the more irritating, and at the same time utterly unhelpful, aspects of the debate on family issues thus far has been the assertion by certain parties of complete ignorance concerning what a family is, or more puzzling still that whatever it is, it is constantly changing. Others have compounded this nonsense by asserting that they know very well what a family is and proceeding to give it a limitless, and consequently meaningless definition which in practice seems to amount to 'whatever you're having yourself'. In the various shades there seems no logical reason within that philosophy why the term should be limited to human beings and not extended to plants and animals, or indeed a mixture of all three. Of course most of them know very well what a family is; no one with the ability of articulated speech could be so stupid as not to know. The attempt to muddy definitions, therefore, is an ideologically motivated attack on the family, and may be understood best as an attack from the rear.

This was not always the case. In the early part of the last century there were many voices raised to explicitly attack the family as an institution. Indeed attitudes to the family were a fair bench mark of political leaning, with ferocious left-wing propaganda designed to undermine it and predicting its imminent collapse. Karl Marx described it as a 'selfish unit' and 'a patriarchal instrument of oppression' which theoretically, meaning in his warped imagination the same thing as inevitably, would disappear with the advent of the communist man and woman in a post-capitalist utopia. The first laws enacted by the Soviet Union after their revolution (supposedly having taken place to relieve economic distress) were not economic measures at all, but instead were directed against the family; specifically the legalisation of abortion, contraception, homosexual acts and divorce. Softer socialists took a softer line but there was, and still is, a general agreement. In private, and occasionally in public, commentators of the leftist variety are still capable to this day of being drawn on this question into pronounced anti-family rhetoric. It goes without saying that they have failed as such, though not without enacting several theories delivering a good deal of damage.

In more recent times the strategy developed, acknowledging that if the institution itself, deriving its durability from immutable natural tendencies in human behaviour, could not be directly attacked or destroyed, then it could perhaps be re-defined. And if such a re-definition could succeed in leaving the term largely meaningless then a partial success could be achieved. The object remains the same: to undermine traditional values and engage in social experimentation for its own sake. The characteristic left/liberal experiment being engaged in is purely and purposefully destructive, which is to say the final construct envisaged as a 'family' is in constant flux and in the end is not really important. What is important is change. Change for the better, for worse, or in between does not feature in the thinking process, constant change is its own fulfilling end. And it hardly requires saying that no thought at all is given to the potential damage inflicted on individuals affected, or on the common good.

Therefore the Committee needs to consider the definition of the family as the most crucial question, and we would submit that such a definition is unchanging and in real terms unchangeable, either by convoluted semantics of by positive law.

The Irish Constitution has established, and there is a significant corpus of precedent law verifying this, that the family is one man married to one woman and their children. In the course of debates surrounding family issues this form has come to be represented as the 'traditional family' though strictly speaking this is not an accurate term. To take an absurd yet revelatory example: If one has an apple which looks like what apples have always looked like, and tastes like what apples have always tasted like, we would not therefore call it a traditional apple. It would remain just an apple. Anyone maintaining that an orange could be an apple too, and more importantly that this was a modern way of thinking, would receive a cool reception intellectually. Though of course if the 'oranges are apples too' people organised politically, with the support of the major media outlets, and a number of parliamentary parties, they might well succeed in obscuring knowledge of the fact.

In short, the family is what it has always been and, until relatively recently, universally understood to be. The salient fact here is that this obvious truth is current in Irish law, as well as common sense.

Further, the definition of marriage is quite clear and every honest person knows it to be. Marriage is the solemn lifelong commitment of one man and one woman to each other, forsaking all others. It involves sexual exclusivity as well as being both the means, and for the purpose, of procreation and subsequent care of children. The bond is consequently indissoluble, though unfortunately with the advent of the divorce referendum of 1995 and subsequent legislation, Irish law has parted company with common sense on this point and reduced its definition of marriage to a temporary arrangement.

We will use the term family here with acknowledgement that there has been some success in confusing matters by malevolent individuals and groups, but it is important that we are understood exactly when defending both the rights and in some cases the justifiable privileges granted in law to the family. As a question for the Committee charged with looking at possible changes to the Constitution, it is quite clear to us that the current definition embodied in the Constitution for the family is the correct one, indeed immutably the only one which is sensible. In the consequence there is no case of imperative necessity for change, nor has one been made. On the contrary, suggestions which have been made, the most commonly quoted being contained in the United Nations definition, are unsoundly based and would set the law at odds with common sense and render the term meaningless.

The current legal definition of marriage, however, is a matter we will return to again.

THE FAMILY DEFENDED

In the first instance, something needs to be stated which properly speaking ought not to be necessary: the family works. As an institution it performs the tasks set before it infinitely better than any alternative which has been suggested by anyone at any time. Reason and experience are the bedrock proofs of both its durability and its remarkable efficacy. This requires to be explicitly stated since, as is perhaps natural but unfortunate, we tend to think of the family when problems arise, and the issues raised in the media are generally those of family failure or dysfunction. Most families, however, are neither failing nor dysfunctional, but rather are the healthy and happy context in which children are born and develop, both physically and mentally toward a maturity which allows them as adults to found their own family, equally healthy and happy.

That the family is a natural institution derived from the most basic of human emotions, desires and societal functioning is evidenced by the fact that it is found everywhere, in every culture around the world, in every part of the world, and throughout history as far back as memory and records exist. (Saving only the exception of polygamy, not properly even a full exception, since cultures which endorsed or endorse polygamy have also provided that precedence is given to the first wife over the others.) In fact it is the only institution still with us which predates the existence of government and as such, government should tread carefully in dealing with it seeing that it is held in greater affection by the people of this and every other state, than the government itself.

If the family occasionally, even often, fails, it is to be remembered that even in societies where this is commonplace, such failure still remains the minority case. And that failure is part of, and directly contributes to, general societal dysfunction. It is the duty of the state, even as a self interest only, to ensure that such failed families as do occur have not had their failure caused by or encouraged by some element of state-sponsored action. *Whither goes the family, thereto goes the nation.*

In that regard, successive Irish governments have pursued an aggressive anti-family agenda involving, *inter alia*, reductions in tax allowance support, specific targeting of single income families through tax individualisation, funding of explicitly anti-family campaigning groups, and negative rhetorical statements. Yet it remains a fact that the two-parent family is the ideal sought by most people and of most benefit in the sound raising and education of children, the next generation. Governments of the future will have to deal with the problems caused by the breakdown of that ideal, while the present government is already dealing with the consequences of its partial breakdown.

Put in direct terms, it is no judgement of individual circumstances and/or behaviour to state that it is not beneficial to Irish society to have more than one-third of births taking place outside the marital family context. While the efforts of single parents, whether male or more usually female, to raise their children soundly, can often be positively heroic, it remains the case that they are at a distinct disadvantage, and that this disadvantage is not wholly or even primarily economic. Nor is this strictly a moral commentary insofar as widowed parents who have never been married, or are divorced/separated. This is not of course a problem which government alone can solve, but an issue for wider societal institutions, such as churches and others.

In fact this is an area where we are inclined to believe that the most positive contribution that can be hoped for, from government, is a negative action. Which is to say *Right Nation* would advocate masterful inactivity on the part of government agencies, since gripped as they are by left/liberal impulses their activity is usually a cause, not a solution, and they have routinely sought to make matters worse.

For example, the endorsement and propagandising by government-funded agencies, of the 'contraceptive culture' has proved most unhelpful. That the state has taken this route is all the more surprising since it has been tried before throughout the world, and in each and every case has proved a failure. The promotion of the use of contraception as 'safe sex' and a means of avoiding, or at least reducing, the instance of unwanted pregnancy has been shown to produce the contrary, a vast increase in the instance of sexually transmitted diseases and births to unmarried mothers. The Crisis Pregnancy Agency is a case in point, achieving only an increase in funding to match the increase in crisis pregnancies. At the risk of appearing old fashioned, it is an unquestionable scientific fact that the only means for a person to practise safe sex is abstinence before marriage and fidelity within marriage. Society, and the state as the legal protector of society, has a vested interest in restoring this as the norm, yet all governmental efforts seem set to the contrary.

The Committee should have the courage to say this and further recommend to government a redress of anti-family financial measures, as well as an end to funding of anti-family organisations, specifically any organisation not upholding the family as the ideal.

Further, while we are reluctant to raise it, since the political parties to which the Committee members belong are hostile, it nonetheless must both be stated and in the long run contemplated by any serious pro-family government: there is the question of prohibiting divorce. The constitutional endorsement of the indissolubility of marriage was the bedrock of sound law in relation to the definition and support of the family, and it is inconceivable that the consequences of divorce will not be visited on Ireland, as with every other country where it is provided for. Indeed the most recent figures for divorce applications show that the predictions, as they related to numbers, made by anti-divorce campaigners in the 1995 referendum have proved accurate, and with them the other consequences must surely follow.

Unfortunately it is difficult to ascertain the extent and nature of such consequences, because at present the workings of the family law courts are secret, itself a disturbing circumstance. Those who are familiar with individual cases first hand are unanimously of the view that this secrecy is not justified as a protection is provided for victims of crime, even when the issues are most sensitive. The practice in the criminal courts has been to protect the anonymity of minors by referring to the participants by pseudonym. There is no reason why this could not be the case in the family law courts as well.

Right Nation is of the view that the only constitutional change or amendment that the Committee should recommend with regard to the family, as a legal entity, is the restoration of indissoluble marriage by the prohibition of divorce. The practical difficulties of having such an amendment approved by the electorate at this time are noted, but in the context of an overarching review of the Constitution, as it pertains to the family, there seems no way around dealing with this issue, whether sooner, or as is more likely, later.

THE ECONOMICS OF THE FAMILY

Right Nation believes that is would be a mistake for the Committee to limit its review of the welfare of the Irish family in the twenty-first century to its moral and sociological aspects alone, as important as they are. The argument for radical action from government in support of the family can also be made in terms of plain economics. The family has indeed become an economic issue, and the biggest one of all, surpassing all others.

All across the western world, fertility rates are declining rapidly and the consequences are being felt in a rapidly ageing population. In the early stages of the process, this produces something of an economic boost because countries with a declining birth rate have a declining dependency ratio. The numbers of returned people are low relative to the working population and that working population has no children, or fewer children, to clothe and feed. Hence they have more disposable income.

However, as the process develops, the lack of growing children becoming young adults and joining the workforce means that over time the workforce is shrinking. At the other end of the age range, yesterday's workforce is leaving to a well-earned retirement. With fewer taxpayers and a growing number of retirees dependent on tax-funded benefits, the problem is obvious. And to cap it all, the retirees are living longer.

For example in Italy where the fertility rate is a shocking 1.2 per woman with replacement requiring 2.1, the population will decline from today's 57 million to 41 million by 2050. The real issue though is that while only 2% of that population will be under five years of age, a full 40% will be 65 or older. One third of all pregnancies end in abortion. In short Italy is dying.

Governments throughout the European Union have woken up in cold sweat. What are they going to do? In the short term, proposals have been brought forward to extend the working life to 75 but that is not a solution. The talk is of cutting state pensions and benefits to the old, restricting health care and forcing the old to prepare their own retirement with less and less state help. And at the same time, raising taxes on those who are working. Euthanasia, voluntary and otherwise, looms in the long-term background. The more advanced and more sensible proposals are for encouraging young families to have more children by increasing child benefits and increasing the availability of services available to mothers.

Ireland today has the lowest dependency ratio of all the EU states, which is to say that relative to the numbers of very young and very old, the working and taxpaying population is quite high. This situation cannot however be maintained. The fertility rate is 1.6, much higher than Italy but much lower than population replacement would require. While the problem is being masked by returning emigrants, and of course immigration, the currently rising population in Ireland will not last.

While we are not suggesting that the state has the right to interfere in how many children an individual family has, they do have a responsibility to society as a whole to ensure that public policy is not in fact causing and contributing to a falling birth rate. This is in fact what is happening. In the mid 1980s the government of the day abolished all tax allowances and benefits available to Irish families which related to the number of child dependants. The talk then was of how it was fairer to pay child benefit based on the number of children since some people were not tax payers, or benefited less from tax incentives. But the money saved was not transferred over to child benefit at all. The total amount of money the government spends on supporting children and their families has steadily declined.

In more recent times the government has introduced tax individualisation in spite of the constitutional requirement that no woman should be forced 'by economic necessity' to work outside the home. This inane attack on mothers working in the home was a direct result of the Lisbon accord signed by the EU heads of government which committed the member states to achieving 70% female participation in the workforce by 2010.

Right Nation are not suggesting that women should be forced to work in the home either, simply that the choice should be available and no financial impediment should be placed in the way of that free choice. Reason, experience, and opinion poll data, suggest that many more women would choose the 'family first' option if they didn't feel that working outside the home was an absolute necessity to make ends meet financially. And families where women work in the home are generally larger.

It will, no doubt, be submitted to the Committee, by some individuals and groups, that this constitutional provision is outdated. This is a common mantra on the liberal/left, who further claim audaciously that it is 'insulting' to women.

Firstly, this common usage of terms such as 'outdated' as opposed to 'modern' falls into a juvenile category of political philosophy. If a thing cannot be argued for on its merits the left/liberal says that it is modern, and what stands at present is out-dated, QED. This is the argument that innovation is its own reward again, and impresses only the weakest of intellects. There is here the refusal to accept the existence of any objective truths that characterises subjective stupidity. Rather, either a thing is true, in which case its merits will be demonstrable, in the here and now, as well as past experience, or it is false and its origins in recent thinking will not preserve it from error.

In presenting the case for changing the Constitution to remove the recognition given to women working in the home, no one has even attempted to present a case of imperative necessity, nor even any single benefit that would accrue to society from doing so. That women who do work in the home perform an enormous and unpaid service to society is obvious, that the emotional well-being of children is vastly improved by them is a given. Why should it not be recognised? Surely in fact, that recognition should involve a more practical acknowledgement, in the form of financial support? And that is what is clearly indicated by the provision that they not be forced out of the home by 'economic necessity'. Thus society would benefit and women would benefit. In fact the only group in society which could possibly uphold a grievance are men, and until such time as they are willing, in any appreciable numbers, to take on the role of homemaker, their case is weak.

In reality of course, each and every government since the foundation of the state has reneged on its responsibilities outlined in Article 41 of the Constitution. In the early years the measures enacted were designed to force women into the home with punitive measures rather than the incentives which were clearly indicated, and in the later years they have sought to force women out of the home by 'economic necessity'.

It is an example of how public policy in this country is dictated by middle-class political mores, without regard to how the majority of ordinary people actually live, that the debate on this Article has largely concerned the issue of women with 'careers'. In fact very few women or men have 'careers', rather they have jobs, and the primary motivation in getting and keeping a job is financial necessity, not some notion of personal fulfilment. For ordinary people, which is to say the real working people of Ireland, personal fulfilment is derived from many sources, very rarely their job, and usually in one sense or another, their family.

The simplest and most objective means of ascertaining whether someone has a job or a career is not based on his/her income level, or type of work, but on what we might call the 'lottery test'. If the person won the national lottery, what are the chances that he/she would continue to turn up dutifully for work? Those who would have careers, those who wouldn't have jobs.

Since all objective evidence indicates that for most women, as with most men, their families are their first priority, there can be little doubt that giving meaningful effect to Article 41 would produce a choice by a majority of women in favour of full-time care of their children. And since society would undoubtedly benefit thereby, the test of imperative necessity, in the view of Right Nation, is met by retaining this provision and legislating to give it meaningful effect.

Right Nation would caution the Committee at this point to also have some regard to the practicalities of change in this provision. Meaningless radical feminist rhetoric aside, does anyone seriously contemplate that the majority of women voters could be induced to vote for 'forced' labour? Under current conditions the Constitution envisages choice, financially supported by the state; the alternative is being forced by economic necessity, often the reality for Irish women, to a workplace into which they do not wish to go. Naturally all socialists will support the latter as George Bernard Shaw wrote, 'Forced labour, with death as the final penalty, is the keystone of socialism', but we are as near certain as it is possible to be that an amendment to give effect to that would not be passed.

On the issue of universal state-funded childcare facilities, we need only one sentence to sum it up – the Irish taxpayer (and voter) will not tolerate the level of taxation required to fund such a system.

A STRAIGHT LOOK AT HOMOSEXUAL 'MARRIAGE'

It is inaccurate to claim, as the homosexual lobby does, that homosexuals are being denied a civil right which is granted to heterosexuals. In reality they have an equal right to marriage, under precisely the same qualification; they must find a person of the opposite sex willing, and competent, to marry them.

The case, however, has been made and doubtless will be presented to the Committee, that homosexual arrangements should be acknowledged as marriages and accorded the full legal rights and privileges previously granted only to the family. Some obfuscation has been attempted by linking this proposal with other relationships such as siblings or mere cohabitees, yet in all honesty it is homosexuality which is the real issue. Here a number of interlocking questions arise. As a first, the role of the state *vis-à-vis* marriage.

The question of whether the state should allow homosexuals to marry is a logically absurd one since it isn't the state which created heterosexual marriage in the first instance, but it is, as earlier pointed out, a natural institution. Correctly put, the state provides by its laws an acknowledgement and a registration of marriage but does not create it. The state, consequently, can no more create a homosexual marriage than it can make the earlier cited orange be an apple.

What is within the power of the state is to engage in the farcical pretence that a given homosexual arrangement is a marriage, and to proceed to the enactment of laws and registration to give effect to the pretence. It is also within its remit to grant certain practical benefits in terms of taxation and inheritance rights etc. as if the homosexual couple were married. That this may be done without the farce, in the form of civil unions, has also been suggested.

Here it must be asked why such practical benefits are granted to married heterosexual couples in the first place. If we were to take religion as our starting point then the question regarding homosexuals has already been answered with a resounding no. But since the Committee is likely to approach the matter from a secular, or even secular humanist perspective, then the case may be made in such terms.

Whenever government grants special tax relief or allowances to particular individuals or groups, it necessarily forgoes revenue, which must be made up elsewhere, either by increasing the tax burden proportionately on everyone else or reducing spending. When there is a direct payment to individuals or groups this must come out of total tax take, in other words be taken from everyone else. The everyone else, in this instance the taxpayer, has a right to ask why. Under what justification does government give to one what it fails to give to all, what goal of the common good is served? Or to put it crudely, the taxpayer may well ask 'What's in it for me?'

In the case of heterosexual marriage, the answer is simple and straightforward: the common good is served by the reproduction of the next generation. Therefore an unalloyed good, even an absolute necessity is promoted and encouraged by special privileges being granted to heterosexual couples making a life-long commitment. Further, through child benefit, we are making an investment more than an open-ended payment.

It has been stated against this that not all heterosexual couples are fertile and even those that are capable of having children may not always intend to do so, yet they receive the benefits accruing to marriage. Here we enter on the issue which should surely be of great importance to the practising homosexual, namely the properly set limits of public policy *vis-à-vis* private morality. It would be a gross intrusion by the state into the privacy of any couple to inquire as to their intention or ability to conceive children. We should then restrict the state in terms of public policy to making general assumptions, the most obvious being that most heterosexual couples are capable of conception and will conceive, whereas it is a certain fact, without any inquiry into personal privacy, that no two men and no two women can conceive a child. The state is entitled to proceed on such a clear assumption.

The contention of the homosexual lobby, which would amount to an even greater violation of privacy, is no less than that the state should subsidise with taxpayers' money the private sexual practices of couples.

Currently the state has no interest in such practices, only noting and rewarding a likely, though uninquired, outcome in the case of heterosexuals. If, however, the homosexual lobby is correct, and the state is drawn thereby into a subsidy of their sex lives, doesn't it follow that the state, through some agency, should have a direct input in some way? Shouldn't in fact the taxpayer, who is subsidising the arrangement, get to say when, where, how and with whom the paid-for-sex takes place? There are more logical deductions we could make from this premise so absurd, but it is likely that the advocates have not given any serious thought to them.

While the Committee is likely to 'deliberate' on the merits of granting homosexuals the rights of marriage and the media is likely to devote a great deal of print space, especially to supporters, Right Nation will take this juncture to submit to yourselves a sobering and salient fact. While this dubious sign of 'progress' from a left/liberal perspective may well be welcome to the chattering classes and media pundits, who decry at length the defenders of marriage and the family with the usual sort of epithets, a legal re-definition of marriage would require a constitutional amendment. It follows that such a legal re-definition is no more possible, and consequently not an option really open for the Committee's recommendation, than an actual re-definition itself. The latter is negated by the natural law, the former impossible to get past the electorate, who have no doubt whatever as to their beliefs concerning the nature of marriage. It may suit a public posturing by some members of the Committee to deny that the electorate would prove recalcitrant on such an amendment, yet it would seem best to privately admit the fact and move on.

Alternatively, an attempt at such an amendment might prove useful in provoking a real debate about the importance of the family as it is traditionally understood. The result would undoubtedly do irreparable damage to liberal morale, still making a shaky recovery from the result of the citizenship referendum, where at least they could console themselves with the notion that the endorsement of the government parties was crucial. It would certainly serve to galvanise the conservative movement which heretofore has proved more latent than active, with the single exception of the abortion issue. In that sense, such a referendum would not be entirely unwelcome to ourselves, though we doubt that the aforementioned taxpayer would share that view.

The Committee will be aware of developments in the United States where the introduction of homosexual 'marriage' had been attempted in several states by judicial fiat. The result, entirely predictable, but obviously not predicted, was the categorical rejection of the idea in eleven states where the issue was put to a referendum, including some of the most liberal and solidly democratic states of the union. Homosexual lobbyists may yet have cause to regret a hubris that was essential for the creation of a large and vocal grassroots movement, which is undeniably hostile to many of their other so-called 'rights', and is now flush from victory. While the majority is inclined to accept the 'It's none of your business' argument that the homosexual movement had previously used, they fail to find the 'life-style choice' as anything other than unattractive, when forced to examine it up close by blatant activism. There is no sound reason to suppose that Ireland would be any different.

As an adjunct point, it is our legal understanding that the provision of the law that only married persons may be allowed to foster or adopt children has constitutional standing. Consequently any discussion of allowing homosexual couples to do so is without purpose. In any case it is our view that children are entitled by right to both a mother and a father, and it is always to be regretted where this is not possible. It is therefore a situation never to be deliberately engineered that a child should be so deprived.

The Committee will be aware of course that the proposed European Constitution provides for a right to marry (Charter of Fundamental Rights), not qualified by a legal definition of marriage in European law and further provides for the supremacy of European law over that of the member states. It is likely that such a right to marry will be interpreted to include homosexual arrangements and consequently bring Irish law as it stands in conflict with the European Union. The Committee in the context of supporting the European Constitution, yet conscious of the impossibility of changing Irish law to conform, is faced with the prospect of a high-profile instance of European Union interference with a fundamental moral precept of the Irish people. This is a conundrum in which you can hardly be envied, although it may be self-solving if the European constitution is not ratified. That is certainly Right Nation's wish and we will strain ourselves to achieving same.

ABORTION – THE PERENNIAL UNRESOLVED

Although this is an area which the Committee unsuccessfully addressed in the Fifth Progress Report it is unquestionably of crucial significance, and the most important way in which Irish law, as it stands, requires pro-family correction. While the Constitution, albeit by judicial fiat rather than appropriate interpretation, holds that the right to life of the unborn child is not absolute and further provides for state-funded killing, albeit in a foreign jurisdiction, there is little point in addressing the rights of the child. Without the right to be alive, all other rights are inaccessible. That much is obvious.

The Committee, we believe, made the great error on the last occasion of assuming that the abortion issue was one similar to other political issues and consequently addressed it as such. The most significant assumption being that there exists on the issue 'a middle ground' of compromise between the view that the unborn child is a human being and the view that he is not. Consequently when the Committee failed to reach a consensus on the matter, the recommendation of the members of the governing party, Fianna Fáil, that an amendment should be proposed to alter some aspects of the X decision, was the one undertaken.

Had the Committee followed the advice of the overwhelming number of submissions made to it at the time, which were in line with all the opinion poll data available, you would have commended to government the complete prohibition of abortion, in which instance a subsequent referendum would have to be passed comfortably. Unfortunately this was not to be, and a thoroughly flawed alternative course failed to receive the assent of the electorate.

That the margin was slim is to miss the point. Certain pro-life organisations sought, and to some extent succeeded, in convincing a large section of the public that the proposal had effects which it did not have, and did not have other effects which it so patently did. However, the attempt to defend the proposal on its moderation and as a middle way had to be abandoned early in the campaign. There is simply no way of winning a referendum on abortion where the proposal alienates both conservative and liberal opinion. Nor does the liberal view command enough votes by itself. The initial error was compounded by an exaggeration of the size and influence of the same pro-life organisations mentioned (who were malleable), and this was a case of wishful thinking.

We are aware of the government's legal opinion on the practical difficulties of legislating for the X decision as it stands, yet this can hardly be satisfactory from anyone's point of view. We shall not belabour the issue here, but would rather refer the Committee to the Youth Defence submissions to the Inter-Departmental Working Group on Abortion, and to yourselves previously. It may further prove useful to read the analysis of the defeated referendum proposal by the Mother and Child Campaign, a copy of which may be provided to you, if it is not already in your possession.

We are aware, of course, that there is no political appetite for another abortion referendum, and at this moment probably not much more among the general public. For the most part, they are satisfied with the real time fact that no legal abortions are taking place in the Republic, and are generally unaware of the use of taxpayers' money for abortions abroad. Notwithstanding, the current legal stasis on abortion is of great concern to many people, who are rightly concerned that in the absence of a specific and unambiguous over-turning of the Supreme Court's decision in the X Case, a future capricious court ruling may move the situation forward in a deleterious way.

The timing and exact wording of a truly pro-life amendment, which protects the life of both mothers and their children, remains obviously within the remit of the government, but that one must be forthcoming from a government which is serious about its pro-family credentials there can be no room for doubt.

CONCLUSION

There is a left/liberal consensus that any institution which has existed for more than twenty minutes is likely to have attempted or succeeded in oppressing and/or exploiting someone. Consequently since the family has been in existence since forever, they are in no doubt that it has had enough time to succeed in oppressing and exploiting everyone. It is, in their view, ripe for dissolution and damn the consequences.

The Committee, on the other hand, has a responsibility to society to protect that which preserves the common good and the best interests of the individual, in proportionate balance. While there is a natural limitation of remit insofar as consideration is really within the realm of what can be done by law and government action, this responsibility is nonetheless grave. Right Nation has attempted in these pages to give voice to what we believe are the views of a great number of Irish people, in some instances the overwhelming majority. On occasion we have been as blunt as we felt was necessary. In no sense do we claim that what we have presented is an exhaustive study of the issues at hand; we have prioritised for emphasis and focused on broad principles meeting the criteria of imperative necessity. Nor do we pretend to fully understand all that needs to be done to preserve, protect, and defend the precious institution, bedrock of civilisation, that is the family.

We have both borne in mind and sought to articulate the principle, commonly though apocryphally, attributed to the Hippocratic Oath: first, do no harm. Right Nation commends the principle to the All-Party Oireachtas Committee on the Constitution as it deals with issues concerning the family.

SINN FÉIN

INTRODUCTION

The 1937 Constitution, and in particular the articles in relation to the family (and the position of women in particular), reflect the dominant religious ethos and political philosophy of 1930s Ireland. These articles were controversial even in the 1930s and were widely opposed by women's groups. They marked a definitive break with the promise of equality for all citizens contained in the 1916 Proclamation.

Sinn Féin's position is that Articles 40, 41 and 42 cannot be usefully considered outside the context of the deficiencies of the whole section of the 1937 Constitution on fundamental rights (Articles 40-44), which is totally inadequate by today's standards – particularly in view of the international instruments and definitions subsequently developed, and also endorsed by the state.

These include but are not limited to:

- the Universal Declaration of Human Rights
- the International Convention on Civil and Political Rights
- the Convention on the Elimination of Discrimination Against Women
- the Convention on the Rights of the Child
- the Convention on the Elimination of All Forms of Racial Discrimination
- the European Convention on Human Rights, and
- the European Charter of Rights and Fundamental Freedoms
- the International Covenant on Economic, Social and Cultural Rights
- the Revised European Social Charter

Taken together, Articles 40-44 also afford significantly fewer protections than other more recently drafted democratic constitutions, such as the Canadian Charter of Rights and Freedoms (1982) and the Constitution of the Republic of South Africa (1993), both of which take greater account of international standards and obligations regarding fundamental rights.

This entire section of the 1937 Constitution needs thorough modernisation. This, however, cannot be adequately undertaken within the confines of a review of Articles 40.3.1, 41 and 42, which is too limited in scope.

Likewise, a review of the fundamental rights section of the 1937 Constitution must not disregard the development of an All-Ireland Charter of Rights, as mandated by Strand 3 of the Good Friday Agreement (Rights, Safeguards and Equality of Opportunity, Human Rights, Point 10).

Indeed, it is arguable that it is also unwise to consider reform of this section separately from the largely superior standards set by the EU Charter of Rights and Fundamental Freedoms which, due to its incorporation into the proposed EU Constitutional Treaty, will become superior to the 1937 Constitution if it is ratified by Ireland and the other member states.

Nor can it be usefully considered separate from Ireland's international obligations. It must be made consistent with these.

Sinn Féin urges the Committee to factor the possibility of a future All-Ireland Charter of Rights into its deliberations. Civil society is already starting to pursue the recognition and delivery of rights on an all-island basis, and – together with Sinn Féin who have embarked on a course of public consultation on this issue – is well advanced on this approach.

PROBLEMS WITH ARTICLES 41, 42 AND 40.3 (AND 40.1)

Article 40 – Personal rights

Article 40 elaborates a narrow set of 'personal rights' reflecting only some of the fundamental rights generally accepted in the 21st century – largely civil and political rights – and even those are incongruously framed by religious sensibilities. A subsequent Article sets out the right to freedom of conscience and religion in greater detail.

Equality rights are almost wholly absent, save for a minimalist protection of the right to equality before the law (Article 40.1).

Socio-economic rights are confined to the right to education and private property enshrined in subsequent articles (42 and 43).

The only group rights set out are those rights accorded to families based on heterosexual marriage in Article 41. Children do not have a subset of specific rights within this group.

In short, the whole of Article 40 and the section on fundamental rights within which it is embedded are problematic and in need of reform in that:

- The right to equality and protection from discrimination are inadequately protected
- Socio-economic rights are virtually absent
- Full secularisation has not taken place, and there remains an unnecessary reference to abortion.

Article 41 – Family rights

Article 41 addresses the family, its rights and protections, along with the role of women, the institution of marriage and the dissolution of marriage.

The problems with Article 41 are as follows.

- The fact that the Constitution contains a definition of the family in Article 41.3.2 is unusual, and serves to unnecessarily limit family rights. It also hampers the realisation of full equality rights.
- The inclusion of a definition of the family in the 1937 Constitution sets it apart from most other constitutions including the 1922 Irish Free State Constitution which contained no definition of the family. Nor is a definition of the family provided in the EU Charter of Rights, the EU Convention on Human Rights in the Universal Declaration of Human Rights. There is no reference to the family in either the main body of the US Constitution or in the Bill of Rights, and there is nothing whatsoever in reference to the family in the Canadian Charter of Rights and Freedoms or in the Canadian Constitution Act, 1982. The only direct reference to the family in the South African Constitution is found in Chapter 3 Article 14 on the right to freedom of conscience, religion, thought, belief and opinion, in which it states that 'nothing in this chapter shall preclude legislation recognising a system of personal and family law adhered to by persons professing a particular religion, and the validity of marriages concluded under a system of religious law subject to specified procedures.' It is therefore questionable as to whether there is any necessity to prescribe in any way what constitutes a family.
- The balance between the rights of the family as a unit and the rights of individual members favours

the family disproportionately, in a manner potentially in conflict with the International Convention on the Rights of the Child, and the consequent implications of this for the rights of children.

We note that

> In the Kilkenny incest case Mrs Justice Catherine McGuinness suggested that 'the very high emphasis on the rights of the family in the Constitution may consciously or unconsciously be interpreted as giving a higher value to the rights of parents than to the rights of children'. The report recommended an amendment to the Constitution which would include a specific and overt declaration of the rights of born [sic] children.[1]

Mrs Justice Catherine McGuinness was charged with heading up an investigation into the Kilkenny incest case, to examine why action was not taken sooner by the health services to halt the serious physical and sexual abuse of a girl by her father over a sixteen year period from 1976 to 1992. Over the years when the abuse occurred, the victim had had a number of hospital admissions for the treatment of serious physical injuries and had been in contact with health professionals, general practitioners, social workers and public health nurses. The report noted that

> The health services are governed by the Constitution, in particular by its provisions dealing with the rights of the family, of parents and of children.[2]

The implication of Justice McGuinness' comments are that the health services' failure to make a timely intervention (i.e. to remove the child from the abusive environment) was influenced by the constitutional provisions in relation to the family which state that it is

> the natural primary and fundamental group of society, and as a moral institution possessing inalienable and imprescriptible rights, antecedent and superior to all positive law.[3]

Because children's rights are not specifically recognised in the Constitution, this creates a situation which favours maintaining the family unit rather than giving precedence to the health and well being of the child. The report further notes that

> The constitutional right of the child seems to render it constitutionally impermissible to regard the welfare of the child as the first and paramount consideration in any dispute as to its upbringing or custody between parents and third parties such as health boards without first bringing into consideration the constitutional rights of the family.[4]

The absence of explicit recognition of the rights, in a separate article, means that the Constitution is in direct conflict with human rights obligations entered into by the state. The outworking of this unacceptable anomaly is that the state is directly implicated in failing to provide the fullest international human

rights protections for Irish children. The Constitution should both reflect and guarantee the fullest protection of children's rights as decreed in international law.

- Constitutional protection for families is only extended to heterosexual families, based on marriage, and this permits discrimination against other family formations. This is inconsistent with rights contained in the EU Charter of Rights and Fundamental Freedoms Article 21.1.[5] In the words of the Constitution Review Group 'The effect of this definition is that neither a non-marital family nor its members are entitled to any of the protection or guarantees of Article 41.'

This has resulted in the courts finding that the rights of the natural father receive no constitutional protection. The courts ruled in the case of *The state (Nicolau) v An Bórd Uchtála [1966]* where an unmarried father sought to prevent the adoption of his child, that the family in the Constitution is the family based on marriage, and that the rights of the natural father accordingly receive no protection. The removal of the restriction of family to family based on marriage would remove this discrimination against unmarried fathers.

Unmarried long-term heterosexual partnerships are also excluded from protections, as are lesbian and gay partnerships.

The refusal to recognise same-sex partnerships, regardless of equivalent permanency, denies lesbians and gays the access to a broad section of rights available to heterosexual married couples. We would like to bring to the Committee's attention that the High Court has cleared the way for a lesbian couple (Katherine Zappone and Ann Louise Gilligan) to bring a legal action to have their Canadian marriage recognised in this state and to have the Revenue Commissioners treat them under the tax acts in the same way as a married couple. Zappone and Gilligan are arguing that the refusal of the Revenue to recognise them as a married couple in Irish law for tax purposes breaches their rights under the Constitution and the European Convention for the Protection of Human Rights and Fundamental Freedoms. In permitting the couple to proceed with such an action, the High Court was satisfied that they had demonstrated an arguable case. The lack of protection for gay and lesbian partnerships has permitted the government to introduce provisions such as that introduced in the Civil Registration Bill 2003, specifically excluding same-sex couples from the benefits of the legislation.[6]

Given the diversity of family formations which exist in the state today, this definition of family is clearly inadequate and discriminatory.

- The references to natural law in the Constitution and specifically in Article 41.1.1 (the Constitution) should be fully secular.

- The references to woman's 'life within the home' and women's 'neglect of their duties in the home' are discriminatory and insulting to women and should be removed. These references promote views with regard to the position of women which are both discriminatory and obsolete. The case for the removal of Article 41.2.1 and 41.2.2 is clear. These articles define women's place as primarily in the domestic sphere and were formulated at a time when the catholic church and the establishment were seeking to prevent women from taking so-called 'breadwinner' jobs. The introduction of discriminatory legislation against women, including the Civil Service Regulation (Amendment) Bill 1925, the Juries Act, 1927, the Conditions of Employment Bill 1935, and the marriage ban against women teachers in national schools (1933), pre-dated the 1937 Constitution and were arguably at odds with the Free State Constitution which, in Article 3, enunciated the principle of equal rights. The provisions in Articles 41.2.1 and 41.2.2 gave cover to those discriminatory laws, however, and enabled the marriage ban to remain in place until the 1970s and this state's accession to the EEC.

We may not be able to accurately quantify the impact of the 1937 Constitution in terms of the inability of Irish women to gain equality in terms of representation in political and civic life but undoubtedly the obstacles erected by the reactionary parties which came to power in the twenty-six counties after partition and endorsed the references to women's place in the home in Article 41, have contributed to the fact that the percentage of elected representatives and those in positions of power, such as the higher levels of the civil service, remain staggeringly low compared to many other states. This state currently ranks 59th out of 120 states in terms of women's parliamentary representation.[7] Only 13% of those currently elected to the Dáil are women. This is below the average in Europe (17%), Asia (16%) and the Americas (16%) and on a par with the average for sub-Saharan Africa (13%).[8] In the twenty-six counties women account for only 9% of managing directors and 7% of high court judges.[9] The feminisation of poverty persists. Nearly one quarter (23%) of women are at risk of poverty. According to the ESRI, one in four women raising children or managing households on their own will experience poverty despite our economic boom. The gender pay gap persists. Nearly one third (33%) of women workers are paid below the minimum wage (compared to 18% of men). Women are also disproportionately represented in the part-time and services sectors.

This is inconsistent with the Convention on the Elimination of Discrimination Against Women (CEDAW) and with the EU Charter of Rights Article 21.1 and Article 23. It is also inconsistent with the EU Convention on Human Rights Article 14 and Article 5 of protocol 7. Explicit protection from discrimination on the basis of gender is a feature of both the Canadian Charter of Rights and Freedoms (Article 15 and 28) and the South African Constitution (Chapter 3 Article 8).

Article 42 – Education and the role of the family

Article 42 deals with education, the family role in education and the right to free primary education.

- This article again reflects the preoccupations of the 1930s regarding education, particularly the role of religion in education. It lacks clarity and is negative and defensive in tone. The role of the state as education provider needs to be central, while also recognising education in the home and in private institutions. The current article does not cover secondary and third-level education and life-long learning.

NEEDED CHANGES IN THE FUNDAMENTAL RIGHTS SECTIONS OF THE CONSTITUTION

- Constitution to represent secular values
- Removal of provisions which discriminate on the basis of gender, marriage or sexual orientation
- Significantly augment the equality provisions
- Inclusion of the rights of the child
- Inclusion of socio-economic rights

SINN FÉIN PROPOSALS

Article 40

Replacement of Article 40.1 with the following:

Everyone in the state shall, as human persons, be held equal before the law.

No person shall be subject to unfair discrimination directly or indirectly.

Without derogating from the generality of this provision, everyone has the right to equality and to protection from discrimination on one or more of the following grounds including race, ethnic origin (including membership of the Traveller community), nationality, colour, gender (including gender identity), sexual orientation, disability, age, social or economic status (including status as a convicted person), marital or family status, residence, language, religion, belief or political or other opinion or membership of a trade union.

The right outlined above does not preclude any law, programme or activity that has as its objective the improvement of conditions of individuals, groups or categories of persons disadvantaged by unfair discrimination in order to enable their full and equal enjoyment of all rights and freedoms.

- In article 40.6.1 delete the references to 'morality' and 'blasphemy' in each instance where they occur.

Article 41

- Delete Article 41 and replace with the following:

  Everyone has the right to respect for their private and family life, their home and their correspondence.

  Everyone of marriageable age has the right to marry and to found a family. All such persons are entitled to equal rights as to marriage, during marriage and at its dissolution.

- Insert an article recognising the work of all carers. *We would only advocate the inclusion of this article where other socio-economic rights were being expressly recognised in the Constitution.*

  The state recognises that those people who work in the home and/or as primary carers have the right to proper recognition of their economic contribution to both individual households and the national economy.

New Article on the rights of the child

The rights of the child to be inserted as a new article:

- The state guarantees to cherish all the children of the nation equally. All children, in addition to the individual rights guaranteed to all persons in this Constitution, are entitled to the special care and assistance essential to childhood. Each child has the right to reach his or her potential as an individual and as a member of the community.

- The state shall ensure, as far as is possible, that every child, for the full and harmonious development of his or her personality, shall grow up in a family environment, in an atmosphere of happiness, love and understanding.

- The state shall ensure the child such protection and care as is necessary for his or her well-being, taking into account the rights and duties of his or her parents, legal guardians, or other individuals responsible for him or her, and, to this end, shall take all appropriate legislative and administrative measures.

- Children have the right to be heard, to be consulted in all matters affecting them and to access information about their person.

- In all actions concerning children undertaken by or on behalf of the state the best interests of the child shall be the primary consideration.

Article 42

- Delete Article 42 and replace with the following:

  1 The state recognises the right to education, and with a view to achieving this right progressively and on the basis of equal opportunity, shall, in particular:

     - Make primary education compulsory and available free to all, ensuring a minimum standard of education for all children whether educated in schools established or recognised by the state, private schools or in the home

     - Encourage the development of different forms of secondary education, including general and vocational education, and make them available and accessible to every child
     - Make higher education accessible to all on the basis of capacity by every appropriate means.

  2 The state shall encourage and promote life-long learning, recognising the right of access for all to human knowledge and skills according to their abilities.

New article(s) on socio-economic rights

Sinn Féin firmly advocates the inclusion of socio-economic rights in the Constitution and has been prominent in campaigning for the right to housing in particular to be inserted into the Constitution. In an equal society, social and economic rights are as important as political and civil rights. Civil and political rights are indivisible from social and economic rights because of the interdependence of both these sets of rights. There are those who would argue that the inclusion of social and economic rights in the Constitution is undemocratic on the basis that social and economic policy are the prerogative of democratically elected and accountable politicians, and that the inclusion of such rights would give the judiciary the power to dictate government spending. This is not the case as can be seen from judicial interpretation of existing constitutional rights, such as the right to education which is currently recognised in article 42 of the 1937 Constitution.

The Constitution of 1937 represents the ideas and priorities of the era from which it dates. Today, social and economic rights are given a recognition by international bodies such as the United Nations and the European Union. We need to reflect in the Constitution this progress in international law since the current Constitution was drafted in 1937. The only obstacle preventing a recognition of socio-economic rights in this state is ideological – the misplaced notion that violations of social and economic rights are somehow less serious than violations of civil or political rights.

It is Sinn Féin's position that the state has a duty to use all means at its disposal to guarantee the social and economic rights of its citizens as elaborated in Article 25 of the Universal Declaration of Human Rights[10] and in Article II of the International Covenant on Economic, Social and Cultural Rights[11] and the Revised European Social Charter.

It is our assertion that socio-economic rights including, but not limited to, the right to housing, healthcare, employment, access to public services and an adequate standard of living, should be included as part of an amended Article 40.

These articles would be similar to the wording in the legislation introduced by Sinn Féin[12] to include the right to housing in the Constitution:

  1 The state recognises the right of all persons to adequate and appropriate housing.

     Where practicable, the enjoyment of this right should

in the first place be ensured by the initiative and effort of each person.

Where persons or their dependants are unable sufficiently to exercise or enjoy the right to adequate and appropriate housing, the state, as guardian of the common good, guarantees, as far as possible, by its laws to defend and vindicate this right, in accordance with the principles of social justice.

Notes

1   Kennedy, Finola. *Cottage to Crèche: Family Change in Ireland*. (Institute of Public Administration, 2001) page 123-124.

2   Kilkenny Incest Investigation. May 1993 Page 25.

3   Article 41.1.1

4   Kilkenny Incest Investigation. Page 31.

5   It is worth noting that Chapter 3 Article 8 of the South African Constitution also explicitly prohibits discrimination on the basis of sexual orientation.

6   Sinn Féin introduced an amendment supporting equal rights of same-sex couples, in opposition to the government amendment specifically excluding them from the legislation. This was opposed by the government parties while Labour and Fine Gael abstained. Amendment No. 5 by Sean Crowe TD to the Civil Registration Bill 2003 was defeated by 63 votes to 10.

7   *Irish Politics – Jobs for the Boys*. Recommendations on increasing the number of women in decision making. National Women's Council of Ireland. November 2002.

8   Ibid.

9   Ibid.

10   'Everyone has the right to a standard of living adequate for the health and well-being of himself and of his family, including food, clothing, housing and medical care and necessary social services, and the right to security in the event of unemployment, sickness, disability, widowhood, old age or other lack of livelihood in circumstances beyond his control.'

11   'The state parties to the present Covenant recognise the right of everyone to an adequate standard of living for himself and his family, including adequate food, clothing and housing, and to the continuous improvement of living conditions. The state parties will take appropriate steps to ensure the realisation of this right, recognising to this effect the essential importance of international co-operation based of free consent.'

12   Twenty-Seventh Amendment of the Constitution (No. 2) Bill 2003.

THE SOCIETY FOR THE PROTECTION OF UNBORN CHILDREN (NORTHERN IRELAND)

INTRODUCTION

The Society for the Protection of Unborn Children (Northern Ireland) is an independent education, research, advocacy and lobby group with active members throughout Northern Ireland. Whilst we campaign as a pro-life organisation rather than a pro-family group, we are concerned about many of the issues raised by the consultation. We also recognise that the legal protection of the family is the best means of defending the rights of the children, in particular their right to life.

Like all 'western' nations, Irish society has seen enormous cultural change in recent decades. Two major aspects of this change are the strengthening role of the state and a progressive lack of cohesion within the family. While the demise of the so-called 'traditional family' has been greatly exaggerated, no one would deny that social trends have changed rapidly in a short period of time.

One result of these changes is the massive loss of early human life through abortion and abortifacients. The Society for the Protection of Unborn Children (Northern Ireland) is committed to promoting the inherent value of human life from the moment of conception. Although the right to life of the unborn is protected by the Constitution, the lives of thousands of Irish children are ended each year through abortion in the United Kingdom, and through the use of abortifacients. The growth of the in-vitro fertilisation industry has also been responsible for the loss of early human life on a massive scale.

Any government policy which undermines the position of the family not only damages individuals but also affects the whole of society; we therefore welcome the opportunity to take part in this consultation. We hope it results in an authentic and evidence-based response with recommendations which are not dictated by ideological agendas or aimed at social engineering.

Throughout this submission the term family is used to refer to the *'natural primary and fundamental unit group'* as envisaged by Article 41.1 of the Irish Constitution. The term 'novel (that is, new) domestic arrangements' is used to refer to so-called alternative structures.

While dealing with the Irish situation, this submission refers to experience in both the UK and the USA, as we believe Ireland can learn a great deal from these societies.

THE STATUS OF THE FAMILY

Article 41.1 of the Irish Constitution states:

> The state recognises the family as the natural primary and fundamental unit group of society, and as a moral institution possessing inalienable and imprescriptible rights, antecedent and superior to all positive law.

> The state, therefore, guarantees to protect the family in its constitution and authority, as the necessary basis of social order and as indispensable to the welfare of the nation and the state.

These obligations were given international recognition by the 1948 Universal Declaration of Human Rights. Article 16 .3 of the UDHR states:

> The family is the natural and fundamental group unit of society and is entitled to protection by society and the state.

There can be no doubt that when Article 41 was drafted, the authors had in mind what has since become known as the 'traditional' family. In recent years some sections of society have claimed this view of the family is outdated and argue that families can be constituted in a wide variety of forms. Policy makers, therefore, may be led to believe that there is no consensus on the nature of the family. This is not entirely correct.

While everyone recognises the legitimacy of the 'traditional' family, this is not true of novel (that is, new) domestic arrangements. The 'traditional' family is therefore the only universally recognised form of the family. As such it deserves the support and respect of government policy and nothing which damages it should be promoted by the state.

Article 40.1 of the Constitution states:

> All citizens shall, as human persons, be held equal before the law.
>
> This shall not be held to mean that the state shall not in its enactments have due regard to differences of capacity, physical and moral, and of social function.

This Article recognises the equality of all citizens as individuals. However, it also acknowledges that the state should not disregard genuine distinctions within society.

Citizens in novel domestic arrangements should have their rights respected as individuals, but novel domestic arrangements should not be equated with the family as envisaged by the Constitution.

THE PARENTAL STATE AND THE FAMILY

> From birth till death it is now the privilege of the parental state to take major decisions – objective, unemotional, the state weighs up what is best for the child.[1]

In some societies the state has become so involved in the lives of its citizens that it has taken over much of the authority formerly held by parents.

The growth of the idea of the state as parent has gone hand in hand with progressive family breakdown. This idea may be best known in dictatorships such as Nazi Germany or Soviet Russia, but it has become increasingly important in western democracies. This is already well documented.

There are now national and global lobbies which view the family as an obstacle to the social changes they espouse. It is not necessary to detail all of these groups or their respective agenda here, except to say they include feminist, eugenic and various economic views of society. The influence of these groups and their followers are active in almost every political field.

In Britain, the writer Anthony Giddens has been a significant influence on Tony Blair's government. Arguing that all forms of the family are unacceptable because they are based on inequalities between men and women, Giddens' book, *The Third Way*, advocates a socially integrated family where children become the subject of parenthood contracts enforced by the state and parental authority is negotiated.[2] Giddens is also credited with bringing about the British government's social exclusion unit which is tasked with cutting teenage pregnancies.

Similar influences can be seen in measures which have been introduced by governments across the globe, although without any explicit international co-operation. This has been true of the promotion of birth control[3] and the liberalisation of abortion, and can currently be seen in plans to introduce euthanasia in several states.

Central to the liberalisation of abortion has been the promotion of birth control through school-based sex education.

Shortly after the US Supreme Court ruled that abortion was a constitutional right, Dr Alan Guttmacher, the president of Planned Parenthood (the American name for the Family Planning Association), delivered a speech which was reported by the *Washington Star-News*.

> The only avenue Planned Parenthood has 'to win the battle' is sex education, Guttmacher maintained. 'I think we're going to establish the individual's complete control over contraception, and that will win the battle for abortion if we act wisely.[4]

Whatever the motives behind the promotion of sex education, the consequences can clearly be seen:

- A rise in conceptions among single teenagers, at progressively younger ages
- Increased levels of abortion
- Increased rates of sexually transmitted diseases (STDs).

The social effects of these changes have secondary results:

- Increased instability in homes and marriages
- Increased infertility rates linked to STDs. With a rise in infertility has come increasing demand for IVF treatment. The IVF industry alone has directly led to loss of early life on an enormous scale. It has also contributed to children being seen as a commodity
- The physical and emotional aftermath of abortion.

Despite a mountain of evidence of the effects of more and more explicit sex-education at progressively early ages, this policy is still advanced both in the UK[5] and in Ireland.

The strategy presented by the Crisis Pregnancy Agency in 2003 demonstrates this.[6] Its recommendations, more sex education and easier access to birth control, are deeply flawed and run counter to all objective analysis. Yet the Agency asked for €22 million of taxpayers' money to be spent over three years on a policy which has proved disastrous.

Concern about child safety and the fear of paedophilia has never been greater. However, government sex education programmes and the promotion of birth control has sexualised children. It has also undermined parental authority and violates Article 14 of the EU

Charter of Fundamental Rights, which states:

> The freedom to found educational establishments with due respect for democratic principles and the right of parents to ensure the education and teaching of their children in conformity with their religious, philosophical and pedagogical convictions shall be respected, in accordance with the national laws governing the exercise of such freedom and right.

While sexual activity of children has risen prosecutions for unlawful carnal knowledge have remained rare. Despite the *de facto* abolition of the age of consent, it is difficult to argue that the children influenced by the policies are not victims of abuse.

ABORTION AND THE FAMILY

By nature abortion is destructive of relationships between mothers and children and between women and men. The emotional and psychological damage to women has been linked to depression, substance abuse and even the neglect and abuse of children. As such, it is a major threat to the family.

Despite the assertions that liberalisation of abortion laws would end child abuse, the opposite proved to be true. Canadian professor of psychiatry Philip Ney, an international authority on both child abuse and post-abortion trauma, believes a clear link exists between the two, stating:

> When I investigated the relationship between child abuse and abortion and reported a direct correlation, people were angry and astonished. It appeared that the rate of child abuse did not decrease with freely available abortions. In fact, the opposite was true. In parts of Canada where there were low rates of abortion there were low rates of child abuse. As the rates of abortion increased, so did child abuse ... Indeed, it is a vicious cycle. That is, parents who have been involved in abortion are more likely to abuse and neglect their children. Mothers and fathers who were abused as children are more likely to abort their child.[7]

Firstly, abortion itself is, of course, the worst form of child abuse. Secondly, it should be noted that we are talking about statistical associations. These connections do not mean that everyone who has an abortion will abuse her children, or that everyone who is abused will have an abortion.

Allowing the abuse of children before birth creates an atmosphere in which the abuse of children after birth is no longer unthinkable.

A second problem is the effect of abortion on fathers. In societies where abortion is easily available, fathers have shown a reluctance to bond with their children. Unattached to their children, they show less support to their partner as well. After an abortion, the alienation worsens. Some studies show as high as an 80% rate of break-up of relationships after abortion. The mother's anger at the lack of support from the baby's father can also be displaced to a born child.

A third reason why abortion can lead to child abuse is also related to bonding. Having an abortion makes it more difficult to bond to a subsequent child, and babies who are not well bonded are more likely to be abused and neglected. A pregnancy following abortion creates more anxiety, caused in part by a fatalistic sense that the child will be abnormal (as a punishment for having aborted the previous one). This anxiety can interfere with bonding.

Moreover, if the grief from the abortion is not adequately processed, it becomes a post-partum depression, which interferes with bonding. When a parent is still grieving a lost baby, it can be difficult to attach to a new baby, because the attachment is still to the one who died. Failure to attach to the one who is alive can lead to abuse and neglect.

There can also be a sense of disappointment in the subsequent child, who is compared to the aborted baby who is often idealised in the mother's mind. Expectations of the new child, sometimes viewed as a 'replacement baby,' are not fulfilled, resulting in anger that can lead to abuse and neglect.

The right to life and the protection of the family are guaranteed by the Constitution, yet successive governments have not only failed to fulfil their duty to uphold these guarantees, government agencies such as the CPA are pursuing policies which actively undermine them.

IVF AND THE FAMILY

The IVF industry has been responsible for the loss of human life on a massive scale through what is euphemistically called embryo wastage. It has produced a climate in which children are considered a mere commodity. It is driven by market forces and the desire of adults to seek their own fulfilment rather than any consideration for rights or well-being of children conceived. Article 3 of the Convention on the Rights of the Child (1989) insists:

> the best interests of the child shall be a primary consideration.

The IVF industry has also succeeded in separating the process of childbearing from the environment of the family. This has given rise to what can only be described as bizarre arrangements involving combinations of biological, surrogate and adoptive parents.

Article 7. 1 of the CRC states:

> The child shall be registered immediately after birth and shall have the right from birth to a name, the right to acquire a nationality and, as far as possible, the right to know and be cared for by his or her parents.

The separation of parents and children is sometimes unavoidable, but the circumstances which arise from IVF are always the result of the decisions made by adults about an elective medical treatment.

Neither the aims nor methods of this industry are compatible with the right to life established in the Constitution or the CRC. The Government should therefore take immediate steps to end the practice of IVF in Ireland.

CONCLUSION AND RECOMMENDATIONS

1 The 'natural primary and fundamental unit group' envisaged by Article 41.1 of the Constitution is the only universally recognised form of the family. No alternative definition can be considered legitimate as none receives the same level of acceptance.

Demands to amend the Constitution on this issue are driven by narrow sectional interests. Furthermore any attempt to amend the Constitution to meet these demands would in itself violate the guarantee given by the state 'to protect the family in its constitution and authority' and would therefore be unconstitutional.

2 The appropriate balance of rights between the family and individuals is already protected by the Constitution. Efforts to alter this balance threaten to undermine the Constitutional protection of the family 'as a moral institution possessing inalienable and imprescriptible rights, antecedent and superior to all positive law'.

The rights of citizens in novel domestic arrangements are already constitutionally guaranteed by Article 40. Amendments to tax, property law or adoption law to treat cohabiting individuals as a married couple would in fact discriminate against individuals (such as siblings) who share a residence without claiming the status of a married couple. It would also fail to give 'due regard to differences of capacity, physical and moral, and of social function,' recognised in Article 40, by treating unmarried couples as if they were married.

3 The government should end its policy of promoting sex education and easier access to birth control. It is deeply flawed and runs counter to all objective analysis. As this policy deals with underage children it also violates the right of parents to educate their children protected by Article 8 of the European Convention on Human Rights and Article 14 of the EU Charter of Fundamental Rights.

4 The preamble of the CRC states:

> Bearing in mind that, as indicated in the Declaration of the Rights of the Child, the child, by reason of his physical and mental immaturity, needs special safeguards and care, including appropriate legal protection, before as well as after birth.

The Constitution offers greater protection of children's rights than the CRC, since the Constitution explicitly recognises the right to life before birth. By giving greater recognition to the rights of the family, it also provides a better guarantee of freedom from state interference. Just as parents have a right to educate and raise their children, children have an equal right to the care and protection of those most concerned with their best interests – their parents. As the Constitution already provides stronger protection of the rights of children than the CRC, no amendment is necessary.

In conclusion, while there are areas in which successive governments have failed to ensure the rights of children and the family, the Irish Constitution provides a level of protection which is balanced and comprehensive. It is difficult to see how any amendment to redefine the family or enhance the rights of children would be necessary.

Attempts at social engineering aimed at changing family life would inevitably promote the power of the state and threaten the rights of all citizens. Such measures would not only be unconstitutional, they would be rejected by the majority of Irish people.

Notes
1 Lady Helen Brook, founder of Brook Advisory Centres. Letter to *The Times* 16 Feb 1980
2 *The Third Way,* Anthony Giddens, Polity Press 1998
3 In this submission the term birth control is use instead of contraception, as many of the drugs and devices currently marketed in Ireland as contraceptives, in fact cause early abortion.
4 *Washington Star-News* 3 May 1973
5 In 1999 the British government's social exclusion unit presented it, report on teenage pregnancy to Parliament. The government's aim is to cut teenage pregnancies by 50 per cent by 2010 with an interim target of 15 per cent reduction by 2004. £15 million was allocated in 2001/02 with similar funding in the following years. This stepped up the policy of the previous Tory government while highlighting the policy's failure.
6 Presented 12 Nov 2003
7 *Deeply Damaged: an Explanation for the Profound Problems Arising from Infant Abortion and Child Abuse* by Philip C Ney, MD, FRCP, MA, R Psych; Pioneer Publishing Co Ltd, Nov 1997, p91.

SONAS

Sonas Housing Association is a supported housing organisation which works with families who have experienced domestic violence. Our mission statement outlines our commitment to the provision of quality, safe accommodation for women and their children made homeless primarily by domestic violence, and to provide a holistic support service to empower women and children to regain control over all aspects of their lives. Furthermore, we strive to influence housing and social policy and decision making as it relates to women and children, out of home due to domestic violence. From our experience of working with families we are submitting the following to the Commission:

DEFINITION OF FAMILY

Family has traditionally been defined as consisting of one man and one woman who are married and have children. However, it is a fact that in modern Irish society, it cannot be so narrowly defined. From information accumulated over many years it is known that there are other forms of family that do not fit this definition, and consequently are denied the protection of the Constitution.

The current definition of family derived from the Constitution, in which family is solely based on the institution of marriage, places the state's needs and objectives at the forefront. Sonas defines the family as an open voluntary relationship based on the mutual and reciprocal benefits participants receive from family membership.

CONSTITUTIONAL PROTECTION

Each citizen of the state is entitled to constitutional protection regardless of his/her position within any type of family. The function of the Constitution is to state and protect these rights, thereby allowing laws to be enacted to support and uphold constitutional principles. Individuals who are not entitled to, or choose not to, marry should not be denied these rights.

BALANCE OF RIGHTS

As stated earlier, the function of any nation's Constitution is to protect the rights of its citizens. In Sonas' definition of family, the needs and interests of individuals are paramount. Sonas considers the total omission of any expressed rights of children in the Constitution to be deplorable in a modern democracy.

The rights of the child deserve full expression in the Constitution. When the child's rights are clearly stated and expressed, the rights of the parent or caregiver should be derived from these rights. Following on from this, if the child's needs are paramount, the rights of the 'natural' mother or father do not need expansion. Where the needs of individuals are in conflict, mediation or a legal intervention may be necessary.

GAY COUPLES

Taking account of the preceding argument, it therefore follows that gay people should not be denied all of the rights and protection which the Constitution affords to every other citizen.

WOMEN IN THE HOME

The Constitution's reference to the woman's life within the home seriously impedes women's human rights, as it contributes to a culture where discrimination is fostered. It is not applicable to modern Irish society and its presence weakens the Constitution.

UN CONVENTION ON THE RIGHTS OF THE CHILD

Sonas believes that the Constitution needs to be updated with reference to the Rights of the Child and brought into line with the UN Convention.

TRAMORE BIBLE FELLOWSHIP

We are a small group of evangelical Christian believers, who base our beliefs on the Bible, which we believe to be God's message to mankind. We share many similar Christian beliefs about the family that are reflected in the present Constitution, because they come from the Bible. We do, however, realise that the world, and Ireland, have changed much since the Constitution was originally drafted.

On the basis of Genesis 2.24 'for this reason a man will leave his father and mother and be united to his wife, and they will become one flesh', we would define marriage as 'the union of one man with one woman, voluntarily entered into for life, to the exclusion of all others' (Lord Penzance 1866). So, contrary to the stream of modern thought, we believe sexual activity is to be for the sole privilege of those who are married – committed publicly to living together for life. That privilege accompanies their responsibilities – to care for each other, to be loyal to each other, and to care for any children that may come as a result of their union. (We see no problem with a married couple using contraceptives to plan their family. Scripture is silent on the issue and leaves us to use the wisdom God has given us.)

It is in this context that the Bible sees immorality and adultery as offences against God and the other people involved. Since God made us as men and women, the biblical injunction is 'Do not lie with a man as one lies with a woman: that is detestable' (Leviticus 18.22). Paul in his letter to the Christians at Rome sees the increase in homosexuality in first-century society as evidence of God's judgment upon a world that refused to acknowledge him. 'Because of this, God gave them over to shameful lusts. Even their women exchanged natural relations for unnatural ones. In the same way the men also abandoned natural relations with women and were inflamed with lust for one another. Men committed indecent acts with other men, and received in themselves the due penalty for their perversion.'

Our belief is that God our maker made us in his image, male and female, and therefore his instructions on how to live as sexual beings is for our good and the good of society. (For example, disregard for these principles has brought AIDS and STDs and widespread abortion in our societies in increasing measure.) In our understanding of marriage outlined above, there can be no such thing as 'gay marriage'. In all the centuries of human history there has never been the demand for such a thing. Do we think that in this area we know more than all our forebears? We seriously doubt that research would show that such relationships last in the way that marriage is meant to – for a lifetime. Procreation is not an insignificant difference between heterosexual marriage and 'gay marriage'. Legislation that undermines the family will ultimately make huge demands upon the state, if it has to pick up the pieces. For example, such partnerships will not produce another generation to pay for the pensions of the elderly.

We believe that to redefine the family (as opposed to making special provisions for exceptional families, e.g. where a spouse is widowed) and to allow gay couples to 'marry' would undermine society and harm the children of future generations.

We are concerned to encourage these sexual standards among our church members and their children. We encourage marriage preparation courses, so that marriage is not entered into carelessly or selfishly but reverently and responsibly.

The message of the Christian gospel means a lot to us. We believe that in Christ, and through his death and resurrection, God has provided a way for sinful people to come back to Himself, and by his Holy Spirit gives the power to live a new life, following him. This pre-supposes that the world in which we live is a fallen world.

Human legislation must provide for the realities of our world, e.g. divorce in certain situations. However, we are concerned that, in our day, governments are in danger of transforming what is abnormal and sinful into what is normal and acceptable. So we urge you to support us in seeking to pass on Scripture's high ideals to our children.

Specifically in response to your questions, we respectfully suggest that you do not:

… contemplate changes in Constitution or law that would further encourage immorality, cohabitation, adultery or homosexuality.

… introduce legislation that allows 'gay marriage'. [A copy of a leaflet entitled 'Gay Spin City' was attached to this submission. For further information, please contact Tramore Bible Fellowship.]

But that you do all you can:

… to support the family financially, so that in the younger years of life at least, children can spend adequate time with their mother. We believe she is uniquely equipped to rear children. (Maybe one change to the Constitution might be to speak of the mother's vital role within the 'family'.)

… to ensure that in the event of separation, fathers as well as mothers can spend time with their own children. Serious consideration should be given to joint custody as the norm, unless there is some serious impediment.

The preamble to the United Nations Convention on the Rights of the Child states several principles upon which those rights are based. These state that the UN is convinced that the family, as the fundamental group of society and the natural environment for the growth and well-being of all its members and particularly children should be afforded the necessary protection and assistance so that it can fully assume its responsibilities within the community. It also recognises that the child, for the full and harmonious development of his or her personality, should grow up in a family environment, in an atmosphere of happiness, love and understanding.

The Rights then go on to assert that state parties shall use their best efforts to ensure recognition of the principle that both parents have common responsibilities for the upbringing and development of the child. Parents or, as the case may be, legal guardians have the primary responsibility for the upbringing and development of the child. The best interests of the child will be their basic concern.

We believe the only way in which these rights are realistically safeguarded is within a committed marriage relationship of one man with one woman. We are concerned that legislation is not enacted that allows for the care of children within a homosexual or lesbian relationship. Such couples cannot naturally conceive their own children, and hence we see it as inappropriate for them to adopt other people's children. We also do not see it as good for the moral formation of children to be reared in such an environment.

TREOIR – FEDERATION OF SERVICES FOR UNMARRIED PARENTS AND THEIR CHILDREN

Founded in 1976, Treoir is the national federation of services for unmarried parents and their children. Its main aim is to promote the rights and welfare of unmarried families in Ireland. Membership of Treoir is open to professional agencies providing services to unmarried parents. They are a combination of statutory and non-statutory bodies, including specialist agencies, health boards, maternity hospitals, adoption societies, self-help groups.

The following are the *core principles* under which Treoir operates:

- Treoir recognises the diversity of family life in Ireland
- Treoir recognises that all families, including unmarried families, have the same rights to respect, care, support, protection and recognition
- Treoir supports and promotes the rights of all children as outlined in the United Nations Convention on the Rights of the Child

- Treoir believes that all children have a right to know, be loved and cared for by both parents.

Current activities of Treoir:

- A national, confidential, comprehensive and free information service for unmarried parents and those involved with them
- A wide range of publications including the *Information Pack for Unmarried Parents*, *Being there for them* (a booklet for grandparents), a series of *information leaflets* etc.
- Organising conferences, workshops and other training sessions for unmarried parents and those who work with them
- Networking with other groups
- Policy development
- Promoting research
- Providing support for workers with young parents through the national resource centre for those working with young parents
- Co-ordinating the teen parent support programme.

RECOMMENDATIONS

Treoir recommends –

1 The enumeration of children's rights within the Constitution using both the UN Convention on the Rights of the Child and the European Convention on Human Rights as a framework. Further, children's rights should be paramount notwithstanding any other article in the Constitution.

2 The protection of family life in all of its forms based on Article 8 of the European Convention on Human Rights which reads:

> Everyone has the right to respect for his private and family life, his home and his correspondence

Treoir further recommends the inclusion of a protection for those rights within the Constitution.

3 That parental rights, if enumerated in the Constitution, apply equally to all parents, mothers, fathers, married or unmarrried and be subject to the principle that children's rights are paramount.

4 The retention of Article 41.2 in a revised gender-neutral form to recognise the contribution of either partner within the home. The revised article would read:

> The state recognises that home and family life give society a support without which the common good cannot be achieved. The state shall endeavour to support persons caring for others within the home.

INTRODUCTION

This submission places children at the centre of reform to the articles of the Irish Constitution concerned with the family. Children's rights are absent explicitly in the

Constitution and this needs rectification. Further, in order for children's rights to be fully protected, there can be no discrimination between children depending on the family form into which they are born.

> It is clear that in accordance with the principle of non-discrimination, the rights of children don't change depending on the nature of their parents' relationship or the circumstances of their admission to the family (Kilkelly: 2003: 1).

Treoir is thus also seeking to have all family forms given equal protection under the Constitution and that the children's rights and best interests are paramount.

CHANGING FAMILY STRUCTURES IN IRELAND

The dynamic sociological changes in Irish life in relation to the family and family life are well documented.[1] Change in this area has been characterised by a decline in fertility and family size, an increase in extra-marital births and cohabitation, and marital breakdown given formal legal expression through the introduction of divorce. Marriage is no longer the primary or dominant gateway to family formation, but there is evidence that extra-marital births are taking place in quasi-marital unions and that many enter into marriage subsequently, pointing to a change in the sequencing of marriage.[2]

Figures from the most recent census reveal that there were some 153,863 lone-parent families in 2002. There has been a significant increase in the number of cohabiting couples who now comprise one in twelve family units. Some 52,000 children now live with cohabiting couples and currently one third of births are outside marriage.

The family can take a variety of forms and these forms depend on a complex blend of economic and social factors. It is no longer the case that marriage forms the basis of family formation or re-formation in Ireland.

Kieran McKeown points out that:

> As in other northern European countries, there is now a trend where births precede rather than succeed marriage. This indicates a decline not in marriage *per se* but in the role of marriage as a gateway to family formation (2002:7).

The attempt to capture family life conceptually or statistically through conflating family with household is also highly problematic as evidenced by the finding in recent research that one quarter of all children (24%) do not live in a household containing both their biological parents.[3]

Finola Kennedy in her seminal work charting family change in Ireland notes that the family is in part a legal construct concerned with the concepts of marriage and dependency. She quotes English family law expert, John Dewar:

> There is now less emphasis on the exclusivity of the legal status of marriage and evidence of a move towards constructing status-like relationships around

new organising concepts. The primary aim, it was argued, is to construct a set of legal-economic relations among family members that are demarcated from, and thereby reduce the financial burden on, the state. In this process, the legal concept of marriage is logically, and is *de facto* becoming redundant (Dewar, 1992:71, Kennedy: 2001: 13).

As a result, Dewar sees parenthood rather than marriage as the significant event in relation to family rights and responsibilities, and a consequent shift from the parental rights to children's rights.

THE FAMILY AND THE IRISH CONSTITUTION

The Constitution is a dynamic document based on broad principles. From Treoir's perspective, the discussion of constitutional reform should take place in the context of the removal of barriers to protection for unmarried families and children generally.

The 1937 Constitution was drafted with the family based on marriage in mind and Article 41 explicitly states that the family to which the special protection applies is the marital family. Article 41.3.1 states that:

> The state pledges itself to guard with special care the institution of marriage, on which the family is founded and to protect it against attack.

The family has thus been interpreted by the Irish courts to be confined to families based on marriage.[4] Although parents who are not married do not benefit from the rights enunciated in Articles 41 and 42 of the Constitution, it has been held that children born outside wedlock have the same 'natural and imprescriptible rights' as children born within marriage. However, the courts have held that in a number of instances, it is permissible to treat children born outside of marriage differently to those born to a married couple. The non-marital family is effectively outside of constitutional protection and an unmarried cohabiting couple cannot, no matter how stable or continuous, bring themselves within the confines of Article 41.1.2.

The report of the Constitution Review Group in 1996 proposed amending Article 41. 3.1 to read as follows:

> The state pledges itself to guard with special care the institution of marriage and to protect it against attack.

The result of the deletion from Article 41.3.1 of the words 'on which the family is founded' would be the removal of the definition of the family based on marriage. The protection for families based on marriage is to be retained. In addition, the Review Group recommended a new section which will give an unmarried person the right to 'respect for family life' similar to that protected in Article 8 of the ECHR.

It is essential and imperative, particularly in regard to protecting children's rights that the definition of the family based on marriage is removed. Mary Daly points out in the report on *Families and Family Life in Ireland* that:

> If one definition of family is used and if that definition is exclusive, such as that in the Constitution, it acts to endorse and perpetuate a hierarchy among different kinds of families (p.25)[5]

There is a recognised need to examine ways of capturing the fabric and realities of family life in legal and other definitions, as mentioned many times during the course of the family fora held around the country:

> Another speaker emphasised the need to think of family not as structure or place or even a definition but, rather, as a set of values, activities, relationships. Such values and activities include nurturing, caring, loving, steadfastness, permanency and consistency (p.26)

The efficacy of defining the family in more expansive terms has already been demonstrated in the Irish legal framework where unmarried families have been equiparated to families based on marriage. The definition of the family in Irish law has been expanded by pieces of legislation such as the Non-Fatal Offences against the Person Act, 1997; Domestic Violence Act, 1996; Parental Leave Act, 1998; Employment Equality Act 1998; Mental Health Act, 2001; and the Residential Tenancies Act, 2004. This displays the need for a more expansive definition of family life in which such structures and relationships can be understood and captured.

Defining the family is a complex task as acknowledged by the Review Group in 1996. Sociological changes discussed above attest to this. These are issues which have been encountered by other jurisdictions. International legal instruments and conventions to which Ireland is a party have attempted to capture the complex social realities of family life within a legal framework which reflects and protects those realities.

The European Convention on Human Rights takes a broad view of family and employs the notion of family life to make sense of diverse family forms. Similarly, the United Nations casts its legal net wide and has adopted a definition of the family which broadly defines the family as:

> Any combination of two or more persons who are bound together by ties of mutual consent, birth and/or adoption or placement and who, together, assume responsibility for, *inter alia,* the care and maintenance of group members, the addition of new members through procreation or adoption or placement, the socialisation of children and the social control of members (Daly: 2004: 23).

THE EUROPEAN CONVENTION ON HUMAN RIGHTS AND THE JURISPRUDENCE OF THE EUROPEAN COURT OF HUMAN RIGHTS

Article 8 of the European Convention on Human Rights states the following:

> Everyone has the right to respect for his private and family life, his home and his correspondence.

On several occasions the European Court of Human Rights has required states to treat non-marital families with the same degree of respect as traditional families. The court will give substantial weight to the functional realities underpinning family life as they appear in 'present day conditions'. In *K and T v Finland*[6] the court held 'that the non-existence of "family life" is essentially a matter depending upon the real existence of close personal ties'.

The ECHR was incorporated into Irish law by the European Convention on Human Rights Act, 2003. Although the ECHR ranks above legislation it has been incorporated at sub-constitutional level. The ECHR Act of 2003 requires the Irish courts to take cognisance of the jurisprudence of the European Court of Human Rights.

Article 8.1 of the European Convention on Human Rights protects, among other things, the individual's right to respect for her private and family life. The article is to be interpreted in the light of present day conditions.[7] It is generally the case that the state enjoys 'a wide margin of appreciation'[8] when balancing the rights of the individual against the interests of the state. There are cases, however, where a higher standard of judicial scrutiny will be applied by the European Court of Human Rights. The Court has in the past required states to treat non-marital families with the same degree of respect as traditional families. In *Inze v Austria*,[9] the court required that 'very weighty reasons would … have to be advanced before a difference of treatment on the ground of birth out of wedlock could be regarded as compatible with the Convention'.

Where the existence of a family tie with a child has been established, the state must act in a manner calculated to enable that tie to be developed; legal safeguards must be established that render possible – as from the moment of birth or as soon as practicable thereafter – the child's integration in her family.[10]

The issue of what constitutes family life was first addressed directly in *Barrehab v The Netherlands*.[11] There the court held that a parent has family life with a child from the moment a child is born; this tie remains in place unless broken by later events. In *Kroon and others v The Netherlands*,[12] the court held that family life existed and that Article 8 was therefore applicable, even in the absence of marriage or cohabitation. The court stated:

> The notion of 'family life' in Article 8 is not confined solely to marriage-based relationships and may encompass other *de-facto* 'family ties' where parties are living together outside marriage. Although, as a rule, living together may be a requirement for such a relationship, exceptionally other factors may also serve to demonstrate that a relationship has sufficient constancy to create *de-facto* 'family ties.

The Kroon decision focused on the relationship between the child's biological parents. Although not married to each other, the fact that they had four other children and had been in a relationship for a number of years was sufficient for the court to hold that family life existed between the father and the child. A child born to such a relationship was *ipso jure* part of that family unit irrespective of the contribution that the father had made to the child's life. Similarly in *Keegan v Ireland*[13] the court held that family life existed between an unmarried father and his biological child even where the child's parents were not cohabiting at the time the child was born. The court instead looked to the '*de-facto*' family ties that existed in the parents' relationship prior to the child's birth.

As pointed out by Ursula Kilkelly, 'the concept of family life, protected by Article 8 of the ECHR, stands in almost complete contrast to the constitutional definition of the family'. The court has found family life to exist between parents and their children, regardless of their marital status,[14] the family's living arrangements,[15] or their apparent lack of commitment to their children.[16] As Dr Kilkelly points out, family life has also been found to exist between children and their grandparents,[17] between siblings[18], between an uncle and his nephew[19], and between parents and children born into second relationships.[20] So, family life is a broad concept which clearly covers the relationship between all children and their biological parents, whether in a committed relationship or not.[21]

In her comprehensive discussion of case-law in this area, including the decision in the case of *X, Y and Z v UK*,[22] in which the court recognised for the first time that family life existed between a child and her social rather than biological father, Dr Kilkelly makes the crucial point that:

> For those who hesitate at this, out of concern that it may not be in the best interests of the child, it is important to remember that the application of Article 8 – finding family life to exist – is only the first step in the process and that all interferences with or failures to respect family life must also be compliant with the second paragraph of the provision. In other words, the safeguard of proportionality is available here.[23]

It would be possible to remove entirely the protection for families based on marriage which would lead to a situation where neither marital nor non-marital families would be favoured. It would still be possible to enter a clause to respect family life in all of its forms which would obviously include families based on marriage.

The preferred option of the Review Group on the Constitution (1996)[24] is to retain a pledge to protect the family based on marriage but also to guarantee to all individuals a right to respect for their family life whether or not the family is based on marriage. One of the reasons which they cited for this was the practical difficulty associated with defining the family. It is our submission that the fact of difficulty in legislating in a particular area is not a sufficient reason for declining to do so where considered necessary. The mere fact that there is difficulty with a definition is not sufficient to deny equal constitutional protection to all families.

Treoir recommends the broad protection afforded to family life in Article 8 of the European Convention on Human Rights and further recommends that these rights should be protected within the Constitution.

CHILDREN'S RIGHTS

In modern social and legal discourse children are no longer viewed simply as chattels, their rights adjunctive to those of their parents. Marital children's rights have been privileged over those of the non-marital child. Children's personal rights are not expressly provided for in Article 41. Certain unenumerated rights have been found to exist in relation to children including the right to an opportunity to be reared with due regard to religious, moral, intellectual and physical welfare. The Review Group recommended enumerating these rights.

It has been argued that:

> the absence of an express provision in the Irish Constitution privileging children's rights over those of other interested parties leaves a gaping hole in the constitutional protection that should be afforded to these most vulnerable of subjects.[25]

Judge Catherine McGuinness, in the report on the Kilkenny incest investigation, observed that:

> the very high emphasis placed on rights of family in the Constitution may consciously or unconsciously be interpreted as giving a higher value to the right of parents than to the rights of children and recommended the amending of the Constitution to give 'a specific and overt declaration of the rights of born children.'[26]

Dr Fergus Ryan suggests that root and branch constitutional reform is required along the following lines:

1 To place the child and his or her interests at the heart of our family law policy and to make practical efforts to realise this aim
2 To displace the privileged position of the marital family by the recognition of alternative family forms
3 To bring Irish law into line with the European Convention on Human Rights by placing an obligation on the state to respect and support family life in all its manifestations.

Treoir is in agreement with this analysis. We also favour giving children the broadest rights possible within the constitutional framework and ensuring that their rights are paramount.

The UN Convention on the Rights of the Child contains many child-specific rights.

For our purposes, Articles 3 and 7 provide particular protection. Article 3.1 of the Convention states:

> In all actions concerning children, whether undertaken by public or private social welfare institutions, courts of law, administrative authorities or legislative bodies the best interests of the child shall be of paramount consideration.

This could be expressly inserted into the Constitution in order to give children a constitutional right to have their best interests respected, particularly in light of the conflict which can arise between their rights as individuals and the right of the family as currently conceived under Irish law. The issue of giving children a voice particularly in family law proceedings also needs to be addressed. Articles 6 and 8 of the European Convention on Human Rights provides for a child's right to participate in legal proceedings.

Article 7.1 of the UN Convention states:

> The child shall be registered immediately after the birth and shall have the right from birth to a name, the right to acquire a nationality and, as far as possible, the right to know and be cared for by his or her parents.

Article 9.3 states:

> State parties shall respect the right of the child who is separated from one or both parents to maintain personal relations and direct contact with both parents on a regular basis, except if it is contrary to the child's best interests.

The Convention does not define a parent in either biological or social terms and Article 2 protects the child from discrimination on the basis of their parents' activities or status.

PARENTAL RIGHTS AND RESPONSIBILITIES

At present a natural mother is considered to have rights in relation to her child which are personal rights protected by Article 40.3.[27] The Review Group recommended in 1996 that these rights should be enumerated, that is made explicit, in the Constitution. However, the Review Group has also pointed out that a general protection to family life, akin to that in Article 8 of the ECHR, gives a natural mother those rights in any event.

Viewed through the prism of children's rights, it is impermissible to allow a specific protection to mothers within the Constitution without a corresponding one for fathers. The potential implications of this are far reaching. As it stands a natural father who is not married to the mother of his child does not have any Constitutionally protected rights to his child. The Supreme Court has held:

i a natural father is not a member of a family within Article 41
ii a natural father is not a 'parent' within Article 42
iii a natural father has no personal right in relation to his child which the state is bound to protect under Article 40.3[28]

Since this pronouncement, the Status of Children Act, 1987 has amended the Guardianship of Children Act, 1964 in order to give the non-marital father the right to apply to the court to be appointed a guardian. This right has been held by the Supreme Court to be distinct from having the right to be a guardian. The European Court of Human Rights has found Ireland to be in breach of Article 8 of the European Convention on Human Rights in this regard. It would be possible to extend to the non-marital father guardianship rights by legislation or by constitutional change.

The Review Group on the Constitution suggests that there does not appear to be justification to giving constitutional rights to every natural father simply by reason of biological links. They feel rather that the solution lies in following the approach of Article 8 of the ECHR in guaranteeing to every person respect for 'family life' which has been interpreted by the European Court of Human Rights to include non-marital family life, but yet requiring the existence of family ties between the mother and father. The Review Group suggest that this may be a way of granting constitutional rights to those fathers who have, or had, a stable relationship with the mother prior to the birth, or subsequent to the birth with the child, while excluding persons from having rights who are only biological fathers without any such relationship. They also point out that it would have to be made clear in the Constitution that the reference to family life is not based on marriage. Treoir is in full agreement with this latter point.

It is Treoir's position that children should have rights to both parents regardless of the family form but dependent on the nature and quality of the family tie, which as we have seen with the jurisprudence of the European Court of Human Rights, allows the court to employ necessary interpretive aids such as that of proportionality and within the context of the principle that children's rights are paramount.

However, Treoir does not support explicitly differentiating between the rights of fathers and mothers in the Constitution, or indeed between those of married and unmarried fathers. In *Nguyen v US*, the son of an American citizen father and a non US-citizen mother was seeking to argue that a statute establishing citizen requirements for individuals born out of wedlock to a citizen father and non-citizen mother violated the equal protection clause of the constitution because it provided different rules for citizenship depending on the gender of the person with citizenship.[29] The Supreme Court ruled 5-4 that there was no violation of the equal protection clause as 'the classification served important government objectives and the discriminatory means employed were substantially related to the achievement of those objectives'.[30]

Justice Day O'Connor, dissenting, pointed out that sex-based generalisations both reflect and reinforce 'fixed notions concerning the roles and abilities of males and females'.[31] Thus, according to O'Connor:

> In upholding the use of a sex-based generalisation to justify the differential treatment outlined in section 1409, the majority's opinion not only perpetuates the myth that men are not as available to establish relationships with their children as women are, but also does a disservice to women and societal perceptions of their roles as well.[32]

The dangers of elevating parental rights to the level of constitutional protection have been well discussed[33] and need to be placed at the heart of a discussion of how those rights interact with those of children, particularly in cases of conflict between the two. Whether elevated to constitutional status or introduced by legislation, Treoir favours an end to the current situation where fathers have no automatic rights to their children, and the rights of marital children to their father are privileged *vis-à-vis* those of non-marital children. There is no reason to make a distinction based on gender or marital status in relation to the rights of fathers *vis-à-vis* mothers in the Constitution. Rights to fathers should flow on the establishment of paternity subject to the discretion of the court to remove them in circumstances where this is warranted.

Article 41.1 confers rights on the family unit as distinct from the rights of individual members of the family and are therefore distinct from personal rights protected by the Constitution. The Review Group itself considers that the present focus of Article 41 emphasises the rights of the family as a unit to the possible detriment of individual members. This is because of the fact that such emphasis may prevent the state from intervening in the interests of an individual within the family unit where necessary or appropriate. This is brought into sharp focus where it is necessary to protect the interests of the child, and has been illustrated in Irish law by the Supreme Court's upholding of the constitutionality of the Adoption (No. 2) Bill 1987 regarding the circumstances in which the adoption of children of marriage may be permissible, having regard to family rights under Article 41 and the child's personal rights. At the centre of our submission is the enumerating of children's rights within the Constitution and their protection as paramount.

THE INTERACTION OF PARENTAL AND CHILDREN'S RIGHTS

The principle of upholding children's rights as paramount has been enshrined in various pieces of Irish legislation pertaining to them. For instance, section 3 of the Guardianship of Infants Act, 1964 and section 24 of the Childcare Act, 1991 stipulate that the court must have regard to the welfare of the child as the first and paramount consideration. The wording of these sections is derived from Article 42.1 and the term 'welfare' is defined in section 2 of the 1964 act.[34]

William Duncan has pointed to the fact that:

> In the context of balancing the claims of different sets of parents, the constitutional provisions have tended to introduce rigidity where flexibility and nuance are called for. Only in one area, that of custody disputes between married parents, has the welfare principle been able to operate without condition, because the constitutional rights of the two parents are of equal standing (1993, 1996: 625).

The issues identified in relation to the subordination of children's rights to those of others relate to the complex interplay between their rights, those of their parents *vis-à-vis* each other and the state, and parental and family autonomy as guaranteed in the Irish Constitution. The problems have been exacerbated by the definition of the family as that based on marriage and the exclusion of non-marital families from constitutional protection.

Commentators have also warned of the dangers of giving excessive power to the state which has proved itself to be 'a lousy parent'[35] in this regard. However, it is imperative that children's rights and welfare be paramount in all decisions affecting them. For this reason, Treoir is recommending that this be explicitly stated in the enumeration of their rights within the Constitution, i.e. that children's rights as enumerated exist notwithstanding any other article in the Constitution which may grant rights to parents or the family as a unit.

ARTICLE 41.2

The Review Group recommended the retention of Article 41.2 in a revised gender-neutral form to recognise the contribution of either spouse within the home.

The Honourable Mrs Justice Susan Denham in a speech to a Law Society/Human Rights Commission conference[36] stated:

> We must bear in mind that the Constitution is a living document. It falls to be construed in our times ... in our time a matter of current debate is life balance ... the aspiration for quality home life (shorn of its inequality) could be found in many Irish homes. (2004: 7)

Treoir does not find the retention of this article problematic as long as the amendment to ensure gender neutrality takes place. The Review Group also suggested a revised form of Article 41.2 in order to recognise constitutionally the role of carers and care work within the home. The Review Group suggested that the revised form of Article 41.2 might read:

> The State recognises that home and family life gives to society a support without which the common good cannot be achieved. The state shall endeavour to support persons caring for others within the home.

References

Daly, Mary. 2004. *Families and Family Life in Ireland. Challenges for the Future*. Report of the Public Consultation Fora. Dublin: Department of Social and Family Affairs.

Duncan, William. 1993. 'The constitutional protection of parental rights' in Eekelaar, JM and Sarcevic, P (eds) *Parenthood in Modern Society*. Dordrecht.

Denham, Susan. 'Leadership in Human Rights Law, Past and Future'. Paper delivered to the Irish Human Rights Commission and Law Society of Ireland Conference, October 16th, 2004.

Fahey, Tony and Russell, Helen. 2001. *Family Formation in Ireland; Trends, Data Needs and Implications*. Dublin: ESRI

Kennedy, Finola. 2001. *Cottage to Crèche: Family Change in Ireland*. Dublin: Institute of Public Administration.

Kilkelly, Ursula. 2004. 'Children's Rights in the Committed Relationships of their Parents'. Paper delivered to the Irish Human Rights Commission and Law Society of Ireland Conference, October 16th, 2004.

McKeown, Kieran. 'Families and Single Fathers in Ireland'. *Administration*, Vol 49, No. 1 (Spring, 2001), 3-24.

McKeown, Kieran, Pratschke, Jonathan and Trutz Haase. 2003. *Family Wellbeing: What Makes A Difference?* Clare: Ceifin Centre.

Rogus, Caroline. 2003. 'Conflating Women's Biological and Sociological Roles: The Ideal of Motherhood, Equal Protection, and the Implications of the Nguyen v INS Opinion'. *Journal of Constitutional Law*. Vol 5:4.

Ryan, Fergus. 2004. 'Child of Our Times': The Child's Place in Family Law and Family Policy' A paper prepared for the One Family Can (Campaigning and Advocacy Network) Biennial Conference 3rd November 2004.

Treoir. 1996. Response to the Recommendations of the Constitution Review Group.

Notes

1. Fahey and Russell, 2001, Kennedy, 2001; McKeown, Pratschke and Haas, 2003.
2. Ibid.
3. McKeown, Pratschke and Haase, 2003: 6.
4. *The State (Nicolaou) v An Bord Uchtála, WO'R v EH and An Bord Uchtála*.
5. This report was on foot of public consultations on families and family life in today's Ireland held around the country.
6. 12 July 2001, Application No 2570/94, Para 150.
7. Marckx v Belgium, 31 Eur. Ct. H.R. (ser A.)(1979).
8. See Lawless Case, 1 Eur. Ct. H.R. (ser B) at 408 (1960-61) (The concept of the margin of appreciation is that a government's discharge of its responsibilities is essentially a delicate problem of appreciating complex factors and of balancing conflicting considerations of the public interest; and that once the commission or the court is satisfied that the government's appreciation is at least on the margin of its powers ..., then the interest which the government itself has in effective government and in the maintenance of order justifies and requires a decision in favour of the government's appreciation).
9. 126 Eur. Ct. H.R. (Ser A) at 18-19 (1979).
10. Eur. Ct. HR. (ser A) at 18-19 (1979).
11. *Berrehab v The Netherlands* 138 Eur. Ct. H.R (Ser. A) (1998).
12. *Kroon and Others v The Netherlands* (1995).
13. *Keegan v Ireland* Eur. Ct. H.R. (Ser. A.) (1998).
14. *Marcyx v Belgium,* no 6833/74, *Johnston v Ireland*, no 9697/92.
15. *Barrehab v The Netherlands*, no 10730/84.
16. *C v Belgium*, no 21794/93.
17. *Marcyx Judgment*, op cit, para. 45.
18. *Olsson v Sweden*, no 10465/93
19. *Boyle v UK*, no 16580/90.
20. *Jolie and Lebrun v Belgium*, no 11418/85.
21. Kilkelly, 2003: 3.
22. *X, Y and Z v UK*, no 21830/93.
23. Kilkelly, 2003: 2. Under Article 8 it must first be established that family life exists, and secondly that there has been an interference with family life which is disproportionate with an aim such as the rights of the child.
24. The Report of the Constitution Review Group 1996.
25. Ryan, 2004.
26. Report of the Kilkenny Incest Investigation.
27. *G v An Bord Uchtála*.
28. *The State (Nicolaou) v An Bord Uchtála*.
29. USC § 1409(a).
30. Nguyen, 533 US at 60 quoting *United States v Virginia*, 518 (1996).

[31] 533 US at 74 (quoting Hogan, 458 US at 725).
[32] Rogus, 2003: 808.
[33] Duncan, 1993, Ryan 2004.
[34] Section 2 of the 1964 act defines 'welfare' as comprising 'the religious, moral, intellectual, physical and social welfare of the infant'.
[35] Ryan, 2004: 5.
[36] Denham, 2004: 7.

UNMARRIED AND SEPARATED FATHERS OF IRELAND

INTRODUCTION

The Unmarried and Separated Fathers of Ireland is a group of men/fathers that was formed approximately ten years ago in response to the inequality that exists in society, the family law courts and the government towards men/fathers. We have lobbied for changes to the present structures that are in place, and it is on this aspect that we make our presentation to the Oireachtas All-Party Committee on the proposed amendments to Articles 40 to 44 of the Constitution in relation to the family. The Unmarried and Separated Fathers of Ireland present the following proposals to the Committee for consideration and implementation within Articles 40, 41, 42, 43 and 44 of the Constitution or any other Articles that adversely affect the family.

Our group have met with ministers associated with our concerns and have been constructive in the way we address the issues that are relevant to unmarried and separated fathers. We have at all times conducted ourselves in an honourable, decent and civilised manner, thus raising the profile of our concerns.

We have protested through the streets of Dublin several times a year for the last number of years and we hold our most poignant protest on the centre island of O'Connell Bridge on Christmas Day every year.

The lack of constitutional rights to unmarried and separated fathers is contributing to and fostering divisions within our people and our society.

As unmarried and separated fathers, we are denied our equal rights to be treated equally before the Irish Constitution and the Irish family law courts, and we are denied the protection of human rights that is afforded the mother of our children. We say that this is discrimination of the highest degree and that as a result our children are also being discriminated against. This discrimination is in breach of the Equality Act, 2000 and in breach of the 1997 Children's Act in association with the UN Convention on the Rights of the Child. It is also in breach of Article 8 of the ECHR findings on the rights to family.

The Universal Declaration of Human Rights under the General Assembly Resolution 217A(111) of 10 December 1948 states clearly in Article 1: 'All human beings are born free and equal in dignity and rights. They are endowed with conscience and should act towards one another in a spirit of brotherhood.'

Article 2 states that everyone is entitled to all the rights and freedoms set forth in this declaration without distinction of any kind such as sex, colour, religion, national or social origin and birth or 'other status'. (We come within the confines of other status). This contradicts the denial of guardianship and access rights to our children.

Discrimination against men/fathers, denying or limiting as it does their equality of rights with women/mothers is fundamentally unjust and constitutes an offence against human dignity, human rights and the elimination of discrimination.

This is being exacerbated and compounded in the family law courts in granting fathers access to children, with the burden of proof being on the father to prove he is a good parent or father and the courts having inadequate training for judges and inadequate time to assess the father's true qualities associated with child-rearing or father and child interaction.

The division of assets and lack of support services for men/fathers is also in breach of Article 16 of our equal rights declarations whereby men and women of full age without any limitations due to race, nationality or religion have the right to marry and to found a family. They are entitled to equal rights as to marriage, during marriage and on its dissolution.

1 This is not the case in the family law courts with the division of assets on a 70% to 30% and 60% to 40% in favour of the wife or mother.
2 This is not the case in relation to the allocation of access rights for fathers to their children.

Article 2, paragraph 2

The principle of equality of rights shall be embodied in the Constitution or otherwise be guaranteed by law.

All appropriate measures shall be taken to ensure men be treated on equal terms with women and *vice versa* without any discrimination; this is not the case in family law.

Without prejudice to the safeguarding of the unity and the harmony of the family, which remains the most fundamental unit of society, whether it be a family in marriage or outside of marriage, fathers and mothers should have a constitutional right to be held to have joint responsibility and to be joint legal guardians to a child from the moment of conception, and this right should be embodied in the Constitution with a special clause that in the 1% of cases of rape, sperm donation and incest, no constitutional protection be afforded to these cases.

All articles should be amended with the insertion of he/she, including where it contains he to have she inserted and she inserted alongside he. Article 12 associated with the President should contain he/she.

THE FAMILY

Article 40.1: should include family law as this is not the case because of the in-camera courts.

Article 40.3.2°: should be amended to remove 'as best it may'.

Article 40.3.3°: should be amended to read 'the equal right to life of the mother and/or the child with consent by the father'.

Article 41.1.1°-2°: should empower all rights within the family on both parents and specify the mother and father rather than the husband and wife.

Article 41.2.1°: should be amended to include men and women; husband or wife, mother or father by their life within the family and the home without which the common good of the state cannot be achieved.

Article 41.3.1°: should read 'the state pledges to guard with special care the institution of marriage, family units outside of marriage through the birth of a child, and including cohabitants with children or adoptive parents and protect them against attack.'

Article 41: should undertake to uphold all members of a family's right to family, whether through marriage or otherwise if there is (are) a child (children).

Biological fathers to be given automatic guardianship with the mother, and give the mother the right to apply to court to remove such right on production of constructive evidence to remove the father as the guardian.

Article 42: should give rights to a natural father in conjunction with Article 8 of the ECHR. Walsh J in the Supreme Court, stated that there had not been shown to the satisfaction of the court that the father of an illegitimate child has any natural rights; this judgment is dated since illegitimacy has been abolished.

Article 42: should give constitutional rights to both parents of the child from conception and this would cover the area of abortion – that both persons would be in consent. Should give particular specification that there are no constitutional rights afforded in the case of sperm donation, incest or rape.

Article 42: should state that where the existence of a family tie has been established with a child, the state and the Constitution should guarantee to safeguard and protect each member of that associated family from the moment of birth, and the integration of that child into that family even if it is a divided unit and there is an absent parent from the home but not from the child's life. This would cater for single fathers and divorcees.

We would recommend a new subsection to any of the above articles that would provide special protection of social and other benefits that are associated with the special care of the institution of marriage.

There is a problem achieving a legal balance offering security and measures of equality when couples separate, whether in a married family unit or a non-married unit in relation to a person's rights to family, when the burden of proof is on the father and he has to apply for his rights to a court whilst the mother is guaranteed her rights.

Both parents should be guaranteed their personal rights. Access to a child or children should be a right through an individual's personal rights. Every man/father who endures separation in a marriage or relationship breakdown is not being guaranteed equality in the family law courts. Children are used as weapons and pawns and this is in breach of the father's and the child's rights when there is nothing contrary to the facts before the courts other than two people who have fallen out of love with each other, and not their child or children.

RECOMMENDATIONS

1 The family should be defined as couples with a child or children; or a couple that have married and have or have not any children.

2 To strike a balance between the rights of the family as a unit and the rights of individual members, incorporate equality in all aspects of family law, and protect equality, as to marriage, during marriage and on its dissolution.

3 It is possible to give protection to the family, other than those based on marriage in accordance with both of the above recommendations, by creating a subsection safeguarding the social benefits and special care within the institution of marriage.

4 The Constitution's reference to the woman's life within the home is dated and should be interpreted and amended as the parents or family members within the home.

5 The rights of a natural mother should have express constitutional protection and equally afforded protection with the father or in consultation with the father, whilst protecting the safeguards of the United Nations Convention on the Rights of the Child. This could be in accordance with Article 8 of the European Court of Human Rights Declaration safeguarding your rights to family.

6 A natural father should have equal rights to his child in conjunction with Article 8 and the protection of his rights; as to marriage, during marriage and on its dissolution. These rights should be guaranteed to unmarried fathers and unmarried mothers because there is no illegitimacy within the confines of the family nowadays.

7 The rights of a child should be afforded special protection by adhering to and implementing the United Nations Declaration on the Rights of the Child in conjunction with Article 8 of the European Court of Human Rights on the rights to family.

8 The Constitution does need to be changed to protect the child through the UN Convention that would interpret that it is the child who has the right to know and love and be cared for by both parents irrespective of what relationship difficulties they

may endure in a marriage or relationship break-down.

9 The Constitution should equally protect the rights of men and fathers to the protection of social welfare, housing, children's allowance etc. in conjunction with the protection of the family and their rights. They should have adequate provisions for food, clothing, housing, medical care and be able to provide for circumstances beyond their control such as sickness, unemployment, death of a spouse or being separated from a spouse through separation or divorce or circumstances beyond their control.

WITH

WITH INTEREST IN MAKING A SUBMISSION

WITH members, unremunerated parents and carers, want constitutional recognition for their role, their work, and their contribution to the economy and society. WITH aims to ensure that family-based care be recognised and financially viable. Article 41.2 represents a key instrument for recognising unremunerated work in a variety of domains and situations and it forms the basis for legal, tax and social welfare provisions of benefit to parents and carers on a full or part-time basis.

Mrs Justice Denham has on a number of occasions ruled that Article 41.2 recognises women's unremunerated work. Mr Justice Murray has ruled that Article 41.2 could be interpreted as extending to men's unremunerated work.

WITH is of the opinion that constitutional protection for unremunerated workers, especially those in the role of parent or carer, should be strengthened and that the wording should be gender-neutral. This position is consistent with the Beijing Platform for Action, the outcome document of the 4th World Conference on Women in 1995. WITH rejects the suggested wording of the Constitution Review Group since the formulation proposed by the CRG has the potential to undermine current and potential future supports for unremunerated workers.

The UN's Commission for the Status of Women will undertake in March 2005 a ten-year review of the Beijing Platform for Action, which calls for the recognition of unremunerated work as a central aspect of ensuring equality for women. WITH will be participating in this process as representatives of our EU umbrella group, FEFAF (la Fédération Européenne des Femmes Actives au Foyer – European Federation of Unpaid Parents and Carers at Home). FEFAF has submitted a statement requesting UN bodies and national governments to implement Strategic Objective H3, on the collection of data on unremunerated work. It is not only in Ireland that this is an important question: the process of changing Article 41.2 will be tracked with interest in other countries by parents, carers and their representative organisations as well.

Professor Gabriel Kiely's study (2004) on valuing unremunerated work in Ireland is annexed to this submission, as are WITH's submission to the CSO on census 2006 and FEFAF's statement regarding recognition on unremunerated work in the Beijing +10 review process.

UNREMUNERATED WORK IN IRELAND

Unremunerated work in Ireland refers to many activities which benefit the economy and society, and more specifically local communities, families and individuals. It is estimated that the total value of this work equals 30%-50% of Gross Domestic Product, or between €40,435,800,000 and €67,393,000,000 (source: calculated on the basis of the CSO GDP figure for 2003, €134,786m, available on http://www.cso.ie/principalstats/pristat5.html.) Unremunerated work includes:

- parenting and other childcare
- caring for dependent elderly and/or disabled relatives
- farming and farm support
- voluntary work in the community
- housework and domiciliary upkeep.

Ireland collects statistics on some of this unpaid work and those who carry it out. Below is a summary of statistics and recent research relevant to this submission.

Homemakers

According to the CSO's most recent figures (Table 21, Quarterly National Household Survey Q3 2004), there are

- 560,000 women and
- 4,600 men

active as full-time homemakers. Generally, a homemaker is considered to undertake all or some of the tasks listed above. Of course, many people undertake some or all of the same work as full-time homemakers on a part-time basis, but there is no method of categorising such a group currently in place at the CSO.

Professor Gabriel Kiely (December 2004) has estimated that the annual value of the work of the average full-time homemaker is €23,540.40. The data also show that the majority of unpaid caring and housework undertaken on a part-time basis is still mostly done by women.

ARK Life, the insurance company, undertakes an annual time-use survey of homemakers to determine the value of the work they do. The rationale for this is that if the homemaker passes away, the work previously done by the homemaker would have to be replaced at market rates. The women in the study worked an average of 142 hours per week for more than 50 weeks of the year. If it were necessary to replace the work of the homemaker at the minimum wage, it would cost the family €49,700 on an annual basis.

Childcare

According to the CSO (Table 5, Childcare Module, Quarterly National Household Survey Q4 2002)

- 22,800 families with pre-school children and
- 31,100 families with primary-school children

rely on an unpaid relative (i.e. not a parent) to care for their children.

Early years' care and education

The EU's Lisbon Agenda, agreed in 2002 and signed by the government, contains targets for pre-primary care and education. It is now government policy that by 2010 33% of children aged 0-3 and 90% of children aged 3-6 should be in non-parental care.

It follows, therefore, that it is government policy that 66% of children aged 0-3 and 10% children aged 3-6 should be cared for in parental care. The OECD has produced a report on Irish early years' care and education. The government has accepted the report. This report suggests, among its recommendations, that paid parental leave should be extended to one year and that supports should be put in place for parents who care and educate within the home.

Carers

According to the CSO (Table 31, Census 2002),

- 57,480 men and
- 91,274 women

over the age of 15 provide various levels of support and assistance to family or friends with a long-term illness, health problem or disability.

In WITH's anecdotal experience, most full-time carers are women. Yet according to the census figures, men make up fully one-third of full-time carers (13,501 out of 40,526). It is not impossible that women under-reported their contribution, especially where they are combining care with other activities.

Farm work

According to European Commission figures (Table: Spouse of Holder, p. 36 in Agriculture: The Spotlight on Women, 1997), Ireland counts some

- 51,000 female and
- 3,000 male

farm spouses, i.e. spouses who are involved in unremunerated farm work on a holding belonging to their spouse. Some of these would also be included in the figures for homemakers quoted above.

Voluntary work

The National Economic and Social Forum produced a report on voluntary work which stated that 10.5% of those who class themselves as being primarily involved with 'domestic duties' also volunteer in the community (*The Policy Implications of Social Capital*, NESF Report No. 28, May 2003, Table 5.1).

One key aspect of volunteering is the scheduling of voluntary services. Any voluntary or charitable activity which takes place between 9-5 generally relies on homemakers, since those in the workforce are generally unavailable between those times. This includes key voluntary activities such as meals on wheels and school support work. Many homemakers pick up, deliver and supervise children and teenagers before and after school. Many pensioners, especially those in rural areas, rely on friends, relatives and neighbours to bring them to the post office and to the shops.

The Joint Committee of the Oireachtas on Arts, Sport, Tourism, Community, Rural and Gaeltacht Affairs has published a report entitled *Volunteers and Volunteering in Ireland* which suggests that voluntary work saves the state up to over €485 million in wage costs to supply the same goods and services.

Although there is no parallel GDP account or regular CSO time-use survey to concretise the value of unremunerated work, it is clear that a large amount of work takes place and that women still do most of it.

ARTICLE 41.2: INTERPRETATION

There are differing interpretations of the thrust of Article 41.2.

Legal recognition and rights

The Constitution Review Group, in their May 1996 report, claimed that:

> Article 41.2 assigns to women a domestic role as wives and mothers.

Mrs Justice Susan Denham disagrees with such an interpretation. In her dissenting judgment on *Kathryn Sinnott v the Department of Education*, Ireland and the Attorney General (July 2001) she wrote:

> Article 41.2 does not assign women to a domestic role. Article 41.2 recognises the significant role played by wives and mothers in the home. This recognition and acknowledgement does not exclude women and mothers from other roles and activities. It is a recognition of the work performed by women in the home. The work is recognised because it has immense benefit for society. This recognition must be construed harmoniously with other articles of the Constitution when a combination of articles fall to be analysed. (p. 33)

Elsewhere, in *DT v CT*, Justice Murray considered that, although specifically referring to women, Article 41.2 could be construed as referring to men also:

It seems to me that [the Constitution] implicitly recognises similarly the value of a man's contribution in the home as a parent. (*DT v CT* [2002] 3 IR 334; [2003] 1 ILRM 321, cited in ¶7.6.94 of J.M. Kelly *The Irish Constitution*, [4th ed.], eds Gerard Hogan and Gerry Whyte, Butterworths (Irl.) Ltd.: 2003.)

Article 41.2 is cited to recognise a spouse's unremunerated contribution to the family in the courts. Murray, in the same judgment, refers to equality of treatment for homemakers:

> The Constitution views the family as indispensable to the welfare of the state. Article 41.2.1. recognises that by her life in the home the woman gives to the state a support without which the common good cannot be achieved. No doubt the exclusive reference to women in that provision reflects social thinking and conditions at the time. It does however expressly recognise that work in the home by a parent is indispensable to the welfare of the state by virtue of the fact that it promotes the welfare of the family as a fundamental unit in society. A [sic] *fortiori* it recognises that work in the home is indispensable for the welfare of the family, husband, wife and children, where there are children. In my view in ensuring that proper provision is made for the spouses of a marriage before a decree of divorce the courts should, in principle, attribute the same value to the contribution of a spouse who works primarily in the home as it does to that of a spouse who works primarily outside the home as the principal earner. (http://www.courts.ie/judgments.nsf/0/01e049f4461fe25480256cc300484411?OpenDocument)

In terms of the breakdown of marriage, Article 41.2 represents a significant instrument for the protection of those who have reduced their participation in the workforce in order to care for home and family.

Entitlements in the tax system

In the Irish tax system, the carer's credit is awarded in direct recognition of the contribution of the at-home spouse to the care of dependent family members.

Social welfare rights and entitlements

Article 41.2 forms part of the basis for

- maternity benefit
- child benefit
- adoptive benefit
- parental leave
- one parent family payment
- carer's allowance
- carer's benefit
- homemakers' scheme (pension disregard for homemakers)
- qualified adult allowance (pension payment for homemakers)

among other payments and income replacement entitlements.

Statistical recognition

Ireland collects census and other data on unremunerated work.

For example, the census (starting in 2002) includes a question on unpaid care. WITH made a submission in 2003 to include other types of unremunerated work in census 2006. The pilot survey in advance of census 2006 included two questions, one on voluntary and charitable work, and another on unpaid childcare and housework.

The census and the Quarterly National Household Survey Q3 report the number of people who undertake unremunerated work on a full-time basis. In Q4 2002, the QNHS included a special module on unremunerated childcare.

European Union perspectives on recognising unremunerated work

Reconciliation of professional, family and private lives: EU Parliament Resolution (2003/2129 INI) Bastos Report excerpt:

> J ... women must be able to choose whether to work, even if they have children, or whether they want to stay at home ...

(full text available on www.euparl.eu.int, website of the Parliament)

United Nations perspectives on recognising unremunerated work

Beijing Platform for Action (1995):

> Paragraph 29
> Women make a great contribution to the welfare of the family and to the development of society, which is still not recognized or considered in its full importance. The social significance of maternity, motherhood and the role of parents in the family and in the upbringing of children should be acknowledged.

> Paragraph 49
> Women contribute to the economy and to combating poverty through both remunerated and unremunerated work at home, in the community and in the workplace.

> Strategic Objective H3
> (e) improve data collection on the full contribution of women and men to the economy, including their participation in the informal sector(s);

> (g) (i) Conduct regular time-use studies to measure, in quantitative terms, unremunerated work, including recording those activities that are performed simultaneously with remunerated or other unremunerated activities;

> (ii) Measure, in quantitative terms, unremunerated work that is outside national accounts and work to improve methods to assess and accurately reflect its value in satellite or other official accounts that are separate from but consistent with core national accounts;

CEDAW protocol

Article 11: specifies the right to social insurance for women in case of retirement, illness, invalidity and old age.

Article 14: concerns the right of women to benefit directly from social insurance programmes.

RELIANCE ON CONSTITUTIONAL SUPPORTS

Although unremunerated workers clearly create value-added goods and services, they lack the protections of other workers and are therefore more reliant on constitutional recognition for their role. Protections other workers enjoy include:

- the structured access to income based on their work
- pension and social welfare contributions and entitlements
- the protection of employment legislation and the Equality Act
- inclusion of the value of their work in the GDP and other statistics.

If the protection afforded to unremunerated workers is weakened through this process, how will they be able to vindicate their rights? How will families access choice in the area of care?

CURRENT WORDING OF ARTICLE 41.2

41.2 1°

In particular, the state recognises that by her life within the home, woman gives to the state a support without which the common good cannot be achieved.

Go sonrach, admhaíonn an Stát go dtugann an bhean don Stát, trina saol sa teaghlach, cúnamh nach bhféadfaí leas an phobail a ghnóthú dá éagmais.

41.2 2°

The state shall, therefore, endeavour to ensure that mothers shall not be obliged by economic necessity to engage in labour to the neglect of their duties in the home.

Uime sin, féachfaidh an Stát lena chur in airithe nach mbeidh ar mháireacha clainne, de dheasca uireasa, dul le saothar agus faillí a thabhairt dá chionn sin ina ndualgais sa teaghlach.

CRG SUGGESTED CHANGES

The Constitution Review Group suggests the following alterations to article 41.2:

> The state recognises that home and family life gives to society a support without which the common good cannot be achieved. The state shall endeavour to support persons caring for others within the home.

This formulation is very general. How is a caring person to be defined and supported? Does it mean that a person looking after a neighbour's child has the same protection as a parent or grandparent?

It also ignores the substantial economic contribution of the parent and carer, whether on a full or part-time basis.

WITH notes that this formulation would not put the state under an obligation to support caring persons; the state would only have to 'endeavour' to support them. Also, any support would only extend as long as persons are actively caring: what is to happen when they are no longer physically able to continue as carers? and what protection have they in the case of marital or relationship breakdown?

The Constitution Review Group's suggested alterations would, in WITH's opinion, weaken the basis of existing supports for parents and carers in the tax, social welfare and legal systems. WITH therefore suggests an alternative formulation.

WITH PROPOSED WORDING

Any alteration to Article 41.2, in WITH's opinion, should not undermine current recognition of unremunerated work or the rights already accruing to those who carry out such work on a full or part-time basis.

WITH's aim is to achieve recognition for all unremunerated parents and carers. WITH therefore suggests the following changes:

> 41.2 1°
>
> In particular, the state recognises that those who care for dependants within the home give to the state a support without which the common good cannot be achieved.
>
> Go sonrach, admhaíonn an Stát go dtugann an té a dhéanann cúram do chleithiúnaithe sa teaghlach cúnamh nach bhféadfaí leas an phobail a ghnóthú dá éagmais.
>
> 41.2 2°
>
> The state shall, therefore, ensure that those who care for dependants within the home shall not be obliged by economic necessity to engage in labour to the neglect of those duties.
>
> Uime sin, cuirfidh an Stát in áirithe nach mbeidh ar an té a dhéanann cúram do chleithiúnaithe sa teaghlach, de dheasca uireasa, dul le saothar agus faillí a thabhairt dá chionn sin ina ndualgais sin.

Appendix 1

Paper read at the FEFAF AGM open meeting 'International Year of the Family + 10: Working for the Family', Dublin Castle, 21/10/2004

THE VALUE OF UNPAID WORK IN THE HOME

Professor Gabriel Kiely
University College Dublin

In this short paper I want to do two things. First I want to examine what we understand about unpaid work in the home and secondly what is the economic value of the work. I will do this by an analysis of the finding of the International Social Survey Programme (ISSP) and other recent research on work in the home and by using data from official statistical sources. The paper will show that unpaid work in the home is of economic value, and that it is primarily undertaken by women but remains hidden in our national official accounts. I will conclude by making some policy recommendations.

Before I begin I want to define what I mean by 'economic value'. All activities can be distinguished as either economic or non-economic. An economic act simply means an act that can be performed for pay by someone distinct from the person who consumes the end result. The act is or can be traded. For example, the preparation of a meal, or cleaning the house, can be performed by someone else on our behalf whether or not we pay for it. A non-economic act is one which cannot be traded, such as eating, sleeping, studying etc. It is clear from this distinction that most of what is termed 'housework' and much of the caring that is carried out within the home is tradable. We can hire a cleaner and pay a carer. Thus most of the work that is undertaken in the home is economic, i.e. economically productive. It has an economic value.

This unpaid economic activity is undertaken primarily by women. While research shows us that men have increased their share of this work, women continue to carry the major burden, even when they are in full-time paid employment. For example, a recent study by the European Foundation for the Improvement of Living and Working Conditions (2001) found that across Europe women in paid employment outside the home do significantly more housework and childcare than their male counterparts as illustrated in Table 1.

Table 1: Who does what at home?

% of respondents doing it for an hour or more per day	WOMEN	MEN
Caring for and educating children	41	24
Cooking	64	13
Housework	63	12

Source: *European Survey on Working Conditions 2000* European Foundation for the Improvement of Working and Living Conditions, 2001

The most recent survey data available show that even with the increased participation by men the burden for women has is fact increased. The ISSP data clearly show this. For example, when family respondents were asked who cares for sick family members, those who responded positively to always or usually caring for sick family members, rose from 55% in 1994 to 61.2% in 2002 as illustrated in Table 2.

Table 2: Care of sick family members

Who does care for sick members 1994	1994 Percentage			2002 Percentage		
	Male	Female	Total	Male	Female	Total
Always Woman/Me	31.5	37.5	34.7	1.3	39.0	22.9
Usually Woman/Me	17.6	17.5	17.5	4.5	22.2	14.7
Equal	49.8	44.1	46.7	42.6	33.3	37.3
Usually Man/Spouse	0.4	0.6	0.5	21.5	1.0	9.7
Always Man/Spouse	0.7	–	0.3	21.8	0.5	9.6
Cannot choose				6.7	3.6	4.9
Total Percentage	100	100	100	100	100	100
Total Count	267	315	582	312	418	730

In contrast the percentage of respondents who agreed that men and women share the care of sick family members equally actually declined between 1994 and 2002 (Rush, Kiely and Richardson, 2004).

Work in the home is usually divided into caring and housework, and studies generally show a different rate of participation by men in these two areas. However, the ISSP data show a similar pattern with housework as illustrated by Table 3. In this table I have selected one task only, i.e. doing the laundry as an example. Again we find that female respondents who answered positively to usually or always doing the laundry has risen, in this case from 87.7% in 1994 to 90.1% in 2002. Similar findings were evident across a range of household tasks including grocery shopping, preparing the dinner and cleaning (Rush, Kiely and Richardson 2004). I should also say that while these are the data for the Irish respondents, similar findings were found across Europe in the same ISSP study.

Table 3: Who does the laundry?

Who does the Laundry 1994	1994 Percentage			2002 Percentage		
	Male	Female	Total	Male	Female	Total
Always Woman/Me	64.3	67.9	66.3	3	67.5	38.8
Usually Woman/Me	23.4	19.8	21.5	3.8	22.6	14.6
Equal	11.5	11.9	11.8	12.1	8.6	10.1
Usually Man/partner	0.4		0.2	31.8	0.5	13.9
Always Man/partner	0.4		0.2	48.7	0.7	21.2
Done by 3rd Person	–	–	–	2.5	0.2	1.2
Cannot choose	–	–	–	0.6	–	0.3
Total	100	100	100	100	100	100
Total Count	269	318	587	314	421	735

Other studies also show that women continue to carry out most of this unpaid work in the home. This is illustrated by the findings of an Austrian study carried out in 2003 by IMAS on behalf of Electrolux as illustrated in Tables 4 and 5.

Table 4: Length of time spent at task

Task	Minutes		Hours	
	Men	Women	Men	Women
Tidying Up	38	49	1.8	4
Wash Clothes	35	45	.8	2.2
Ironing	55	71	08	2.4
Washing Up	31	38	2.5	4.3
Hoovering	26	27	.1	1.8
Cooking	53	64	2.2	6.1
Make Beds	9	11	.9	1.4

Source: IMAS/Electrolux, Austria, 2003

Table 5: Frequency of doing the tasks

Task	Women		Men	
	Weekly	Seldom	Weekly	Seldom
Tidying Up	96	4	69	31
Wash Clothes	86	14	35	65
Ironing	80	20	25	75
Washing Up	96	4	74	26
Hoovering	88	12	59	41
Cooking	92	8	51	49
Make Beds	97	3	55	45

Source: IMAS/Electrolux, Austria, 2003

Earlier studies show similar results such as the 1993 Eurobarometer study on Europeans and the family, and a study by the Family Studies Centre, UCD, published in 1994 (Kiely).

There are two points I want to emphasise here, both of which are quite obvious. The first is the extent to which women carry out these tasks within the home. The second is that contrary to popular belief, stability rather than change characterised the gender division of unpaid labour, with female respondents suggesting that their share of the unpaid labour is increasing rather than decreasing (Rush, Kiely and Richardson, 2004). This increase is due in large part to the demand being placed on family members to provide care for dependent relatives over a larger period of time, arising from the so-called 'community care' approach in public policy which really means care by women in the family. This of course raises an important policy question, i.e. how should the state support families in providing this service for the community at large. I will return to this question later.

Earlier I said that unpaid work in the home is an economic activity. However, when compared to paid work outside the home it is seen to be of low status and to a large extent of no monetary value. One approach to addressing this imbalance is to place a monetary value on it, just as is done for other forms of economic activity. Although there is no consensus in the economic community about the conceptual and methodological issues involved in the measurement and valuation of unpaid work in the home, a monetary value can be estimated. One approach is to calculate the value based on GDP. It is generally estimated that

the output of private households in terms of goods and services is equivalent to between 30% to 50% of GDP (Keppelhoff-Wiechett, 1993:9). Based on the GDP estimate for 2003 (latest figures available) of €135.2Bn (Budget 2004) the monetary value of the unpaid work is between €40.6Bn and €67.6Bn, or if we use the GNP estimate of €109.8 it works out at between €33Bn and €55Bn.

According to a study carried out by Ark Life, the value of Irish women's work in the home is equivalent to an annual salary of €49,700. This rather high figure is based on 142 hours per week over 50 weeks and pay the minimum wage of €7.00 per hour. The 142 hours is based on the number of hours worked in the home by women working full-time in the home given by the women who participated in the study. However, the women themselves estimated the value of their work at €17,800.

A more realistic approach would be to base the calculation on average female industrial wage and estimates of hours worked derived from international studies. It is generally estimated that women who work full-time in the home spend 45 hours per week doing this work. In 2002 the average female industrial wage was €10.06 per hour. Based on these figures we can estimate that the value of this unpaid work was €23,540.40 per woman per annum. If this were included in the annual GDP figures, it would add a further €9.8Bn i.e. €23,540.40 multiplied by the number of women working full-time in the home, which in 2002 was 417,633 (census 2002). This is an unrecognised contribution to a GDP, which is invisible and unrecorded. You will not find it recorded in any official statistics. From an official perspective it seems that the production of these goods and services in the home do not exist. In addition these workers are not covered by employment legislation or entitled to the benefits their counterparts in paid employment receive.

Ten years ago I calculated the monetary value of work done by women in the home which also included women with children who were active in the paid labour market (Kiely, 1995). At that time I was simply attempting to cost, rather crudely, the value of women's work in the home as a percentage of the GDP. My interest here is more on women who are working full-time in the home and not attached to the paid labour market.

I am not including men because this is primarily an issue that affects women and especially mothers. According to the latest data available, only 4,500 men compared to 551,900 women reported their principal economic status as 'home duties' (Quarterly National Household Budget Survey, 7/9/04). As we can see many women are choosing to work at home full-time. This is about making life choices between full-time work at home and paid employment.

Catherine Hakin (2000) in her analysis of women's work-lifestyle balance preference says that in any society about 20% of women (varies from 10% to 30%) will choose to stay, as she describes it, as 'home-centred'. These women see family life and children as their main priority, and are not responsive to employment policy. This does not mean that those women who try to balance work and family life are any less concerned about family. It simply means that they are making different life choices. She goes on to say that, 'Policy research and future predictions of women's choices will be more successful in future if they adapt the preference theory perspective and first establish the distribution of preferences between family work and employment in each society.'

It is now clear that policies aimed at enabling mothers to remain attached to the paid work force or to return after a period of absence, no matter how generous they are, will not attract a substantial number of these women back into the paid work force. A Eurobarometer (1991) study found that 66% of Irish women who did not return to the paid work force after a long period of interruption stated that they did not do so for family reasons, such as bringing up children or caring for an adult family member. This was only slightly higher than the European average which was 64%.

I would now like to address some policy issues. Caregiving extends across the life cycle of the family from care of children to care of dependent older people. Measures to support families should reflect this. For example, income foregone to care for a child is no different to income foregone to care for an adult dependent member of the family. At present there are schemes in place to help some families with young children and schemes to help some families with the care of dependent adults. From a family policy perspective these schemes should be integrated in terms of their social value.

Also there should be no preference between measures to support those who are full-time in the home and those who combine work in the home with employment. However, in the current climate where there is great pressure on mothers of young children to participate in the paid labour market, measures to help them to combine employment and work in the home may have a broader appeal. The measures should not be solely employment based. Women in the home constitute a unique perspective on family policy. They care for the young, for the old, for other family members and for non-family members. This provides a unique overview of the different elements of what is family policy. What women in the home provide us with is a clear rationale of why family policies, that is, care of the young, care of older people, care of adults for adults, should not be subordinated to labour market policy. The point being made here is that we need policies for both constituencies of care which recognise the different life choices being made by parents and families.

The Commission on the family in its final report *Strengthening Families for Life* (1998) did try to address some of the policy issues. In chapter five the report sets out the various options in supporting families with children but did not reach agreement on what options to recommend. The lack of agreement points up the complexity of the issues involved. The Commission was established in 1995 as one initiative arising from the Year of the Family in 1994. It is now ten years on and time to revisit these issues.

The OECD in a report published in 1991 identified two approaches to caregiving within families, i.e. the maximum private responsibility model and the maximum public responsibility model. In the first model, the problem of family life and labour force participation are entirely left up to the individual to solve as a purely private concern. The second model defines the problem as an important state concern. States across the European Union differ with regard to which model they follow. The northern European countries tend towards the second model, while Ireland, the UK and the Mediterranean rim countries tend towards the first. Given the declining birth rates to below replacement level in all member states including the ten new member states (Eurostat, 2004), combined with the rise in old age dependency ratios, the question has to be asked, 'can we afford the maximum private responsibility model any longer?'

References

Commission on the Family (1998) *Strengthening Families for the Future*, Stationery Office, Dublin.

Central Statistics Office (2004) *Quarterly National Household Budget Survey, March – May 2004*, Stationery Office, Dublin.

Central Statistics Office (2004) *Census 2002*, Stationery Office, Dublin.

Eurobarometer (1991) *Family and Employment Within the 12*, European Commission, Luxembourg.

Eurobarometer (1993) *Europeans and the Family*, European Commission, Luxembourg.

European Foundation for the Improvement of Living and Working Conditions (2001), *Ten Years of Working Conditions in the European Union*, European Commission, Luxembourg.

Eurostat (2004) *The Social Situation in the European Union 2004*, European Commission, Luxembourg.

Hakim, C. (2000) *Work-Lifestyle Choices in the 21st Century*, Oxford University Press, Oxford.

IMAS/Electrolux (2003) *Umfrage Hausarbeiten*, Austria, (unpublished).

Keppelhoff-Wiechett, H. (1993) *Report of the Committee on Women's Rights on the Assessment of Women's Unwaged Work*, European Parliament Session Document.

Kiely, G. (1994) 'Fathers in Families' in I. Colgan-McCarthy ed. *Irish Family Studies: Selected Papers*. Family Studies Centre, Dublin

Kiely, G. (1995) 'Paid and Unpaid Work in Families: Ireland' in T. Willemsen et al eds. *Work and Family in Europe: The Role of Policies*, Tilbury University Press, Tilburg.

Kiely, G. (1998) 'Caregiving Within Families', in K. Matthijs ed. *The Family: Contemporary Perspectives and Challenges*. Leuven University Press, Leuven.

Rush, M., Kiely, G. and Richardson, V. (2004) *Family Policy and Unpaid Reproductive Work*, Department of Social Policy and Social Work, University College Dublin, (unpublished).

Appendix 2

WITH Submission to the CSO (2003)
Questionnaire content for the 2006 Census of Population and on outputs

Proposal: Inclusion of question on unremunerated work

Proposed changes

Question 36 (currently: How many hours in total did you work last week?) Change to read:

Last week, how many hours did you spend:

in paid employment _ _
in unpaid care and/or supervision* of children (your own and/or others) _ _ _
in unpaid care and/or supervision* of an elderly and/or disabled person _ _ _
in unpaid farm work _ _ _
in unpaid housework _ _
in volunteer work for the benefit of the community _ _
*care and/or supervision, meaning that someone else would have to look after the person/s if you were unavailable

Other changes required: **Q19:** if you are under 15, skip to Q36 (currently skip to Q37); **Q23:** can be eliminated if new wording on care is inserted into Q36.

Rationale

The social economy has supported the market economy in ways which are not fully understood and therefore cannot be taken properly into account by research bodies and, ultimately, public policy. The social economy consists of activities which are undertaken not for profit but often support, directly or indirectly, the market economy. These activities include: unpaid caring work, including unpaid childcare, eldercare, and the care of people with disabilities; unpaid farming work; and unpaid voluntary work, including unpaid work for charities.

If, for example, an at-home carer takes up paid employment, that care must be replaced. Such a change has implications for the person being cared for as well as for the state. The implications for the state can include the provision of a bed in an institution, insurance costs, staffing costs etc. If the state is to plan the replacement of those active in the social economy, then the state needs to know how much work is going to need to be replaced. If, on the other hand, the state chooses to support care in the social economy, the state will need to have clear information on what activities it would like to support.

A recent CSO study on childcare pointed up the necessity to consider the social economy in terms of forward planning and the implications of policies, such as that of the Lisbon agenda, for full employment. Nearly 31,000 families with school-going children used unpaid relatives for their childcare services. If those unpaid relatives are instead to take up full-time paid employment, the government will have to consider the provision of alternative arrangements for those 31,000 families. It is essential for the government to recognise the implications of such a move well in advance.

There is a lack of information on other types of caring as well as on farming and voluntary work. The census collects data on the numbers of people involved in 'home duties' on a full-time basis, but there is little hard data on what these 417,633 people actually do. Also, it is necessary to collect data on those who are active in the social economy on a part-time basis. They may well carry out essential support services which would otherwise have to be replaced.

EUROSTAT has set up a task force to formulate proposals towards the development of a harmonised methodology for the establishment of satellite accounts for households and to account for the economic value of family-based work. This is in recognition of the importance of the social economy. The CSO has the opportunity to be a leader in this area by including a relatively simple question which would provide a clear basis for satellite accounts.

Appendix 3

FEFAF (EU umbrella body of WITH) Statement submitted for the Commission for the Status of Women's Beijing +10 Review in March 2005.

Beijing + 10

Subject: Strategic Objective H3:

Generate and disseminate gender-disaggregated data and information for planning and evaluation

FEFAF – Fédération Européenne des Femmes au Foyer – the EU umbrella NGO of national and regional associations representing at-home parents and carers, calls on national governments and the United Nations, respectively, to implement Strategic Objective H3 of the Beijing agreement in national, regional and international statistical services and relevant governmental and United Nations agencies.

The unremunerated work carried out within the family – education, supervision and care of children and elderly and/or disabled relatives – still mainly undertaken by women, has an economic value and is therefore essential to society and economy. This work must be undertaken as a matter of free choice; and neither those who undertake such work nor their families should be penalised in any way. Furthermore, such work should be facilitated so that women – and men – can freely choose their preferred life path.

There can be no clear planning or cost-benefit analysis for the care of children, elderly and disabled without *reliable data* on *all types* of care: community-based care, institutional care *AND* unremunerated family-based work carried out within the family.

Where the contribution of unremunerated work is recognised, structured methods for rewarding such work – such as personal social welfare rights awarded equally to all those who provide the same service without or with remuneration – can be developed.

Therefore FEFAF requests the implementation of § 11 and 14 from CEDAW and 165g, 206 (f, g, o, p) and 209 from PFA Beijing,

- particularly collecting data on:
  - the economic value of unremunerated family-based work for the benefit of dependants
  - the impact of national and community policies on the basic unit of the family and all its members, notably in the domain of the elimination of discrimination, the struggle against domestic violence, the risk of poverty of female heads of households, pensions policies for unremunerated parents and carers.

- Methods of data collection on unremunerated work should be internationalised and include:
  - headings in the census and all relevant statistics for unremunerated work and workers, unremunerated agricultural and food production; unremunerated childcare, eldercare and care of the disabled; unremunerated community and NGO support work
  - parallel GDP accounts for unremunerated agricultural, family caring and voluntary work
  - gender- and age-disaggregated information on unremunerated workers.

Bruxelles, le 6 décembre 2004

WOMEN IN MEDIA & ENTERTAINMENT

ARTICLE 41.1.I

Amend to read as follows:

> The state recognises the family as the primary and fundamental unit of society, understanding the word 'family' to denote a group of people who define themselves as a family, irrespective of gender or marital status, and who are as a unit committed to one another emotionally and/or financially and who respect and support one another.

ARTICLE 41.2.I

Amend to read as follows (incorporating an amended version of Article 25 of the Universal Declaration of Human Rights):

> The state recognises that home and family life give society a support without which the common good cannot be achieved, and recognises work done within the home as productive work which is to be measured and valued as part of the Gross Domestic Product. Every family has the right to a standard of living adequate for the health and well-being of its members, including food, clothing, housing, and medical care and necessary social services, and the right to security in the event of unemployment, sickness, disability, widowhood, old age, or other lack of livelihood in circumstances beyond their control. Motherhood and childhood are entitled to special care and assistance. All children, whether born in or out of wedlock, shall enjoy the same social protection.

ARTICLE 41.2.II

Amend to read as follows:

> The state shall therefore ensure that mothers, and others, who carry out caring work in the home be financially remunerated at the rate of the average industrial wage, and are entitled to independent pensions in recognition of such work.

ARTICLE 45.2.I

Amend to read as follows:

> That the citizens (all of whom, men and women equally, have the right to an adequate means of livelihood with pay equity between men and women) may through their occupations find the means of making reasonable provision for their domestic needs.

'Occupations' shall include the hitherto unwaged caring work of mothers, and others, in the home.

The Constitution should adopt all the provisions of the UN Convention on the Rights of the Child.

If the phrase 'natural mother' is employed in the Constitution, it should be amended to read 'birth mother'.

Gay marriage should receives constitutional recognition with same rights as heterosexual marriage.

THE WOMEN'S HEALTH COUNCIL

The Women's Health Council is a statutory body established in 1997 to advise the Minister for Health and Children on all aspects of women's health. Following a recommendation in the Report of the Second

Commission on the Status of Women (1993), the national *Plan for Women's Health 1997-1999* was published in 1997. One of the recommendations in the Plan was that a Women's Health Council be set up as 'a centre of expertise on women's health issues, to foster research into women's health, evaluate the success of this Plan in improving women's health and advise the Minister for Health on women's issues generally'.

The mission of the Women's Health Council is to inform and influence the development of health policy to ensure the maximum health and social gain for women in Ireland. Its membership is representative of a wide range of expertise and interest in women's health.

The Women's Health Council has five functions detailed in its statutory instruments:

1 Advising the Minister for Health and Children on all aspects of women's health

2 Assisting the development of national and regional policies and strategies designed to increase health gain and social gain for women

3 Developing expertise on women's health within the health services

4 Liaising with other relevant international bodies which have similar functions as the Council

5 Advising other government ministers at their request.

The work of the Women's Health Council is guided by three principles:

• *Equity* based on diversity – the need to develop flexible and accessible services which respond equitably to the diverse needs and situations of women

• *Quality* in the provision and delivery of health services to all women throughout their lives

• *Relevance* to women's health needs.

In carrying out its statutory functions, the Women's Health Council has adopted the WHO definition of health, a measure reiterated in the Department of Health's 'Quality and Fairness' document (2001). This definition states that

> Health is a state of complete physical, mental and social well being.

EXECUTIVE SUMMARY

The Women's Health Council submits its views only on matters which it considers to be within its competency. It approaches all issues from the standpoint of its mission and values, and considers all matters with a view to ensuring the maximum health and social gain for women.

In recent European surveys, good family relations were found to be a key demand for good quality of life (Krieger, 2004). Irish participants in public consultations were also in unanimous agreement on the importance of the family in Irish society and on the vital role and function the state plays in meeting the needs of families (Daly, 2004). Therefore, it is crucial that state recognition of the reality of contemporary family life in Ireland goes beyond theory and moves into the realm of practice at all levels, from policy formation to service delivery. However, as argued in this submission, none of these changes can be fully achieved and implemented without the endorsement of the fundamental law of the land: the Constitution. Thus, the Women's Health Council calls on the All-Party Oireachtas Committee on the Constitution to propose amendments which will provide an updated, and less discriminatory legislative framework for Irish families. A revised framework, which truly recognises the diversity of family life in Ireland and removes the discriminatory principles behind current legal and social provisions, would benefit all families, and aid them in giving the state 'a support without which the common good cannot be achieved'. A revised framework would hence ultimately benefit the whole of Irish society.

The Women's Health Council believes that amendments in relation to the articles on the position of women in society, and on the family, are necessary, and proposes the following:

1 The Family must be defined in terms of what it does rather than on how it is constituted. Moreover, constitutional provisions must reflect the reality of family life in contemporary Ireland. This revised framework will enable the government to reduce the direct and indirect discrimination experienced by non-marriage based families.

Article 41.3.1 should be deleted or amended in such a way as to guarantee respect of their family life, whether based on marriage or not, to all individuals and the right for all persons to marry within the requirements of law and to found a family.

2 Legislation should be introduced to impose certain legal rights and duties on cohabitees, including same-sex couples.

3. Article 41.2.1 and 41.2.2 should be deleted and replaced by the following: 'The state recognises that family life gives to society a support without which the common good cannot be achieved. The state endeavours to support caring for others within the home'.

The revised policy framework that would stem from such a constitutional provision would enable both women and men to embrace more fully their many social roles as carers and workers.

4. There should be recognition of children as separate entities with rights distinct from those of their families, and children's constitutional rights should be expanded accordingly.

RECOMMENDATIONS

The Women's Health Council therefore wishes to recommend the following constitutional amendments:

Amendments to Article 41 The Family

The deletion of Article 41.2.1 and 41.2.2 to be replaced by the following:

> The state recognises that family life gives to society a support without which the common good cannot be achieved. The state endeavours to support caring for others within the home.

This amendment has also been suggested and supported by the All-Party Oireachtas Committee on the Constitution in 1997, and by the Second Commission on the Status of Women in 1993 (Government of Ireland, 1997, 1999).

The deletion of Article 41.3.1 to be replaced by

a) an amended article which guarantees respect of their family life, whether based on marriage or not, to all individuals and the right for all persons to marry within the requirements of law and found a family or

b) its replacement by an amended article which guarantees respect of their family life, whether based on marriage or not, to all individuals and the right for all persons to enter into civil partnerships within the requirements of law and found a family.

The Constitution Review Group also made some of these recommendations (Government of Ireland, 1996), as did the National Economic and Social Forum (2003), and the Equality Authority (Mee and Ronayne, 2000).

Articles 41 and 42

Adjectives similar to *inalienable* or *imprescriptible* should be deleted from the description of rights or duties cited in Articles 41 and 42.

Legislation

The introduction of legislation to impose certain legal rights and duties on cohabitees, including same-sex couples. These provisions have also been recommended by the Law Reform Commission (2004).

Rights of the Child

The Constitution should be amended to expand children's constitutional protection. These amendments would be in accordance with the European Convention on Human Rights (ECHR), which came into force in Ireland on 31 December 2003, and the UN Convention on the rights of the child, ratified in 1992. Family law experts have highlighted the fact that more than in any other area of law, the development of conflict is now likely between the Irish domestic concept of the family and concepts set down in the European Court of Human Rights (One Family, 2004).[1]

INTRODUCTION

In relation to family rights, the Irish Constitution may be viewed as a document of its time. It is clear even from a cursory reading of the Constitution that, in relation to the family, this is a document of its time. It reflects strongly held and widely accepted views on the role of women and men in society in post-independence Ireland (Kennedy, 2001; Scannell, 2001). It is generally agreed that these views were greatly influenced by Catholic teaching and morality (Government of Ireland, 1996; O'Connor, 1998; Byrne and McCutcheon, 2003). However, they are no longer commonplace, and social practice is now broadly divergent from that envisaged in the Constitution, as clearly evidenced by current statistics on marital status, living arrangements and women working outside the home (Central Statistics Office, 2003b, 2004a). Constitutional change, one might argue, is unnecessary in order to reflect the changing values and mores of a society. This can be done through the legislative functions of the Oireachtas, the judiciary, and the policy-making and regulating work of the relevant State Departments.

The Women's Health Council wishes to argue against this approach and demonstrate that constitutional amendments in relation to the Articles on the position of women in society and on the family are indeed required. The Constitution 'provides the foundations for social citizenship in Ireland' (Daly and Clavero, 2002: 180), and, as Connelly emphatically stated:

> is the fundamental law of the land. Not only is it meant to give expression to society's fundamental values but the making, interpretation, and application of the ordinary law takes place within the set framework of these constitutionally endorsed values. Legislation will be interpreted in so far as possible to comply with these values, and, in the case of unavoidable conflict, will be held by the courts to be invalid for failure to comply with the provisions of the Constitution.
>
> (1999: 25)

While legal experts have sustained that constitutional change is unwarranted due to the courts' capacity to interpret the Constitution in an historically-sensitive manner (Byrne and McCutcheon, 2003), the state, and especially the Supreme Court, have so far refused to read the Constitution in such a way in relation to the articles on the family, and continue to understand its provisions in a literal fashion (Casey, 2000; Ryan, 2002).

These provisions, which adopt a biologically deterministic approach to women's and men's roles, and proclaim marriage as the only valid path to family formation, have had significant negative repercussions not only for women and children, but also more surprisingly for men. These will be detailed further in the following pages, but, briefly, the strong male breadwinner model (Lewis, 1992 in Daly and Rake, 2003) on which the Constitution is based is underpinned by a gendered model of care. The belief that caring abilities and responsibilities should be the responsibility of women has had a detrimental effect on the emotional well-being of both women and men, in their role as parents (O'Connor, 1998; Ferguson and Hogan, 2004), and also has been found to especially affect the physical and mental well-being of mothers (Wiley and

Merriman, 1996; Holmshaw and Hillier, 2000; Strazdins and Broom, 2004).

Moreover, the official endorsement and promotion of one type of family has created a discriminatory policy framework which has given rise to numerous inequitable circumstances: the higher risk of poverty in lone parent families (Combat Poverty Agency, 2002), the lesser legal and financial safeguards for cohabitees and their children (Ryan, 2002), and the lack of recognition of same-sex couples and their children (Mee and Ronayne, 2000; NESF, 2003) to name but a few. Constitutional amendments to reflect the changed and changing nature of Irish society, first recommended by the Constitution Review Group in 1996, are now long overdue.

HOW SHOULD THE FAMILY BE DEFINED?

Historically and cross-culturally, family life has never remained constant. Kennedy contends that in Ireland it was not until the post-war economic boom that marriage became both possible and popular on a scale comparable to other European countries (2001). Hence, this 'traditional' form of family formation actually only started to dominate Irish society a few decades ago.

However, 'any discussion of contemporary family life must begin from the lived experience of actually existing families, whose hallmark is variety and change' (Carling, 2002: 3). Participants at recent public consultations on the family organised by the Department of Social and Family Affairs echoed this statement, claiming that: 'diversity ... is the reality of contemporary Irish society and it would be remiss of policy makers not to take account of it' (Daly, 2004: 25). Recent statistics clearly indicate a changed family landscape: divorced persons have trebled, from 9,800 to 35,100 between 1996 and 2002, the number of separated (including divorced) persons increased from 87,800 in 1996 to 133,800 in 2002. Cohabiting couples accounted for 8.4 per cent of all family units in 2002 compared to 3.9 per cent in 1996. The number of children living with cohabiting parents increased from 23,000 in 1996 to 51,700 in 2002 (Central Statistics Office, 2004a). There has also been a 20 per cent increase in the number of lone parent households with children in the state, from 125,500 in 1996 to 150,600 in 2002 (Central Statistics Office, 2003a). These are predominantly and increasingly headed by a woman (91%) (Central Statistics Office, 2004b). Growing acceptance and recognition of assisted human reproduction procedures, which may necessitate the use of gamete donation, have been further highlighting the distinction between biological vs. social parenthood, and introducing new family types. Anecdotal evidence also points to the rising number of same-sex couples who are parents through divorce or separation, adoption and artificial human reproduction procedures.[2] Finally, the growing multicultural nature of Irish society (NCCRI, 2002; Immigrant Council of Ireland, 2003), also calls for a more inclusive approach to family forms.

The definition of family implied in our Constitution as that based on marriage no longer reflects the reality of Irish society. However, once one rejects this narrow approach, finding a working framework for the definition of family can be quite complicated. In this regard, Lynch's proposal to look at what the family does, i.e. caring for and supporting activities of family/personal life, especially the caring of children and other dependent persons, rather than what it is, proves critical (1996). Lynch reasons that 'the notion of protecting the institution of the family *qua* institution without regard for its substantive work seems to signify a very narrow and limited approach' (Ibid.: 628). On the contrary, one must look at the purpose of family life in order to legislate and formulate policies which will protect and support it. Again, this view was also representative of general public opinion. Participants at recent public consultations expressed their desire for official policy to see the family 'in terms of what it does – caring – and the kinds of relationships and values that comprise it rather than seeing the family in terms of structure or a group of people who are defined by a legal relationship' (Daly, 2004: 27). So, if one agrees that the main purpose of family life is to care for close personal relationships and especially children, then the state must encompass all family forms that carry out this task without discriminating on the basis of how they were constituted.

Nevertheless, the current situation is far from that described above. Daly (2004) refers to a 'hierarchy among different kinds of families', with planning focused around the core constitutionally endorsed family which is in all intents and purposes privileged by official policy. This hierarchy discriminates against non-marriage based families in both tangible and not so tangible ways. Real discrimination occurs in terms of taxation, legal recognition and social policy measures (Ryan, 2002), despite the fact that the state is perfectly capable of recognising non-marital 'family units' for the purpose of denying social welfare entitlements (Casey, 2000), showing an approach which is not based on principle but on convenience. Furthermore, lack of legal recognition, as in the case of the absence of 'next-of-kin' status in relation to medical procedures for cohabiting partners and non-biological parents, can result in harmful and even fatal delays.

Discrimination also affects members of non-marriage based families on an emotional and psychological level. As previously seen, lone mothers have been found to be at greater risk of experiencing mental health problems. Children also suffer from this familial hierarchy. Hayes argues that 'children are more than able to evaluate whether their family is "different" from the model promoted by public consent, and translate this covert discrimination into a negative perception of their family and themselves' (2002: 11). Hence, it is paramount that difference in family forms is not perceived and understood as a deficit.

In fact, international studies comparing parenting outcomes for families formed in different ways have found that it is the quality of parenting rather than how the family came into being that most influenced child development (Golombok, 2000). Similar findings were also reported in Ireland by McKeown *et al* (2003) who claimed that once socio-economic environment, personality characteristics and family processes are controlled, the particular type of family in which one is raised has little or no impact on well being.

Legal and social provisions must be updated in order to end this official discrimination of different families. Moreover, any new provisions must acknowledge and reflect the fundamental role that family life plays in Irish society regardless of marital status, so that they may adequately cater for the needs of all Irish families within a contemporary updated context. The diversity of family forms will make it more difficult to define 'the family', and will require constitutional change and more thoughtful social policies, but in the end will be more beneficial to the well being of families and all their members (Hayes, 2002).

HOW SHOULD ONE STRIKE THE BALANCE BETWEEN THE RIGHTS OF THE FAMILY AS A UNIT AND THE RIGHTS OF INDIVIDUAL MEMBERS?

The Council believes that the main purpose of family life is to care for close personal relationships especially children. When the family unit cannot, for whatever reason, fulfil these functions the protection of the human and social rights of the individual family members, and especially of children, must take precedence over the maintenance of the *status quo*.

IS IT POSSIBLE TO GIVE CONSTITUTIONAL PROTECTION TO FAMILIES OTHER THAN THOSE BASED ON MARRIAGE?

An amended Constitution would not preclude the state from offering constitutional protection to family forms other than that based on marriage. As previously stated, the European Convention on Human Rights (ECHR) came into force in Ireland on 31 December 2003. Article 8 of the Convention provides that everyone has a right to respect for private and family life. In compliance with the ECHR, the European Court of Human Rights stated that the notion of the 'family' is not confined solely to marriage-based relationships and may encompass other *de facto* 'family' ties where the parties are living together outside of marriage, and related the existence of 'family life' to the *real existence in practice of close personal ties* (Government of Ireland, 1996: 322).

Moreover, Article 12 in the ECHR states that men and women of marriageable age have the right to marry and to found a family, according to the national laws governing the exercise of this right. This has been construed by the Court as permitting a state to treat families based on marriage more favourably than ones not so based, provided treatment for the latter does not conflict with those individuals' rights to family life under Article 8 of the Convention, quoted above.

The Women's Health Council calls for Article 41.3.1 to be amended to ensure guarantees and respect of family life, whether based on marriage or not, to all individuals and the right for all persons to marry (or form officially recognised civil partnerships) within the requirements of law and to found a family.

Finally, the introduction of formal legislation in relation to cohabitation is also recommended, and the Council welcomes the Law Reform Commission's proposals for legal provision of maintenance, property and rights under succession laws on 'qualified cohabitees' (2004). These would be people who, although not married to one another, have lived together in a 'marriage-like' relationship for a continuous period of three years, or two years if there is a child of the relationship (Ibid.:1). The inclusion of same-sex couples in the definition of cohabitees within the Law Reform Commission suggestions is welcome.

SHOULD GAY COUPLES BE ALLOWED TO MARRY?

Lesbian women and gay men have been found to suffer from discrimination and prejudice resulting in disadvantage and exclusion from full participation in society (Gay and Lesbian Equality Network and Nexus Research Co-operative, 1995). They also experience poorer mental health because of the chronic stress associated with being a member of a stigmatised minority group (Meyer, 2003). This situation has been recently further exacerbated by the Irish government. Through the introduction of the Social Welfare (Miscellaneous) Bill 2004, which restricts the definition of 'spouse' or 'couple' to a married couple and to an opposite sex cohabiting couple for state welfare schemes, Ireland is now in breach of Article 14 (obligation not to discriminate) and Article 8 (right to respect for private and family life) of ECHR, and is the only EU country to have introduced deliberately discriminatory legislation against lesbians and gays for over a decade (Equality Coalition, 2004). Hence, legislative amendments are urgently needed to reverse this situation and to promote and support their full participation in all aspects of society, including legally recognised relationships and families.

Being able to marry would reduce the inequity currently experienced by gay couples and go some way towards eliminating discrimination on the basis of sexual orientation in the realm of family formation. While not as satisfactory a solution as the legal provision for gay marriages, the introduction of civil partnerships for same-sex couples would be a positive stepping-stone towards equality. The case for the establishment of civil partnerships for same-sex couples has already been comprehensively argued by two government agencies: the National Economic and Social Forum (NESF, 2003), and the Equality Authority (Mee and Ronayne, 2000).

IS THE CONSTITUTION'S REFERENCE TO WOMAN'S 'LIFE IN THE HOME' A DATED ONE THAT SHOULD BE CHANGED?

The domestic role envisaged for women in the Constitution has been described as dated (Government of Ireland, 1997), patriarchal, or at least, paternalistic (O'Connor, 1998), and offensive (Connelly, 1999). De Valera had defended these constitutional provisions on the basis of their protective aim (Kennedy, 2001). However, his intentions did not ever translate into practice in relation to tax or social policy purposes (O'Connor, 1998; Kennedy, 2001), rendering them of no real assistance to women working in the home.

Furthermore, the constitutional vision of clearly defined and confined gender roles was based on a biologically deterministic understanding of women and men. This vision was never fully accurate, but social and economic changes in the last decades have now further curtailed its relevance to Irish society. Women are increasingly joining the labour market (Daly and Clavero, 2002; Central Statistics Office, 2003b), due to a desire for economic independence and personal fulfilment outside the home, and also driven by the rising cost of living in the Republic. On the other hand, men are starting to desire greater involvement in the parenting of their children as well as demanding greater recognition for their social identity as fathers (Ferguson and Hogan, 2004).

The constitutionally envisaged 'model family' based on the male breadwinner model, therefore, is now hindering the ability of both women and men to embrace fully their many social roles. The expectation that women will remain in the home to care for their family on a full-time basis has created a chronic under-provision of childcare services. During a national public consultation, the reconciliation of work and family life was an issue more for women than for men, and women felt that they are being forced to make difficult choices between earning money and caring for their families (Daly, 2004). The constant struggle to balance their role as mothers and workers has been found to cause women high levels of emotional and psychological distress (Holmshaw and Hillier, 2000; Lasswell, 2002; Shrier, 2002).

This situation is further aggravated in the case of lone mothers. Lack of economic resources and the absence of a co-parent to share even a part of the workload results in particularly stressful lives for single mothers (Lasswell, 2002). In addition, the prohibitive cost of childcare and the dearth of educational and training programmes which cater for the needs of lone mothers are further barriers to their ability to access the labour market (Women's Health Council, 2003), locking them into a 'poverty trap' from which it is very hard to escape.

On the other hand, men, and especially fathers, have also suffered at the hands of prescriptive family policy practices based on gender stereotypes. The definition of women as carers has underpinned the marginalisation of men as emotionally significant in their children's lives (O'Connor, 1998), as well as their discrimination in relation to social welfare entitlements as carers (Kennedy, 2001). This marginalisation has recently been found to be even more significant in the case of vulnerable fathers, including unmarried and separated fathers (Ferguson and Hogan, 2004).

The replacement of Article 41.2.1 with a more encompassing outlook, which focuses on the caring role of family, without any gender assumptions, would prove beneficial to both women and men, and, ultimately, also to their children.

SHOULD THE RIGHTS OF THE NATURAL MOTHER HAVE EXPRESS CONSTITUTIONAL PROTECTION? WHAT RIGHTS SHOULD A NATURAL FATHER HAVE, AND HOW SHOULD THEY BE PROTECTED?

The common understanding of the definition of the terms 'natural mother'/'natural father' could exclude adoptive parents and, as mentioned earlier, the growing use of assisted human reproduction procedures, in which biological and social parenthood may be dissociated, further complicates any clear-cut analysis of the rights of any 'natural' parent.

SHOULD THE RIGHTS OF THE CHILD BE GIVEN AN EXPANDED CONSTITUTIONAL PROTECTION? DOES THE CONSTITUTION NEED TO BE CHANGED IN VIEW OF THE UN CONVENTION ON THE RIGHTS OF THE CHILD?

Historically children's rights have been taken into account and assessed within the familial framework set out in the Constitution. However, the Child Care Act, 1991, the ratification of the UN Convention on the Rights of the Child in 1992, and the launch of the National Children's Strategy in 2000 heralded a shift away from a family-based approach and the recognition of the child as a separate entity with rights distinct from his/her family (Office of the United Nations High Commission for Human Rights, 1996). In light of these recent developments, references to the 'inalienable' rights of parents should be deleted from Article 42.1.

Moreover, the rights of children as separate social entities should be more strongly affirmed in the Constitution. Furthermore, any amendments in this area should be formulated in such a way as to encompass all children resident in Ireland, irrespective of the child's ethnic origin, in accordance with Article 2 of the UN Convention, and regardless of whether they are Irish citizens or not.

CONCLUSION

In recent European surveys, good family relations were found to be a key demand for good quality of life (Krieger, 2004). Irish participants in public consultations were also in unanimous agreement on the importance of the family in Irish society and on the vital role and function the state plays in meeting the needs of families (Daly, 2004). Therefore, it is crucial that state recognition of the reality of contemporary family life in Ireland goes beyond theory and moves into the realm of practice at all levels, from policy formation to service delivery. However, as initially argued, none of these changes can be fully achieved and implemented without the endorsement of the fundamental law of the land: the Constitution. Thus, the Women's Health Council calls on the All-Party Oireachtas Committee on the Constitution to propose amendments which will provide an updated and less discriminatory legislative framework for Irish families. A revised framework, which truly recognises the diversity of family life in Ireland and removes the discriminatory principles behind current legal and social provisions, would benefit all families, and aid them in giving the state 'a support without which the common good cannot be achieved'. A revised framework would hence ultimately benefit the whole of Irish society.

References

Byrne, R. and McCutcheon, J. P. (2003). *The Irish Legal System*. 4th Edition. Dublin: Butterworths.

Carling, A. (2002). 'Family Policy, Social Policy and the State' in *Analysing Families: morality and rationality in policy and practice*. (Ed, Edwards, R.). London: Routledge.

Casey, J. (2000). *Constitutional Law in Ireland*. 3rd Edition. Dublin: Round Hall Sweet and Maxwell.

Central Statistics Office (2003a). *2002 Census of Population – Volume 3 – Household Composition and Family Units*. *Press Statement*. Cork: Central Statistics Office.

Central Statistics Office (2003b). *Quarterly National Household Survey: second quarter 2003*. Cork: Central Statistics Office.

Central Statistics Office (2004a). *Statistical Yearbook of Ireland 2004*. Dublin: The Stationery Office.

Central Statistics Office (2004b). *Women and Men in Ireland 2004*. Dublin: The Stationery Office.

Combat Poverty Agency (2002). *Poverty Briefing No. 13: Poverty in Ireland, the Facts*. Dublin: Combat Poverty Agency.

Connelly, A. (1999). 'Women and the Constitution of Ireland' in *Contesting Politics: Women in Ireland, North and South*. (Ed, Wilford, R.). Oxford: Westview Press.

Daly, M. (2004). *Families and Family Life in Ireland*. Dublin: Department of Social and Family Affairs.

Daly, M. and Clavero, S. (2002). *Contemporary Family Policy: a comparative review of Ireland, France, Germany and the UK*. Dublin: The Institute of Public Administration.

Daly, M. and Rake, K. (2003). *Gender and the Welfare State*. Cambridge: Polity Press.

Equality Coalition (2004). *Submission on the Social Welfare (Miscellaneous) Bill 2004*. Dublin: The Equality Coalition. http://www.iccl.ie/minorities/gayles/04swelf_submission.pdf

Ferguson, H. and Hogan, F. (2004). *Strengthening Families Through Fathers: developing policy and practice in relation to vulnerable fathers and their families*. Waterford: The Centre for Social and Family Research, Waterford Institute of Technology.

Gay and Lesbian Equality Network and Nexus Research Co-operative (1995). *Poverty, lesbians and gay men: The economic and social effects of discrimination*. Dublin: Combat Poverty Agency.

Golombok, S. (2000). *Parenting: what really counts?* London: Routledge.

Government of Ireland (1996). *Report of the Constitution Review Group*. Dublin: The Stationery Office.

Government of Ireland (1997). *First Progress Report on the Implementation of the Recommendations*. Dublin: The Stationery Office.

Government of Ireland (1999). *Third Progress Report on the Implementation of the Recommendations of the Second Commission on the Status of Women*. Dublin: The Stationery Office.

Hayes, N. (2002). 'Who is Family?' at Biennial Conference on Family Diversity: exploring issues, reflecting reality, challenging assumptions. Cherish. Dublin, 12.10.2002.

Holmshaw, J. and Hillier, S. (2000). 'Gender and culture: a sociological perspective to mental health problems in women' in *Women and mental health*. (Ed, Kohen, D.). London: Routledge.

Immigrant Council of Ireland (2003). *Labour migration into Ireland*. Dublin: Immigrant Council of Ireland. http://www.immigrantcouncil.ie/labour.pdf

Irish Centre for European Law (2004). *The Communitarisation of Family Law: key implications of the revised Brussels II Regulation (Council Reg. No. 2201/2003)*. http://listserv.heanet.ie/cgi-bin/wa?A2=ind 0411&L=irish-law&T=o&F=&S=&P=3459 accessed on 03.12.2004.

Kennedy, F. (2001). *Cottage to Crèche: family change in Ireland*. Dublin: Institute of Public Administration.

Krieger, H. (2004). 'Family Life in Europe: results from recent surveys on quality of life in Europe' at Irish EU Presidency Conference on Families, Change and Social Policy in Europe. Dublin, 13-14.05.04. http://www.eu2004.ie/templates/news.asp?sNavlocator=66&list_id=708

Lasswell, M. (2002). 'Marriage and Family' in *Women's mental health: a comprehensive book*. (Ed, Clayton, A.H.). New York: The Guildford Press.

Law Reform Commission (2004). *Consultation Paper on the Rights and Duties of Cohabitees*. Dublin: The Law Reform Commission. http://www.lawreform.ie/Cohabitees%20CP %20%20April%202004.pdf

Lynch, K. (1996). 'Defining the Family and Protecting the Caring Functions of Both Traditional and Non-Traditional Families' in *Report of the Constitution Review Group*. (Ed, Government of Ireland). Dublin: The Stationery Office.

McKeown, K., Pratschke, J. and Haase, T. (2003). *Family well being: what makes the difference?* Dublin: Kieran McKeown Limited.

Mee, J. and Ronayne, K. (2000). *Report on the Partnership Rights of Same Sex Couples*. Dublin: The Equality Authority.

Meyer, I. H. (2003). 'Prejudice, social stress, and mental health in lesbian, gay and bisexual population: conceptual issues and research evidence'. *Psychological Bulletin*, 129 (5), pp. 674-697.

NCCRI (2002). *Migration policy: reform and harmonisation*. Dublin: National Consultative Committee on Racism and Interculturalism.

NESF (2003). *Equality Policies for Lesbian, Gay and Bisexual People: implementation issues*. Dublin: National Economic and Social Forum.

O'Connor, P. (1998). *Emerging Voices: women in contemporary society*. Dublin: Institute of Public Administration.

Office of the United Nations High Commission for Human Rights (1996). *Initial Reports of State Parties due in 1994; Ireland 17/06/96. CRC/C/11/Add 12*. Geneva: Office of the United Nations High Commission for Human Rights. http://www.nco.ie/upload_documents/First_Report_of_Ireland1.pdf

One Family (2004). One Family call for legislative and policy change to confer equal rights on all family types. Dublin: One Family. Press Release 01.03.04

Ryan, F. (2002). 'Legal Rhetoric, Social Reality: towards a new legal concept of family for the 21st century.' at Biennial

Conference on Family Diversity: exploring issues, reflecting reality, challenging assumptions. Cherish. Dublin, 12.10.2002.

Scannell, Y. (2001). 'The Constitution and the Role of Women' in *The Irish Women's History Reader*. (Ed, Urquhart, D.). London: Routledge.

Shrier, D. K. (2002). 'Career and workplace issues' in *Women's mental health: a comprehensive book*. (Ed, Clayton, A. H.). New York: The Guildford Press.

Strazdins, L. and Broom, D. H. (2004). 'Acts of love (and work): gender imbalance in emotional work and women's psychological distress'. *Journal of Family Issues*, 25 (3), pp. 256-378.

Wiley, M. and Merriman, B. (1996). *Women and health care in Ireland: knowledge, attitudes and behaviour*. Dublin: Oak Tree Press in association with the Economic and Social Research Institute.

Women's Health Council (2003). *Women, Disadvantage and Health*. Dublin: The Women's Health Council. http://www.whc.ie/publications/31657_WHC_Disadvantage.pdf

Notes

1 Following the increased 'communitarisation' of family law (Irish Centre for European Law, 2004), this situation is likely to give rise to increased legal conflict between Irish and European family law.

2 These are currently not available in Ireland for same-sex couples, but can be easily obtained in other countries, such as the United States of America.

THE WORKERS' PARTY OF IRELAND

INTRODUCTION

The family is an established institution in Irish society. It commands special protection in the Constitution. However, no institution exists in isolation. The basic structure of society is dependent on the relations of people to each other in the process of production. The types of relations that people enter into always correspond to a definite stage of development of the forces of production. These relations of production, the economic foundation of society, are consolidated and reinforced by social institutions, political systems, social ideas and theories, legal and cultural institutions.

Family and tribe were among the earliest forms of community. As economies developed, as the division of labour grew, the primitive mode of production was destroyed. As the instruments of labour improved the amount of products increased. The division of labour inevitably led to an exchange of products. Needs could only be met through exchange. Gradually, as there was no longer a need for the whole community to produce the means of subsistence, families gained control of the means of production, and control over property was exerted by the head of the family who apportioned that property among the members depending on the degree of kin. This laid the grounds for private ownership of property. Primitive society was replaced by slave-owning society which was, in turn, replaced by feudal and later capitalist society. In undertaking social production, human beings entered into relations with each other and these evolved into property relationships.

The nature of ideas, views and notions is dependent on the level of production of material benefits and the place these occupy in the system of social production. Accordingly, the basis of any social or political theory of the family is rooted in the sphere of social being. In order to produce and distribute the necessities of life, human beings create a social organisation that permits them to do so most effectively. The form of ownership of the means of production determines the position of social groups in production and the manner in which the products of labour are distributed. History has demonstrated that factors such as population growth and changes in the environment force human beings to increase and improve production. This, in turn, is accompanied by development both in the productive forces and production relations. The institutions of any society can only be explained on the basis of the relations of production and the class interests of those involved in those relations.

The family, under capitalism, is an economic unit based on the social relations of production. It does not stand apart from the relations of exploitation. On the contrary, the concept of the family, as envisaged and idealised by the Constitution, the family based on the monogamous heterosexual couple, developed and is based on private property relations. It is not possible for every member of the working class to sell his/her labour and for many, the family provides access to a wage that is essential to survival. It also performs an ideological function, socialising children into the prevailing cultural and social values and norms. While women have found new opportunities to enter the labour market, in the case of many working class women they have entered the public labour market not as a result of the expression of individual choice but as a consequence of economic necessity. Those women remain chained to the double or triple shift. Connolly's observations in *The Reconquest of Ireland* remain valid today.

There is no universal consensus on the definition of 'the family'. However, the family as contemplated and understood in the Constitution is the nuclear family consisting of an adult male and adult female, married to each other and living with their biological offspring or adopted children and presented as an ideal to which members of society should conform.

However society develops and changes and within the context of those developments, it is necessary to revisit established definitions of human relations. Ireland in 2005 is very different from Ireland in 1937. Increased industrialisation and the shift from a predominantly rural based economy in conjunction with the lessening of the influence of the Roman Catholic

Church created the possibilities for changed family roles and family life. Increased geographical mobility and an exposure to different cultures, views and values created a new environment for change.

THE FAMILY AND INDIVIDUAL MEMBERS – A REVIEW OF THE PRESENT CONSTITUTIONAL AND LEGAL POSITION

There are now two-parent families where both partners work, where one partner works or where neither partner works – with or without children. There are more people living alone than before, more single-parents, more people cohabiting, separating, divorcing and remarrying and re-entering 'reconstituted' marriages. This is the social reality that the law must reflect.

The Constitution does not define 'the family'. However, the courts have made clear that the family described in the Constitution is the nuclear family – the family based on marriage between heterosexual adults (*State [Nicolaou] v An Bord Uchtála [1966]*). A cohabiting couple and their children are not regarded as a family under the Constitution, as interpreted by the Irish courts – a clear breach of Article 8 of the European Convention on Human Rights and Fundamental Freedoms. Social reality cannot be made to fit early twentieth century moral precepts. Irish law must confront and give effect to social reality. Accordingly, The Workers' Party believe the definition of family must be sufficiently wide to encompass the types of well-recognised relationships in which people live as families today.

Although Articles 41 and 42 of the Constitution provide strong family rights, these rights attach to the family as a unit rather than to individual members of that family (*Murray v Ireland [1985]*). Further, the courts have taken the view that the family is 'endowed with an authority which the Constitution recognises as being superior even to the authority of the state' (Keane CJ in *North Western Health Board v H.W. and C.W. [2001]*). This emphasis leads to a conflict between the rights of the family as a unit and the individual rights of a family member to the detriment of the latter. It is necessary to strike a greater balance between those rights, and this will require a clearer constitutional recognition of the rights of the individual members of the family unit, such as a child of the family, than currently exist.

The Constitution Review Group recommended that the rights which derive from marriage, family, parenthood or childhood should be guaranteed to, or imposed on, individuals. Subject to a wide definition of family, we would endorse that view. Although it has been conceded by the courts that the state may intervene in the decision making authority of the family in the interests of the common good and where such intervention is not construed as disproportionate, the idea that the institution of the family has an authority

which is superior to the authority of the state is, of itself, a questionable concept worthy of reconsideration given that this provision may be called upon to defeat progressive social legislation on the grounds that it is a disproportionate intervention by the state and repugnant to Article 41.

The judgement of Henchy J. in Nicolaou stated that Article 41 of the Constitution did not protect a family other than that based on marriage. He took the view that for the state to award equal constitutional protection to the family founded on marriage and 'the family founded on an extra-marital union' would be 'a disregard of the pledge which the state gives in Article 41.3.1 to guard with special care the institution of marriage'. It is not satisfactory in 2005 that a non-marital family is not afforded the protection of the Constitution and is, in effect, compelled to trawl other articles of the Constitution and various pieces of legislation to establish its rights.

The decision of the European Court of Human Rights in *Keegan v Ireland (1994)* to the effect that the notion of 'family' under Article 8 of the Convention is not confined to marital relationships should provide sufficient impetus to amend the Constitution to reflect the social reality that there are many families other than those based on marriage. In many respects, this approach is consistent with the view expressed, on occasion, in the case law, that the courts must take into account the extent to which ideas and values have changed or developed, and that the Preamble to the Constitution recognises that the rights provided by the Constitution must be considered in accordance with concepts which may change or develop as society changes and develops, and which fall to be interpreted from time to time in accordance with prevailing ideas (*McGee v Attorney General (1974)* and *The state (Healy) v Donoghue (1976)*). Where the Constitution cannot be interpreted in a manner which attempts to give effect to 'family' and individual rights, accorded for example under the European Convention, amendment is necessary.

SAME-SEX COUPLES AND MARRIAGE

Article 40.1 of the Constitution provides that 'All citizens shall, as human persons, be held equal before the law'. Domestic law and/or the jurisprudence of the European Court has increasingly recognised the need to prohibit discrimination on grounds of sex (including trans-sexuals), marital or family status, sexual orientation (including gay, lesbian and bisexual). In this context, it is important to consider that there are many same-sex couples living in stable family relationships that are deprived of legal rights and entitlements in respect of property, succession, pensions and tax and social welfare benefits. There can be no justification for excluding same-sex couples from the enjoyment of those rights. The question of whether such couples should be permitted by law to marry does not conclude the issue. There may be many couples, same-sex or otherwise, who do not wish to enter a formal state or church endorsed institution of marriage. This should not disentitle those couples from the benefits of the protection afforded to a family under the Constitution.

Gay or lesbian couples should be entitled, by law, to avail of a civil marriage if they wish. Whether they elect to do so, or not, should not predetermine their constitutional entitlements as members of a family unit or as individuals.

CONSTITUTIONAL RIGHTS OF CHILDREN

The adoption of the UNCRC in 1979 represented a paradigm shift regarding the rights of children. The old ideology, as faithfully reproduced in the 1937 constitution, was based on the dual foundation of paternalism and on the role of the 'family' as the central unit within the Catholic Church's vision of the corporate state. The new thinking is based on equal rights and respect for difference. Our vision, similar to the vision of the UNCRC is that children, *qua* children, have rights and that these rights neither derive from, nor are subsidiary to, the rights of the parents/ family unit.

It is important here to state that the Workers' Party believes that, as guaranteed by the UNCHR and the ECHR, individuals have the right to marry, to have children and to be a family. Each member of that family has rights individually and collectively, but the family, *qua* family, does not have rights superior to the rights of the individuals who, for the time being, may constitute that family.

We believe that the three guiding principles as set out in the UNCRC should be incorporated within the Irish Constitution. These principles are: non-discrimination (Article 2), best interests of the child (Article 3) and right to be heard (Article 12). In order to give effect to these new principles within the Constitution we believe there will have to be widespread legislative change. Change will also be required within the state bureaucracy and the administration of many state agencies. We refer here to just one example. In legal disputes over child custody, the overriding principle must be 'the best interests of the child'. However, the present operation of the 'in camera' rule within the family courts (which, as a principle, we fully support) means that there are no statistics, much less information to inform the statistics, as to the outcome of these thousands of cases. While we welcome Section 40 of the Civil Liability and Courts Act, 2004, we greatly doubt whether this, on its own, will be sufficient to remedy the problem (a problem, incidentally, highlighted and brought to the government's attention in the mid-1990s by the Law Reform Commission).

We believe that children with disabilities need special constitutional protection. We believe that Article 23 of the UNCRC should be the basis for this new portion within our Constitution.

Article 42 deals with education. It is the view of the Workers' Party that this article is deeply defective. The entire ethos of the article is paternalistic – dealing with the rights of the parents over the education rather than with the right of the child to an education. We also believe that Article 42.2, which merely commits the state to 'provide for free primary care' to be much too restricted. Once again we believe that the rights and vision outlined in Articles 28, 29 and 42 of the UNCRC should be the foundation stone of our Constitution in this area. We believe that our legislature must take account of the decisions of the European Court of Human Rights, which has interpreted the guarantee of free primary education within the ECHR as being 'effective' education.

The Workers' Party believes that Articles 41 and 42, as currently exist, need to be completely deleted and rewritten. We believe that the amended articles should be so drafted that, while absolutely guaranteeing certain fundamental rights as outlined in the UNCRC (and detailed above), they do not prevent legislative development aimed at the protection of children and the promotion of the common good.

ARTICLE 41.2.1

The Committee asks specifically our opinion on article 41.2.1. The reference in Article 41.2.1 to woman's 'life within the home' is paternalistic and out-dated. While the Constitution does not necessarily require a woman to be the homemaker, and theoretically places no restrictions on a woman to choose otherwise, the interpretation of this article has been oppressive. The infamous 'marriage ban' was just one of the consequences that flew from this article. It is a mere tokenistic recognition of the unpaid labour of women which confers no rights on women, but instead perpetuates gender inequality and reinforces a patriarchal ideology that is already deeply embedded in Irish social, economic and cultural life. The reference should be removed.

However, we do recognise that the care of children imposes great responsibilities on parents. We therefore propose that constitutional provision must be made whereby parents must be positively supported, and not discriminated against, in carrying out their responsibilities with regard to their children.

SHOULD THE RIGHTS OF A NATURAL MOTHER HAVE EXPRESS CONSTITUTIONAL PROTECTION? WHAT RIGHTS SHOULD A NATURAL FATHER HAVE, AND HOW SHOULD THEY BE PROTECTED?

These questions must be seen in the context of social progress. The formation of families with children through adoption and medical advances are very much part of society today. Providing the natural mother or natural father with express constitutional protection can in effect establish a right that conflicts with that of the non-biological mother or non-biological father to the detriment of the child. We believe that neither the natural mother nor the natural father should be given express constitutional protection but that their rights should derive from that as individuals as set down in the Universal Declaration on Human Rights and in accordance with the Convention on the Rights of the Child.

ARTICLE 40.3

The All-Party Committee on the Constitution is also reviewing Article 40.3, which sets down personal rights. Article 1 of the Universal Declaration of Human Rights recognises that all human beings are born free and equal in dignity and rights. Currently the Constitution gives equal protection to the unborn and the mother. The Constitution in providing an equal right to life of the unborn and the mother is balancing a woman's right to life against that of the unborn. This can physically and/or psychologically diminish her right to life. The Workers' Party believes that this constitutional provision is ambiguous and that in a modern democratic state this is an unnecessary interference by the judiciary, and that the Constitution should not replace the role of legislators. We therefore recommend that Article 40.3 be removed from the Constitution.

CONCLUSION

As outlined in our introduction, both the legal and social conceptions of family change with time and circumstances.

Ireland now, and indeed the world in general, is radically different from that which existed in the mid-1930s.

The constitutional provision for the family and children in the 1937 Bunreacht na hÉireann, based as they were on victorian property values and Roman Catholic social teaching of the previous thirty years, have proven woefully inadequate and have not stood the test of time.

We are pleased to have had this opportunity to make our views known and to highlight specific proposals, and we hope that the committee include our proposals in your final submission to the Houses of the Oireachtas.

YOUNG GREENS – ÓIGE GHLAS

THE CASE FOR SAME-SEX MARRIAGE

Recent developments in the UK, the US and in Europe have led to increased questions being asked as to why in Ireland same-sex couples are barred from the civil institution of marriage. The Young Greens/Óige Ghlas feel that this is a blatant example of discrimination against homosexuals and seek to have changes enacted in law and the Constitution, to rectify this situation.

This discussion document sets out the grounds for our beliefs and our proposals for reform.

The document sets out the current position regarding civil marriage in Ireland, and then outlines the discrimination faced by same-sex couples (and married heterosexual couples). It then outlines the current position regarding same-sex marriage in other jurisdictions in Europe and the wider world, and presents the arguments why Ireland should proceed to legislate for change here. Finally, the document makes some tentative proposals as to legislative and constitutional change that would rectify the current inequalities faced by same-sex couples in Ireland.

Some who oppose the notion of same-sex marriage regard civil unions, which contain many of the benefits of marriage, as an acceptable alternative. This policy sees the introduction of a form of civil union as part of the solution to the current problem. Such unions would allow for a greater degree of stability and security for those in relationships, either homosexual or heterosexual, who, for whatever reason, do not wish to enter into a marriage. However, we firmly believe that, under principles of equality and democracy, those in the same-sex relationships should be able to avail of the full rights and responsibilities of marriage, and not merely have to content themselves with civil unions.

It should be noted that 'civil marriage', as mentioned throughout the policy, refers to marriages taking place in registry offices.

1 CIVIL MARRIAGE IN IRELAND

Article 41 of the Constitution deals with marriage. Article 41.3.1 states:

> The State pledges to guard with special care the institution of marriage, on which the family is founded, and to protect it against attack.

As can be seen, this statement does not define marriage as a union solely between a man and a woman. This issue has been alluded to in some case law. In *B v R* [1995] 1 ILRM 491, Costello J. defined marriage as 'the voluntary and permanent union of one man and one woman to the exclusion of all others for life'. In *Murray v Ireland* [1985] IR 532 at pp. 535-6, Costello J. stated that 'the Constitution makes clear that the concept and nature of marriage, which it enshrines, are derived from the Christian notion of a partnership based on an irrevocable personal consent, given by both spouses which establishes a unique and very special life-long relationship.' The implication of this statement would be that the Christian notion of marriage, as interpreted in the Constitution, would be restricted to one between two people of the opposite sex. These conclusions that marriage must be between a male and a female were recently restated by McKechnie J. in the case of *Foy v An tArd-Chláraitheoir* (Unreported), where the judge rejected a claim by a post-operative transsexual that she had the right to marry someone of her former gender.

The fact that the Constitution must 'protect [marriage] against attack' has led to questionable definitions as to what actually constitutes such an 'attack'. In the case of *Ennis v Butterly* [1996] 1 IR 426, an unmarried couple who had been cohabiting for many years broke up. The woman claimed that she had undertaken all the household duties as her male partner had promised to provide for her, even in the event of the relationship breaking down. In the High Court, it was held that such an agreement could not be upheld by the courts as it would undermine the special constitutional protection of marriage.

2 PRESENT INEQUALITIES

The failure of the state to recognise a right for same-sex couples to marry results in such couples facing a large number of difficulties. Many of these difficulties also apply to non-marital heterosexual couples.

a) Succession: under the Succession Act, 1965, the spouse of the deceased is entitled to a significant portion of the deceased party's estate (two-thirds where they have children, the entirety where they have none) if the deceased dies without making a valid will.

b) Next of Kin: in the event of surgery or a medical emergency, partners in a same-sex relationship are barred from acting as next of kin. Thus, a partner is prevented from making life-altering decisions that spouses in a marriage would take for granted.

c) Tax System: while the individualisation of the tax system has gone some way to alleviate the discrimination that occurs in the tax system, it remains firmly biased against non-marital couples. Inheritance tax is significantly higher between the recipient and his/her deceased partner than it would be between the recipient and his/her deceased spouse. The exemptions granted to married couples in respect of capital acquisitions tax, capital gains tax and stamp duty do not apply to same-sex couples.

d) Maintenance: when a married couple split, either by separation or divorce, there is a large body of legislation governing the division of the couple's assets, and providing for the payment of maintenance and child support. Such protection is not readily available to same-sex or non-marital couples, regardless of the length of their relationship. Indeed, it was held by the High Court in *Ennis v Butterly* that even if a non-marital couple had made an agreement concerning maintenance in the case of the relationship breaking down, such an agreement could not be enforced by the courts as it would undermine the special constitutional protection of marriage.

e) Family Home: the Family home Protection Act, 1976, provides for the division of the marital family home in the case of marriage breakdown. Such protection is not available to those in same-sex relationships, where, irrespective of the length or nature of the relationship, the partner who does not own the house must prove that he/she made a direct financial contribution to its purchase or he/she will receive no interest in the property.

f) European Convention on Human Rights: Ireland has now incorporated the European Convention on Human Rights into domestic law. In the recent case of *Foy v An tArd-Chláraitheoir*, it was held in the High Court that according to the Constitution, a post-operative transsexual does not have the right to marry in his or her assumed gender. Days after this decision, the European Court of Human Rights held in the case of *Goodwin v UK* 2002) 35 EHRR 18 that prohibiting a transsexual from marrying in his or her assumed gender is a breach of the European Convention on Human Rights. As such, the present constitutional situation as interpreted by the courts leaves Ireland in breach of the European Convention on Human Rights.

3 RECOGNITION OF SAME-SEX MARRIAGE IN OTHER STATES

Currently, only two states, the Netherlands and Belgium, permit civil marriage for same-sex couples. The Spanish parliament is currently discussing legislation allowing for same-sex marriage in Spain, and the Swedish parliament has also engaged in the process.

In Canada, courts in five of the country's provinces have ruled that same-sex marriages should be permitted. The Canadian Supreme Court has declared constitutional a bill that would permit same-sex marriage to be legalised across the country. The bill will soon come before the Canadian parliament. In the United States, the Supreme Judicial Court of Massachusetts has ruled that same-sex couples should be allowed to marry under state law, though attempts are currently underway to change this ruling via an amendment to the State Constitution.

Civil unions, which have many of the characteristics of marriage, are available to same-sex couples in a greater number of countries. A Civil Partnerships Bill is currently before the UK houses of parliament. This bill would provide that the partners would have certain rights and obligations towards each other in issues including tax, inheritance and succession of tenancy.

In the US, the state of Vermont has legalised civil unions for same-sex couples. Civil unions for same-sex couples are relatively widespread throughout Europe, being recognised in France, Norway, Denmark, Sweden, Switzerland, Finland, Iceland and Germany.

Finally, it is relevant to note that Article II-9 of the Charter of Fundamental Rights of the European Union, which is part of the recently signed Constitution for Europe, states that:

> The right to marry and found a family shall be guaranteed in accordance with the national laws governing the exercise of these rights.

Recently, in the case of *Goodwin v UK*, the European Court of Human Rights compared this provision with the similar provision contained in the European Convention on Human Rights. It stated:

> [t]he Court would also note that Article 9 of the recently adopted Charter of Fundamental Rights of the European Union departs, *no doubt deliberately*, [our emphasis] from the wording of Article 12 of the Convention in removing the reference to men and women.

4 JUSTIFICATION FOR CHANGE

Section 3 of this document highlights the increased legislative recognition that is being granted to couples in same-sex relationships. It also points to the fact that this is an international trend, occurring in both strongly secular societies (Netherlands) and those where religious faith remains influential (Spain). Indeed, Article II-9 of the draft European Constitution is indicative of this less traditionalist approach which is now being taken to the definition of marriage.

In light of these developments, and the wide ranging discrimination outlined in Section 2 facing same-sex couples, the Young Greens/Óige Ghlas firmly believe that Ireland should enact whatever changes are necessary to allow same-sex couples enjoy the rights and responsibilities of civil marriage. We do not see any of the arguments against this development as being strong enough to justify the present inequality.

While extending the right to marry to same-sex couples would have financial implications for the exchequer, such considerations cannot be used to trump the basic equality argument. Same-sex marriage can in no way undermine religious rules as regards marriage, as it would only apply in the civil sphere. Indeed, some of the countries that allow same-sex couples to marry permit individual registrars to refuse to perform such ceremonies if it is against their personal beliefs.

Further, at a time of falling marriage rates, the Young Greens/Óige Ghlas believe that by opening the institution of marriage to a group of previously excluded, the concept of marriage will be made firmer.

5 ACHIEVEING CHANGE

Having surveyed the current state of the law, it is the opinion of the Young Greens/Óige Ghlas that currently the Irish Constitution does not rule out the possibility of allowing same-sex couples to marry. Official provision for this could be ensured by enacting a bill that would replace all gender specific terms in current legislation regarding marriage, with gender-neutral terms. This bill would also define marriage as being available to same-sex couples. It would probably be necessary to refer such a bill to the Supreme Court, to confirm its constitutionality.

It is our belief that any such legislation would survive scrutiny by the Supreme Court, as in all previous case law mentioned in Section 1 the definitions of marriage used were linked to outdated notions of marriage being solely a Christian institution. We believe that in light of the developing notion of what constitutes marriage across Europe, and the commitment to equality in our own Constitution, the Supreme Court should hold that marriage as outlined in the Constitution is not restricted to couples of the opposite sex. This finding would involve overturning the decisions in *B v R* and *Foy*. As such, Ireland would be recognising that marriage is a human right, as is acknowledged in the International Convenant on Civil and Political Rights. Indeed, the fact that Ireland now permits divorce is evidence of the fact that marriage as defined in our Constitution is not solely the traditional concept.

Should the Supreme Court decide that same-sex couples are excluded from marriage as described in our Constitution, the Young Greens/Óige Ghlas would then advocate a referendum to rectify the situation. We would tentatively suggest the insertion of the phrase 'The right to marry will be governed by laws surrounding the exercise of this right' into Article 41 of the Constitution. This would permit the government to legislate as to who could actually avail of marriage, making a decision as to whether same-sex marriage is permitted in Ireland one for the Oireachtas. In addition to this, we would also support adding the phrase 'the Oireachtas may provide for institutions and arrangements containing some of the benefits and responsibilities of marriage, by law' into Article 41. This would allow the government provide for civil unions by law for those who do not wish to avail of the institution of marriage, and thus avoid the issue of civil unions being interpreted as 'attacks' on the institution of marriage, similar to the decision in *Ennis v. Butterly.*

APPENDIX 4

APPENDIX 4

The Doha Declaration

PREAMBLE

Reaffirming that the family is the natural and fundamental group unit of society, as declared in Article 16(3) of the Universal Declaration of Human Rights;

Noting that 2004 marks the 10th Anniversary of the United Nations' 1994 International Year of the Family and that the Doha International Conference for the Family was welcomed by UN General Assembly Resolution A/RES/58/15 (December 15, 2003);

Acknowledging that the objectives of the 10th Anniversary of the International Year of the Family include efforts to (a) strengthen the capacity of national institutions to formulate, implement and monitor policies in respect of the family; (b) stimulate efforts to respond to problems affecting, and affected by, the situation of the family; (c) undertake analytical reviews at all levels and assessments of the situation and needs of the family; (d) strengthen the effectiveness of efforts at all levels to execute specific programmes concerning the family; and (e) improve collaboration among national and international nongovernmental organizations in support of the family;

Taking into consideration the academic, scientific and social findings collected for the Doha International Conference, which collectively demonstrate that the family is not only the fundamental group unit of society but is also the fundamental agent for sustainable social, economic and cultural development;

Recognizing the need to address the challenges facing the family in the context of globalization;

Realizing that strengthening the family presents a unique opportunity to address societal problems in a holistic manner;

Reiterating that strong, stable families contribute to the maintenance of a culture of peace and promote dialogue among civilizations and diverse ethnic groups; and

Welcoming the announcement by Her Highness Sheikha Moza bint Nasser Al-Missned, Consort of His Highness the Emir of Qatar and President of the Supreme Council for Family Affairs, State of Qatar, to create an international Institute for Study of the Family.

In this regard, we reaffirm international commitments to the family and call upon all governments, international organizations and members of civil society at all levels to take action to protect the family.

Reaffirmation of Commitments to the Family

We reaffirm international commitments to strengthen the family, in particular:

1   We commit ourselves to recognizing and strengthening the family's supporting, educating and nurturing roles, with full respect for the world's diverse cultural, religious, ethical and social values.

2   We recognize the inherent dignity of the human person and note that the child, by reason of his physical and mental immaturity, needs special safeguards and care before as well as after birth. Motherhood and childhood are entitled to special care and assistance. Everyone has the right to life, liberty and security of person.

3   We reaffirm that the family is the natural and fundamental group unit of society and is entitled to the widest possible protection and assistance by society and the State.

4   We emphasize that marriage shall be entered into only with the free and full consent of the intending spouses and that the right of men and women of marriageable age to marry and to found a family shall be recognized and that husband and wife should be equal partners.

5   We further emphasize that the family has the primary responsibility for the nurturing and protection of children from infancy to adolescence. For the full and harmonious development of their personality, children should grow up in a family environment, in an atmosphere of happiness, love and understanding. All institutions of society should respect and support the efforts of parents to nurture and care for children in

a family environment. Parents have a prior right to choose the kind of education that shall be given to their children and the liberty to ensure the religious and moral education of their children in conformity with their own convictions.

CALL FOR ACTION

Taking into account the above commitments, we call upon all governments, international organizations and members of civil society at all levels to:

Cultural, Religious and Social Values

1 Develop programs to stimulate and encourage dialogue among countries, religions, cultures and civilizations on questions related to family life, including measures to preserve and defend the institution of marriage;

2 Reaffirm the importance of faith and religious and ethical beliefs in maintaining family stability and social progress;

3 Evaluate and reassess the extent to which international law and policies conform to the principles and provisions related to the family contained in the Universal Declaration of Human Rights and other international commitments;

Human Dignity

4 Reaffirm commitments to provide a quality education for all, including equal access to educational opportunities;

5 Evaluate and reassess government policies to ensure that the inherent dignity of human beings is recognized and protected throughout all stages of life;

Family

6 Develop indicators to evaluate the impact of all programs on family stability;

7 Strengthen policies and programs that will enable the family to break the cycle of poverty;

8 Evaluate and reassess government population policies, particularly in countries with below replacement birthrates;

9 Encourage and support the family to provide care for older persons and persons with disabilities;

10 Support the family in addressing the scourge of HIV/AIDS and other pandemics, including malaria and tuberculosis;

11 Take effective measures to support the family in times of peace and war;

Marriage

12 Uphold, preserve and defend the institution of marriage;

13 Take effective measures to strengthen the stability of marriage by, among other things, encouraging the full and equal partnership of husband and wife within a committed and enduring marital relationship;

14 Establish effective policies and practices to condemn and remedy abusive relationships within marriage and the family, including the establishment of public agencies to assist men, women, children and families in crisis;

Parents and Children

15 Strengthen efforts to promote equal political, economic, social and educational opportunities for women and evaluate and assess economic, social and other policies to support mothers and fathers in performing their essential roles;

16 Strengthen the functioning of the family by involving mothers and fathers in the education of their children;

17 Reaffirm that parents have a prior right to choose the kind of education that shall be given to their children;

18 Reaffirm and respect the liberty of parents and, when applicable, legal guardians to choose for their children schools, other than those established by the public authorities, which conform to such minimum educational standards as may be laid down or approved by the State and to ensure the religious and moral education of their children in conformity with their own convictions.

We request the host country of the Conference, the State of Qatar, to inform the United Nations General Assembly of the proceedings of the Conference, including the Doha Declaration, in particular during the celebration of the 10th Anniversary of the International Year of the Family to be held on 6 December 2004.

APPENDIX 5

APPENDIX 5

Extract from
Report of the Constitution Review Group
[Ireland, Whitaker, T.K. (chairman), *Report of the Constitution Review Group* (1996), Stationery Office, PRL 2632]

INTRODUCTION

Article 41 contains the main provisions relating to the family. Article 42 is closely linked with Article 41 and has been construed by the courts as containing in Article 42.5 a guarantee of children's rights which go beyond education (*In re The Adoption (No2) Bill 1987* [1989] IR 656). Article 40.3 is also relevant, because the rights of an unmarried mother in relation to her child and the rights of a child born of unmarried parents have been held to be personal rights protected by Article 40.3 (*The State (Nicolau) v An Bord Uchtála* [1966] IR 567 and *G v An Bord Uchtála* [1980] IR 32.

Article 41 was a novel provision in 1937. The Constitution of 1922 contained no provision relating to family and marriage. It is generally considered that Articles 41and 42 were heavily influenced by Roman Catholic teaching and Papal encyclicals. They were clearly drafted with only one family in mind, namely, the family based on marriage.

The family in Irish society has been profoundly affected by social trends since 1937. The mores of Irish society have changed significantly over the past six decades. The traditional Roman Catholic ethos has been weakened by various influences including secularisation, urbanisation, changing attitudes to sexual behaviour, the use of contraceptives, social acceptance of premarital relations, cohabitation and single parenthood, a lower norm for family size, increased readiness to accept separation and divorce, greater economic independence of women.

The most striking changes in the family in Ireland since 1937 are the 30% drop in the birth-rate from 18.6 to 13.4 per 1.000, the rise from 3% to 20% in the proportion of births outside marriage and the increase from 5.6% to 32.4% in the proportion of married women who work outside the home. The traditional family consisting of a husband, wife and four to five children has dwindled to husband, wife and two children.

The absence of divorce in Ireland and the significant increase in marital breakdown has meant that there are many couples living together, some with children, who may wish to be married. This has distorted attitudes to non-marital families and, in particular, has resulted in anomalies in the tax and social welfare codes.

These social changes call for amendments in the Constitution, some of which raise difficult issues that require the achievement of delicate balances for their resolution.

PROVISIONS

At the time of drafting the report the litigation on the divorce referendum is proceeding. The Review Group is in a position where the current provisions of Article 41.3 are unclear. The provisions of Article 41, Article 42 and Article 40.3 as they have been interpreted by the courts and in so far as they relate to the family might be divided as follows:

i) recognition and protection of the family based on marriage and the rights of such family units

ii) protection for certain rights of parents and children resulting from a family based on marriage and for other relationships recognised by the natural law, that is, those of natural mothers and children

iii) recognition and support for a particular role of women and mothers within the home

iv) protection for the institution of marriage and consequent prohibition of (or limited permission for) divorce and recognition of certain foreign divorces.

ISSUES

The Review Group has identified eleven issues which need to be addressed:

1   the constitutional definition of 'family'
2   the balance between the rights of the family as a unit and the rights of the individual members
3   constitutional protection for the rights of a natural father
4   express constitutional protection for the rights of a natural mother
5   expanded constitutional guarantee for the rights of the child
6   the relative balance between parental and children's rights
7   the description and qualification of family rights
8   the continued constitutional protection of the institution of marriage and any necessary constitutional limitations to be placed on it
9   whether there should be an express right to marry and found a family

THE ALL-PARTY OIREACHTAS COMMITTEE ON THE CONSTITUTION

10   the reference to the role of women and mothers or other persons within the home

11   whether the Constitution should continue to regulate the position of foreign divorces and, if so, how

1   constitutional definition of 'family'

The family recognised and protected in Articles 41 and 42 is the family based on marriage. In *The State (Nicolaou) v An Bord Uchtála* Walsh J in the Supreme Court judgment stated that it was:

> ... quite clear ... that the family referred to in [Article 41] is the family which is founded on the institution of marriage and, in the context of the Article, marriage means valid marriage under the laws for the time being in force in the state.

Support for this view derives from Article 41.3.1°:

> The state pledges itself to guard with special care the institution of marriage, on which the family is founded, and to protect it against attack.

The effect of this definition is that neither a non-marital family nor its members are entitled to any of the protection or guarantees of Article 41. Likewise, they are probably not comprehended by the terms of Article 42: see *G v An Bord Uchtála*. As indicated above, rights of an unmarried mother and of a child of unmarried parents, which some might consider as rights resulting from a family relationship, have been held to be personal rights which the state is obliged to protect under Article 40.3. An unmarried father has been held to have no personal rights under Article 40.3 in relation to his child (*The State (Nicolaou) v An Bord Uchtála*). In that case the father sought to challenge the provisions of the Adoption Act 1952 which permitted the adoption of his child without his consent.

The Review Group has received many submissions to the effect that Article 41 should be amended so as to recognise in the Constitution family units other than the family based on marriage.

In Irish society there are numerous units which are generally regarded as family units but which are not families based on marriage. There are differences in the treatment of such family units for different purposes. For certain Social Welfare purposes heterosexual couples cohabiting are effectively treated as a family unit. They are not in general so treated for the purposes of tax laws or succession laws.

The Review Group appreciates the point of view of those who feel that persons living in family units not based on marriage should have constitutional recognition. However, the constitutional protection of rights of any family unit other than a family based on marriage presents significant difficulties.

The first and obvious difficulty is that once one goes beyond the family based on marriage definition becomes very difficult. Thus the multiplicity of differing units which may be capable of being considered as families include:

> a cohabiting heterosexual couple with no children
> a cohabiting heterosexual couple looking after the children of either or both parents
> a cohabiting heterosexual couple either of whom is already married
> a cohabiting heterosexual couple either of whom is already married, whose children (all or some of them) are being looked after elsewhere
> unmarried lone parents and their children
> homosexual and lesbian couples.

Questions will also arise such as what duration of cohabitation (one month? six months? one year? five years?) should qualify for treatment as a family. Furthermore, certain persons living together either with or without children may be deliberately choosing to do so without being married, that is, choosing deliberately not to have a legal basis for their relationship. Would it be an interference with their personal rights to accord in effect a legal status to their family unit?

The Review Group has considered the provisions in relation to family and marriage in many of the European constitutions, in the European Convention on Human Rights (ECHR) and the International Covenant of Civil and Political Rights (CCPR). None appears to attempt a definition of a 'family' in terms other than one based on marriage. Some clearly link family with marriage. Others are silent on the matter. Macedonia and Slovenia refer expressly to non-marital cohabitation in apparent distinction from the family. Some refer to the equal rights of children born 'out of wedlock' with those 'in wedlock' or 'of marriage' (Poland and the Slovak Republic) or the equal rights of children born 'outside matrimony' with those born 'in matrimony' (Slovenia).

If an amendment were made so that the family referred to in the Constitution was not confined to the family based on marriage, it would seem necessary to leave to the judiciary, on a case by case basis, the definition of the form of units which might constitute a family within the meaning of any such amended provision. While this could create uncertainty, it is essentially the approach of the ECHR, Article 8(1) of which provides:

> Everyone has the right to respect for his private and family life, his home and his correspondence.

The focus of the Article is, however, on the protection of an individual's right to family life as distinct from protection of the rights of a family unit.

The European Court of Human Rights and the European Commission of Human Rights have interpreted 'family life' within the meaning of Article 8 as extending beyond formal or legitimate arrangements. The Commission in *K v UK* No 11468/85 50 DR 199 stated:

The question of the existence or non-existence of 'family life' is essentially a question of fact depending upon the real existence in practice of close personal ties.

In *Keegan V Ireland* (1994) 18 EHRR 342 the court stated:

> The Court recalls that the notion of the 'family' in this provision is not confined solely to marriage-based relationships and may encompass other de facto 'family' ties where the parties are living together outside of marriage. A child born from such a relationship is ipso jure part of that 'family' unit from the moment of his birth and by the very fact of it. There thus exists between the child and his parents a bond amounting to family life, even if at the time of his birth the parents are no longer cohabiting or if their relationship has then ended.

The present emphasis of Article 41 is the protection of rights of the family as a unit rather than the protection of rights of individuals resulting from a family relationship (see Issue 2 below). The Review Group considers that this approach presents particular difficulties if the family unit is extended beyond the family based on marriage by reason of the uncertainties referred to above as to the existence at any given time of any such family unit.

An alternative approach is to retain in the Constitution a pledge by the state to protect the family based on marriage but also to guarantee to all individuals a right to respect for their family life whether that family is, or is not, based on marriage. For the reasons that appear later in this section of the report, this is the preferred option of the Review Group.

2   the balance between the rights of the family unit and those of the individual members

The rights referred to in Article 41.1 are the rights of the family as a unit as distinct from the rights of individual members of the family. In *Murray v Ireland* [1985] IR 532, Costello J stated:

> The rights in Article 41.1.1° are those which can properly be said to belong to the institution itself as distinct from the personal rights which each individual member might enjoy by virtue of membership of the family.

A similar approach was taken by Finlay CJ in *L v L* [1992] 2 IR 77 where he said:

> Neither Article 41.1.1°–2° purports to create any particular right within the family, or to grant to any individual member of the family rights, whether of property or otherwise, against other members of the family, but rather deals with the protection of the family from external forces.

The Review Group considers that the present focus of Articles 41 and 42 emphasises the rights of the family as a unit to the possible detriment of individual members. Giving to the family unit rights which are described as 'inalienable or imprescriptible', even if they are interpreted as not being absolute rights, potentially places too much emphasis on the rights of the family as a unit as compared with the rights of individuals within the unit. It is desirable that the family should retain a certain authority and autonomy. However, this should not be such so as to prevent the state from intervening where the protection of the individual rights of one member of the family requires this or to prejudice the rights of the individuals within the family. Professor William Duncan (see Appendix 22 – 'the constitutional protection of parental rights') has identified the problem as follows:

> The problem seems to be essentially that of achieving a legal balance which will offer security and a measure of equality to individual family members in a manner which does not devalue or endanger the family as an institution.

The history of adoption legislation in the state and the reluctance of the Oireachtas until recently to permit the adoption of legitimate children undoubtedly was influenced by a fear that any such provision would conflict with the rights of the family in Article 41.1.1°. The circumstances in which the Adoption Act 1988 permits the adoption of legitimate children are extremely limited, essentially those envisaged in Article 42.5, namely where parents for physical or moral reasons have failed in their duty towards their children. It was primarily in reliance upon that Article, while referring also to the obligations of the state under Article 40.3 to vindicate the personal rights of a child whose parents had failed in their duty to it, that the Supreme Court upheld as constitutional the Adoption (No2) Bill 1987 in the relevant Article 26 reference.

From the Review Group's consideration of the family and marriage provisions in many of the European constitutions and in the ECHR and CCPR, it appears that with the exception of Luxembourg, none guarantees expressly the rights of the family unit as such. Many recognise the family as a primary or fundamental unit in society and some state that it is entitled to the special protection of the state or society but the rights or duties which derive from marriage, family, parenthood or as a child are guaranteed to or imposed on the individuals. The Review Group considers that this would be the better approach in any revised form of Article 41.

3   constitutional protection for the rights of a natural father

A natural father is considered not to have any constitutionally-protected rights to his child. This arises from the decision of the Supreme Court in *The State (Nicolaou) v An Bord Uchtála*. In that case the child of a natural father had been adopted pursuant to the Adoption Act 1952 without his consent. He challenged the provisions of the Adoption Act which permitted that to be done. The Supreme Court held:

i)   a natural father is not a member of a family within Article 41

ii) a natural father is not a 'parent' within Article 42

iii) a natural father has no personal right in relation to his child which the state is bound to protect under Article 40.3

The basis for the third conclusion is stated by Walsh J:

> It has not been shown to the satisfaction of this Court that the father of an illegitimate child has any natural right, as distinct from legal rights, to either the custody, or society of that child and the Court has not been satisfied that any such right has ever been recognised as part of the natural law. If an illegitimate child has a natural right to look to his father for support that would impose a duty on the father but it would not of itself confer any right upon the father.

Since the decision of the Supreme Court in *The State (Nicolaou) v An Bord Uchtála*, there have been two significant developments in relation to the legal as distinct from the constitutional position relating to the rights of a natural father.

Firstly, section 12 of the Status of Children Act 1987 amended the Guardianship of Infants Act 1964 by the insertion of the following section:

> 6A(1) Where the father and mother of an infant have not married each other the court may, on the application of the father, by order appoint him to be a guardian of the infant.

The above section has been construed by the Supreme Court as giving to an unmarried father a right to apply to the court to be appointed a guardian as distinct from giving to him a right to be a guardian which is capable of being annulled, that is to say, a defeasible right (*K v W* [1990] ILRM 121).

There are two particularly important consequences for an unmarried father who is appointed a guardian of his children. Under section 10(2) of the Guardianship of Infants Act 1964, he is entitled, as against every person who is not a joint guardian of the children with him (normally the mother), to the custody of the children. Also, under the Adoption Acts his child may not be adopted without his consent unless the court makes an order dispensing with his consent. However, a father who is not appointed the guardian of his children has no such defeasible

right to custody nor to have to give his consent for the adoption of his child.

The second important development is the finding by the European Court of Human Rights that Ireland was in breach of Article 8 of the ECHR in that it failed to respect the family life of an unmarried father who had had a stable relationship with the mother of his child in permitting the placement of the child for adoption without his knowledge or consent: see the *Keegan* case.

Ireland is, therefore, now obliged to give natural fathers to whom children are born in the context of 'family life' as interpreted by the European Court of Human Rights, a legal opportunity to establish a relationship with that child. This obviously requires a legal entitlement to be consulted before the child is placed for adoption; also it would seem to require that he be entitled at a minimum to rights of access to the child and possibly defeasible rights to joint guardianship or joint custody with the natural mother. The European Court of Human Rights expressly declined to consider whether Ireland was in breach of Article 8 by reason of its failure to grant to Mr Keegan a defeasible right to be the guardian of his child. It expressed its approach to these issues as follows:

> According to the principles set out by the Court in its case law, where the existence of a family tie with a child has been established, the state must act in a manner calculated to enable that tie to be developed and legal safeguards must be created that render possible as from the moment of birth the child's integration in his family.

There is of course no requirement that these rights be constitutional rights. It would be sufficient for Ireland in order to comply with its obligations under the ECHR to grant such rights by legislation.

There has been much criticism of the continued constitutional ostracism of natural fathers. This can be readily understood in relation to those natural fathers who either live in a stable relationship with the natural mother, or have established a relationship with the child. However, there does not appear to be justification for giving constitutional rights to every natural father simply by reason of biological links and thus include fatherhood resulting from rape, incest or sperm donorship.

The Review Group considers that the solution appears to lie in following the approach of Article 8 of the ECHR in guaranteeing to every person respect for 'family life' which has been interpreted to include non-marital family life but yet requiring the existence of family ties between the mother and the father. This may be a way of granting constitutional rights to those fathers who have, or had, a stable relationship with the mother prior to birth, or subsequent to birth with the child, while excluding persons from having such rights who are only biological fathers without any such relationship. In the context of the Irish Constitution it would have to be made clear that the reference to family life included family life not based on marriage.

4 express constitutional protection for the rights of a natural mother

A natural mother is not considered to have any rights protected by Articles 41 or 42. She is considered to have rights in relation to her child which are personal rights protected by Article 40.3 (*G v An Bord Uchtála*).

The Review Group is recommending that rights previously identified by the courts as unenumerated personal rights protected by Article 40.3 should now be enumerated in the Constitution. It would be appropriate that the rights of a natural mother be specified in Articles 41 and 42. If as suggested above a new section were inserted in Article 41 giving to everyone a right to respect for their family life, this would clearly include the rights of a natural mother in relation to her child.

Consideration should also be given to whether any modified form of Article 42.1 which refers to parental rights should expressly include unmarried parents. If this were done, care would have to be taken with the drafting to avoid giving rights to natural fathers who have no relationship with the natural mother or no relationship, other than a biological one, with the child.

5 expanded constitutional guarantee for the rights of the child

There is no express reference in Article 41 to the child. As already indicated, the focus of this Article is on the rights of the family as a unit and on protection of it from intervention by the state rather than on the rights of the individual members of the family. Only Article 42.5 makes reference to the rights of the child and imposes any specific obligation on the state.

The *Report on the Kilkenny Incest Investigation* chaired by Judge Catherine McGuinness observed that 'the very high emphasis on the rights of the family in the Constitution may consciously or unconsciously be interpreted as giving a higher value to the right of parents than to the rights of children' and went on to recommend the amendment of the Constitution to include 'a specific and overt declaration of the rights of born children'.

unenumerated rights

Over the years judicial interpretation of the Constitution has revealed certain unenumerated rights to which the child is entitled:

4   the judgments of the High Court and the Supreme Court in *G v An Bord Uchtála* [1980] IR 32 identify:

i)   the right to bodily integrity

ii)   the right to an opportunity to be reared with due regard to religious, moral, intellectual and physical welfare.

The judgments went on to emphasise that the state, having regard to the provisions of Article 40.3.1°, must by its laws defend and vindicate these rights as far as practicable.

O'Higgins CJ in the Supreme Court added to the list when he pointed out that a child, having been born, has the right 'to be fed and to live, to be reared and educated and to have the opportunity of working and realising his or her full personality and dignity as a human being and that these rights must equally be protected and vindicated by the state.'

1   the Supreme Court returned to this issue in *In re Article 26 and the Adoption (No 2) Bill 1987* [1989] IR 656.

In this reference to the Supreme Court to test the constitutionality of the Bill, the court was required to construe Article 42.5 and in doing so stated that the rights of a child are not limited to those contained in Article 41 and 42 but include the rights referred to in Articles 40, 43 and 44. This important statement confirms that the child is entitled to all of the personal rights identified in Article 40.

2   *FN (a minor) v Minister for Education* [1995] 2 ILRM 297 was a High Court case dealing with child care and the detention of a child with very special needs caused by a hyperkinetic conduct disorder. It was held that 'where there is a child with very special needs which cannot be provided by the parents or guardian there is a constitutional obligation on the state under Article 42.5 of the Constitution to cater for those needs in order to vindicate the constitutional rights of the child'.

However, it was stated that this was not an absolute duty. Later in the judgment it was stated by Geoghegan J:

> ... the state is under a constitutional obligation towards the applicant to establish as soon as reasonably practicable ... suitable arrangements of containment with treatment for the applicant.

This is a strong affirmation by the High Court of the constitutional obligation on the state to make proper provision for the welfare of a child suffering a psychiatric illness. This is consistent with the judgment of the High Court in *G v An Bord Uchtála* which identified the child's constitutional right to be reared with due regard to her religious, moral, intellectual, physical and social welfare. This wording follows closely on Article 42.1 with the important distinction that the word *welfare* is included instead of *education*.

Consistent with the view already expressed by the Review Group relating to the specific inclusion in the Constitution of identified unenumerated rights, the Review Group recommends the express inclusion of the unenumerated rights of the child set out above. A child is, of course, a person, and therefore the general constitutional rights shared by adults, such as the right to bodily integrity, will be protected elsewhere in the Constitution. Article 41 should contain an express guarantee of those rights of a child which are not guaranteed elsewhere and are peculiar to children, such as the right to be reared with due regard for his or her welfare.

United Nations Convention on the Rights of the Child (CRC)

In September 1992, Ireland ratified the CRC. It constitutes a comprehensive compilation of child-specific rights, many of which have already been identified by the superior courts as unenumerated rights under the Constitution. They include the right to education, freedom of religion, expression, assembly and association.

However, two separate and distinct issues are of interest and may inspire constitutional amendment.

3   The first of these is contained in Article 7 of CRC which states

> The child shall be registered immediately after birth and shall have the right from birth to a name, the right to acquire nationality and, as far as possible, *the right to know and be cared for by his or her parents* (emphasis added).

The Review Group recommends that a child ought to have a right as far as is practicable to his or her own identify which includes a knowledge and history of his or her own birth parents. The child ought to be entitled to this information not only for genetic and health reasons but also for psychological reasons. The Review Group recognises that in the case of adoption it may be desirable in the child's interests to regulate the time and manner in which the child should be entitled to this information. There may be other situations where such regulation is also desirable. Thus, the protection of any such right in the Constitution should be subject to regulation by law in the interests of the child.

In addition, the child should have a right as far as is practicable to be cared for by both parents. This is particularly so where the child is a non-marital child. It has already been pointed out that a natural father has no con-

stitutionally protected rights in relation to his child. However, the judgment of Walsh J in *The State (Nicolaou) v An Bord Uchtála* seems to imply that such a child may have a constitutional right to know and be cared for by his or her natural father where it stated:

> If an illegitimate child has a natural right to look to his father for support, that would impose a duty on the father but it would not of itself confer any right upon the father.

4   Throughout the text of the CRC, reference is made to the concept of the 'best interests of the child': see *inter alia* Articles 3, 9 and 18. These Articles deal with different situations such as actions concerning children where the best interest of the child shall be 'a primary consideration' (Article 3), the prohibition of a separation of a child from his or her parents against his or her will, except in certain circumstances, and where 'such separation is necessary for the best interests of the child' (Article 9), where it provides that both parents shall have common responsibilities for the upbringing and development of the child and that 'the best interests of the child will be their basic concern' (Article 18).

Section 3(2)(b) of the Child Care Act 1991 provides that the Health Board, in exercising its function in the care and protection of children, shall 'have regard to the rights and duties of parents, whether under the Constitution or otherwise and shall regard the welfare of the child as the first and paramount consideration'. Accordingly, it appears that the operation of the Child Care Act will closely coincide with the principles set out in CRC.

Section 3 of the Guardianship of Infants Act 1964 also provides that the court shall regard the welfare of the infant as the first and paramount consideration.

However, in *In re JH (an infant)* [1985] IR 375 the Supreme Court held that section 3 of the 1964 Act must 'be construed as involving a constitutional presumption that the welfare of such a child is to be found within the family unless the Court is satisfied that there are compelling reasons why this cannot be achieved or the evidence establishes an exceptional case where the parents have, for moral or physical reasons, failed, and continue to fail to provide education for the child'. In this instance the child was returned to his natural parents who had married subsequent to his birth and placement for adoption but before finalisation of the adoption.

The Review Group considers that, notwithstanding the above legislative provisions, it is desirable to put into the Constitution an express obligation to treat the best interests of the child as a paramount consideration in any actions relating to children. Any such provision might be modelled, with the appropriate changes to suit an Irish context, on Article 3.1 of the CRC which provides:

> In all actions concerning children, whether undertaken by public or private social welfare institutions, courts of law, administrative authorities or legislative bodies the best interests of the child shall be of paramount consideration.

The existence of such a provision would oblige those making decisions in relation to children to take into account not only the child's right to be cared for by his or her parents (which the Review Group suggests should now be constitutionally protected) but also such matters as the desirability of continuity in a child's upbringing. This is expressly recognised by Article 20.3 of the CRC and referred to by Professor Duncan (See appendix 22).

6   the relative balance between parental and children's rights

Closely linked with issues relating to the balance between the rights of the family unit and of the individual members are the issues relating to the correct balance between any constitutional protection of family autonomy or parental rights and the rights of the child. Professor Duncan has discussed these fully.

Express constitutional permission for state intervention is limited at present in Article 42.5 to 'exceptional cases, where the parents for physical or moral reasons fail in their duty towards their children'. If a decision is made to amend Article 41 so as to grant express rights to children and also maintain an express guarantee of parents' rights and duties, it would appear necessary to expand the circumstances referred to in Article 42.5 so as to include a situation where the protection of the constitutionally guaranteed rights of children require intervention. A re-wording of the state's duty to the child under this Article is necessary in the light of the Review Group's proposed amendments to guarantee expressly certain rights of the child and elsewhere remove adjectives and phrases which appear to refer to natural law which have been a source of some difficulties (see Issue 7 below).

Further, if parental rights and children's rights are both being expressly guaranteed, it would be desirable that the Constitution make clear which of these rights should take precedence in the event of a conflict between the rights. One can envisage, for example, a situation where a child has lived for, say, ten years with foster parents and a natural father or mother seeks to recover the custody of that child. The natural mother might well have a constitutional right to the custody of the child but the best interests of the child might require it to remain with its foster parents. If, as suggested above, there is an express statement included in any revised Article 41 that in all decisions affecting a child its best interests should be a paramount consideration, then this would resolve any conflict in favour of the child.

7   the description and qualification of family rights

Article 41.1.1° recognises the family as 'a moral institution possessing inalienable and imprescriptible rights antecedent and superior to all positive law'. Article 42.1 refers to the 'inalienable right and duty of parents', Article 42.5 refers to the 'natural and imprescriptible' rights of the child. These are clearly references to natural law. As Mr Justice Walsh has stated (See 'The Constitution and Constitutional Rights' in *The Constitution of Ireland 1937 to 1987*, IPA, Dublin 1988):

> The Constitution does not claim to confer or bestow any of the rights set out [in Articles 41 to 44] but rather expressly acknowledges them as having existence outside the law and beyond the law.

Notwithstanding this, no clear meaning of these terms has emerged from the judicial consideration of them. In *Ryan v Attorney General* [1965] IR 294 Kenny J interpreted 'inalienable' as meaning 'that which cannot be transferred or given away' and 'imprescriptible' as 'that which cannot be lost by the passage of time or abandoned by non-exercise'. However, in *G v An Bord Uchtála* Walsh J referred to some inalienable rights being 'absolutely inalienable' and others as 'relatively inalienable'. Moreover, notwithstanding the absolutist language of this subsection, Costello J in *Murray v Ireland* [1985] IR 532 considered that the rights of the family under the Constitution may be validly restricted by the state. Further in *In the Matter of The Matrimonial Home Bill 1993* [1994] ILRM 241, the Supreme Court, in holding that the Bill, which gave rights to a spouse to a joint tenancy in the family home, was unconstitutional, stated:

> ... the court is satisfied that such provisions [of the Bill] do not constitute reasonably proportionate intervention by the state with the rights of the family and constitute a failure by the state to protect the authority of the family.

The Review Group, as already indicated, considers that there should continue to be express protection for the rights of the family based on marriage. It recognises that it would not be possible to set out comprehensively in the Constitution what are the rights of the family and the precise interpretation of such rights will fall to the courts. However, it considers that the rights protected should not be described as 'inalienable' or 'imprescriptible'. These words have given rise to judicial decisions which some consider as tilting the balance in favour of the autonomy of the family to the possible detriment of individual members: see, for example, *In re JH (an Infant)*. Others consider that the present Article 41 has prevented some of the excesses of state intervention in family life experienced in other jurisdictions: see Professor Duncan – Appendix 22. The Review Group considers that the protection of the family in its constitutional authority together with the express guarantee of certain rights of the child (see Issue 5 above) and specific criteria for state intervention as suggested below should provide a reasonable balance.

Apart from the necessity for the state to act where the rights and welfare of a child requires this, there may be other circumstances in which the state should be permitted to interfere with the exercise of family rights or restrict their exercise. The situation which arose in *Murray v Ireland*, where convicted criminals are imprisoned and deprived of the ability to exercise their conjugal rights, is one such example. Notwithstanding that the courts have interpreted even the rather absolutist wording of the existing provisions of Article 41 as not preventing certain restrictions on the exercise of family rights by the state, it appears desirable to set out in the Constitution the relevant criteria which should apply to any such restriction by the state. Article 8.2 of the ECHR might provide a useful model for any such qualifying clause. It provides:

> There shall be no interference by a public authority with the exercise of this right (to respect for, *inter alia*, family life) except such as is in accordance with the law and is necessary in a democratic society in the interests of national security, public safety or economic well-being of the country, for the prevention of disorder or crime, for the protection of health or morals, or the protection of the rights and freedoms of others.

Article 8.1 of the Convention guarantees respect for private life, home and correspondence in addition to family life. Hence not all the above criteria may be relevant to guarantees in relation to family life alone.

8 the continued constitutional protection of the institution of marriage and any necessary constitutional limitations to be placed on it

The issue to be considered here is whether the Constitution should retain Article 41.3.1° or a revised form of it. The Article provides:

> The state pledges itself to guard with special care the institution of marriage, on which the family is founded and to protect it against attack.

The effect of this Article is that the state may not penalise marriage or the married state. This Article has been relied upon successfully to challenge a number of provisions which had the effect of penalising the married state: see for example, *Murphy V Attorney General* [1982] IR 241 – the challenge to the prejudicial taxation of married couples. It would also appear to provide constitutional justification for legislation favouring the married state.

The retention of a pledge to protect marriage similar to this Article would not appear to conflict with Ireland's obligations under the European Convention on Human Rights, Article 12 of which provides:

> Men and women of marriageable age have the right to marry and to found a family, according to the national laws governing the exercise of this right.

This has been construed by the European Court of Human Rights as permitting a state to treat families based on marriage more favourably than ones not so based, provided treatment of the latter does not conflict with those individuals' rights to family life under Article 8 of the Convention.

The Review Group considers that a revised Article 41 should retain a pledge by the state to guard with special care the institution of marriage and to protect it against attack but that a further amendment should be made so as to make it clear that this pledge by the state should not prevent the Oireachtas from providing protection for the benefit of family units based on a relationship other than marriage.

While the Review Group favours an express pledge by the state to protect the family based on marriage, it does not favour the retention of the words 'upon which the family is founded' in Article 41.3.1°. These words have led to an exclusively marriage-based definition of the family which no longer accords with the social structure in Ireland.

9 express guarantee of the right to marry and found a family

Such rights have been held to be amongst the unenumerated personal rights guaranteed by Article 40.3 (*Murray v Ireland*). The Review Group has recommended elsewhere in this report that Article 40.3 be replaced by a comprehensive list of rights. A majority of the Review Group consider that the right to marry and to procreate or found a family should be included among the rights guaranteed in Article 41 as distinct from Article 40. It appears more appropriate to have all the family rights in the one Article.

If, as recommended by the Review Group, Article 40.3.1° is amended to include a comprehensive list of rights, an express right to marry and to procreate or found a family should be guaranteed in Article 41. Such rights have been held by the courts to be personal rights guaranteed by Article 40.3.

10 the reference to the role of women and mothers or other persons within the home

Article 41.2 assigns to women a domestic role as wives and mothers. It is a dated provision much criticised in recent years. Notwithstanding its terms, it has not been of any particular assistance even to women working exclusively within the home. In the *L v L* case the Supreme Court rejected a claim by a married woman who was a mother and had worked exclusively within her home to be entitled to a 50% interest in the family home. At common law, it has been held that a married woman who makes a financial contribution directly or indirectly to the acquisition of a family home is entitled to a proportionate interest in it. However, this principle is of no help to the significant number of women who do not have a separate income from which they can make financial contributions to a family home but who contribute by their work within the home and in many instances relieve their husbands of domestic duties thereby permitting them to earn money. The Supreme Court considered that, while Article 41.2.2° imposed an obligation on the judiciary as well as on the legislature and the executive to endeavour to ensure that 'mothers should not be obliged by economic necessity to engage in labour outside the home to the neglect of their duties within the home', this Article did not confer jurisdiction on the courts to transfer any particular property right within a family.

These provisions have also been cited by the state in support of legislation which appeared to discriminate on grounds of sex. In *Dennehy v The Minister for Social Welfare* (1984) Barron J used Article 41.2 to support his conclusion that the failure of the state to treat deserted husbands in the same way as deserted wives for the purposes of Social Welfare was justified by the proviso in Article 40.1 (the recognition of a difference in capacity and social function).

The Review Group considered whether this Article should simply be deleted or whether section 2.1° should be retained in an amended form which might recognise the contribution of each or either spouse within the home.

The Review Group is conscious of the importance of the caring function of the family. It considers it important that there is constitutional recognition for the significant contribution made to society by the large number of people who provide a caring function within their homes for children, elderly relatives and others. On balance, therefore, the Review Group favours the retention of Article 41.2 in a revised gender neutral form. The retention of Article 41.2.2° may not be appropriate to a gender neutral form of the Article. The revised form of Article 41.2 might read:

The state recognises that home and family life gives to society a support without which the common good cannot be achieved. The state shall endeavour to support persons caring for others within the home.

11 whether the Constitution should continue to regulate the position of foreign divorces and, if so, how

Article 41.3.3° may be regarded as complementing the provisions of the divorce prohibition contained in Article 41.3.2°. The language of this subsection is not easy to interpret. However, the following extract from the judgment of Kingsmill Moore J in *Mayo-Perrott v Mayo-Perrott* [1958] IR 336 has been subsequently accepted as authoritative:

> The general policy of the Article seems to me to be clear. The Constitution does not favour the dissolution of marriage. No laws can be enacted to provide for the grant of a dissolution of marriage in this country. No person whose divorced status is not recognised by the law of this country for the time being can contract in this country a valid second marriage. But it does not purport to interfere with the present law that dissolutions of marriage by foreign courts, where the parties are domiciled within the jurisdiction of those courts, will be recognised as effective here. Nor does it in any way invalidate the remarriage of such persons.

The judge went on to hold that it was open to the Oireachtas to regulate the question of the recognition of foreign divorces by law, as the operation of Article 41.3.3° is essentially contingent on their being 'a subsisting valid marriage under the law for the time being in force.'

At the date of the enactment of the Constitution, the law in force for the purposes of Article 41.3.3° was a common law rule by which it was provided that a foreign divorce would only be recognised if both parties were domiciled in the foreign state where the divorce was granted. That common law rule interacted with another common law rule whereby the wife was presumed to take her husband's domicile and the operation of both rules had peculiar consequences. It meant, for example, that an English divorce obtained by a husband who previously acquired an English domicile of choice would have that divorce recognised in this state because (a) the wife was taken to have an English domicile of dependency and (b) it satisfied the criteria for recognition at common law as both parties were domiciled in England.

These common law rules have been overtaken by two significant developments within the last decade. In the case of divorces granted after 2 October 1986, the recognition criteria have been relaxed by section 5 of the Domicile and Recognition of Foreign Divorces Act 1986. This provides that a divorce granted after that date will be recognised in the country where either spouse is domiciled or, where neither spouse is domiciled in the state, if it is recognised in the countries where the spouses are domiciled. The recognition of divorces granted *prior* to 2 October 1986 is now governed by the rules formulated by the Supreme Court in *W v W* [1993] 2 IR 476. In that case, the court first ruled that the common law rule regarding domicile of dependency was unconstitutional as it discriminated against wives, contrary to Article 40.1. The court went on to hold that the common law rules of recognition required to be modified in the light of that finding of unconstitutionality and ruled that a divorce granted prior to 2 October 1986 should be recognised if granted in the country in which either of the parties to the marriage was domiciled at the date of the proceedings. However, a foreign divorce granted to a couple where *both* of the parties were domiciled in Ireland will never be recognised in this state.

Since at the date of the submission of this report it was unclear as to whether the divorce prohibition had been validly deleted and replaced by the 15th Amendment of the Constitution, the Review Group has decided to approach the foreign divorce issue from two perspectives. The first assumes that Article 41.3.2° has been deleted, the second assumes that it has not.

whether Article 41.3.3° should be retained if the original Article 41.3.2° is deleted and replaced by the 15th Amendment

It might be thought that because Article 41.3.3° complemented the original prohibition on divorce, it was rendered redundant by the deletion of that prohibition. The Review Group is not persuaded by this suggestion and considers that Article 41.3.3° might still have a relevant role even in the wake of the enactment of the 15th Amendment. The 15th Amendment provides for the granting of divorce in certain limited circumstances, including proof that the parties to the marriage 'have lived apart from one another for a period of, or periods amounting to, at least four years during the previous five years'. If Article 41.3.3° did not expressly provide the Oireachtas with the capacity to enact legislation providing for the recognition of foreign divorces, even where they did not satisfy the requirements specified by the 15th Amendment in the case of divorces granted in this state (for example, foreign divorces granted after one year), it might mean that legislation providing for the recognition of such foreign divorces could be held to be unconstitutional as being contrary to, *inter alia*, Article 41.3.1° whereby the state guarantees to protect the institution of marriage against attack.

By international standards, the requirements specified by the 15th Amendment are highly restrictive. Accordingly, in order to avoid the prospect of 'limping marriages' (that is marriages which remain valid in one country but considered to have been dissolved in another country), the Review Group considers it appropriate that the Oireachtas should retain an express capacity to provide for the recognition of such divorces, even where the criteria for the granting of such divorces (for example, one year's separation) would not in themselves satisfy the requirement of the 15th Amendment had the divorce been sought in this state.

whether Article 41.3.3° should be amended if the divorce prohibition remains in place

If the divorce prohibition remains in place, it is appropriate that the Oireachtas should retain an express capacity to recognise the circumstances (if any) in which a foreign divorce should be recognised. In the absence of Article 41.3.3°, there would be a danger that all foreign divorce recognition rules would be held to be unconstitutional. Such a development would not only lead to striking anomalies, but it would not be in harmony with the general principles of both public and private international law.

Conclusion

The Review Group considers it important that there is a coherent approach to the family provisions in Article 41 and to the education and religion provisions in Articles 42 and 44 in so far as they affect the family. As indicated at the outset of this section of the report, the Review Group considers that Articles 41 and 42 were drafted with only one family in mind, namely, the family based on marriage with children. For that reason and notwithstanding that the recommendations retain many of the elements of Article 41, they necessitate significant amendment of the Article. It is to be noted that the recommendations set out below are interdependent. They involve delicate balances such that, if any part of the recommendations were not acceptable, a change might be required in the remainder of the recommendations.

Recommendations

1   All family rights, including those of unmarried mothers or fathers and children born of unmarried parents, should now be placed in Article 41.

2   Delete existing Articles 41.1.1°, 41.1.2°, 41.2.1°, 41.2.2° and 41.3.1°.

3 The description of any rights or duties specified in Articles 41 or 42 should not include adjectives such as 'inalienable' or 'imprescriptible'.

4 A revised Article 41 should include the following elements:

i) recognition by the state of the family as the primary and fundamental unit of society

ii) a right for all persons to marry in accordance with the requirements of law and to found a family

iii) a pledge by the state to guard with special care the institution of marriage and protect it against attack subject to a proviso that this section should not prevent the Oireachtas from legislating for the benefit of families not based on marriage or for the individual members thereof

iv) a pledge by the state to protect the family based on marriage in its constitution and authority

v) a guarantee to all individuals of respect for their family life whether based on marriage or not

vi) an express guarantee of certain rights of the child, which fall to be interpretated by the courts from the concept of 'family life', which might include:

a) the right of every child to be registered immediately after birth and to have from birth a name

b) the right of every child, as far as practicable, to know his or her parents, subject to the proviso that such right should be subject to regulation by law in the interests of the child

c) the right of every child, as far as practicable, to be cared for by his or her parents

d) the right to be reared with due regard to his or her welfare

vii an express requirement that in all actions concerning children, whether by legislative, judicial or administrative authorities, the best interests of the child shall be the paramount consideration

viii) a revised Article 41.2 in gender neutral form which might provide

The state recognises that home and family life give society a support without which the common good cannot be achieved. The state shall endeavour to support persons caring for others within the home

ix) an amended form of Article 42.5 expressly permitting state intervention either where parents have failed in their duty or where the interests of the child require such intervention and a re-statement of the state's duty following such intervention

x) an express statement of the circumstances in which the state may interfere with or restrict the exercise of family rights guaranteed by the Constitution loosely modelled on Article 8(2) of ECHR

xi) retention of the existing provisions in Article 41.3.3° relating to recognition for foreign divorces.